Dr Macnamara

Born in Montreal in 1861 the son of a soldier, T. J. Macnamara
was educated in Exeter and at Borough Road College. From
1882 to 1892 he was a teacher, first in Lancaster, then in
Huddersfield and then in Bristol. Elected to the Executive of
the National Union of Teachers in 1890, he became Editor
of its weekly journal the *Schoolmaster* in 1892, a member of
the London School Board in 1894, President of the Union in
1896 and a Member of Parliament in 1900. In the period
1907–1922 he progressed from Parliamentary Secretary to the
Local Government Board (1907–1908), to Financial Secretary
to the Admiralty (1908–1920) and finally Minister of Labour
(1920–1922)

Dr Macnamara
1861–1931

ROBIN BETTS

LIVERPOOL UNIVERSITY PRESS

First published 1999 by
LIVERPOOL UNIVERSITY PRESS
Senate House, Abercromby Square
Liverpool, L69 3BX

British Library Cataloguing-in-Publication Data
A British Library CIP record is available

ISBN 0–85323 863 4 *cased*
0–85323-873 1 *paper*

Typeset in Monotype Plantin by Carnegie Publishing,
Chatsworth Rd, Lancaster
Printed and bound in the European Union by
Bell and Bain Ltd, Glasgow

Contents

List of illustrations

Acknowledgements

For access to their archive and/or journal material I am indebted to the Librarians of the Birmingham Central Library; the Bodleian Library, University of Oxford; the British Library; the British and Foreign School Society Archive at the West London Institute (Brunel University); the Churchill Archives Centre (Churchill College Cambridge); the Devon County Record Office, Exeter; the City of London Guildhall Library; the Liverpool Central Library; the University of Liverpool Sydney Jones Library and Department of Education Library; the London Metropolitan Archives; the National Union of Teachers' Library, and the Public Record Office.

Copyright permission to quote from documents from the Lloyd George and Davidson Papers in the custody of the House of Lords Record Office has been granted by the Clerk of Records on behalf of the Beaverbrook Foundation Trust. It is acknowledged with thanks, as is the permission of Curtis Brown Ltd, London (on behalf of C&T Publications Ltd. Copyright C&T Publications Ltd.) to quote the Winston Churchill letters on pp. 274–7. I am grateful to the University of Liverpool for two periods of study leave which materially advanced the progress of the work and, for their assistance, to Col. J. A. C. Bird OBE, Mr Robin Bloxsidge, Mr Ian Cook, Ms Janet Friedlander, Dr Rob Gibson, Ms Frances Hackeson, Mr Bob Hunt, Professor Bill Marsden, Ms Alma Mason, Ms Audrey Massey and Major N. J. Perkins.

Some of the material used in Chapters 1, 5, 8 and 9 has previously appeared in articles published in the *History of Education Society Bulletin*, *History of Education* and the *Journal of Educational Administration and History*. I thank the editors and Taylor and Francis Ltd, publishers of *History of Education*, for permission to deploy the material here.

1 The London School Board offices, 1895–6.
The original building on the Victoria Embankment was designed by G. F. Bodley
and opened in 1874. It was extended by R. W. Edis (who added the clock tower)
in 1891–3. In the gardens, facing the river, stood a statue of W. E. Forster.
The Offices were demolished in 1929.
Reproduced by permission of the London Metropolitan Archives

2 'Back from the holidays', from *The Board Teacher*, 1 October 1895.
From left to right: Mr Riley, Mr Macnamara, Canon Bristow, Mr Diggle,
Mr F. Davies, the Rev. Stewart Headlam, the Rev. J. Coxhead. In less than a
year Macnamara had established himself as one of the leading members of the
London School Board.

3 Composite of portraits by Francis Carruthers Gould, from *London*, 30 April
1896 and 21 May 1896. From left to right: Rev. J. Coxhead, Mr A. Riley,
Mr Macnamara: the leading protagonists in the London School Board
religious education struggle 1893–5.

4 Dr Macnamara, from *The King*, 11 November 1905.
After the coming General Election, *The King* predicted,
England and the world at large would hear more of this brilliant speaker
and vehement advocate of social reform.
Reproduced by permission of the British Library

5 Mrs Macnamara, from *The King*, 11 November 1905.
'The best I could wish any man is that he should have at his elbow so sound a
counsellor as I have'. (Dr. Macnamara, 1899). See also p.21
Reproduced by permission of the British Library

THE
PRACTICAL TEACHER

A
MONTHLY MAGAZINE
AND REVIEW

FOR
THE SCHOOL-ROOM
AND THE STUDY

Vol. XXVII. No. 10.   APRIL, 1907.   Price 6d.

DR. AND MRS. MACNAMARA.
(Photo by Weston, Poultry, E.C.)

6 Dr and Mrs Macnamara in court dress, from *Practical Teacher*,
April 1907. See p. 250

7 'The Two Macs', from *Punch*, 22 April 1908. The original caption read '"THE TWO MACS" (CHAMPION KNOCKABOUTS) AT THE ADMIRALTY. Being a timely caution to Admiral Sir John Fisher and other eminent persons who may be interested in making the acquaintance of their new political chiefs. (The Rt. Hon. Reginald McKenna, and Dr. Macnamara.)'

8 Dr Macnamara debating at the Peckham by-election, by Francis Carruthers Gould, from *Picture Politics*, August 1908.

9 'Driving power' portrait of Dr Macnamara by Francis Carruthers Gould, 'Occupying a seat below the gangway and speaking with tremendous force and energy, he was one of the prominent figures in the Parliament of 1900–06', from *Picture Politics*, August 1908.

10 'An Ex-Admiralty Crichton. Dr. Macnamara effects a Labour Exchange', by A. W. Lloyd, from *Punch*, 21 April 1920.

11 'Who Goes Home?', by A. W. Lloyd, from *Punch*, 24 August 1921. The
Coalition Liberals stand firm against the blandishments of the Asquith minority.
From left to right: Mr Asquith, Sir D. Maclean, Mr Lloyd George, Mr Neal,
Dr Macnamara, Mr Churchill, Sir Alfred Mond, Sir Robert Horne,
Sir Eric Geddes, Col. Amery, Mr Chamberlain, Mr Macpherson.

12 'The Unemployment Question: The Three Graces Get to Work', by
A. W. Lloyd, from *Punch*, 16 November 1921. From left to right: Dr Macnamara,
Sir Alfred Mond, Sir Arthur Griffith-Boscawen.

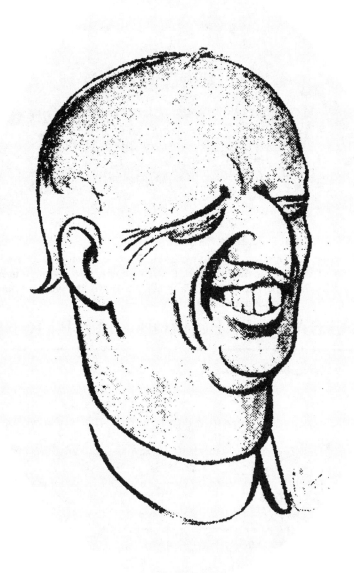

13 Dr Macnamara as Minister of Labour, portrait by Matt, from *Daily Sketch*,
28 July 1921.

14 'Off for the holidays', by A. W. Lloyd, from *Punch*, 9 August 1922. From left to right: Col. Amery, Sir Alfred Mond, Dr Macnamara, Lord Winterton, Mr Chamberlain, Sir Robert Horne, Mr Churchill, Mr Lloyd George, Sir Laming Worthington-Evans, Mr Neal, Capt. Guest.

WALSALL ELECTION CAMPAIGN.

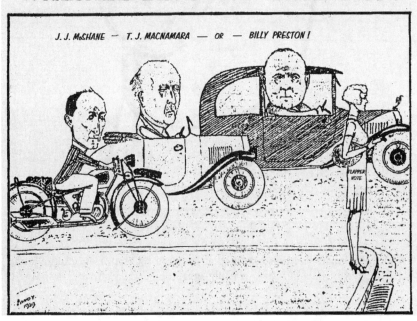

15 'Walsall Election Campaign', by Pandy, 1929.
McShane, Macnamara and Preston in pursuit of the flapper vote.

1

Apprenticeship in Education

On 15 June 1861, two months after the outbreak of the American Civil War, the 47th (Lancashire) Regiment of Foot, known as 'Wolfe's Own', set sail from the Irish port of Kingstown in the SS *Golden Fleece* for Canada. An invasion by the Federal forces seemed possible; Hamilton, Toronto, Kingston and Montreal were completely undefended. The Regiment reached Quebec on 2 July. Three days later it arrived, in steamers, at Montreal. Six companies were marched to temporary accommodation at Logan's Farm, four to St Helen's Island. By the end of August the Regiment was reunited in the Quebec Gate Barracks.[1] Here, on 23 August 1861, Thomas James Macnamara was born. He was baptised eight days later by the Reverend Edward J. Rogers, a Presbyter of the United Church of England and Ireland and Chaplain to the Forces.[2] Of Macnamara's mother, formerly Elizabeth Harvey, little is known. Thomas, his father, a Crimean veteran, now a Colour Sergeant, was an Irishman from County Clare.

The 47th Regiment remained in Canada until well after the Civil War was over, taking part in the repulse of the Fenian invasion in June 1866. Macnamara's earliest memory was of being on sentry-go at the age of five, with a toy rifle (the bayonet fixed) guarding Danny, his father's batman, who was asleep in the grass near the barracks' outer wall. 'At an early age', he wrote in 1898,

> I notified my father that I intended to join 'the drums'. In reply he gave me one of the only three serious thrashings I ever received at his hands. The second occasion was one on which he found me at the back of the cook-house as drill-instructor to an imaginary squad of exceptionally awkward 'cruities, and swearing – well – like an old-time drill-instructor.[3]

His education was affected by the limitations of army life. The only books available were *Gil Blas* and *Don Quixote*, both of which, he claimed later, he learned by heart.[4] In 1869 the family returned to Great Britain on the SS *Orontes*, settling briefly at Pembroke Dock. Here the young Macnamara was enrolled in the Depot School. One afternoon his mother called at the school to take him to some sort of entertainment. He was not to be found, having gone off with some other boys playing truant:

> I was duly thrashed (this was the third time) when I got home; but this thrashing

has not left so big an impression upon me as the fact that I lost the entertainment. I never played truant again, probably for fear of losing another good thing. The motive is, perhaps, not a lofty one, but there it is.[5]

Later the same year the Macnamaras settled in Exeter. The father had been appointed a Militia staff sergeant in the 4th Battalion of the Devonshire Regiment. The son was sent to the Wesleyan Elementary Day School in the Mint. Then, in the autumn of 1871, he was moved to the National School in the outlying parish of St Thomas the Apostle.[6]

As Macnamara arrived in England, plans for the system of public elementary schools which was to be created under Forster's Education Act of 1870 were under discussion. Unlike most advanced European countries, including Scotland, England had resisted the establishment of a national system of education. In 1833 John Arthur Roebuck, MP for Sheffield, had advocated such a system, but the House of Commons had decided that subsidisation of existing schools (with £20,000 per year) was preferable to assuming the national responsibility for which Roebuck was pressing. Religious societies, Anglican and Nonconformist and, as time went on, Roman Catholic and Jewish, were awarded Treasury grants to help maintain their schools. From 1839 these grants were monitored by a small off-shoot of the Privy Council designated the Committee of Council on Education, under the nominal control of the Lord President of the Council, a Cabinet peer who had a large number of other duties. In 1856, in response to growing interest in education (and also the expenditure that it incurred) in the Lower House, the creation of the post of Vice-President at last provided a House of Commons spokesman for what was henceforth also referred to as the Education Department.

In its early days this Committee was concerned with expenditure rather than policy. Exceptionally and almost surreptitiously between 1839 and 1849 its Secretary, James Kay (later Sir James Kay-Shuttleworth) sought to extend its responsibilities. Teacher training, an essential attribute for an expanding educational system, was his special interest. It was he who, having experimented in association with his friend Edward Carleton Tufnell at their College in Battersea with the training of young teachers, provided the model for training colleges which the religious groups (the Government's efforts having failed) took up in the 1840s and 1850s. He, too, had introduced from the Netherlands the idea of the pupil-teacher, which enabled heads to apprentice promising pupils as teachers before their schooling was complete. At the end of the apprenticeship successful pupil-teachers would be awarded a certificate and could then compete for a Queen's Scholarship, which would meet most of the costs of a course at a training college.[7]

Successive British governments remained sceptical about the value of elementary education. In the period of retrenchment following the Crimean War, educational expenditure was reduced and Payment by Results, whereby grants were dependent on pupils' regular attendance and success in annual examinations in reading, writing and arithmetic, was introduced. By the late 1860s, however, attitudes were changing. The Paris Exhibition of 1867, the counterpart of Britain's Great Exhibition of 1851, seemed to demonstrate that the British lead in industrial development was being overhauled by continental rivals and that the success of these rivals was based not only upon scientific and technical education but also upon universal elementary education. Gladstone's first ministry, assuming power in December 1868, also discovered that, in London and other cities, a large vagrant child population was abroad, a potential threat to public order.

Forster's Education Act of 1870 did not introduce the exclusively State-run system of public elementary schools that some members of his own party, for example A. J. Mundella, who was familiar with American and German provision, had been demanding. The religious societies' schools (the 'voluntary' schools) remained, losing after six months the building grants that had sustained them since 1833. Where no such schools existed, or where they existed in insufficient quantity, local boards, with men and women members elected by male and female ratepayers, were to be established to fill up gaps.[8] Over the next thirty years 2,568 of them came into operation, ranging in size from the London School Board, serving a population of 4,000,000, to the Board of Dunton, in Essex, with a population of 140 and six children of school age. What distinguished the new board schools and their voluntary counterparts over this period was that the latter had no access to rate-based income to which, under clause 54 of the 1870 Act, the former were entitled; also that in board schools, under clause 14 (the Cowper-Temple clause) no religious catechism or religious formulary distinctive of any particular denomination was taught.

School boards often excited suspicion; between 1870 and 1873 their creation was resisted in nearly 600 districts in England and Wales. In retrospect they are sometimes depicted as nests of Radicals keen to challenge the local political, territorial and ecclesiastical establishment.[9] Often, however, the establishment was too entrenched to be overturned or even influenced by the new administrative units. Traditions of public service, coupled with an unquestioning assumption that they were the people best fitted to fill posts of public responsibility, enabled local worthies to view the boards with equanimity.

In Exeter the recently appointed Bishop, Dr Frederick Temple, was known to be greatly interested in education. From his fellowship at Balliol he had moved to become an Examiner (the rank from which Assistant Secretaries and the Permanent Secretary were chosen) at the Education Department in Whitehall. From 1850 until 1855 he had been Principal of Kneller Hall, a short-lived training college for masters of workhouse and penal schools, where he had dug potatoes alongside his students in order that garden labour (which he judged to be an essential part of the system) might not be undervalued. For three years he had functioned as HM Inspector of Schools before becoming Headmaster of Rugby.[10] Macnamara, who was to encounter him in London in the 1890s, recalled that his arrival in Exeter had caused apprehension among the beer-loving brotherhood in the Ever Faithful City, since he was known to be a militant temperance advocate. On one occasion an attempt was made to storm the platform of the Victoria Hall in Queen Street and 'flour' the uncompromising prelate.[11] This was unwise. Dr Temple was a muscular Christian who knew how to retaliate.

The new bishop viewed with disapproval the disbursement of government financial aid to elementary education, an enterprise customarily regarded as charitable. Two pounds raised locally, he considered, would always go as far as five pounds from central funds.[12] He had no objection to the creation of school boards, but he felt that religious education would be endangered if board schools stood alone in any district. He acted quickly in commissioning an enquiry into the school buildings already available in the diocese and, giving 500 pounds himself, made a public appeal for financial support to replace the building grants to voluntary schools, for which no applications were to be accepted by the Education Department after 31 December 1870. In the Bishop's view even if, eventually, a school had to be handed over to a board there would be a good claim for having it back on Sundays if it had been received by its new owners in good repair.[13]

A school board was soon set up in Exeter. Another was established in the parish of St Thomas, on the opposite bank of the River Exe. Amongst its first members was Miss Jennetta Octavia Temple, an older sister of the Bishop, who had managed her brother's household when he was Headmaster of Rugby and who continued to preside at the Palace. Described as a homely lady of strong character and sterling qualities, keenly interested in education,[14] she had narrowly and accidentally won a seat on the Board. Voters were given votes equal to the number of candidates and were permitted to plump all of them for the candidate of their choice. One voter plumped his five votes for Mr Reed, but then (this was a year before the Secret Ballot Act) signed the name Reed instead of his own. The returning officer declared the paper null and void, with the result that Miss Temple was elected.[15] She held office for one three-year term.

As far as the Bishop's educational plans were concerned, the St Thomas National School proved to be a disappointment. 'The attendance in this school is very irregular', it was noted in the log book in November 1870. 'Attainments generally are poor. The lower classes appear to be the more successfully taught ... HM Inspector reports that the accounts are kept in a very slovenly fashion. HM Inspector also observes that the supply of books is not sufficient.'[16] Little improvement had occurred in attendance by the following March and the number of children presented for examination under Payment by Results was very small compared with the number on the books.[17] There was evidence not only of low attendance but also of low attainment.

By now the St Thomas Board had begun its meetings. Its main tasks were to determine how many children there were between the age of three and thirteen in the parish and, having done so, to decide what school accommodation was needed. At the meeting held on 20 July, when accommodation was being discussed, the Chairman read a resolution from the subscribers to the National School. They wanted to transfer it to the Board. The decision to accept was taken a month later and approved by the Education Department on 7 December.[18]

During the debates on Balfour's Education Bill, in July 1902, Macnamara recalled the effects of the transfer of his voluntary school to a 'godless' school board. Immediately, the equipment for the teaching staff was improved and, curiously, while there was one Bible for every three boys under the old régime, under the new each boy was given a brand new copy.[19] But the school did not improve. The Inspector reported a year later:

> This School continues in an unsatisfactory condition. Making every allowance for irregular attendance and past ignorance, I cannot think the results of the examination this year give much prospect of improvement. My Lords hope that the Boys' school will deserve a better Report from HM Inspector next year, otherwise they will be compelled to enforce Article 32b.[20]

In July, when the school year ended, William Henley took over the responsibilities of headmaster.[21] He was appalled. The school, he wrote, was in utter disorganisation. The boys were 'so far from being orderly that they do not seem to have the remotest idea of what order means'. For the first two days of the new term they ran out of their places to the cupboards for books, pencils and slates whenever they pleased. 'Their behaviour', he concluded, 'was insufferable in every way and the noise deafening ... to make them fit for the coming examination seems almost a hopeless task.'[22] To assist him he had two pupil-teachers, Courtney Williams and George Smith, and a candidate pupil-teacher, James Jackman. On 11 August a further appointment was made. Henley noted in the log book: 'In accordance with directions received from the Board, I set Thomas MacNamara at work as Monitor this day'.[23] The directions, it was always asserted afterwards, came from Miss Temple herself.[24]

Macnamara was to spend six more years at the St Thomas Board School. It was a valuable experience. As he consolidated his own basic education and acquired the classroom skills of a teacher, he was able to observe the process by which a bad school was transformed into a good one. Henley found the task hard. The boys objected to military drill, then in vogue amongst educationists as a means of inculcating habits of obedience and discipline.[25] Their parents shared their aversion. 'During the holidays', the headmaster noted at the beginning of 1874, 'roughs have frequented the yards etc at pleasure.' As the Bishop had intended, the premises were also used as a Sunday school but 'the Sunday scholars have been equally bad within the school. Ink has been deliberately poured into the master's desks and damage has been done thereby to books and paper.'[26]

Nevertheless, some progress was made. In March the Inspectors commented that there was evidence of care and sound teaching. Discipline was thought to be much improved and both in attainments and in numbers there was considerable advance.[27] In December, content with the general arrangements, they turned to details. Failures in arithmetic were attributed to former defective teaching. Drill was satisfactory. The special subjects, chosen by the Headmaster in addition to reading, writing and arithmetic, were 'weak as yet, as might have been expected'.[28]

Macnamara recalled his schooldays in an article entitled 'The Schoolboy of To-day and of Yesterday' in the *Daily Chronicle* thirty years later. Mathematics, he concluded, had not changed; neither had the fiction chosen for reading, but there was more of it: 'the boy of yesterday read Captain Marryat, Fenimore Cooper, G. P. R. James, Jules Verne and Ballantyne; to-day he reads these and Henty, Kingston, Rider Haggard, Stephenson, Manville Fenn, Talbot Baines [Reed], Mayne Reid, Gordon Stables and so on'. History he claimed to loathe because in his time it had been a dry list of accessions and deaths of kings and dates of battles. Geography consisted of the heights of mountains and the lengths of rivers, Grammar was parsing and analysis, Composition comprised the spelling of tricky words such as *receive, necessary* and *fulfil*. Fighting was a daily occurrence; a real scrap, arranged in advance, was much enjoyed. There were practically no out-of-school activities or games. The school teacher shut the schoolboy out with the closing of the school door.[29]

Macnamara was indentured as a pupil-teacher on 11 April 1875. 'The calling is not that which I should myself have chosen at the time', he remembered in 1899.[30] It was certainly an unpropitious moment. Henley had failed to win the support of the local inhabitants. 'More glass has been broken during the holiday', he wrote as the summer term began, 'either by the rough fellows who take every opportunity of entering the yard or by the Sunday scholars.'[31] Attendance was very bad. At the end of April there were nearly fifty absentees. This could be explained, he suggested, by inability to pay the fees.[32] Other entries, however, indicated that attendance was affected by local events like the Militia marching to camp[33] or by changes in the weather. On 9 June he noted that there had been a violent thunderstorm: 'Only eighty boys in school this morning, ie fifty-seven less than yesterday morning'.[34] Pupil-teachers, according to the Education Department's Code of Regulations, were boys and girls employed to serve in a school under certain clearly defined conditions:

(a) That the school is reported by the Inspector to be
    1. Under a duly certificated teacher

    2. Held in suitable premises

    3. Well furnished, well supplied with books and apparatus

    4. Properly organised and skilfully instructed

    5. Under good discipline

    6. Likely to be maintained during the period of engagement

(b) That the pupil-teachers be not less than thirteen years (completed) of age at the date of their engagement.[35]

The St Thomas School Board and the headmaster were interpreting some of these conditions rather freely.

After the summer holidays the school was reopened by Edward Burnet, Henley's replacement. Absenteeism remained a serious problem. 'Attendance 125', he wrote on 25 July. 'Thirty boys on the register have been absent all the week.' The next day there were only 118: the Marsh Barton races and Gala were due to take place in the afternoon and evening. At the end of August attendance was a little better: the approach of the School Treat supplied the reason. On 20 October the morning attendance was forty-three, the afternoon sixty-three. The cause, Burnet noted, was the excitement consequent upon the flood in Cowick Street, Okehampton Street and Alphington Street. A week later water had come through the walls of the school and of the master's house.[36] Not surprisingly, the Inspector's report in December was unenthusiastic:

> the School has passed fairly in Reading. Writing is not good in the Upper Standards. Arithmetic is unsound in all Standards except the second. Singing is very fair. The answering in the special subjects, Geography, Grammar and Analysis was not good. Discipline is not so good as heretofore.[37]

Three of the pupil-teachers had been examined. Macnamara had been giving a spelling lesson. 'He should improve generally', the report stated bleakly.[38]

Burnet was replaced in the new year.[39] For the school in general and the pupil-teachers in particular the new appointment proved to be a turning point. 'It was my good fortune', Macnamara recalled later, 'to have been trained by Mr George Robins, one of the best teachers that ever used chalk.'[40] Robins, a Devonian, had taught for many years in the North Devon village of Merton. Then, in 1874, he moved with his family to London where for over a year he occupied the post of assistant master at the Cottage Row, Bermondsey, Permanent School under the London School Board at £100 per year, increased by £10 the following May. At the St Thomas Boys' School he was to receive £80 per year and half the grant.[41]

The new headmaster was energetic and determined. Since the grant depended mainly on pupils' attendance, truancy needed to be vigorously dealt with. He reported on 25 January: 'Mr James, a member of the Board, brought a boy to school in the afternoon called Rd Oatway, who was truant playing. Two others were found with Oatway, Ed Godbeer and

Saml Kidwell – noted truant players'. The next day's comment was brief: 'Yesterday's truant players severely punished.' Though the culprits repeated the offence, for example when the Races took place, Robins pursued them relentlessly. On 31 October he noted: 'For the past few days Godbeer, Oatway and Kidwell have been playing truant: they were severely caned, and kept in without dinner'. To check the attainments of both pupils and pupil-teachers he instituted a weekly examination. 'Dictation and Arithmetic still very weak in all the classes', he wrote at the beginning of June. 'Gave the usual examination to the school by Standards – work in all the classes below the average', he observed as the summer holidays ended. But, by September, progress was taking place: another weekly examination showed that Robins and his pupil-teachers were beginning to prevail.[42]

The Inspectors were impressed. 'There is a complete revolution in the school since it has been under the charge of the present teacher', their report stated. 'The boys are now in good order and pay attention to their work. The subjects of the Standards (Reading, Writing and Arithmetic) are very much improved ...' Robins was planning to extend the curriculum. He chose Physical Geography and Literature as the two optional subjects for the next examination. He also required the pupils to take the Drawing examinations organised from South Kensington by the Science and Art Department. When the gratifyingly long (and grant-earning) list of success-ful candidates was published, the names of the erstwhile truants Godbeer and Kidwell were included. Later in the year the Inspector declared:

> This school has passed a very good examination. Out of 161 boys presented ... 160 passed in Reading, 154 in Writing and 155 in Arithmetic ... 115 were presented in Grammar and 108 in Geography ... thirty-five boys were presented in Literature with twenty-eight passes and twenty-three in Physical Geography with seventeen passes. Singing is very fair. Discipline is good. Drill is good. J. Jackman, T. J. Macnamara and J. Merrifield have passed well.[43]

The pupil-teachers were benefiting from Robins' régime. Each of them took charge of a large class and taught all the subjects. At 7.00 am they themselves took instruction from the headmaster, in the school in the summer, in his house in the winter. In 1896, Macnamara wrote:

> Those who were of that happy circle of ambitious youths will not forget the picture around the kitchen fire in the early winter morning, they struggling, right down to the youngest candidate, with Quadratics – for it was Mathematics from Monday morning till Saturday night – kindly George Robins roundly reproving this one or that for not completing the squaring process at the right moment, whilst quite as fully occupied himself with the task of whipping, also at the psychological moment, a fuming coffee pot from the fire. And it used to boil over nine times out of ten when Quadratics were going forward.[44]

In November 1876 Courtney Williams heard that he had won a First Class Queen's Scholarship, with a place at Culham College. He left school in January, returning for a week at the beginning of July 1878 when James Jackman was in London to take the examination. Though Jackman's performance during the inspection immediately on his return was judged by HM Inspector to be merely fair whilst Macnamara passed well, Robins was able to report that Jackman too had been awarded a First Class Queen's Scholarship. He left for Borough Road College in London in January 1879.[45]

Macnamara was now the senior pupil-teacher. In November he took his blackboard examination at St Luke's College, Exeter. In July he, in turn, travelled to London to take the Queen's Scholarship examination at Hawkstone Hall. The Inspector's report on the St Thomas Board School, entered in the log book in September, commended his practical teaching and stated that, on the termination of his apprenticeship at the end of the month, he would be qualified to take up a post as an uncertificated teacher. But like his friend Jackman he had decided to go to College. St Luke's was nearby and he would have been high on the Exeter list, but he did not care to become a member of the Church of England; the non-denominational Borough Road College was more attractive and he had already applied for a place there.[46] Robins, in a reference dated 7 March 1879, recommended him as a most successful and ready teacher; Her Majesty's Inspector had reported very favourably on him and for the last two years the school had received the full grant of £3 on his account. The vicar of St Thomas, the Rev. Maurice Swabey, described how he had taken part in Sunday School instruction for some four years and given satisfaction and how he had attended the church (though not as a communicant) and assisted in the choir. The St Thomas School Board clerk was asked: 'Can you recommend him strongly as a person likely to value and benefit by the training given at the College?' 'Is he, as far as you know, truthful and conscientious?' 'Are his manners agreeable, and indicative of good feeling and kindliness?' All three questions were answered in the affirmative.[47]

Hence in January 1880 Macnamara left Exeter. He, too, had won a First Class Queen's Scholarship and been accepted by Borough Road College. He never forgot what George Robins had done for him. 'A man who, in any but the elementary school teacher walk of life, would have won the laurels of lasting fame at the hands of a grateful community', Macnamara wrote of him when he died in January 1896, a few months into his retirement on the pension of £30 a year that was all the State was then prepared to offer. 'His was singularly the teacher's life ... He made men, they passed through his hands, all to honest citizenship, some to high success. He alone stood where he began.'[48]

Macnamara's four companions on his journey to London were all second-year 'Old B's'. They included James Jackman, now known as Marshall Jackman, who had already won a reputation at Borough Road as the ever-dauntless champion of the always ill-treated and badly fed student. The train, on the old Great Western broad gauge, was very slow. Even in the early 1880s you might luxuriously run from Exeter to Paddington in four-and-a-quarter hours, Macnamara recalled in 1903, but the timetable, with the all-sufficient words 'First and Second Class only', ruled out the Training College student. London, when they eventually arrived, was deep in fog. The cab drew up wheezily before a black, gaunt, jail-like building. This was the famous College of the British and Foreign School Society, on the corner of Lancaster Street and Borough Road, Southwark. It had begun as Joseph Lancaster's Elementary School in 1798 and had been expanded to contain the British and Foreign School Society's teacher training institution in 1809. At first the College had been an adjunct of the School; in the course of time the School became an adjunct of the College, employed as its educational laboratory. It was funded by Quakers as an undenominational foundation, its doors being open to male teachers of promise whatever their creed. In 1877 the Committee responsible for its operation resolved to admit students of every religious persuasion on exactly equal terms, provided they were able to meet the requirements of the College. This, one commentator observed, 'was intended to open the College to Mohammedans and Jews, though they had, I think, never been excluded'.[49]

Educationally, Macnamara knew, he was on sacred ground. But if the outside of the building was forbidding, inside it was worse:

> I find the eighth landing. How cold and clammy! The newly scrubbed floor is not even dry, and the nauseating smell of disinfecting soap pervades everything. My bedroom, a cheerless cubicle, six paces by three ... Downstairs a hopeless maze of half-dark corridors and brutally cheerless rooms. One of these poverty-stricken chambers serves a double purpose. It is a classroom in working hours and a common room out of them ... Thank the Giver of all Mercies it has a fire ... up the sepulchral stone stairs, past the convict-like iron gates ... Let me seek what comfort there is in a very tough mattress and very cold and shiny sheets ...[50]

It was certainly gloomy. James Runciman, incorporating his experiences there at the beginning of the 1870s in his *Schools and Scholars*, published in 1887, described it as:

> unspeakably forbidding ... The stairs were bare, and the hoarse winds that moaned around the building forced their way in and swept shrieking over the cold stones ... No grounds were attached to this melancholy place, but at the back there was a narrow, flagged yard, like the square in which Millbank prisoners take exercise ... There was not a picture or an ornament in any room; the asceticism of a workhouse was blended with the solidity and ugliness of a jail.[51]

In 1880 there were 130 students. The best training each man received, Macnamara considered, was from the other 129:

> As for the College itself, life in it was a hard experience. It didn't much matter

in summer, for there were Clapham Common, Battersea Park and the then rural charms of Honor Oak, the old village of Dulwich, and so on. But in winter it was hideous. How I used to look in at the front windows of the little residences along the road to Clapham, and envy the comfort of the neatly tied curtain, the little choice plant in the window, the knick-knacks upon sideboard and mantel, the cheery little fire, and the inviting armchair. All this meant home and the touch of a woman's hand. College hopelessly lacked these.[52]

At the end of his first year some 300 British and Foreign School Society teachers gathered in the Memorial Hall for a celebration presided over by A. J. Mundella, Vice-President of the Committee of Council on Education. Dr Joshua Fitch, one of Her Majesty's Inspectors of School, gave an address. It had been his duty as an Inspector, he said, to visit all parts of the country and to see schools of all kinds:

> I find old Borough Road students at the heads of the greatest of our elementary schools ... Wherever I go I find three characteristics of Borough Road men. I find, in the first place, an intellectual life and vigour which distinguishes them as a rule from others I know ... There is a certain enthusiasm, a certain intellectual brightness, what one may call a certain 'go', which seems to me mostly to characterise Borough Road men ... The second characteristic ... is a great facility ... in the handling of large numbers ... And the third ... is an affectionate loyalty to the institution.[53]

Fitch had been successively pupil, pupil-teacher and assistant at the Borough Road School; then tutor, Vice-Principal and Principal of the College. After he was appointed to HM Inspectorate in 1863 the famous institution had begun to decline. Payment by Results affected colleges as well as schools. Instead of reaching out towards a liberal cultivation of future teachers they were obliged, for over twenty years, to restrict themselves to mechanical, low standard work.[54] Borough Road continued to attract some of the best young men in the kingdom, since no candidate had a chance of admission unless he were high up on the Queen's Scholarship list, but the quality of the staff was not the same. Past students were to recall Fitch's successor, J. C. Curtis, with affection for his transparent honesty, sincerity and conscientious discharge of his duties, but he himself acknowledged that his position had been won by perseverance rather than by brilliance. Macnamara recalled how he would set the students pages of dates to memorise. These were then repeated round the class of 130. So mechanical was the process that on one occasion when a student had taken his turn and apparently ended the session by calling out the last date in the book, his neighbour sprang up mechanically with 'Printed and published for J. C. Curtis BA by Smith and Son, Stamford Street SE'. Runciman, too, had experienced what he called the silly torture, in which 'to omit a semi-colon was culpable; to leave out a preposition was worse, to substitute a word for one of those used in the book was worse still'. Curtis, he thought, was well aware of the lines which an intelligent teacher should follow, but he was cramped by the requirements of the Education Department with the result that he passed the best years of his life in starving the minds of some of the cleverest young men in England. Nevertheless, in February 1880, fifteen books by Curtis were available under the imprint of Simpkin, Marshall and Co. His six-penny *Outlines* had sold well: *English History* was in its 184th thousand, *English Grammar* in its 173rd and *Geography* in its 130th. He may have become, under orders, a hidebound pedant, but he was probably a rich one.[55]

The Vice-Principal, Alfred Fish Smith, was a fine mathematical scholar. Absorbed in his subject he would rush his classes along at high speed. When one side of the great board in the lecture theatre was filled, he would move behind it and write on the other. Nine years before Macnamara had arrived at Borough Road, Smith had suffered a misfortune. The manuscript of his book on mathematics was destroyed in the great fire at the College. The effect of the disaster on him was tragic and permanent. Sometimes he would speak about the imminent publication of his book, though he must have known now that it would never appear. Sometimes he would not deliver the lecture assigned to him but instead would sit down in front of the class and dreamily examine his beard for white hairs.[56]

Though in retrospect Macnamara judged the Teachers' Certificate course to have been absurdly unintelligent, wearisome and unfruitful, the formal test with which it ended was, he thought, as stiff as that required for a degree at the average British university. Over two years he had followed courses in Arithmetic, Algebra, Geometry, Grammar, Composition, Geography, History, School Management, Reading and Recitation, Penmanship, Political Economy, Music, Teaching, Latin, French, Mathematics, Theoretical Mechanics, Physics, Chemistry, Animal Physiology, Art and Drill. He had been placed fifteenth in the College entrance examination. In the examination at the end of the first year he rose to seventh, with distinction in History, Geometry and Geography. In the final examination, a year later, he was placed fifth and awarded the Teachers' Certificate with Distinction in School Management, Higher Mathematics and Music.[57] His provisional testimonial stated that 'Mr MacNamara is a very intelligent, industrious and well-conducted young man and a thoroughly efficient teacher and disciplinarian. We have no doubt that he will successfully perform his duties and we recommend him with confidence.'[58] He now needed to earn two good reports as a practising teacher before he received the so-called 'parchment', the diploma of professional competence, through the issue and annual revision of which the Education Department maintained Whitehall's unwavering control over the teaching profession.

Even more urgently, he needed a job. The number of certificated schoolmasters was to rise throughout the 1880s but employment was not automatic. School managers realised that to provide the mechanical teaching required under Payment by Results two ex-pupil-teachers could be employed for the cost of one certificated teacher.[59] Back at the Exeter Barracks Macnamara wrote to the Principal:

Dear Sir,   3rd January 1882

I am extremely sorry to trouble you with correspondence but could you inform me whether the College Authorities have, as yet, been successful in finding Schools for those who left College unappointed? I myself, up to the present, have been utterly unsuccessful in finding a School and I can ill afford to remain longer dependent upon my parents. I should feel satisfied with the existing state of affairs had I wasted my time at College but on the contrary I worked hard and am disappointed with the result. Undoubtedly you will think it absurd of me to write thus, and I offer no excuse beyond that of being thoro'ly disappointed at not having a School.

I am, Sir,

Yours obediently,

Thos J MacNamara [60]

Within a matter of days he was appointed, on a temporary basis, as assistant master at £45 per year at the Friends' School Lancaster [61] which, with ninety boys on the roll, was apparently prospering under George Aldridge, headmaster since 1863. Macnamara's appointment was extended till the summer. A year later catastrophe struck. In October 1883, to the horror of the Lancaster Friends, Aldridge filed a petition in bankruptcy. At the creditors' meeting, held in Lancaster at the end of the month, he admitted that he had never kept books of accounts and simply paid money away as he received it. He thought he must have been living at a rate above his means, spending a shilling where he ought to have spent elevenpence. As a result he had run up a debt of something between £2,000 and £3,000. His estate was liquidated and he resigned his headship. Nevertheless his reputation was such that when he set up a new school in a house on Castle Hill he was able to recruit most of his former pupils. At the Friends' School only twenty-four boys remained.[62]

Macnamara had left just in time. Aware of the risks a voluntary school could run, he prudently secured employment under the Huddersfield School Board. It was in board schools that the remainder of his teaching career was to be spent.

2

The Board School Teacher,
1882–1892

On 21 August 1882 Macnamara took up an appointment as an assistant teacher at Spring Grove School, Huddersfield. The previous December the town's schools had been the subject of a report by A. P. Graves HMI.[1] The board schools, in his view, were

> exceedingly handsome ones and are now in a thoroughly efficient condition; they are well-staffed, well-disciplined and well-taught and possess a larger proportion of children in the upper standards and have earned a larger government grant than almost any other set of board schools in the country ... The scholars are, on the whole, keen about their work. Prizes for proficiency and regular attendance are well contested. The examination is looked forward to with positive excitement, and during it listless faces are rare, whilst over-eagerness rather than inattention causes most of the lapses in order ... I have noticed that the natural common sense of Yorkshire children, when it is guided by a capable teacher, produces a class feeling which is a strong support to him against insubordination.[2]

The difficulty in discipline lay in the roughness of the children, who needed firmness combined with kindness: 'The teacher has, as a rule, a hard time of it for the first few months. He is rarely able to dispense with the rod ...' Fifteen years later Macnamara confirmed this: 'I remember looking around me –... every boy had his pockets stuffed with stones – for a stick wherewith to coax order. (I knew the Regulations and had taken the oath. But I argued that this was a crisis in which Regulations must go to the wall).'[3]

Spring Grove was a new, co-educational school. Still performing its original function, it stands to this day at the end of Water Street overlooking the Colne Valley. Times had changed since the Committee of Council had expressed the view that a barn was a good example of how a school should be built and that a barn could easily be converted into a school.[4] The new building, designed by Edward Hughes of Huddersfield, had been planned on the German model. The classrooms, fourteen in all, were situated on two sides of a central hall eighty-five feet long and thirty-two feet wide. The upper rooms, approached by a balcony, were reserved for the girls, the lower ones for the boys. Girls and boys could assemble in a large gallery at the end of the hall. The most striking feature of the building was that the whole school could be supervised by one head teacher.[5]

On 1 December 1880 it had been officially opened by A. J. Mundella, the new Vice-President of the Committee of Council. English people, he declared in his celebratory speech, were very conservative. They liked even the forms of their ancient buildings, they liked the old, old schoolroom, they liked to have five or six classes all making a noise one against another. He confessed that all his predilections were in favour of the classroom system and he thanked God that he had lived to see in England as good a school as the one he was in at Huddersfield that day.[6]

The headmaster from 1 February 1883 was George Sharples, A keen footballer (he was to be captain of Bolton Wanderers in 1884), Sharples possessed what the *Practical Teacher* described later as splendid powers of organisation, indomitable energy and remarkable will power.[7] Another of the assistant teachers was Richard Waddington, a former colleague of Sharples at Pikes Lane, soon to become nationally known as the champion of half-timers, the children the law permitted to spend half the day in factory work, if they spent the other half in school. Macnamara and Waddington became close friends; at lunch time Sharples, sandwiched between his two assistants, underwent what he later called his liberal education.[8] They also made him ambitious. All three of the Spring Grove schoolmasters were to become Presidents of the National Union of Teachers. Sharples, the oldest, was to hold the position last.

Twenty-five years later Macnamara could remember the beginning of the Spring Grove day. 'From 9 to 9.15 the children were gathered together as one family; the teachers read a Bible lesson and the Lord's Prayer was recited, and then the children went to their classes and entered upon their work: this was said to be a Godless Board School'.[9] There was a choir of 300 pupils; he became its conductor. A programme for the Annual Distribution of Prizes and Children's Concert for Monday 10 March 1884 has survived. The proceedings began with the hymn 'How shall the young secure their hearts?', and included part songs by Mendelssohn and Reichardt and the old English air 'When the Rosy Morn'.

Having been awarded his teaching certificate or parchment as a result of the annual inspection, Macnamara began to look for promotion. At Calverley with Farsley, near Bradford, he was called for interview. He was asked whether he smoked or drank; he replied that he would please himself whether he smoked or got drunk. Later, after he had not been appointed, the members of the Committee admitted that he was too good; they had fears that he might end up in charge of the Board as well as the school.[10] But, on 10 April 1884, Sharples recorded in his Log Book:

Mr Thomas J. Macnamara terminated his duties this morning as First Assistant. He was presented yesterday with a splendid 'Baton' mounted with sterling silver as a 'Mark of Esteem' from Standards VI and VII. He leaves with the best wishes of myself, staff and children.

At the age of twenty-two, Macnamara had been appointed headmaster of the boys' division of the Avon Vale School at Barton Hill, in Bristol, under the St George's School Board. Barton Hill, on the eastern edge of the city, was a dingy, dilapidated and depressing industrial area. But again the school was new, standing with its counterparts for girls and infants on the corner of Cotton Factory Lane and Beam Street.[11] Macnamara, like George Robins in Exeter, discovered that his first task was to secure pupil attendance. Seventy per cent of the parents were real, downright, earnest and self-denying toilers, for whom no trouble was too great and no sacrifice too exacting that would serve to further the welfare of their sons. 'For the remainder', he wrote in 1891,

> no word of reprobation that I can find is strong enough. It is one long struggle between them and those who would do a good turn for their youngsters. They are actively and intensely hostile to the school and its work – in fact, they want neither your schools nor your teachers. Their ingenuity is largely directed to the frustration of the aims of the Education Acts. The whole thing, to them, is an unwarrantable and presumptuous interference with their indisputable right to do as they like with their own.

In that year, free elementary education first became available for the majority of children. Macnamara monitored the effects on attendance during the first four weeks of the autumn term. Every child had taken home leaflets headed 'No More School Fees' at the beginning of the three weeks' holiday on 31 July. In the week before the new term, attendance officers made house-to-house visits distributing further copies. The result was that in the first week, the average attendance reached eighty-five per cent, higher than in any previous opening week in the seven years' existence of the school. Over the next three weeks, however, it fell to eighty-three, eighty-one and finally seventy-nine per cent. On the Monday of the last week at 9.15 am, only 190 of the 287 boys on the roll were present. Twenty-six more were assembled by sending out fifty temporary juvenile attendance officers in search of them. Sixty-one remained unaccounted for. Macnamara sent a message of enquiry to each house and tabulated the replies:

In seven cases:	'No one home'
	(Both parents at work. Boys probably sent to school.)
In five cases:	'Truanting.'
	(The following are the sort of replies in these cases:- 'He got up before it was light and ran away.' 'He has been out all night sleeping in railway trucks.' 'He hasn't been home since last Wednesday; we don't know where he is.' And so on.)
In ten cases:	'Gone to shop.'
	(A euphemism that needs no explanation.)

In seven cases: 'Gone on an errand.'

In five cases: 'Bad in bed.'

In six cases: 'Minding the baby.'

(An occupation by no means confined to the little mothers of the alley home.)

In six cases: 'No one up yet.'

(It is a striking fact that on Monday mornings the whole neighbourhood appears to oversleep itself. I suppose the fathers are in their places at 6 am as usual; but the statement comes in very generally up to 10 am on Mondays that there is 'no one up yet.')

In four cases: 'No boots.'

(This is scarcely a legitimate excuse, as there are always several bare-footed boys present, and on no account would the lack of shoe-leather constitute a reason for non-admittance.)

In eleven cases: 'Not coming this morning. Shan't tell you why.'

(In several such cases as these the message comes back, 'Tell the b____ schoolmaster to be d___d!' In two of these cases the child is at work – illegally, of course.)

Over seven years in the school Macnamara had admitted 1,348 boys, but, he calculated, at the very outside not more than 400 had attended with sufficient regularity to reach Standard IV. Children living within a biscuit-throw of the school had never entered it or any other school. Scores of others had attended irregularly so that by the age of thirteen they had learned no more than the alphabet. Unfortunately the law was unenthusiastically enforced by the magistrates. Peppercorn fines were paid out of children's wages and the parent walked off jingling the substantial difference in his pocket.[12]

Nevertheless, progress was made at the Avon Vale Boys' School. In 1889 the *Teachers' Aid* included Macnamara in its series entitled 'Peeps at the Successful Pedagogue'. 'He mainly owes his success to the fact that he is willing to learn from anybody and everybody and to a keen appreciation of the theory that the art of teaching is made up of innumerable details', it commented. Macnamara in his leisure moments was depicted with a note-book, ever on the look-out for rare shells, stones, fossils and the like which could be used in geography lessons; at the railway station jotting down the names of advertisers who might provide him with a colourful poster for the school, gardening, cycling, fishing or playing cricket. His interest in music had taken him to the local Philharmonic Society; now, not infrequently, he would entertain his staff at home and, with the windows ablaze with light from basement to roof, an assistant teacher's voice could be heard trolling forth some bass melody.

Within the school Macnamara was seen as an exponent of the personal approach. He always greeted the assembled pupils. Each boy's name was placed in a cardboard plan hung before each class so that absentees could be noticed at once; each teacher addressed his pupils by their Christian names. Even without his note-book the headmaster remembered where older brothers had gone to work and enquired about their progress. Pupils were motivated by prize tokens for regularity and punctuality. Homework of an attractive kind, usually requiring artistic embellishment, was set; cricket and swimming fixtures were organised; a museum and library had been created with the assistance of parents and pupils. All the teachers were fond of asking – how far can you jump? Span? Stride? How tall are you? Am I? This room? Industrious pupils were permitted occasionally to go to the front of the class and question their fellows; not infrequently pupils could be seen busily disentangling some abstruse problem upon the blackboard.

The *Teachers' Aid* correspondent scrutinised the Christmas breaking-up at the Avon Vale School. In turn, groups of twenty boys were assembled on a cleared floor space on to which some 200 wooden blocks the size and shape of bricks had been tumbled. One boy was chosen, placed in the middle of the space and blindfolded. The teachers now built a castle round the chosen boy, placing bricks one upon the other so as to leave every alternate brick space vacant. When the bricks reached the boy's head small prizes, a ball, an orange, a packet of sweets, a penny, a top, a penknife, a stick of blacklead, a pencil case, a nine-inch rule were placed in nearly every space; the boy inside was then invited to forage about and stow away the plunder until he displaced a brick. Then down came the edifice, out rolled the valuables and a scramble ensued. When every set of twenty had participated, the whole school would transfer to the play-ground. The closing scenes included an address by the headmaster:

> For once his originality forsakes him ... He tells his boys (1) to keep out of trouble (2) not to bother their parents (3) to come back prepared to work like giants refreshed and (4) ... not to eat too much pudding, and then he dismisses them with his blessing, and with a profound sigh of relief relinquishes himself to the *otium cum dig*: that he above all workers needs, and knows how to enjoy.[13]

In 1904, as a witness before the Inter-Departmental Committee on Physical Deterioration, Macnamara was told by J. G. Legge, HM Inspector of Reformatory and Industrial Schools (which dealt with children who were vagrants or found associating with criminals) that there was a good deal of evidence that the elementary school did not fit a large number of children for the part they had to play in life. Perceiving the implication that a school curriculum in poorer districts might benefit by taking on a more industrial character involving (for example) making brushes and boots, or carpentry, Macnamara resisted strongly:

> Because a child happens to be born in a very poor part, I do not think you are entitled to rob him of the foundation – which will not be very deep in any

case, because he will have to leave school very early – of a really thorough general education. I think you do him the greatest wrong if you do that ... I should shrink from restricting the curriculum in such a way as would increase the difficulties of the upward and onward movement of the poor child simply because he was born in a poor locality.[14]

Another account of Macnamara the schoolmaster was published by the *Practical Teacher* in its series 'Well-Known Teachers at Work' in February 1892. The walls of the Avon Vale School were bright with pictures; the home-made apparatus included a miniature Mount Vesuvius which functioned realistically when lit by a match; plants stood on the window sill, the ledge beyond served as a showcase for little models of mill-wheels, churches and cottages, all neatly put together from paper and card. The report continued:

> But the boys! Lean shaggy, hungry-looking urchins, the bulk of them, with highly-ventilated elbows and aerated boots. Here one catches the gleam of a solitary clean white collar; but there, on the other hand, protrude a brace of bare feet. And yet ... the demeanour of the youngsters, quiet and attentive, speaks volumes for the training they receive at school.

As he sat pondering on the school and its achievements, Macnamara arrived:

> a keen, alert face ... a broad-shouldered, wiry form, above the average height; a young man, devotee of the razor, who does not even look his lightly-carried thirty years; a quick long gait, an unconventionality of garb, somewhat of the American accent ... a *tout ensemble* breathing of force and individuality, and a personality original and picturesque, such is the T. J. Macnamara whose name is 'writ large' ... upon the annals of our elementary education of to-day.

Off they went to face the boys of the First Standard. There were seventy of them with a dozen or so of them already twelve years old. Macnamara said:

> The Government makes the tremendous mistake of expecting all sorts and conditions of schools to reach the same standard ... When will it be acknowledged that in good localities teacher and parents join hands to make for one end; whilst in such districts as East Bristol many of the parents are actually hostile to the teacher and his work?

He described how, in the summer months, most of the boys who spent the dinner hour at school had only dry crusts to eat or, as an occasional alternative, a raw turnip. In winter, halfpenny dinners were provided by the Children's Help Society: 'During the last three months of last winter I bought 2,167 halfpenny dinner tickets from the Society. But as even a halfpenny toll bars the way to so many of the hungriest mouths, 1,516 of the tickets had to be distributed gratis.'

Macnamara was too realistic to oppose Payment by Results. The school needed money. When he opened it in 1884, he said, there were about 130 of the roughest samples of boy material that ever teacher gave up in despair. He had devised a scheme whereby the work in each subject was divided into nine parts. One part was dealt with by the teacher and examined by the headmaster each month. By this system the year's work was thoroughly got through in nine months, leaving the last three months before HM Inspector's visit for revision. In November 1884 eighty-nine per cent of the pupils passed the annual examination, while a year later the figure had risen to ninety-seven per cent. More emerged from this scheme than the results and the grant. Inexperienced teachers and pupil-teachers could be assisted and the progress of classes could be monitored. Its success, as far as the pupils were concerned, could be seen from the Honours Board. Boys were winning scholarships at secondary schools. Nevertheless, Macnamara admitted, the eagerness of many parents to pack their children off to work at the earliest possible age made progress unnecessarily difficult.

Macnamara began to talk about his writing. His first serious effort had, he said, been a pamphlet denouncing Payment by Results: 'It contained more adjectives than any book of its size I ever came across. Most of the copies, I believe, went to wrap butter up.'[15] He had also a number of text-books to his credit. Three years earlier the *Practical Teacher* had reviewed his *Mental Arithmetic: Teacher's Complete Syllabus, Standards I and II*:

> If his directions and plans are followed systematically children will become, as a rule, ready and accurate in their calculations, the slate and paper arithmetic will show signs of intelligence and the sums involving thought will be oftener attempted and successfully worked.[16]

His *Periodical Examination Report Form* derived from his monthly examinations at Avon Vale drew less favourable comment: 'Mr Macnamara has spoken and written against this method of estimating the work of a teacher as much as anyone during the past few years, and yet he perpetuates the fallacy in this broad sheet'.[17]

After two years at Avon Vale, aware that in the teaching profession rewards go mainly to the ambitious, Macnamara sought an appointment within HM Inspectorate. Inspectorships were reserved for graduates of the ancient universities, but since 1863 an additional post, that of Inspector's Assistant, had been available. Macnamara had secured the support of two Inspectors[18] but, as it turned out, at twenty-five he was too young to be accepted. Without doubt this was a piece of good fortune. Inspectors' Assistants were regarded with suspicion by the teaching profession and, as a rule, the job was a dead end.

A more promising way forward lay in the National Union of Elementary Teachers. During the controversy caused by Forster's Bill in 1870 the Liberal MP J. W. Whitwell had convened a conference of fellow MPs of his party and invited some teachers to give their opinions on the religious issue. The result of the exchange of views was unexpected. What had for so long been a cause of strife at the political level became to teachers a means of unity. The isolation preserved by the different categories of teachers, Church of England, Wesleyan, Roman Catholic and undenominational which had encouraged ignorance of each other, sectarian animosity and bitterness of feeling was at last perceived to be undesirable. A series of meetings at King's College London resulted, on 25 June 1870, in the union of the various existing teachers' associations in a national body. At the first general meeting of the new union, J. J. Graves, the newly-elected President, explained what its aims should be:

> We ought to leave off servility, and take a more manly position in matters educational ... We must trust our own leaders, place ourselves under our own banner, follow our own tactics, fight our own battles against ignorance and crime on the one hand, and personal opponents and prejudicial interference on the other.[19]

The Union began with 400 members. Numbers rose gradually throughout the 1870s, to reach 13,716 in 1881. Then, with the annual subscription increased to three shillings, membership began to fall. It was not until 1887 that the 1881 figure was recovered.[20] The Bristol Association, which Macnamara joined in 1884, was run by old men, some of whom looked with surprise at the clean-shaven boyish-looking young man who had something to say on most matters. Soon, it was observed, they began to chastise him a bit. But if they could chastise with whips, Macnamara could chastise with scorpions. The Association came to life.[21] In 1885–86, as he became Secretary, there were 108 members. By 1889, when he was President, the number had risen to 189.[22]

At rehearsals of the Bristol Musical Festival Society in 1885, Macnamara met Rachel, elder daughter of Angus Cameron, formerly of Aberdeen. They were married the following year.[23] Though, according to Waddington, Macnamara could pass as a Devonian or Scotsman, as well as an Irish-Canadian,[24] he was always proud of his Irish descent. When he moved to London he gave the name 'Clontarf' to two of the houses he lived in, recalling the battle in 1014 at which the power of the Danes in Ireland was effectively broken. Later, at the hustings, he raised no objection to being greeted as an Irishman by T. P. O'Connor, the Nationalist MP.[25] His wife claimed to be a descendant of Lochiel. But neither of them, despite the rediscovery of the Celt which was a feature of the 1880s and 1890s, made a public display of their connections. 'It looked as if our marriage would mean a very real Union of Hearts', Macnamara wrote in 1899. 'And so it has been. The best I could wish any man is that he should have at his elbow so sound a counsellor as I have.'[26] Their daughter, Elsie Cameron, was born in 1887; their sons Neil Cameron, Brian Cameron and Terence Cameron in 1891, 1894 and 1905 respectively. Rachel Macnamara soon discovered that she was married to the NUT nearly as much as to her husband. To do him justice, she recalled in 1907, he never mentioned the Union during their honeymoon, but, once they returned home, she found herself virtually the co-secretary of the Bristol Teachers' Association.[27] Local meetings would end with tea and a concert, with Rachel presiding at the piano.[28]

Elizabeth Burgwin, the distinguished headmistress of Orange Street School, Southwark, and a member of the Union Executive from 1885 till 1896, liked to recall her first encounter with the young man with a keen face and an eagle eye who got up at the back of a meeting she had been sent to address on the Code and who 'wanted to know'. 'Put that boy into office', she said to the Chairman. 'It will do him good.'[29] In 1887 he attended the NUET Annual Conference at Portsmouth. Having silently absorbed the procedural rules he was able to make his mark at Cheltenham the following year. With Charles Hayward of Fox Street Board School, Birmingham and James Yoxall, of Sharrow Lane Board School, Sheffield, he had written to the *Schoolmaster* (the weekly journal of the NUET), before the Conference, suggesting that since the flower of the successful organisers of the local associations – the Indefatigables as they called them – would be gathered together at Cheltenham, it would be a pity to miss the chance of comparing notes about how to increase membership:

> Far be it from our minds that we should interfere with any of the authorised sessions; but as only 140 can be accommodated at dinner, and as about 200 will be fuming with disappointment because there is no room for them at the festive board, we think that such a meeting might be advantageously held on Tuesday evening.[30]

A week later the letters columns of the *Schoolmaster* showed how popular the idea had been.[31] From now on, to many supporters in the Union, 'the Indefatigables' meant the organisers of that meeting. It was a name which, over the next few years, Macnamara and Yoxall would exploit. The event itself, at the Belle Vue Hotel, was a great success. 'Mr Macnamara', the *Schoolmaster* reported, 'having explained the objects of the symposium to the general meeting, adjourned to conduct the overflow meeting'.[32] Two hundred representatives were present at the two meetings 'which were very animated throughout'. Macnamara, in a letter published in the *Schoolmaster* on 14 April, commented:

> This should be an annual gathering; and that we may always get the real pithy experiences and suggestions of 'the fighting men', it must continue to be a friendly and informal meeting; many of the most valuable hints were given by those who would have hesitated to address the representatives 'in annual Conference assembled'.[33]

No further symposium took place, but thereafter the dinner was replaced by a public meeting.[34] The Union, for another reason, was never to be the same again. Until the Cheltenham Conference its leading figures, having secured its existence, had scarcely changed over seventeen years. The Executive and the Union officers had been almost perfunctorily elected at the Annual Conference.[35] Now a constitutional amendment, providing for the election of the Executive in advance by the entire Union membership, proved revolutionary:

> Three conspicuous late members [wrote 'Greenwich' to the *Schoolmaster*], Mr Langler, the only representative of the training colleges, a late President too; Mr Smith, the late Chairman of the Finance Committee, a man respected by the whole of London for his temerity in the cause of our profession; Mr Clark, a man who has for sixteen years past worked like a slave for the Union – were ruthlessly sent to the wall to the lasting disgrace of those who brought about the calamity, and to the deep regret of all men who have a spark of gratitude in their constitution.[36]

Macnamara took the opposite view: touting for the Executive on Monday and Tuesday at Conference was over, and, more than that, the waste of time consequent upon the windiness of candidates for election was likewise ended. As for the means by which the new Executive elections were conducted:

> It would be well to agitate for the printing of the list of candidates for the Executive in alphabetical order, instead of giving the retiring members the front page of the voting paper. Members of the Executive seeking re-election should be distinguished by an asterisk, and then leave it to the voter to show a proper sense of gratitude for services rendered by picking them out from the alphabetical list.[37]

Macnamara returned to Bristol to participate in the inaugural meeting of the Bristol Education Council, held on 12 April 1888 at Clifton College. This body, to which members were to be nominated by the Professors of the University College, the masters of Bristol Grammar School, Clifton College and the Merchant Venturers' School; the Headmasters and Headmistresses of the Bristol Endowed Schools; the mistresses of the Clifton and Redland High Schools and the Bristol School Board, with seven representatives of elementary schools, had arranged a programme which was to include an address by the former Borough Road Principal, Dr Joshua Fitch who, it was suspected, owed his appointment as HM Inspector to his relentless loyalty to the rules laid down by the Education Department and his devotion to Payment by Results. The *Schoolmaster* reported:

> We are informed that the lecturer pointed out that a comparison between the laws which governed the world of the naturalist, and those which prevailed in the world of the schoolmaster, was full of encouragement. It brought home to the teacher the conviction that every effort he made for his own personal cultivation, every good lesson he gave, every right habit he formed, every true aspiration after better things he could excite, was in its own way a distinct contribution to the improvement of the race, for it helped to make the condition

of life more favourable, and to make the development of right character more easy, not only among his own scholars, but among all who might come after them.

No opportunity was given for a full discussion of the paper, the *Schoolmaster* noted, even though many of the audience were anxious to offer a word of comment.[38] A letter from Macnamara, however, appeared in the *Western Daily Press*:

> ... the elementary teachers of this country will rejoice and give thanks that the high priest of the 'Inspectarchy' has become so thorough and complete a convert to the crusade against Payment by Results, an illogical code and an irrational system of classification. If seems but yesterday that Mr Fitch was ready to champion the present system ... against all comers ... but a more powerful denunciation of the monstrosities of the system has, I venture to say, rarely been uttered than that delivered ... last night.
>
> ... We may confidently expect, therefore, that the teacher who casts aside the craving for grand results on paper, sums correct, dictation right, and glib parrot-like answers with the lip, and tries to follow out the heroic and noble ideal pictured by Mr Fitch ... will receive his reward and be paid for the true results he has obtained. He may receive a bad report on the mechanical results, he may pass only fifty per cent of his scholars through the ordeal of examination, his schooling may be classed 'fair' or even 'bad' by the tangible-result-requiring officials, his managers may regretfully request him to resign, because his ennobling moral influence does not extract enough money from the imperial coffers to allow them to work the school comfortably. But what are all these? Mere trifles compared with the satisfaction he will feel at having helped to make the condition of life more favourable, and to make the development of right character more easy, not only among his own scholars, but among all those who might come after them ...[39]

When the Union, redesignated the National Union of Teachers, held its Conference in London in 1890, Macnamara put up for the Executive. There were twenty-four places and forty-seven candidates: Yoxall came first, with 6,309 votes, Macnamara was tenth with 4,398.[40] His elevation gave him the opportunity to comment on national policy issues. Supporting a resolution on the management of schools, he took up the issue of the future of the school boards. In the great centres of urban population (in two of which he had direct experience) they had done well. Small boards were another matter. Their members were often elected simply to starve education. Clerical intolerance was nothing to the intolerance of illiterate board members. Later, he moved a resolution 'that in the opinion of this Conference the areas of small school boards should be materially increased in order to ensure efficient administration'. T. E. Heller, the Union Secretary, seconded, and it was carried unanimously.[41]

The fact that H. J. Walker, the President for 1890–91, was also a Bristol teacher, soon caused it to be said that Union and Executive business was being discussed and even prearranged in the Bristol-Paddington express.[42] What may well have emerged from the hours spent on the train was the idea that Union meetings should be rescheduled. Macnamara first appeared at the headquarters at 71 Russell Square on 19 April 1890. He was appointed, as were all members of the Executive, to three committees; in his case those dealing with Education scheduled for the first Friday and the third Monday of the month; the Organisation Committee, on the first and third Saturday, and the so-called Parliamentary Committee, concerned with lobbying MPs, which met on the first Friday and the third Saturday. The Executive itself met fortnightly, on the first and third Saturday.[43] On 19 September Macnamara successfully moved that one Executive meeting per month was sufficient. The President's attention was drawn to the fact that Standing Orders would need to be rescinded.[44] A fortnight later, with this in view, Macnamara stated his case. Business, he said, could be despatched by the Executive monthly; the previous evening could be occupied with committees. Costs of travel, which had increased from £188 to £404 over the previous ten years, made the change particularly desirable. Heller agreed. Union work would be strengthened, he said, if the Executive dealt with general questions of principle and policy and left the operative part to large committees with increased powers.[45]

At his first conference Macnamara had noticed that the proceedings had little or no interest either for the local inhabitants or for the country at large.[46] By 1891 all this had changed. Members of Cardiff's new County Borough Council, expressing traditional Welsh enthusiasm for education, bade the teachers a most cordial and hearty welcome and the proceedings were reported nationally.[47] During the fourth session the issue of small school boards reappeared. Yoxall, who had just been elected Vice-President, moved that the practice of creating and maintaining school authorities for small districts had proved to be injurious to the interests of national education and that both the Education Department and Parliament should be petitioned 'to make the areas of all school boards to correspond with those of the administrative counties of the country'.[48] This was by no means a new idea. When the Local Government Act of 1888, which was to set up the county councils and county boroughs, was before Parliament, John Morley, one of Gladstone's closest advisers, suggested in a speech at Newcastle that the school boards should be consolidated in the new Local Authorities. The *School Board Chronicle* had been taken aback:

> The School Board differs exceedingly from all other Local Authorities in character and functions. The man who will be a good town councillor will probably be a good Poor Law Guardian, a good Board of Works man, a good Paving Commissioner, a good Assessment Commissioner – or a good anything connected with public business – but he may be a bad or altogether unsuitable member of a school board. All other local public functions are more or less

homogeneous – but the work of the school board is a thing apart, as to which the ratepayers ought to have the opportunity of separately choosing their representatives.[49]

Now Macnamara, who had been re-elected to the Executive, this time at the top of the poll, seconded Yoxall's motion. It was carried unanimously, though by a bare quorum. The small school boards, he said, brought discredit to the system. Quoting from the reports of HM Inspectors, he showed how, in the north of England, small boards were apathetic in administering the bye-laws on compulsion. In the south, expenditure was grudged on heating apparatus. One school in Devonshire had not been scrubbed for sixteen years, because the operation would cost five shillings. Small boards, he said, were abominably tyrannical to the teacher.[50]

Again, during the sixth session there was evidence that the sympathies of the Union were moving towards the county councils and away from the school boards. By the Technical Instruction Act of 1889 the new county authorities, rather than the boards, had been given powers to develop institutions for technical education. The following year funds originally designated for compensating the owners of compulsorily closed public houses (the so-called whisky money) were diverted to these authorities either to finance technical education or to reduce the rates. Now Seth Coward (Southwark) moved 'that this Conference is of opinion that in large towns the funds derived from the beer and spirit duties, available for technical education, should be administered by the school board'.[51] Yoxall spoke strongly against the motion. It would, he said, give school boards large and small the power of using this money simply to lighten the rates. Macnamara moved an amendment proposing to strike out the words 'administered by the School Board' and add the words 'in every instance devoted to educational purposes'. Ernest Gray (Executive) seconded, urging that power of this kind should go to the county councils. So soon after the debate on the shortcomings of small boards the move to transfer new financial responsibilities to boards failed to win support.[52] Scarcely noticed, a decisive moment in the history of educational administration had been reached. The substitution of the school boards by the county authorities had been signalled.

The Union was growing confident. Instead of responding to government initiatives, it was now seeking more effective means to apply pressure to politicians. At the Cheltenham Conference of 1888, after eleven years' intermittent discussion of the topic, George Girling (President 1887–88) had proposed that the annual subscription be increased by the sum of one shilling to six shillings to secure the election of a practical teacher to the House of Commons.[53] 'When we have a spokesman at Westminster', the *Schoolmaster* declared, 'we shall have a speedy change of front in the regions of Whitehall; and when the wrongs of the country in regard to education are duly exposed among the law-givers, we are confident of a rapid redress'.[54] Macnamara, however, was doubtful. He supported a hostile amendment on the grounds that the move was divisive, but it was defeated on a show of hands.[55] In March 1890, just before his election to the Executive, the matter arose again. Ernest Gray, headmaster of St Gabriel's, Pimlico, who was spending a good deal of time at Westminster, urged the Executive to place a motion on the Conference Agenda adding a further two shillings to the subscription.[56] One shilling yielded £700 per year, sufficient to support one candidate. Hence, he argued in the *English Teacher*, 'no other case can be taken up, no matter how good, no matter how small the cost, simply because we have no funds to meet it. Directly negotiations are opened with any one constituency, work has to be stopped in every other quarter.'[57] Macnamara again resisted the move. The matter, he wrote to the *Schoolmaster*, should be discussed at local association level by the rank and file of the Union.[58] Having secured the point at the Conference, he put his views to the Bristol association: 'Increase the Parliamentary Fund by all means', he said, 'but let it be by an increase in membership rather than an increase in subscription'. He asked the members to make up their minds which they wanted – 'a small Union and an exclusive Union with but little influence in the country and the House of Commons, or a large Union and a representative Union having weight and influencing public opinion'. The association was persuaded, voting against the increase by forty-five to seven.[59] He developed his argument in an article entitled 'The Future Policy of the NUT' published in the *Schoolmaster* the following March. The future task of the Union was, he thought, to secure the welfare, socially and professionally, of the teacher. At a recent conference of members of Parliament with the Union on the question of superannuation, the President had been asked how many members the Union had. 'Sixteen thousand', he had answered. Then came the inevitable poser: 'There are, I believe, something like 45,000 teachers in the country; how do you know that the 29,000 outside your ranks seek a scheme of superannuation?' In Macnamara's view it was by numbers alone that he and his colleagues could put the educational machinery straight. Most of the disabilities under which teachers suffered could be removed in the twinkling of an eye if the membership were 45,000. It was by an increase in membership, especially in rural areas, rather than an increase in subscription that they would prevail.[60]

It was Gray, however, who prevailed, both at the Executive and at the Leeds Conference of 1892, though he had to make do with a seven rather than an eight shilling subscription. 'Mr Gray was tremendously in evidence', the *Board Teacher*, the monthly journal of the Metropolitan Board Teachers' Association, commented acidly, 'and wrought most artistically towards his great aim. No effort was spared by Mr Gray to get Mr Gray put forward as candidate for Parliament on the Conservative side. He succeeded. He is now the only possible Tory Teacher MP.'[61] Unfortunately for Gray, the general election came too soon for him to make the necessary preliminary arrangements. Yoxall, now President of the Union, contested Bassetlaw for the Liberals: here all he could do was to reduce the majority of the sitting member.

Gray's efforts had opened up a new opportunity for Macnamara, but he was not yet ready to claim it. Instead, encouraged in the first instance by Walter Reid, the editor of the *Western Daily Press*, he was transforming himself into a journalist. By the beginning of 1892 he had contributed to many of the education journals and, most recently, to *Macmillan's Magazine*, the *Pall Mall Gazette* and the *Westminster Review*.[62] On 18 March he was interviewed for the post of editor of the *Schoolmaster*. The edition of 26 March announced that he had been unanimously appointed and that he would move to London and take up his duties after the Easter Conference. The *Bristol Mercury* commented:

> ... Mr Macnamara has been one of the most prominent figures in local educational circles ... As headmaster of the Avon Vale School, he has won the highest encomiums from the St George School Board and from the local Inspectors. But more important than this, he has essayed to be considerably more than a mere schoolmaster to the hundreds of poor youngsters with whom he has had to work. As an exponent in the public press of educational questions, he is widely known ... his removal to London will be hailed with regret.[63]

Even the *School Board Chronicle* which, in protecting the interests of the boards, tended to regard teachers with suspicion, was generous: 'The board of directors of the *Schoolmaster* appear to have been fortunate ... Mr Macnamara is a brilliant and energetic writer, young and full of resources, and promises to make his mark in education journalism'.[64]

For the next thirty-five years Macnamara was to live in London. Honor Oak and Dulwich had appealed to him as a student and it was in this area that he and his family settled, first in Montem Road, Forest Hill, then in Turney Road, West Dulwich, and finally in Rollscourt Avenue, near Herne Hill station.

3

The *Schoolmaster*

In March 1892, when he moved to London from Bristol to edit the *Schoolmaster*, Macnamara was well placed to comment on the entire range of educational institutions provided by public authorities in England, with more than ten years' experience in the classroom, eight years as a headmaster and Union activist and two years on the NUT executive (which put him in line to become Vice-President, then President of the Union). He took over the editorship, he recalled in 1922, 'consumed with the fierce zeal of the wholly convinced propagandist: "Better education for the children of the people; fairer treatment for the teacher". I can honestly say I lived for nothing else.'[1]

The *Schoolmaster* had been adopted as its official journal by the National Union of Elementary Teachers in April 1872. The year before, George Collins and T. E. Heller, both members of its Standing Committee, had concluded that without press coverage the new Union was handicapped and comparatively inarticulate. Reports in the press on educational matters appeared haphazardly. Out of their slender salaries they therefore raised capital of £500 and in October 1871 set up the Educational Newspaper Company, allotting some of the shares not for cash, but as payment in advance for journalistic or other work. With William Binns they began to publish the *Schoolmaster* on 6 January 1872 from offices at No. 14, Red Lion Court, off Fleet Street.[2] Gilbert Christian, who became a reporter for the journal in 1878 and a member of its editorial council in 1891, described the premises in his memoirs as a ricketty old place more suited for a tripe shop. No teacher connected with the new publication received a single penny for his services during the first year or so of its existence, but soon, perhaps as a result of this initial sacrifice, it achieved a conspicuous commercial success.[3]

The first edition consisted of twenty pages and cost one penny. With the appointment of Heller as Secretary of the Union in 1873, editorial policy was placed in the hands of Collins, John Russell, who had been the correspondent of the Ayrshire Observer in London at the time of the Great Exhibition and was now headmaster of the Presbyterian School (known as 'the Scotch School') at Woolwich, and J. W. Grove, who had been headmaster of All Souls' Boys' School, Langham Place since 1865. As news and advertising expanded, the journal was permanently enlarged to thirty-two pages in October 1884. But between April 1891 and January 1892, Collins (who had just become President of the Union), Russell and Grove all died. The directors decided to appoint a sole editor and their choice fell on Macnamara.[4]

He was young, capable and full of enterprise, Christian recalled, and with the aid of the shrewd and capable manager, William Shellard Latham, he made things hum. The Company also published the *Teachers' Aid* ('The Working Teacher's Indispensable Companion') founded in 1885; this too was his responsibility. In September 1893, exploiting printers' new skills with illustrations, he added a new magazine intended for children at school entitled the *Scholars' Own* ('The Favourite School Newspaper and Children's Delight').[5] But it was the *Schoolmaster* with its important topical element which provided the pivot of his activities. The timetable of work suited him. The *Schoolmaster* was published on Fridays. He was then available for his Union commitments.

As soon as he arrived in London, Macnamara assembled a complete set of the Blue Books on education published since 1839.[6] With this collection, kept up to date by the addition of every new code, circular, report and bill, he established his reputation as an expert. Whilst the *School Board Chronicle* of the 1890s, essential reading though it was for school board members, was known to be dull, the *Schoolmaster* under Macnamara's editorship was entertaining as well as accurate. He and his colleagues energetically attacked administrators and managers who displayed what he was fond of describing as a 'pettifogging' and 'shabby' spirit. In May 1892 a brief article appeared under the title 'Exchanging a Teacher for a Drainpipe'. At the board school in Crondall, Hampshire, there were 224 children. It was, however, staffed for 260. The Chairman concluded that the school could do with one teacher less and by this means save a little money towards paying for the new drains. One board member protested; then, Macnamara commented:

> ... comes in one of those delightful sentiments so delightfully worded which make Arcadia and its school board members a joy forever. It fell from the lips of a Mr Britton. Here it is in all its delicacy of touch: 'I'll undertake that the efficiency of the school does not come down. If it does somebody will have to shift'. When alas, when, will the country 'shift' out of the educational arena men like this?[7]

Under 'Items and News' in September 1893, the *Schoolmaster* provided an alarming account of the Board election at Roydon, near Diss. It had resulted in a serious riot:

> The effigy of one candidate would have been burned with the usual circumstance attending this time-honoured custom, but the police interfered, so the effigy was instead torn limb from limb. Windows were smashed and the police, trying to prevent further damage, came into collision with the disturbers, and after receiving several volleys of stones, were compelled to charge the crowd, several

persons being injured. The police received serious injuries from stones, several cutting completely through their helmets, and inflicting severe wounds. One policeman sustained a severe injury to his spine. The disturbance was not quelled until after midnight. Of course, police-court proceedings followed, and in the evidence of one constable we read that, after the declaration of the poll, he went to the window of the inn, and saw an effigy in a chair, and a room full of men, who were shouting, halloaing, singing and drinking. He afterwards went into the house, and, looking into the doorway, saw one man slapping the effigy on the side of the head. Mr Anness, who was there, said 'Let the ____ have it'.[8]

At the Dreghorn School Board in the summer of 1898 a proposal to install a bath in the teacher's house was made. 'Would any sensible person ask to get water introduced into a teacher's house when there is a tap not ten yards from the door?', the Chairman was asked by a Scottish member named Hunter, who added that a bath could be had in the sea: teachers had plenty of time on their hands, especially on Saturdays. Another added that teachers could bathe as much during the holidays as would do them all year.[9] The artless observations of a complacent upper class provided another source of anecdote. In June 1896 under 'An Honourable's Opinion' it was reported that the Hon. H. B. T. Strangways, of the Bridgwater Rural District Council, had declared himself no enemy of education, but, he said, he found difficulty in getting labourers who could go and lay a hedge and do a ditch properly. He was therefore strongly in favour of putting a veto on the School Board rate. He also expressed the view that schoolmasters were overpaid:

> It did not require more natural ability or more natural intelligence to make a good schoolmaster than it did to make a good mechanic (Hear, hear). Each had to learn his trade, but the schoolmasters were paid by the State for learning their trade, whilst the artisan and mechanic were not. What was the comparative work that they did? Country schoolmasters, as a rule, had to work for five hours a day five days a week, and they got from six weeks to two months' complete holiday during the year. That was not a bad billet in his opinion.

'We apologise to our readers', the *Schoolmaster* commented in Macnamara's unmistakable tones, 'for troubling them with the Hon H. B. T. Strangways' opinions, but it is just as well that the working-men of this land should understand the quarter from which arises such opposition to the extension of their children's education.'[10]

At a meeting of the Executive in March 1893, a year after he had taken up his post on the *Schoolmaster*, Charles Bowden, the Union Vice-President, moved that the best thanks of the Executive be given to Macnamara for his able services to the Union as Editor. The paper had become vastly more interesting in his hands and was now taken and read where it was never seen before, he said. The resolution, seconded by Mrs Burgwin, was cordially adopted. Macnamara, in reply, said he had succeeded distinguished and capable men; his aim was to make a living commission week by week into the difficulties which beset teachers of all ranks and hindered the work of national education.[11] A further compliment arrived obliquely in a letter published the following month in favour of women inspectors, which referred to the new editor as a man of candour and capability who had made the *Schoolmaster* pleasant reading for schoolmistresses.[12]

The year 1892 was a promising one for an editor of an educational journal. The Conservative government, already in power for over five years, was beginning to prepare for a general election which could not be held any later than 1893. The Liberals, recovering from the defection of Joseph Chamberlain, Lord Hartington (now the Duke of Devonshire) and their followers over Irish Home Rule, seemed likely to offer a formidable challenge. Leading figures in both parties were taking up national education as a major issue. This was a very recent development. Until the 1880s few ministers had pursued educational objectives with enthusiasm. When Lord John Russell, one of the few exceptions, had tried to set up a Ministry for Education in 1839, he had been obliged to resort to Orders in Council and settle for the establishment of the much less significant Committee of Council to avoid House of Commons hostility. In the 1840s, Lords President of the Council began to establish a tradition of inertia in educational matters (which Kay-Shuttleworth had exploited to camouflage his innovations). Robert Lowe, Vice-President of the Committee between 1859 and 1864, became notorious for his determination to reduce expenditure through Payment by Results, under the 1862 Revised Code.[13] Even W. E. Forster, when, in February 1870, he spoke of filling the gaps, also expressed the hope that this might be achieved 'sparing the public money where it can be done without'.[14] When at last an educational enthusiast, A. J. Mundella, was appointed Vice-President in 1880, he found his plans for reform thwarted by an economy drive directed by Kay-Shuttleworth's successor Ralph Lingen who, after twenty years administering education, had transferred to the Treasury.[15]

Now attitudes were changing. Mundella had brought about the appointment of a Royal Commission on Technical Instruction (the Samuelson Commission) which, in 1884, made a strong case for government intervention in the provision of both technical and secondary education. Public interest was maintained by the commissioners through the National Association for the Promotion of Technical Education, a pressure group founded in 1887, consisting of the Liberal peers Granville, Ripon, Rosebery and Spencer; Dr Temple, now Bishop of London; the MPs Henry Broadhurst, Sir John Lubbock, Mundella, Lyon Playfair, Bernhard Samuelson, James Stuart and Sir Richard Temple and the scientists T. H. Huxley and John Tyndall, with two further MPs, Arthur Acland and Sir Henry Roscoe, as joint secretaries.[16] It finally secured the passage of an act to establish technical instruction in 1889, through the County authorities created the previous year. Then at the beginning of 1886, the Conservatives, realising that voluntary schools, in comparison with the schools run by the larger boards, were under-financed, had set up the Royal Commission on the Elementary Education Acts (the Cross Commission). Intended by its sponsors to make out a case for increasing financial aid to voluntary schools, it failed to reach unanimous conclusions, but its Majority Report concluded that it did not seem just or expedient to allow the voluntary system to be gradually destroyed by the competition of board schools with unlimited resources at their command.[17] The detail that the commissioners elicited and the debate that emerged through the publication of the Majority and Minority reports had the advantageous effect of establishing that country-wide school provision was one of the duties of government and not merely an expensive innovation introduced by the Liberals. In Macnamara's view the change was guaranteed by the appointments of Sir William Hart Dyke as Vice-President of the Committee of Council in 1887 and of George Kekewich as Permanent Secretary to the Education Department three years later.[18] A whole range of issues began to be discussed and acted upon: as the *Schoolmaster* put it in March 1894: 'out of the gloom of the long night of Distrust and Dissatisfaction began to dawn the day of Confidence and Cheerful Service'.[19] Teachers and their Union representatives began to regard their problems as soluble; their future as promising. The Cross Commission had taken evidence from over thirty teachers in public elementary schools, both board and voluntary, and it showed itself genuinely concerned about their day-to-day experiences. The Majority Report expressed the view that the system of Payment by Results was carried too far, was too rigidly applied and that it ought to be modified and relaxed in the interests equally of scholars, of teachers and of education itself. The First Minority Report referred to it as a far from satisfactory method of securing efficiency; the Second, whilst recognising the difficulties for the Education Department of relating expenditure to efficiency, described its effects as injurious. Heller (the NUET Secretary) and his colleague Dr Dale added a note in which they observed that it led to the degradation of teaching.[20] In the next year or so Lord Cranbrook (the Lord President), Hart Dyke and Kekewich began the process of dismantling it, placing emphasis on establishing more cheerful, innovatory schools.[21] Relations between the Education Department and the National Union of Teachers became warmer. At the Annual Conference in Cardiff 1891, Hart Dyke was the guest of honour at the dinner held at the Royal Hotel and was received with cheers. He refused to receive a local deputation of Inspectors, saying that he had come to Cardiff for the sole purpose of showing his friendship for the Union and the profession.[22]

Parliament was dissolved on 29 June 1892; from the election the Liberals emerged with 273 seats, their allies the Irish Nationalists and Labour gaining eighty and two respectively. They thus had a majority of forty over the 269 Conservatives and forty-six Liberal Unionists. Lord Salisbury's government lingered till Parliament met on 11 August when it was defeated on a vote of no confidence. On the Vice-President of the Committee of Council's departure Richard Waddington wrote in the *Practical Teacher*: 'Whig, Tory, Unionist, Radical, Conservative and Liberal pedagogues regret to lose you'.[23] The *Schoolmaster* agreed: 'no Vice-President, in recent years at any rate, did so much in so short a time to put the cause of Popular Education on a really rational and healthy basis as Sir William Hart Dyke'.[24]

His successor was Arthur Acland, whom Hart Dyke had described in 1889 as 'a bitter little Rad, but still an ardent educationist'.[25] The second son of Sir Thomas Acland, who had long been a great friend of Gladstone, he had renounced holy orders on the news that Mundella had been appointed Vice-President of the Committee of Council in 1880; in 1885 he had become MP for Rotherham; five years later he had been instrumental in securing the allocation of the so-called whisky money for the promotion of technical education under the Technical Instruction Act. He had recently been a member of the Select Committee on Superannuation; the *Schoolmaster* quoted approvingly his comment to the joint education committee of Wales and Monmouthshire (of which he was Chairman) that the sooner some scheme was found for all young teachers appointed in elementary schools the better, and concluded that not only educationists, but politicians, and especially Radical politicians, would hail his appointment with delight.[26] Because the Lord President (Lord Kimberley) was also Secretary for India, Acland was to be in sole control of educational matters. He was given a seat in the Cabinet, an honour bestowed on only two of his predecessors;[27] also, perhaps, a move on Gladstone's part to avoid (after abortive House of Commons investigations in 1865 and 1883) the issue of whether a single Education Minister was needed.

Macnamara was always keen for a scoop, so on 16 August, when the appointment became official, Christian called at Acland's Chelsea home for an interview. The article in the *Schoolmaster* that resulted was, however, as Christian later admitted, an example of spinning *multum ex parvo*.[28] Acland declared that since the educational policy of the new Government had not been discussed, he was not to be drawn on any of the educational issues of the day. Having secured a portrait of the new Vice-President, which was duly published on 3 September, Christian found his way back to the station impressed, gratified, yet none the wiser. With Parliament having been prorogued for six months on the formation of the new administration, Acland left England almost immediately for a holiday which lasted until the middle of October.[29]

Once he took up his duties, the new Vice-President proved to be gratifyingly energetic. He was determined to make further progress on school attendance legislation. In the early 1890s the efforts of teachers were still being hampered by pupil absenteeism. It not only affected classroom practice, because the size of Parliamentary grant to a school was influenced by it; the supply of equipment and even the provision of teachers was affected. Compulsory attendance at public elementary schools for children aged between five and thirteen had been advocated by W. E. Forster as he introduced his Bill of 1870.[30] Insufficient schools had made compulsion impracticable; also a number of HM Inspectors expressed the view that school attendance was best achieved by legislation levelled at employers rather than parents. Mundella, at a meeting of the National Education League in October 1869, took the opposite view:

> to neglect a child until he is eight, nine or ten years of age and then, when he first commences work, to insist on his going to school is the most objectionable and unreasonable form of compulsion I think it is possible for the human mind to devise.[31]

In its final form Forster's Act permitted boards to require parents of children of such age, not less than five nor more than thirteen as might be fixed by bye-laws, to cause them to attend schools.[32] Sandon's Act of 1876 extended the obligation to voluntary schools by means of school attendance committees. Mundella, when he became Vice-President of the Committee of Council in 1880, immediately piloted through a Bill which established the principle of compulsion on a national scale, but the results were disappointing. Heller, representing the NUET, told the International Conference on Education held in London in the summer of 1884 that only 58 per cent of the children aged between five and ten for whom the Act had been passed were in regular attendance.[33] Four years later, as a member of the Cross Commission, Heller dissociated himself from the complacent observations of the Majority Report on what had been achieved since 1870:

> the vast increase in the school population receiving regular instruction ... is ... most satisfactory ... the absence of any serious opposition on the part of the wage-earning classes to compulsion, not withstanding its grave interference with their homes, is largely owing to the gradual steps by which it has been introduced ... accordingly we cannot endorse any general condemnation of the manner in which compulsion has hitherto been administered.[34]

This, too, was not an approach that the Indefatigables within the Union could countenance. At the Annual Conference of 1892 held in Leeds, Yoxall, soon to be Heller's successor as Union Secretary, took up the issue in his presidential address. From the Education Department's own figures, he said, it could be seen that 5,800,000 children should have been in attendance in the previous year at public elementary schools. The actual number was 3,700,000. Hence there were 1,000,000 children of the poorer classes who never entered the public elementary school at all; and of those who ever entered, 1,100,000 were absent every day.[35] Macnamara followed this up with a specially prepared paper on the subject. Emphasising again the figures that Yoxall had provided, he commented:

> So far ... from having succeeded in filling each school place with the child for

whom it was designed, the existing state of the facts twenty-one years after Mr Forster's project was launched may thus be put in brief: 'Of every three of the children whose names should be on the rolls of the elementary schools, the registers show the names of two only; and of every four of the children actually enrolled, one is always away'.

He blamed, in the first place, the magistracy. Some parents 'long ago found out that the machinery of compulsion is cumbrously slow in movement, erratic in incidence and ludicrously inadequate in effect. They therefore break the law and chance the result.' Next he cited the ineffectiveness of many of the rural school boards and school attendance committees. Usually they were made up of farmers and others who were far more interested in obtaining cheap child labour than in education. Some of them did not bother to appoint an attendance officer to check up on irregular attendance in their district. Finally, however, he held the Education Department responsible. The Department, he pointed out, was invested with executive powers under the Acts of 1870 and 1876; it could declare Local Authorities failing to administer their own bye-laws in default. But, he said, 'it is possible to count on the fingers of one hand the cases in which such powers have been exercised for failure to perform the particular duty under reference'. The Department had in effect washed its hands of the question of school attendance.[36]

When, under the new Liberal government, raising the school leaving age from ten to eleven was treated as a priority, Macnamara took the opportunity to point out the difference between passing laws and applying them. In the *Schoolmaster* he drew attention to the *Rotherham Advertiser*, published in Acland's constituency. The teachers of the town had complained that there were children of school age 'who attended no school, and cases were not rare of children from seven to twelve years old being entered on a school register for the first time'. Various excuses were sent to explain non-attendance: 'minding house', 'looking after baby', 'fetching water for mother to wash', 'gone for medicine' (sometimes identical with a visit to the pawnbroker's) or working for a farmer. 'Our farmers are a constant source of hindrance to our schools and scholars', the teachers commented:

> Scholars are useful at all seasons, even in winter. Who can take a cow to market as cheaply as a schoolboy? The schoolboy drives the drill, he sets the potatoes, he and the schoolgirl single the turnips and swedes, he turns and leads the hay, he makes bands for the reapers (but for this the school holidays are fixed) and after the holidays he picks potatoes. One school is half emptied at times by farmers at potato-picking season. Any children will suit these offenders, who think not of the strain upon boys under ten years and upon girls of poor physique ...

Macnamara added: 'There is nothing new in all this. It has long since passed into an accepted state of things that attendance became supremely optional in practice from the day that it became compulsory in theory.'[37]

Acland's new Act was to come into effect on 1 January 1894. On Saturday 16 December 1893 the *Schoolmaster* reported that the Union had sent a strong deputation, bristling with appalling facts and figures, to the Education Department, to point out the limitations of the new legislation: '... as the miserable tale was unfolded both Messrs Acland and Kekewich listened with the air of men who fully appreciate the gravity of the situation, but feel little better than helpless materially to improve matters'. The Department had issued a circular concerning the new Act. Copies of this had been sent to HMIs together with a memorandum urging them to communicate any infringements to the Department. The *Schoolmaster* concluded:

> We sincerely hope that, in the interests of the children, HM Inspectors will speak out plainly and courageously in response to this invitation, for it is an open secret, with which all of them who work in the Rural districts are intimately acquainted, that wholesale infractions of the Bye-Laws are taking place under their very noses every day of the week.[38]

Children above the age of ten (beyond which Mundella's 1880 Act had not reached) could claim exemption from bye-laws and go out to work. On 25 July 1891 Richard Waddington was giving evidence to the Royal Commission on Labour. 'A child may work full-time when he reaches thirteen if he has passed Standard IV?', Mundella, the Chairman, asked. 'Yes', Waddington replied:

> '... under the Factory Act, but under the Education Act he may work full-time at any place not under the Factory Act after he has passed the local exemption standard which in some cases is lower than Standard IV ... A large proportion of children will attain Standard IV at ten years of age comfortably'.
> 'And clever children will attain it sometimes before?'
> 'Very much before'.
> 'So that if a boy or a girl is a promising child, the earlier he or she attains the Standard the sooner he or she is exempt from attending school?'
> 'That is so'.[39]

What Waddington (now Headmaster of St James' National School, Bolton) was particularly concerned about was the practice of half-time education. Quoting from the official returns, he described how in Lancashire two thirds of the children between ten and thirteen were working half the day in the mills under the Factory Act, or in workshops, or in some other employment under the Education Act, and attending school in the other half. Mundella enquired about the effects on their physical condition. 'In the afternoon, when the children have been working in the morning, we find very often that they are drowsy, very sleepy, their receptive power is impaired', Waddington replied. 'You may use all your powers as a teacher and you will find that some of the very best of them are gradually dozing off, especially in this warm weather.'[40]

Two months before, in an article in the *Practical Teacher* entitled 'The Half-Timer – Hard Swearing Somewhere', Macnamara described how Henry Matthews, the Conservative Home Secretary, had recently introduced a government Bill to amend the Factory Act of 1878. In 1888, the Cross Commission Majority Report recommended that the minimum age for half-time exemption should be raised from ten to eleven and that the minimum age of full-time exemption should be thirteen. At the Berlin International Congress of 1890, Great Britain, along with all the other participants, had undertaken to end the half-time system once and for all. But Matthews maintained that half-timers were sharper and more intelligent than full-time scholars, and that they made equal progress. In a parallel column Macnamara quoted Hart Dyke, who had made clear that half-timers lagged behind. Their health, the Home Secretary said, introducing the Bill, was as good as those who spent their whole time in school. Again, Macnamara showed how Dr Torrop, Factory Surgeon of Heywood, Lancashire, took the opposite view: 'the healthy, bright child of ten degenerates into the sallow weakling of thirteen and the deterioration of our industrial population, especially in mills, has become a real source of danger to the nation'. Matthews justified the system as a combination of technical education with scholastic or literary education. Macnamara quoted Mundella: 'the idea that a child of ten obtains technical education by being driven to the mill as a half-timer is one of the most preposterous fallacies ever trotted out by an interested class to hoodwink the community'. He ended by expressing the hope that the Government would think again before the Third Reading was reached.[41] It did so, excluding children below the age of eleven from factories.[42] They could still, however, leave school and secure employment elsewhere.

When the Conservatives' Factory Bill of 1891 was being debated, the Home Secretary had been severely criticised by leading Liberals, among them John Morley and Mundella, for not redeeming the pledge given at the Berlin Conference of 1890 to raise the age limit of child labour to twelve. In May 1894 the Liberal government introduced a new Factory Bill in the House of Commons. 'Today, three years later', the *Schoolmaster* commented:

> with Mr John Morley and Mr Mundella in the Cabinet, a Factory Bill is introduced which leaves the age a year behind the Berlin pledge, and two or three years behind most of the great nations of Europe. We hope the stifling atmosphere of the Ministerial Benches has not erased from Mr Mundella's memory the words he used in the debate of 1891, when he said, 'What did the doctors think about the condition of these children? They said their state of health was such that they were a weak, debilitated and stunted race, nervous and highly strung'. Since 1891 the Royal Commission on Labour, and the

Report of the Departmental Committee, have strengthened the case for the children. Is their cry to go unheeded because parties have changed sides in the House?[43]

The following February, with another Factory Bill in preparation, the *Schoolmaster* presented its readers with a special ten-page report on the half-timer.[44] Germany, France and Switzerland, the accompanying editorial commented, had redeemed the promise made in 1890 in Berlin. England still lagged behind. Nevertheless, it was too easy to blame the Government. 'The poor widow will once more be depicted as trudging off to the workhouse because of the withdrawal of the earnings of her eleven year old child', it observed. 'If poverty is at the root of the half-time system, Lancashire must be the poorest county in England.' An account was included of how the previous week the Textile Operatives' Hall in Bury was thrown open to the public so that the new £150 Bechstein drawing-room grand pianoforte could be admired. 'Which side will the Textile Operatives take?', it enquired: 'In 1875 they opposed the raising of the age from eight. In 1891 they strenuously opposed raising the age to eleven. And in 1894 we find them once more barring the progress of the nation, for at a meeting in Manchester they have decided that the proposed reform is uncalled for.'[45]

At the NUT Executive meeting on 7 March, Macnamara referred to the Commons debate on child labour the previous evening with satisfaction. As usual, he said, Matthews, the former Home Secretary, had been on the wrong side but Asquith, his successor, had agreed that the minimum half-time age should be twelve. He moved

> that the Executive note with extreme pleasure the sympathetic attitude of the Home Secretary and several other speakers on the question of raising the age from eleven to twelve, for child labour in factories and workshops, discussed on the First Reading of the 'Factory Acts Amendment Bill'. In view of the admitted need of this reform, and in the interests of the physical, moral and educational well-being of the children, the Executive earnestly ask all friends of the children to support amendments to the Bill which propose to raise the minimum age.

Waddington, who had been elected to the Executive in 1892, seconded the motion. He observed that the one remnant of the party which used to eulogise to the skies the system which turned children into school on one half of the day and into the mill the other was Mr Hanbury, who still argued that a valuable technical education was obtained within the factory wall, adding, however, 'that he expected to be laughed at'. His expectations, Waddington added, had been realised. The resolution was adopted unanimously.[46]

At the Annual Conference at Manchester in April, Waddington pleaded for the complete abolition of the school and factory conditions militating against the physical, moral and intellectual welfare of children. The Mayor of Bacup, a town in which half-timers were numerous, had recently asserted that the factory was not only a useful source of technical education but 'a very palace of delight'. Macnamara, supporting Waddington, suggested that the Mayor probably took very good care not to subject his own child to the 'peculiar pleasures' of the monstrosity he delighted to praise. He concluded with a strong appeal for the emancipation of the young factory worker.[47]

The Second Reading of the Factory Bill began on 22 April. Though the *Schoolmaster* affirmed that everything seemed to be going well for the raising of the age of the half-timer, it emerged that the Government had made no specific provision for it, merely promising that if a proposal were made during the debate, it would not be opposed. Asquith told a deputation of Master and Operative Cotton Spinners that he himself desired it, but if a movement in this direction should jeopardise the Bill then, because of the many other beneficent reforms it would secure, the matter would have to be postponed. In May, the Executive was still hopeful. At a meeting organised by the Lambeth Teachers' Association, John Burns (MP for Battersea) commented that the country had been flooded with facts about what he called the half-time iniquity through the efforts of Macnamara and the *Schoolmaster*. If every father who had a half-timer at work would put by one-tenth of the money he spent on beer, betting and upon football, he went on, he would be able to keep his child at school not only until he was thirteen years of age but fifteen: if all the child workers were turned into the schools or into the county council playground, twenty-five per cent of men and women at present unemployed would be able to find work.[48]

Macnamara maintained the pressure. At the beginning of June he described the problem in the *Westminster Gazette*:

> And inside the mill do they learn a trade? Are their fingers trained to nimbleness? Nothing of the sort. They are little *scavengers*. They run and carry and brush and dust and oil … At meal times they are packed off to fetch hot water, tea and the like for adult workers … What strikes me as most pitiable about the whole business is not the technical education and 'happy as young chickens' arguments of those who want to retain juvenile factory labour *because it is cheap* – one expects these things. *I* am most disheartened at the selfish and short sighted policy of a section of the operatives themselves, who do not seem to see that the employment of the children is in a considerable measure responsible for their own unemployment.[49]

Later in the month the defeat of the Rosebery ministry made it necessary for ministers to act quickly to salvage outstanding legislation. When the amendments to the Factory Bill as it stood had been cleared, Asquith begged that all further suggestions might be withdrawn. The *Schoolmaster* reported that the half-timer's chance was gone: 'either the half-timer or the Whole Bill had to go by the board, and we confess the alternative offered, if the claims of the half-timer were pressed, was one no person with the vestige of a thought for the toilers in factory and workshop dared entertain with unconcern'. Burns had announced that he intended to bring in a bill in the next session dealing with the whole question of juvenile labour.[50] Unfortunately, however, the prospects of the private member as an initiator of legislation were poor. All the efforts of the half-time movement, both in and out of Parliament, had, apparently, come to nothing.

Twelve years later Waddington was still campaigning against what he called the baneful effect of the wretched half-time system. 'All the steps which have been taken in the past thirty years by which the age has been raised from eight to twelve have been opposed by the textile workers', the *Schoolmaster* reported in August 1908 when, at last, a new feeling seemed to be emerging at the United Textile Workers' Association.[51] The *Report of the Inter-Departmental Committee on Partial Exemption from School Attendance* (published a year later) still concluded, however, that the main obstacle to the disappearance of half-time was the custom of the textile districts. 'The children themselves like going to the mills', it asserted:

> At first at any rate, they enjoy the sense of becoming grown-up and independent, and of having money to spend. We were not surprised to hear of a case where out of 300 children questioned only seven replied that they would have preferred not to have gone to the mill. The regrets come later, when the young person of eighteen or twenty begins to miss the schooling that might have led to a better position in life and better wages in the long run.[52]

Already, before the Cross Commission was appointed, Lord Salisbury had perceived that compulsory school attendance made the introduction of free education unavoidable. Even though the Majority Report expressed the view that the existing system should not be altered,[53] Salisbury pressed ahead, both to secure the financial position of poorer voluntary schools and to attract working-class voters. The Fees Act took effect on 1 September 1891 and provided subject matter for Macnamara's first ventures into national journalism. Managers of public elementary schools might accept or reject the fee grant (ten shillings per year for each child aged between three and fifteen) though a refusal to accept it, when the Act came into force, did not bar those who were suspicious of the conditions that might be attached from accepting it at a later date. 'The line of cleavage between the parties will not be over the principle of free education', Macnamara pointed out in *Macmillan's Magazine*: 'that is already conceded. The fight will, of course, be over the character of the management of the schools; over the extent to which Education should be assisted; and possibly over the source from which the compensating fund should be drawn.'[54]

Acland's task was the interpretation and application of the Act. As Macnamara had foretold, difficulties arose. In November 1892, the Vice-President received a deputation from Liverpool led by two local MPs who informed him that, in their opinion, the School Board was administering the Act in a dilatory and unsatisfactory way. Parents who wished to avail themselves of the benefits of the Act had been marked down as paupers. Managers who wished to implement it were being threatened with dismissal. Acland responded that the example of the London School Board, which had decided to free all its schools, was the one that he had in mind.[55] Section Five of the Act had allowed parents to petition the Education Department about deficiencies in free places. The Vice-President encouraged this process, even inviting parents to write to him personally. Boards which supplied too few free places could be declared in default. Where free places were not made available in voluntary schools a board would be established, threatening their future.[56] 'Sir William Hart Dyke's beautifully simple Act of 1891 is still calling for no end of rulings and decisions', Macnamara commented on 18 March 1893. A Memorandum had been published on 6 March to clarify the position. It concluded that the law did not give parents a right to free education at the school which their children were attending, if that school had a right to charge fees, but it did give them a right to demand free education for their children at some school which was free, or which provided free places, and which was within a convenient distance from their homes.[57] A further Memorandum followed in May. It stated again that all parents in England and Wales had a right to free education for their children between the age of three and fifteen and provided instructions how it might be claimed. No charge was to be made for books, slates, or anything else.[58] Asked by Sir Richard Temple in the House of Commons on 12 June whether he intended to press for the extinction of all school fees, Acland replied that there was no intention on the part of the Department to deviate from the strict administration of the Act of 1891.[59]

In June 1895, in what proved to be the last weeks of the Liberal government, the *Schoolmaster* examined what had been achieved by free education. Thirty-four out of every forty scholars in public elementary schools now paid no fees. Of the remaining six at least three paid only a penny a week or less. Free education had brought about an increase of nearly 240,000 on the roll, and an addition of close on 350,000 to the average attendance since 1891. The percentage of scholars over ten had only slightly increased, but some 185,970 older children had been retained over the last three years.[60]

As Payment by Results gradually disappeared, other injustices derived from Robert Lowe's administration began to be discussed. The system by which appointments were made to Her Majesty's Inspectorate particularly annoyed teachers. HM Inspectors, appointed since 1839, formed a caste drawn from Oxford and Cambridge graduates who had been to one of the so-called great public schools. The Royal Commission of 1858–61, enquiring into Popular Education, had picked up teachers' resentment at their exclusion. The Commissioners, however, considered it justified:

As to the specific complaint that they are not made inspectors, we think that they would not be fit for the office. It is absolutely necessary that the inspectors should be fitted, by previous training and social position, to communicate and associate upon terms of equality with the managers of schools and the clergy of different denominations. It is one of the alleged grievances of the school-masters that these persons do not recognise them as social equals; and that state of things, with which no public authority can interfere, is itself conclusive against the suggestion that they should be made inspectors.[61]

Two years later the creation of the post of Assistant enabled HMI to draw on the knowledge and expertise of ex-teachers, whilst maintaining them in a position of inferiority.[62]

In the 1870s the issue of promotion resurfaced, this time in Parliament. Mundella pointed out in 1878 that in England, good men were always offered the prizes of every profession. He was unable to see why this should be the rule in the Army, at the Bar, and in the Church, and not in the profession of teaching.[63] Once in office he was instrumental in the creation of a new category of Sub-Inspectors, drawn like the Assistants from elementary teachers.[64] Apparently he had intended that promotion might follow. The Cross Commission Majority Report noted that there had been so far no instance of this and concluded: 'while the public service requires inspectors to be men of wide and liberal training, it is neither fair nor wise to prevent elementary teachers from rising to the rank of inspectors'. The First Minority Report argued more firmly. Its signatories stressed that all ranks of the inspectorate should be thrown open to elementary teachers, adding that it was also important for inspectors to have had practical experience as teachers.[65]

Yoxall, in his presidential address to the NUT Conference in April 1892, renewed the attack on the Inspectorate:

taken as a whole Her Majesty's Inspectors of Schools are not the practical, sympathetic, enlightened, just and successful school-tasters that they should be ... English education suffers, the teachers suffer and the children suffer most of all ... Why should the School Inspector come from a class and from surroundings foreign to the inhabitants and occupations of the public elementary school?

After a period during which no appointments had been made, 'three Varsity men, two of them without any experience of the work of public elementary schools, and the third without any adequate experience, have been appointed to examine and inspect such schools, and to report on the skill of teachers whose lives from boyhood or girlhood have been devoted to the work. The appointments are lamentable ...'[66] The fact that the third new appointment had taught in board schools for two-and-a-half years, first in Oxford, then in Bow, could well have been regarded by Lord Cranbrook and Kekewich, who selected him, as something likely to placate or even please the Union.[67] If so, they were mistaken. Yoxall made clear what the Union wanted. It was that in future all Inspectors should be drawn from two sources; partly from the Sub-Inspectors and Inspectors' Assistants now in the service, 'partly from the best, most experienced, most cultured, sympathetic, and estimable teachers in public elementary schools'.[68]

In January 1893 the *Schoolmaster*, under the headline 'From the Ranks – At last', triumphantly announced that, as his first appointed Inspector, Acland had selected Mr Wilkinson Northrop, a former elementary school headmaster, who had served twenty years as an Inspector's Assistant and nine years as a Sub-Inspector.[69] A gap had appeared in the charmed circle, 'and the sky has not fallen, the powers of darkness have not seized upon the schools, and up to the hour of publishing we have not heard that ruin has crashed upon the fabric of the educational system of England and Wales'.[70] Unfortunately a second appointment was of the traditional type. 'Cannot even Mr Acland, educationist and democrat that he is, get rid of the prejudices of caste in a matter such as this?', a further article demanded. The place the new HMI (P. A. Barnett, late Principal of Borough Road College) filled

> ... should have been occupied by a certificated teacher, by right of the special qualifications possessed for it by many such teachers, by reason of the recommendation of the Royal Commission, and by consent of the Press and members of Parliament – who represent a public opinion on the subject which is almost unanimous in support of the teachers' claim.[71]

At the February meeting of the NUT Executive, Macnamara, seconded by Waddington, successfully moved a resolution that

> whilst congratulating Mr Acland upon the selection of so eminently capable and experienced an educationist as HM Sub-Inspector Mr Wilkinson Northrop, for the post of Inspector of Schools, this Executive begs respectfully to express its regret that the first appointment has not been followed by the promotion, direct from the teaching ranks, of one of the many distinguished and long-tried experts at present at work as primary teachers – such promotion being distinctly recommended by the recent Education Commission. At the same time, this Executive, relying upon Mr Acland's keen desire for the best interests of National Education, begs to express the sincere hope that such a step will be taken by him when next a vacancy in the Inspectorate is at his disposal.[72]

In December, Acland promoted John Foster, another former Sub-Inspector, who had been connected with public elementary schools for twenty-five years, as teacher, headmaster and both Assistant and Sub-Inspector. He had studied at Battersea College then, evidently to the approval of the Vice-President, at Christ's College, Cambridge.[73] But the appointment of L. J. Roberts in February 1894 provoked consternation. Roberts, it was discovered, was only twenty-seven years old. His origins were unexceptionable: he had been a pupil, then a pupil-teacher, at the British School, Aberayron; he had then studied at Lampeter and Oxford before taking up a post at the Grammar School at Lampeter. But he lacked experience as a teacher in the schools that he would inspect.[74] Macnamara and his Union colleagues were incensed. An editorial headed 'Snubbed!' in the *Schoolmaster* on 10 February opened with the observation that 'the scion of a county family, the son of a distinguished baronet, erstwhile Reverend, sometime Don, and now and henceforward Rt Hon, Mr Acland finds it difficult, no doubt, to be as democratic in instinct as in thought, in deed as in word'.[75]

The matter had been discussed at a meeting of the Executive the previous Saturday. Tom John, the Welsh member, found no difficulty in obtaining leave as a matter of urgency to introduce a resolution that 'This Executive record their emphatic protest against the recent appointment to the Inspectorate in Wales, and hereby re-affirm their frequently expressed opinion that it is essential that Inspectors of School should possess extensive practical knowledge of the work of primary schools'. The principle of promotion from the ranks was, he said, as essential amongst teachers as in any other department of life. He had no quarrel with Mr Roberts, who was a splendid Welshman, but his practical experience was insufficient. Moreover, although he would be receiving the full salary of £400 from the first, the work would be done by the Sub-Inspector until such time as Mr Roberts became capable of doing it himself. Macnamara declared that he had stood by Mr Acland zealously on every possible occasion, but he was absolutely disgusted with the appointment. Tom Clancy, a voluntary school headmaster from Portsmouth, declared that if they did not tell Acland that they were disgusted with his conduct, they would be neglecting their duty to their constituents. John's resolution was carried unanimously and, on Macnamara's initiative, it was resolved to send the resolution to Lord Kimberley, Acland, members of the House of Commons, NUT Parliamentary correspondents and the Press.[76]

Nevertheless, when a month later the Rosebery ministry was appointed on the retirement of Gladstone, the *Schoolmaster* admitted that a pretty universal sigh of relief was to be heard that the Vice-President had not been removed:

> We have not, unfortunately, been able on every occasion to agree with Mr Acland's policy. We think he was wrong, pitiably wrong, and lamentably false to his own best instincts, in the appointment of Mr Roberts to the Inspectorate. But we are all very fond of Mr Acland, and all recognise the great zeal and devotion he has brought to the office of director of our common schools.[77]

Reverberations from the Roberts case continued to sound throughout 1894. In May the *Schoolmaster*, with a trenchant editorial entitled 'In a Democratic Administration', apparently written by Macnamara, argued that the social disabilities experienced by teachers as regards the Inspectorate were replicated within the Education Department itself, where Examiners were differentiated from Clerks by social origin and university background and by a considerably higher salary when, in practice, they were doing the same work. 'Put it selfishly if you like', the editorial concluded: 'How can teachers ever hope to secure an open Inspectorate with the patronage system flourishing so prolifically inside Whitehall itself?' [78] A week later the appointment of another former Sub-Inspector was announced.[79] The principle of promotion from the ranks seemed to have gone by default. But support came for the cause from an unexpected source. On the last day of May an address entitled 'The Position and Influence of the Schoolmaster' was given at a meeting of the Teachers' Prayer Union by Dr John Percival, Headmaster of Rugby School and a future Bishop of Hereford. His expressed support for the NUT was made even more welcome by his comments on the Inspectorate which, the *Schoolmaster* suggested, Acland, as a former pupil of Rugby School, might take as a lesson he was not too old to learn. Dr Percival urged:

> There must be in the great army of certificated teachers many individuals of distinguished ability who are both by natural endowment and by self-culture as well fitted to fill those higher and well-remunerated posts in the Education Department as are some of the young men to whom they fall as prizes at the very outset of their working life.[80]

Acland's fifth appointment was carefully chosen. 'We Hail Mr Holman's Elevation with nothing short of delight', the *Schoolmaster* commented at the beginning of July. Henry Holman was a Cambridge graduate, but this time the new Inspector, just under thirty-five years old, had a long career in the education service. He had been a pupil-teacher at Hurstpierpoint National School, won a second class Queen's Scholarship to Battersea College and worked as an assistant in East London, Devonshire, Hampshire and Sussex before studying at Gonville and Caius College, Cambridge. He had then taken up the post of normal master at the University of Aberystwyth in 1892 and advanced to the post of Professor of Education. 'He is one of us', the *Schoolmaster* continued: 'the story of Mr Holman's career should be read over to every pupil-teacher in the land as a genuine incentive to steady labour and as an assurance that an ounce of solid purpose will go further in the long run than much flashy skill or brilliant alertness of intellect.'[81] At the Executive meeting on 7 July Macnamara professed himself delighted with the appointment. But, he said, what the Union should avoid was giving countenance to the impression that an Inspector needed a degree from Oxford or Cambridge. In the year that Holman was at Battersea College there were men better qualified than he was, but because they did not give up teaching and go to one of the older Universities they were unlikely to win promotion.[82]

When Rosebery's government fell in June 1895 the *Schoolmaster* provided a balance sheet of the Vice-President's inspectorial appointments. It was plain that progress had been made. 'Five of them had been certificated teachers, three not. Seven had been university men, one not. Five had worked in an elementary school, three not. Four were promotions of Sub-Inspectors.'[83] The progress that Acland had been prodded into making did not continue. In 1902 the *Schoolmaster*, appraising eighteen new Inspectors, reflected that under Acland's successor patronage and influence had reasserted themselves. The series of appointments culminating in the new list had been nothing short of a public scandal. 'In education as in commerce we support the policy of the open door', it concluded, 'and in the interest alike of professional fairness and public efficiency we claim as a common act of justice that in future appointments the services of the experienced Sub-Inspector and the expert knowledge of the qualified teacher shall be properly recognised.'[84]

Teachers have always been aware of the importance of good school buildings. As boards in large towns began to deal with the problems involved in maximising urban sites for large numbers of pupils, new designs began to emerge, some, like the Spring Grove School, Huddersfield, drawn from abroad. The Cross Reports pointed out that a large number of older schools were structurally below any proper standard of efficiency and concluded that the time had come when the State might 'justly claim for all children that amount of air and space, that suitability of premises, airiness and lightness of site and reasonable extent of playground' which only a minority of boards were providing. Within defective buildings heavy benches and desks which converted into tables were often supplied so that the schoolrooms could be used for parish meetings, tea parties, and other enterprises with the result that 'it is a piteous sight to see ... infants with their legs dangling in the air and children kept for a long time sitting on benches with no back to them'.[85]

By 1892, as Macnamara pointed out in the *Schoolmaster*, little or nothing had been done. Board schools, most of them built since 1870, were mainly sound. The older voluntary schools, however, were being neglected:

> The great bulk of the Inspectors seem to be exceptionally long suffering in their attitude towards the quality of the accommodation offered by many of the older schools to the youngsters attending them ... They find Voluntaryists struggling hard to keep afloat ... They know full well if these managers are pushed hard they will be compelled to relinquish the struggle and give place, in the rural districts at any rate, to that abomination of all abominations, the pettifogging school board ... we should be far from advocating the harsh treatment of those who have done valiant service in the cause of popular education long before the State troubled its head about the matter. Yet here are hard facts to face ... there stand many ... buildings ... their fabric generally old and dilapidated, their floors ancient and uneven, their walls mildewed and damp in winter, their windows and doors badly placed and badly fitted, their apparatus rickety and age worn, and their antiquated apologies for desks perfect tortures to the children who are condemned to sit in them.[86]

Ventilation, lighting, heating and drainage were also of a very low standard.

Most of the examples Macnamara quoted from came from the report for 1891–92 by Scott Coward, HMI for the north western division of England comprising Cumberland, Westmorland, Lancashire and the Isle of Man. He concluded:

> no true friend of the voluntary system will ask sufferance for such things as Mr Scott Coward depicts. There are the National and other societies ... and the Diocesan Boards of Education. These must be appealed to in this matter and must come to the rescue of the older of their schools; for board or voluntary, the least a State which compels its children to undergo a course of educational training can do, is to see that proper schools for that purpose are provided for them.[87]

Conditions in schools preoccupied Acland more than any of his predecessors. In January 1893 he issued his so-called 'Fabric Circular' [88] which laid down that HM Inspectors were to report on the condition and facilities of the schools that they visited. Board schools, none more than twenty-one years old, might well have defects, but the main target was the inadequate buildings in which voluntary schools operated. Acland threatened withdrawal of grants if the terms of the Circular were not met. Lighting, heating and sanitation all needed to be checked. Such detailed investigations created hostility. In the Lords the Marquis of Salisbury complained that it was 'very cruel' to force upon the voluntary schools standards which they could not attain; still more cruel, if the Department did not intend to make them compulsory, to frighten them into the belief that it did.[89] In a letter to the *Standard* signed by 'a Grandmother', an attempt was made to belittle Acland's efforts by sarcastic humour. A few additional questions were suggested:

> (14) Have any black beetles been seen on the premises? (15) Is Pears' soap regularly used in scrubbing the floors? (16) Do any of the chimneys smoke? (17) Is there an ample supply of screens to keep off the draught, if a window should be accidentally broken during school hours? (18) Is Liebig's Extract of Meat administered freely to the pupils whenever they get fagged? (19) Are there plenty of warm water bottles during the winter months? (20) What about comforters for the children's throats? (21) Who is held responsible for the measures to be adopted, if one of them should arrive with damp shoes?

Macnamara reprinted this in the *Schoolmaster*, merely adding, 'This is poorish funning after all, isn't it?' [90]

Not all Voluntaryists opposed the Circular. Dr Temple, Bishop of London since 1885, referred to 'an emergency which has come upon us suddenly in consequence of the demand of the Education Department – a just demand, a righteous demand, I must call it'.[91] The Bishop of Rochester thought it 'fair and right that we should be compelled to meet modern requirements'. The Rev. Arthur Jephson, a member of the London School Board, wrote later that Acland's directions

... were probably the most beneficent plan man ever carried through for the children's sake. I know it put the Church managers to grave inconvenience, myself among the number. We had to raise money and ventilate and enlarge and make suitable old and dilapidated buildings. But the children benefited, and looking back now on the dust and tumult then aroused, one cannot but feel that Mr Acland was right, and untold good was done to the children in our Church schools. I never could be a party to excuse bad drains, on the ground that sound Church teaching was being imparted.[92]

Another urgent issue for Acland's attention was superannuation. When by means of the Minutes of 1846 Kay Shuttleworth had set up his system of teacher training, it was promised that a retiring pension might be granted by the Committee of Council to any schoolmaster or schoolmistress who should be rendered incapable by age or infirmity of continuing to teach a school efficiently. A minimum of fifteen years' satisfactory service needed to be completed, whereupon up to two thirds of the teacher's salary would be paid as a pension. Lowe had brought this arrangement to an end at the same time as he instituted Payment by Results; since then teachers, especially since the creation of the NUET in 1870, had striven for its revival on a nationwide basis. Nothing had been achieved, however, except the establishment of a fund in 1876 from which Vice-Presidents could draw in deserving cases.[93] The Cross Commission had concluded that a superannuation scheme should be established by means of deferred annuities supplemented by the Education Department through Treasury grants.[94] This idea seemed likely to become the basis for future action. When Macnamara took over the *Schoolmaster* a Select Committee of the House of Commons, with Acland as a member, was reaching its conclusions. Macnamara, who had contributed an article on the subject just before his appointment as editor,[95] appeared in his new capacity at a Grand Educational Demonstration, organised by the Lambeth District Association of the NUT at Peckham Public Hall on 14 May 1892. He pointed out that all the Union had been able to wring from successive governments were meagre retirement allowances of between £20 and £30 for 650 teachers. He found that there were twenty-nine masters and twenty-seven mistresses over seventy years of age still at work 'clinging on to their posts with seriously impaired faculties because there was nothing before them but the workhouse'. Only five countries in Europe had failed to establish superannuation schemes: Norway, Sweden, Spain, Turkey and Great Britain. The teachers were not asking the State to superannuate them, but they were asking the State to help them superannuate themselves.[96]

The Committee's Report was published on 27 May. Though several of his Union colleagues had given evidence, Macnamara found it disappointing. In an editorial on 4 June he recalled that two of the greatest arguments in favour of a Superannuation Scheme had been 'in the first place the need for a means of compulsory and honourable retirement for those teachers whose advanced ages make efficient service entirely out of the question, and in the second place, the equally pressing need for the opening up of something like a reasonable flow of promotion for the younger teachers'. The Report did not meet those needs. It brought superannuation one step nearer, but it made clear that the State would not yet pay for a compulsory scheme. 'We would urge teachers', he concluded, 'as a general election may be upon us any day, to study the problem carefully.'[97]

The superannuation issue, checked by the change of government, appeared to be making progress again by the end of 1892. NUT representatives, calling at the Education Department on 3 December, had been assured beforehand of the deep interest and warm sympathy felt both by the Vice-President and the Permanent Secretary. The former, in reply to the deputation, admitted the pressing need for the establishment of a Teachers' Superannuation Fund. He had just completed his first adjudication of pension applications. 'One hundred and thirty-nine aged teachers had come up craving a crumb from the table of the Nation's gratitude', the *Schoolmaster* commented in its editorial, 'and of these eighty-five were sent empty away.' As far as immediate Parliamentary action was concerned, the Treasury was the bugbear. Hence the chances of finding a Superannuation Bill in the immediate government programme were not worth very much.[98] This view was confirmed when on 24 February Sir Richard Temple, who had chaired the Select Committee, introduced a motion to establish a national State-aided system of superannuation for teachers in public elementary schools in England and Wales at an early date. Though the House was unanimously in favour of moving forward, the only occupant of the front benches on either side was Acland.[99]

In May, selection processes were gone through again. The Vice-President considered 155 applications. This time 141 were agreed, the teachers receiving pensions of £20, £25 or £30. The Government decided it needed more information and a Departmental Committee was appointed under the Chairmanship of Kekewich.[100] Its progress was slow. The financial issues had been dealt with by 20 June 1894; the Report was agreed and signed on 28 November, but it was not made public till March 1895. The *Schoolmaster* found it a step in the right direction. Henceforth all certificated teachers recognised under the Minutes of the Education Department, including those certificated before the establishment of the scheme, would qualify for a pension or annuity. Male teachers would contribute £3 per annum, female teachers £2. The Government would contribute to the funds in respect of each future teacher reaching the age of sixty-five whose service amounted to not less than half that teacher's possible service, the sum of ten shillings per annum; the fund for existing teachers receiving for men 10s 3d and for women 10s 2d for each complete year of service at the date of the establishment of the scheme. Auxiliary pensions would be available for those who retired for health reasons before sixty-five.

'Everything', it concluded, 'now rests with the Chancellor of the Exchequer and the Government.'[101]

A special meeting of the NUT Executive took place the same day under the Chairmanship of Gray, the President. It unanimously adopted a resolution, to be forwarded to the Treasury, that the scheme afforded a suitable basis for legislation. Macnamara commented that the scheme was not all it would have been if all their wishes had been met, and he could not forget that an Assistant Inspector received a subsidy of £5 a year for every year of service. He realised that the answer to his objection would be that there was only a small number of Assistant Inspectors and that there were 50,000 certificated teachers, but he considered this argument no answer at all. The best thing about the scheme was the idea of the auxiliary pension, but, he said, it needed a liberal interpretation: when men or women at fifty or sixty years of age could not keep up the pace, and were reported upon as inefficient by the Inspector, the pension should be made available. Like his colleagues he felt it best to accept the scheme as it was, with a view to improving it later.[102]

At the Annual Conference at Manchester in April 1895 Macnamara reminded his colleagues that when superannuation had been debated in the House of Commons in February 1893, Leonard Courtney, the MP for Bodmin, had admitted that a person paying into a retiring fund should be given reasonable security in his office. Reasonable security of tenure was, he said, all they were asking for; they did not for a moment desire to endow inefficiency or to perpetuate incapacity (Applause). What they said was that so long as a teacher was doing good service he should not be liable at any moment to dismissal for altogether extraneous and, very often, scandalously unjust reasons (Cheers). The danger lay, in particular, with one-man managers of voluntary schools or microscopically small school boards. To leave the teacher at the mercy of administrations of this sort was to court tyranny and persecution of the worst type (Hear, hear). In March 1893 Acland, answering for the Education Department over a case in which a Sussex village schoolmaster had been dismissed because he had involved the board in the expense of providing a proper water supply, admitted that the Department had no power to require a teacher's reinstatement. Though the Vice-President had pronounced against setting up the Department as a Court of Appeal, Macnamara said, the Union offered him the simple, fair, and businesslike alternative of an appeal to the Law Court: 'Let teachers have a memorandum of agreement; let there be every possible ground for dismissal included in that memorandum; let teachers have a right to know the grounds of the dismissal; and let them have a claim to go to the Law Courts in extreme cases in order that the reasons for dismissal might be judicially reviewed'.[103]

As for the superannuation issue itself, the Executive's resolution received the Conference's unanimous approval.[104] 'Nothing now remains', the *Schoolmaster* commented on 27 April 1895, 'but for the Chancellor to tell us in his Budget speech of next Thursday night that he has earmarked the trifle necessary in the first year for starting the machinery.'[105] But the Chancellor, Sir William Harcourt, did not do so. Instead, he said that a very considerable expenditure, amounting to between £600,000 and £700,000 a year, was involved and as this was a charge upon posterity, it was all the more necessary that they should most carefully consider the subject.[106] Another three years were to pass before the required legislation was secured.[107]

At Manchester, Macnamara assumed the Vice-Presidency of the Union. The result of the election for the post, announced at the Executive meeting on 2 February, gave him 11,001 votes; his opponents, the veteran C. J. Addiscott and the young Irishman Tom Clancy (both future Presidents) won 1,176 and 1,074 votes respectively. It was a crushing victory. Gray, the outgoing President, congratulated him. The Union, he said, had secured an able, energetic and valuable Vice-President.[108] The last meeting of the old Executive took place on 6 April. Here a vote of thanks was moved to Macnamara by Cyrus Heller for the services he had rendered as editor of the *Schoolmaster*. As members of the Union, they owed much of their present position to the *Schoolmaster*. In the old days they were groping about simply because they had no unity and no means by which they could express their opinions. The vote was seconded by Marshall Jackman, who had been elected to the Executive in 1893. He spoke, he said, both as a personal friend and as a member who recognised the brilliant work the editor of the *Schoolmaster* had done. Macnamara was wholly absorbed in making the paper the very best possible, putting before them the latest information in a form that it was a pleasure to read.[109] After the Conference Macnamara was again singled out for praise, this time by the *Board Teacher*:

> Mr Macnamara (we feel inclined to drop the Mr) is sweeping to the front. His speech at the temperance breakfast was the only lively performance. He was very fine on the tenure problem and now we have him rapiering the half-time system with the zest of a Coeur de Lion and the skill of a Gaston de Marsac.[110]

For over a year another major issue, the provision of a national system of secondary schools, had been occupying the attention of educationists. In March 1883 Lord Norton, formerly (as C. B. Adderley) Vice-President of the Committee of Council in 1858–59, called for the appointment of a Select Committee to enquire into the working of the higher schools being established by the Bradford, Manchester, Leeds and Sheffield School Boards which were extending elementary education for older pupils and placing a scientific emphasis upon it. These institutions, he suspected, would affect the development of independent schools in the cities concerned. Lord Carlingford, the Lord President, correctly credited the previous Conservative administration with the innovation. The higher schools, he said, were greatly approved of on all sides and he quoted reports and letters from Sheffield and Bradford in proof of the excellent, needful and unobjectionable work they were doing. The motion was withdrawn.[111]

The further development of what became known as the Higher Grade Schools was investigated by the Cross Commission. Its Second Minority Report declared that they were an important and necessary element for the completion of the popular schools of the country, but the Majority Report concluded that however desirable they might be, a decision to add them to the system needed to be openly arrived at. Their indirect inclusion in the present system was injurious to both elementary and secondary instruction.[112]

By the 1890s able pupils from Higher Grade Schools were winning scholarships to universities which, in response, began to interest themselves in the development of post-elementary education. Through the efforts of Michael Sadler, then a young graduate active in adult education, a conference was held at Oxford in October 1893 to discuss the issue. It recommended that a Royal Commission be appointed. Acland, who had already, just before the resignation of the Conservatives in 1892, demonstrated his enthusiasm for secondary education by introducing what proved to be an abortive bill designed to create an adequate national provision of these schools,[113] responded with alacrity, perhaps aware that the Liberal government was unlikely to survive for a seven-year term. The commission, under the Chairmanship of James Bryce MP, who had been a member of the previous commission on secondary education (the Taunton Commission of 1864–67), was appointed in March 1894. Though it worked rapidly, it survived the Government.

The NUT was now established as a respectable public body, representative of the majority of teachers in public elementary schools. A breakdown of the Executive membership published in the *Schoolmaster* at the end of the month showed that it was made up of three elements: the Old Guard of the 1870s, Surviving Stalwarts from the 1880s and the Young Bloods of the 1890s, who included Macnamara with four years' service, Waddington with two years and Jackman with one year.[114] Yoxall, the General Secretary, was duly invited to serve on the Bryce Commission alongside (among others) Sir Henry Roscoe MP and Henry Hobhouse MP, both of whom had assisted Acland in presenting his 1892 Secondary Education Bill. The appointment was not universally approved. The *St James's Gazette*, displeased by the absence of representatives of the private school interest, commented: 'the secretary of the remarkably well-organised union of elementary teachers is an excellent official ... But his appointment as a Royal Commissioner on education higher than the most elementary kind is at its best a mere impertinence – at its worst, a low bit of vote-catching pandering'.[115]

Furthermore, Bowden, a former NUT President, and Macnamara, as Chairman of the Technical and Secondary Education Committee of the

Union, were invited to give their views on secondary education to the Commissioners at Westminster Hall on 6 and 11 July 1894. They had been invited to 'consider what are the best methods of establishing a well-organised system of secondary education in England'. The existing system of elementary schools would need to be amended. On his second appearance Macnamara strove to make plain the difficulties under which teachers in public elementary schools were already working. He was asked whether there were any difficulties which had struck him with regard to the kind of control which was exercised over elementary schools which he desired to see avoided in whatever control the State might in future exercise over secondary schools. This was a promising opening. Macnamara replied cryptically: 'Yes, I think it is most desirable that many of the evils of the present State administration should be avoided if the State is to take control'. He then provided a list:

> I am thinking of the evils of the system of assessing grants upon the results of examinations; the infliction of a rigid code of regulations affecting the plans and routine of the schools, and the aims and functions of the teachers; the system of endeavouring to test progress by set examinations; and the most glaring evil of endeavouring to inspect schools by unqualified persons.

What he intended to convey by 'unqualified persons' was, of course, Her Majesty's Inspectors of Schools, 'persons who have had no practical experience of the work of elementary school education'. 'You think it should be an essential precondition for the appointment of anyone as an inspector that he should have had practical experience as a teacher?', he was asked. 'It is most essential', he replied. Later he was able to raise the issues of extraneous duties and unfair dismissal:

> Large numbers of our rural schoolmasters are compelled, as a condition of appointment, and as a condition of retention of their office, to do certain other matters, such as play the organ, train the choir, be secretary of various village clubs, and so on. I am anxious that they should have liberty to do those things if they wish, but that it should not be made a condition that they should do them.

Local managers, he added, denied teachers the ordinary civil and religious liberties of English people. As an example he quoted a teacher who, whilst nothing was alleged against him as a teacher, was dismissed for canvassing for a political candidate. 'Surely that would be an offence which would be the subject of censure by the Central Authority?', Bryce enquired. 'The Central Authority has no control over the dismissal of teachers by the Local Authority', Macnamara replied. 'Mr Acland was thoroughly well assured of that, and had to say in the House ... that the central authority is absolutely helpless.' Nor, he added later, could an appeal be made to a court of law. When asked about secondary education, Macnamara voiced his concern about the difficulties of involving the State in the operation of institutions traditionally closed to the lower classes. In every secondary school aided by the State there should, he thought, be a proportion of free places. In general, however, he felt that the time had not yet arrived for State-supported secondary education:

> I observe that where school boards are very anxious to establish free Higher Grade Schools, however desirable that may be, they cause a feeling against the movement, and when you sum it up it comes to this, that they have by that endeavour put back educational progress. Many of the ratepayers, however wrong they may be, object to the Higher Grade education being entirely free, and the consequence is that the movement is retarded.[116]

The appointment of the Bryce Commission, with its implications for a rapid establishment of a national system of secondary education, involving increased expenditure and the reform of local administration of education, confirmed the Conservatives' apprehensions about the educational policies of the Liberal government. Acland's encouragement of free education and his determination to improve school buildings had already provided a threat to the declining income of voluntary schools. Lord Harrowby, formerly (as Lord Sandon) Vice-President of the Committee of Council between 1874 and 1878, concluded, on the publication of the Fabric Circular, that the Government intended to destroy the voluntary schools.[117] At the end of 1893 the *Schoolmaster* noted that a group of Conservative MPs including Lord Cranborne and his brother-in-law Lord Wolmer had formed a committee for keeping an eye on Acland.[118] He began to encounter obstruction in the House of Commons. In the course of 1893 he was referred to as 'Apostate', 'Demagogue-Tyrant', 'Despot', 'Bengal Tiger' and 'Monophysite'.[119] In January 1895, when the Bryce Commission was completing its investigations, his creation of the Office of Special Inquiries and Reports, intended to be the Department's research unit, suggested that the process of reform would continue, made permanent by a civil service department devoted to drawing comparisons with national systems abroad and introducing expensive innovations. By now Cranborne and his friends in the House of Commons were attempting to wear him down in the House by means of questions on trivial matters.[120] He survived till the fall of the Government but then suffered a breakdown in health. In July 1898 he resigned his seat.

The fall of the Liberal government was sudden, though it had been long predicted because of Rosebery's erratic leadership. On 21 June 1895 the so-called Cordite Vote, over an allegation that the country possessed an inadequate supply of cordite and small arms ammunition, left the Government in a minority of seven.[121] Rosebery resigned, a Conservative-Liberal Unionist coalition took over and a general election was called. The *Schoolmaster* expressed the despair of the teachers: hopes of a Superannuation Bill had revived; the raising of the age of factory employment of half-timers by one year had seemed to be within their grasp, but now Acland was to leave the Education Department.[122]

For this election the Union's candidates were Yoxall, who was now contesting West Nottingham, and Gray, who had been adopted as Conservative candidate for West Ham North in 1893. The Union took the view that education should not be treated in partisan fashion and the two candidates were pledged to take a non-party line on the issue.

In the meantime a new Vice-President of the Committee of Council had been selected. The *Schoolmaster* announced the appointment of Sir John Gorst. The new Vice-President was not to be in the Cabinet, and, as further evidence of the new Government's view of his office as an inconsiderable and paltry one, it had taken twelve days of Ministry-making before the name of the new Vice-President had been released: 'After twelve days' babble, and when things have got down to the Junior Lords of the Treasury, the Masters of the Horse, and the Under-Secretaryships, one looks for some little interest even in England in 1895 on behalf of the future "First Schoolmaster of the Land" ... But one looks in vain.'[123]

In the same edition of the *Schoolmaster* a third NUT Parliamentary candidature was announced by means of a letter signed by Gilbert Christian, Marshall Jackman, W. J. Gilham and Arthur Thomas:

> At a moment's notice Mr Macnamara has consented to contest the Deptford Division at the general election. But eight or nine days remain for us for this stiff fight. As there will be plenty of clerical work, ladies' help will be highly acceptable. A long day's work on Saturday and the campaign will have been well begun. Teachers ready to assist one who has spent himself so unstintingly should write or call at once on either [sic] of the undersigned at Portland House, 202 New Cross Road (opposite New Cross LB & SC Railway Station).[124]

Another appeal appeared a week later. The correspondents added in deference to Union policy: 'Mr Macnamara specifically asks us to say in any appeal we may make on his behalf that he does not for a moment desire that any solicitation should be made for the help of any teacher whose views on the great political questions may be different from his own'.[125]

Macnamara spent ten days in the constituency. Jackman and his colleagues had secured the support of hundreds of teachers: there were eighty or ninety at work during the week, 150 on Saturday and over 200 on election day.[126] Macnamara wrote on 6 July to John Burns, who was contesting Battersea:

> Dear Burns,
>
> This *is* a place. Politics don't go beyond the smoking-concert. Principles are lost sight of in the geniality of a man's exterior. The Railway men will vote Tory, I understand! Can you squeeze in ten mins next Friday specially for Railway workers and Dockers? I am ashamed to ask; but it is infernally disheartening to see these chaps selling their liberties, wives and families in a blind helpless fashion ...

Burns appears to have agreed and asked for a *quid pro quo*. Macnamara wrote again on 11 July:

My dear Burns,

God bless you, I wish I cd come over, but I'm doing eight years' work here in eight days. My voice is gone and I'm electioneering by dumbshow. If I'm at all audible I'm coming over. (Deptford is too respectable for a Sunday meeting). [127]

The 1895 election proved disastrous for the Liberals. The Conservatives won 340 seats, their allies, the Liberal Unionists, seventy-one, the Irish Nationalists eighty-two and the Liberals 177. Gray was elected with a majority of 704, Yoxall with a majority of 513. Macnamara's opponent, the future Judge Darling, increased his majority from 565 to 1,229. The *Schoolmaster* declared:

Let us most heartily, in the name of the 30,000 members of the union and on our own behalf felicitate our new MPs and felicitate Education and the teachers of the country upon the brilliant service the Union members of Parliament are bound to render as time goes on. Messrs Gray and Yoxall are men inconceivably superior to the average party man on either side of the House, not only in their knowledge of general politics and especially of the subject nearest to their hearts, but also in their ability as public exponents and administrators.[128]

When the Executive met on 20 July on the morrow of the election it was clear that the members were pleased with their third candidate. Thomas, Macnamara's supporter, pointed out that while the Conservative-Unionist gain in London had averaged fourteen per cent, in Deptford it had only been six per cent. Macnamara, seconding a motion of congratulation to Yoxall and Gray, reminded the Executive of Union policy on party politics. Both men would have to say things as politicians with which sections of the Union would disagree, but he hoped teachers would remember that with the politics of the two new members they had nothing to do (Applause). What they had to expect from their representatives was straight and loyal action upon educational problems. He knew, he said, that they would not be disappointed.[129]

4

The London School Board, 1894–1897

In July 1895 Macnamara was not quite thirty-four years old. The next general election would take place, at the latest, in seven years' time. In the meantime his responsibilities were heavy. First there were his editorial duties on the *Schoolmaster* and its associated papers. Since April he had been Vice-President of the Union. Also, since the previous November, he had been a member of the London School Board.

The idea of establishing the London School Board had emerged almost accidentally during the debates over the 1870 Education Act. Forster had intended to make metropolitan education the responsibility of the City Corporation, the Boards of Guardians, the vestries and the district Boards of Works. On 4 July 1870, however, William McC Torrens,[1] the member for Finsbury, successfully introduced an amendment in favour of an elected Board for the whole of the Metropolis.[2] Section 37 of the Act provided for the immediate establishment of the Board and the first of the elections which were to be conducted triennially under the cumulative vote (whereby each ratepayer elector, male and female, had as many votes as there were seats in the division) took place on 29 November 1870. Forty-nine members, male and female, were elected representing ten divisions: the City, Chelsea, Finsbury, Greenwich, Hackney, Lambeth, Marylebone, Southwark, Tower Hamlets and Westminster. The first meeting took place in the Guildhall on 15 December. From 1871 until 1874 the Board continued to meet there; then, in October of that year, it took possession of the building designed for it on the Victoria Embankment.[3]

The Board faced immense tasks. Of the child population of London in 1871, only two out of five attended any sort of school. Buildings were needed, both to house new scholars and to replace unsuitable premises (among them the arches under railway viaducts) previously used for educational purposes.[4] Habits of attendance needed to be created, often in the face of parents hostile enough to attack a building site on which a school was being erected[5] or to drop a dead cat from an upstairs window on to the head of a school attendance officer.[6] A curriculum needed to be devised, the task being taken up by a committee chaired by the eminent scientist T. H. Huxley. Fortunately the new body proved, under the

chairmanship of Lord Lawrence, the former Viceroy of India, to be energetic and non-party. Its early achievements made clear to the ratepaying
public what school boards were intended to do.

The duties of a London School Board member took up a good deal of
time. Weekly meetings of the Board took place on Thursdays throughout the year with breaks at Christmas, Easter and in the summer. Few
functions were delegated to school managers. Board members were
expected to make policy decisions, serve on sub-committees and keep
themselves informed in detail about the Board institutions within their
constituencies. 'Our proceedings would have been much more cumbrous',
Lord Reay, the last Chairman of the Board commented, 'if Members of
the Board had relied only on official reports, and not also on their own
supervision. Questions could be quickly settled in Committee and at the
Board, notwithstanding elaborate agenda, because members were fully
acquainted with their merits'.[7]

From the election of the second Board two parties began to develop:
the Progressives, devoted to the expansion and efficiency of the Board's
schools, and the Moderates, containing a number of clergy (some of whom
were mainly concerned to protect the voluntary schools from Board school
competition) and also a group devoted to keeping the local rate below the
3d in the pound estimated as sufficient by Forster in 1870.[8] Thomas
Gautrey, secretary of the Metropolitan Board Teachers' Association and
a member of the Board for its last ten years, recalled:

> there was a running fight inside and outside the Board, the objectors trying to
> prove that most, probably more than half, the project places were unnecessary.
> The clerical opponents inside fought in the committees, wrought up deputations
> and engineered petitions chiefly to protect their own Church schools from
> competition. Vestries and Ratepayers' Associations sent protests and deputations
> because they objected to the cost.[9]

Party divisions were, however, rigorously observed only between 1885 and
1894, the year in which Macnamara was elected.[10] During this period the
Chairman was the Rev. J. R. Diggle, leader of the Moderate Party who,
according to Gautrey:

> dominated the Board by his personality ... He packed every committee and
> sub-committee with his own followers ... [he] was himself a prodigious worker,
> adroit, cautious, almost cunning at times, clever and expert on committees ...
> He believed in providing good school buildings and playgrounds, capable
> teachers, competent inspectors and organisers; always, of course, keeping a keen
> eye on the cost.[11]

Towards the end of the Diggle régime it began to appear that the days
of initiative and enterprise on the London School Board belonged to the
past. It had become committee-ridden. Diggle, in his annual statement in
September 1892, dilated upon the magnitude of the Board's work. It

administered an area with a population larger by 200,000 than the whole of Scotland. It directly managed the work of three quarters as many schools and children as were supervised by the 979 school boards north of the border. This task, the *Schoolmaster* commented, had taken, during the first eight months of the current Board, ninety-eight hours of Board time and 436 hours of committee time. This amounted to two-and-a-half hours per working day for every Board member.[12] These lengthy sessions were being employed, according to a report in the *Daily Chronicle*, in a programme of cost cutting. The previous Board's decision to make evening schools free was rescinded; the swimming bath building programme was cut short; the movement in favour of providing pianos was brought to a halt; girls' departments were mixed with infants' under one head teacher. The article concluded:

> Londoners must wake up about this School Board business ... Labour leaders must keep the question to the front and the parents must go to the poll ... Meanwhile ... a proper interest in this matter on the part of the workers would make things warm at the next School Board election for the 'Moderates'.[13]

The majority party's zeal for economy had unfortunate results. In December 1892 the Board's Clerk was summoned to attend the Southwark Police Court on the ground that, as the legal owner of the Johanna Street Board School, he had failed to comply with a notice served upon him to place the school in a proper sanitary condition after reports by the Medical Officer of Health and the Sanitary Inspector had been ignored, and cases of scarlet fever and diphtheria had occurred.[14] Nevertheless, Diggle and his supporters had the backing of certain newspapers. The *Echo* commented on the budget in May 1893:

> The present Board may be bigoted in its religious tendencies, may have been slow to repair defective drainage and structural defects, may have been unduly tardy in providing for the educational necessities of particular neighbourhoods, but it has one redeeming quality – it does not ask for more money, and it actually closes the year with a balance in hand. Ratepayers who are smarting under increased demands ranging from threepence to sixpence in the pound upon inflated assessments will readily forgive many shortcomings in view of this important fact.[15]

Early in 1893, however, Diggle made a serious misjudgement. He permitted the Board to become involved in a theological debate which, as time went on, gave opportunities for the expression of religious bigotry, sapped the cohesion of his party and brought ordinary business to a halt. In March 1871 a formula for religious teaching, based on the Cowper-Temple clause of the 1870 Act and devised by W. H. Smith, bookseller, Board member and later Cabinet Minister, had been adopted:

> In the schools provided by the Board the Bible shall be read; and there shall be given therefrom such explanations and such instruction on the principles

of religion and morality as are suited to the capacities of children; provided always:

(1) that in such explanations and instruction the provisions of the Act in Sections 7 and 14 be strictly observed both in letter and spirit, and that no attempt be made in any such schools to attach children to any particular denomination;

(2) that, in regard to any particular school, the Board shall consider and determine upon any application by managers, parents or ratepayers of the district who may show special cause for exception of the school from the operation of this resolution, in whole or in part.[16]

In 1892 the Rev. John Coxhead, in one of his infrequent visits to a Board school, discovered a teacher dealing with the events of the life of Christ and, as he reported in the *Guardian* on 16 November 'not a word was said to imply the existence of his Divine nature'. This incident provided his fellow Board member Athelstan Riley with an opportunity to challenge the approach to religious education supported by the Board.[17] For the next two years, as a result of his activities, the proper work of the Board was neglected and, as Macnamara recalled in 1900, the weekly meeting would very nearly have justified the reading of the Riot Act, and the number of memorials and protests received ran the printer's bill for 1894 up to £10,000.[18]

Athelstan Riley, born in 1858 and educated at Eton and Pembroke College, Oxford, was a religious enthusiast. Having travelled in the Near East, Persia and Kurdistan, he published an article in the *Contemporary Review* championing the Christians of Eastern Turkey. In his house in Kensington Court he and his wife (the eldest daughter of the Rt Hon. and Rev. Viscount Molesworth) had installed a private chapel. He had become a member of the London Diocesan Conference and of the House of Laymen of the Province of Canterbury.[19] In Gautrey's recollection, he was more clerically minded than most bishops and clergymen. Once, at a social gathering, he approached a bishop, fell on his knees, and requested an impromptu blessing.[20] Elected to the Board as a member for Chelsea in 1891, he was openly hostile to school boards, commenting two years later that they were the greatest enemy of the Christian religion in the land.[21]

'First Thursday in the month, "close time" for routine business – gala day for private motions ... a most violent outbreak of the Religious Diffi-culty', a report on the London School Board in the *Schoolmaster* in Macnamara's characteristic style recounted at the beginning of February 1893: 'Mr Riley would have it laid down that the children should distinctly be taught "that Christ is God". Moreover, he would lay it upon the Board to appoint only such teachers as "may be reasonably supposed to possess capabilities for imparting elementary religious knowledge".' Before the meeting Riley had circulated a printed statement of his criticisms of religious teaching under the Board. Applicants for teaching posts could not be asked whether they were Christians. School managers and local inspectors could be of any or no religion. As for the Board itself, 'it is composed of Churchmen and Roman Catholics, heretics and schismatics, agnostics and atheists, in different proportions according to each triennial election'.[22] A month later the *Schoolmaster* reported:

> Fifth weekly dose of Theology. School Board for London now thoroughly transformed into a useful medium for the preliminary rehearsal of the weekly sermons for the succeeding Sunday. Everybody, except perhaps Mr Riley and two or three other fanatics, sick and tired of the whole thing and anxious to get back to ways of educational sanity.[23]

By mid-May it was plain that the Chairman was losing control. The Board meetings were being largely wasted in wrangling, its agenda papers congested with correspondence and petitions on the religious issue. As the *Schoolmaster* put it, the Board Room 'had become the area for theological thrust and parry between the members of the Board themselves and between members of the Board and outsiders who have entered the lists under the style of deputationists ... What makes the matter the more pitiable is the fact that *it has only just begun!*'[24] Riley had now set himself the task of altering the Smith formula of 1871 so that the word 'Christian' was inserted before 'religion and morality'.[25] In July the matter was referred to the School Management Committee (SMC). But when in January 1894 the Committee's conclusions were placed before the Board, the dissension broke out once more.[26] The Smith formula was duly amended, but protracted Board meetings took place for weeks, during one of which Riley and his supporters refreshed themselves with oysters and chablis as the long hours passed.[27] On 1 February, after a session ending at 11.55 pm, the Board resolved to implement the new regulations by sending a circular to all the Board's teachers, the closing sentence of which indicated that, if there were those who could not conscientiously impart Bible instruction in the new spirit, means would be taken to release them from the duty of giving Bible lessons.[28] This raised the possibility of religious tests.[29] The *Board Teacher* (the journal of the MBTA) expressed alarm:

> Every fresh appointment and every case of promotion will inevitably be preceded by questions put to every candidate as to conscientious scruples ... it will require but one or two trivial cases (made big by the usual exaggeration and distortion) to bring down the deluge under which will disappear that great confidence which has hitherto been reposed in the teachers' judgement and disposition.[30]

The Council of the Association decided to petition the Board for relief from religious teaching.[31] 'In this great crisis', the *Board Teacher* commented, 'it is of incalculable value as a tonic to have the support of the NUT.'[32] On 21st April the *Schoolmaster* in an editorial entitled 'Stand To', apparently written by Macnamara, had concluded:

It is with feelings of profound sorrow we have to announce the failure of all endeavours to establish a modus vivendi on the question of the 'Test' Circular between the present majority of the London School Board on the one hand, and all reasonable persons on the other. The Board teachers of London – over seventy per cent of them, it is worth remembering, trained in Church Colleges, have been most patient in this matter. They have listened with shame to the many ignorant and scurrilous things said about them and their work, they have looked on amazed and pained for nearly two years whilst those to whom they should have looked for support have spent their frenzied efforts in bringing ridicule and contumely upon their work; they have eloquently pressed upon the Board the utter needlessness of all this deplorable agitation ... the undertaking not to add the Circular to the Board's Code of Regulations has been very properly put on one side as scarcely worthy even of contempt.

As for Coxhead and Riley, it asked:

Do these gentlemen flatter themselves that teachers are altogether so simple as to place their professional futures meekly in their hands – especially when it is remembered how persistently these selfsame theologists mix up their eagerness for dogma with their zeal for a secular education which shall be cheap and nasty? ... these zealous theologists ... must be taught a pretty sharp lesson. And we rejoice to think, inspired as we are simply and solely by a desire for wider, more universal, and more highly efficient Christian schools, that the teachers of the country will not shrink from the painful duty of administering the lesson.[33]

At the Board meeting on 3 May, Coxhead argued that the circular had a limited objective, to make clear the freedom and the duty of the Christian teacher to teach the Christian religion and to relieve at his own request the non-Christian teacher from giving this instruction.[34] But a week later it emerged that, as Chairman of the Scripture Sub-Committee, he had asked specific questions about the circular to candidates for appointment to head teacherships at the Brockley Road School:

1   Have you read the Rules of the Board, in reference to Bible Instruction and Religious Observances?
2   Have you read the Board's Circular in reference to these subjects?
3   Is it your intention to give Bible instruction in accordance with the Rules of the Board?
4   Are you a member of the Metropolitan Board Teachers' Association?[35]

The Board, after discussion, found these questions inappropriate. A motion, expressing disapproval of his conduct was passed by thirty-nine votes to three.[36]

By the beginning of May, the *Board Teacher* reported, 3,000 teachers had signed the petition.[37] It commented on 1 June: 'Every society has its crank, who is rarely taken seriously by his colleagues. As a rule a pint of ridicule swamps his stupid proposals. But at the London School Board the awesome faddist pegs on and gets his way, more or less.'[38]

A fortnight later the SMC reported to the Board that the MBTA petition, to which some 3,130 signatures were attached, had been delivered by Gautrey. Its request that its signatories should be granted relief from the duty of giving religious instruction could not possibly be met for so large a number, so the Committee recommended that it be authorised to address a letter to each of them asking whether they meant what they said.[39] Eight, in reply, persisted in the request for relief; 230 stated individually that they had no objection to continuing Bible lessons; the rest, 2,886 in all, sent a general communication, dated 11 July, to the Board respectfully objecting to its action in treating their applications as if they were not *bona fide* because they were sent through the MBTA. They added that they much regretted to have been obliged to assume an attitude of apparent opposition to the Board's wishes, and still earnestly hoped that the Board would withdraw the circular and permit the instruction to continue on the same lines and with the great success that had hitherto attended it.[40]

The triennial election was now approaching. Diggle, as if to dissociate himself from his extreme colleagues, resigned as Chairman of the SMC.[41] After the summer recess he took the opportunity in his Annual Report as Board Chairman to remind the electorate how economical the Board had been. In March 1892, four months after the 1891 election, there had been 362,585 scholars; two years later there were 390,812.[42] Instead of demanding more money, the Board had demanded less, yet the results were undeniably satisfactory:

> Every recognised public elementary school is examined annually by HM Inspectors ... In making their reports, the Inspectors omit scarcely any detail which affects the working of the school. We are told, for example that 'stones are wanted to sharpen pencils upon'; that 'the unexplained smell in the large room should be cured'; 'that the stoves, when the fires are hot, apparently burn the air' ... It can scarcely be imagined, when these things are deemed worthy of mention, that so important a state of things as schools left without sufficient teachers would go passed by without notice ... It must be a satisfaction to all of us to receive reports from HM Inspectors such as these: 'An excellent school' or 'this is a perfect school', and it matters not what test is applied, the same kind of answer is given.

Diggle attempted to play down the circular. Once the word 'Christian' had been inserted into the specifications for religious instruction, he declared, the Board had been obliged to indicate to the teachers within what limits the teaching should be given and offer them the opportunity, if they so wished, to withdraw from such teaching.[43]

Nevertheless the religious circular became the main issue in what the *School Board Chronicle* described as the most momentous election of a School Board for London since 1870. In the event its fear, that abstentions would confirm Rileyism and encourage denominationalism on school boards all over the country,[44] proved unfounded. By comparison with 1891 the number of voters increased sharply. Macnamara, in his election address at West Lambeth, declared that under Diggle:

> dogmas have so occupied the Board's time and energy that drains have only received attention after pressure from the Education Department, from vestries, and even from magisterial benches. Schools have gone unheated at midwinter, unventilated at midsummer; and dirt instead of cleanliness has been the accompaniment to the Diggleite cry for godliness. Children have been habitually crowded in eighties and nineties into 'sixty' rooms; and teachers have had to struggle hopelessly and singlehanded with great unteachable classes of eighty, ninety and even 100 pupils ... My policy from first to last is, a fair chance for the child of the toiler. I want (1) the withdrawal of the religious 'test' Circular; (2) the maintenance of the Compromise; (3) an end put, once for all, to theological wrangles at the Board; (4) good schools, well staffed, well equipped, and giving a generous training; (5) a straight trade union policy for all labour employed by the Board.[45]

Not only was he elected; he was top of the poll in West Lambeth with 48,255 votes, the highest number in all London and the highest number ever cast for any individual in any London School Board election.[46] 'One of the best fighters in this campaign has been Mr Macnamara, the editor of the *Schoolmaster*', reported the *Board Teacher*. 'No one knows the duties to be performed better than he, and doubtless he will devote himself with energy to the work of the Board.'[47]

Among the new members was a selection of the clergy, retired officers from the armed services and the moneyed young men whom the London School Board had traditionally attracted: Canon Ingram, Rector of St Margaret's Lothbury; Colonel the Hon. Cecil Hubbard of the Grenadier Guards, who had served in Egypt and won the medal and bronze star and was thoroughly convinced that Church of England principles had a firm hold upon the working classes; Gerard Fiennes, Resident of the University Settlement at Oxford House, Bethnal Green; the twenty-seven-year-old Viscount Morpeth, a JP for Cumberland and Vice-President of the North of England Temperance League, who had been Assistant Secretary to the Royal Commission on the Aged Poor; and Evelyn Cecil, the twenty-nine-year-old nephew of Lord Salisbury, who had been called to the Bar in 1889.[48] The young Duke of Newcastle, who had been co-opted to the Board earlier in the year, was now elected for the first time for the City. 'It cannot be said that he has taken a very active part in the Board's work, although he is a pretty regular attendant', the *Board Teacher* reported later, adding that he was an enthusiastic amateur photographer who had recently made a tour of Kent, Sussex and Hampshire in a gypsy caravan in pursuit of his hobby.[49]

Apart from Macnamara there were two other members amongst the

Progressives with school experience: Graham Wallas, a leading Fabian, and Thomas Gautrey of the MBTA. Commenting on how the Diggleites had endeavoured to break up the Association, the *Board Teacher* added somewhat defensively: '... There is no reason in the world why Mr Gautrey, although an official of the teachers, should not have a position on the Board, just as John Burns and other representatives of trade unionism have been elected to public bodies and to Parliament'.[50]

The Moderate Party of which Riley and Diggle were members still had a majority, but it was reduced from fifteen to three. The *St James's Gazette* (a Conservative journal) commented:

> The Rileyites and the Diggleites have thrown away the fine surplus the Moderates gained in 1891 ... The accidents and 'flukes' of the cumulative voting system and the bad organisation of their opponents have given them this nominal majority; but if you count up votes, they are smitten hip and thigh. The Progressives cast somewhere about 130,000 votes more, and in every constituency except one, their men, or women, head the poll in most cases with thousands of votes in hand ... The electors have left us in no doubt as to their meaning.[51]

The *Schoolmaster*, warmed by these comments and by similar conclusions expressed in *The Times* and the *Pall Mall Gazette*, took a restrained, constructive view:

> For the future we most earnestly hope that there may be an end to the bitter struggles of the past two years. They have served no purpose save to bring Religion itself into disrepute, and to distract the attention of the Board from the real work which it was elected to perform. And we hope the Circular may quietly and peaceably be got out of the way once and for all.[52]

The new Board assembled on Thursday 6 December 1894. Its premises had recently been enlarged for the second time.[53] The new Board Room, with a radius of fifty feet, had a polygonal domed ceiling with lunette lights in each division of the polygon.[54] 'Today the Board Room had more resemblance to a "first night" at a theatre than a meeting called for the transaction of business', the *Schoolmaster*'s correspondent reported. 'As each member entered he was received with cheers or groans from the public, the demonstration being specially marked in the case of Mr Riley, where the groans predominated.' The first task was to appoint a provisional Chairman to replace Diggle. The Hon. Lyulph Stanley, leader of the Progressive Party, proposed Macnamara, on the grounds that he had received the greatest number of votes, but he was defeated by the longest-serving member, Coxhead. For the Chairmanship the candidates were non-members: the Rev. T. W. Sharpe, the distinguished HMI, and Lord George Hamilton, who from 1878 till 1880 had been Vice-President of the Committee of Council on Education. Over this matter Macnamara's first public encounter with Diggle occurred. In proposing Lord George, Diggle was obliged to speak against uproar from the gallery which, as an onlooker remarked, was as overcrowded as the London schools. He tactlessly observed that Sharpe's calling, 'like that of a schoolmaster', was unlikely to qualify him to deal properly with a body of men like the members of the London School Board, because a schoolmaster had always to do with pupils who knew so much less than himself, and his authority had to be backed up with the possible alternative of corporal punishment. The editor of the *Schoolmaster*, unabashed by this discourtesy, delivered a speech in favour of Sharpe, pointing out that Lord George, who was politically partisan, had voted in 1891 in favour of the status quo for half-timers.[55] Eventually Lord George was elected by twenty-nine votes to twenty-six.[56] He was to remain Chairman for only eight months; in November 1895, he was succeeded by the Marquis of Londonderry.

The following week Macnamara, who had been appointed (as were all members of the Board between 1894 and 1896) to the SMC as well as to the School Accommodation and Attendance Committee,[57] moved his first resolution. His immediate purpose, he said, was to place before the public an up-to-date statement on the number of children who were attending school under-fed, and the number of cases dealt with by voluntary agencies. Surprisingly, he received support from Diggle, who nevertheless objected to the rapidity with which Macnamara sought to obtain the return. Since, however, as Macnamara pointed out, winter was approaching, action was agreed. Both men were appointed to a Special Committee to consider the issue.[58]

His second initiative concerned Higher Grade Schools. 'If it offers a prospect of a decisive movement in the direction of placing London more nearly on an equality with great provincial school board towns in the matter of provision for Higher Grade Teaching', the *School Board Chronicle* commented, 'we welcome it most cordially.'[59] Macnamara's motion involved consultation with the Technical Education Board of the London County Council set up under the terms of the 1889 Act. The Technical Education Board had made progress in an area that the London School Board had neglected during the Diggle years. In Macnamara's view there was still time to make up the backlog. His motion, however, was referred to the SMC, where it was blocked.[60]

Two further early interventions by Macnamara marked him out as an enemy of the 'economists'. On 14 February he successfully moved that the SMC be authorised to make an inquiry into the number of pianos already supplied to the Board's schools, with a view to supplying more of them.[61] A fortnight later, he proposed that the Committee be instructed to arrange that fees should no longer be charged in the Board's evening schools. In the previous year, he said, only 0.4 per cent of pupils past the school leaving age (then eleven) had attended. In Nottingham and Bradford where the courses were free, the figures were 5.5 per cent and 5.9 per cent respectively. 'When the Free Education Bill was passing through

Parliament', he recalled, 'the London School Board passed a resolution to free both their day schools and evening schools, but one of the first acts of the late Board was to rescind that resolution so far as the evening schools were concerned.' But the debate was adjourned.[62]

When Diggle had proposed Lord George Hamilton as Chairman he had promised that no attempt would be made to reopen the religious discussion.[63] But the fact that no answer had been sent by the Board to the teachers' letter of the previous July emerged on 24 January. A proposal containing a suggested reply was referred to the SMC for consideration and report. It was accompanied by a second, 'that it be an instruction to the SMC that no question is to be put to any candidate for appointment as teacher, whether the candidate does or does not belong to any particular association of teachers'.[64] No report was produced. Hence, on 14 March, Lord Morpeth, alluding to the case of a teacher who had applied to be relieved from Bible Instruction because he could not accept the terms of the circular, suggested that the circular was dead. Riley immediately objected. He declared that they could not rescind the circular for one teacher without rescinding it for all. Recalling the whole history and course of the circular controversy at the Board, he argued that his party's action had been approved by the London voters who had returned it with a majority. Diggle, by swiftly and successfully moving the previous question, put an end not only to the hilarity that this view occasioned but also to the discussion.[65]

The religious issue was beginning to stir once more. On 2 May the SMC's Chairman suggested to the Board that the second proposal of 24 January be discharged. Macnamara disagreed. To discharge it, he said, would encourage undesirable questions about teacher associations. Coxhead, still determined to justify his action of a year before, joined in. Gautrey responded provocatively, alleging that Coxhead's questions were likely to lead to a system of terrorism. Riley could not resist expressing his support for Coxhead, saying that he was right to ask the question because at the time the teachers were behaving with gross impertinence. 'We are not here in the interest of the teachers', he concluded; 'we have a duty to perform to the parents and children.' 'You do it very badly', commented Macnamara.[66]

There the matter remained until the Board meeting of 18 July when the Chairman of the SMC moved to discharge the first of the tasks it had been set in January, on the grounds that no reply to the teachers' letter was necessary. The Rev. Arthur Jephson (East Lambeth) proposed an amendment, that the Board should state that 'it recognises the faithfulness and tact which the teachers have shown in their Bible teaching, and trusts that, in the future as in the past, such explanations and instructions in the principles of Christian religion and morality as are suited to the capacities of children will continue to be given; and that a copy be sent to the Metropolitan Board Teachers' Association'. His aim, he said, was that the hatchet should be buried. Riley reacted sharply to this well meaning suggestion. He repeated his previous accusation that Macnamara's purpose as a member of the Board was merely to support the interests of the teachers. Macnamara demurred. 'The religious question will never be settled except upon our terms', Riley responded.[67]

At the next meeting the motion and Jephson's amendment were discussed further. George Whiteley (East Lambeth) said that he believed the Board was heartily sick of the whole subject. It was all very well for those who came there fresh as new members, but old members would be glad to let it alone. Coxhead responded that there were but two courses: either to reaffirm the circular or to go back on it. Of the teachers, he added, only 3,000 out of 7,000 had objected to it. The rest, apparently, had understood and accepted it.

Macnamara spoke next. If Riley wanted peace, he said, he was acting in a curious manner. As for Coxhead's argument, it was mistaken to suppose that the teachers who did not sign the letter to the Board agreed with the circular. The teachers had been faithful and tactful, as the amendment put it, in giving religious instruction since 1870; and, until Riley came, members on the other side had been ready to say so, from Diggle downwards. Had it not been for the teachers, hundreds of parents would have withdrawn their children from the religious instruction given in the schools. Major Skinner (Westminster) disagreed. He was prepared now to put the sword back in the scabbard, but he did not mean to break it or lay it aside. The action of the teachers had been insubordinate and insolent. 'Mr Macnamara', he said, 'has told us that the teachers, servants of the public, snapped their fingers in the faces of the Board ... And now we are asked, by the amendment, to go down on our knees and beg the teachers' pardon.' Diggle again endeavoured to bring the debate to a close. The amendment, he said, would reopen the controversy. On his second attempt the Board voted to proceed to the next business, but not before Riley had promised that before the term of the Board was over he would have had plenty of time to discuss the issue further.[68]

When the Board reassembled after the summer recess, what the *Schoolmaster* now referred to as 'the perennial religious difficulty, which one hears so much of out of school and nothing in', arose immediately. Stanley introduced a motion on behalf of two teachers asking for the cancellation of their application to be relieved from giving Bible instruction. Faced with the contention that they should first declare themselves ready to teach in accordance with the circular, he responded that, to be consistent, the Board should obtain the same declaration from the 3,000 teachers giving religious instruction not in accordance with the circular. Macnamara took the opportunity to raise another matter. Having enquired why the Board did not take the same action with all the 3,127 teachers who had resisted the circular, he reminded the Board that it had been agreed that teachers' requests to withdraw from religious instruction should not prejudice their position. When a teacher's promotion was being discussed at the SMC on 1 July, however, Riley had gone privately to see whether this teacher was one of the 3,127. 'Can anything be more dishonest?', Macnamara asked. Not surprisingly, Riley found this question provocative. He declared that he did not pay much attention to being called dishonest by Macnamara. 'The 3,000 teachers alluded to', he said, 'have been grossly insubordinate to the Board who pay their salaries. They have treated the Board with contempt, and I will never consent to place in the Board schools a teacher who has been insubordinate and who leaves us in the dark as to whether he is a Christian man or not.' Admitting Macnamara's charge, he added that he intended to use every legitimate means to prevent any one of the 3,000 from securing any position of authority under the Board. This speech, the *Schoolmaster* commented, created a considerable sensation; Edmund Barnes (Marylebone) announced that he would table a motion in favour of Riley's withdrawal from the SMC.[69]

On the Monday of the following week Riley issued a memorandum, prepared in April but not previously made public, in which he concluded that the 2,886 teachers who had not replied personally to the Board's individual letters had adopted a course of action 'which necessitates the greatest vigilance over them and their promotion, on the part of those members of the Board who are pledged to do their utmost to protect the little children of Christian parents in our schools from receiving their Bible instructions at the hands of those who do not believe the cardinal doctrines of the Christian Faith'. On Tuesday, a letter over his signature appeared in the London dailies attributing the non-cooperation of the teachers to the influence of Macnamara and Gautrey.[70] Macnamara's response was published the next day. Having recalled the chief events in what he referred to as 'this deplorable controversy', he went on:

> Now, what is Mr Riley's position today? As I understood him last Thursday ... his expressed intention was to use every legitimate means to prevent any one of these protesting teachers from attaining a position of responsibility under the Board. Concerning 5,000 of the teachers, roughly, he is satisfied ... But 3,000 of them have been grossly insubordinate, and they have left him in the dark as to whether they are Christian men or women or not ... What I want Mr Riley to tell me is this: how have these Board members and local managers who are doing the 'vigilance' business over these teachers got to know who they are? Does not the statement admit my contention that Mr Riley is armed with a list of the petitioners, and that he is following them up? I may remind Mr Riley that on 22nd February 1894 the Board resolved by thirty-four votes to none, ten not voting, that 'the religious opinions of candidates will not in any way influence their appointment or promotion'. I may also ask Mr Riley to recall the fact that he was one of the thirty-four. I may further remind Mr Riley that in his presence on 15th March 1894 the Board resolved without a division, 'nor are they (the teachers) to be subjected to any questions with reference to their religious beliefs'.[71]

Two days later the public gallery was filled to overflowing in what the *Schoolmaster* described as 'great expectations of scenes between Mr Riley and other members of the Board concerning his utterances of last week'. Macnamara moved, as a matter of urgency:

> that in consequence of the statements made by Mr Riley at the meeting of the Board on 3rd October, and in the memorandum issued by him on 5th October ... it is the opinion of the Board that Mr Riley should no longer remain a member of the Teaching Staff Sub-Committee of the SMC, and that it be referred to the SMC to give effect to this decision.[72]

Diggle opposed this, saying that there was no case for urgency but, on the vote, Macnamara prevailed by twenty-four votes to twenty-two. He then proceeded to make his case. A most critical situation had been created in the past few days, he said, by the extraordinary statements of Riley. He recalled the arguments about the teachers who, in Riley's view, had accepted the circular and those who had, by means of a general letter, resisted it. Riley's hand was confessedly against these 2,886 and he had decided that he must test them before they could be received into the light of his countenance. Because, in his opinion, they had disregarded the circular, he could disregard its safeguards. Then, Macnamara went on, they came back to the Rules of the Board. Rule 15 specifically forbade inquiries into teachers' religious beliefs, whether they were up for selection, nomination, appointment or promotion. At least 700 new teachers had been appointed since April 1894; many hundreds would be appointed during the life of the present Board. Riley was plainly determined to test them. Hence, with regret, he felt compelled to move his resolution for the removal of Riley.[73] Diggle in a long, discursive speech argued that the issue at stake was the rights and liberties of members. As soon as Riley's name was mentioned, he said, away flew the sanity of the Progressive Party, and if Riley announced his support of anything it was at once supposed to be as chock full of Jesuitry as a sardine tin should be of sardines. He attempted to move the previous question. This was no answer, Wallas declared. Riley had given definite evidence of his intention to break the Rules of the Board, and the Progressives' action had been forced upon them. Those who voted for the previous question would make themselves responsible for Riley's action.[74]

The debate was adjourned to the following week. In the meantime it continued in the press. On Saturday 12 October a letter from Macnamara appeared in a number of papers:

Mr Riley and the London Board Teachers

I see from your columns today that Mr Riley complains that I 'confuse a plain issue'. My impression is that he must be pretty well alone in his inability to see where this thing stands. To the vast majority of the people of this city the issue, I believe, is painfully clear. It is whether or not Mr Riley is to carry on a private inquisition into teachers' religious opinions – thereby disregarding the honourable pledge of the Religious Circular, violating Rule 15 of the Board's Code (which rule, by the bye, Mr Riley helped to frame), and snapping his fingers at a vote taken by the Board on 10th May 1894, when it was decided by thirty-nine to three that certain questions Mr Coxhead had put openly and publicly to candidates for promotion at the Teaching Staff Committee were improper, Mr Riley himself publicly stating that for once he was bound to disagree with his friend Mr Coxhead. The Rule of the Board is specific in this matter. It reads:

Religious Opinions of Teachers

15. The religious opinions of teachers are not to influence their selection, nomination, appointment, or promotion, nor are teachers, or candidates for appointment as teachers, to be subjected to any questions with reference to their religious belief, or, as to the possession or otherwise of certificates, which might be taken as indicative of belonging to any particular denomination, nor are inquiries to be made into the religious beliefs of teachers, either by committees of the Board, Local Managers, or by any other person having any connection with the Board'.

I pass over Mr Diggle's preposterously flimsy argument yesterday that his rule *was not intended by its terms to apply to the action of an individual member of the Board* as being altogether unworthy of a man of Mr Diggle's position.

The plain issue which Mr Riley will not face is whether or not he has violated that rule, putting aside the Circular and the vote of 10th May 1894.

Now Mr Riley is wont to pose as a very much misrepresented man. I suppose, however, he will scarcely charge the 'Church Education and Voluntary Schools Defence Union,' which publishes a weekly record of the Board's debates, with having unfairly reproduced his admissions on this critical question. At the meeting of the Board of 3rd October, I charged Mr Riley with having on 1st July looked out whether or not a teacher then before the Teaching Staff Committee, was one of the protesting 3,000. I take the following from the published record before mentioned:–

Mr Athelstan Riley: 'Mr Macnamara says that on a certain occasion I looked to see which teachers were numbered amongst the 3,000. Quite so'.
Mr Macnamara: 'Do you admit that?'
Mr Athelstan Riley: 'Of course I admit it'.

What I want to know is whether this is not a violation of the spirit of the Board's rules ... Later on in the same debate Mr Riley is reported in the same voluntary school record:–

Mr Athelstan Riley: '*All I have done, and I shall do it again, is to make careful inquiries about these doubtful teachers* (the 3,000) before placing them in a position of importance in a school, a position of superintending the religious instruction ...'

For Mr Coxhead's action I have the utmost respect. He openly and publicly asked certain questions of a candidate for promotion. The Board thought these questions improper. He at once desisted, and I can imagine nothing more unlikely under the sun than the spectacle of the Rev John Coxhead running about privately instituting inquiries into the position of the protesting teachers with a list of them stowed away in his pocket. Mr Coxhead and the great number of his colleagues would be above such action. To me it was most reassuring to hear the Rev Allen Edwards say yesterday that he was '*shocked beyond power of words to express, when he heard Mr Riley's words last week*'.

That, I believe, represents the feeling of the great bulk of the Moderate Party on the Board, and the sooner Mr Riley realises that he will either have to leave the Teaching Staff Committee or give an undertaking to stop this 'vigilance' business of his the better for everybody concerned.

T. J. Macnamara
School Board Offices, 11th October.[75]

'The School Board meeting has once more become one of the sights of the city', the *Schoolmaster* commented on 19 October, 'and claims its share of public patronage with Cleopatra's Needle, the Zoo, the Big Wheel and the Empire of India Exhibition. Today, when the door of the public gallery turned on its hinges, there came in a rush like that which takes place at a first night at the Lyceum, and in a few seconds it was packed as it was never packed before.'[76] On this occasion 'Riley and the Teachers' was to occupy four hours of debate. He himself, at an early stage, moved for precedence to deal with the teachers who had not replied to the letter of July 1894. Members would not be diverted and the motion was not seconded, but Walter Key, a City of London member, took up the teachers' behaviour as a means to return to Macnamara's motion of the previous week. Macnamara, he said, was more responsible than anyone for the misguided actions of the teachers. 'It appears', he declared, 'to be but part of a campaign to raise the status and influence of the teachers, to, in fact, give them a predominating voice in things educational, and enable them to set their feet upon the necks of the ratepayers by dictating the policy of the Board.'[77] The Rev. Andrew Drew (East Lambeth) was also disposed to blame Macnamara who, he said, wanted to persecute Board members, when at the same time he was blaming Riley for persecuting the teachers. It was almost an insult to pass such a resolution as that proposed.[78] Stanley, the next speaker, drew attention to an amendment proposed by the Rev. Rowland Plummer, of which notice had already been given, which was intended to reaffirm Article 15 and, consequently, to avoid making a victim of Riley who, Stanley said, was not alone in selecting teachers on their reputation as Christians. Major Skinner had written to *The Times* describing his approach to promotions. Col. Hubbard had expressed similar views. The best thing would be for Riley to withdraw from the Committee in question. The Board would have an increased respect for him and, he concluded, 'there was not one of them who wished to lose sight of Mr Riley' (Macnamara: Hear, hear) 'who had very amiable qualities'.[79]

Riley had carefully prepared his speech. The torrent of abuse with which he had been assailed over the previous fortnight proved, he said, that great interests and principles were at stake. He now denied expressing the intention to use every legitimate means to prevent any one of the 3,000 teachers from securing any position of authority under the Board and blamed Macnamara for diligently spreading the idea throughout the press. 'Be they Christian, Agnostic or Atheist', he said, 'I have never made any difference between them in the matter of promotion, and any allegation to the contrary is deliberately false and proceeds either from ignorance or from a wilful desire to misrepresent my action.'

Over the teachers' circular the Board had been guilty of drift. Riley went on:

> If I had to put this speech into a single sentence I would say that the whole of the dispute in which we now engaged arises from the fact that there are at least half-a-dozen different views current amongst Board members as to the exact position the 2,886 teachers occupy at this moment with reference to the Board, and that it is for the Board in its corporate capacity to face the question boldly and settle it once and for all, instead of seeking to fasten the responsibility for its hesitancy upon one of its members.

As for Rule 15 he reminded the Board that though it stated that the religious opinions of candidates should not in any way influence their appointment, members made a practice of selecting Jewish teachers for Jewish children.[80]

When Macnamara responded, he expressed regret that Riley had not stuck to his guns with respect to the statements he had unquestionably made. He was interrupted by Major Skinner on a point of order. Riley had distinctly denied using the words attributed to him and now Macnamara had practically said that the denial was a lie. He had never heard such a thing done on a public board before. Macnamara, however, substantiated his statement. Though he could not regard its publications as official he had quoted the report of the Church Education and Voluntary Defence Union which, whilst it condensed the speeches of other people and presented them in the third person, gave Riley's speeches at great length and in the first person. Now if Riley did not use those words, he went on, why had various Board members protested against them? Even if he had not done so, there was sufficient evidence in his written statements, including the memorandum published the week before, that he intended to maintain the controversy and carefully watch the teachers. Would Riley stand upon the memorandum, or would he repudiate it too?

Regarding the insubordination of teachers, dealing with which Riley now found so urgent, Macnamara reminded members that no-one had been more ready than Riley to avoid settling the question: 'if the teachers were insubordinate fifteen months ago, what Mr Riley should have done was to table a resolution to put that matter in order, and it is preposterous for him to charge himself with a commission of privately carried-on inquisition, partly into these teachers' religious opinions, and partly with regard to their insubordination and run about with a list of their names in his pockets'. In conclusion, he suggested that Riley should tabulate a resolution rescinding Rule 15, or leave the Teaching Staff Sub-Committee, or give up his private vigilance and inquisition for, he said, the people of London would not tolerate it. Finally, he expressed support for the Plummer amendment.

When the Plummer amendment was discussed it became plain that a number of his fellow Moderates were not going to support Riley. Cecil said that he understood that Macnamara himself and most of his colleagues accepted the amendment. As for Riley's motion, it should have been moved fifteen months ago. J. W. Sharp (Finsbury) declared that at the recent election he, Canon Ingram and Benson Clough had all told the electors that the protest against the circular would not prejudice the position of the teachers who made it. Riley was absent from the Board Room at this moment, but Sharp continued meaningfully: 'If I went against that promise I should be a man devoid of all honour and integrity'. When finally the vote on the amendment was taken, ten of the Moderates did not vote; seven, including Plummer and Cecil, joined the Progressives and voted in favour.[81] Nobody voted against. Reproof, the *Schoolmaster* commented, had been administered in a less direct form than in the original motion, 'but it is pretty safe to say that every one of the twenty-six voting in favour of the resolution finally carried, mean it to have a very direct and specific reference to Mr Riley's conduct'. 'And', it went on, the replication of its phraseology suggesting its author, 'we rather fancy that when Mr Riley comes to think over the situation he will feel bound to do one of three things -either table a resolution to rescind Rule 15; or give up his inquiries, or leave the Teaching Staff Committee.'[82] The *Board Teacher* expressed the relief of the London teachers:

> that amendment, to men guided by ordinary canons of honesty, would in effect be the same as that of Mr Macnamara's motion ... To Mr Macnamara, as all liberal-minded men and women must be, we are deeply grateful for the able manner in which he has championed the cause of religious freedom and secured, we hope, the protection of conscientious teachers from secret persecution by Mr Riley and his friends.[83]

'Surely', concluded the *Evening News*, 'we have had enough of Mr Riley now, and if he will not resign he may, at least, give London a rest from Rileyism.'[84]

Riley, however, did not resign. He wrote to the Board from St Pitrock Minor, Cornwall, on 23 October:

> ... As the Circular of April 1894 is not rescinded, I assume that the Circular

and the Rule are equally in force and still govern both the religious instruction and the selection and promotion of teachers; otherwise, as I maintained in the debate last week, the Board will have committed itself to the proposition that the religious opinions of teachers not only are not to influence their appointment and promotion, but are not to be a hindrance to their giving the religious instruction to the children – a proposition for which I firmly decline to be in any way responsible.

If the majority of the Board are of opinion that my interpretation of the Board's regulations and resolutions on the subject is admissible, the matter need go no further; if the contrary, they can say so by a straightforward vote. In the latter case I shall feel bound at once to reconsider my position as a member of the Teaching Staff Sub-Committee ...

The letter appeared at the next meeting of the Board, the following afternoon. Members were not, however, disposed to continue the debate on Riley's terms. Discussion of it was postponed and it was not even acknowledged till the following March.[85] A matter of privilege remained. Stanley called attention to the fact that Riley's memorandum on the Progressives' alleged retaliation on the Christian teachers had been issued at the Board's expense. Not only was it a charge that was entirely false, mean and unworthy, but it had also violated the Rules of the Board. Riley withdrew it to cheers, whereupon Jephson asked for precedence to move a resolution that the present Board declined to renew any debate or discussion on the religious question. Seventeen voted in favour, seventeen against, but the Chairman, perceiving that this amounted to a dangerous precedent, let the matter drop.[86]

In its review of the educational year, the *Schoolmaster* concluded that even though progress at the London School Board had been scarcely perceptible, the present position was better than expected:

> Thanks to Mr Riley, religious intolerance at the Board is, to put it forcibly, smashed up – for a time at any rate. The 'Circular', it is true, is still unrepealed, but the crushing exposure of Mr Riley's methods has for a long time branded what is popularly styled 'Rileyism' as a 'nasty, ugly, misshapen beast' – to quote one of Mr Riley's pet phrases.[87]

But this was by no means the end of Riley. He had discovered another way to undermine the undenominational religious instruction purveyed in the London Board Schools. As a member of the Industrial Schools Committee he found himself in charge of a project intended to establish a London Day Industrial School. The terms on which pupils were to be given religious instruction within this school offered promising possibilities which he was already exploiting.

The Industrial Schools movement, providing board, lodging and training for vagrant children, began in Aberdeen in 1841. Legislation for the provision of Industrial Schools in Scotland passed in 1854 provided a model taken up for England in 1857 and 1861. The Scottish and English Acts were consolidated in 1866 when rules for the committal of children below the age of fourteen who were beggars, vagrants, orphans or found frequenting the company of reputed thieves were laid down. Forster's Act of 1870 conferred on school boards the powers, which prison authorities already possessed, of contributing to the establishment of Industrial Schools or of founding them. Sandon's Act of 1876 introduced the idea of Day Industrial Schools in which industrial training, elementary education and one or two meals a day, but no lodging, were provided. Again, prison authorities and school boards were given powers to set them up, aided under the Act by a Parliamentary grant of one shilling per week for each child committed by order of a court.[88] Whilst the London School Board had established an Industrial Schools Committee, it did not at first possess any such institution. Then in 1874 it founded the Brentwood Industrial School and, in 1878, a training ship, the *Shaftesbury*.

Despite the provisions of the 1876 Act no Day Industrial School had been founded.[89] In March 1890 the Industrial Schools Committee at last recommended that action should be taken. Consequently in June 1894 the Goldsmith Street public elementary school off Drury Lane was closed and plans were made to open it as a Day Industrial School for 200 children. At the Board meeting on 28 February 1895 it was reported that the school buildings were being adapted.[90] Rules and regulations were adopted for the new institution on 21 March, with one ominous exception, Article 18 on religious instruction. Debate on the issue was adjourned[91] so that the Board's Solicitor could offer an opinion and the matter did not recur until 2 May, when it became clear what the Moderates had in mind. 'Each day shall be begun and ended with Divine worship consisting of hymns and prayers', the proposed regulation began. Then the provisions of Article 23 of the Order in Council of 20 March 1877 were to be strictly observed, making it clear that religious instruction was to be carried out according to the rules laid down for Industrial Schools. The proposal ended:

> No child shall be required to attend any religious observances or instruction, or shall be taught the catechism or tenets of any religion to which his (or her) parents or guardians object, or other than that to which he (or she) is stated in the order of detention to belong. The managers shall, as far as practicable, make arrangements that the children shall, during the times set apart for religious observances or instruction, attend religious observances or instruction conducted by ministers of such persuasion or by such responsible teachers of the school or other persons as are delegated by such ministers with the approval of the managers.

John Sinclair (West Lambeth) and Roston Bourke (Finsbury) immediately moved an amendment to the effect that religious instruction should be given under the provision of the 1870 Act. It was immediately clear where the debate might lead. In the religious climate of 1895, made sensitive by the teachers' circular issue, a decision to support denominational religious instruction in a Day Industrial School could be understood as a move away from the accepted public elementary school practices under the Cowper-Temple Clause. Even though it was dealing in this case with a special type of school, the choice between denominational and undenominational religious instruction within it was a crucial one. The Board could, according to its Solicitor, adopt either course.

Whiteley, the first speaker, moved that the question should be referred back to the Industrial Schools Committee with an instruction to consider counsel's opinion and to bring the teaching as nearly as possible into harmony with that given in the day schools of the Board. It did not get any easier the more they considered it, he observed. As a School Board it was almost accidental that they had anything to do with this Industrial School work. Now the trouble they had experienced with the religious difficulty in the day schools was leading to a corresponding problem with the Industrial Schools. A compromise was needed but, he admitted, there was a need for something more in the way of religious teaching than was given in the ordinary schools, because if the parents of these children were all that they should be, their children would never be sent to Industrial Schools. Ominously, Diggle took up this point. The kind of religious teaching Whiteley desired for Day Industrial School children, he said, was what some of them would like to see in the Board schools. It did not always follow that the religious teaching given there was supplemented at home. Macnamara intervened. What Whiteley would like was a common basis for religious teaching, with provision made for parents who wanted more or less than that. He was afraid that what Diggle wanted was to extend his principles as to religious teaching in the Day Industrial Schools to the ordinary day schools. His fears were confirmed when Riley spoke. The Day Industrial Schools, he said, should be treated in the matter of religious teaching and observance exactly as the residential schools were.[92]

The recommendations for the Day Industrial School which appeared before the Board on 30 May showed that some attempt to compromise between the two positions had been made. The religious observances and teaching were to be given by, and under the direction of, the head teacher. They were to include simple family worship, hymns and the reading of the Scriptures, and 'a minister of the religious persuasion which, as the case may be, is specified in the order of detention or attendance order as that to which the child appears to ... belong ... may visit the child at the school on such days and at such times as are from time to time fixed by regulations made by the Secretary of State.[93] Again it was plain from the beginning of the debate that difficulties lay ahead. The Chairman of the Committee, dissenting from the proposals, had refused to present them. Six notices of amendment had been given, four of which were intended to ascertain that children were given religious instruction by the ministers of religion appropriate to their beliefs. Drew and Fiennes both inserted the phrase 'as far as practicable' but Riley's amendment, specific to Church of England and Roman Catholic children, was intended to make certain that they did not receive any religious teaching other than that of their own Church or from teachers not of their own faith. His ally, the Duke of Newcastle, called attention to letters from the Vicar of Holy Trinity Church, Great Russell Street and from the priest of the Corpus Christi RC Church, Maiden Lane, both claiming teaching responsibilities in the new school. A letter from Cardinal Vaughan, Archbishop of Westminster, supporting the principle of differentiated instruction, concluded: '... I may perhaps add that what is called undenominational religion will not be a religion that Catholics can accept for themselves or for their children'.[94]

When the Board met again after the Whitsun recess, a further two hours was spent on the topic. Cecil's amendment, seconded by Riley, laid down that children whose religious persuasion had been designated in the Order of Detention should attend religious instruction conducted by appropriate ministers or responsible teachers; children without such affiliation would be instructed by responsible teachers. Another hour was needed to discuss Fiennes' amendment, seconded by Macnamara, which made the requirements even more precise. No child was to attend any religious instruction to which his parents objected. Boys belonging to a particular religious persuasion were to be given religious instruction by appropriate ministers or responsible teachers or other persons delegated by the ministers and approved by the managers. The fundamental principle of the amendment, Macnamara said, was undenominational teaching, for that was what it would eventually resolve itself into, as time elapsed. Others, including Riley, thought the opposite. Nevertheless it was passed by twenty-six votes to one, Cecil and Riley, Fiennes and Macnamara voting on the same side.[95]

At the Board meeting on 1 August, the Industrial Schools Committee reported that the necessary steps had been taken to implement the decision. In response to the applications from the local clergy it had passed resolutions recognising them as the ministers responsible for the children whose religious persuasion was specified in the order of detention as Church of England and Roman Catholic on the understanding that teachers of these faiths would be appointed in due course. Then, having also concluded that the principal teacher should be a member of the Church of England and one of the assistants a Roman Catholic, the Committee had appointed Miss Mary Stansfield, who had for thirteen years been an assistant at the Tower Street Board School, to the former post, and Miss Annie Swann, most recently an assistant teacher in a Liverpool public elementary school and formerly an assistant in Day Industrial Schools in Liverpool and Blackburn, to the latter. The Board confirmed the appointments, Miss Stansfield at a salary of £135 per annum, Miss Swann at £80, both with partial board, but not until there had been considerable discussion which raised the religious question anew.

Once more the issue of religious tests for teachers was emerging; once again it was Riley who was responsible. During the debate Macnamara read out a letter which, he said, had been written to Miss Stansfield on the orders of Riley, as Chairman of the Committee of Managers of the Drury Lane Day Industrial School, making reference to the Board's rules on religious instruction in Industrial Schools. It stated that the Industrial Schools Committee, as managers of the school, would, in all probability, appoint as principal teacher a member of the Church of England. Miss Stansfield was asked whether she was a member of the Church of England, and, if so, requested to forward as soon as possible some further testimonial or testimonials as to her capability, if appointed, of acting as the delegate of the minister of the Church of England, who would be responsible for the religious instruction of the children.[96]

Riley appeared to have found a way of introducing the religious tests so long feared by London School Board teachers. During the summer break he sought to consolidate his advantage. At the Board meeting of 10 October the Rev. William Hamilton (West Lambeth) asked him whether he was correctly quoted in *Church Bells* as saying:

> We are establishing our first Day Industrial School in London this month. I took the Chairmanship of it in order to see that it was established on proper lines, because if this succeeds, we shall probably put them all over London. The school is to be worked entirely on Denominational lines. As affecting the whole school board system this is of indirect, as well as direct importance; because if it be found possible to work a Day School on Denominational lines, this would prove an irresistible argument for working the Board's ordinary day schools on the same lines, should an alteration of the law permit it. The two kinds of schools are practically on all fours with each other, being both day schools, and both being supported out of the rates.

Riley, who the same day was weathering one of the most serious of the attacks on him over the circular issue, replied airily: 'I cannot remember the exact words I used on the occasion of this interview, but the report seems fairly accurate. It may interest Mr Hamilton to know that I referred to the same matter in a letter which appeared in *The Times* of last month.'[97]

With his activities over the circular and the Day Industrial Schools, Riley had made himself into a national figure in the Church of England. For the next few months he was occupied as a member of the Archbishops' Committee, the purpose of which was to advise the new Government on the action that needed to be taken to restore the voluntary schools after the exigent demands of the Acland era. On 20 November it presented the 'Principles to be kept in view in all Legislation affecting Public Elementary Schools' to Lord Salisbury, the Prime Minister. Under principle No. 8, it sought what it called 'reasonable facilities' for separate religious instruction in board as well as voluntary schools, in the spirit of the Industrial Schools Act of 1868. Macnamara, writing in the *Echo*, pointed out that this modification to the 1870 Act might well be in the interests of the Nonconformist children living in the 10,000 English villages possessing only a Church of England school as it was of Church of England children attending the many urban and rural board schools of the country. 'For myself, however', he went on, 'I do not see the need for any change whatever. The board school system of religion is thoroughly Christian, thoroughly wholesome, and such as ought to satisfy parents of all denominations.' Riley's idea, however, was to place in every board school in the country first a permanent teacher who was an Anglican, then a permanent teacher who was a Roman Catholic, then, probably, Free Church teachers, 'and a pretty state of things we should then have arrived at', Macnamara concluded: 'Our teachers would in each case be subjected not only to religious tests, but to *denominational* religious tests; their fitness as teachers would be an entirely secondary consideration; and within the four walls of every board school in the United Kingdom we should have the elements of a very promising theological warfare'.[98]

When the issue of the Day Industrial School in Drury Lane arose again at the Board the following June, Macnamara related how Riley had interpreted the compromise reached in 1895. Riley had made certain that Miss Stansfield, the headmistress, was a member of the Church of England. He had then, without any instruction from the Committee, placed an advertisement for an assistant teacher in only one newspaper, the *Catholic Times*, accompanying it with a letter in which he indicated that since he and his friends had received such generous support from the Roman Catholics in the 1894 election, its readers could understand that their interests were safe in their hands. The subsequent appointment of Miss Swann was agreed unanimously by the Committee with Riley as Chairman. It was, however, open to a number of objections. Miss Swann was an uncertified ex-pupil-teacher, whose salary should have been £26 per annum, not £80, plus three meals a day. This exceptional treatment, Macnamara suggested, had been agreed not so much because of the longer hours she had to work but because of her obligation to be available to meet the demands for Roman Catholic teaching at all times.

By now, however, Riley had a new answer ready. For many years, he said, the London School Board had, in relation to Industrial School teachers, made their fitness to give denominational teaching a condition of appointment, at any rate as far as Roman Catholic teachers were concerned. Diggle, ending the discussion for the time being, pointed out that an earlier section of the Industrial Schools Act of 1866 made Riley's action perfectly acceptable. What was done at the Drury Lane School was not outside the law. This proved to be the last word on the subject. Diggle was interrupted by the six o'clock rule and the debate was adjourned.[99] Later in the month the failure of the Government's Education Bill[100] put an end to Riley's hopes that the Drury Lane School would set a pattern for the whole of London.

In November 1897, in the last weeks of the Board, Macnamara drew attention to yet another of Riley's attempts to undermine undenominational education. Riley had put down a motion for the Board to close the Board schools on Ascension Day. Having failed to gain precedence, he withdrew it and began his efforts afresh on the SMC. A rule had been established by which children might be awarded the 'early mark', which qualified them for prizes and medals if they were away from school for a scholarship examination at a manual training, cookery, laundry, art or swimming class or at the Board's Scripture examination. On 14 May this was extended to include punctual attendances at a religious service. The clergy then became active: at Sunday schools on 23 May forms were given to children to be taken home, filled in by parents and handed to the Board school teachers, demanding permission to be absent from school on Ascension Day to attend a church service. The result, Macnamara went on, was that on 27 May 1,967 children were late for school, 3,012 left early to go to 11.00 am services and 674 were absent altogether. This had been only the beginning. The parish clergy were then sent a circular, signed by influential churchmen, advising them to seek permission for children to be withdrawn from the school's religious instruction on one or two days a week so that they could receive it elsewhere under the direction of their own clergy. Some teachers, having received requests for absence from their pupils, consulted the SMC. They had been informed that such requests should be granted.

As Macnamara pointed out, the extension of the rule of 14 May had not been sanctioned by the Board. Frederick Davies (Chairman of the SMC) had chosen to regard the matter as a question of interpretation. Efforts to bring it to the Board for discussion had been put off by procedural moves. But it was not a question of interpretation, it was a principle: 'the extreme Church party had obviously been assured that they could get all they wanted in the way of "facilities" for denominational instruction "within" and "without" the school under "existing rules" – which was very far from being a complete or accurate statement of existing facts'.

Davies attempted to justify his action in terms of the Board's prize and medal policy. The rule had emerged, he said, from an SMC session, lasting nearly an hour, on 14 May, at which it had been agreed that punctual attendance at a religious service, commencing at such an hour as would preclude punctual attendance at day school, would, with satisfactory proof, count as the equivalent of an attendance. It was a rule capable of different interpretations. Cases were brought forward day after day requiring settlement. He had acted as he was bound to do and, in his opinion, Macnamara had raised the matter for vote-catching purposes.

This view failed to convince the Board. A. W. Shepheard (a new member for Marylebone) said that Davies must be either mentally deficient or deficient in honour if he meant to suggest he did not know the difference between religious instruction and a religious service. Stanley, who had been present at the meeting of 14 May, said it was clear that Davies' arrangement would not hold water. The action he had taken was underhand and dishonest. At this point Colonel Hubbard moved the previous question, adding that Davies had taken an improper way of stealing a party victory for the Church. In his own opinion a man should either work inside the School Board for the good of the people, or take up his position outside if he wanted to destroy the system. A double-faced attitude was to be deplored. He considered it a great waste of time to take the matter any further.

But Riley could not resist joining in. 'Oh, what a tangled web we weave, when once we practise a deceit', he observed. They did not know where they were because the Board had always shown a disposition not to be perfectly straight on the religious difficulty. He also, he added, objected to the principle of a 'Chairman's gloss' upon the resolutions of Committees. At this point the debate was interrupted by the five o'clock rule.[101] The next meeting of the Board, at which Riley resumed his speech, was the last one before the triennial election. If this kind of instruction were to be substituted for the kind at present given, then the Board needed to institute a far-reaching and drastic reform which, he said, should be brought about by straightforward means, not by a Chairman's gloss upon his committee's interpretation of a Rule of the Board dealing with cookery and laundry classes. 'Probably this is the last piece of advice I may ever offer to this Board', he added, 'and I will conclude by saying to one and all, "Be true and just in all your dealings".'

Diggle, speaking a little later, said that he regarded the whole matter as an election ploy devised by Gautrey and Macnamara. The former, in 1895, had stated that the Progressives intended to keep the religious question alive till the next election. The teacher who had written the question to Davies had been prompted by Gautrey; the interpretation decided upon by the Committee had been decided upon when there was a majority of Progressives upon it. It was a red herring.

The debate continued until 5.00 pm when the Board passed on to the reports of committees, to disband later in the evening for the election. Diggle came under attack. Gautrey commented that he was sorry to see a man of Diggle's ability and experience deteriorating so rapidly since his Chairmanship. Instead of taking a broad view, he now constantly descended to personalities and trivialities. As for his charge of collusion with the teacher concerned, he denied it emphatically. Macnamara opened with a personal complaint against Diggle, whose tactics he described as contemptible. Rather than wait to hear a reply to the charges he had made, Diggle had left the Board Room. As usual, Macnamara said, the teachers and their leaders had been denounced; the teacher in this particular case had been bitterly and unfairly attacked. He reminded the Board in Diggle's absence of a sentence in the first of the manifestos that the former Chairman had issued. It ran: 'no policy can succeed which is not directed by abiding principles based upon permanent and settled convictions'. It was about time, Macnamara said, that Diggle learned to act upon it.[102]

The religious question was to be one of the main issues of the 1897 election. The other was money. Here, again, Macnamara and Riley clashed. Whilst Macnamara regarded the Board as an instrument by which the taxpayer and the ratepayer could assist the children of less fortunate parents to develop their talents, not only in their own but also in the national interest, Riley took a much more limited view, that board schools were charity schools for pupils who, because they were born into a low social class, were fated to stay there. Taxing him with hypocrisy over the circular issue at the Board in February 1894, Ruth Homan (Tower Hamlets) commented that Riley and his friends were certainly not among those who were willing to give up everything to follow Him whose word they preached: talk to them of the poor and they would tell you they should be kept in their proper places.[103]

The 1870 Act had laid down that the boards would receive part of their income from the Treasury, any deficiency being met through the proceeds of a local rate. Riley regarded it as a duty to defend the interests of ratepayers. Board school facilities, he believed, needed to be basic, their curricula limited. In April 1890, the year before he was elected, the Board had passed to the SMC the proposal that pianos would be beneficially used in schools. It had provoked a public outcry and a petition signed by the Duke of Westminster, the Earl of Wemyss and Dr Temple, Bishop of London, which declared that education should not be made to stink in the nostrils of the ratepayers by making it a serious burden unless there was a positive necessity for doing so.[104] Riley took up the issue. At the end of 1892 the journal *Church Bells* quoted from a letter he had written to the newspapers explaining to the ratepayers what heroic efforts he was making as a Board member in the cause of economy. 'Everybody by this time knows that', the *Board Teacher* commented in its new year edition, 'and how, amongst his other economies, Mr Riley is opposed to having pianos in schools.' On the day that the letter appeared, it went on, invitations were issued by Messrs John Broadwood and Sons, asking people to come and see, at their premises in Great Pulteney Street, a decorated grand pianoforte, designed by T. G. Jackson Esq ARA for – Athelstan Riley Esq. 'Truly it is a beautiful piano, and must have cost some hundreds of pounds' the *Board Teacher* concluded:

> We have not a word to say against it. Mr Riley is a rich man, with dainty tastes. He is doing an admirable thing in having fine pieces of furniture made which gratify his taste and give good artists and workmen their opportunity. But it is a little dangerous game this, perhaps, of surrounding yourselves with luxuries and grudging in the cause of the education of less fortunate brethren, the expenditure of a few pounds whereby some sort of pleasantness may be brought into their lives also. One has to be very careful with oneself – self-deception is so easy.[105]

The precept for the rate contribution, discussed six months in advance, presented opportunities for members to express their opinions on Board policy. In July 1895 Walter Key, Chairman of the Finance Committee, disclosed that the precept for the half year till 25 March 1896 would be £897,023, adding that it was, unfortunately, the largest which the ratepayers had ever yet been called upon to pay. Macnamara described the educational tone of Key's speech as a discredit to the school board of Little Pedlington.[106] Riley, having moved the adjournment, took up the issue the following week:

> Everyone knew the London School Board had long been a bye-word for extravagance and callous disregard for the unfortunate ratepayer ... Mr Diggle, Mr Stanley and the rest 'taken asunder', to use the words of an old English philosopher, seem men and the reasonable creatures of God; but confused together, make but one great beast, and a monstrosity more prodigious than hydra ... Mr Macnamara and Mr Gautrey were there to force up teachers' salaries and to weaken the Board's control over them ... The Board, and apparently the Education Department too, under the late lamented Mr Acland ... thought a school building erected twenty years ago, out of date and unsuited to modern requirements ... [107]

The growing financial difficulties of the voluntary schools, made more acute by Acland's measures (particularly the fabric circular) brought a further element into Riley's campaign. Church leaders were complaining about school board expenditure, making comparisons between the level of teacher salaries in board and voluntary schools not with the aim of raising the latter but of reducing the former. 'I am certain that a considerable portion of the expenditure is simply wasted', Dr Temple wrote in December, 'and that the schools might be made quite as good as they are at much lower cost.' The provision of secondary type education was one cause: 'But there is waste beside this which ought to be checked. And the expenditure both in salaries and buildings might be diminished without hurting the board schools at all ... There are men in the board schools who are doing work which could equally be done by men inferior to themselves.'[108]

The agenda paper of the London School Board was now crowded with the complaints of the vestries, the rate-collecting agents. The *Schoolmaster* quoted at length a letter from the Precinct Clerk of the Parish of St Sepulchre which appeared on 19 December 1895. It expressed the desire of the parishioners to place on record an emphatic protest against the extravagant and unnecessary expenditure of the London School Board. Referring to the 1870 Act it added that 'in the opinion of Mr Forster, its illustrious founder, the Act was to be applied only where there was educational destitution ... it was intended as a rule for the waifs and strays or gutter children'. Elementary education amounted to reading, writing and arithmetic, but, the letter continued, 'the education now given is of the most elaborate character, and ... Board schools are filled with the children of well-to-do people as a rule, whilst the waifs and strays are outside the schools and swarm the markets and the streets of this huge metropolis'.[109] At the same session Riley called attention to the fact that the Board's debt on loans, which amounted to £8,500,000, was not far short of the National Debt of Denmark, namely £10,000,000. It was £1,500,000 more than the National Debt of Norway and three or four times as much as that of Switzerland.[110]

Earlier in the month the Chairman of the Finance Committee had announced that to meet the next deficiency £831,155 would be needed from the rates. The ensuing debate about the effectiveness of the expenditure enabled the Nonconformist JP, William Winnett, to introduce, not for the first time, his tale of the boy who had passed the Seventh Standard but could not do a sum in rule of three. This brought in Macnamara, who was as sceptical about the existence of this boy as was Betsy Prig about the existence of Mrs Harris. Riley in turn moved to express regret that the expenditure of the Board had exceeded even the lavish estimates presented twelve months before. There was, he said, no likelihood of any reform on the part of the School Board unless Parliament imposed upon some other public body the duty of watching and controlling the Board's expenditure. When put to the vote, however, his amendment was defeated by twenty-five votes to three, with seven abstentions. Apart from Riley, those in favour were the Duke of Newcastle and Thomas Huggett, the Kensington builder whose main contribution to Board debates was to complain about waste.[111]

Riley and Huggett took up the subject again in the new year. The *Schoolmaster* reported on the Board meeting of 13 February 1896:

> The garrulity to which this unique collection of bores is always so prone finds its subject today in a question of expenditure raised by Mr Riley and Mr Huggett in an amendment to the Finance Committee's 'formal' proposal to make arrangements for borrowing money from the County Council. There are bewailments of 'grievous cost', lamentations concerning schools which it is said are not needed, and much chagrin that the Board has bound itself to pay trades' union wages ... Each party charges the other with extravagance, and then comes a childish wrangle about the closure ... the debate continues an hour and three quarters before there is a division ... More pure obstruction follows of one sort and another, Mr Riley chirping about the room in high glee. Net result of work done, so far as we can see – nil! [112]

In July when the next deficiency was announced, Riley again moved that some external controlling body should be appointed and suggested that the Board accompany its precept to ratepayers with a letter of apology. He continued with a long attack on its administration:

> Everybody who has rates to pay knows that this hateful thing called a 'precept' is about to be issued and that the School Board rate has gone up as usual; everybody is asking when it is going to stop going up ... The rate which was

8¾d in the pound in 1886, 11d in 1891 and 11½d in 1895, has now passed the shilling ... What is the cause of this increased rate? The old story – reckless expenditure in nearly every department ... Trusting the School Board with the rates is like shutting up a cat in a dairy.[113]

Riley's amendment was taken up by Macnamara. The struggling ratepayer Riley was so anxious about was, he said, the struggling West End ratepayer. He ridiculed the idea that there was no control over School Board expenditure. It was the ratepayers with whom ultimate control rested.[114] Diggle, the following week, blamed the individual members of the Board for what he said was an abnormal precept. They voted the money away in driblets and when they saw the grand total they were astounded. When Macnamara went to speak with the working men at Clapham he told them that all the excessive expenditure was the necessary oil to lubricate the machine. If this were so then the machine needed a great amount of lubricating. His contention was that the Rules of the Board were systematically and regularly evaded by a majority of members. Stanley had suggested that a Special Committee should inquire into expenditure. This Diggle regarded as absurd. What was needed, he said, was a body of men determined to do their best for the welfare of the children but determined to do so with the conviction that any money they spent for the purpose over and above what was absolutely necessary for the work was creating outside a spirit of antagonism to the Board's operations.[115]

The proposal that a Special Committee be appointed to examine the whole question of expenditure and to discover where, if at all, economies could be effected was agreed without difficulty on 3 December. Among the members were Stanley and Coxhead, who between them had proposed its establishment, Diggle (who had changed his mind about the idea), Davies, Key and Macnamara.[116] It proved to be a disappointment. Its report, published the following May, showed a division of opinion among the members. The majority (including Macnamara) proposed to entrust the Board Accountant with the responsibility of drawing up estimates: 'The only way to get the estimate absolutely untinged with partisanship and a genuinely workable allowance', Macnamara argued, 'was to have on record somewhere the expert opinion of the permanent official.' Diggle, however, maintained that it was wrong to move the responsibility from elected members to non-elected members.[117]

The last Estimates of the ninth Board were discussed in the wake of Queen Victoria's Diamond Jubilee. 'The real question', Macnamara commented, 'was, did they get value for money?' This was a question to which *The Times* had recently given an unqualified affirmative. The gross total expenditure had been £2,956,879, the cost of three ironclads. Since the British people had just been given one of these, they might well pay up the costs of the schools cheerfully (Hear, hear and laughter). Some day one of the colonies would help them by sending a present of half-a-dozen board schools (Laughter). Three millions was, no doubt, a large sum. But London's share of the cost of the army was nearer four millions, her share of the cost of the Navy five millions and, as Diggle had told the Duke and Duchess of Connaught at the recent Albert Hall Display, 'If their Royal Highnesses had been able to see the behaviour of the people of London during the Jubilee celebrations, they might have attributed the order and good humour that prevailed not to the police or military, but to what the schools had done for the people' (Hear, hear). The Chairman of the Finance Committee, Mr Key, had reminded them: 'a country is rich in such a degree as its children are strong in that which makes for righteousness and truth; and poor, however much of land or gold it may possess, if its children lack these qualities'. If he wanted this idea realised, Macnamara said, he should not grumble so bitterly at the cost (Hear, hear). He could not have it both ways. The teachers cost £1,216,826; in the same area the police cost £1,361,975. So long as its policemen cost any community more than its pedagogues, that community need not fear that it was spending too much on laying down the solid foundations for the superstructure of the children's lives which Mr Key had talked about (Cheers).[118]

Macnamara's speech drew a response from Riley which failed to find the mark. Macnamara, he said, had made his usual speech and said that the ratepayers received good value for money (Macnamara: 'I quoted that from *The Times*'). He and others were there to do their best to see that teachers' salaries were put up; it was not for people of that kind to talk about value for money (J. C. Horobin: 'Why not? We were elected in the same manner that you were'). He had gone on to say that the good humour of the crowd at the Jubilee celebrations was due to the work of the London School Board (Macnamara: 'No, that was Mr Diggle' [Laughter]).[119]

Riley's interest in the Board and its affairs was now on the wane. In April he had announced that he did not intend to offer himself for the third time as a candidate for election. Both religious instruction and expenditure, he had decided, could only be dealt with by means of legislation and he was convinced that the special work he had set himself to accomplish on the School Board had been done. In the future he would work for the cause from an independent position.[120]

As Riley withdrew, it was plain that the reputation of Diggle, his patron and associate, had been fatally compromised. As the ninth Board began he had persuaded himself that the small majority by which the Moderates had been returned to power was a temporary setback occasioned by the religious issue, about which he himself had since been circumspect. During the course of the Board his administrative and educational expertise had been increasingly eclipsed, not only by Stanley, an old antagonist, but by a new one, Macnamara. Finally, his reputation amongst the teachers was destroyed by what appeared to be his personal vendetta against one of them.

His distaste for teachers had been made clear in his objection to the Rev. T. W. Sharpe as his possible successor as Chairman of the Board in 1894. Sharpe, however, was a university man. Teachers from Board schools constituted an even more objectionable species. In March 1895 Diggle and Davies were interviewed for the *St James' Gazette* on the influence of school board education on the morals and manners of the rising generation. In response to a question about the provenance of Board school teachers, one of them replied that such people were, first, pupil-teachers in the Board schools and afterwards educated in training colleges.

'And *are* they educated?' the interviewer enquired.

'No, they are not educated', came firmly, if reluctantly from both gentlemen. 'The teachers have a great deal to learn. They have to learn that public respect comes from conscientious discharge of duty, whereas they think it is to be won by self-assertion, and they do assert themselves. We are constantly lectured by our own servants.'

'Then the teachers are not likely to inculcate the duty of ordering oneself lowly and reverently to all one's betters?'

'No, because they do not consider that they have any betters'.[121]

In October 1896 a new President of the Metropolitan Board Teachers' Association assumed office. It was Macnamara's friend Jackman. The subject of his presidential address, the expenditure of the London School Board, he discussed with fourteen years' experience as a London teacher. He had been an assistant master at Webber Row, then at Holland Street, Southwark, and he was now headmaster of a temporary school recently opened in a disused Baptist Chapel in Horsley Street, Walworth. Referring to his address as 'lucid and able' in an editorial entitled 'Value for Money', the *Schoolmaster* added: 'We do not think it would be easy to find, within an equal compass, so many proofs that, enormous though the expenditure is and must of necessity be, yet, compared with that of other cities, it is certainly not "extravagant" when the vastness of the work is considered'.[122]

Jackman had been active in the circular affair and had also attacked Riley for depriving children of pianos and swimming baths.[123] When a permanent building was ready for his school, his two assistants were immediately appointed to it. Jackman applied for the headship. The Board's Teaching Staff Committee put his name on the shortlist of three. At the Committee's next meeting, however, Diggle, who did not approve of automatic transfers, called attention to what he termed an irregularity, raised the issue at the SMC and, when Jackman's appointment was proposed, referred the proposal back for reconsideration.

The matter reached the Board on 20 May 1897. Diggle, moving that the proposed nomination be referred back, said that the appointment of a head teacher was as serious as any subject they had to consider. He reminded his colleagues of the procedures that should be followed.

He could understand a motion that a teacher having done admirable work should, without competition, be put in charge of a school, but notice would be given. A precedent for this case did not exist in the history of the Board. Macnamara intervened. 'There are several', he said, but Diggle pressed on, comparing Jackman with one of the other candidates and arguing that the latter had spent longer in the service of the Board and had better qualifications. Admitting, however, that Jackman's qualifications were good, he added meaningfully that he did not seem to have given his undivided allegiance to teaching. This observation failed to impress the Board. Speaker after speaker referred to Jackman's achievements at Horsley Street. When he finally intervened, Macnamara said that it was merely to clear up the matter upon which Diggle had laid such stress. Having dealt with the precedents with the assistance of a list prepared for him by the Clerk, he went on: 'It is difficult to believe, and I say this deliberately, that Mr Diggle has nothing personal against this man ... I want Mr Diggle to be open and frank with us, and I invite him to tell us what it is that he has against this teacher – [Dissent] – for his arguments based on the question of precedent do not hold'. Diggle did not reply. Consequently, Jackman's appointment to the Faraday Street School was confirmed.[124]

Diggle's defeat at the triennial election of November 1897 was almost universally forecast. In September the *Board Teacher* commented:

> Mr Diggle's position as leader of the 'Moderate and Unionist' Party is not enviable. One section of the party will not support him till he declares in favour of assimilating the religious instruction given in Board schools to that given in voluntary schools; another section refuses to follow him when he is trying to assimilate the secular education given in Board schools to that given in voluntary schools. What wonder, therefore, that his manifesto contains no clear statement of an intelligible and consistent policy ...?[125]

In October the right-wing *Pall Mall Gazette*, referring to his second manifesto, observed:

> ... The cry of 'economy' which Mr Diggle has raised is a mere trick to catch votes. He must know that a reversion to the 'economical' policy of 1891–94 is the most ruinous step to the cause of elementary education that could be taken ... It was just this spurious economy of 1891–94 that led to the increased expenditure of the succeeding triennium ... If any one is responsible for the increased expenditure of the present Board it is Mr Diggle.[126]

The Conservative Party was also treating Diggle with disdain. In 1895 at Brighton, and in 1896 at Rochdale, he had appeared as spokesman on education at the annual conference of Conservative Associations. This year, a week or so before the Board election, the *Schoolmaster* reported that Lord Salisbury, addressing the conference at the Albert Hall, had made no mention of him or his policies:

> The Prime Minister, our readers do not need to be reminded, is pretty keen

upon the education question; but after dealing with foreign affairs his Lordship markedly omitted all reference to the London School Board election, which takes place within a few days, and passed directly to the London County Council elections, which will not take place for many weeks.[127]

The *Schoolmaster* described the Board election results as startling. The central feature in what it called 'this historical contest' was the defeat of Diggle: that he should have given fifteen of the best years of his life to the Board only to be rewarded by rejection and defeat, it concluded, was intensely pathetic. Of the fifty-five seats the official Progressives won twenty-nine; they had the additional support of four Independent Progressives. The Moderates won only twenty-two; of these, five were judged, on previous form, to have Progressive tendencies.[128] 'London has done magnificently', the *Board Teacher* concluded: 'It has elected a School Board that is vastly superior to nearly all its predecessors. 1870 gave us a sprinkling of clever thinkers, 1897 gives us a host of resolute and capable workers.'[129]

Nevertheless the damage done to the Board by Riley and his friends between 1894 and 1897 proved to be mortal. The religious question became a national question. 'Mr Riley represents a great party in the Church', the *School Board Chronicle* had commented in November 1894. 'He is not a mere London adventurer in this business. He is not working for a mere local triumph, however great and important the area in which he is personally a combatant.'[130] The issue of denominational religious instruction, taken up at Church Congress and then in the House of Commons, would bring down the first major attempt to reform the local administration of education in 1896 and prolong the debates over the Bill of 1902. In the meantime the Board of 1897–1900 aimed to restore its reputation. But the energetic and purposeful efforts that were made proved to be self-defeating. As well as his claims about religious instruction, Riley's charges of extravagance had also received wide publicity. Between 1894 and 1897 they could not be substantiated. When Macnamara and his colleagues began once more to extend the activities of the Board, the charges were renewed. Taken to the courts they brought about the end, not only of the London School Board, but also of the board system itself.

5

President of the NUT

As the Conservative-Unionist government assumed power in the summer of 1895 it was plain that, within the life of the new Parliament, education would be a major issue. The Bryce Commission, set up to examine how a national system of secondary education could be created, was completing its report. The financial difficulties of the voluntary schools, exacerbated by Arthur Acland's initiatives, were becoming increasingly difficult to ignore. Ominously, echoes of the debate on religious instruction begun at the London School Board by the Rev. John Coxhead and Athelstan Riley were beginning to be heard in Parliamentary circles.

The National Union of Teachers had long been dissatisfied with the administration of elementary education. The voluntary bodies, in existence long before 1870, had redoubled their efforts to earn building grants during the six months' grace that they were permitted under Section 96 of Forster's Act. In the 1870s and 1880s their efforts to establish schools without these grants and without rate aid did not slacken. Hence a nationwide, though incomplete, network of voluntary schools existed. Intermeshed with it, a system of schools provided by boards was developing. In urban areas voluntary schools and board schools might compete and thereby improve. In the country isolated schools, voluntary or board, often lacked any such motivation. At the Bryce Commission, in July 1894, Macnamara and the previous year's Union President, Charles Bowden, pointed out that the local administration of elementary education in rural districts needed improvement before any expansion into secondary education provision could be considered. Bowden expounded the Union's view that the best area would be an administrative county as defined by the Local Government Act of 1888. Within such an area he envisaged an authority funded by the county council but elected *ad hoc* to assume control of all education, primary and secondary, within the district. School boards would be absorbed and it would be possible also to absorb the managers of voluntary schools. Macnamara was asked whether he had any observations to add. He replied:

> I quite agree with Mr Bowden as to the absolute essentiality that all forms of education in each locality shall be under one control. That is the beginning and end of the whole problem. Unless you do secure that, you fail to secure a proper linkage of schools and a proper passage for bright children. But, having said that, I disagree with Mr Bowden as to the constitution of the Local

Authority. I think the *ad hoc* election is a most desirable one, but I think it is not at all practicable. I say that what we want to do is to take all the existing Educational Authorities and from those establish a composite board in each locality.[1]

James Yoxall, from his position as a Commissioner, sought to resolve the disagreement between his colleagues on their second appearance. 'I take it', he said to Bowden, 'that the view of the Union you represent is that the Local Authority shall be an elective body for preference, with a composite body created by existing bodies as an alternative?' 'First an elective body *ad hoc*', Bowden replied firmly. 'Then, if that were found utterly impracticable, a composite body composed of the bodies in existence at the time.'[2]

Of the bodies in existence at local level, the school boards, entrusted in 1870 with elementary education, had apparently achieved a great deal. Because they were elected, however, they were variable. In large cities and towns they tended to be progressive. In smaller urban areas and especially in the country they could easily, through the exercise of the cumulative vote, be packed by elements hostile to educational endeavour. 'What is your objection to taking the school board and making it the Local Educational Authority?', the Chairman asked Macnamara. 'I do not think the school boards are competent, as at present constituted, to deal with all forms of local education', he replied.[3] On his second appearance when the issue of rural education was raised, he agreed that small school boards could be less progressive, in some cases, than even the clergy. 'I have', he said, 'no words strong enough to say against a small school board.'[4] He put the same view in a letter to *The Times* in September the following year: 'If the school is under a small school board then, three times out of four, God help the mistress, for nothing is more exquisite than the torture inflicted by the pettifogging, ignorant and illiterate school board member'.[5]

The Bryce Commission Report, published on 1 November 1895, laid out detailed recommendations about education administration. At the centre a consolidated Ministry for Education was advocated. At the local level a general and representative body to take charge of secondary education had been sought. The Report concluded that the county councils and county boroughs created by the Local Government Act of 1888 and given the opportunity by the Technical Instruction Act of 1889 to organise schemes of technical education, were appropriate for the purpose. If these recommendations were followed, elementary and secondary education would be under different kinds of administration: the former under an *ad hoc* system, the latter under bodies with a variety of local functions.[6]

Macnamara, writing in the *Fortnightly Review*, expressed general approval of the Bryce conclusions but referred to its local administration recommendations as an egregious blunder:

to call into being new State secondary schools, and place them under management entirely apart from the State work already accomplished, is to contradict very materially our supposed desire for co-ordination ... I very sincerely hope that all the friends of national progress will strongly oppose the keeping apart, in any way whatever, of the local management of the primary and the secondary State schools.

Urban school boards, Macnamara considered, could be expanded so as to take on post-elementary education. In the counties 'the proper course to have taken ... would have been to have recommended the direct election of a County Board of Education hereafter to supervise every branch of education in the county, from the infants' school desk to the University College lecture-room'.[7]

Changes in the administration of education were also being discussed by the Church of England. In the autumn of 1894, mainly in response to Acland's building circular, the Archbishops of Canterbury and York took the initiative in setting up a special committee under the chairmanship of Lord Cross, to make recommendations for safeguarding the financial future of voluntary schools. Members included Frederick Temple (Bishop of London), Edward Talbot (future Bishop of Rochester and ex-principal of Keble College, Oxford), Lord Cranbrook (the former Lord President) and Lord Cranborne, eldest son of Lord Salisbury and MP for Rochester. The so-called Archbishops' Committee reported in January 1895, concluding that whilst the main cause of the difficulties of voluntary schools was the building circular, the pressure had been greatly aggravated in many of the manufacturing and mining districts by the operation of the Fees Act of 1891. Rate aid, which might involve local popular control, was rejected as a solution by a majority of the committee. If financial aid was to be sought it was considered better to apply to the Exchequer.[8] Arthur Balfour, appointed First Lord of the Treasury and Leader of the House in the Government, duly made clear during the election campaign that he and his colleagues were anxious to relieve the financial difficulties of the voluntary schools, though he was not yet decided on what their policy was to be. 'Are we not bound to do something to preserve the voluntary school, and to do that something quickly?', he asked his constituents. 'My belief, at all events, is that this is one of the questions which we can least afford to neglect and which we least ought to neglect.'[9] In September, an exchange of letters with Cranborne was published in *The Times* in which Balfour repeated his intention to take action on the voluntary school question. 'I am extremely anxious', he wrote, 'that something effectual should be done to relieve the almost intolerable strain to which these schools are now subjected, and this is, I believe, the general wish of the party and of the Government.'[10] Again no concrete proposals were made.

Balfour, at least, made no move to reduce expenditure on education. The Bishop of London regarded this as the solution to the voluntary schools' financial problem. Dr Temple declared:

Looking not to the church schools, but to our whole system, I have no hesitation in expressing my own opinion that ... a good deal of the money spent on elementary education is wasted ... Mr Forster, in 1870, openly declared his belief that a rate of 3d in the £ would entirely cover the expenses of the school boards and their schools. If that limit had been imposed it would not have involved so hard a strain on the resources of Churchmen to maintain church schools at the same cost as that incurred by the boards ... If Mr Forster had held fast to his principle, and had fixed even so high a limit as 6d in the pound, I believe the education would have been quite as good and the trouble to the church schools would not have arisen.[11]

Macnamara, quoting the Bishop's view at the NUT Executive meeting on 21 October, commented that such education, as far as it went, might have been good, but it would have been of the most elementary character. It was the duty of the Union to do its best for both teachers and children in the voluntary schools, but it was impossible to work with those who with one breath asked the Government for aid and with the next advocated spending less money on education.[12] At a conference on education at Bristol the following January he reversed the Bishop's argument. 'Did anyone present', he asked, 'say too much money was spent on board school education? Then if not, too little was spent on children in voluntary schools.' Of every five children attending elementary schools, three were in these schools. Blue Book returns showed that the average cost of educating a board school child was 10s 8d higher than the cost in a voluntary school. The salaries of board school teachers averaged £1 17s 9¼d per child in average attendance. In voluntary schools the average was £1 9s. Balfour, he said, had talked about the 'almost intolerable strain' resting upon the managers of voluntary schools, but of the 10s 8d difference in costs, 8s 9¾d, or nearly five-sixths, was borne by their teachers. Concerning the 3,000,000 children and 70,000 teachers in voluntary schools, he did not care, he declared, what the politics of the members of his audience might be. It was the right thing to see that these children got the right education and the teachers the right treatment.[13]

These arguments reappeared in an article in the *Schoolmaster* on 22 February. Everybody knew, he declared, that both board and voluntary schools had the same pull on the Exchequer. It followed that the financial weakness of the voluntary schools was derived from the fact that the subscriptions they received did not match the rates available to board schools. As he repeated the view that he had advanced in Bristol, that it was the teachers in voluntary schools who were bearing the 'intolerable strain', the underlying argument, implied rather than stated, was that rates should be universally set and that voluntary schools should share in them.[14]

It was Lord Salisbury who had begun the national debate on religious instruction. In May 1893 the *School Board Chronicle* had reported a sparsely attended Second Reading of the Bishop of Salisbury's eventually unsuccessful Elementary Education (Religious Instruction) Bill in the House of Lords. During the debate the Conservative leader had declared that the Cowper-Temple clause, the lynch pin of non-denominational religious education in the board schools, was 'an absolute failure'.[15] Now, five months into the new Ministry, the Archbishop of Canterbury placed before Lord Salisbury the memorial entitled 'the Principles to be kept in view in all legislation affecting Public Elementary Schools'[16] which had strengthened Riley's determination to end non-denominational religious education under the London School Board. In the January edition of the *Nineteenth Century*, Riley congratulated himself on what he saw as the change in public opinion over the voluntary schools in the four years since 1891, when they had seemed doomed to gradual and painless extinction and undenominationalism 'appeared destined to bind the next generation of Englishmen together not in Christian unity, but in a hideous indifferentism to the principles of the Christian faith'.[17] Now the 1870 education settlement could be reconsidered. Macnamara, in the *Contemporary Review*, admitted that it could be argued that those who were advocating a modification of the excellent system of religious instruction which the country had enjoyed over twenty-five years were as much activated by the interests of the Nonconformist children living in the 10,000 English villages possessing only a Church of England school as they were on behalf of the Church of England children attending the board schools of the country. But he did not think this was the case. The demand came 'from those who least of all have any claim to speak on behalf of the working class parent; who are not working class parents themselves; who do not love or use the public elementary schools, and whose acquaintance with the life of the working classes is of an extremely exiguous character'. He was not prepared to overturn the existing system in response to their claims, because they were impracticable:

> The schools do not lend themselves to the simultaneous inculcation of differing denominational tenets to a dozen or more little pens of denominational juveniles under the care of amateur teachers who are far from being distinguished either for the genius of simple elucidation or for the power of maintaining discipline amongst youngsters.[18]

The Conservatives had never attempted a radical reform of national education. Having set up the far-ranging Royal Commission on the Working of the Elementary Education Acts (the Cross Commission of 1886–88), their response to its recommendations had been muted. Now, Salisbury's appointments to the education posts in the new Government made progress difficult. The new Lord President was the Liberal Unionist Duke of Devonshire, whom Queen Victoria had wished to appoint as Prime Minister, instead of Gladstone, in 1880. The details of educational administration, however interesting to the enthusiast, were 'frankly distasteful to the Duke's temperament', his private secretary admitted.[19] Gorst, the Vice-President, had been one of Great Britain's representatives at the Berlin International Conference on Child Labour in 1890 and had served on the Departmental Committee on the Maintenance and Education of Poor Law Children of 1894–95. 'We heartily testify, to his especial fitness for the post of Vice-President of the Council', the *Schoolmaster* declared on 27 July. 'As a man of the highest intellectual and academic distinction, it is impossible for him not to respond with a touch of fraternity to the aspirations of teachers. We therefore look forward with a considerable measure of confidence and hope to Sir John's rule at Whitehall.'[20]

Gorst's appointment proved, however, to be unfortunate. He was already nearly sixty years old. Since graduating in 1857 as Third Wrangler in the University for which he was now a member of Parliament, he had expected to attain high office. He had been Solicitor General (1885–86), Under Secretary for India (1886–91) and Financial Secretary to the Treasury (1891–92). His interest in education centred on the reform of local administration. But already it had been noted that he was a natural enthusiast turned by the ingratitude of his party into a cynic.[21] Now, growing increasingly bitter, he was to be subjected to interference from Salisbury, Balfour and other members of the Cecil family whose priority was the defence of the voluntary schools.

Whatever emerged from the conflicting views of the various members and supporters of the new Government, the probability that the education settlement of 1870 would be changed was sufficient to stimulate the recovery of the Liberal Party, dispirited after its electoral defeat. At the end of January 1896 at the Queen's Hall, Langham Place, a great meeting was held organised by the National Education Emergency Committee and the National Education League of the Evangelical Free Churches, under the presidency of H. H. Asquith. In his address, Asquith emphasised that the meeting was not intended to have the character of a party demonstration. There were, in the hall, habitual and loyal supporters of the Government. It was not the intention of the organisers to attack the Government's educational policy because, he said, they had not the faintest idea what that policy would be (Laughter). The Duke of Devonshire had already hinted that there were differences of opinion in the cabinet over education. He himself was quite willing, whilst the delicate process of adjusting the focus was still going on (Laughter), to set off the Duke's relatively reassuring declarations against the sinister and reactionary dicta of the Prime Minister. Asquith went on to present a measured and persuasive defence both of the compromise of 1870 (which he implied was in danger from the ill-informed views of Lord Salisbury) and the achievements of the school boards. These, he said, had, over twenty-five years, done their work well: 'there is no department of our national expenditure which the people of this country are entitled to regard with more solid and unmixed satisfaction, nor is there any which has yielded a more remunerative social dividend' (Cheers). The Prime Minister, however, was disposed to consider that the requirements of these elected responsible bodies were adequately met by the proceeds of a threepenny rate (Laughter) whilst demanding further resources from the Exchequer for the voluntary schools, the managers of which were responsible to nobody. Asquith reminded his audience that, in 1870, it had not been expected that the voluntary system would be indefinitely extended, and that it had been enacted that voluntary schools should not receive more in government grants that they received from local sources. Instead, more schools had been built and, since the 1876 Act, they had been able to earn 17s 6d per pupil without any corresponding local contribution. If, as seemed likely, the Government was planning to relieve the 'intolerable strain' then, he declared, the principle of local control should be extended.[22]

These arguments in favour of the boards furnished an advance warning of the opposition that could be expected if the Government, acting on Bryce Report recommendations, made any move to displace the boards from the local administration of education. As a bill began to take shape, the administrative framework was taken care of by Gorst and Kekewich. Financial assistance for voluntary schools and religious education were dealt with by Balfour and his personal advisers.[23] What finally emerged was a patchwork document.[24] Gorst, responsible for only part of it, was, however, given the task of piloting it through the House of Commons.

The Vice-President introduced it on 31 March as a measure for decentralisation. Public education provision, both elementary and secondary, was now to be supervised by the county councils and county boroughs set up under the Local Government Act of 1888. Because the Education Department was overwhelmed by detail (as the century ended it was dealing individually with 2,568 school boards and 14,238 bodies of school managers), there was a good deal of justification for this move which, in principle, had already been recommended by the Newcastle Commission of 1858–61, the Taunton Commission of 1864–67 and the Samuelson Commission of 1881–84 before it was taken up by Bryce. Nevertheless, the Bill was only superficially innovatory. It left untouched the school boards, both large and small. Despite the urgent advice that had been received from church interests on the subject of financial aid, the Government did not propose to make rates available to voluntary schools. Under Clause 4, a special annual grant was now to be paid both to needy voluntary and board schools, based on the principle laid down in Section 97 of the 1870 Act which had formerly only applied to the latter. Finally, after the detailed administrative provisions, Clause 27 was designed to bring about the changes in religious instruction which the Prime Minister and his family judged to be so important. It stated that one of the regulations in accordance with which a public elementary school would now be conducted was that reasonable arrangements would be made for separate religious instruction, if it was required by the parents of a reasonable number of scholars.

Gorst's tactics suggest that he sensed difficulties ahead. In a speech of some eighty minutes he spent seventy on education in general, leaving only ten to explain the rationale that lay behind the Bill.[25] This left no time to discuss Clause 27. The House then adjourned for Easter.

Easter week was the traditional time for the Annual Conference of the NUT. This year it was to take place at Brighton in the Royal Pavilion, which the Corporation had purchased from the Office of Woods, Forests, Land Revenues, Works, and Buildings in 1850 and was (until 1948) accustomed to let for miscellaneous purposes. The presence of royalty attested to the distinction of the occasion. In February it had been announced that the Duke and Duchess of York (later King George V and Queen Mary) would attend the Conference on Thursday 9 April. They had consented to receive the purses of money collected from members for charity. 'Collect your little towards that big sum of £15,000, which we hope to see placed in the hands of the Duke and Duchess', urged 'Breezy Brighton' in a letter to the *Schoolmaster*. 'What a practical proof it will be of the generosity and unselfishness of the members of our grand Union!'.[26] 'Teachers throughout the country will appreciate the compliment which this royal patronage of their charitable work means', wrote T. B. Ellery, the retiring President, in April. 'This Orphan and Benevolent work is dear to the hearts of thousands of teachers, and the encouragement and support which this royal visit will give to those who are labouring in a truly noble cause can scarcely be over-estimated.' The conference was to begin on Easter Saturday with a reception in the Banqueting Room of the Royal Pavilion. Business was to begin on Monday. Whilst the Dome was to be used for the main sessions, the various reception rooms of the Pavilion were to be employed for teachers' meetings. On Wednesday evening a soirée and ball were to take place. The proceedings would end on the Thursday evening with a reception from the Mayor. On Friday excursions had been arranged to Hastings, Arundel and Chichester.[27]

In all these proceedings Macnamara was to play a leading part. Still four months short of his thirty-fifth birthday, he was due to assume the Presidency of the Union at the first session, on Easter Monday. In March the *Schoolmaster* reproduced part of an interview he had give to the magazine *Young Man*. He was asked, as a young man who had succeeded, what his advice would be to young men wanting to make their mark in the world. He replied:

> I do not know whether I can be said to have succeeded. I cannot lay claim to any exceptional cleverness, but this I can say frankly – I am an indefatigably hard worker. Whatever I have tried to do I have done for all I have been worth. I have worked too hard, some of my friends say. What I should recommend a young man to do is to make himself indispensable in his post. The only way to do that is to put your back into it for all you are worth. Let a man find out what he can do and then do it. I do not consider I did much worth talking

about till I got married ... When I married my aims seemed to be crystallised, and I should like to say that I attribute in a very considerable measure any success that I have achieved to my wife. But I hope all the young men won't rush off and get married on that account.[28]

As he began his presidential address, Macnamara reminded the Conference of the great responsibility placed upon him. There had never been so many members of the NUT and it was his task to speak on behalf of the 33,000 at a moment when it appeared that the education machinery of the country was on the point of complete reconstruction. So he appealed to his audience to remember that although they were of many and divergent schools of religious and political thought, they had established a tradition of unity over the past twenty-six years, and that they were at Brighton merely as teachers – 'teachers in the schools of the people, anxious only for the betterment of the great national work upon which it is our privilege to be engaged'.

His purpose, he said, was to provide a strictly educational view of the changes which Sir John Gorst had outlined. Unfortunately, as it turned out, his interpretation was based on Gorst's somewhat misleading House of Commons speech, not on the as yet uncirculated Bill; he had also not had time to do more than informally consult his colleagues on the Executive. He began his appraisal with the new Local Authority. This commended itself, he said, because for the first time a paramount Education Authority, albeit of a merely supervisory nature, was being created. He would have preferred an *ad hoc* Authority but, he declared (pursuing the line of argument he had followed before the Bryce Commission), he was willing to compromise in the constitution of the Authority for the sake of its function, which was the disbursement of additional financial assistance to needy board and voluntary schools. Admittedly, non-educationists would be put in charge of education, but the Bill left it open to the council members of the Authority to coopt whatever elements they might deem necessary. Amongst the coopted elements, Macnamara said, he hoped to see representatives of persons engaged in the actual work of teaching and of managing schools of all classes in each locality.[29]

The ultimate effect of the new arrangements would be the extinction of the school boards and the greater municipalisation of all forms of publicly assisted education. This admission, lightly passed over, was to provoke dissension. The NUT Executive, as Yoxall, Bowden and Macnamara had shown at the Bryce Commission, was prepared to face the replacement of the school boards. The rank and file, as resolutions about local administration published in January should have warned the new President, still regarded the establishment of these boards on a national basis as the most desirable development.[30]

Macnamara went on to examine the financial features of the Bill. These included the creation of a new Special Aid Grant from the Exchequer amounting to four shillings per annum for each child in every voluntary school and in every board school already receiving assistance under the 1870 Act. This he regarded as Gorst's attempt to meet the contention that he himself had advanced on numerous occasions, that four fifths of the 'intolerable strain' in the voluntary schools had been borne by the teachers. Hence, he said, it was most desirable that the Bill should make it impossible for the money to be spent in any other way than that suggested by the Vice-President. The abolition of the so-called seventeen and sixpenny limit was also proposed. This limit, introduced in 1876, allowed a voluntary school to earn up to this amount a year per child in grant from the Exchequer before it became liable to deductions intended to balance the grant with income from local subscriptions. Macnamara advised caution. 'It is most essential', he commented, 'that when the House of Commons agrees to the removal of this limit, it shall also devise some means of securing that the existing income from voluntary subscriptions shall, on no account, be allowed to fall off.'

Pausing to congratulate Gorst on the clause aimed at preventing the employment of juveniles below the age of twelve, Macnamara moved on to what, in his view, had been left out. Nothing was being proposed about the abolition of compulsory extraneous tasks; nothing about establishing an appeals procedure for teachers who felt they had been unjustifiably dismissed; nothing about superannuation. Amongst these long-standing grievances he inserted his observations about Clause 27. He tried to minimise its importance:

> As I understand it, the proposal of the Government is in effect to extend the Cowper-Temple clause of the Act of 1870, so as to give the parent not only the right to withdraw his child from the Scripture lesson but to have facilities offered him for the separate instruction of the child in the definite denominational teaching of his particular Church.

He was prepared to admit, he said, that there might be something in the claim about the 'undeniable rights' of parents to determine religious instruction, though in his view the demand for exceptional treatment was not likely to be at all general. Therefore, he was prepared to agree, 'in the profound belief that the opportunity would be seized in a very few and rare cases' that teachers should accept the move. But, he added:

> I must point out in the most emphatic manner possible that if it be agreed to make this change in order to set at rest the disturbed conscience of this fabulous parent, it should be clearly understood, at the very outset, that the provision of the teaching power for this exceptional religious instruction cannot be undertaken by the school authorities.

His fear, derived from what he had observed in London, was that the concession could be used to subordinate the selection of teachers to the requirements of specific religious teaching: 'I suggest to you that to allow

ministers of religious or their delegates to come in and give denominational teaching is one thing, to select board school teachers because of their adherence to particular forms of religious faith – whatever those forms may be – is another thing entirely'.[31]

The practice at NUT conferences was to regard the Presidential address as an expression of personal views, which was not subjected to criticism. The topicality of the Bill made it impossible on this occasion to treat Macnamara's comments in the customary manner. The debate on the Bill was introduced on Tuesday morning by Robert Wild, formerly twice President of the Union and now Chairman of its Education Committee. He moved that conference approve the proposed creation of Education Authorities by county and county borough councils, pointing out that in this respect the Bill followed closely the Executive's own proposal of 1888 that the country should be divided into school districts of not less than 50,000 people. Small school boards and school attendance committees would disappear. He admitted, as Macnamara had done, that an authority elected *ad hoc* was preferable, but, he said, they must aim at what was practical and possible. Wild was seconded, but W. J. Gilham, the next speaker, moved an amendment asking for authorities appointed for education alone. Gorst's new statutory authority would, once appointed, be practically independent of the county councils, he said. It would conduct its operations in secret. Moreover, county councils were elected for a variety of purposes, to look after sewers, bridges, lunatics, swine fever and muzzling. Education would be neglected: 'let such a committee get to work and the muzzling order will not be confined to dogs in the future', he concluded.

Gilham had begun diffidently, but it was soon plain that he had wide support among the board teachers of the Union. Ernest Gray, like Macnamara, argued that they should make the best they could out of the Bill. It was the inefficient school boards and the inefficient voluntary managers that would be interfered with. But Marshall Jackman resisted this argument. The Bill would do more than create a new statutory body, he said. It would kill the school boards. When the vote was taken it was evident that this division between two members of the Executive reflected a division between the voluntary and board teacher members of the Union. Gilham's amendment was passed by 14,479 votes to 9,255.[32]

The debate over the seventeen and sixpenny limit worsened the situation. Macnamara had assumed it would go; Jackman however, moved that conference oppose its abolition. Its retention was necessary, he said, to secure for voluntary schools their share of the extra grant to be paid: to abolish it when subscriptions were already going down would be to invite their closure. But the voluntary teachers agreed with Macnamara: Dr George Beach pointed out that nothing was more galling to a teacher than to work hard, earn grants and then be deprived of them. The most common method of increasing subscriptions was by calling upon the teacher to promote a concert or a sale of work; consequently anyone who voted for the retention of the limit was voting for additional demands upon the time and energy of voluntary teachers. But when Jackman's motion was put to the vote it was carried by a large majority.

Finally Macnamara's advice on Clause 27 was rejected completely. The principle of the withdrawal of a board school child for denominational instruction proved to be so objectionable to board teacher members that a motion against revision of the 1870 Act, introduced by Bowden, was adopted *nem. con.* amidst cheers. Cyrus Heller, brother of the former Secretary of the Union, supporting it, spoke regretfully of the line Macnamara had taken. He had known the new President as a candidate for the London School Board and as Radical Parliamentary candidate for Deptford, he said, and it had given him intense pleasure to assist him in both these elections. This week, however, he had been brought face to face with another Macnamara, one who was a shadow of his former self (Hear, hear). Macnamara had fought their cause well at the London School Board (Applause). But what did he advocate now? He advocated the acceptance of Clause 27 as a compromise, because he saw the impracticability of working it. People wished them to allow every sect to have its own peculiar doctrines taught within the school. This was utterly impracticable. If it were done by outsiders the teachers would lose much of their influence with the children. If, on the other hand, teachers were to give the instruction, they would be selected for religious reasons alone. The Union had pronounced against the selection of teachers for other than professional qualifications – for organ playing, choir training and so on – but it was ten times worse to hold out a premium to a man's religious views, and take him, not for what he was, but for the sake of the amount of religious dogma he was content to swallow (Applause).[33]

'The Bill, and nothing but the Bill' had been the call at the beginning of the week. By the time the Conference ended, the Government's proposals, at least as far as the board teachers were concerned, were in shreds. Macnamara was obliged to summarise what they had done. Against his advice, two major issues had emerged. The paramount authority, far from being adopted, had given rise to a strongly supported movement to defend the boards. Similarly the religious question had once again demonstrated its capacity for engendering passion. Fortunately, good humour had prevailed. Jackman, in moving a vote of thanks to the President, said he was proud to do it because he had been associated with Macnamara as a boy, as a pupil-teacher, as a fellow-student in the training college, and as a colleague on the Executive. This, he said, had been the most brilliant of all conferences. The President's address had been distinguished by tactful judiciousness which rendered it impossible for anyone to say that on certain questions he had led the Conference. It must have cost him an effort which, in the immediate future, would be highly appreciated. Macnamara, having heartily thanked his colleagues for their great kindness during the week, responded a little ruefully. Conference, he said, had left him high and dry. Nevertheless it was a source of immense satisfaction to him to feel that it had distinctly given itself its own lead.[34]

Fortunately a diversion was at hand. On Tuesday the *Schoolmaster*'s correspondent commented on the fact that the Royal Pavilion had been given a coat of paint in honour of the Royal visit. 'Even that cannot conceal its extreme ugliness', he added: 'one marvels exceedingly at the grotesque taste, or lack of it, exhibited by the royal builder.'[35] Venetian masts had been set up in the main streets: along the front was an apparently endless vista of Royal Standards, Union Jacks and banners of every shape, size and hue and on the corner of East Street, near the entrance to the Pavilion grounds, a triumphal arch of fire escapes had been erected. Macnamara and his wife, having, in company with the Mayor of Brighton and other dignitaries, greeted the Duke and Duchess of York at the railway station, then drove in the carriage procession through the streets to the Royal Pavilion. After luncheon, the party transferred to the Dome where the Duchess ceremonially received the purses containing the charitable donations, amounting to £9,000, made by the local associations. Speeches were made by Macnamara, Mrs Burgwin, Yoxall and the Duke, who indicated that he and the Duchess had agreed to become Patron and Patroness of the Union's charities. The party then returned amid cheering, the Duchess taking the arm of Macnamara and the Duke conducting Mrs Macnamara to the reception room. 'The brilliant ceremony is the crowning glory of a conference which can only be described as momentous, episodical, startling, and royal', the *Schoolmaster*'s correspondent reported triumphantly. 'As night closes in, the noble front becomes one dazzling array of rainbow light. There are fireworks and a bonfire, a carnival of cyclists, a battle of confetti – a kaleidoscopic revel of bewildering fascination ... Thus, in wonderful brilliance closes the grandest conference the Union has ever beheld.'[36]

The coincidence of the introduction of Gorst's Bill and the NUT Conference caused the views expressed at Brighton to receive extensive press coverage. The unexpectedly moderate speech by the President followed by the opposition of the rank and file provided irresistible opportunities for speculation. *The Times*, referring to Macnamara as 'one of the most active and conspicuous among the Progressive members of the London School Board', found him 'compelled to play the part of Balaam ... he welcomed the Bill precisely for doing what has been denounced by the organs of Radicalism, for establishing in every organised district throughout the kingdom whether county or borough, an independent Educational Authority'. The (Liberal) *Westminster Gazette* was puzzled:

> Mr Macnamara falls, so to speak, on Sir John Gorst's neck, thanks him for his sympathetic speech, and appears to be struggling with himself to say every word

that is possible in favour of the new Bill, and to soften and suppress all criticisms, though in substance these criticisms may far outweigh the good which he discovers in the Bill. This is a strange spectacle which we cannot pretend to explain, but we can hardly believe that the teachers as a body will take this Bill in quite the same spirit of uncritical gratitude which appears to inspire Mr Macnamara.[37]

The next day it noted that the Executive's resolution to approve the supervisory authorities had been amended by a large majority. 'So it appears that Mr Macnamara does not carry the teachers with him in the enthusiastic affection with which he seems to regard Sir John Gorst's Bill.'[38] the *Manchester Guardian* commented:

Every reactionary, every enemy to popular education will quote – is indeed already quoting – Mr Macnamara, and we confess he appears to us to have deserved the pillory of their approval: but the general body of teachers have saved the situation ... the Conference was at once wiser and more courageous than its leaders, and allowed no doubt of its views of the attack upon school boards, which is the real origin and explanation of the Bill.[39]

The wisdom of Macnamara's cautious approach began to be perceived as soon as the conference with over. It became clear that the voluntary school teachers had been deeply offended. On 25 April a meeting of the National Association of Voluntary Teachers was called at King's College, London, following a notice stating that the conference at Brighton had shown great hostility to the Bill which the Government had framed for the special assistance of voluntary schools, and that members should attend and show the House of Commons and the public that the Brighton conclusions were reached in opposition to their views. One speaker, seconding a motion hostile to the seventeen and sixpenny limit, declared that hitherto he had felt himself a Unionist first and a voluntary teacher next. He doubted very much whether he still had that feeling, though even now he would not wish to weaken the Union. Still he would have the Union know that they had strained their relations almost to breaking point (Loud cheers). They called themselves a National Union of Teachers but they were only a National Union of Board Teachers.[40]

The teaching profession momentarily faced disruption. Its reconsolidation was effected at the Queen's Hall, Langham Place, on 29 May, by means of what the *Schoolmaster* described as the greatest Union meeting ever held. Even though the resolutions submitted were open for general criticism and discussion, and supporters given ample opportunity to express their views, the proceedings were carefully organised as a public demonstration. From 7.15 p.m., 4,000 teachers trooped in to the music of the splendid organ. At 8.00, Macnamara, accompanied by his wife and the appointed speakers, appeared on the platform. Macnamara spoke first. The task he and Yoxall had set themselves was to persuade their teacher colleagues, both board and voluntary, of the advantages to be secured through a county-based system of education administration. Macnamara appealed first to the board teachers. He was, he said, one of those who thought national education of sufficient importance to call for the direct and exclusive election of its controlling authority, and he viewed with suspicion more or less irresponsible statutory committees which might work in secret and without reporting to their council (Loud cheers). But, he added, genuine municipalisation might deal with a number of the teachers' long-term grievances:

> Let the municipal Authority have very direct powers over every school it assisted, the power to insist that the teachers should be paid a fair wage, (Cheers) to insist that the teaching staff should not almost entirely consist of unqualified juveniles, (Cheers) to insist that the teacher should be at liberty to utilise his dearly bought leisure as he pleased, and not be compulsorily tied to the church organ stool, the conductorship of the choir, and the superintendency of the Sunday-School (Loud cheers) and to insist that to every teacher dismissed his office should be secured the right of appeal (Loud cheers).

Yoxall spoke next, taking up Macnamara's points. Under the Bill, he said, the Education Department was to be superseded by Local Authorities. Such Authorities needed to be strong educationally. He therefore moved:

> If the Authority be appointed as is proposed in the Bill it should invariably include representatives of school boards, governing bodies and managing committees of schools, teachers working in schools and other educationists. The Authority should be required to appoint representative managers on all committees of voluntary schools. There should be a protection for teachers against extraneous tasks and unjustifiable dismissal.

The advantages for voluntary teachers of having a Local Authority able to intervene in their interests were obvious. To secure the support of the board teachers he prefaced the main motion with an expression of the Union's desire that county authorities (if set up) should administer both primary and secondary education, coupling it with the demand that they should be directly elected *ad hoc*. Put to the vote, his resolution won overwhelming support.

Gray, the Union's Conservative MP, dealt with the financial proposals his party was putting forward. He concentrated upon the imposition of statutory limitation on Parliamentary grants, included in Clause 19. That this was altogether objectionable, he said, was a point on which all friends of education could unite. He was supported by Waddington, who warned, as a voluntary teacher, that the abolition of the seventeen and sixpenny limit would cause the withdrawal of public subscriptions and (as Jackman had said at the conference) weaken the voluntary schools. Interventions by voluntary school teachers who were anxious to establish the principle of equality of grants from public funds for both board and voluntary schools, a much larger issue with which the Bill was not concerned, were headed off.

It now remained to amplify the criticism of Clause 27. Here board and voluntary teachers were unquestionably at one. C. J. Addiscott, the Vice-President, explained how his own school was in Upper Clapton, close to the Headquarters of the Salvation Army. The majority of his pupils, under the Government's proposals, would be taught by the Salvationists, but there would also need to be teachers from the Church of England, the Wesleyans and the Primitive Methodists. Tom Clancy, Headmaster of St John's Roman Catholic School, Portsmouth, supported him, emphasising the virtues of the existing dual system in which the voluntary schools had been distinctly erected for denominational, the board schools for undenominational, education. Finally Mrs Burgwin, seconded by Jackman, paid tribute to the positive aspects of the Bill, in relation to raising the school leaving age, improving attendance and amending the education facilities open to children resident in industrial and Poor Law institutions.[41]

The purpose of the Queen's Hall meeting had been to repair the unity of the Union. Macnamara, bringing the proceedings to a close, expressed the hope that what had been said would also be of some value in shaping the Bill in the right direction. By now the Government's proposals had excited active opposition by the Liberal Party. Acland, in a speech at Rotherham on 15 April, had pronounced that the substitution of county council for Departmental influence could not anywhere raise, while it would certainly in the great majority of districts depress, the standard of efficiency in the schools.[42] Asquith, giving his presidential address to the Walsall Liberal Association on 20 April, took the same view. Powers would be transferred from the Education Department to a local county committee which he designated as amateur, ill-qualified and not elected for educational purposes. Whilst the Bill contained changes for the better it also, he said, contained a great many changes which, in the opinion of the party, would be for the worse. These so largely exceeded both in number and in weight the changes for the better that it was not worth purchasing the one at the price of the other. The Bill would certainly and gratuitously reopen the door, so long and so happily closed, of religious and sectarian controversy, so that in the course of time not only the Local Authorities, but even the schools themselves, would become battlegrounds for the competition and rivalry of discordant sects.[43]

Gorst moved the Second Reading of the Bill on 5 May. 'Since the First Reading', Macnamara wrote in the *Pall Mall Gazette* of 12 May, 'Clause 27 has undergone an alarming development. Now Sir John Gorst talks about desiring that "it should be the duty of every school board and of the manager of every school to give that instruction which is most in accordance with the wishes of the parents".' This, he pointed out, involved the application to the teaching staff of a denominational test in order to secure the particular class of religious teaching required. Athelstan Riley had made no secret of how he would carry out Clause 27. A petition from the parents of children attending each board school would be vamped up, and when next an appointment to the permanent staff was made, the main and prime test would be not the applicant's skill, experience and aptitude as a teacher, but whether he or she would subscribe completely to the doctrines of the Church. Macnamara saw that his efforts to find a compromise had failed: 'there is one thing that will be fought against to the bitter end – and that is, that the best interests of education and the children should be subordinated to the needs of denominationalism in the selection of our board school teachers'.[44]

In the Commons, Asquith poured scorn on the Bill and promised obstruction.[45] Balfour taunted the opposition by emphasising that the paramount authority had been designed to prepare the way for the abolition of the school boards. He declared:

> I rejoice to think that a step has been taken under this Bill which may put both primary and secondary education under one municipal Authority, which shall prevent overlapping and waste, and be able to superintend, from the highest to the lowest stage of primary and secondary education, the whole curriculum which the children may be expected to pass through.[46]

With a majority of 267, enlarged by the support of the Irish Nationalists, the Government still seemed secure, but within hours of the close of the debate, amendments, amounting eventually to 1,355, began to crowd the order paper. As the national debate developed, the idea of the Bill's paramount authorities, which were intended to supervise (and therefore duplicated) existing administrative machinery, began to lose its attraction. On 8 June, at Birmingham Town Hall, a meeting of the local Liberal Association passed a resolution declaring that the Bill would lower the quality and efficiency of education; would fail to relieve elementary teachers from theological tests; would place elementary education in the hands of the clergy and priesthood at the expense of the taxpayers; would degrade and weaken school boards and add to the burdens already borne by the ratepayers.[47] By now some of the county borough and county councils were expressing their unwillingness to take on the new burdens, while spokesmen of the Municipal Boroughs and Urban Districts began to complain that they were denied independent Educational Authorities of their own.[48]

As the Bill was about to go into Committee, Asquith, speaking at Abingdon on 10 June, renewed his attack on the paramount authority, arguing that a high standard of education was the most valuable of national assets which was not to be left to the hazards of a body elected for purposes of another kind. As for the religious issue, the Liberal Party would never consent that the system built up and supported by the money of the taxpayer in the highest interests of the community at large should be warped and diverted to secure the interests of particular sects (Loud cheers).[49] In the Commons, it was Clause I (which defined the constitution of the proposed county education authorities) which proved the Bill's undoing. On the evening of 11 June Sir John Gorst was attempting, with some success, to deal with the objections of Sir Albert Rollit, the representative of the municipal councils, which had been resentful about their exclusion from the decentralisation plans. Balfour, appearing unexpectedly in the Chamber, accepted, as the *Schoolmaster* put it later, 'with extraordinary want of consideration for the views of the Minister in charge and even more extraordinary lack of appreciation of the aims of the Bill', Rollit's proposal that Municipal Boroughs with populations of over 20,000 should have, like county boroughs, independent Education Authorities.[50] From that moment any defence of the Bill in its original form was impossible. On Monday 22 June it was withdrawn. The *School Board Chronicle* was triumphant. Reasons innumerable had been offered to account for the wonderful collapse of a measure which it, almost alone at first, had refused to describe as Statesmanlike. Gorst, Balfour and Macnamara came under attack:

> Politicians, organs of the Government, and others committed by their position, or by their first ill-digested utterances, to an approval of the Bill have, for the most part, sought to account for its failure by a reference to Parliamentary tactics. All such explanations are as unjust as they are wide of the mark. The Bill has failed ... because it was a thoroughly bad Bill.[51]

The issues it raised had been very dangerous to the NUT. As the *Schoolmaster* recalled at the end of the year, the Union had been tried as in a furnace:

> It came into existence after the battles of 1870 had been fought. As an organisation it knew nothing of the strain that inevitably comes when religion and politics get mixed up with professional affairs. In all its many struggles there had been nothing to set friend against friend with all the bitterness of party and sectarian enmity. The experience of the late campaign was a new one and to those ... who would sacrifice almost anything rather than see the good old ship go under, one of the utmost momentousness.[52]

By now, however, a new campaign was under way, one which this time was to unite rather than divide. Macnamara, in the *Schoolmaster*, began to draw attention to the plight of rural schools, where the interests of voluntary and board teachers were at one, sectarian and party differences submerged by poor conditions and low pay. Already, just before he became editor, the *Schoolmaster* had shown how different rural life was from the poet's fancy. Old-fashioned, defective school buildings, insufficient resources, lack of support from managers and of any opportunity to pursue additional qualifications, put the rural teacher (whom it assumed to be male) at a disadvantage by comparison with his urban counterpart.[53] A year later, he pointed out that of the 1,300 village schools with forty or fewer pupils and the 4,000 with an attendance of between forty and sixty, the greater number were under the care of schoolmistresses, 'and a more shamefully underpaid, overworked, and generally unfairly-treated body of public servants it would be difficult, if possible to conceive'. The management, board or voluntary, was often genuinely willing to advise and encourage: 'But how often a coterie of mean and vulgar illiterates ... how often, too, a high stomached autocrat, betwixt the wind and whose nobility the village schoolmistress dares only go with trembling'. Pay was poor: 'Here are today 314 rural headmistresses, at least a third of whom are fully certificated, working for less than £40 a year, or under fifteen shillings and four pence per week. Why, the Factory Hand would laugh at it!' [54]

At the NUT Annual Conference at Oxford in April 1894, Macnamara presented a paper, entitled 'The Village Schoolmistress', which attracted the attention of *Punch*. Since his *Schoolmaster* editorial he had instituted an enquiry into life and conditions of service. He showed that whilst the Church of England, the dominant employer in country districts, paid its certificated headmistresses least well, low school board salaries were also common. Some of the so-called school houses were a disgrace to nineteenth-century civilisation. One was overrun with rats and insects: it had been used as a coach-house and store-room for wool fleeces. In another the schoolmistress had no wash-house and no pump; she had to fetch water down a steep hill. Lodgings were often as bad. He quoted the case of mistress who could hire only a bedroom.

> She spends all day in the school, cooking her own meals at the school stove. She sits in the dreary, empty schoolroom during the evening, and then retires to her bedroom lodgings. I ask you to picture for yourselves the condition of this woman in winter, sitting all the black frozen evening through in her solitary schoolroom, and will not venture to intrude upon your reflections with a single word of my own.

Then there was 'that abomination of all abominations, the pettifogging school board'. He described how a schoolmistress sent a child two miles to the house of the board clerk for a box of chalk. She received six pieces of chalk wrapped in brown paper with a verbal message that under the board's instructions, all school material was to be dispensed in that way. Another asked for a blind for the southern window of the school and was told that a guano bag was good enough. A third asked for materials to teach drawing. She was recommended to get up an entertainment to raise money and did so. What was required, he concluded, was a larger grant for small schools, a more careful control of teacher supply and above all more efficient boards of local school management. [55]

In July 1895 the NUT Executive had set up a special committee, which included Macnamara (then Vice-President) with the aim of reducing the overpressure upon scholars and teachers and alleviating the special anxiety of rural teachers. In its report (in December) it concluded that the chief difficulties of rural schools were inadequate staff, inadequate salaries, insufficient funds, undue pressure through the Code, irregular pupil attendance, the extraneous duties required of teachers by their employers, insecurity of tenure and unsuitable school houses.[56] Now, three months after the failure of Gorst's Bill, the *Schoolmaster* published a special supplement entitled 'The School Board in the Villages'. The author, recognisably Macnamara, trod carefully, warning the reader that no general attack against the school board system was intended: 'we may say frankly that we rejoice that the great school boards have come so triumphantly out of the insidious designs which some of those obviously responsible for the late Bill were – and possibly are still – harbouring'.

The small school boards were another matter:

> If the Bill had wiped out all the little rural school boards – thereby saving vast sums now uselessly frittered away upon needlessly multiplied school board microcosms, immensely improving the character of the administration, and equalising the local charge for education – and had given us effective County Boards of Education in their stead, it would have gone down in the educational history of the country as a ·reform at least as great as that of 1870. But it conspicuously failed to do this.

The original error had been made by the Forster Act which, outside the boroughs, designated the parish as the unit of school administration. The result of this decision was that in the school year 1895–96 there were 181 borough-based boards in England and Wales and 2,271 parish-based boards. Of these, 585 contained fewer than 500 men, women and children, and 150 of the 585 were administering the education of parishes with less that 250 souls. Grotesque instances were provided. At Mallerstang, in Westmorland, there were seventeen children in average daily attendance, with five elected members and a paid clerk to operate the functions of the board. At Biggin (Yorkshire) there were twenty-one children in the board schools. It cost £3 per child per year for administrative machinery only, when the average annual cost of educating a board school child was £2 8s 9¾d. The most recent school board election at Keyham, in Leicestershire, a parish of 137 people, cost £8 8s and increased the rate by more than a penny in the pound. And what, he asked, 'does Devonshire want with 152 little school boards, and an official expenditure on this machinery of something like £9,000? Wouldn't the Devonshire schools be the better [for] ninety additional assistant masters at £100 a year apiece?' Macnamara charged the members of small school boards with being 'in a considerable number of cases neither competent to discharge, nor desirous of carrying out appropriately, the work of the important office to which they have sought election'. Their members often objected to paying the rate, especially when, because the small number of children could earn only a small Exchequer grant, it was high; some were openly hostile to education:

> We could tell many a tale of tyranny on the part of some of these little coteries of narrow-minded ruffians: tales of teachers dismissed for such offences as

buying their tea at a shop other than that kept by the Chairman of the Board; of teachers dismissed for objecting to members of the Board illegally employing children of eight and nine years of age during school hours; of teachers dismissed for almost every conceivable reason except the one for which alone dismissal is just – viz neglect of duty.

He quoted HMI Reports on small school boards. W. Scott Coward, then Chief Inspector of Schools in the North Western counties, had written:

The apathy and often wilful neglect of the small school boards in ... the administration of the law compelling regular attendance, are responsible for most of the irregularity in country districts. I see little remedy for this ... My hope is that sooner or later we may have larger bodies acting over wider areas, with larger views of their office ...

S. R. Wilson HMI had reported in 1893–94 that some of the smaller boards in Lincolnshire did not even pretend to enforce the law, giving election pledges not to prosecute irregular attenders. C. G. Colson, HMI for the York District, incorporated a log-book extract in his report showing that, in one rural school, one third of the children were nearly always absent, with, not infrequently, one half in the summer months. The great reform necessary, Macnamara concluded, was the extension of areas of administration. New larger units were needed so that the local financial burden could be equalised and public-spirited men and women secured to administer them.[57]

The case that Macnamara had assembled against the rural school boards was republished in penny pamphlet form and followed up by a series of articles in the *Schoolmaster*.[58] The *School Board Chronicle* was at once suspicious, perceiving, despite Macnamara's protestations, another direct threat to the existing board system:

Substantially the pamphlet repeats ... the attack upon the rural school boards which was the one feature of Sir John Gorst's argument on the great Reactionary Bill of 1896 that made, for a time, an impression upon Parliament. The *Schoolmaster* has been indicated as the source of Sir John Gorst's one effective inspiration. By its ... pamphlet reprint it now comes forward to rekindle the animus against the school board system in the villages.

The attack was short-sighted, narrow in spirit and unserviceable as a guide for public policy. The *Chronicle* itself agreed that the principle of the school board system was defective where the population was too small. This was a fault of detail, remediable by enlarging and combining the petty areas. But if the boards were replaced by county authorities there would be no effective local control, no conscious parental responsibility and little or no public interest in the management of village schools.[59]

In the December edition of the *Nineteenth Century* Macnamara surveyed the question of rural finance. Whilst voluntary and, later, board schools might benefit soon from increased State grants, the defects of the existing rating system remained, affecting board and voluntary schools alike. Only two thirds, approximately, of the rateable value, population and area of the country were being taxed locally for the purposes of education. Within that two thirds, owing to diversities in the size of administrative areas, the value of property and what was decided were educational needs, the rate was charged in the most grotesque and uneven manner. In the remaining third, voluntary schools alone existed: 'This preference enables it to escape a local tax for education. In some cases no doubt, as much is raised locally by voluntary subscriptions as would reach the average level of the compulsory education rate.' But, especially in rural districts, the voluntary school too often existed 'simply and solely that the locality may entirely or almost entirely "contract itself out" of its proper obligations towards the education of the people'. In 1895, supplementary to the Treasury grants, £3,750,000 had been drawn from the rates for the 2,310,253 children enrolled in board schools. Supplementary to the Treasury grant only £750,000 had been raised by subscriptions for 3,015,605 children in the voluntary schools. He concluded the article with three questions. Why should not every ratepayer, urban and rural, take his share in the local support of education? Why should not this local support be equalised in such a way as to render the incidence of the burden fair and equitable throughout the country? And why should not all public elementary schools be adequately and fairly financed, not only out of the central but out of the local purse as well? [60]

In the new year the NUT began what was to become a national campaign on rural education, with a conference at Exeter Hall in the Strand, the former home of the anti-slavery movement. As Chairman, Macnamara was supported by four past Presidents of the Union, J. J. Graves, Robert Wild, James Yoxall MP and Ernest Gray MP. Opening the proceedings, he commented that nobody could do other than rejoice at the achievements, over recent years, of the State as a schoolmaster in the municipal centres. In villages, especially obscure villages, where there was no driving force of public opinion, it was another story.

More money was the first requirement of rural schools. They were assisted by the Exchequer in exactly the same way as their urban counterparts, the grants being calculated upon the attainments and attendance of pupils. 'Thus', he said 'you teach ten rural children grammar for a year; they do well; you receive (under Article 101(e)(l)) two shillings per head ... On the other hand, you teach a class of fifty children in the urban school the same subject for a year; *they* do well; you receive two shillings per head of your fifty. Hence the average amount spent on each scholar, taking board and voluntary schools together in London, was £3 17s 11d. In Wiltshire it was £1 19s 5d, in Suffolk £1 18s 2½d and in Cornwall £1 17s 5½d. What was needed was an entirely different system of aid, especially since the task of raising supplementary local resources in rural areas was so much more difficult. The effect of under-financing was felt in both the quality and quantity of teachers. In London seventy per cent of teachers were fully qualified adults and fifteen per cent were juvenile pupil-teachers. In Cambridgeshire the percentages were thirty-nine and twenty-five, in Norfolk thirty-nine and twenty-eight, in Durham thirty-two and thirty-two. In London three per cent of teachers were unqualified women; in Oxfordshire the figure was twenty per cent and in Herefordshire twenty-eight per cent. In London board schools the certificated teacher-pupil ratio was 1:58, in all London schools 1:71. In Cumberland it was 1:107, in Kent 1:109 and in Worcestershire 1:115. 'Of course', Macnamara commented, 'this pitiable neglect of the village school has its fruit, not only in the inefficient and insufficient character of the staff and the lack of suitable appliances, but in the disgraceful stipends paid to most of the village teachers.' Here, he went on, he had chosen to concentrate upon the voluntary school because, by now, his charge of incompetency against the average village school board had been freely admitted, even by school board supporters. The average salary of a headmaster in an English or Welsh public elementary school in 1896 was £137 16s 10d; of a headmistress £87 11s 9d. In rural schools there were forty-four headmasters earning less than £50 and eighty-one headmistresses earning less than £40. Rural headships often included a rent-free house but falling subscriptions for voluntary schools sometimes meant that salaries were reduced. Often applicants for headmasterships were expected to bring a wife or sister to help in the school without pay. Macnamara quoted an advertisement for a Master for a Mixed Country School at Bransdale, Kirbymoorside: 'Wife or Sister for Sewing. Average twenty-two. Salary £60, with house.' In another the Rector of Hartley, near Alton, Hants, displayed a singularly enlightened estimate of the social status or the village school teacher: 'Certificated Mistress for small Mixed School (country). £50, furnished house, and fuel. Widow with son, of sister and brother, who could be employed as outdoor servant, preferred.' Macnamara commented: 'I look forward to the time when the village parson, the village doctor and the village schoolmaster will rank together – and I am not going to say who should be put first'. Similarly, extraneous duties were demanded, sometimes for a few pounds extra per year, sometimes free:

> Kenton National School. WANTED, immediately. Master and Mistress, married couple. Certificated. Church Communicants. Good testimonials and references. Husband harmonium and choir. Salary £75 and unfurnished house. Apply, stating age, Vicar, Kenton, Debenham.

In exchange for low salaries, long hours of work, inside and outside the school, were expected. 'Mr C' taught fifty-seven children at seven different levels and infants as well, aided for the last nine months of the year by a monitress. His extraneous duties comprised arranging for school cleaning, Sunday-school (morning and evening), playing the organ (he was paid extra for this), conducting the choir, running the savings bank and assisting with Band of Hope meetings.

The second requirement of rural schools was better management. In country districts the one-man clerical manager was the rule. 'In the majority of cases', he said, 'he is sympathetic and kindly. ("No, no" and cheers) ... but occasionally he is something entirely different ("Hear, hear") ruling the teacher in an exceedingly offensive and autocratic manner and casting him aside heartlessly when old age creeps on ... he very often subordinates, in the selection of "his teacher" for "his school" the well-being of the school and its pupils to the exigencies of outside parochial affairs.' A responsible body of managers, never less that six, was needed for every village school. Because public grants were paid, public accountability should be recognised. Hence the board of management should include a representative of a Local Authority.[61]

The Conference attracted a good deal of attention from the press. The *Guardian*, agreeing that many rural school boards deserved censure, reminded its readers that the NUT had failed to support the Gorst Bill which would have extended education areas and improved conditions. *The Times* expressed doubt about whether there was a need to bring rural education up to the level of the best urban schools. The opposite view was put in the *Echo*:

> A boy living in a village, and attending a village school, is as important to the State and our social well-being as a boy living in Birmingham or London ... A reform is demanded, and must be accomplished; and if the Government would show a quarter of the zeal they manifest in building new battleships, that may not be required, in improving our educational machinery, which is required daily, they would deserve well of the country.

The *Daily Mail*'s conclusions were downright:

> Our rural education is a disgrace. Men of all parties and all creeds will do well to mark the facts rehearsed to the National Union of Teachers yesterday. These facts are discreditable enough – starved teachers, useless plant, slack and incompetent management. What wonder that the produce of a well-educated peasantry like that of Denmark knocks ours out of every market?[62]

The rural campaign, which lasted into the new century, secured the future of the Union. Emphasising the defects of village board schools (meanwhile avoiding the question of the survival of the large urban boards, which had proved so sensitive an issue in 1896), the Executive secured support for a new system of local education administration based on the counties. Evidence of the defects of village voluntary schools pointed in the same direction. Once it was agreed that further public resources were needed to support them, administrative reform to replace the dominant clergyman could not be avoided. At the NUT Conference in Cambridge in 1899, Macnamara moved that:

> whilst expressing gratitude for the efforts of benevolent societies and individuals in the past as voluntary subscribers in support of public education, this

Conference is of opinion that the time has now come when the whole of the finances necessary for the support of public education should be provided from public sources, and should be expended subject to public control.

They must give up the idea of partly supporting national education by charity, he said (Cheers):

... The thing is an anachronism (Cheers). Education is a line of National Defence – by far the cheapest of the three (Cheers). Now with regard to the first line, the Navy, they didn't say 'We will maintain the men-of-war entirely out of public funds; but we will send the hat round for the torpedo flotillas' (Loud laughter). With regard to the Army, they didn't say 'We'll maintain the Infantry as a public charge; but we'll open subscription lists for the Cavalry' (Loud laughter). Why, they didn't even do that for the Militia! (Loud laughter).

The following day the resolution was carried almost unanimously and with cheering.[63] Later in the year, evidently with some relief, he recalled the anxieties of 1896: 'good sense kept us all together happily, though the experiences of that time took a good deal of the hair off my head, I remember'.[64]

Macnamara was emerging as a national figure. In February 1896 he had published his *Schoolmaster Sketches*, a humorous and satirical collection of short stories about the functionaries of the education world. 'Every incident in the sketches', he wrote in the preface, 'has actually occurred within the past few years in connection with our State system of elementary schools, and many of the incidents are typical.' It included an account of a new teacher who tried to make more flexible the mechanical methods of teaching that were expected. She was paid off. 'Faddy HMI' was a portrayal of the kind of Inspector that the Education Department had for so long foisted on public elementary school teachers: 'transformed ... from the Graduate in Arts, with his eye-glass, his lackadaisical insipidity, and his aristocratic drawl, by one single "Hey presto!" into a full-blown journeyman Inspector'. His comments about the attitude of the rural school board member towards the provision of education annoyed the *School Board Chronicle*:

He doesn't believe in it; he has done splendidly – in his own estimation – without it himself: he objects to paying for it for other people's children, and he makes the life of the teacher under his sweet rule in very many cases a thing grievous to be borne ... the cheaper and the nastier school work can be made, the better he is pleased.[65]

When the Education Bill was abandoned, the *Chronicle* contended that 'there was only too plain evidence ... that ministerial impressions of the school board system had been too exclusively derived from sources identical, or very closely kindred, with those to which we owe the serious purpose of these sketches'.[66]

This was a great, if exaggerated, compliment for Macnamara. Another came from the *Phrenological Magazine*, which featured him in its series 'In

the Public Eye'. 'His head is developed in the fore region, which favours
intelligence of a special order', it opined:

> The brow is well filled out in the central line, and is exceptionally active,
> which ... gives him his immense power of criticism; ready memory of com-
> parisons; keen intuition regarding character; and a clear discernment of facts,
> incidents, truths, and principles. The second characteristic is the breadth of
> the head in the Perfecting faculties. He has a ready command of language, a
> fluency of expression and an ideal sense of the appropriateness of things whether
> he is dealing with dry facts or making a critical survey of artistic work. A third
> characteristic is to be noticed in the breadth of the upper arch of the head,
> which gives him broad sympathies, a wonderful grasp of the circumstances that
> go to make up life, and an interest in the brotherhood of man from a
> humanitarian standpoint. He should therefore be known for the sincerity of his
> views and the earnestness which he puts into everything he does. His concen-
> tration of mind is not so great as to prevent him from taking a deep interest
> in many subjects, far more that the public are likely to know of, and his mind
> is capable of passing from one subject to another with remarkable ease and
> ability. He has inherited his courage from his father, only he has shown it in
> the educational Crimea ... [67]

In June 1896 *Philo* of the *New Age*, contributing to the series 'Men who
Ought to be in Parliament', took Macnamara as the subject and retold
the story of the conference speech in complimentary terms:

> Recognising the Union comprised men and women of every shade of political
> and religious belief, and appreciating the power of a strong Parliamentary
> majority pledged to assist the voluntary schools, he accepted the decentralising
> clauses and endeavoured ... to mould the Bill rather than condemn it wholesale.
> The President's attitude of caution was not observed by conference, which in
> Mr Macnamara's own phrase 'left him high and dry' ... he has been wrong in
> assuming that it is possible to democratise the Bill in Committee. Mr Macna-
> mara made a mistake, but as Abraham Lincoln said 'the man who can't make
> a mistake can't make anything!'

The Editor and President can only have been delighted to reproduce *Philo*'s
conclusion in the *Schoolmaster*: 'As a speaker, journalist, administrator, and
teacher he has sought success only to find it, and in our opinion his seat
at St Stephen's is already waiting for him'.[68]

Two years later, a public honour of immense value was conferred on
him. Whilst English universities had looked askance at the study of Education, Scottish foundations, following central European examples, had
taken up the subject with interest and enthusiasm. On Friday 25 March
1898 Macnamara was invested, alongside J. M. Barrie, with the degree of
Doctor of Laws at the University of St Andrews by Professor Meiklejohn,
who had occupied the Chair endowed by the trustees of the educationist
Andrew Bell for the previous twenty-two years, and who had proposed the
award. Women as well as men were robed in the far-famed scarlet gowns.

In the Library college songs were roared out, penny trumpets squeaked, animals were let loose. Finally the doctorates were presented. Meiklejohn introduced Macnamara:

> editor of the *Schoolmaster*, the most powerful educational journal in Great Britain. He is also at present member of the London School Board and was – in 1896 – the President of the National Union of Teachers. He is the author of several books on the present condition of education and of many able articles on educational subjects in the leading monthly and quarterly reviews of the country. A teacher among teachers, he has always been the friend of teachers, has upheld their cause and fought their battles, and given his life to the spread of thought and light.[69]

Though it was an honorary degree, the title of doctor was too good to overlook. For the rest of his career the man previously known as 'T. J. M. ' or 'Mac' was usually referred to as 'the Doctor'.

The rural campaign had made it almost certain that when major legislation on education was again essayed, the teachers would be united, but, as the century ended, prospects for such legislation looked bleak. Balfour, the Prime Minister's representative in the House of Commons, had been shocked by the hostility that Gorst's Bill had provoked. Nothing in his Parliamentary experience, he admitted in July 1896, had caused him more pain than the degree and character of the opposition that it had encountered.[70] Financial aid, first for voluntary schools, then for needy board schools, was secured in piecemeal fashion the following year; he was unwilling, he declared, to risk opposition to financial subventions by combining them with other cognate but alien subjects.

The ministers responsible for education, both of whom had been expected to act upon the Bryce Report's recommendations for State-supported secondary education, found themselves incapacitated by this approach. Little was expected within the Education Department of the Lord President. 'The Duke', Kekewich (the Permanent Secretary) recalled in his acrimonious memoir:

> came to the office at Whitehall comparatively rarely; in such intervals, no doubt, as he could spare from social engagements and the pleasing diversions of racing and bridge ... As he so seldom did any work, and as he so rarely gave himself the trouble of serious discussion his influence certainly was the reverse of stimulating ... he seemed to consider that his principal duty was to pour cold water upon every proposition that was made to him.[71]

Nevertheless the Lord President, who had concluded that the prerequisite for adequate secondary provision was an effective central authority, secured the establishment of a full-scale government department for education by means of the Board of Education Act of August 1899. 'So far so good', Macnamara observed in the *Nineteenth Century*:

> but what bewilders me not a little is the fact that the vital and urgent problem

of 1896 is quite untouched in 1899 ... practically all educationists of all shades of political thought are agreed that the problem of the Local Authority must be faced, and that the scope of the Board of Education Bill must be so far extended as to include the treatment of that great feature of the whole question which, in 1896, was held by the Government to overshadow in importance all others ... as far as I can see, the aim of the Government is to keep the question of the Local Authority away from Parliament in the hope that it will muddle itself into something like shape in each locality and after much civil war. This may or may not be first class political expediency, but in the way of Statesmanship it scores but a poor place.[72]

Balfour's piecemeal policy was disastrous for Gorst. The two men had, in the early 1880s, been associated in the ginger group known as the Fourth Party. Now they were on bad terms. Annoyed by the treatment he had received in 1896, and aware that, at his age, he would be offered no new post if he resigned, Gorst persistently drew the attention of the House of Commons to the manifold defects of the national education system. His colleagues, however, afforded him no support. Instead they fled from the Treasury bench to avoid his damaging speeches.[73] In December 1896 he set up a Departmental Committee on the Pupil-Teacher with a view to winding up the system of apprenticeship. Its report, published in March 1898, recommended that the age at which pupil-teachers were indentured was to be progressively raised and that the number of them employed in a school should not exceed two for the principal teacher and one for each additional certificated teacher.[74] But the Church of England found pupil-teachers invaluable in staffing its elementary schools; hence, in November, the National Society set up its own investigating committee under the Chairmanship of the Archbishop of Canterbury. Among the witnesses was Macnamara. He argued that pupil-teachers should not be counted on the staff at all. All regulations should be made with a view to fitting them for their future profession and for nothing else. The large additional costs should be met by the Government. Not surprisingly, the Committee found no use for what it called his ingenious suggestions, but as he completed his evidence Dr Temple stumped down the room, grasped him by the hand in a way that made him wince and said 'Good-bye. I've disagreed with nearly everything you've said. But I like the way you've spoken to us.'[75] The effect of the Committee's report[76] on the unfortunate Gorst was instantaneous. He had been planning to introduce new pupil-teacher regulations in the Code of 1899. Now, under pressure from the National Society, rural school managers and rural MPs, he announced that he would not force them upon a reluctant House of Commons. 'And so these reforms go out of the Code!', the *Schoolmaster* reported. 'Dear Reader, please make your own comments on this extraordinary speech and pitiable surrender. The situation is beyond us!'[77]

Early in 1899 Gorst perceived an opportunity to achieve amendments to the regulations dealing with child employment, thereby raising the school leaving age to thirteen, through a Private Member's Bill introduced into the House of Commons by W. S. Robson QC, Liberal MP for South Shields, who had been induced by Gray and Yoxall to take up the issue.[78] At the beginning of the Second Reading, on 1 March 1899, Macnamara, Jackman, Clancy and Waddington were all to be seen under the Gallery. The Opposition Front Bench was crowded but upon the Government Bench Sir John Gorst sat, for most of the afternoon, alone.[79] Unsupported by any ministerial colleague, he spoke as a private member giving no indication of the Government's view and, in his anxiety that the Bill should succeed, he made a suggestion to conciliate the agricultural interest in the House, that rural children over a certain age might absent themselves from school, or even that the schools might close during the harvest as they did in Switzerland, so that the children could work in the fields. Asquith, the next speaker, assailed the Government for its silence. 'Did they mean to redeem the Berlin pledge?', he asked. 'Did they even mean to stand to the clause of their own Bill in 1896?' Still, by 5.25 pm, when the division was taken, nobody had spoken for the Government. The Second Reading was carried by 317 votes to fifty-nine, to great cheers. Outside, the NUT contingent met Gray and Yoxall, their Parliamentary representatives, in jubilation. Only Macnamara, who had been ready to bet anybody and everybody that there would not be sixty votes against the Bill, was a trifle distressed at the nearness of the number to his estimate.[80]

When the amendments were tabled for the Committee stage it was clear that Robson had taken up Gorst's suggestion about rural schools. He proposed that the Local Authority for any rural district might, by means of a bye-law, fix thirteen as the minimum age for exemption in the case of children to be employed in agriculture; such children would not be required between the ages of eleven and thirteen (if they had passed the local standard for partial exemption) to make more than 300 attendances per year.[81] Macnamara attacked the proposal. 'Why should rural youngsters, who were, just as much as town youngsters, the future heritors of Imperial greatness and responsibility, be done out of their schooling simply to furnish the 'depressed agriculturalist' with the cheapest form of child labour?', he asked a large gathering of rural teachers at Matlock Bath on 17 June.[82] 'It is a thousand pities', he wrote in an editorial at the end of the year, just as the Act was to come into force:

> that Mr Robson, in his desire to score the biggest victory of the session, feverishly rushed to make terms with those whom, he well knew, have no special love for the cause of education and are conscientiously of the belief that even today the village child is getting more than is good for him. However, Sir John Gorst has assured us that attendance in the village schools shall be 'real' during the time that the children under the permissive clause of the Robson Act are supposed to be in attendance at school. To this miraculous end some wonderful

'Bye-laws' for the working of this ill-starred plan are in the process of incubation. The Act comes into operation on Monday. But of those marvellous bye-laws we have as yet seen nothing.[83]

Here, however, Gorst ended his run of failure. His Elementary Education (Attendance) Act, which came into force on 8 August 1900, was intended to stiffen bye-laws on attendance through increased fines. It included a clause by which the school leaving age could be raised to fourteen.[84] At the NUT conference, held in York, Macnamara declared that Gorst's little Bill was one for which they ought to thank the Government very cordially (Cheers). Raising the maximum penalty for absence from school from five to twenty shillings brought England and Wales in line with Scottish practice. The Conference, he said, recognised that there was a small minority of thriftless, indifferent parents who left the police-court every time they were prosecuted for not sending their offspring to school jingling in their pockets the substantial difference between the small fine they had paid and the children's wages. To deal with them, State-appointed attendance officers were needed. Many Local Authorities openly defied the bye-laws. Even after repeated pressure from HM Inspectorate, one small school board, obliged at last to appoint an attendance officer, had, he related, selected the turnpike toll-gate keeper. The board members perceived that, in consequence of his duties, he was quite unable to run about looking after the children.[85]

Generally unsuccessful inside the House of Commons, increasingly reviled outside it, Gorst had never abandoned his determination to bring about a major reform in local education administration. As Parliamentary prospects faded, he turned to covert means. Aiming to destroy the system set up in 1870, he had begun a plan to undermine the largest school board in the country. When, in November 1897, Macnamara submitted himself for re-election in West Lambeth, the days of the London School Board were already numbered.

6

The London School Board,
1897–1900

'The Progressive majority of the new School Board for London has a great opportunity before it', commented the *Schoolmaster* at the beginning of December 1897:

> ... an opportunity for quiet useful work of genuine educational value and of far-reaching consequences ... If it desires a short life and a merry one its members will rush ahead at breakneck pace ... if it desires three years hence to receive back from a grateful community the charge with which it is now entrusted ... it will move forward steadily and with prudence ... and it will be exceedingly chary of adding fresh burdens to those already upon the ratepayers' shoulders.[1]

This was good advice. Few members of the new majority party were, however, disposed to take it. The new Chairman, drawn (as was now customary) from non-members, was the Progressives' candidate, Lord Reay. A descendant of the Mackays who had taken up residence in the Netherlands in the seventeenth century, he had abandoned his career as a diplomat and politician there on the death of his father (a former Prime Minister) in 1875 and entered British public life. Created a peer of the United Kingdom in 1881, he had been Governor of Bombay between 1885 and 1890. Keenly interested in education, he was to use the occasion of his annual report as an opportunity not only to appraise the achievements of the Board, but also to reprove the Government for its obstruction and hostility.[2] The Vice-Chairman, the Hon. Lyulph Stanley, Leader of the Progressive Party, had first been elected to the Board in 1876, and with the exception of the sixth Board (1885–88) had been a member ever since. Unlike those Board members who used their power for religious, party or personal ends, Stanley worked single-mindedly to improve the quality of education provision. He was activated by an apparently boundless personal energy which was mainly deployed for practical measures like the improvement of buildings and the reduction of class size, though his industry and wonderful memory were combined with a nervous irritability which often daunted opponents and supporters alike. He was the driving wheel of the whole machine, the *Schoolmaster* concluded: 'Go into whatever department of the Board's work and the genius and activity of Mr Stanley at once confronts you. And whatever may be the dictates of expediency it is always full-steam ahead with Mr Stanley.'[3]

Macnamara, described as a Progressive at Board elections, retained some independence from the Stanley line. But at the first meeting of the new Board his enthusiasm for action accorded less with the *Schoolmaster*'s call for prudence, and more with Stanley's forward policy. He raised the subject of revenue, challenging the Government to make more Treasury money available. Since a Royal Commission on Local Taxation was in the process of collecting evidence, Macnamara advocated placing before it a specific claim for more aid accompanied by a memorandum comparing the contribution made to Board education by the Treasury and by local rates. Throughout the country, he said, boards received half their resources from the Treasury. London, however, received only a quarter, yet it was obliged to contribute to both voluntary and board schools in the provinces under the Acts passed in 1897. The Finance Committee was duly instructed to prepare evidence for the Royal Commission;[4] as it did so, Macnamara prepared the memorandum in which he quantified his observations on the Board's sources of income. London raised seventy-two per cent of its education costs by local rate, receiving only twenty-eight per cent from the Exchequer, while the figures for the rest of England and Wales were fifty-three and forty-seven per cent. This disproportion was intensified by the fact that, under the recent legislation, London was obliged to assist areas which raised little or nothing by means of rates. Giving evidence on 18 May 1898 to the Royal Commission, he placed emphasis on to the London School Board's resolution that a more equitable relation should be secured between the cost of elementary education borne locally and centrally, adding the observation that a much larger proportion of the cost of education could be met by the Exchequer.[5]

The wisdom of these representations may be doubted. Members of the Unionist government, especially Salisbury and Balfour, had already shown themselves hostile to the school boards. In the Commons the Church Party of Conservative MPs which had harried Acland during the lifetime of the Liberal governments of 1892–95 was still active. In the summer of 1896 Lord Cranborne, Salisbury's eldest son, had become its leader: another member was his brother Lord Hugh Cecil, even more zealous in what he took to be the service of the Church of England. Their cousin Evelyn Cecil, elected to the London School Board for Marylebone in 1894, was able to provide them with information about its operation. In February 1896 Balfour told a Unionist meeting at Bristol that the London ratepayer was paying a School Board rate on a scale of extravagance which, to his knowledge, surpassed anything in Great Britain or Europe.[6] From the moment the Progressives took over, any expansion of the Board's expenditure would therefore be eyed critically at government level. Even a proposed change in the allotment of resources would be viewed with suspicion. 'Why do you select cost as the test upon which the Imperial contribution is to be given?', Macnamara was asked by Lord Balfour of Burleigh, Chairman of the Royal Commission: 'I suggest to you that taking cost as the test is about the most efficient means you could devise of running the cost up greater than it need otherwise be.' He refused to be drawn: 'I should have thought there is no grant made which is so carefully surrounded by safeguards as the education grant', he replied.[7]

Before Christmas, Macnamara had also taken up once more the issue of the hungry child. 'Free half-penny and penny dinners have been supplied of late years in many schools', the Final Report of the Cross Commission had observed in 1888, 'and there is no doubt that the regular feeding of the poor children in schools is a great aid to their regular attendance and to their progress in their studies.'[8] In the *Schoolmaster* of 8 December 1894, just after he had first been elected to the London School Board, Macnamara had written a fierce editorial about the horrors of winter for the children of the destitute poor:

> For a teacher in the slums to have to stand up morning after morning before a class of more or less ill-clothed and half-fed children, and to be expected to cram their minds with instruction to be negotiated for government grants on the examination day, is an experience that no one who has tried it will care to talk much about. The parsing of the complex sentence is doubtless an agreeable feast of reason in its way ... but there are times when the pinched faces, the sharp features and tightly drawn rags of the hungry philologists enjoying its pleasures seem to call for something of an entirely different nature.[9]

Instead of the instant action he had called for, however, the Board had set up a Committee under the Chairmanship of Graham Wallas (with Macnamara among the members) to ascertain the number of children who were attending school insufficiently fed and to recommend remedies. Information was collected about food provision in a range of large cities, including Bristol, Cardiff, Glasgow, Liverpool, Manchester, Sheffield, Belfast and Dublin. People engaged in the voluntary agencies supplying meals were interviewed separately. They included Macnamara's old friend Mrs Burgwin, who, amongst her other activities, was Secretary of the Free Meals Fund run by the newspaper the *Referee*, Sister Gertrude Bromby, of St Philip's Mission, Plaistow, and W. H. Libby, Hon. Secretary to the Lambeth Teachers' Association Scholars' Free Meal Fund and headmaster of Victory Place Board School, Walworth. Not all witnesses were in favour of the provision of meals. The Rev. Benjamin Waugh, Director of the National Society for the Prevention of Cruelty to Children, observed that the great bulk of the starving children of the country were starving either through the idleness or the vice of their parents.[10] When the Committee's report was discussed at the Board, nearly a year later, no enthusiasm for action among the majority was evident. It was accepted that head teachers should keep continuous records of all children receiving charitable meals, together with the names of the associations providing them, the prices (if any) and the places where the food was consumed, but it was not considered appropriate for the Board to supply meals. It was the duty of parents to secure food for the children, Thomas Huggett commented, not the Board.[11]

Under the new Board an opportunity soon arose for the discussion of the question. On 16 December business was transacted with such rapidity that the last page of the agenda was reached within a quarter of an hour of the start of the meeting. Father Brown (the newly elected Roman Catholic member for Southwark) moved a resolution that the Board should assume powers to supplement voluntary efforts to deal with under-feeding. Since the previous Board report, he said, some excellent and impartial work had been done by the London Schools Dinner Association. On an inadequate income of £1,400 some 12,000 meals were provided each week, but this worked out at only two-and-a-third meals per week per child. When the tickets ran out, teachers were under the painful necessity of turning the needy children away. He was supported by Frank Costelloe, another new member (also one of the leaders of the Progressive Party on the London County Council) who pointed out that the Board had already begun to play a rôle by erecting dining rooms for the use of the promoters of the Free Meals Fund. Where was the difference in principle, he asked, between providing a dining hall and a crust of bread to put upon the tables? The Rev. Copeland Bowie, one of the Progressive Whips, dismissed these arguments. At all new Boards they had newly elected members filling the paper with fireworks and letting them off, he said. One of his own canvassers had encountered a bright Board school boy in a block of buildings in Southwark who had said: 'We are for Father Brown, not Bowie. He will give us sausages, and save our souls' (Laughter). The London School Board, he went on, had not been elected for the management of the world, nor for the solution of all social problems. Macnamara, speaking next, deplored the tone of Bowie's speech. As a principle, he declared, they should not have any hungry children in the schools. He knew from experience that it was impossible to teach children who were in want of food. From a national point of view their present easy optimism was very shortsighted. 'We used to boast of our physical superiority over the French', he added, 'but this will soon be reversed unless we are careful, for already France undertakes such work as this.' The discussion continued for nearly three hours; finally a decision not to proceed was taken by twenty-eight votes to fifteen.[12]

Expressing doubts about the propriety of Father Brown's motion which, it commented archly, came all too hot from the oven of the Triennial Election to serve as fit and wholesome food for the constructive thoughts and debates of a young Board, the *School Board Chronicle* nevertheless concluded the following week that:

the question remains with us, and will remain, so long as, from any cause whatever, children are brought to school hungry, unfit to profit by the teaching ... The Board will do well, for the present, to offer no handle to its enemies, and to avoid needlessly disturbing the susceptibilities of those who have been loading it with advice about keeping to its proper business and generally being little seen and less heard. Yet we should be sorry to think that the London School Board ... should be precluded, by any pedantic conception of the limits of its function and responsibility, from using any great opportunity of public service that presents itself.[13]

The following July another investigation began. Costelloe, supported by Macnamara and Brown, moved that the General Purposes Committee should consider and report whether any and what enquiry could be made before the next winter about the number of children attending public elementary schools in London who were probably under-fed, and how far existing voluntary provision for school meals was effective. The motion was approved by thirty-one to six. On 3 October, the General Purposes Committee appointed a sub-committee, the investigations of which lasted until November the following year and included the collection of information from France, Germany, Italy, Belgium, Sweden and Switzerland. Under the Chairmanship of Costelloe, the members included G. C. Whiteley (Chairman of the General Purposes Committee), Mrs Bridges Adams, Edmund Barnes, Sir Charles Elliott, the Revs J. S. Lidgett and Russell Wakefield (all members of that Committee) and Brown, Mrs Dibdin and Macnamara.[14]

The report, prepared by Costelloe, concluded that compulsion to attend should involve ascertainment of which children went to school unfit to derive normal profit from school work. The idea that the existence of a scheme of school dinners pauperised parents or destroyed the sense of parental responsibility was dismissed as a mere theoretical fancy, entirely unsupported by practical experience. The existing system was not ineffective. As against the 55,050 children reckoned as under-fed, there was an enormous aggregate of meals, porridge breakfasts, breakfasts consisting of cocoa or coffee, with a currant roll or bread, dinners in some places consisting of soup and bread and a bun, in others Irish stew or vegetarian food. But they were available only from the beginning of December till mid-March; in some places four days a week, in others only three or two. The sub-committee had been convinced, both by consideration of the subject and by special information collected by Wakefield in Paris, that the whole question of the feeding and health of children compulsorily attending school should be dealt with as a matter of public concern. But as the report showed, its conclusions had been made tentative by financial considerations. Elliott, Barnes and Mrs Dibdin in a minority report suggested that the Voluntary Associations could deal with the question; the main report advised the Board to take Counsel's opinion before assuming any specific responsibilities.[15]

Whiteley presented the final version of the report to the Board on 17 November 1899. The *Board Teacher* found his speech disappointing. Though he moved that a special Under-fed Children Committee be set up, it appeared that his aim was to minimise the effect of the proposals which he described, to laughter, as 'only a few simple and moderate resolutions', intended not to feed children out of the rates, but only to supplement existing efforts. Thus encouraged, Bowie struck out against the report, conjuring up visions of demoralisation of parents and an alarming tide of socialism overwhelming all and sundry. But he was followed by Costelloe, who had risen from a sick bed with the symptoms of a mortal illness. Received with sympathetic cheers, he attacked Bowie's arguments without mercy. The matter did not touch the question of parental responsibility, he said. He did not see how it was good for the moral fibre of parents to see their children starve. The thing that impressed him was that 55,000 children (a figure supplied by their own teachers) continued to go to school on a dark January morning unfed or insufficiently fed, while the Board shilly-shallied with the question. The Board spent anything in every direction on aids to education, even to the provision of a flower for the school-room windows, and what was proposed was an aid worth all the others put together. He called for immediate, courageous action. At the close of this remarkable speech there was general cheering, but after two hours the debate was adjourned.[16]

It was continued the following week. J. W. Sharp, the Moderate leader, lugubriously prophesied that the proposals would, if implemented, increase the rates by 1½d in the £. Voluntary contributions, he concluded, would meet the needs of the case. The London Schools Dinner Association was quite equal to the emergency, to say nothing of other valuable organisations. Let it be known that government or local aid was being received for the purpose and the streams of benevolence would dry up. Macnamara, sensing defeat, recalled how, ninety years before, when Samuel Whitbread had advocated a national system of education, his proposal had been regarded as mischievous and dangerous. But his proposal had come to pass. No doubt the proposal for an Under-fed Children Committee would be beaten: some time in the future when State intervention with regard to the physical needs of children was a fact, everybody would be amazed at the opposition that the principle met on its first enunciation. One point of general agreement had already emerged, that it was cruelly impossible to attempt to teach a hungry child. It was perceived that to attempt to do so wasted money spent on educational resources; also that more needed to be done. The real question was whether the State should take over responsibility from the charitable agencies. In his view it was charity, not State intervention, that demoralised. He was astonished by Progressive educationists who were opposed to such intervention. They had swallowed the camel and were straining at the gnat. They voted for pianos, for window boxes, for chemical and physical laboratories, for dark rooms to develop lantern-slides, and the previous week they had voted to supply children with spectacles. Yet their economic stomachs revolted at the thought of a basin of State-aided soup. Members of the Moderate Party who opposed the scheme were similarly astonishing. Flamboyant references to Britain's greatness were always on their lips; they had decided that the Union Jack might be hung in schools. But, he said, Britain's greatness was not to be secured by merely waving the Union Jack and singing songs with loud choruses. Britain's greatness would depend on the fitness of her people.[17]

The views expressed by Stanley, as leader of the Progressive Party, confirmed Macnamara's appraisal of its intentions. He fell upon the report, the *Board Teacher* commented, with all the vigour and sarcasm at his command. The existence of destitution, he said, was recognised by the community in the operation of the Poor Law; poverty, short of actual destitution, was best met by well-organised charity. The recommendations of the report were pestilent heresy. They would break down just that self-respect which stood between the independent poor and the sponging, cringing, pauperised poor. The Board's function was education. Mrs Bridges Adams, the Socialist member for Greenwich, spoke last before the adjournment. Stanley, she said, was a true, sturdy democrat in the matter of the provision of education for the children of the people, but his attitude over this question was deplorable. She warned that society stood upon a mine: while they slept in smug security, quiet street-corner meetings were being held at which these very questions were being discussed.

Macnamara, like a number of his fellow sub-committee members, had appended some specific suggestions to the report. He proposed that a dining hall should be furnished at the Johanna Street School for the three North Lambeth schools (Johanna Street, Waterloo Road and Addington Street) with a school kitchen provided under the direction of a public official. Dinner coupons, paid for or free according to the necessities of the case, would be procurable by parents at a convenient public office. Similar arrangements could be made in the other parts of the division and ultimately throughout London. 'This is the system which I have frequently pointed out is in force in many Continental cities, and which works with the most excellent results', he declared:

> Bye and bye I should hope that practically all the parents would avail themselves of these midday meals for their children. It would mean a great economy of time and money to them, and the meal provided would, in all probability, be a good deal more nutritious and satisfying to the children than that at present prepared in the home ... I insist that it is equally essential to our future prosperity as a nation, to see that no child lacks warm clothing and comfortable housing ... I say, too, that the medical examination from time to time of the children especially with regard to the condition of their eyes, and indeed, their general physical state, is a matter of communal obligation ... As a Christian

and civilised community, I urge that we should not allow an appreciable section of our youth to slouch through lives of suffering and destitution into ricketty, misshapen and very frequently evil-minded adults. I cannot blame these social derelicts, if they ultimately become a ruinously heavy charge upon the public purse as inmates of the public workhouses and gaols.[18]

With most of the members of both parties agreed that rate-supported intervention was not to take place, a further effort was made to deploy the voluntary agencies in the relief of under-fed children. On 1 March 1900, the Board resolved that a permanent committee should be appointed to supervise the work of organising relief for them. Labelled 'the Joint Committee', it had two representatives from both the London and the Rochester Diocesan Boards of Education, two from the Roman Catholic Voluntary Schools, two from the Committee of Representative Managers of London Board Schools, one each from the London Schools Dinner Association, the Board School Children's Free Dinner Fund, the Destitute Children's Dinner Society and the *Referee* Fund, and eight, including Macnamara, from the Board itself. The *Referee* member was Mrs Burgwin; the London Schools Dinner Association member was J. R. Diggle. After three years' work, the majority of the Committee was to conclude that the relief of under-fed children in London could no longer be effectively dealt with by organising the resources of private charity, which involved periodic appeals to the public. One to the London Press on behalf of the London Schools Dinner Association by Lord Reay in January 1901 serves as an example. 'The Association and its Committee during last winter provided more than 600,000 meals for underfed children', Reay related:

> The work of investigating the needs of the children and of providing the meals was performed by seventy-two local committees, who had under their charge 165 very poor schools. The winter was one of exceptional freedom from distress; but nevertheless, the Association was obliged to provide a sum of £1,233 in grants to these committees. In a less favourable season the sum would be larger. To meet this necessary expenditure only £870 was received in subscriptions. The result is that the current account of the Association is now considerably overdrawn.[19]

Macnamara was still deeply concerned about pupil attendance at school. In his paper delivered to the NUT Conference in 1892 he had shown that legislation to bring it about was not working. Twenty-one years after Forster's Act had permitted attendance bye-laws to be passed, twelve years after Mundella's Act had made them obligatory, an appreciable minority of English parents still placed so low an estimate upon the value of education that they would suffer little or no inconvenience and make few or no sacrifices to ensure that their children were kept in regular and continuous attendance at school.[20]

The first London School Board of 1870–73 had not hesitated to pass attendance bye-laws despite the fact that, by taking this step, it greatly increased both the extent and the cost of its work. Its territories were divided into more than 300 districts, to each of which a visitor was appointed whose job was to check up on absentees and, occasionally, to participate in a street raid when all the visitors of one of the Board's divisions would cooperate in interrogating children found at large. Parents whose children had not attended school would first be issued with a warning; if the offence was repeated they could be called before a divisional sub-committee. If the absences continued, prosecution could follow. But, as Macnamara had shown in his 1892 paper, the result of all this effort was unsatisfactory. During the half year ending 30 June 1891, 147 of the fines imposed at the Southwark Police Court alone were still outstanding, and what was more, they were likely to remain so. Knowing the temper of the Bench, the attendance officer was therefore often compelled to give up. The establishment of special petty sessions in Hackney (in 1894) and in Kensington (in 1896) proved to be a more effective method of dealing with these cases.[21]

On his election to the Board in 1894, Macnamara had been appointed to the Accommodation and Attendance Committee. Despite the devotion and zeal of Sharp (the Chairman) and all the officials, he pointed out a year later, twenty per cent of children were absent from school. What this meant was that ninety per cent of children made a good attendance, perhaps nine out of ten possible, whilst ten per cent made a thoroughly bad attendance. Hundreds of prosecutions were awaiting a hearing at the Clerkenwell Police Court alone. The following year the story was similar. The Board had provided 754,614 places. There were 738,930 children on the rolls. Yet of these, 144,257 on average were away every time the school was open and at least 100,000 of these were the most neglected of the children of the metropolis. An improvement of one per cent in average attendance would have the advantage of increasing the annual Treasury grant by £10,000. But in November 1897 Sharp warned that although the percentage attendance had been increasing by less than one per cent since 1891 and had reached 80.4 the previous year, over the previous twelve months it had declined to 80.2 per cent.[22]

'Attendance! Oh, the attendance', the *Board Teacher* exclaimed, referring to the annual reports of the Managers of the London Board Schools:

The dolorous strain runs through nearly the whole series. Yet to right the matter is so easy. In some of the wretchedest quarters of the East End are schools in which each department obtains ninety per cent throughout the whole year. One Headmaster points out exceptional troubles in his case that will prevent his ever getting a much higher percentage than ninety-six. Yet grinding poverty is all around him. How is it done then? Let easy-going Board members and case-hardened superintendents of visitors travel eastward to see. Their complacent excuses of poverty and sickness will be forced out of them. Not far from the heart of wealthy Marylebone comes this recital of scandalous fact:

'Nearly fifty children, from over seven to twelve years of age, have been admitted to the boys' department this year, totally unfit for first standard, the majority of them scarcely knowing their letters'.[23]

Macnamara urged the new Board to set up a special committee to concentrate on attendance. Not only were improved figures desirable in themselves, he declared; they also meant that revenue would increase. At the end of February 1898 a sub-committee was duly set up under Macnamara's Chairmanship; it included Brown, Bowie, Sharp and Charles Bowden (Macnamara's former NUT colleague, elected for Finsbury in 1897) and, ex officio, the Chairman and Vice-Chairman of the Board. In October, after six meetings and the analysis of evidence given by witnesses from both in and outside schools, it submitted to the Accommodation and Attendance Committee what the *Board Teacher* described as an exceedingly interesting and valuable report which was discussed at the Board on 17 November. If they had lost two battleships, Macnamara said in the course of the debate, they would regard it as a great national loss, but the communal loss involved by the gross irregularity of a certain class of children was, in the long run, far greater. In 1891 the attendance percentage was 77.1; now it was only 80.7. The report's recommendations were not much, but a move in the right direction. They had to peg away without the assistance of magistrates who did not believe in educating children out of their proper stations.[24]

The report's main conclusion was that attendance enforcement failed because the law was not taken seriously. The *Board Teacher* commented:

Everybody knew it. More than a thousand times it has been proclaimed from the house-tops, in the public streets, on all sorts of platforms, and from all kinds of pulpits. Still the declaration is timely – most timely ... it is only in educational matters that our magistrates feel themselves above the law they are paid to administer ... Every true educationist must pray for more power to the elbows of the members of this excellent sub-committee, which asks to have its commission renewed.[25]

A related question was the employment of children out of school hours. In July, the Board had carried a resolution by Major Skinner, a Westminster member, that Board teachers should be instructed to supply details of the extent to which this occurred. Macnamara was asked to draft a report from the returns. This was submitted to the Board on 16 February 1899. It provided evidence of 1,143 children who worked from nineteen to twenty-nine hours per week; of 729 who worked from thirty to thirty-nine hours; and of 285 who worked more than forty hours. Shop, factory work, errands, newspaper and milk delivery brought in 1d per hour; house work and domestic work ½d per hour. The employment of girls, judging from two schools, one in Greenwich, the other in Hackney, was less customary or systematic than that of boys, schools for whom were investigated in

Chelsea, Finsbury, Greenwich, Hackney, West Lambeth, Marylebone and Tower Hamlets. One boy at the Baker Street School, Stepney was employed by a local greengrocer every weekday between 8.00 am and 9.00 am, 12.30 pm and 1.45 pm and 4.35 pm and 10.00 pm, on Saturday from 8.00 am until past midnight and on Sunday from 11.00 am till 2.00 pm for 1s 6d per week. Another at the Aldenham Street School, Marylebone, worked for an undertaker for twenty-three-and-a-half hours per week. He helped in measuring corpses and his weekly wage was a shilling. The Headmaster of the Lillie Road School, Chelsea, reported that boys delivering milk were up, as a rule, by 5.00 am. They presented themselves late at school and, as a consequence, they were more asleep than awake in the afternoon session.

Macnamara added some general comments. Out-of-school labour was a monstrous injustice. Recreation and rest would seem to be almost unknown terms, to the boys especially. It was impossible to over-state the extreme unwisdom, from a purely communal point of view, of submitting children to this kind of physical strain. The employment of children was in many cases probably the result of thoughtlessness consequent upon established custom, not only in London; elsewhere young children were still drafted off to factories, workshops, mills, pit banks, even the coal pits themselves. No doubt the extreme poverty of many of the parents made the few pence that the child earned a material consideration but, no doubt again, the necessity to secure those few pence was the result in some cases of parental thriftlessness, drunkenness and worthlessness.[26]

Two courses seemed to him to be open: Parliament could be approached to introduce legislation to prohibit the employment of school children or the existing bye-laws could be extended and reinforced.[27] A fortnight later, it was decided to consult the London County Council. But when in 1900 Macnamara reviewed the three years of the School Board, he regretfully admitted that nothing practical had yet been achieved in mitigating the evil. The question of reform was still being considered by both bodies. The Board had, in fact, lessened its demands. It had yielded to a request in April 1899 from the Retail Newsagents' and Booksellers' Union that boys employed in the news, milk and other trades by responsible tradesmen for the purpose of delivering goods between 5.00 am and 8.00 am and 5.00 pm and 8.00 pm should be permitted to continue their work. All it had done was to address a letter to the London County Council, asking it to consider framing bye-laws.[28]

The daily attendance problem remained deplorable and alarming. He had worked pretty hard at the problem, Macnamara told the Board on 12 October 1899, but he was almost giving it up. There were 758,377 children enrolled on the registers of the London elementary schools, but the daily attendance was only 616,378. Thus 142,000 children were absent from school every time the schools were open. If they accepted that 42,000 abstentions were necessary and unavoidable, they had a daily abstention of 100,000 which was contumacious and unjustifiable, and some 50,000 of these were the same children pretty well every time, the wretchedly neglected children of careless and indifferent parents. He believed that the Board's attendance officers did their best, but the parents whom they were especially required to look after simply laughed at them.[29]

Macnamara had made clear his interest in Higher Grade Schools for London as the 1894 Board began. Already in the early 1870s it had become plain that some children wished to extend their education beyond the six standards which existed when the Forster Act was passed. This aspiration began to be met by the creation of a seventh standard in 1882 and by the consolidation, with the encouragement of Vice-Presidents of the Committee Council from Lord George Hamilton (1878–80) and A. J. Mundella (1880–85), of Higher Grade Schools and Organised Science Schools, mainly in the north of England. Financial support came from the Science and Art Department at South Kensington, which had been encouraging science and art teaching on the Payment by Results principle since 1859. These new schools, which enabled elementary school boys (and less often, girls) to advance to the new university colleges and higher technical institutions, were considered by their teachers to offer better opportunities than the old-established secondary schools. 'When you have caught your elementary school boy and passed him through the secondary school to the older university, what have you gained?', John Bidgood, President of the Association of Headmasters of Higher Grade and Organised Science Schools asked at the Association's Conference in 1895:

> A youth with some knowledge of classics, mathematics or, very rarely, pure science, who recognises too late that what he has gone through is merely learning the capabilities of a few tools and that his real preparation for earning a living is yet to come. At the age of twenty-two or twenty-three he finds that he has no money to keep him whilst he is learning a business or profession and that the only thing he can do is to go and swell the already over-crowded ranks of amateur, untrained, and unqualified secondary school teachers.[30]

London had resisted the tendency to create Higher Grade Schools because, it was argued, they were less suitable for the commercial metropolis than for industrial centres. Nevertheless, in 1887 the Board had decided to establish so-called Higher Standard Schools where special attention could be given to older pupils and had added to them from time to time until in the year 1894–95 there were forty-nine. But, as Macnamara argued at a conference on Higher Grade Schools organised by the NUT in London in May and June 1895, what was needed were special schools in each division of the Board area devoted entirely to Higher Grade work, to which the cleverest of the boys and girls among the day school pupils could be drafted for a three or four years' course of modern commercial and practical training. Manchester had five such schools accommodating 5,256 pupils; Nottingham five; Bradford four; Hull three; Leeds two;

Birmingham two; Bolton two; and Salford two. Through these schools, he told the conference, the children of the workers won distinctions at Oxford and Cambridge (including Girton and Newnham colleges), which would make their mouths water, and apart from winning scholarships and exhibitions the practical, technical and commercial training given in these Higher Grade Schools offered those who passed through them a fine chance in life.[31]

Still, at the end of 1894 the London School Board had not regarded the matter as urgent. Macnamara's motion had been blocked, on the grounds that the Secondary Education Commission Report was expected the following July.[32] In the event Bryce and his colleagues did not publish their recommendations until 1 November 1895. Then it was at once clear that the Technical Education Board of the London County Council (LCC), set up in 1893, had, under Sidney Webb and Dr William Garnett, established itself as a powerful force. Outlining a constitution for a Secondary Education Authority for London, the Report suggested that, of the forty-two members, the County Council should appoint eighteen, the School Board seven, the City and Guilds Institute two, the City Parochial Charities' Trustees two, the University of London two, the Universities of Oxford and Cambridge one each, to whom nine coopted members would be added. Garnett took up the point at the Conference of the Association of Headmasters of Higher Grade and Organised Science Schools at the end of the month. Speaking enthusiastically about the achievements of the schools, he added pointedly that if these schools were to be raised to the level hoped for by their supporters, school boards, which were elected chiefly for the purpose of carrying on theological discussions, should not be the sole governing authorities.[33] The warning was plain. Higher Grade Schools were to be regarded as institutions of secondary education and the LCC intended to take up the powers that the Bryce Commission had recommended should be conferred upon it.

Sir John Gorst's Bill of 1896 had been an attempt to put both secondary and elementary schools under a new Local Authority. After its failure he returned to the question of how a future national system of secondary schools could be separately administered. As Vice-President of the Committee of Council he was the House of Commons spokesman not only of the Education Department, which administered elementary education from Whitehall, but also of the Science and Art Department at South Kensington. On 28 October 1896 a Committee of Inquiry was appointed under his Chairmanship to investigate how grants to science and art schools were distributed. Its report, published the following May, included a recommendation that:

> In counties and county boroughs in England possessing an organisation for the promotion of Secondary Education, the authority so constituted may notify its willingness to be responsible for the science and art instruction within its area.

In such cases, while the rights of the managers of existing schools and classes will be preserved, no managers of a new school or class will, except under special circumstances, be recognised unless they are responsible to such authority.[34]

Within the Blue Book which contained the report, the Revised Science and Art Directory was also to be found; the recommendation appeared as Clause VII. Though Gorst denied any intention of setting up a new authority by extra-Parliamentary means and explained the innovation as a move towards decentralisation from which Higher Grade Schools might benefit, the idea was greeted with suspicion. 'Another attack on the Board School', commented the *Board Teacher*, 'a cunning scheme for making the effete and ludicrously incapable Science and Art Department the central authority for the higher education of the brightest children in our elementary schools.'[35]

Once a Progressive majority had been secured at the London School Board election of November 1897, the educational journals began to press for immediate action on the Higher Grade School question. 'We are not only behind the provinces', the *Board Teacher* declared as 1898 opened:

> ... we have not even entered the race ... the time has arrived when we should seriously face the competition of our great provincial rivals. The young Londoner is at the present moment at a distinct disadvantage, compared with his provincial cousin. In most of the great cities the boy whose circumstances are favourable steps from the primary school to the Higher Grade School, and thence to the Technical College as a matter of course. In London alone he finds himself blocked at the seventh or ex-seventh Standard; and while the country boys are being fitted for the best positions in the labour world, the children of the capital are thrust in the background, to become the hewers of wood and drawers of water ... [36]

As soon as the Board reassembled after the Christmas recess, Macnamara, seconded by Bowden, secured a motion that the provision of Higher Grade Board Schools should be taken up by the School Management Committee. They intended that the Board should seek a conference with the Technical Education Board of the London County Council, to settle the secondary school administration question by discussion. On 12 May the lines upon which the SMC had been working became apparent. Wallas moved on its behalf that the Board concur in a memorandum received from the Executive Committee of the Association of School Boards to the effect that borough school boards should be treated as conjoint and co-equal authorities with town councils in the constitution of Local Authorities for secondary education. In response Cecil moved an amendment, quoting the Bryce Report and protesting against any attempt to associate the elementary school authority with the secondary school authority. The ambition of the Board to deal with matters not concerning it was ever growing, he said. He put this down to misplaced zeal.[37]

Macnamara, opposing the amendment, congratulated Cecil on the advance in his position since, two years before, he had objected altogether to State organisation of secondary education for the people. But neither Wallas nor Cecil, he said, seemed to grasp the importance of the issue. The Bryce Commission had proposed only a very small board representation upon the Secondary Education Authorities. At the time the Board was not a body of much weight (Laughter). Nevertheless both Moderates and Progressives had been agreed that the Board should be the nucleus of the Secondary Education Authority. He would propose, he said, that they should associate themselves with the school boards of county boroughs in a deputation to the Committee of Council to point out that it was desirable to secure the proper representation of the School Boards upon the twenty new bodies already created under Clause VII of the Science and Art Directory. But if they could not get election *ad hoc*, he concluded, or the School Board for London as the authority, at least they should secure its proper representation. Stanley agreed. Cecil's amendment would give them one-sixth representation. They must make a stand for nothing less than equal representation. With the amendment lost by thirty to ten, Macnamara replaced it with one making a specific claim for equal treatment for the London School Board. This was approved by thirty-two votes to six.[38]

In the Queen's Speech in February 1898 the Government had undertaken to deal with secondary education. Hence the Board, when addressing the question during the summer, took care to claim representation in advance on whatever authority was set up, whilst still emphasising its views about what it regarded as the provisionally appointed Local Authorities being created under Clause VII of the Science and Art Directory.[39] In fact, the Bill, introduced in the House of Lords by the Duke of Devonshire, the Lord President of the Council, on 1 August, showed that what he regarded as the priority was not secondary education but the creation of a full-scale government department to replace the Committee of Council.[40] Meanwhile applications for recognition under Clause VII of the Science and Art Directory continued to arrive for Gorst's attention. In the House of Commons on 8 July he announced that thirty-three had been received and twenty-one had been granted. In November, the Technical Education Board of the London County Council began to consider whether to apply. Macnamara, at the London School Board meeting of 24 November, recalled what had been decided on 12 May and moved:

> That, as steps are now in course of progress for the recognition, through the agency of Clause VII of the Science and Art Directory 1898, of the Technical Education Board of the London County Council as the Secondary Education Authority for London, representations be made to the County Council and the Lord President of the Committee of Council – in order that Elementary and Higher Public Education in London may be properly co-ordinated, and that,

as far as possible, overlapping and consequent waste of effort, may be avoided – in favour of the recognition of the principle adopted by the School Board on 12th May 1898, to the effect that the representation of the School Board upon the Secondary Education Authority should be equal to that of the County Council.

'The School Boards have got to be there', he added, 'although the School Board should be the nucleus, not the fraction.[41]

The following Monday the Technical Education Board reached its decision to seek recognition. 'Now this proposal affects us directly and immediately', Stanley declared as the Board resumed its debate on the question on 1 December:

> ... the claim put forward by the Board last summer is a just claim. But now let me say that while we are perfectly entitled to ask for what we think fair, I do not think it is wise or just to approach the County Council with an ultimatum. We are both, according to the official statements of the Science and Art Department, Local Authorities competent to set in motion the machinery of Clause VII ... It is by co-operation, not by antagonism, that education will prosper.[42]

A letter, proposing discussions between the two bodies, was subsequently dispatched.

At the next Board meeting on 8 December the London County Council's reply was discussed. The proposal for a conference had been acceded to, a date and place offered and ten members of the Council nominated. The Board responded. Twelve members were appointed, including Wallas, Macnamara, Stanley and Lord Reay, and empowered to take any action that might become necessary over the issue.[43] But these brisk exchanges were the preliminaries of disagreement. When the parties met at Spring Gardens on 14 December the Board representatives asked the County Council to delay its application on the grounds that legislation, upon which both Boards and County Councils would be consulted, would shortly be initiated. The County Council refused. Its members were determined to make application immediately on their own behalf for recognition under Clause VII.[44]

The Board was aware from a previous ruling by the Education Department in December 1897 over the Derby Technical Education Committee application that a local organisation under Clause VII needed to be generally acceptable to all the various educational authorities of the district.[45] It was therefore proposed at its meeting on 15 December that letters be sent to the Lord President of the Council and to Major-General Sir John Donnelly, Secretary to the Science and Art Department, requesting an inquiry into the issue, so that the Board could have an opportunity of expressing its opposition to the County Council's policy. The motion was agreed by thirty-four votes to ten. Opposition to the decision, and (once again) to the Board's ambitions regarding secondary education, was expressed by

Cecil. Some time ago, he said, Stanley had likened the action of the Board in the matter of secondary education to the action of the French at Fashoda. Just as the French had planted their flag at Fashoda, so the Board was going to plant their flag on the domain of secondary education. They were now beginning to witness the spectacle of the School Board flag being hauled down just as the French flag was hauled down. Macnamara responded. He understood that Cecil approved of the action of the County Council. 'Everyone here is fond of Mr Cecil', he added, 'but he has the characteristic of hereditary hostility to the development of national education.' The action of the County Council would prejudice the question of future legislation.[46]

Donnelly's reply to the Board's request was dated 19 January 1899. The inquiry duly took place on 1 February at the Science and Art Department, South Kensington. Donnelly presided; the seven School Board delegates included Wallas, Macnamara and Stanley. At the opposite side of the table sat Edward Bond, Chairman of the Technical Education Board of the London County Council, and five colleagues, including Dr William Garnett. In the background, observing the proceedings, was Gorst. It was soon plain that the two parties were at cross purposes. The London School Board delegates had anticipated an exchange of views on the legality of the procedures following Gorst's initiatives under Clause VII. The County Council representatives, fortified by a twenty-page memorandum prepared by Garnett, were disposed to raise questions about the Board's plans to develop, not only its secondary school provision, but its evening schools as well. Stanley duly rehearsed the argument that the granting of powers under Clause VII was improper, but Bond responded that the Technical Education Board's application was merely intended to avoid overlapping between the two authorities. The School Board, he suggested, was preternaturally suspicious. Macnamara dissented. Nominally the scope of Clause VII might well be as exiguous as Bond had stated, but the clear and obvious intention was to effect, through Departmental minute, what the Government had failed to achieve through its Bill of 1896. If the London County Council's application were granted, he added, the London School Board would bring about still further overlapping and would deliberately open new schools and classes in the proximity of existing institutions.[47] But in the midst of the discussion of the various courses that the Technical Education Board and the School Board were offering, a sudden inquiry by Donnelly dropped like a bomb into the proceedings. 'By what right do ye do these things?', he asked the School Board representatives. In an instant it became clear that the question at issue was not the possible cooperation between two competing agencies but the future existence of one of them.[48]

Once the inquiry was over, Gorst asked Garnett to accompany him to the Education Department building in Whitehall, where a meeting of the Department of Science and Art was to take place. Here it was decided to accept the London County Council's application. A fortnight later, after Cabinet approval had been secured, the parties were informed of the decision. Macnamara, at the Board meeting on 16 February, commented that Donnelly had sat as both judge and advocate on the inquiry and his animus against the School Boards had been obvious. The County Council had said they had no desire to prejudice the future of the organisation of secondary education, but they could not make the application they did without prejudicing the future of the Secondary Education Authority for London. Nevertheless the conference with the County Council Authorities should be renewed so that an effective and permanent Secondary Education Authority could be created.[49]

Gorst, however, now had other plans. At the Education Department on 1 February he had taken the opportunity to discuss with Garnett how the Board's evening school activities, mounted under the Education Code Act of 1890, might be restrained. Garnett recalled, thirty years later: 'The answer, of course, was that it was the function of the High Court to interpret an Act of Parliament and that the simplest way to bring the matter before the Court was to obtain a surcharge on the School Board by the District Auditor against which the School Board would be sure to appeal'.[50] What appeared to be a campaign against the London School Board began before the end of the month in the House of Commons. Cecil, who was to retire from the Board on 27 February, having been elected member of Parliament for Hertford, asked Henry Chaplin (President of the Local Government Board) on 20 February when Board expenditure could be challenged. Chaplin replied that the accounts were audited half-yearly, usually in February and August, the audit was held at the offices of the School Board, and whilst it continued any ratepayer might, at any time, attend and object to any item in the accounts. The *Schoolmaster* commented at the end of the week:

> ... the attack upon the upward development of the school board system ... is obviously directed by official knowledge and skill. Questions are put in Parliament designed to secure the answer that school boards cannot legally come upon the School Fund for the cost of instruction which is not under the Day or Evening School Code of the Education Department. And the necessary assurance is given. Then comes a palpable hint to objectors to attend on the occasion of the Public Audit and direct the attention of the auditor to expenditures on account of Science and Art Instruction, so that he may 'surcharge' ... the cause of the London School Board in this context is the cause of every one of the large urban school boards. Those who hate the popular schools and their success have failed in the frontal attack. They are now trying new and far more dangerous tactics.[51]

In fact Cecil's efforts were superfluous. Garnett, as before, had made all the arrangements. He had ascertained that headmasters of Metropolitan Schools of Art preferred the LCC as a controlling authority. He had enlisted the support of Francis Black, Principal of the Camden School of Art, and William Hales, a solicitor who was also a member of its governing body. Black had set up his school in 1892. By 1898 it had 300 pupils. With the expansion of Board activities he discovered that, within a mile radius, fifteen Board evening schools, six of which took advanced subjects, were functioning. All fees were now remitted by the Board and the materials were provided free of charge. No school, the Camden Governors concluded, could long withstand so severe a competition and they contended that the overlapping was caused by the Board exceeding its statutory powers and misapplying public funds for purposes not justified by the Codes. Objections to rate expenditure needed to be made by ratepayers. Black and Hales willingly took on rôles as objectors, the former searching the registers of the Medburn Street Higher Grade School, Camden Town, the latter enthusiastically undertaking to contest the Board's evening class expenditure.[52]

The audit, under T. B. Cockerton, began at the London School Board offices on 26 April. Three months later to the day, seven specific items of expenditure were duly surcharged.[53] As Gorst had anticipated, the Board took the matter to the High Court where the so-called Cockerton Judgment was delivered in December 1900. Meanwhile, shaken by what had occurred, the Board reviewed the expansion that had taken place in its activities. Macnamara had admitted at the end of February 1899 that the decision to give free admission to evening schools had been a mistake, in view of the fact that in some of the classes they were teaching very advanced work. What he did complain about, he said, was that the government departments should have such grotesque lack of knowledge of their own position that they had misled the Board in the past. That fact, however, did not exonerate the Board if it had been acting illegally. In July the Board, in consultation with the Technical Education Board, agreed that it would limit evening instruction in science and art and that it would not conduct classes in technological subjects nor offer instruction intended for university degrees or for specific trades. The two bodies agreed to cooperate in the production of an annual course list.[54]

The future of Higher Grade Schools could not be decided so easily. On 3 November the annual meeting of the Association of Higher Grade Schools and Schools of Science took place at the Society of Arts rooms in London. Among the visitors were Bond and Garnett of the London Technical Education Board; Bowden and Macnamara from the London School Board; Yoxall and other members of the NUT Executive; and, from the Education Department, Michael Sadler and Robert Morant, the latter soon to move rapidly to the forefront of the Government's policy-making in education. The new President of the Association, Joseph Dyche of Halifax, described how the schools fitted naturally on to elementary schools, how they were staffed by trained teachers, a very large proportion of whom were graduates, how their discipline was admirable and how their pupils were fitted to move on to technical colleges and universities. Their defects, the abnormal size of classes, the shortness of the holidays and the insufficient salaries of assistant teachers could not, he said, be remedied till the legal and financial position of the schools was settled. The following week, in the *Schoolmaster*, Macnamara described the policy of the Education Department over the issue as calamitous to the last degree: 'The brief chance of thousands of the brightest and best of the children of the nation [is] slipping away, and slipping away for ever – and some of our educational leaders, so far as we can see, chuckling! It is a humiliating picture; and one can only put up a fervent prayer that relief may soon come.'[55]

On 1 April 1900 the Education Department and the Science and Art Department were merged to form a new government department, the Board of Education. It at once issued a minute purporting to settle the Higher Grade School question. Higher Elementary Schools which would provide a complete four years of instruction for boys and girls up to the age of fifteen were to be established. 'It is a *leetle* late in the day to talk of 'establishing' these schools', Macnamara commented in a *Schoolmaster* editorial. The Higher Grade Schools had begun eighteen years before with the encouragement of Mr Mundella: they 'struggled into existence, often the object of partisan conflict and latterly the victims of the vicious hostility of a moribund and discredited Department of State'. The Organised Science Schools were plainly excluded from a minute which did not cater for pupils over fifteen. Their future and the future of such pupils was obviously in doubt. More generally, many boards had provided extra classes for older pupils in the elementary school building. 'What is to become of these Higher Elementary Classes?', he asked:

> Apparently the Higher Elementary School must be entirely separated from the ordinary Elementary School ... there will be many small urban areas where a separate Higher Elementary School would be quite out of the question and where this practical difficulty has been to a large extent removed in the past by the zeal and enterprise with which the teachers have devoted themselves to their Upper Standards.[56]

As the year progressed the Board of Education's interpretation of the minute gave further reasons for disquiet. In May the London School Board decided to apply for recognition of its seventy-nine Higher Standard Schools (redesignated Higher Grade Schools in 1898) as Higher Elementary Schools. The application was turned down on the grounds that, in all but four of them, the curriculum was a commercial not a scientific one, though the Board of Education conceded that it would be ready to entertain a proposal regarding the four science schools. In October Ellery, in the *Practical Teacher*, described how in Bradford the School Board had established a new commercial school:

> One would have thought the Board of Education would have helped such an

institution by every means in its power. But no! It has decided that the school is not eligible for grants under the Minute ... Is this the way England is to be assisted in the attempt to compete with the foreigner? It seems clear there is to be as little advanced education as possible in the primary schools, all the 'plums' being reserved for the secondary schools of which one has heard so much of late.

Macnamara, as the London School Board considered a reapplication on behalf of eleven of its Higher Grade Schools, complained that the minute had been a confidence trick. He himself had earlier in the year induced the Board to thank the Government cordially for it, but, he added, he did not intend to be deceived again. He recalled an old Quaker saying: 'If thy friend deceive thee once, shame on thy friend. If thy friend deceive thee twice, shame on thee!' [57]

As the year ended teachers' suspicion of the minute had become general. The *Practical Teacher* commented:

The Board of Education has put an entirely different construction upon this Minute from what was generally accepted. It was supposed to be a Minute in favour of the higher education of the children of elementary schools, to be used for the purpose of lengthening the school life of promising children, and giving free education to those who could not afford secondary school fees, and who could not be supplied with scholarships at secondary schools. The Board of Education, however, has laid it down that these schools must be of the nature of schools of science, notwithstanding the unsuitability of such a course in many localities, both as a means of general education and as providing for the wants of localities.

Finally on 29 December the *Schoolmaster* admitted:

One is almost driven to say that the Minute must have been deliberately intended to deceive the House of Commons and the country ... As to the desire of the Government to save the Higher Grade Schools, and to put them on to a legal footing, that too, is difficult to believe. The clear purpose of the Minute is to restrict their scope. [58]

The Cockerton Judgement, delivered on 20 December in the Court of Queen's Bench, made clear that wherever future initiatives to develop public secondary and continuation schools were to come from, it was not to be from the school boards. According to Mr Justice Wills the London School Board had exceeded its powers. To argue, he concluded, that it was free:

... to teach at the expense of the ratepayers to adults and to children indiscriminately the higher mathematics, advanced chemistry (both theoretical and practical), political economy, art of a kind wholly beyond anything that can be taught to children, French, German, history, I know not what, appears to me to be the *ne plus ultra* of extravagance. If the Acts of which the primary object was elementary education and the whole object was education for children are to be transformed into Acts for the higher education – education of a kind usual rather in a college or a university than in a school – of grown-up men and women, it must be done by Act of Parliament.

A week before the decision was known, Gorst was triumphant. His plans for paramount Local Education Authorities could at last be revived. He wrote to the Duke of Devonshire on 13 December:

> I have never regarded it as possible that school boards could be a permanent institution ... they are a modern anomaly in Local Government, which would never have been created if county councils had existed in 1870 ... There should be one Administration for all local purposes.[59]

Evidence of public sympathy and support at a time of uncertainty would have been welcomed by London School Board members of all persuasions. The Board election at the end of November conspicuously failed to deliver it. The Progressives retained their majority, reduced from thirteen to five, but it was the size of the poll which was to prove disastrous for the Board's reputation. In 1897, 1,098,733 people had voted; in 1900 the figure was reduced to 821,719, the smallest poll on record. Macnamara's empty Committee Rooms provided evidence of the apathy that prevailed. For the second time he received more votes than any other candidate in London, but his 23,059 was less than half the 1894 figure. The most deplorable feature of the whole situation, the *Schoolmaster* concluded, 'is the Londoner's expressed and supercilious unconcern of the School Board and all its works'.[60]

As the new year began it was clear that major changes in the national system of education now needed to take place. The Government, confirmed in office through the khaki election of October, could, it seemed, no longer avoid the legislative task that it had avoided since 1896. Against the national trend, Macnamara had been returned for North Camberwell, adding the responsibilities of a member of Parliament to his duties on the NUT Executive, on the *Schoolmaster* and on the London School Board. Previously a spectator and critic of national policy-making in publicly provided education, he was now, as the local administration issue reached its climax, able to participate in the framing of the most important Education Act since 1870.

7

Parliament, 1900–1902

As the 1900 general election approached, Ellery made a confident forecast, in the *Practical Teacher*, that both the NUT members of Parliament would be re-elected.[1] This time Gray was faced by J. H. Bethell, the former Mayor of West Ham; Yoxall by Sir Lepel Griffin, the ex-arbiter of the destinies of Afghanistan. To speculate on Macnamara's chances at North Camberwell was riskier. In 1885 and 1892 a Liberal member had been returned, in 1886 and 1895 a Conservative. Major Dalbiac, the retiring member, had been popular. Had he remained, Ellery thought, he would have been a hard nut to crack. But the new Conservative candidate was J. R. Diggle, Macnamara's old antagonist at the London School Board. Locally, Liberal and Conservative were considered to be evenly matched. The Conservative *South London Observer and Camberwell and Peckham Times* declared that

> the issue of the dramatic 'fight' in North Camberwell between ... Diggle and Macnamara – old time foes in public work, and avowed dissentients in all matters of opinion – must devoutly be left to the will of the gods – and the chances of the ballot box. North Camberwell has a chequered reputation for fickleness, and must be left to decide for itself to which of two brilliant candidates for its favour, the glove will be thrown.[2]

Macnamara was well satisfied to compete against Diggle. Afterwards he told his colleagues on the NUT Executive that he had been fortunate in many things but perhaps most fortunate in his opponent.[3]

In September 1900, when the election campaign opened, the second Boer War had already run for nearly a year. British pride, shaken in December 1899 when a rapid series of defeats had occurred in 'Black Week', had by now been restored through the successful campaign of Lord Roberts, who had secured the surrender of Pretoria in June. The Liberals, in their election manifesto, challenged the Government vigorously on their conduct of the war:

> now this Government are scheming that, in the achievements of a great General and a brave army, their own negligence, miscalculation and manifold misdoing shall be forgiven and forgotten. They are seeking to prostitute the sacrifices of a whole people to the interest of one political party ... Not Lord Roberts and his soldiers, but Lord Salisbury and his colleagues ask for the Nation's confidence ... What have they done to deserve it?[4]

In his election addresses, Macnamara sought to connect the patriotic ardour of the moment with his own specific aims. 'The British Empire can only be truly and permanently great', he asserted, 'through the adequate equipment of the children who are its heritors, and the comfort and happiness of its citizens, and especially those of the homeland – the heart of the Empire. I desire to see a generous development of our educational facilities so that the citizen of to-morrow may be appropriately equipped for his stewardship.'[5] At an election meeting at the Credon Road Board School on 25 September he put his own patriotism beyond doubt. He had heard it said that the return of the Liberal government would undo the work of Lord Roberts in the Transvaal. A statement of that kind in respect of himself, a man born and brought up in the ranks of the regiment that defended Kimberley, a man whose father went through the Crimea with the same regiment, was, he declared, simply ludicrous (Loud cheers).[6]

On 3 October the *Observer and Times* instructed the local electorate in its duty. Both Dr Macnamara and Captain Hemphill (the Liberal candidate for Peckham) had achieved deserved popularity and respect, it admitted:

> but on the single and imminent question of Imperial policy in the coming settlement of South Africa; in just intention to reap the reward of England, Ireland, Scotland and the Colonies' tribute of blood and treasure to the call of Empire, to-morrow the men of Peckham and North Camberwell must vote straight, and decisively, for the Unionist candidates.[7]

The Unionist government's majority at the dissolution had been 128; the election gave it 131. Gray and Yoxall were duly re-elected. Macnamara secured a majority of 1,335.[8] His friends and supporters were delighted. 'No man enjoyed himself more in this election than did Macnamara', recalled Waddington, who had spent nearly a fortnight in the constituency: '"Fighting Mac" the Old Kent Road designated him ... that Macnamara knocked Diggle in the Old Kent Road is now historical.'[9] Diggle's candidature, Jackman told the Executive, was a direct challenge to the teachers of London. 'We teachers took up the challenge', he added, 'and the result is a splendid evidence of our power and organisation.'[10] Macnamara, in a letter to the *Schoolmaster*, related how messages of the most touching character had come from his old scholars, his old fellow students at college, his colleagues in the NUT all over the country, and political friends and opponents everywhere. He concluded:

> For all these I, my wife and my little children (whose determination to see their father an MP was almost pathetic) are deeply grateful ... My election confers upon me a very great honour. It lays upon me also a responsibility the magnitude of which almost frightens me. All I can endeavour to do is to make my recognition of the responsibility the measure of my appreciation of the honour.[11]

Parliament assembled on 3 December. With the Boer War its priority, there appeared to be no programme of home affairs to which the new Government was pledged. 'There is one certainty, however', the *Schoolmaster* commented:

> ... the power inside the House of Commons that induced the large amount of attention which the last Parliament gave to scholars' and teachers' affairs will again be at work – stronger than before indeed, for Messrs Gray and Yoxall will be reinforced by the presence of Dr Macnamara ... The remarkable success which attended the political candidatures of three members of the National Union of Teachers has struck the imagination of others than teachers alone; the public have not failed to note that neither the flowing tide of party, nor any local peculiarities, can overcome the candidature of men capable of working skilfully and speaking eloquently – picked men belonging to the profession of teaching, and champions of the cause of the child.[12]

As the century ended the Parliamentary Reform Acts of 1832, 1867 and 1884 had not yet finally overturned the patrician rule that had flourished since the Glorious Revolution of 1688. Hence the arrival of three teachers who were both products of, and former practitioners in, the schools of the poor could not escape notice. Payment by Results, R. B. Haldane was to observe in 1903, had made elementary school teachers too business-like and narrow. There were brilliant exceptions, he went on, and there were no better examples than the three representatives of that body of teachers in the House.[13] But Gray, Yoxall and Macnamara had no need for compliments of this kind. As the old century ended, the disappointing performance of officers in the Boer War brought the independent boarding schools, the by now traditional educational institutions attended by the vast majority of leading public figures, under the scrutiny of a Parliamentary Committee. Macnamara discussed its conclusions in the *Schoolmaster*: 'The Secondary Schools are supposed to train those who are to be the brain of the army; they have failed ... will they, their teachers and their pupils, cease to vaunt themselves and contemn the schools which prepared the rank and file who saved the credit of the army?'[14]

Criticism of the independent boarding schools spilled over into the universities. H. G. Wells took his opportunity in the *Fortnightly Review* to attack the ordinary Oxford, Cambridge or London BA. This, too, was quoted in the *Schoolmaster*:

> He has a useless smattering of Greek, he cannot read Latin with any comfort, much less write or speak that tongue; he knows a few unedifying facts round and about the classical literatures, he cannot speak or read French with any comfort; he has an imperfect knowledge of the English language, insufficient to write it clearly, and none of German, he has a queer, old-fashioned, quite useless knowledge of certain rudimentary sections of mathematics, and an odd little bite out of history ... if he knows anything of evolutionary science and heredity it is probably matter picked up in a casual way from the magazines, and art is a sealed book to him.[15]

Meanwhile Gray, Yoxall and Macnamara were establishing their Parliamentary reputations. Practised as public speakers, with a cause that few would publicly dismiss, they found that the House of Commons, like the NUT, yielded to those who mastered its customs. Gray, known as the Union's Demosthenes, its silver-tongued orator, was fluent in both French and German. He enriched his observations on educational matters with information acquired abroad. Defeated in the general election of 1906 he was to become a leading member of the London County Council, returning to the House of Commons as member for Accrington between 1918 and 1922. In his retirement he became a successful broadcaster for the BBC from Savoy Hill.[16] Yoxall, the Union's Ulysses – the man many-sided – had first known Westminster as a student at the Training College in 1877–78. As General Secretary of the NUT he was already serving as a member of the Bryce Commission when his Parliamentary career began. He divided his time between the union offices at 71 Russell Square, the Board of Education in Whitehall and the House of Commons. He was an ambitious and prolific writer, publishing a series of novels including *The Rommany Stone* (1902), *Smalilou* (1904) and *Chateau Royal* (1908), all of which won critical admiration.[17] Macnamara, the Mercury of the Union, attracted attention through the detail and energy of his speeches. Delivered in a voice that sounded like a pistol shot, with a vestigial North American accent, they were judged to be practical, full of point, crammed with illustration and often remarkable for their humour.[18] Pressure of work caused him to take up golf. His health was soon restored and he also reaped the social rewards of the pursuit, encountering other Parliamentarians, including Balfour and Lloyd George, on the links.[19]

The three main educational issues of the 1890s, the poverty of the voluntary elementary schools, the insufficiency of post-elementary education and the establishment of an effective local system of educational administration linking elementary, secondary and post-secondary institutions, all remained to be dealt with. During the week ending 22 December a letter above Macnamara's signature appeared in a number of daily newspapers including the *Standard* and the *Morning Post*. He alluded ironically to the surge of patriotism that had secured the Unionist government in power. 'I imagine', he observed, 'that it is now generally conceded that the intellectual equipment of our people represents a first-class factor in National Defence and Advancement ... is it not an anachronism, having regard to the vital importance of efficient education, to expect to maintain education in any degree from voluntary contributions?' What was needed, for board and voluntary schools alike, was that the great bulk of running costs should be met by the Exchequer. The remainder would be provided by a universalised and equitable rate. As a condition of receipt of this money, voluntary schools, now receiving 10s 6d per child less than board schools, should admit to their management representatives of Municipal Authorities, town and county. By this means a series of regulations for voluntary schools, regarding buildings, equipment and staffing, could be introduced.

There remained, of course, the religious question. Personally, Macnamara observed, he was sorry to refer to it. Three years of squabbling at the London School Board would last him his lifetime. Yet it was this question which was obstructing the measures that were needed. The towns raised no difficulty: parents could choose the school for their children. In the country the Church of England was dominant. His suggestion, which he admitted was a crude one, was that for four mornings a week undenominational religious instruction should be given, leaving the fifth for teaching the Church catechism.

Macnamara's letter, reproduced in the *Schoolmaster*, provoked comment. The *School Board Chronicle* suspected that his proposal carried with it the end of the school boards: 'Did the electors of North Camberwell understand this to be the line of action he would take … if they sent him to Westminster? They might perhaps have known, if occasion had been taken to recall the NUT Conference of 1896.' The *Morning Leader* was encouraging:

> Dr Macnamara has gone to the House of Commons full of a brave determination to worry his fellow members into an attitude of attention. We wish him every success. Our educational defences are neglected. We spent in 1897 40⅓ millions sterling on armaments to Germany's 32¾, 10½ on education to Germany's 12¼, while the United States spent 16½ millions on war and thirty-seven on their schools. Our whole system is in a hopeless muddle.[20]

The Cockerton Judgement had both highlighted the muddle and made it more difficult to deal with. Higher Grade and evening school provision had been declared illegal,[21] but, for the moment at least, both continued in operation. The Judgement could be taken to appeal and, in fact, Mr Justice Wills had commented that the importance of the subject demanded that the question should be decided by the House of Lords. But to practising teachers the Judgement was a disaster: 'The Court of Queen's Bench has given a decision that more than cripples much of the valuable work done by the school boards', the *Board Teacher* complained: 'The vital question for educationists on school boards and off is to decide speedily whether they will agitate for an improvement of the law, or wait perhaps a couple of years for a verdict … that will in all probability confirm the present decision.'[22] The *Journal of Education* agreed:

> Now is the opportunity for the Duke of Devonshire. Things cannot remain as they are. Fresh legislation is inevitable. Either the school boards must have further powers given them or they must be absorbed in the one Educational Authority, whose advent seems at last near … The Duke must go back to the principles of Sir John Gorst's Bill of 1896.'[23]

The London School Board debated the matter on 31 January. A motion, that steps be taken to obtain the decision of the highest tribunal, was eventually passed by twenty-nine votes to fourteen. Macnamara argued that they were bound to appeal, to maintain the status quo. Lyulph Stanley agreed. Whether the appeal went for or against them, Parliament would legislate on the subject with greater knowledge. He spoke with feeling of the loss of the opportunity to educate adults, men, women, Polish Jews, the Italians of Saffron Hill, policemen who wanted to improve their position and the workmen at Woolwich Arsenal. On appeal it might be that this part of the judgement might be set aside. W. W. Thompson took the opposite view. The proper arena for the settlement of this question was Parliament. It was not right to spend ratepayers' money to secure a reversal of the decision.[24]

From speculation about the future, the Board turned to the difficulties of the present. At the next meeting, in an attempt to rectify the financial arrangements upon which the evening schools were still being run, Sharp moved that the abolition of fees be rescinded. The Moderate Party, he argued, had always taken the position that abolition was a gigantic mistake. He was intensely anxious that the ratepayers of London should not be saddled with an expense which had been declared, on an authority high enough for him (Laughter) to be illegal. The Rev. J. Scott Lidgett moved the Previous Question. It was obvious, he said, that until the result of the appeal was known, the status quo must be rigidly maintained. They must neither extend nor limit their work until they were sure exactly what the law was. Macnamara supported him. He could not see, he said, what the Cockerton Judgement had to do with the remission of fees. The total number of evening students was 79,897. Of these 67,203 were young people continuing their elementary education. These had not figured in the Judgement. Put to the vote the Previous Question won a majority of two, putting an end to Sharp's initiative.[25]

Whilst the Queen's Bench decision on the Cockerton case had been long awaited, the appeal was dealt with rapidly. On 1 April 1901 the Master of the Rolls, in the Court of Appeal, confirmed the verdict. On 25 April the London School Board voted to abandon further appeal.[26] Unmistakably its initiatives and those of all other boards in regard to post-elementary education had to come to an end.

For post-elementary education after Cockerton, Macnamara wrote in the *New Liberal Review*, two things were needed immediately:

(1) For the Higher-Grade Day Schools: a liberalising of the Higher Elementary Minute, especially in the matter of the 15-year age limit, and the character of the curriculum designed for these schools: and an assurance that Rate-expenditures on these schools shall be legalised.

(2) For adults in the Night Schools: legislation that shall make it competent for the Elementary School authorities to proceed with the work they are now doing.

He concluded with a discussion of the form that the Local Authority for education should take. What was needed was a paramount Authority in each area exercising general supervision over all grades of school. The great school boards could not be abolished, as the Government had discovered in 1896. Instead, the Technical Education committees of the town and county councils represented the principle that would ultimately prevail in local government, the principle of electing one strong council for all municipal purposes. In the meantime, he asked:

> Why not try Local Option? Why not leave the constitution of the Local Education Board to the locality itself? If it desires an *ad hoc* authority, well and good. If it desires to merge all its local Boards of Education in a grand Education Committee of the Municipal Council, why not? I commend the suggestion to those who will draft the Government Bill.[27]

In Parliament immediate prospects for educational reform remained discouraging. In the previous *New Liberal Review*, Macnamara had contrasted the activity one evening in the House of Lords, when Army Reform was being discussed and the steps of the throne were thronged with Cabinet Ministers, and the same period in the Commons, when Sir John Gorst sat alone upon the Treasury bench:

> A dozen very serious and very deadly monomaniacs sat on one side, listening to another dozen, equally serious and more deadly monomaniacs, on the other. Above, a handful of strangers. They yawn decorously behind bowler hats. There is profanity in their very silence. For they are cursing the fate that brought them into the Gallery on an Education night! The situation is an illumination. John Bull, all agog about Army Reform; supremely unconcerned about Educational Reform.

The supreme power of the British Empire had been built up by brute force, great endurance and fine intrepidity. What was needed now was an Imperial Policy in Education:

> From the commercial and mercantile point of view we are blundering along with the cross-bow and arquebuse ... Our people must learn that their reward will be according to their capacity. If their attainments qualify them to become the captains of commerce and the master-craftsmen of industry, those posts are open to them the world over. If, on the other hand, their lack of training fits them to be merely the hewers of wood and the drawers of water to the more highly-equipped peoples of the world, it is into these subordinate positions which a fierce and relentless competition will drop them.[28]

In the King's Speech of 14 February (Queen Victoria had died on 22 January), reference to the possibility of the introduction of a bill had been, as the *Schoolmaster* put it, cryptic and tantalising. 'The most likely thing that emerges', its Parliamentary reporter commented, 'is that the Bill will be made as comprehensive as the Government dare. The fate of the Bill of 1896 is ever before their eyes.'[29]

By the time the Easter recess approached, no proposals for a bill had yet been made. Nor had the Code for 1901–02 been laid on the table. Macnamara was concerned that the time set aside to discuss it would be reduced, if not lost, when it was now particularly important that authorities supplying post-elementary education should know where they stood.[30] On 2 April, the day after the rejection of the appeal against the Cockerton Judgement was made known, he enquired whether, pending the passing into law of any proposals that the Government might be prepared to make, the *status quo ante* might be maintained. But Balfour was not prepared to answer.[31] Yoxall raised the question again later the same day, during the Adjournment Debate. The need for legislation, he said, was doubly acute now that the verdict of the Master of the Rolls was known. Gorst, however, replied that he had not been able to grasp the whole effect of the Judgement as rapidly as the hon. member, and that he was glad to have the Easter recess in which to digest it.[32]

Even after the Easter recess there seemed at first no sign of any Education Bill and hardly any hope if its introduction before Whitsun. This seemed to end all prospects for the time being. 'Rumours go about the Lobby', the *Schoolmaster* reported:

> ... and whispers that there has been a hitch over the Bill; that the Duke of Devonshire and Mr Chamberlain have been checkmated over it by Lord Salisbury and Mr Balfour; that the Bill would have proposed the absorption of school boards and the unification of Local Authority; that Mr Balfour's argument was the furious action which Irish members would take against a bill that might do away with the cumulative vote and remove the opportunity for Roman Catholics to get on school boards; and that when the disastrous results that will accrue to school boards, board schools, and evening education, unless they are pulled out of the Cockerton hobble by a bill this session, were pointed out, some members of the Cabinet said in effect, 'So much the better'.[33]

Whilst the Government itself was inactive, a measure of agreement was emerging amongst Unionist and Liberal educationists in the Commons. For this Evelyn Cecil, now MP for Aston Manor and Parliamentary Private Secretary to Lord Salisbury, was responsible. He had read Macnamara's letter in the press in December 1900 and, though formerly a keen supporter of his cousin Cranborne's Church Party, perceived the significance of the compromise on the religious question that it contained. On 26 March 1901, when he convened his Parliamentary Education Committee, he included not only his Unionist colleagues Sir Richard Jebb (the Chairman), Sir William Anson, Edward Bond, Ernest Flower, Sir Michael Foster, Ernest Gray, Henry Hobhouse, J. F. Hope, J. T. Middlemore, W. R. W. Peel and A. F. Warr, but also Sir John Brunner, G. Harwood, C. P. Trevelyan, Macnamara and Yoxall, all of whom he described as Radicals. Convinced of the need for a single comprehensive bill, they were all prepared to discuss the education question in a non-partisan manner. Though he had resigned from the London School Board with a view to attacking its expansionist policies, Cecil, now that its end appeared to be in sight, was prepared to make concessions about popular representation on voluntary school management boards. Macnamara, certain as he had been in 1896 that voluntary schools needed rates, was now keen to investigate as well any move which might advance the cause of secondary education for the masses.[34]

By the beginning of May the Committee had completed its consultations. Agreement had been reached on a number of related issues. In its final statement it put the case for a single Local Authority for elementary, secondary and technical education, adding the recommendation that an Authority should serve a county, a county borough or any area approved by the Board of Education (which covered the issue that had caused the failure of the 1896 Bill). Where voluntary schools applied for connection with the new Authority, they were to be accepted provided that the Authority appointed not more than one third of the managers. Only the *ad hoc* question was left unsettled. In the third of his reports which were forwarded from his office in Downing Street to the Duke of Devonshire, Cecil commented that the Radical members were still anxious about it, adding that the question must give rise to discussion in the House.[35]

But the indefatigable Gorst was still possessed by the ambition to secure comprehensive education legislation. Referring, not without pride, to his efforts in 1896, he introduced a new Bill on 7 May, designed, he told the House, 'to establish in every part of England and Wales a Local Education Authority which is intended to supervise education of every kind, and which may ultimately have the control and supervision of all schools, whether elementary, secondary, or technical'.[36] On the means of achieving this aim, however, Gorst was vague. Like Macnamara he took up the idea of the local option. The object of the Government and of the Board of Education, he said, was elasticity. They were not prepared to impose a scheme prepared at Whitehall on every part of the country. They wished the county councils themselves to take the initiative and propose schemes suitable to their particular circumstances.[37] Neither the educational press nor the House was impressed. The *Practical Teacher* concluded that Gorst's career was over: 'The man who was the yeasty brain of the "Fourth Party" from 1880 to 1885 might have expected a better FINIS than to go down to memory as the most injurious or impotent Vice-President of the Committee of Council since Robert Lowe'.[38]

Macnamara treated what was indeed to be Gorst's last attempt to move major education legislation through the Commons as an empty performance. He complimented the Government on their Board of Education Act of 1899, which had provided a central, unified executive, but seized on the main defect of the proposals that, for the foreseeable future, the new Local Authorities were to deal only with technical and secondary education. 'It is fatal to keep primary schools outside this scheme of control', he told the House: '... the educational ladder should be a reality ... You cannot get that unless schools of all grades are under one Local Authority.' Turning to the Cockerton Judgement he recalled that it had forbidden the expenditure of school board rates upon Higher Grade education in the day schools and upon the instruction of adults in the night schools. What Gorst was proposing was that the boards, specifically elected for educational purposes, would now go to the municipal councils to ask permission to become their agents in this educational provision. No money was to be made available, he said:

> I suppose the cupboard is now bare for educational purposes. I am sorry for this, because our position depends upon sound finance, and sound finance depends upon good trade, and good trade depends on the equipment of the people, and unless we spend money on that we cannot expect them to be properly equipped.

Intimating that in his opinion the Bill might fail, he added that what was essential was a little measure to legalise boards' activities for the coming year. Yoxall took up this point. There was now insufficient time for the school boards to seek permission from the county councils to spend money on educational plans for which they had already incurred financial responsibilities. What was needed was a short suspensory bill permitting their now illegal activities to continue.[39]

In mid-May, Macnamara moved the education resolution at the National Liberal Federation at Bradford. He spoke of the confusion and disorganisation in national education and of the pressure of competition from better educated foreign nations. The whole work of public education, elementary, secondary and technical should, he said, be entrusted in each district or area to one responsible and popularly elected local body. Since the Education Bill entirely failed to satisfy this essential condition, measures should be taken to enable school boards to carry on their pre-Cockerton work. 'Dr Macnamara is not yet so well known outside London as within, and this was, I believe, his first important appearance at a Federation meeting', the *Daily News* reported:

> He took the meeting by storm ... He has a good presence, a clear-cut face, a fine voice and a simple, lucid way of making his points, which he probably learnt as a teacher; but he is, above all, a hard hitter. He never spares a word, and the dishonest, un-English trickery of the Government in hamstringing the higher schools of the people deserved every word he spoke. He never turns his back on the necessity of a constructive educational policy in the future – the need of a central authority controlling all education from top to bottom; but he denounces the present tinkering with an expert's scorn.[40]

A month later the Education Bill was *in extremis*. 'The ebbing tide of Parliamentary time is like to leave it stranded', 'Ferula', Parliamentary correspondent of the *Practical Teacher*, concluded. 'Common decency causes it to be kept on the programme a little longer. But up in the Press Gallery we regard it as almost moribund.'[41] Balfour had reached the same conclusion. In the presence of the Duke of Devonshire and Gorst, he received a deputation of nearly 100 Unionist MPs on the evening of 27 June at the House of Commons and told them that the ten-clause Bill would be withdrawn.[42] 'With a sigh of relief many true educationists received the joyful news that Sir John Gorst's wonderful and marvellous Bill was dropped', the *Board Teacher* reported:

> But that is only the artfulness of the wreckers. They mean at least to cripple the school boards. They have discovered that their lumbering Bill, which resembled chaos (being without form or void) is altogether too clumsy a thing to force through the House this Session. So they just drop the innocuous portions and preserve the vicious part – the clause that contains the deadly virus.'[43]

Clauses 8 and 9 were removed from the expiring Bill and re-presented as Education Bill No. 2. What it amounted to was a measure, intended to pass rapidly through the legislative process, which would enable the county authorities to empower school boards to mount certain classes on a temporary basis. Gorst's interventions slowed down its progress so that, intermittently, it occupied the Commons till 30 July. At the beginning of the Second Reading he quoted the terms of the Cockerton Judgement, making clear as he did so that he regarded it as decisive and, as far as he was concerned, unalterable. There were, he said, forty-eight Higher Grade Schools with a science top educating between 900 and 1,000 boys and girls. These were the only day schools affected by the Judgment; the greater part of their pupils could easily be provided for in the secondary schools by means of scholarships. They would receive, in his view, as good, or rather a better education in that way than in the Higher Grade Schools. Turning to evening schools, he told the House that he had recently made careful inquiry into the case of London, because in London were to be found nearly half of the registered students. His tone became unmistakably sarcastic. Attendance, he said, was quite phenomenal. In the Battersea Park Road School, book-keeping was taught for seventy-two hours over the year; on the roll there were thirty-eight students, but only ten attended even for twelve hours. Commercial geography was taught for sixty-four hours; there were 152 on the roll, yet only twenty-nine students attended as much as twelve hours. The same kind of discrepancy appeared in every school. 'I should, however, be very sorry if the House carried away the idea that I am saying that all these schools are of an ineffective character', he went on:

> There are some very good schools carried on by the London School Board. They have schools for the metropolitan police, in which constables are prepared for the examinations which they have to undergo for promotion and in these

schools you may hear a school board teacher instructing police officers how they are to answer questions on the life and duties of a policeman. Then there are schools in which telegraph boys are prepared for their examinations. There are other schools in which instruction is given to teachers of board schools themselves. In these schools the parts are interchanged – the pupils of one night become the teachers of another night; they teach each other.

Most of the other schools, he continued, were purely recreative. Dancing was taught under the name of physical exercise: 'The education which you are spreading amongst the people is cheap, shoddy education instead of the better and higher education which we wish to promote'. The authorities which, in his view, should be supplying advanced and adult work were the county authorities.[44] Pressed on this point by James Bryce (Aberdeen South) and Sir John Brunner (Cheshire, Northwich), he made a scathing attack on the school boards which created great merriment on the government benches.[45] 'Are we to keep up in this House the farce that school boards are elected for educational purposes?', he asked:

> Everybody knows that educational purposes are the very last ideas in the minds of the members of school boards [Opposition cries of 'Oh']. I have heard that they are elected, some on religious grounds, some on party grounds, but I have never heard of anyone being elected on educational grounds.

Even the idea that ratepayers cared at all for board elections was a pretence:

> Why, everybody knows that in London, whereas about eighty per cent vote at Parliamentary elections and between fifty and sixty per cent vote in county council elections, there is, I think, only some twenty to twenty-five per cent who can be got to go to the poll in school board elections.[46]

This was a highly damaging point. Nevertheless, Macnamara, speaking next, gave Gorst, in the opinion of the *Practical Teacher*, a tremendous trouncing.[47] The Government, he said, had not found time to pass its Education Bill. It had withdrawn it but in doing so had taken out its essential principle and placed it in a one-clause temporary expedient. He asked:

> What, Sir, is the vital principle the Government desire to see vindicated by this temporary measure? It is to subordinate the school boards to the county councils in the matter of education, so that they may be at once truncated as to their operations, and ultimately entirely superseded ... I venture to say with all respect that it is not quite fair or honest ... to work the essential principle of the municipalisation of the local control of education into a measure of this sort, which is, as the rt hon Gentleman says, a temporary expedient to meet an unforeseen emergency.

Further, Gorst was already anticipating Commons' approval of the Bill. The previous week he had sent a circular informing county boroughs of their new supervisory rôle over school boards, with hints of restrictions to come. On 3 July he had issued a minute on evening continuation schools, seeking to remove the boards' apprehension about rate expenditure at the cost of their future independence. 'I do not see why we should accept the Cockerton Judgement', Macnamara declared. 'We are here to alter that Judgement.' Already, over evening schools the Government was exceeding its requirements: 'First of all the law says "You shall not use the rates for pupils over 16½ years". Then the rt hon Gentleman goes further and says, "You shall not have grants either for pupils over fifteen".' Gorst's minute was not yet law. He hoped the House of Commons would agree to modify it. He concluded:

> I want to say in the most deliberate manner possible that I marvel at the colossal contradiction between the rt hon Gentleman's precepts and his practices. And I marvel more at rt hon and hon Gentlemen opposite who take so paltry a view of the importance of national education from the point of view of national defence and national advancement ... what is the good of adding new areas to the British Empire, painting fresh areas red, if the only purpose you serve is to find new markets and new spheres of influence for more highly equipped foreigners? [48]

Gray, from the government benches, attacked the Board of Education for its lack of foresight. Everybody knew, months before the Cockerton Judgement, what the decision would be, he said, but the Board had, apparently, sat quietly by. Now, at a time when the Educational Authorities up and down the country were seeking to make provision for the winter months, seeking not merely to give young men and women, boys and girls, some education, but also to keep them out of the streets, trying to keep them out of mischief, and to prevent them becoming occupants first of the police dock, and then of the prison cell, the Board of Education remained idle. As for the Government itself, he expressed astonishment at the way in which Education Bill No. 1 had been introduced. It was a Bill of a magnitude which, he said, was sufficient to constitute the work of a material portion of a session. What could possibly have been their object in introducing such a Bill and spending the time they did over it if they had no intention to go on with it? It was apparently but another evidence of the continual uncertainty and timidity which marked the Government in dealing with the question of popular education. He continued with an attack on Gorst:

> The rt hon Gentleman's speech yesterday was a long string of jokes at the expense of those who have as honestly laboured as the rt hon Gentleman himself to advance the cause of education. I am very sorry indeed to find anyone at the head of the educational system of this country descending to methods of that kind. I noted it with the keenest regret ... [49]

The Parliamentary session was by now almost over. As it ended, 'Ferula', in the *Practical Teacher*, summed up:

Let me record that the little Bill was passed and the Evening School Minute discussed; that upon the first Mr Yoxall nearly defeated the Government, reducing their majority to seventeen; and that upon the second Dr Macnamara's speech repeated upon Sir John Gorst the disintegrating effect of Mr Gray's unforgotten onslaught.

The 1900 Parliament, he concluded, had struggled under the almost paralysing burden of the Boer War:

... one watches for earnestness and hopefulness about education in vain ... Mr Balfour is sick of it himself ... For him the letters of the word 'Education' spell humiliation. I daresay that he has already registered a vow that, for the rest of this Parliament, Education shall be given a very wide berth.[50]

But the Parliamentary Education Committee's reports had reassured Balfour. Now he could be confident that legislation need not end in disaster in the House of Commons. What he needed in the summer of 1901 was expert assistance and confident advice. Gorst, who could supply neither, had brought forward the man who could offer both. Robert Morant had returned to England in 1894 after his appointment as a tutor at the Siamese court had ended in acrimony and he had failed to secure a position in the British Legation at Bangkok. After a few months' social work, based at Toynbee Hall in the East End of London, he was appointed in 1895 to Acland's Office of Special Inquiries and Reports, contributing a significant article on Switzerland to its 1898 edition. Perceiving that the future of the Office under a Unionist government was a limited one, he had become Gorst's personal assistant in June 1899, then, in November, his personal secretary, even though he had already expressed the greatest contempt for the Vice-President of the Committee of Council and his 'rotten ideas'. Now he was able to observe the ineffectiveness of the Government's education policy at close quarters. Then on Palm Sunday, 31 March 1901, at a luncheon given by his friend Edward Talbot, Bishop of Rochester, Morant encountered Balfour. It was the day before what was to be the final judgement on the Cockerton issue. By the end of June he was taking his place as one of the First Lord of the Treasury's closest advisers, beginning a personal campaign to persuade Balfour that a comprehensive Education Bill was both desirable and practicable, a campaign that, apart from its legislative result, was to yield for Morant the post of Permanent Secretary to the Board of Education.[51]

Hence, at the end of August, when Balfour wrote to the Duke of Devonshire informing him that he had seen Lord Salisbury the previous evening at Hatfield, and had been told that the Prime Minister was very anxious to have some sort of bill actually in print by the time the Cabinet met on 5 November, he added that he had promised rough drafts of two bills, one dealing with secondary education alone, the other with both secondary and primary. A third, settling secondary education alone but including clauses reforming school board voting and safeguarding religious teaching in primary schools, might, he concluded, be worthwhile. All three would serve as a basis for discussion. He ended, referring to Morant's now central rôle. 'It does not occur to me at the moment that there is anything further into which it would be desirable to get enquiries going during the holidays. If any ideas occur to me perhaps you will allow me to communicate direct with Morant during your absence.'[52] Cecil, observing the new development, wrote to Morant on 19 September: 'Personally I have no hesitation in strongly advocating a large constructive measure dealing with both Elementary and Secondary Education in preference to a more partial Bill, and I believe I may truly say the same view would be taken by all Parliamentary friends'.[53]

But the Duke of Devonshire was still not convinced. Opening the new Central Technical School in Liverpool on 26 October, he offered the view that majorities in Parliament would not avail. What the Government needed was the conviction that public opinion was in favour of it. Whilst he fully recognised the responsibility of the Government in making new proposals, 'whether they launched a small craft or a large one, it was they who were responsible for the lines upon which it was built ... but no vessel, however built, or however navigated, could sail its course unless it had a breeze behind it. Without a breeze the vessel would probably drift on the rocks and reefs and shoals'. He wanted the people to provide them with that breeze.[54] The *Board Teacher* commented ironically:

> In these humane days, when societies for the protection of the lower animals abound, why does not someone start a society for the protection of Dukes? A concrete illustration of its need is furnished by the cruelties inflicted on the Duke of Devonshire. Not only is the poor fellow called names and made to do something – he is called Minister of Education, and made to draw a salary – but he is actually expected to find a policy. His wails at Liverpool were pitiful ...[55]

Yoxall, in the *New Liberal Review*, showed some sympathy for the Duke,[56] but Macnamara, in a letter to *The Times*, had already reacted critically:

> It is painfully clear from the Duke of Devonshire's speech ... that the Government means to let the education question drift unless sharply pulled up by the force of public opinion. Of course there will be another Education Bill, and of course that Bill will deal with the creation of Local Authorities for education. But unless I am very much mistaken neither will be worth the Parliamentary time that will be spent on them ...

What was needed, if a national system of secondary education was to be organised, was rationalisation of administrative authorities:

> Separate authorities for each grade of education mean waste of time and money, mean local friction, mean unnecessary overlapping, and mean an insuperable barrier to that linkage of schools without which we cannot get such educational

harmony and co-ordination as will make it possible for the child of poor parents to move uninterruptedly from grade to grade ... linking together is absolutely out of the question unless the authority that controls the elementary school is also the authority that controls the Secondary School.

The function of the Local Authority was far more important than the question of whether it was constituted *ad hoc* or was set up as a committee of the municipal council. This was a question which the locality might very well be left to determine for itself. He concluded with a call for government initiative which would be heard, decade by decade, throughout the twentieth century:

Sound finance depends upon prosperity in commerce. Prosperity in commerce depends mainly upon the intellectual equipment of the people. To-day the nations of the world are feverishly active sharpening their intellects for the struggle into which they will immediately be plunged. Great Britain's attitude of indifference and unconcern is admirably typified in the Duke of Devonshire, the Lord President of the Board of Education, the Chairman of the Defence Committee of the Cabinet. Placidly he folds his hands in sleep ... [57]

Stung by Macnamara's reference to the local option, the *School Board Chronicle* responded instantly:

Few men in public life are more swift or more able than Dr Macnamara to seize an opportunity. His letter to *The Times* ... put the case for administrative unity in our educational system very forcibly. All the more pity that the value of the letter should have suffered detraction from the unfortunate tag concerning local option. In that, it shares misfortune with nearly every other speech upon the subject which the brilliant member for North Camberwell has made during the Recess ... At the risk of being tedious we feel bound, while welcoming the Doctor's decisive and vigorous espousal of the principle and practice of the one Authority ... to repeat again the warning, first given when this idea was sprung upon the Teachers' Conference at Yarmouth. It is just one of those plausible suggestions which might well have proceeded from the arch-enemy himself of local representative control. It plays directly into the hand of those who have fought the school board system inch by inch ... [58]

In December Macnamara attended a public meeting promoted by the Sheffield and District Teachers' Association for the discussion of the education question on a neutral platform. Seconding a resolution calling upon the Government to 'institute such legislation as shall place our public Day and Evening Continuation Schools on a thoroughly efficient basis', he presented a detailed and critical account of the Unionist Government's record on the education question. Having failed to reform central and local administration at the same time by the 1896 Bill, they had approached the issues by sectional action. The 1899 Act had unified the central executive authorities, and done it, he said, very well indeed. It had, however, appointed a Consultative Committee of experts including Sir William Hart

Dyke, Mr Acland, Dr Sophie Bryant, Sir Michael Foster, Sir Richard Jebb, Mrs Sidgwick and others, to advise the Board. This had been at work for twelve months but nothing appeared to have emerged from its deliberations, nor had the Government consulted it. Central administration was nevertheless a simple matter by comparison with local, where the 14,000 non-representative Boards of Voluntary Managers worked side by side with the 2,544 school boards set up under the terms of the 1870 Act and 120 County and Borough Technical Education Committees. These, he said, had to be reduced to something like unity. The resolution proposed in general terms to put the whole of this hotch-potch into the melting-pot, and to bring out something entirely new and different. Educational institutions also needed to be coordinated so that an educational ladder could be provided. It was the hereditary pride of Scotland that every opportunity was offered to every lad of parts to work his way to the highest positions in the country. The first Scotsman he ever knew, a professor at a University, was the son of an old woman who sold milk from door to door. England could never furnish such opportunities as long as there were differing Local Authorities.

What provided the greatest obstacle to the Local Authority question, Macnamara concluded, was the acute interest of the Church. Questions of popular control, of Boards of Management, the upkeep of buildings and the appointment and dismissal of teachers needed to be settled. What he could foresee was that the Government, failing agreement, would shrink from legislation at all. Then country, children and teachers would find themselves unable to escape from what, educationally speaking, was a terrible muddle.[59]

The new year was to be Coronation year, the first since 1838. Parliament was to open a month earlier. 'What chances for the schools in this pre-dated session?', asked 'Ferula':

> Is the 'big Bill' that educationists look for, to make his obeisance to Big Ben? ... What ... is being devised by the Great, Wise and Eminent who consent to manage our national affairs for us? Is it a cockboat or a cruiser that lies on the stocks in Whitehall? ... A 'comprehensive Bill' last year would have been one dealing with Secondary, technical and board schools; but the meaning of the word 'comprehensive' has been extended since then to cover the voluntary schools as well.[60]

For the first time, perhaps, in the history of England, he mused, the thinking part of the nation would be hanging on the lips of the Lord Chancellor to discover whether the King's speech contained a promise of an Education Bill. In the event it was the King himself who read the speech, but 'Ferula' was not disappointed. A promise was duly made: 'My Lords and Gentlemen, proposals for the co-ordination and improvement of primary and Secondary education will be laid before you'.[61]

8

The Education Act, 1902

A promise had been made, but, at the beginning of March 1902, it was by no means certain that it would be kept. 'Ferula' conceded that, with the Boer War still in progress, the toga was likely to yield to the sword. No bill had been tabled and Mr Balfour only 'hoped' to table it before Whitsuntide. Nevertheless, the King's promise and Balfour's hope had been sufficient to prevent the moving of an amendment to the Address:

> Otherwise an amendment, affirming the principle of One Local Authority for all kinds of schools in each local government area of suitable size, must have polled three-fourths of the House of Commons. It is wonderful how popular that idea has become. Six years ago it could count but one set of supporters. But that was a numerous and persistent set: it was the NUT.[1]

Macnamara made clear what the NUT intended in an article in the March *New Liberal Review*. He began by claiming that if the Bill lived up to the promise of the Speech from the Throne, it would have no more ardent supporter than himself. The duplication of educational effort by boards and county authorities was wasteful, overlapped and failed to provide coordination. What the Government would attempt to do was to insist that the municipal councils would be the Education Authorities in each locality. But what would happen to the school boards?, he asked. He answered his own question by referring to the local option, already introduced to the House of Commons by Gorst the previous May; this, for the time being at least, would damp down any strong feelings about the municipal take-over. As for the future of the voluntary schools:

> Bring the voluntary schools under the general public authority for their area; accept their offer to admit representatives of the public to each local board of managers; levy your rate universally by counties and county boroughs; dispense the proceeds together with your government grants – which should form the greater proportion of your 'maintenance' expenditure – subject to public audit and under regulations local and central; and the thing ought to work smoothly enough.[2]

Balfour introduced the Education Bill in the House of Commons on 24 March. He began with a review of the operation of Forster's Act. There had been no organisation for voluntary schools, no sufficient provision for teacher education and no connection between elementary and secondary schools. A single authority, namely the county council or county borough, would deal with these problems:

> Our reform, if it is to be adequate, must in the first place establish One Authority for education – technical, secondary, primary – possessed of powers which may enable it to provide for the adequate training of teachers and for the welding higher technical and higher Secondary Education on to the University system. In the second place I conclude that this One Authority for education, being, as it is, responsible for a heavy cost to the ratepayers, should be the rating authority of the district. In the third place, I lay down that the voluntary schools must be placed in a position in which they can worthily play their necessary and inevitable part in the scheme of national education.[3]

This position was to be within the system of local education administration, drawing, as the board schools had done since the implementation of the 1870 Act, on the rates.

What was being proposed exceeded by far the administrative innovations incorporated in Gorst's Bill of 1896. Then the county authorities were to supervise. Now they were to appoint education committees and raise rates. Then voluntary schools were to be financially assisted. Now they were to be put on the same financial basis as the board schools. It was a bold, far-reaching scheme. Having sketched it, Balfour added, apparently contradictorily, that the new authorities could exercise an option not to administer elementary education.

This was a move of value both to the Government and to their known supporters on the opposition benches. Not to insist that the elementary schools were included in the new administrative structure provided the opportunity for members representing constituencies incorporating successful school boards to speak up in defence of them, as many had done in 1896; also for members disinclined to put voluntary schools on the rates to claim the exclusion which the permissive clause put on offer. If the elementary school proposals excited hostility, Balfour and his colleagues on one side of the House, Yoxall and Macnamara on the other, could withdraw in good order leaving behind a less ambitious bill which would at least settle the future of technical and secondary education.

> Members of the Parliamentary Education Group spoke early on the significance of the new administration structure. In the absence of Cecil, who was chairing a Select Committee on steamship subsidies, Sir Richard Jebb, from the government benches, almost invited board supporters to challenge the proposals, referring to the permissive clause as the great blot on the Bill.[4] The control of secondary education, he stated, could not be efficiently managed by a Local Authority which was not responsible for elementary education as well. Macnamara, speaking next, repeated the challenge. The permissive feature was futile to the last degree; as for the voluntary schools, he stated baldly, he had no

objection to providing them with financial assistance from the rates. He was very glad that the issue had been raised:

I am a voluntary school manager, and I am grateful to the voluntary contributor for what he has done. He has done work which the State was either unwilling or too selfish to do. I submit that the time has come when we should no longer maintain in operation the educational work of working class children out of money collected at jumble sales and ping-pong tournaments. It is a proper thing to raise the question of the form of local financial aid, and to lay down definitely that in all schools, board and voluntary, money must be forthcoming from public sources, central and local, under proper conditions ... [5]

Before the Second Reading, the NUT Conference took place at Bristol. Confident that the teachers employed by the large boards now accepted that the county authority system was necessary to remedy the deficiencies experienced by their disadvantaged colleagues, the Executive offered for debate a resolution approving the principle of 'wide areas' for administrative purposes. Macnamara, carefully prefacing his speech with the comment that he parted company with many of the features of the Bill, said that he was bound to recognise in it one great principle for which he had worked for many years on that platform and throughout the country – the creation in each locality, of suitable area, of 'One Authority' capable of controlling all grades of education: 'From the point of view of the nation, whose brain was its best asset, the essential thing in the first place to fight for was the linking together of all schools under one and the same authority' (Hear, hear).[6]

'One Authority' unquestionably involved, sooner or later, the abolition of the boards, but no hostile reaction from the board teacher representatives manifested itself, either to the new authorities or to the new status of voluntary schools under them.[7] So far encouraged, Macnamara's Parliamentary colleagues, responding, at the annual dinner, to the toast 'the House of Commons', emphasised the breadth of agreement that existed. Yoxall asserted that in the House there was a large body of opinion, not limited to one side or the other, or to one creed or the other, in favour of sinking old controversies and acute differences and of compromising and arranging in order to produce for the country at last a satisfactory system of National Education (Cheers). Gray hoped that amendments to the Bill might be amendments purely and simply of an educational character, and that no amendment would find a place on the paper which would arouse needlessly the great religious controversy (Cheers). He trusted that the House would bend its best energies to advance and improve the Bill (Hear, hear). With the Conference over, the Union's Parliamentary representatives were able to return to their duties confident that, as far as the Union was concerned, they could press ahead in support of the main principles of the Government's measure.[8]

Still apprehensive about a campaign from his own party in favour of the boards, Macnamara published an article in the *Pall Mall Gazette* on 21 April on the origins of the *ad hoc* system. Contrary to popular belief, the Gladstone Cabinet had not introduced the idea. What had been intended in 1870 was that the Local Education Authority was to consist of a number of persons selected by the town council in urban areas and by members of the vestry in the country. When Sir Charles Dilke had moved the replacement of this scheme by direct election by ratepayers, he had been enthusiastically opposed by Liberal educationists, among them Mundella, the future Vice-President of the Committee of Council, who maintained his attitude even when his party altered its Bill in favour of the *ad hoc* principle. 'It was thus that we came by the school boards', Macnamara concluded, 'and in the light of the present position of the Liberal Party towards the municipalisation idea, and of the Conservative Party towards the *ad hoc* idea, the whole story strikes me as being exceedingly interesting.'[9]

Macnamara returned to Westminster for a busy session. He had been appointed to the Joint Select Committee on the Housing of the Working Classes which began its meetings on 2 May and the Second Reading of the Education Bill began the following Monday. 'Ferula' again reflected, when it was over, on the influence that the NUT now exerted:

> The power of an organised body of units, individually weak, but compact and purposeful, and represented ably at St Stephen's, was never before so clearly seen ... the Bill is the direct result of the policy of the elementary school teachers. The One Authority idea is almost solely due to them ... It was the representatives of the National Union of Teachers who pressed the idea on the Royal Commission on Secondary Education; it was Mr Yoxall who appended to the report ... a memorandum urging that nothing should be done legislatively which would hinder the ultimate realisation of the One Authority principle ... In 1896 the government Bill on Education contained the germ of the same idea. In 1901 a Bill which went against it was killed from the moment of its First Reading. In 1902 a Bill triumphantly passes its Second Reading, which affirms that principle at all costs ... For good or ill, the school boards are to end; for good or ill, a municipal committee is to come into play in the elementary education world; for good or ill, the voluntary schools are to come under local public control.[10]

The implementation of the 'One Authority' was, Sir William Hart Dyke (the former Vice-President of the Committee of Council) declared on the second day of the debate, a matter of national importance:

> The question we really have to ask ourselves is, how long is this grievous stigma to rest upon our shoulders, this confession of impotence before the whole world, this confession of inability to proceed on safe and secure lines towards the end we all have in view ... I have long since come to the conclusion that the real kernel of the solution of our difficulty rests in the appointment of a single Local Authority to supply and supervise education.[11]

From the Opposition benches Macnamara supported this view: 'I shall venture to assume that the Government will strike out the permissive clause', he began, 'and I shall venture to assume that they will make it compulsory on Local Authorities to take over elementary education; because if that is not intended by the Government, then the scheme is absolutely grotesque, and scarcely worth discussing'. The creation of 'One Authority' capable of controlling all grades of education was the first great principle of the Bill.[12] He went on to remind the House of the chaotic state of the local administration of education in the country. To complement groups of voluntary school managers, 2,544 school boards had been created under the 1870 Act; Technical Instruction Committees had been added since 1889. The result was a hotch-potch of educational machinery. He observed:

> So long as each grade school is under a separate authority you cannot have the schools linked together; you cannot have that community of aim and purpose, that dovetailing of the curricula of various schools, which will enable a child of capacity but of humble parentage to move from one school to another without hindrance. From the point of view of the working classes that is the most serious problem of this time.[13]

As for the Government's proposals about the local administration of education, Macnamara again sought to uncover support for school boards by suggesting that, within the new municipal councils, the boards might still find a place. Gray, from the other side of the House, duly marshalled the arguments in favour of all-purpose county and county borough councils and (no doubt by prior arrangement with Macnamara) pointed out the inconsistency of the argument. He said:

> It struck me that the member for North Camberwell was somewhat illogical when he suggested that in some of the large boroughs the school board should be allowed to remain ... in the earlier part of his speech my hon friend declared that this Bill would be grotesque if the option were allowed to remain, and yet he is claiming that there should be option to continue two authorities.[14]

Macnamara moved on to what he called the second great principle embodied in the Act, the frank abrogation of the endeavour to maintain education by voluntary contributions. From amongst his Liberal colleagues, accustomed to the idea that it was the Conservative Party which was indulgent to the voluntary schools, he expressed, as he had done during the First Reading, his gratification that the question had been raised. 'I consider it a dangerous anachronism to endeavour to maintain education by charitable contributions', he said. 'Education is too vital a matter to leave its maintenance to the fluctuating hand of charity ... I have always thought that education should be entirely maintained from public sources.' He showed, as he had done many times before outside the House, how disadvantaged voluntary schools were by their inability to call on the rates.

Their staffs were less qualified; the teacher-pupil ratio which in board schools was 1:76, was 1:103; and while the pay per child of a board school teacher was 45s 2d, for a voluntary school teacher it was 35s 2d. He continued:

> I will give no more facts. I could give hundreds that would speak eloquently as to the lamentable condition of these voluntary schools. I am concerned about this, because these schools educate much the same class as board school children. They are the citizens of to-morrow, and I cannot shake off responsibility for these unhappy children and teachers, because of the anachronism of endeavouring to obtain education by voluntary contributions.

He wondered, however, what the reaction of ratepayers was going to be:

> To put the whole of the voluntary school children on the rates, at the very moderate estimate of 15s a child, will increase the aggregate rate maintenance from £5,000,000 to £7,250,000. Is the educational zeal of the country sufficiently high that the mass of the people will gleefully and cheerfully contemplate such an increase in the rate maintenance as that? ... I am very doubtful indeed whether the ratepayers will pay, not alone in the agricultural districts, but in the much more enlightened urban districts ... I am a school board member; I have fought three school board contests; and I tell the Vice-President that the ratepayers make it pretty hot for us if we raise the rate by even a halfpenny.

The answer, he thought, was that the great bulk of the cost of maintenance should fall on the national Exchequer rather than the rates. He recalled that Balfour, in his election campaign of 1895, had made rather a prominent feature of the fact that he believed in the nationalisation of the charge for education and that since then he had, on more than one occasion, expressed the same view.[15] In reality, as Macnamara must have suspected, the likelihood of the Government adding to the burdens of the Exchequer in the last months of the war was small, but to first-time, unwilling ratepayers the prospect of eventual complete Treasury funding would be an attractive one.

Macnamara's advocacy of financial support for voluntary schools was supported by Yoxall, who added a warning that it might come about at the expense of ex-board schools:

> I may liken the voluntary schools to a gap, and the board schools to a hillock. What is more simple and obvious than to pare off the top of the hillock in order to fill up the gap? ... To my mind, it should be compulsory to take over the elementary schools in an area, and there should be an Exchequer grant for the purpose of meeting the additional expense of administering the area.[16]

'Ferula' found their efforts convincing: 'Educationalism would have them partly bless the Bill, party would have them wholly ban it'. While they gave the impression of being torn by conflicting loyalties, Gray, amongst the Unionists, appeared to be on velvet.[17] But he, too, had an NUT task to fulfil: to emphasise the advantages that would accrue when the Bill was passed. 'A new idea has grown up in the popular mind', he observed on 7 May:

> The education of a poor man's child is not now regarded as a charity to the child, or a gift to the family. The idea now is that the education of the poor is the preservation of the State and we *MUST* teach these children in order that the nation may have the full benefit of their mental activity. It is national insurance. It is the development of the best wealth the country has.[18]

Curious eyes turned towards Macnamara and Yoxall when the division came. Doing their party duty they voted against the Bill, but it was carried by a majority of 237. 'The fact is', 'Ferula' concluded, echoing Gray, 'that on both sides of the House of Commons opinion has softened, and neither theological nor party views now suffice to check a general longing for efficient national education.'[19]

When the House reassembled after Whitsun and education was again being discussed, little of this longing appeared to remain. But now the issue was Gorst and the Estimates, not Balfour and the Bill; the Government's past neglect, not its future plans, were under attack from the NUT members. Macnamara questioned the Vice-President on evening schools. Gorst maintained that the Minute of 3 July 1901, introduced so hastily towards the end of the previous session, was a necessary reform and that since then attendance had very much increased:

> Dr Macnamara: Where?
> Sir John Gorst: All over the country.
> Dr Macnamara: Including London?
> Sir John Gorst: Yes, everywhere, including London. I should be very much surprised if the first year of this new system does not show that a very great deal more good, honest, solid educational work has been done than in previous years ... [20]

Macnamara thought otherwise. The evening continuation branch of the education question had been disastrously dealt with by the present administration, he said. Through the efforts of school board and technical instruction committees, attendance had been rising. Since Gorst's minute, school boards had been unable to spend rates on any evening instruction and neither rate nor Exchequer grant could be spent on any person over fifteen years old. Gorst had said that nobody would be excluded; Balfour had supported him, but Macnamara had sent forms to the clerks of 400 school boards to find out how they were getting on under the Cockerton Act and the minute. Classes had ceased, numbers had fallen: on a rough estimate they would fall by 100,000. In London, about which Gorst had answered so confidently, enrolments had fallen by 8,000; the special grant for physical exercise had been discontinued because the Vice-President suspected that a ball had taken place at the end of a course on dancing;

even swimming had been restricted so that a grant was only available for teaching on land, not in the water. In Scotland, the Education Department permitted Local Authorities to make their own decisions on evening school provision; in England, it was the deliberate policy of the Vice-President to put down night schools. He moved the reduction of the vote by £100.[21]

Yoxall followed Macnamara; Gray spoke a little later, and Gorst was criticised on Higher Grade Schools, pupil-teacher centres, the inspectorate, the relations between elementary and secondary education and plans for a teachers' register. Gray hit on the most important question of all. He wanted, he said, to invite the representative of the Government to clear the Government from the charge which had been made against them for the last two or three years, that they had instigated the Cockerton crisis; fortunately for Gorst he moved on to further items and the moment was lost.[22] 'Ferula' was impressed:

> As I listened I could not help thinking that it was a pity that no such members, skilled by experience, and apt and smart in speech, should exist to deal with the administration of other great departments of State. If the military members were as fluent, informed and industrious – or the rural members, or the postal or financial members – as are the educational members, ministers for these departments would not have so good a time, and things might be managed better.[23]

The Committee stage (which had provided the occasion for the destruction of Gorst's Bill in 1896) lasted from 2 June to 8 August (when Parliament adjourned), then from 16 October to 21 November. In 1896 suspicion that the Government intended to press ahead stimulated opposition. In 1902 fears began to be expressed that the Government would run out of time. Progress, haphazard and piecemeal, was interrupted by a vote of thanks to the army on the successful conclusion of the war (the peace treaty was signed on 31 May) and by the Finance Bill.[24] At one time it seemed uncertain whether the Education Bill would be taken up again before the Coronation, planned for the last week in June. In the event the fell news of the King's illness, on 24 June, proved to be a boon. Some unexpected extra days for Commons business became available.[25]

Clause 1 occupied the sessions of 2, 3, 4 and 17 June. In its final form it established that the county councils and county boroughs would take over the local administration of education, with autonomy for the purposes of elementary education being given to municipal boroughs with populations of over 10,000 and urban districts with populations of over 20,000. During the debate on 2 June, with Gray as his foil, Macnamara made what he called an appeal to the First Lord of the Treasury on behalf of the great county boroughs, in which he again made out the case for the survival of the large school boards from whose teachers the NUT drew a vital proportion of its members. He referred to a letter Balfour had written to a correspondent when the 1896 Bill was being discussed, in which he stated that the aim of the Bill was not to destroy the school board system in the great county boroughs, and gone on to say that though 'One Authority' was desirable, it was not intended to force a change on reluctant Local Authorities. Now, Macnamara argued, the great school boards did not want the happy despatch, and did not desire to see their duties extinguished. Moreover, a number of the city councils, among them Cardiff, Gloucester and Manchester, had made it clear that they did not want education added to their present responsibilities. If the city council and the school board desired continuance of the *ad hoc* body for the purpose of education, the Government should agree to give them that option. He developed his argument the next day, suggesting that the work of the Leeds, Birmingham, Manchester and Liverpool School Boards, each of which had 100,000 elementary school children to deal with and 2,000 or 3,000 school teachers in their service, when added together with the responsibility for voluntary schools, to the cities' existing responsibilities, might well cause a breakdown. This educational leap in the dark was the most portentous this country had ever taken without consulting the localities concerned.[26]

A last opportunity for members in favour of school boards, who in 1896 had been so vehement in their opposition to a reduction in the power of the boards, had been offered. It was not taken up: 'Ferula' commented:

> Very extraordinary seems to me the apathy or the incompetency of the great school boards or the Association of School Boards to take a hand in the game. Certainly I have never known a drastic change in educational policy so soon commend itself to educationists as this has done. And had the question not been complicated by theological differences and the war between churches that consensus of opinion would have declared itself long ago.[27]

Macnamara's objections, on behalf of the school boards, to Clause 1 had been hollow. Its further provisions he found genuinely annoying. When he asked that the county boroughs should have their school boards, he was told, he said the next day, that he was a two-authority man, and that they must have only 'One Authority'. Here, on the other hand, was a proposal to grant separate authority to small local units, boroughs with populations of over 10,000 and Urban Districts of over 20,000. The Bill, he said, would take out of the rural areas the 'fat' rating districts for the purposes of elementary education, and leave the residue of the counties with a large number of children and with a large number of small schools. In Kent, Canterbury and sixteen other areas would be removed from the county administration; in Staffordshire they took out fourteen; in Middlesex and the West Riding of Yorkshire thirteen.[28]

Balfour did not give way. He thought it was true, up to a certain point, he said, that the full benefits of the 'One Authority' principle were diminished by the scheme of the Bill but to nothing like the extent represented by the hon. Gentleman. In his view the system which the Government had suggested would work perfectly. As for the argument that the Bill would deprive the counties of the most valuable areas within their limits, his own investigations had persuaded him that no general law could be laid down. In these circumstances, the most practical course was to adopt the scheme of the Bill.[29] But when the House took up the Bill again on 17 June, Macnamara repeated his arguments in more detail. Balfour responded:

> The hon member for North Camberwell pours contempt on any man who is influenced in the structure of an Education Bill by any but purely educational considerations. He approaches the Bill purely in the spirit of a theoriser and professor. In my opinion the man who approaches a question like this in that spirit may produce an excellent paper scheme, but it will be a scheme destined to remain a paper scheme for all time ... though I do not contend that this clause as it stands ... reaches that theoretical finish and perfection which all of us in our speculative moods might desire, neither do I admit that it destroys the principle of the Bill, or that it will seriously impair that co-ordination of primary and Secondary Education which it is one of our great objects to attain.[30]

The debate was ended by the closure. The *School Board Chronicle* commented:

> ... The weight of evidence, argument, experience, authority marshalled against Clause I in particular as against the Bill in general, constituted a case to which no reply could be offered within the limits of the professed purpose of the measure. Yet the closure and the clause were voted practically without defence, and for reasons which no one has dared to offer in debate ... If this clause becomes law, a vital force has been taken out of our national education.[31]

Clause 2, passed on 30 June, consolidated the powers of the new authorities. It was now laid down that they should 'consider the needs and take such steps as seem to them desirable, after consultation with the Board of Education, to supply or aid the supply of education other than elementary'; they were to act in the coordination of all forms of education, including teacher training, and for that purpose they 'shall apply all or so much as they deem necessary of the residue under Section I of the Local Taxation (Customs and Excise) Act 1890' (the 'whisky money'). This was much to Macnamara's satisfaction. If they were really anxious to promote non-elementary education, he said, they must lay upon the Local Authorities an obligation to start the organisation and development of that branch of work. If the Bill were left in a permissive form he had no hope of action in the English counties: the member for Thanet (the Rt Hon. James Lowther) had spoken of too much money being 'wasted on so-called education', while the member for Sleaford, the Rt Hon. Henry Chaplin, had declared that they wanted to keep the agricultural labourers on the land, and the more they were educated the more they were inclined to desire to settle in towns.[32]

Clause 3 was designed to enable the non-county boroughs and urban districts to spend rate-raised sums on aiding non-elementary education, to carry on, as Macnamara put it, the good work they had been doing subject to effective county control. His objection to the clause rested not on the need to support these schools but on what now emerged as the implementation of Clause 1. The original scheme of the Bill, which he had cordially supported in principle, was, he said, that of a single authority for all grades of education. He now found that, in addition to the 330 authorities set up under the interpretation of the First Lord of the Treasury, there were to be 853 authorities for Secondary Education, making 1,183 educational authorities in all. In Devon, apart from the administrative county, there would be the three county boroughs of Devonport, Exeter and Plymouth; three non-county boroughs, Barnstaple, Tiverton and Torquay, which would be autonomous for elementary education and also for non-elementary education up to a limit of one penny in the pound; and thirty-four urban districts which would not be autonomous for elementary education but would be so for non-elementary education up to one penny in the pound. 'There was a spectacle!', Macnamara exclaimed: 'Forty-one different authorities in one county!' He commended the proposals to Mr W. S. Gilbert.[33]

'When the House got into the consideration of Clause 4', 'Ferula' related, 'at once the fat was in the fire, for this clause deals with the eternal religious difficulty.'[34] The new Local Authorities were to be responsible for post-elementary institutions in which the issue of religious education would arise. Balfour accepted, from his own side of the House, an amendment from Sir William Anson applying the Cowper-Temple clause to any school, college or hostel provided by any council under the Higher Education clauses of the Bill.[35] Macnamara took the opportunity, when the establishment of Local Authority teacher training colleges was being discussed, to air the NUT's long-standing grievance (already raised by Lloyd George during the Second Reading) about the operation of the existing colleges with which, he said, the First Lord of the Treasury did not deal at all. At the end of their apprenticeship 12,000 young pupil-teachers submitted themselves to the King's Scholarship Examination. If they secured a place in the first or second class they were normally entitled to go to a college largely maintained by the State and to proceed to the full teacher's certificate by means of State assistance. In fact, however, not only were there only half the required number of places available for those who secured first or second classes, but of the existing 3,000 places 2,000 were in the hands of denominationalists and of the remaining 1,000 not more than 200 were open at any moment to Nonconformists. He hoped that if the future authorities had the money and the right to provide undenominational training colleges, the insufficiency of places might be met but, he added, considering the large amount the denominational colleges received from public funds, they should admit other students on a conscience clause. This suggestion alarmed Lord Hugh Cecil, who expressed the fear that such an innovation would seriously alter the character of church colleges and their religious influence. Balfour, supporting his cousin, said that if they were to indulge in the most extensive system of spoliation tomorrow and deprive Roman Catholics, members of the Church of England, and Wesleyans of their training colleges, the matter would remain much as it was at present. The only way in which the difficulty could be met was not by redistributing the accommodation in the existing colleges, but by increasing the number of these colleges. This the final version of Clause 4 was intended to facilitate, though as Samuel Evans (Mid-Glamorgan) observed, it would be the work of years to add to training colleges out of the limited amount of money that was to be given to the county councils.[36]

It was Henry Hobhouse, a member of the Parliamentary Education Committee, who, when Clause 5 was discussed on 9 July, moved an amendment to omit the power of option and thus oblige every Local Education Authority established by the Act to assume responsibility for elementary education.[37] Macnamara reminded the House that the existing categories of public elementary schools were financed differently. The finances of both came, to a certain extent, from the central Exchequer, but the Exchequer grants were not sufficient to conduct the schools properly. The board schools received an essential supplement from local public funds, the voluntary schools from charitable contributions which in the previous year had produced a disability of about 20s per voluntary school. If this option remained, he asked, would Local Authorities rate themselves for elementary education? He himself did not think for a moment that they would do so. There were eight county boroughs, 500 other urban districts and practically half the entire agricultural area of the country, which had never yet had a rate for elementary education. Did the Committee think that in those districts they would now tumble one over the other, if left to themselves, to impose a rate for education? The interests of education demanded that Parliament should not shilly-shally any longer with the matter. They should apply the Act all round without any option, with a proviso that they must improve, perfect, stiffen and strengthen the public control over these authorities.[38]

Politically this was the most controversial section of the Bill, encapsulating two vital issues, the future of the boards and the future of the voluntary schools over which the two main parties had clashed repeatedly over the past ten years. Now Macnamara, from the Liberal benches, was putting the case both for placing the control of elementary education under the new Local Authorities and for supporting the voluntary schools from the rates. J. W. Philipps, the Liberal member for Pembrokeshire, put a contrary view. The hon. member for North Camberwell, he said, appeared to be anxious to make education more expensive and to increase the rates. It was a great pity that his constituency was not affected. London did not come within the scope of the Bill, yet here was a London member making an eloquent speech to make everybody else outside London pay for something which they did not want.[39]

Gray seized on this contribution. The member for Pembrokeshire, he said, had taunted the member for North Camberwell by stating that he did not represent a constituency affected by the Bill. He himself represented a division of West Ham which he believed paid a higher sum than any other throughout the whole country for the support of elementary schools. In that heavily rated district, he believed, the preponderance of opinion was in favour of making the Bill compulsory.[40] Educational progress made it essential that, in every administrative county and county borough, 'One Authority' should obtain charge of all the elementary and Secondary Schools. He concluded with a plea well calculated to win support on his own side of the House for voluntary school children. He was not prepared, he said, to leave it in the power of any administrative county, governed by a feeling of parsimony, to condemn these children to the life of educational poverty which they had too long endured. No sane man of whatsoever creed or party could believe that it was possible to work this Bill with the option clause in it.[41]

As the debate on this clause drew to a close, Sir Henry Campbell-Bannerman, the Opposition leader, pointed out the importance of the vote that the House was about to cast. It involved, he said, nothing less than consenting to, or protesting against, the slaughter of the school boards. But he was unable to provide any argument for keeping them.[42] The needs of the voluntary schools as presented by Macnamara and Gray had made the case for a take-over by larger units inescapable, and into these new units the boards, as well as the voluntary agencies, would have to fit. When the vote was taken, Campbell-Bannerman was supported by Bryce and Lloyd George, with McKenna, Runciman and Trevelyan, three future Presidents of the Board of Education. But amongst those voting with the Government were Macnamara, Yoxall, Haldane and Asquith.[43]

The cancellation of Clause 5 secured the future of the Bill. Its opponents recognised this. J. Hirst Hollowell, the fiery Rochdale Nonconformist, in a letter to the Press, gave an early intimation of the resistance which would trouble the first few years of its operation. Referring to the fate of the school boards and the placing of what he called every Sectarian, Ritualist and Romanist Day School on the rates, he concluded: '... the decision was arrived at with the help of the Irish members, and with the help also of Dr Macnamara, who has crowned his past services to Sectarian Schools by helping the Government to destroy the school boards'.[44]

The consolidation of the Bill coincided with the resignation of Lord Salisbury which, though not unexpected, came at last with a startling suddenness. The following day (12 July) Balfour became Prime Minister. 'Perhaps the most striking of the changes due to Lord Salisbury's retirement and Mr Balfour's accession to the Premiership have taken place at the

Board of Education', the *Schoolmaster* reported a month later. The Duke of Devonshire's departure was not regretted:

> His Lordship probably made a very painstaking effort to master the labyrinthine technicalities attaching to the Education Office, but it cannot be said that he succeeded very well.. Indeed he flaunted with some ostentation his entire lack of acquaintance with the details of his work. How it is possible to make this policy conform with the receipt of a large official salary we have never yet been able to understand. In any other walk of life the servant who revelled in an ignorance of his duties would be promptly dismissed. But, apparently, the rule doesn't apply to Cabinet Ministers – in this country at any rate.

The disappearance of Gorst, the last Vice-President of the Committee of Council, was judged to be another matter:

> With all his faults – surely no man was so full of promise and so barren of performance – Sir John did a number of good things. He religiously carried forward the Acland-Hart Dyke policy in favour of Inspection as against Examination. He fought hard for the emancipation of the factory half-timer and the juvenile coal-miner; and he passed an admirable little Attendance Act the fruits of which are already apparent. We take leave of him, when all comes to all, more in sorrow than in anger.[45]

The new education ministers were odd choices. The President of the Board of Education was to be the Marquis of Londonderry, who, having been Chairman of the London School Board between 1895 and 1897, could now expect to preside from Whitehall over its dissolution. The new Parliamentary Secretary, Sir William Anson, one of the MPs for Oxford University, apparently wished to crown a career as Warden of All Souls by presiding over the national education system. 'Probably Sir William Anson has never crossed the threshold of an elementary school', the *Schoolmaster* commented: '... Still, we hail Sir William as the first of the Parliamentary Secretaries with a good deal of satisfaction. He is a quiet, precise, good-natured, rather liberal-minded little man with a large amount of that very uncommon sense – common sense.'[46]

The Government could now move on to settle the future of the public elementary schools or, as Anson strove to label them, the council schools. Only two more clauses were passed before the summer recess. The new Clause 5, laying down the means by which the various pieces of legislation framed between 1870 and 1900 could be recast to place the powers in the hands of the new Local Authorities, proposed, in its original form, that all secular education in public elementary schools, whether provided by them or not, should be under their control.[47] Macnamara intervened on what he called a point of ambiguity. What was needed, he said, was to establish a distinction between publicly maintained schools, where the authority would have both control over secular instruction and the power to give unsectarian religious education, and the former voluntary schools over which its powers would be confined purely to secular instruction.[48] In its final form the clause allowed for this point, but in removing one ambiguity it established another, for, as the West Riding case of 1906 was to show, it had not been made clear how the teachers of religious education were to be paid.

Clause 6, concerned with the management of schools, took much longer. It was first discussed on 16 July; twelve days later Balfour intimated to the House that during the first four evenings of the week the evening session should not be interrupted by the twelve o'clock rule and it was finally voted through at 12.30 am on 8 August, enabling Parliament to be adjourned in time for the delayed coronation of King Edward VII and Queen Alexandra the next day. On 9 August the *School Board Chronicle* commented:

> It involves the first instance of departure of English local government from the constitutional principle that rate-aid and ratepayers' government must exist together ... Clause 6 being passed, it has become a question not of setting one Local Authority to destroy another, but of denying to the survivor the rights which the former had represented, and for representing which its life was forfeit. The councils are resolving to be masters in their own sphere, and if voluntary schools are forced into that sphere, in virtue of their maintenance from the rates, the councils will master them or will know the reason why not.[49]

The issue emerged over the appointment of managers. As a rule, bodies not exceeding six managers had been allowed for. In the voluntary schools the question was whether the majority four out of the six should come from the public authority or the private agency.

On 21 July, Macnamara expressed again his satisfaction that voluntary schools had been put on the rates. But there were swift and certain consequences of that course of action, he said, which the Government was endeavouring to avoid, and that was public control to the full of the public funds voted for those schools. The Government must know well that, having placed the voluntary schools on the rates, they must give the control of those schools to the ratepayers. Estimating that only one eleventh of the cost of maintenance would come from voluntary sources, it was unreasonable to give the voluntary agencies a two-thirds majority.[50] The Government, however, persisted in its intention, which gave what were now called the 'non-provided' public elementary schools a degree of independence from the new administrative bodies.

Over four months in the Commons, the Education Bill had provoked much discussion but little passion. Members on both sides of the House restrained themselves (as they had not done in 1896) from making extreme statements.[51] Lloyd George was the exception. The consensus presented him with an irresistible opportunity to re-establish his public reputation, which had suffered a decline over his attitude to the Boer War. Like the NUT members, he made the most of his specialist knowledge (of

Nonconformity, of Wales and of the law). The Nonconformist grievance made its appearance during the Second Reading associated (in the hope of gaining Irish support) with the 'sacred cause of small nationalities'.[52] Discussion of voluntary schools opened up the subject. By the August adjournment the issue of the popular control of these schools had been inflated into a quasi-constitutional question. Macnamara had spoken of public control of public funds. In Lloyd George's view there was no obligation for Nonconformist ratepayers to contribute to those funds at all if they were to be disbursed for the benefit of religious groups of which Nonconformists disapproved. Reminding the Government that, over Irish Home Rule, a number of its members had approved of the idea that Ulstermen should refuse to pay levies imposed by an Irish Parliament, he warned that the whole body of Welsh Congregationalists, on the same principle, would resist the payment of rates for voluntary schools. If the Government really meant to press the matter through, the county councils in Nonconformist districts would defy the pressure of the central government and no power in the land could coerce them.[53]

Though these promises were immediately dismissed within the House as stage thunder,[54] outside it the debate began to grow warm. On 29 July the North Leeds bye-election brought defeat for the government candidate. A majority of 2,517 was overturned and a Liberal returned with a majority of 758. The Liberal Unionist MP for Orkney and Shetland, J. C. Wason, disowned his party's association with the Government and crossed to the Opposition benches.[55]

Macnamara grew concerned that, after all, the Bill would fail. In the last week of August a letter from him appeared in the principal daily newspapers. The defeat, or the withdrawal, of the Education Bill was now a contingency which must be reckoned with, he wrote. Anyone who cared for the country's future could see the disadvantages under which voluntary schools had been working. Despite its manifold faults, the Bill sought to sweep away once and for all the dangerous anachronism of endeavouring to equip the children by voluntary contributions:

> Why cannot this urgent reform be accomplished? Partly because of sectarian rancour, but partly also because the Government has not been ready to accept frankly the concomitant to its policy of rate-aid for the Denominational schools. The concomitant is obviously full and complete public control, and no matter how carefully it may be hedged around by all sorts of expedients, it is bound to come ... In the meantime, will the Government take note of the signs of the times and concede a larger measure of public control? If not, will its Bill be beaten? And if so, what then? Will the Unionist policy be that of another small Exchequer dole for those starving 'voluntary' schools? Will the Liberal policy be that of allowing the 'voluntary' schools slowly and painfully to be squeezed out of existence by competition with the 'board' schools? And are these latter schools to continue in their now truncated and Cockertonised condition? ... These are, as it seems to me, questions which call for immediate

answer. It is not enough ... for Progressive Educationists to confine their efforts to the endeavour to kill the present Bill.[56]

From among the many responses, both editorial and individual, the *Schoolmaster* selected for reproduction one from the *Manchester Guardian*:

> The member for Camberwell ... is not a partisan on the question, otherwise his forecast of the probable course of events would scarcely have commanded so general an interest. Probably then, I am right in saying that Dr Macnamara's fears rather than his wishes are to be traced in his anticipation of a fiasco which, if it were to happen, would shatter the Unionist Party for years. Are the Unionists likely to court such a fate? The more widely accepted view is that, at any rate in the first instance, they will concentrate their energies on an effort to bring Mr Balfour to reason – in other words, to secure such an expansion of the principle of popular control in the management clauses as may render the Bill acceptable ... Mr Balfour must give way or he must make up his mind to a prolonged struggle, attended by instant risk of disaster.[57]

Balfour, however, was confident and did not give way. He announced his intentions at a mass meeting held on Tuesday 14 October as part of the conference of the National Union of Conservative Associations in Manchester. 'Now there is one preliminary question which I find often asked by those who have but slightly followed this controversy', he observed:

> They say to me, 'Why did the Unionist government ever start this unhappy dispute? Why have you, by bringing forward an Education Bill, filled the land with these insensate clamours from north to south, and from east to west? Why have you disturbed the social peace which might have lasted, had you not taken the course you thought fit, for an indefinite period?' It is a perfectly fair question. I will give it a direct and, I hope, an intelligible answer. The answer is this, that the existing educational system of this country is chaotic, is ineffectual, is utterly behind the age, makes us the laughing-stock of every advanced nation in Europe and America; puts us behind not only our American cousins, but the German and the Frenchman and the Italian, and that it was not consistent with the duty of a British government to allow that state of things longer to continue ... I tell you there are at stake issues more important than the fortunes of any political party ... There is at stake the education of your children for a generation, and if ... through a desire to avoid a little extra trouble or the fear of a few loud mouthed speeches or mendacious pamphleteers ... we hesitate to do our duty and carry through this great reform, then I say we shall receive the contempt of the parents of the children living and to be born for the next generation, and the contempt which we shall receive we shall most justly and richly earn.[58]

Thus when Parliament reassembled, there could be no doubt that the Government would persist in its endeavours. The *School Board Chronicle* concluded regretfully:

With Mr Balfour's Manchester speech died the last hope – if any hope had lingered – that, out of the reflections of the Recess, the Government might have extracted counsels of moderation. Instead of peace the Prime Minister sends a sword. His only answer to argument or protest, or appeal, is a bitter defiance, and a hard refusal to negotiate on any basis but one of absolute submission.[59]

The first issue for discussion, under the new Clause 7, was the extent of the powers proposed for the new Local Authorities over both kinds of elementary schools. The NUT members took the opportunity to press for the inclusion of safeguards against long-held teachers' grievances. Their determination to settle details was evidence of their continued support for the Bill; they found the Prime Minister receptive. The tenure issue was settled as a result of an amendment introduced on 27 October by Lloyd Morgan which was in turn replaced by a formula devised by Balfour himself. Dismissal by managers would no longer be effective (except in voluntary schools on grounds connected with the giving of religious instruction). The consent of the Local Education Authority would be required. This, Macnamara said, was a simple act of justice to a very deserving body of public servants.[60] The next day he introduced an 'extraneous tasks' amendment, seeking to render it unlawful to make it a condition of appointment that a teacher should perform, or abstain from performing, any duties outside ordinary school hours or unconnected with the ordinary work of the school. His purpose, he said, had been affected by the Prime Minister's tenure amendment. No doubt if a teacher was dismissed for refusing to perform these duties, the veto of the Local Authority would apply. But the need to deal with conditions laid down at appointment still remained. Teachers generally were ready to cooperate generously with the managers out of school in anything which affected the well-being of the children and the community, but it should not be expected of a teacher that, in order to secure a post in a public elementary school hereafter to be maintained entirely from public funds, he should undertake to perform duties extraneous to his work. He quoted from the Blue Book for 1842–43 on the training of teachers. It was then assumed that the new incumbent 'should be accustomed to the performance of those parochial duties in which the schoolmaster may lighten the burden of the clergyman. For this purpose he should learn to keep the accounts of the benefit club. He should instruct and manage the village choir, and should learn to play the organ.' A great deal of water had run under London Bridge since those days. His point was that if the teacher wished to do these things, he should do so, but he should not be compelled to do them and he should be able to give them up if he thought fit (Hear, hear).[61] The Prime Minister, the *Schoolmaster* reported, agreed in warmly sympathetic terms. He thought, however, that the Bill as it stood would do a good deal to remedy the evil.[62] Member after member then endorsed Macnamara's plea, but Gorst and then his successor, Anson, offered the alternative of dealing with the problem by means of the Code. Macnamara's supporters pressed the point even when he himself accepted Anson's undertaking: the matter was then put to the vote and lost.[63] 'The Board of Education's execution of the pledge is not likely to be any less thorough and effective than it would otherwise have been', the *Schoolmaster* concluded: 'It is with the liveliest satisfaction that we recount the story of this remarkable double victory which, we are quite sure, will be received with intense gratification in every schoolhouse in the country.'[64]

The Bill, assumed in advance to be Church-inspired, was yielding surprising advantages. The *Practical Teacher* commented:

> Generally speaking, it may be said that day by day the Bill has been made a better instrument for its real function, which is NOT the support of denominational schools ... The real function of the Bill is to bring about an enormous and undenominationalising change in the English primary school world.[65]

The powers granted under the new Clause 7 to managers of former voluntary schools over religious instruction at first appeared to consolidate the influence of the parson. But Colonel Kenyon Slaney (member for Newport, Shropshire) produced an interpretation which, whilst apparently retaining the managers' powers, added that such education should be in accordance with the provisions of the institution's trust deed.[66] The *Practical Teacher* commented:

> It represents a certain antagonism general among members of Parliament – among Unionist members as much or more than among the others – towards the fussy, pompous, interfering, unctuously professional parson, who insists on being regarded as 'THE person of the parish' ... it represents also a side-hit at Ritualism in the Established Church. 'You may say and do what you like in the pulpit and at the altar', the clause means, as an utterance of the average MP, 'but you shall not introduce your aping of Roman Catholicism into the schools.' [67]

During the Third Reading, Macnamara was to provide an example of the kind of case that the Kenyon-Slaney formula would settle. At Billesdon (Leicestershire) the vicar, who had developed High Church tendencies, began to interfere both with the schoolmaster's religious instruction lessons and with his superintendence of the Sunday School. Formerly the schoolmaster would have had to resign; now he could resist. Not only was he employed by the Local Authority; the vicar was officially one of six managers and personally unable to change the religious practices of the school at his own whim.[68]

Five more clauses dealing with the relationship between the Board of Education and the new Local Authorities were examined and amended in the first ten days of November. In Balfour's view, however, progress was too slow. On 11 November he proposed a scheme of closure by compartments whereby the Committee Stage would be brought to an end within nine days:

> I believe that I have now exhausted every conceivable plan by which the House would be enabled to do that which everybody must admit it must do – namely, to carry an important Bill in a session which has not been unduly crowded by other work.

Campbell-Bannerman, in reply, recognised the amiable and philosophic tone which the Prime Minister had employed. There was nevertheless a suggestion that the Opposition had been involved in obstruction. His party took a different view:

> we say that these numerous amendments would not have been necessary if the Bill had not been introduced in such an elementary condition that it had to be patched and mended in order that it might hold together at all ... my hon friends, who are, many of them, experts in education, who are thoroughly masters of the subject, who know it in its practical working, have been doing their best to improve your Bill and make it more workable.[69]

Macnamara, plainly one of the friends to whom Campbell-Bannerman referred, emphasised the importance of the Bill, which, he said, would settle the principle of education in the country for the next twenty or thirty years. The impatience shown by the Prime Minister was therefore a little bit unpatriotic. 'I venture to protest against the policy of rushing this Bill at this stage', he concluded: '... We should go on and do the best we can, and give all the time that may be necessary to the full and complete discussion of this Bill, so that we may make a great and effective measure of it.'[70]

Once Balfour had secured his intention (by a majority of 152), the programme he had laid down began to take effect. Nine clauses were voted through within the next two days. What made the process more objectionable was the introduction of new clauses on finance, endowments, the management of voluntary schools, and fees. It was now much more difficult for the Opposition to secure amendments, but on fees Macnamara took a stand. 'The new clause which I have now to propose', announced Anson on 20 November, 'gives to the Local Authority power to continue the charging of fees in respect of a public elementary school not provided by the Local Education Authority, and the Local Authority will have power to apportion the school fees between itself and the managers.'[71] Macnamara called it a very impudent proposal. It was an attempt by the Church of England, supported by the Government, to shake off the obligations it had undertaken at the beginning of the controversy. Every day revealed some amendment on the Paper showing that the Church desired to whittle away some part of the obligation. He did not know which he was more amazed at – the cupidity of the Church or the pusillanimity of the Government.[72] Sir James Fergusson (Manchester NE) expressed his surprise at what he called Macnamara's extravagant language. He could only attribute it, he said, to sectarian animosity. The hon. member and his friends would like to strip the voluntary schools of every possible means of support, so that they might fall helpless victims into the hands of those who wished to sweep them away.[73] But Macnamara received backing from his own side. Lloyd George congratulated him for pointing out the results of the guillotine resolution. The Bill was being changed without any opportunity being given to discuss it. He was amused to hear Sir James Fergusson denounce Macnamara as a narrow sectarian bigot. He himself had never been able to discover what his hon. friend's convictions were, though he believed he was a manager of a voluntary school in conjunction with the Archbishop of Canterbury. J. H. Whitley (Halifax) declared that Macnamara's words were not in any way too strong for this proposal. He concluded that the avarice, the grasping nature of the claims which the Church had put forward, would do that Church more harm than it had suffered in any of the controversies of the last 100 years. Walter Runciman (Dewsbury) said that Macnamara's denunciation was absolutely justified. Any sober-minded man, whether in the Church or out of it, must see that the continued cry by the Church for more money was detrimental to its best interests.[74]

With the clause approved by 207 votes to 116, Macnamara introduced an amendment to provide that fees, if continued, should be credited as a relief of the charge upon the rates of all elementary schools. The Church of England, he said, had repented of the bargain it had agreed to in Clause 8 to keep their schools in good repair. Now the Government had come forward with a proposal to raid, to commandeer, the pence of the children amongst other things, to enable the managers to meet this obligation. Again he was strenuously supported from his own side. But both Anson and Balfour denied the existence of a bargain. The amendment was voted down by 182 votes to eighty-five. Macnamara's intervention proved to be the last involving any debate at the Committee Stage. It was already 10.14 pm. Between 11.00 pm and 12.15 am the last clauses and schedules were voted through by means of the Closure.[75]

When the Report stage, also according to Balfour's timetable, began on 25 November the first item, a clause introduced by C. P. Trevelyan, proved to be an attempt to deny fees to the voluntary schools by abolishing fees altogether in public elementary schools with effect from 1 January 1904. 'Why was it', Trevelyan asked, 'that now that all these schools will be on the rates a certain section of the population who are fee-payers and ratepayers should continue to be fee-payers? There was only one possible reason why the fee-paying system should be maintained: it was because part of these fees as the Bill stood might go in lieu of subscriptions in assisting voluntary subscribers to maintain the fabric. Macnamara and Lloyd George again took up the argument: the former repeating that the Secretary to the Board of Education had undertaken that the fabric should be repaired and maintained by the owners, the latter arguing that parents who paid fees were really subscribers who should be given a voice in the management of the schools. But the Trevelyan clause was lost by 167 votes to 101.[76]

The opportunity to insert new clauses which the Report Stage provided proved irresistible to Lord Hugh Cecil, as enthusiastic in the House of Commons as Athelstan Riley had been at the London School Board to introduce Church of England religious teaching into board schools. He attempted to revive the idea of both 'outside' and 'inside' facilities involving the withdrawal of pupils for denominational as opposed to non-denominational instruction. The case against inside facilities was made by Yoxall. Where it had been tried, he said, the experiment had failed and an experienced teacher had been called in to maintain order. He added that it was impracticable to try to make children understand theological distinctions. They would leave no impression upon children's minds which was at all comparable to the effect that could be produced by the broad religious teaching which could be given by a skilled teacher. The Cecil clause was defeated by 243 votes to 59.[77]

The next day the needs of Nonconformist pupils in Church of England schools were similarly set aside. Runciman introduced an amendment intended to place schools in single school areas (which tended to be Church of England institutions) under the Local Authority, whatever the previous rights or conditions of the denominations to which they belonged. Macnamara argued that the Government should have done more for the grievance of the single school area. The issue was whether they should continue to compel people to send their children to a school the religious instruction in which would be distasteful to them. He urged that where there was one school, the six managers should consist of two representing the parents, two the public, and two the trust. This Lord Hugh Cecil regarded as no remedy at all. The inalienable right of parents, he said, was only over their own children. No parent had rights over other people's children. The amendment was voted down by 209 to 117.[78]

The question of the composition of boards of managers in voluntary schools recurred the same evening. The Government, Macnamara said, was trying to create a body of managers which would do two things at one and the same time: preserve denominational instruction and secure public control. It was an impossible task under this Bill. He himself had suggested a scheme by which the schools would be placed under full public control and the denominational buildings rented back to the religious groups for religious teaching in out-of-school hours. Despite his energetic exposition the Bill remained unaltered on this point.[79] The idea was to emerge again within a matter of months.

The principle of democratic control of public education was given emphasis by Campbell-Bannerman in his final speech on the Bill during the Third Reading, which began on 2 December. He said:

The Bill appears to endeavour to reconcile two things which are incompatible with each other, namely the national system of education and the denominational system ... The only permanent system must be the national system ... We believe that ... when Parliament has declared that education is the business of the State itself, it becomes inevitable that sooner or later State education must be in the hands not of individuals, but of representatives of the people.[80]

Macnamara, in a much longer speech surveying the entire Bill, begun the same day and completed the next, supported this view. The last word, he said, would not be spoken until every public school was under full and complete public control. Campbell-Bannerman had also been critical of the lack of provision, within the Bill, for the creation of an educational ladder from the elementary school to the University for poor but able pupils. Macnamara commented:

I do not think we can pay the present Ministry the credit of being enthusiastic on the subject of elementary education. The last of the Vice-Presidents of the Council will tell you frankly that the members of the Government are composed of an aristocratic class who do not believe in higher education for the children of the people, being perfectly convinced that there are certain functions in civilised life which are best performed by ignorant people.

But in general his tone was constructive, even congratulatory. He expressed his sincere admiration of the manner in which Balfour had acted during the proceedings. 'His exquisite courtesy and unfailing good temper', he said, 'will always remain a pleasant memory, although they must be associated with a matter on which we sincerely differ.'[81]

Macnamara had received a good deal of public attention since the Bill had been introduced in March. Now, nearly nine months later, the *Journalist and Newspaper Proprietor*, beginning a series entitled 'Journalists on the Floor', claimed that he had proved himself to be the one man in the House of Commons who knew all about the Education Bill in the whole of its ramifications and in respect to each of its possible consequences:

This is one of the reasons why some members have declared that he bores them. Charles Fox said that he made it a duty never to miss a day of the Parliamentary session without speaking at least once. Men in the Gallery ceased to number the speeches made by Dr Macnamara. There was always another to come. But the speeches were practical, full of point, crammed with illustration, and often remarkable for their humour. The great point was that they were evidently sincere, the expression of the mind of a man with whom the education of the people is a passion. They are delivered too rapidly, in a voice somewhat nasal, with abundant but rather monotonous gesture. But they impressed the House, which always listened when Dr Macnamara rose. For which reasons the close of the session leaves him in possession of a considerable Parliamentary reputation. And he is still young.[82]

December had brought no respite. Macnamara set to work at once, in partnership with Jackman, to interpret what had been achieved to *School-master* readers in a series entitled 'How to Work the Education Act', which was later to be published in shilling pamphlet form.[83] It was well received. Among the plaudits came a note from Gorst: 'I have read your book with the greatest interest and pleasure. Of course you do not expect me to agree with all your observations about the Education Act, but in your advice to Local Authorities I can heartily concur.'[84]

Also, one school board, the greatest of all, remained to be reformed. England and Wales had been provided for, but London had been excluded from Balfour's Act. As 1903 opened, the issue of the administration of education in the capital rose inevitably above the Parliamentary horizon.

9

The End of the
London School Board

On 7 April 1903, replying to an NUT Executive vote of thanks for his work on the *Schoolmaster*, Macnamara confessed that, as time went on, he did not find the duties any easier. It had been a heavy year. He had attended the House of Commons, day by day, for eight weary months, and when he got home about 1.00 am it was to do several hours of editorial work.[1] Afterwards, in a series of public meetings, he had striven to publicise and elucidate the new legislation for the benefit of teachers, especially those who were taking their places on the new Education Committees. Throughout he had maintained his attendance both on the Executive and on the London School Board.

From the Board, Macnamara had taken with him to the House of Commons a reputation as an expert on the employment of school children. Parliamentary investigations had begun as a result of an article by Edith Hogg, of the Women's Industrial Council, in the August 1897 edition of the *Nineteenth Century*.[2] The following May she headed a deputation to Sir John Gorst. After a preliminary inquiry, Gorst had set up an Inter-Departmental Committee of the Board of Education and the Home Office; it collected evidence between 22 February and 22 July 1901. Among the witnesses, with Macnamara, were his former colleagues at Huddersfield, George Sharples and Richard Waddington; Marshall Jackman, now President of the NUT and Sir Charles Elliott of the London School Board. Macnamara, who had consulted Mrs Hogg, handed in a document replicating some of the information he had reported to the School Board in February 1899 about children who worked more than nineteen hours a week out of school. They included a boy who assisted an oil seller for forty-two-and-a-half hours, another who assisted a barber for thirty-nine hours and a third who worked in a boot shop for thirty-six-and-a-half hours. The first two earned two shillings, the third three shillings and sixpence. Amongst the girls, one spent thirty-five hours a week on cracker work, for which she received twopence or threepence. Under the Education Act of 1876, Macnamara noted, no child might be legally employed between the ages of five and fourteen so as to interfere with its education. Unfortunately the law had been involved merely to determine whether the child had been present at or absent from school.[3] Hence new statutory powers were needed, in addition to effective bye-laws.[4]

The absolute non-employment of children, Macnamara said, was his ideal.[5] The Committee, however, seemed doubtful. 'You would admit that there are hardly occupations enough, clubs and things of that sort, for boys after they have left school at 4.30 – how would you have them fill up their time?', he was asked. He responded firmly:

> I think it would be most desirable to establish boys' clubs and social institutes, where they can be profitably engaged, but I am prepared to see them do nothing rather than being subjected to the extreme physical toil which they are now.

He was equally emphatic about rural employment:

> I should say that some of the most severe toil at present is in the agricultural districts. Under the guise of healthy surroundings there is a monotonous course of labour thrown upon little children, which is bound to blunt their intellect.[6]

The report had been published in November 1901. Its main recommendation was that the overworking of children in those occupations which were still unregulated by law should be prevented by giving powers to make labour bye-laws to the county and borough councils; as the *Schoolmaster* commented, 'precisely what we have been urging ever since June 1898'.[7] On 20 January 1902 Macnamara secured an assurance from C. T. Ritchie, the Home Secretary, that a bill was being prepared. It was duly introduced in July, but withdrawn. Macnamara renewed his enquiries. With the Education Act secure, the Government took up the issue. Legislation was announced in the King's Speech of February 1903[8] and a Bill based entirely on the report of the Inter-Departmental Committee was introduced by Aretas Akers-Douglas, Ritchie's successor, on 4 March.

It was warmly received. Gorst reminded the House that a very great number of children went to school in such a state that it was cruelty to compel them to engage in intellectual labour.[9] Macnamara provided examples from his own experience: boys dragged at 3.00 am to the Covent Garden flower market, who got back to the East End at 9.00 am, ran errands during the whole of their dinner hour, sold flowers or newspapers till 10.00 pm and slept all through school. He recalled the Marylebone boy, now dead, who had spent all his leisure time as an undertaker's assistant, measuring corpses. He hoped that the Bill might go to a Grand Committee, to strengthen it.[10] Here he was supported by John Burns: 'Some of the newspapers will oppose it', he said: 'some of the parents will obstruct it, and shopkeepers will say that it goes too far. I ask the rt hon Gentleman to stiffen his back on the matter.'[11]

Akers-Douglas agreed that the Bill would benefit from examination by a Grand Committee. Consequently, following the Second Reading, it was committed to the Standing Committee on Trade, augmented for the purpose by fifteen extra members including the Home Secretary, Gorst, Gray, Macnamara, and two future Prime Ministers, Asquith and Bonar Law. Its report was completed on 7 May. 'The Bill has been very appreciably stiffened up', the *Schoolmaster* reported:

> ... The member for Camberwell has secured quite a number of useful amendments, including one that will make it impossible to engage any factory half-timer in either out-of-school or out-of-factory labour and another which will reduce the number of hours that a child may be employed to a maximum of twenty-five hours in any one week.[12]

These were among the universal statutory prohibitions. The Bill was also to give powers to Local Authorities to make bye-laws with respect to specific occupations, ages and hours. Macnamara wrote in the *Schoolmaster*:

> The employment of school children for profit out of their school hours, and even school children not yet in their teens, will of course still be possible even under the aegis of this very moderate but yet withal very beneficent little measure. But the real cruelties and the real injustice involved in heavy physical toil of an exacting character and covering hours of protracted suffering ought to be and will be abolished for ever ... No longer will it be legal for any coster to hale his little son out of bed before 5 am – winter and summer – to take him to Covent Garden in his 'little donkey shay' ... No longer will it be possible for the child of the agricultural labourer to pitch turnips into a cart or to lead horses in the harvest field for ten or even fifteen hours a day. No longer will it be possible to send the British citizen of to-morrow around with milk cans at dawn, or to compel him to cry 'Xtra Speshul' along the gutters even up to the hour of midnight.[13]

The Inter-Departmental Committee had suggested that opposition to the measure might be expected. Macnamara had suddenly been asked whether he would prohibit the employment of all children employed in theatres under the age of fourteen. He replied that they should be in bed.[14] Between March and June Akers-Douglas received representations from Sir Henry Irving and other theatre managers. He therefore moved that Section 3 of the Prevention of Cruelty to Children Act of 1894 should have effect as if re-enacted in the new Bill, so that no licence should be granted to a child under nine. 'The Grand Committee had rejected a clause similar to the one now moved by the Home Secretary', the *Practical Teacher* reported, 'and Messrs Gray and Macnamara had done excellent work on that Committee in this respect as in others. The House was now asked to do, and compelled to do, what the Committee had deliberately refused to do – namely allow children henceforth to work or act in theatres after 9 pm.'

This proved unpopular; the Government's majority fell to twenty-three and the Home Secretary, a former Chief Whip, raised the minimum age to ten. Instead of the statutory enactment outlawing child employment which Macnamara pressed for again at the report stage,[15] the Government carried permissive clauses which, over the next two years, were only marginally acted upon. 'Thus slowly do the mills of Parliament grind out reform', the *Practical Teacher* concluded sadly.[16]

Whilst the Bill which was to produce these exiguous results was being shaped, the Government approached the question of the future administration of public education in London. In 1870, London was judged to require the insertion of a specific clause in Forster's Act.[17] In introducing his Bill of March 1902, Balfour indicated that the omission of London was a matter of convenience, not of policy.[18] Had the comprehensive Bill failed and the education legislation of 1902 dwindled to a measure dealing only with post-elementary education, the Board might have survived. Once the other boards were abolished, however, London's fate was certain.

The achievements of the Board were monumental, but the fact that its public reputation had declined made it appear, to a Prime Minister keen to finish with the troublesome issue of education, an easy target. The teacher resistance consequent on the Riley affair had brought its management effectiveness into question; the Cockerton case had made it seem reckless. Even its standing as an example of democracy in action had been damaged by the fact that in 1900 only eighteen per cent of its electorate bothered to vote.[19] Nevertheless Macnamara was determined not to surrender without a struggle. 'When the Government proposes to apply this Bill to London', he promised during the Third Reading, 'I will do my level best to show that London presents a case which can only be efficiently dealt with under the *ad hoc* principle.'[20]

On 19 June 1902 the Board had appointed a Special Committee under Lord Reay to consider and report as to what should be the constitution and functions of the future Education Authority for London. The twenty members, including Macnamara, unanimously reached the conclusion, moved on 27 November

> that whether for primary or other form of education, the Authority should be for London as a whole, and that the charge should fall upon London as a whole; that, both for primary and other forms of education, there should be one controlling Authority for London as a whole, providing that the constitution of that Authority be thoroughly representative of the electorate of London.

The motion was agreed. It omitted, however, recommendations about the constitution of the future Authority, about which the Committee had failed to reach a conclusion. Macnamara added an amendment which incorporated the argument that he was to employ over the next few months in his attempts to ensure the Board's survival:

> ... Having regard to the large population of London and to the very great extent of the work which is to be performed in connection with primary education, and, further, to the large amount of work which will be entailed in developing and organising technical and higher education, it is the opinion of

the School Board for London that this work cannot be adequately discharged by any body attached to, or subordinate to, any Local Authority elected for London and charged with other and onerous duties.

He attached a recommendation for direct election by the ratepayers for which all persons already eligible to serve on school boards should continue to be eligible, triennial elections taking place on the same day, by the same electorate, as elections for the London County Council. He was not against the municipalisation of education, he said, but he was against administration by a subordinate body.[21] When his motion was carried by thirty-one votes to seventeen, amid cheers, Macnamara declared that the *ad hoc* principle might well be vindicated as far as London was concerned. The following week a delegation to petition the Prime Minister was appointed.[22]

On New Year's Day, the *Board Teacher* declared:

> The School Board ... is taking the right line. It is not going to meet its fate lying down. It has wisely decided to seek direct approach to His Majesty's Ministers ... The deputation will represent a properly elected Board, which sees as clear as in noonday light that the educational needs of London are so vast and so intricate that by no possibility can they be effectively met save by a directly elected body ... Surely the bitterest enemy the LCC has ever had to contend with is the subtle foe who now seeks to make all its machinery ineffective by clogging its wheels with the minutiae of Education. What has London's beneficent CC done to the Fabian Society that they thus seek to kill it?[23]

Balfour passed the responsibility of interviewing the deputation from the Board to the President of the Board of Education, the Marquis of Londonderry. He extended a friendly welcome to his erstwhile colleagues, expressing his extreme pleasure at meeting again, even for business purposes, those with whom he had been associated for two years and from whom, he said, he had received such kindness and consideration. Not surprisingly, the mission was fruitless. Lord Reay presented the Board's case expertly, adding, in the presence of Mrs Bridges Adams, Mrs Homan and the Hon. Maude Lawrence, a plea that women should remain eligible for the new Authority for London. Macnamara pressed the Board's own scheme. Of course it was idle to disregard the fact that the Government had declared war on the *ad hoc* principle, he said, but if it really intended to promote the well-being of London there were only two courses open. One was the *ad hoc* principle with cooption; the other was the application of last year's Act, by which the Technical Education Board would be made the Education Authority. But Lord Londonderry, referring to these and other contributions, could only assure the delegation that he and his colleagues would keep a very close and watchful eye on the matter to see that no injustice was done. Dr Macnamara, an education authority second to none, wished to impress on them the great magnitude of the task and, he said, the Government had not disregarded London's importance.[24]

'Nothing could have exceeded the warmth and cordiality with which Lord Londonderry received his old colleagues of the London School Board. Nothing could have overpassed the emptiness of his reply', the *Schoolmaster* reported.[25] Curiously, however, the Government felt that in Scotland, education should have its basis in popular election. At a dinner at Frascati's in honour of Thomas Gautrey on 31 January, Macnamara commented that what was good enough for the Scottish gander ought to be good enough for the Cockney goose. Since London was a sort of colonial dependency of Scotland (Laughter) he thought they might claim the Secretary of State for Scotland as a cordial supporter of the *ad hoc* cause.[26]

Again the King's Speech announced an Education Bill. The *Practical Teacher* observed:

> Education bills are now a standing dish in the sessional bills of fare; education bills seem likely to stretch along the path of time up to the very crack of doom. English legislation is patchwork and piecemeal; each Act omits something, leaves something over for another session's debates. The Education Act of 1902 left a good deal over, and hence the Education Bill of 1903 ... Sir John Gorst and his friends, three years and more ago, with their Clause VII and their Cockerton judgments unredressed, and all the manoeuvres they perpetrated ... against the really popular and efficient schools of the country, made the Act of 1902 inevitable, and a London Education Bill in 1903 a certain corollary.[27]

Whilst the 1902 Act had established the principle of Education Authorities appointed by county councils and county boroughs, it was still by no means certain that it could be applied to the London County Council. On 1 March, the *Board Teacher* commented:

> Mr Sidney Webb, who has remarkable ability as an ingratiating negotiator, lightly asserts that the LCC could easily add the duties of School Authority to the tasks it already discharges. Great as is the LCC, its makers – the citizens of London – desire to restrict its services to the work it has undertaken on their behalf. They don't want a swollen-headed body giving them scraps of its time and shreds of its thought ... The fact is, Mr Webb has no mandate ... he is a meddler, not an ambassador ... a magnified Technical Education Board, reposing on the pasteboard caryatids of officialism overpasses the power of imagination to conceive.[28]

A week later the NUT showed that the idea of an *ad hoc* Authority was far from dead. Five thousand people assembled in Queen's Hall to hear the President, Allen Croft, with Macnamara, Gautrey, Gray, Jephson, Jackman and Yoxall. Yoxall summed up. What they aimed at was not the continuation of the old School Board. New arrangements were necessary to meet the needs of the voluntary schools. The old electoral divisions and the cumulative vote were not worth fighting for. But the principle of a directly representative Board to which women as well as men could be elected was one that should be preserved. The resolution, that a directly elected body was the only body that could be entrusted with the administration of education in the metropolis, was carried unanimously.[29]

Nevertheless, even within the teaching profession some doubts about the Board existed. The great Queen's Hall meeting was very *à propos*, the *Practical Teacher* commented, at an hour when the Government was vacillating. Many deputations of teachers had interviewed the London MPs, and much ingenuity had been expended; nevertheless *ad hoc* meant the London School Board and, it concluded:

> ... the objection to it is not cogent or rational; it is one of prejudice: the London School Board has not made itself liked ... With Mr Lyulph Stanley for engine driver and Mr Graham Wallas as stoker, it has been an engine driven without wisdom, tact, or avoidance of danger and offence. Hardly anybody in Parliament will say a word for its continuance.[30]

The Government kept its intentions secret till Sir William Anson introduced the London Education Bill in the House of Commons on 7 April. Its object, he declared, was to abolish the London School Board and to place the London County Council to a great extent in the position in which councils were placed under the Act of 1902. But the constitution of the Local Education Authority he proposed was at once objected to as unsatisfactory. Of its ninety-seven members, thirty-six were to be members of the LCC, thirty-one were to be Metropolitan Borough Councillors, twenty-five were to be coopted experts, and (on the first Education Committee) five were to be members of the old School Board. A curious feature was that while the ex-voluntary schools were to be managed under the terms of the 1902 Act, the former Board schools were to be controlled not by the new Authority itself but by the councils of the newly created Metropolitan Boroughs. 'We propose to give them the appointment and dismissal of the teacher', Anson continued, 'the custody of buildings and, where a new school is to be provided, subject to the determination by the Local Authority of the area to be provided for and the amount to be expended, the selection of the site.'[31]

Campbell-Bannerman, the Leader of the Opposition, attacked the proposals vigorously. There had been no demand for change. But if the London School Board was to be rejected it should be replaced by the London County Council. He said:

> I admit that it would impose a tremendous amount of duty on the London County Council, which its present members could not possibly discharge. But you might double the members of the London County Council, or in some way you might still keep the direct responsibility to the people. But now there are only to be thirty-six members of the County Council on this Committee out of ninety-seven. And this is called making education part of a municipal duty![32]

Macnamara also addressed the question of the constitution of the

Education Authority. There was nothing essentially anti-democratic in giving the full and complete control of education to a municipal council wherever that was physically possible, as it might be in a town of 10,000 people, he said. The education of London, however, involved 2,000 separate institutions, 20,000 teachers, the instruction of 1,000,000 pupils, and a public expenditure of £4,000,000 a year. The thirty-six County Councillors, having all their other duties to attend to, would not be able to attend to the work of the Education Committee. That work would, therefore, fall into the hands of the thirty-one borough councillors and the thirty outsiders. 'This scheme cannot be tinkered with', he declared: 'It is inherently bad.'[33]

The following Saturday the *School Government Chronicle* (formerly the *School Board Chronicle*) expressed itself offended by what it described as a hostile Bill, which had dealt a shattering blow to the system built up by a generation of devoted and patriotic labour on the basis of the Victorian Education Acts.[34] The *Schoolmaster*, after Macnamara's arguments about overloading the LCC had been repeated and amplified, declared that 'the present Bill has already been laughed out of existence ... There can be no shadow of doubt that if the friends of progress will only make an effort, an Education Bill for London based on *ad hoc* lines will yet be secured.'[35] A warning followed about how voluntary school teachers were likely to be treated if the LCC assumed responsibility for education. The Fabian Tract entitled 'The Education Act 1902: How to Make the Best of It', advised new Local Authorities to obtain reports by their Inspectors on the qualifications and efficiency of the teachers in the voluntary schools they were taking over, with a view to granting permanent appointments only to those who were appropriately qualified, educationally efficient and otherwise suitable. 'This ought to be particularly interesting to the London voluntary school teachers just now', the *Schoolmaster* commented:

> One of the leading lights of Fabianism, and we should not be far out if we described him as its chief educational exponent, is Mr Sidney Webb, whose untiring energy has so far managed to pave the way for the control of London's education nominally by the London County Council, but actually by Mr Sidney Webb and his immediate entourage. We do not suppose that this cold-blooded advice will be followed at all generally throughout the country. But if the Sidney Webb policy to capture education in London succeeds, then our friends will know what to expect.[36]

Parliament adjourned for Easter and, as usual in Easter week, the NUT Annual Conference assembled, this year in Buxton. The Union was celebrating the election as its first honorary member of Sir George Kekewich, Permanent Secretary to the Education Department and the Board of Education since 1890, who had been unceremoniously ousted by Balfour in October 1902 to secure the future of the Education Act. In the course of a controversial speech Kekewich touched briefly on the London Bill.

He was, he said, absolutely in accord with the letters and speeches of Dr Macnamara (Cheers). He hoped that the Government would hesitate before it introduced a bill which intensified all the objections to the Education Act of last year, and a good many more. He hoped that the County Council would be put in charge, though he would have preferred an *ad hoc* Authority, the only body that could take the place of that splendid School Board which had done more in a shorter time for a larger number of people than any other authority in the world (Cheers).[37] These observations provided an ideal introduction to a motion on the Bill introduced by Jackman, that:

> This Conference is of opinion that the London Education Bill contains proposals fraught with the greatest possible danger to educational progress, will lead to inefficiency and extravagance in administration, is unworkable, and is incapable of being satisfactorily amended ... While not opposed to the municipalisation of education where the amount of work to be accomplished makes this possible, the Conference believes that the magnitude of London's educational operations is such that no scheme of administration can be satisfactory which does not place primary and higher education under the effective control of one Authority, directly elected, exclusively for that purpose.[38]

Macnamara, supporting the motion, said that the Bill in its existing form was as dead as Queen Anne. His ideal was an *ad hoc* body consisting of fifty-eight members (one elected for each of the divisions) to which coopted members would be added. The motion was passed with only one dissentient.[39]

Back in the House of Commons, Macnamara accused the Prime Minister of moving too rapidly. The Second Reading of the Bill was taking place but neither the County Council nor the School Board, both in recess over Easter, had been able to discuss it.[40] He concentrated on the question of the constitution of the proposed Local Education Authority for London:

> The thirty-six County Councillors will be there by direct election ... Thirty-one persons will be there by secondary election, chosen from the borough councils. Not one of those sixty-seven members can be a woman. As a colleague of nine women members of the School Board I can speak of the admirable work and devoted service they have given to the public ... Of the remaining thirty members, of whom some may be women, not one will be elected on behalf of the ratepayers either directly or secondarily; they will be selected by the County Council. I have only one comment to make on that scheme. We need not bother about it; it was killed at its birth.[41]

There were, in practice, two possibilities: 'Either an *ad hoc* Authority or genuine municipalisation; but as the second alternative shuts out women who have done so much good work for education, I prefer the *ad hoc* principle'.[42]

Balfour, speaking next, confessed himself rather surprised at the degree of opposition which Macnamara and his friends had expressed. The constructive approach that the educational expert had displayed all through the debates of 1902 had apparently caused the Prime Minister to assume that the principles underlying the new Education Act could be effortlessly applied to London. He commented:

> The Bill is intended, and solely intended, to apply the principles of the Bill already on the Statute-book to the metropolitan area. I cannot quite understand the feeling of the hon Gentleman. It perhaps arises from an idea – an entirely mistaken idea – that the framers of this Bill have some special animus against the great body of which he is a distinguished member, the London School Board.

The question, he went on, was not really now whether the London School Board had or had not been an efficient body for the administration of education in London, but how best they were to administer education as the problem presented itself in London after the Act of the previous year. In his view neither the old School Board, appropriately augmented, nor the London County Council, could deal with this problem. He was in favour of a central authority and the delegation of part of its work to other authorities.[43]

As the current of the debate moved away from the compromise arrangements introduced by Anson, it became plain that the London County Council rather than an *ad hoc* authority, would prevail. R. B. Haldane, already working with Webb on the establishment of what was to become the Imperial College of Science and Technology, suggested that the Government should take the County Council, give it the power of cooption (to include experts and women) and eliminate the borough councils.[44] Gorst supported this view, saying that though it was the opinion of the hon. member for North Camberwell that the County Council would be unable to perform the duties cast upon it by the Bill, many of its experienced members did not agree. 'If I were able to have my own way about this matter', he declared, 'I would leave the London County Council absolutely free to appoint its own Committee.'[45]

Yoxall, speaking next, expressed his surprise at the way in which the issue was being handled. To all appearances the House had resolved itself into a sort of amiable and non-partisan Committee to recommend the bases of a totally new Bill:

> What we are now supposed to be discussing is the London Education Bill, brought in by a great government with an immense majority, a government which knew for more than twelve months that they must submit such a Bill to Parliament, and had had many months to prepare it. I submit that it is hardly respectful to the capacity and industry of this House that a debate of this kind should be allowed to go on.[46]

Nevertheless, the Bill passed its Second Reading by 137 votes. When it was reintroduced for the Committee stage on 18 May, it emerged that while the Prime Minister's view of a central authority with partial delegation still prevailed, Anson, in conference with the London Unionist MPs, had devised, by a process described by Yoxall as 'botching and tinkering', a compromise by which the County Council was to have forty-two members on the new authority and the borough councils twelve.[47] Twenty-five or thirty coopted members would be added. 'Never was known such a case in Parliamentary history', the *Practical Teacher* reported. 'According to all canons of House of Commons tradition and etiquette, a government measure so used ought to have been withdrawn: according to most precedents, the Government responsible for the Bill ought to have resigned.'[48]

Macnamara took the opportunity early in the debate over what he called 'this undigested scheme', which the Government was 'passing at a speed illegal for a motor car', to introduce an amendment designed to revive the *ad hoc* issue. He was the only member of the London School Board with a seat in the House, he said, and if his authority was to go down he meant to go down with his flag flying. He proposed a variation on the scheme he had advocated at the London School Board on 27 November, a body directly and triennially elected from both male and female candidates in London's fifty-nine Parliamentary divisions with fifteen additional coopted members. He had no quarrel with municipalisation in small towns, he said, but in the great county boroughs it had resulted in all sorts of outsiders being called in, with no responsibility whatever to the ratepayers. They and the paid officials did the work. This is what would happen in London. Already the Board was dealing with 500,000 children. Now it was proposed that these, as well as 220,000 voluntary school children, were to be added to the London County Council's existing educational responsibilities. 'Did any hon member believe that the London County Council could spare forty-two men who would be taken exclusively away from their work as County Councillors?', he enquired. The one thing the Government's proposals would do would be to destroy the London County Council.[49]

The prospect of the continuation of the London School Board even in altered form drew Gorst into the debate. He dismissed Macnamara's amendment, arguing that they would never have proper local self-government until there was one body alone able to rate the people and be responsible to the people for local finance and general expenditure. He then took the opportunity to hold Anson, who had supplanted him as the Commons spokesman for education, up to ridicule. He was going to vote for a real municipal body in London as elsewhere, he said, not for any sham supreme municipal body. He would do everything in his power to make the control of the County Council over the education of London absolutely real, and secure for the Council all the powers and opportunities of carrying out the great work placed upon it. As for the difficulty, or as some thought, the impossibility of the existing County Council being adequate for the work, he repeated the view that he had expressed during the Second Reading. The best judge of that question was the County Council itself.[50]

The significance of this observation became apparent almost at once. Responding to James Bryce's taunt that the Government had given no reply whatever to the criticisms of the Bill, many from its own supporters, Walter Long (President of the Local Government Board) disclosed that he had been involved in negotiations with members of the London County Council, both Moderate and Progressive, over a very considerable time and they had said to him: 'Add to our duties and we will reduce our committees, and we shall bear this burden with the utmost ease'. Hon. Gentlemen, he continued, were entitled to the view which the hon. member for North Camberwell had always consistently held, that there should be an *ad hoc* authority for education in London. That was a perfectly reasonable proposal; but manifestly they could not support it by the contention that the County Council was overworked.[51]

Long's intervention destroyed any lingering hope that the London School Board, or any *ad hoc* body, could survive. It also destroyed the Government's case for the partial delegation of the London County Council's educational functions to the borough councils. Finally it was agreed on both sides of the House that, as the Prime Minister put it, instead of repeating the discussion and arguments over and over again on different amendments, one full and adequate discussion on borough council representation should take place. On 25 May Balfour duly admitted that the Government's efforts to find a compromise which would leave the boroughs some representation on the Education Committee without giving them that very great authority on the Committee which a representative of each borough would necessarily do, had failed. 'I never refuse to accept the facts of a situation when they are presented to me clearly', he said, 'and it is quite evident, not only that the great body of the House, unconnected directly with London, look with considerable suspicion and dislike on this plan, but the majority of London members themselves, for one reason or another, very often for different reasons, do not approve it.' The Government concluded, therefore, that the best plan was to put the London County Council, regarding the constitution of its Education Committee, precisely in the position of the other county councils in the country. It would itself have to produce a scheme, Balfour pointed out, which would have a majority of members of the County Council (unless the council itself determined otherwise) and which would provide for the inclusion of women and the appointment of some experts and also some members of the London School Board, if the first Committee considered it desirable.[52]

Balfour appended the hope that more harmonious progress could now be made on what he called 'this thorny topic'.[53] But the disadvantages of postponing the issue of Education Committee membership till the new Committee met became at once apparent over the question of women's membership. The abolition of boards by the 1902 Act had cancelled women's membership rights, allowing them to participate on Education Committees only through cooption. Sydney Buxton (Tower Hamlets, Poplar) and Thomas Lough (Islington) attempted to raise the issue, the latter pointing out that ever since 1870 there had been a distinguished band of women who had rendered most excellent service to the cause of education in London, but that most county councils had appointed only one woman on their Committees, or at most two.[54] But having spent so much time on London's education administration, the Government was not disposed to spend any longer on it. Balfour responded:

> I hope the hon member and others will not persist in discussing this question ... the London County Council will be in the same position as all other county councils as regards fixing the number of women that should be appointed and I have no reason to believe that they will fail in their duty to the cause of education or deprive themselves of the services of an adequate number of the accomplished ladies of whom the hon member has spoken in terms not the least too strong. But we are only wasting time by discussing a clause which is not to be proceeded with.[55]

Macnamara rejoined that the Prime Minister was probably correct in thinking that the London County Council would appoint a sufficient number of women. The present Council certainly would, but that body would not last for ever. Balfour was not to be moved. 'We have found after prolonged experience the futility of the attempt to lay down in this Bill precisely what the constitution of the Committee of the London County Council is to be', he concluded.[56]

'The County Council is supreme', the *Schoolmaster* observed on 30 May:

> It appoints its own Education Committee. That Committee will devolve upon the local managers just as much and just as little as it pleases. The borough councils practically disappear from the education administration of London save that they nominate a proportion of the membership of each group of managers. All that ridiculous farrago relating to their appointment and dismissal of board teachers and the choice of sites has been relegated to [the] limbo of the utterly discredited.[57]

In the Commons, Macnamara had described the Government's conduct of the Bill as grotesque.[58] The education journals shared his view. 'All the goals were kicked by its antagonists, none by its supporters', the *Practical Teacher* commented, 'and still it remained a government Bill.' Perhaps unfairly, Anson's performance was rated low:

> he was too untried to know how to prepare against the sudden changes of Westminster weather ... Very pitiable it was to see this refined, Oxford-donnish, dried-up, precise little gentleman cast hither and thither in the rough-and-tumble of hot controversy ... Many members of the House of Commons used to be pupils of his at All Souls, and they particularly lamented the spectacle. He was so clearly a fish out of water.[59]

The *Board Teacher* developed Macnamara's remark in the Commons that it would have been better if the debates on the Bill had been acted out in the Savoy Theatre:

> The history of the London Education Bill is sheer delight to anyone with an appreciation of Gilbertian humour. There may possibly be yet one or more diverting incidents to record. But even as it stands the tale is hardly to be equalled for drollery in the whole range of Parliamentary proceedings.

Its humour was mixed with bitterness:

> The existing London School Board has been sentenced. The execution day is fixed. On an early day in May of next year the authority directly elected for purely educational purposes ceases. It will disappear with all its grand record of a well-spent and devoted life left behind it as a guide and an example to its successor.[60]

In the meantime the strength of feeling provoked by the threat to its existence had been manifested by a demonstration in Hyde Park on 23 May, preceded by a procession with bands from the Embankment led by Macnamara. Arrangements were in the hands of Jackman. In the Park, there were a dozen platforms with 100 speakers representing Nonconformity, the Trade Unions, Parliament, the LCC, the London School Board and the NUT. It was estimated (probably over-estimated) that there were 250,000 protesters. A. G. Hales of the *Daily News* described the scene:

> When the time for the cessation of speeches came, a bugle rang out sharp and clear; every man who was addressing the multitude stopped with words upon his lips, a fine display of party discipline, and certain proof of able organisation and leadership. The resolution was put from every platform. It was in these terms:- 'That this mass meeting of citizens of London emphatically condemns the Education Bill now before Parliament, because it destroys the London School Board, excludes women from election to the Education Authority, imposes religious tests upon the teachers, and does not provide for the free teaching of Elementary, Technical and Higher Grade Education in suitable day and evening schools entirely controlled and administered by a body directly elected for that purpose'. Thereupon from all that great and enormous array there broke such a volume of sound as men have seldom heard even in that famous spot, a deep long roar that had a mingled note of triumph and of menace in it, for the crowd had condemned the Bill, and with the Bill those who begat it.[61]

For all the drama of this occasion, the Board was now a condemned institution. In August, Macnamara provided a valedictory account of its members and the policies that it had pursued for the *Daily News*. From the first Board which contained a number of educational giants, among them Lord Lawrence, Mrs Garrett Anderson, Professor Huxley, W. H. Smith and Lord Sandon, the Board had attracted men and women of distinction. He recalled, however, how in the 1880s Londoners had grown apathetic and the Board had passed into the hands of the Diggleites, first with their cry of economy, later into a furious religious controversy. Finally, in 1897, with a Progressive majority, the Board had recovered its zeal and discrimination. 'Probably', he concluded, 'had there been no Progressive majority, the London School Board would not be in the condemned cell.' For the thoroughness with which the Board's work had been pursued had brought about a conspiracy against it in which, Macnamara alleged, Lords Hugh and Robert Cecil had played leading parts and which had culminated in the Cockerton Judgement.[62]

Paradoxically the Board continued in vigour. On 22 October, Macnamara moved the acceptance of the Report of the School Accommodation and Attendance Committee for the year ended 25 March 1903. The estimated number of children for whom London had, within that period, to find accommodation numbered 784,355. There were already in existence 771,286 permanent elementary school places, 554,198 in Board schools and 217,088 in voluntary schools. To meet the deficiency of 13,069 the Board was providing 18,451 places in temporary schools, so that there was an apparent excess, necessary to allow for the migratory habits of Londoners, of 5,382. As for the attendance figures, in October 1901 he had commented on the excellent effects of Gorst's Act of 1900 under which the magistrates were cordially assisting the Board with the result that the attendance percentage reached 82.5. A year later it was 83.7 per cent, passing that for the whole of England and Wales.[63] Now, with a school roll of 762,974 London showed an average daily attendance of 653,124, which yielded a percentage of 85.6. At last, Macnamara reported, Scotland's figure had been beaten. To find himself in a position to make this announcement had been one of his fondest hopes, he added:

> that we should be compelled to drop this extremely difficult and delicate social and educational problem when we have so industriously and successfully surmounted so many almost overwhelming obstacles is to me a matter of intense regret ... much as I respect and admire the administrative zeal and capacity of the London County Councillor, I cannot disguise from myself that it may very well be that, whilst he is feeling his way with this highly technical, deeply complex and acutely susceptible problem, things may easily slip back from the fine position in which we leave them.[64]

Webb, the Board's residuary legatee, took a different view. In an account of fifty years of London education in the October edition of the *Nineteenth Century and After*, he began by attributing the largest share in what he called 'one of the most remarkable chapters of social history', the transformation effected in half a century in the manners and morals of the London working class, to the School Board. He contrasted the frowsy, dark, insanitary rooms, practically destitute of apparatus, and their mainly untrained teachers, fifty years before, with the admirable buildings and professional teachers of 1903. There was now a school place for every child and attendance had reached 83.7 per cent. Much had been done by the School Board of late years, mainly at the instigation of Dr Macnamara, to look after these children and various improvements were already in progress. More could be accomplished when the voluntary schools, where the attendance was much below that of the Board schools, were brought under the same central control. On the quality of the education given, Webb suggested that, since Payment by Results had been abandoned, no common measure had been applied to all the schools. Nor was there any statistical evidence to appeal to. The contrast between the best and the worst, even of the Board schools, was considerable. Amongst the voluntary schools even greater divergencies existed. Nearly all the 100 Roman Catholic schools and perhaps 300 of the 331 Church schools were calamitously behindhand. This, an implied criticism of the Government's real education policy which had been masked by the administrative and financial legislation of the so-called Education Act of 1902, was made sharper by an international comparison:

> Putting together what little is really known of all the 1,000 public elementary schools of London, including both board and voluntary, there are competent observers who declare that nearly half of them, containing about a quarter of all the children, would probably be condemned as inefficient, either in respect of buildings or sanitation, of staffing or equipment, of curriculum, of real success in child training by a Swiss, a Danish, a Saxon, a Prussian, or a Massachusetts school inspector.

So, Webb concluded, the London County Council was left with a daunting array of tasks: to level up the elementary schools, to multiply and improve the Higher Grade Schools, to establish training institutions, extend the secondary schools scholarship schemes and recast evening class provision into a single harmonious organisation. Macnamara had often stated that the administration of education would be too much for the London County Council. Webb, by contrast, seemed to be relishing the prospect. 'Now that Parliament has decided', he concluded, 'the sooner the new education Committee grapples with its great task, and makes the necessary reorganisation of the administrative machinery ... the better it will be for London's children.'[65]

The Webbs remained suspicious of Macnamara. After the LCC elections in early March 1904, Beatrice Webb commented that the Progressives were romping back with practically undiminished numbers. But as for Macnamara, she added, 'there has not been a whisper of having him on in any capacity – not even as a co-opted member'.[66]

On Thursday 28 April 1904 the last meeting of the London School Board took place. 'An historic scene', the *Board Teacher* (now re-named the *London Teacher*) reported:

> The Board Room and galleries are filled to their utmost capacity ... On the

dais behind Lords Reay and Stanley of Alderley sit past Chairmen: Mr J. R. Diggle ... and Lord George Hamilton ... Old-member guests sit in a long row to the right of the chair ... the Rev J. J. Coxhead ... Mr Athelstan Riley, Mr Benson Clough ... The new possessors of the goodly heritage -the LCC Education Committee – are also invited guests who come in force ... the President of the MBTA, Mr W. D. Bentliff, sits near the old members as the invited guest representing the huge teaching staff ... the Dowager Lady Law-rence, widow of the first Chairman – whose fine portrait overlooks the room – adds a pathetic interest.

The agenda was dealt with in twenty minutes. Then votes of thanks were carried, the chief of them by Lord Reay and Lord Stanley, to the teaching staff of the schools who, the latter declared, 'have not looked upon them-selves as mere civil servants, but have tried to gain access, not only to the minds, but to the hearts of the children, and through their hearts to the consciences of the parents'. Forty minutes were spent listening to Lord Reay providing a résumé of the Board's work.[67] Then at 5.45 the proceed-ings ended with the singing of the National Anthem. So the Board made 'a swan-like end, fading in music'.[68]

Though for the next few years Macnamara continued to fight a rearguard campaign on behalf of the *ad hoc* principle,[69] it was soon clear that the issue belonged to the past and not to the future. Some two weeks after the Board's ceremonial end, he attended a meeting of the Kennington Liberal and Radical Association, which had supported him in the three Board elections he had fought and won since 1894, to receive a presentation in recognition of the services he had rendered London education over the previous ten years. J. Williams Benn, recently appointed Chairman of the London County Council, speaking warmly of his achievements, observed that when the story of education in London came to be written, the name of Macnamara would be at the head of the roll of fame. Thanking him, Macnamara made it clear that he regretted the loss of the Board. Its destruction, he said, was a crime. He hoped yet to see a directly-elected body governing London education. The number of members of the Council was not only too small. They were to meet behind closed doors. So far as he could help it, he said, he would not allow London's education to be governed in other than the fullest publicity and under the direct sanction and gaze, day by day, of the people who paid for it (Loud cheers). If circumstances made it possible he would very much like to fight this matter out as a candidate for the first bye-election vacancy (Loud cheers).[70]

Already he must have been aware that circumstances would not make this practicable. As the LCC successfully absorbed its new educational responsibilities, Parliament was providing new opportunities to occupy his time.

10

The Decline of the Unionist Government, 1903–1905

In November 1902, when the Education Act was passing through its final stages, Macnamara was interviewed for the magazine the *World*, which was running a series entitled 'Celebrities at Home'. On the wall of the drawing room of his house in Rollscourt Avenue, Herne Hill, hung two portraits, one of his father-in-law, clad in the plaid and tartan of the Camerons, the other of Sergeant Macnamara. In the study was an old tin pipe case which, Macnamara said, had been compulsorily sold to soldiers for two shillings and sixpence. His father had used it for months in the trenches before Sebastopol. The tale evoked an expression of regret that in the House of Commons circumstances had tied him to one subject. He was particularly anxious to speak up for the private soldier: 'Now if I had my own way, I should like to be heard on the subject of Tommy Atkins and his condition of life, but no-one would listen to me ... There is much I could say on the wrongs of poor speechless Tommy.'[1]

Sponsored by the NUT and the Educational Newspaper Company[2] to advance the cause of education, Macnamara had never disguised his interest in the Army. 'Are you a pro-Boer?', he had been asked at a constituency meeting during the khaki election, when the Liberal Party's reservations about the conduct of the war were being exploited by its opponents. He answered:

> Nobody has ever heard me say an unkind word about our soldiers in South Africa. I have said many nasty things about the War Office, and they deserve it. Let me tell you a story. In 1866 there was a rebellion in Canada, and some English regiments took part in putting it down. Last year, thirty-three years after the event, the War Office notified all the surviving men who had taken part that it was proposed to give each of them a medal. A certain poor old man was extremely delighted at the letter. Six months after its receipt he died, never having received the medal. Three months after his death, the medal was received by his son. There is the medal, my friends, and I am the son.[3]

His father's exploits caught the ear of the Whips before the new MP took his seat. 'Macnamara?', one of them said, as his name was taken. 'It can't be. You couldn't have been in the Crimea!'[4] And the Sergeant would

have approved of his maiden speech. Delivered on 10 December, it contained a series of questions about the war. Was it true, he asked, that the wives and children of Irish soldiers were now in Irish workhouses? Was it true that soldiers on transport ships to South Africa had been given biscuits thirty years old, and beef that had been in casks twenty-seven years?[5] In the course of it he told the House that he was a soldier's son; afterwards the Unionist member for Pembroke and Haverfordwest approached him. It was General Laurie, late of the 47th. To Macnamara's pride and pleasure, he claimed the Sergeant as an old comrade.[6]

As the Blue Books on the South African War began to appear, Macnamara perceived a melancholy similarity between the conditions described in them and the tales he had heard as a child in the barracks at Montreal about the Crimean War. In the *New Liberal Review* of December 1903 he compared the Parliamentary reports on the supply failures of the two campaigns. Then the men's clothing had been hopelessly unsuitable; stores lay piled up in Balaklava harbour (if they got that far); the wounded were transported to ships on the backs of mules; the trained medical orderlies were insufficient and the men pressed into the Service from the ranks were grossly ignorant and often fiendishly selfish and cruel. He observed:

> It is little wonder that the men upon whose knees I sat as a boy would always wind up the recountal of their sufferings in the Crimea with the pathetic assurance that after Roebuck's committee, Sidney Herbert's Hospital Commission, Russell's letters to *The Times*, the public indignation and concern, and so on and so on, these things could never happen again.

Yet the stories told by the two reports were absolutely similar. The Government had been warned in the most categorical and specific manner by its military advisers in South Africa, month by month from 1896 till the opening of the war, about the nature of the struggle ahead and about the Boers' stupendous military preparations, yet the country had been allowed to drift into war precisely in the same hopeless state of unpreparedness as it had done in the Crimean campaign. Four million defective rounds of Mark IV cartridges were sent home on 17 October 1899; thousands of Reservists fought at Graspan, Modder River, Stormberg, Magersfontein and Colenso with Lee Enfield rifles of which the sighting caused a truly aimed shot to be delivered eighteen inches to the right at 500 yards; cotton clothing was not warm enough, boots collapsed, ammunition pouches were unsuitable, entrenching spades were almost useless, bad stores of hay, flour, oats, bran etc. were sent out under contract. Sick and wounded were transported from Swarzkopfontein to Kimberley in oxcarts mostly without shade from the scorching sun. At the Newton Base Camp Hospital at Kimberley, patients' property disappeared. Orderlies cornered supplies of delicacies including eggs, brandy and port. 'And of course, it will all happen again next time', he concluded, 'which may very well be the LAST time for the homeland of the British Empire.'[7]

The supply failures of the war had been matched by failures of leadership. Defects in education were held to be responsible. Soon after the end of the war, the *Schoolmaster* published two editorials, the first on the men, the second on the officers. 'The men', 'Linesman', an officer eye-witness had written, 'were splendid'. 'Education', the *Schoolmaster* concluded, 'has strengthened and bettered them ... If it was the German schoolmasters who won the campaigns in Austria and France, it was the British public elementary teachers who saved from shame and ultimate defeat the forces of the Queen in South Africa.' But the best plea 'Linesman' could make on behalf of the officers was: 'We have done our best; no man can do more; many might not have done so much; and we are sorry it has not been good enough'. The *Schoolmaster* associated his comments with the recent report of the Committee on Military Education dealing with Sandhurst: 'The witnesses are unanimous in stating that the junior officers are lamentably wanting in military knowledge, and, what is perhaps even worse, in the desire to acquire knowledge and in zeal for the military art'.[8] The disclosures continued. In January 1904, Dr Thomas Miller Maguire, a celebrated Sandhurst entrants' crammer, who had provided evidence for the Committee in June 1901, unburdened himself to the *Daily News*. To the Committee he had commented crushingly on the ineffectiveness of sports and particularly games as preparation for the arts of war; now he denounced the so-called great public schools. 'I have proved that the cult of ignorance by soldiers is a recent absurdity, and that the worship of boyish games by grown men is utter frivolity', he concluded. He had often been obliged to inform parents who had spent hundreds of pounds on public school fees that their sons were too ignorant to pass an examination either for a commission or to qualify as a sergeant. 'Quite so!' the *Schoolmaster* commented. 'And wasn't it one of the Boer generals who said that if the sergeants in South Africa – the products of the despised elementary schools – had all been promoted to the command of companies, regiments, brigades, and divisions, the war would have been over in half the time?'[9]

While the public elementary school products had performed so creditably, another factor about them had emerged. A large percentage of men offering themselves for recruitment into the Army had been rejected for medical reasons. The percentage of rejections at the St George's barracks in London had been 37.4; at Belfast, 37.6; at Newcastle on Tyne 38.1; at Liverpool 38.8; at Hounslow 39.5; and at Manchester 49.0.[10] At the beginning of 1903, the *Schoolmaster* published correspondence between Lord Charles Beresford MP and the Duke of Devonshire on the issue of physical and military training in public elementary schools. Beresford pointed out that when the Education Bill had been before the House of Commons, he had advocated that physical and military instruction should be made compulsory in all schools supported by public funds. He had been ruled out of order but advised that his proposal could be introduced into the Education Code. He argued:

Compulsion of any form is only possible in the schools. Training boys and lads to become healthy must help towards the efficiency of the Empire ... by the words 'Military Instruction' ... I mean that youths should be taught to march, swim and give orders. I also advocate that every boy capable should be taught to fire a rook or small-bore rifle at a target ...

The Duke's secretary replied that Lord Londonderry, the new President of the Board of Education, was considering some of these suggestions; others could only be dealt with by the War Office.[11]

The outcome was the so-called Model Course for schools. A village school-mistress wrote to the *Schoolmaster* describing how it was introduced:

The Inspector of this district is determined to have the new drill taught according to the most approved methods, and for this purpose a class has been started under his auspices *at the barracks at X*. All teachers are expected to attend, young and old ... Has the Government the right to demand such a sacrifice? If the War Office wish to improve the physique of our village population let them employ itinerant sergeants ... What is the NUT doing to help us poor village teachers in this crisis? Has the Executive taken up the matter? What are the teacher MPs doing ...?[12]

The letter was published on Saturday 21 February. Two days later Macnamara asked Sir William Anson to replace the Model Course. Anson refused.[13] An NUT deputation supported by Gray and Yoxall failed to move the Board of Education.[14] Hence at the end of March, on the grounds that the Model Course was inappropriate, Macnamara moved the reduction of the vote by £100 during the Supply debate. In the Course, he said, he recognised an old friend. It had been very unintelligently prepared from the earlier part of the infantry drill book for Army recruits which had simply been adopted with a few verbal alterations to suit scholars in elementary schools. Several of the exercises were harmful. One, known as 'pressing from the ground', required a child to lie prone resting on the palms of his hands and the tips of his toes.[15] To laughter, the *Schoolmaster* reported, he invited Anson to step out into the lobby and show hon. members how the exercise could be done. The idea that it was necessary to associate the school with the Army, he said, was one that he objected to very strongly. They had no right to compel a working man to send his children to school with the object of recruiting them for the Army in the school playground. At the end of the drill programme was a letter signed 'T. Kelly-Kenny, Adjutant General'. What had the Adjutant-General got to do with the Board of Education? He asked for a small expert committee consisting of a medical man, a practical school inspector, a practical teacher, an instructor of gymnastics and a woman to draw up a thoroughly good system of physical training for the schools. He was supported by Sir John Gorst, their differences about the discontinuance of suitable physical exercises in London School Board evening classes consigned to the past, and by John Burns, who suggested that if the Course under discussion were imposed on schools some parents would withdraw their children from its operation.[16]

The small Inter-Departmental Committee set up as a result of this intervention was selected on the principle that Macnamara had suggested. The 'instructor of gymnastics' was Col. G. M. Fox, enthusiastically recommended by Burns; one of the practical teachers was Marshall Jackman. In its report, published at the end of April 1904, the Committee rejected the Model Course, chiefly because it did not seem to be constructed on well-defined general principles 'educed from a consideration of the function of physical exercise as a necessary element in a well-ordered course of general education for children'.[17] The *Schoolmaster* offered its congratulations:

> The Committee not only condemn the 'Model Course', but have freed themselves and us from many of the evil traditions which have grown up in connection with physical training in schools ... The 'classified list' of exercises, as it is called by its authors, consists not of show exercises, but of such as will really improve the physique of our children.[18]

The issue of recruiting created another connection between education and the Army. In July 1903, in the House of Lords, the Earl of Meath drew the Government's attention to the Report of the Inspector-General of Recruiting for 1902, in which it was stated that 'the one subject which causes anxiety in the future ... is the gradual deterioration of the physique of the working classes from which the bulk of the recruits must always be drawn'. He asked whether the Government would be prepared to appoint a Royal Commission or a Committee of Inquiry to investigate whether the poorer populations in large towns were exposed to conditions which, if continued, would contribute to a low national standard of physical health and strength and constitute a grave national peril. Drawing also on the evidence collected by the Royal Commission on Physical Training in Scotland, he pointed out that in Edinburgh nearly thirty per cent of elementary school children were badly nourished, 19.17 per cent were in poor health, 12.33 per cent were mentally dull and 78 per cent were more or less physically weak and suffering from some kind of disease. If the children of Edinburgh were in this lamentable condition, he enquired, 'what must be the condition of those of Glasgow and of some of the more crowded cities of England?' The principal requisites in the production of a physically capable population were first, healthy parents; second, sanitary homes; third, good, abundant and well-cooked food, including a cheap supply of fresh milk; fourth, pure air and water; fifth, facilities for exercise and healthy recreation; and sixth, a good educational system, combining physical with mental and moral training. The British had founded the mightiest Empire the world had ever known, he concluded, in a characteristic peroration; they should not, by indifference and carelessness, hinder nature in her efforts to people that Empire with an Imperial race.[19]

The Duke of Devonshire, whose ministerial responsibilities since 1895 had included both education and aspects of defence, concentrated in his response on the issue of enlistment. Undoubtedly it was a serious fact that more than one in three of those who offered themselves were pronounced medically unfit. This and questions relating to deterioration had been brought to the attention of the Secretary of State for War and the Home Secretary, both of whom, he said, proposed to consult the medical profession (through the Councils of the Colleges of Physicians and Surgeons) about the need for a Royal Commission.[20] Subsequently, on 2 September, an inter-departmental committee, upon which the Board of Education secured representation, was appointed to decide on the terms of reference for such a Commission.

Questioned the following March by Gorst on the progress of this committee, Anson agreed that it had moved away from the recruitment issue to consider the physical condition of children from infancy to adolescence, placing particular emphasis on nutrition.[21] Gorst, whose growing enthusiasm for social reform was eventually to lead him into the Liberal Party, was interviewed by the committee on 25 April. Asked about the teacher as a source of information on hungry children, he recommended that the question be put to Macnamara.

Macnamara, appearing two days later, had been called to give evidence because of his experience as a member of the London School Board and his direct connection, as a teacher, with elementary education. He argued that, as a result of the influence of thirty-three years of compulsory education, the habits of discipline formed in school, the physical training given, the organised games of playgrounds and playing fields and the elevating effect of the school system upon the home, eighty per cent of working-class children had never been better off. It was the other twenty per cent that they were concerned with. Did those twenty per cent come to school habitually hungry?, he was asked. He gave a cautious answer:

> I should not put it so high as that. There are twenty per cent who come to school habitually improperly fed ... Of course the proportion would vary with the time of year. The proportion would run up in a hard winter when the building trade and allied trades are out of employment.

He recalled his days as a teacher in Bristol of 300 boys:

> I knew in a very short time the children who were hungry, by their appearance ... when the school was disbanded at midday, day after day, winter or summer, there would be twenty or thirty boys out of say, 300, who would hang about the playground ... there was nothing to go home to. I know they had nothing to eat at all ...

What he would like, he said, was that every underfed child would get a breakfast. If a meal was only provided at midday, the morning was one of torture if he was absolutely hungry:

Of course a midday dinner is more practicable, but there are lots of children coming to the poor elementary schools with regard to whom I should feel easier in my own mind if they got a breakfast as well as a dinner.[22]

Questioned about the work of the London School Board (now in the last weeks of its existence) Macnamara recalled how three committees had been set up, in 1889, 1894 and 1898. The majority of the last one (of which he had been a member) came, he said, to the very definite conclusion that voluntary effort was not enough and it had recommended that the attendance officers should ascertain which children came to school unfit to profit by school work by reason of physical disability or underfeeding. The former, he said, needed a medical inspection. For the latter, attendance officers and teachers would suffice. Then it should be the duty of the authorities to see that they were provided with food: voluntary efforts should be supervised and supplemented by the Local Authority.[23]

'Perhaps you had better give your practical suggestions in full?' he was asked.

'I can put it very shortly', he replied: 'I propose that a dining-hall should be furnished at the Johanna Street School for the three North Lambeth schools: Johanna Street, Waterloo Road and Addington Street.'

'This is a model for the treatment of the problem in every great urban centre?'

'Yes. I take those three very poor schools, and propose to provide them with a dining-hall and kitchen.'

'Would not the halls in most schools be utilisable?'

'I should object to that.'

'Why?'

'I do not think you should disorganise the school hall.'

'It is used now during the interval when the school is not utilised for educational purposes?'

'I know that, but there would be a considerable amount of dislocation. The children would come from various schools. You might have 1,000 children dining off soup in the hall. There would be a great many objections.'

'I think there would, but do you not think that we should be prepared to meet and overcome these objections from the point of view, if this plan is to be adopted, that it should be done at the least possible cost to the community?'

'I would rather have them dine in the school hall than not at all'.

The Committee was preoccupied by questions of cost. Macnamara, quoting schemes in Paris, Brussels and Vienna, explained how in 1897 the Parisian municipal school canteen system distributed 8,250,000 meals, at a cost of £70,000. He advocated that dinner coupons should be available at a convenient public office, for example the town hall or the district council office. In Paris, payments for coupons amounted to about £30,000; the rest of the cost was met from the rates. Therefore, because its child population was three times larger, London would need to raise £120,000, which was about three farthings in the pound on the rateable value. 'Assuming nothing was recovered from the parents, but that the parents paid for tickets voluntarily where they could?', he was asked. 'We hope, of course, that a great deal would be recovered', he replied, 'but that is assuming that nothing was recovered.' The Committee saw that the assumption of food provision functions might affect voluntary effort and might even sap it at its source. Macnamara acknowledged the possibility.[24]

Regarding medical inspections, Macnamara (in his documentary evidence) had drawn on the article in the second volume of Special Reports on Educational Subjects (published through the Education Department) which described the system in operation in Brussels where the eyes, teeth, ears and general physical condition of every child were overhauled every ten days. Again the Committee reacted to the financial implications. 'The cost of applying such a system to London upon that scale would be very considerable, would it not?', Macnamara was asked. He pointed out that the medical men involved worked part-time and agreed that once every ten days was over-frequent. 'Then there are a great many schools where that would be wholly superfluous?' 'I think in every elementary school every child ought to come under medical supervision', he replied.[25]

The Committee's report was published at the end of July. The *Schoolmaster* commented:

> It is the best bit of Imperialism that has come our way for a long time. It is a deeply suggestive sermon preached to our own text that 'True Imperialism should begin at home' ... Many of the recommendations deal with the betterment of condition of adult life, particularly in our great Urban Centres ... not less far-reaching and comprehensive is the valuable list of recommendations affecting child life ...[26]

Medical inspection of school children was emphatically recommended on the grounds that in a country without compulsory military service, the period of school life offered the State its only opportunity for taking stock of the physique of the whole population and securing, to its profit, the conditions most favourable to healthy development. Referring to the striking consensus that had been reached about the effects of improper or insufficient food in determining physique, the report recommended, under the heading 'Feeding of Elementary School Children', that definite provision should be made by the various Local Authorities: the school to supply the 'machinery' or accommodation and benevolent agencies to supply the food. This was described as a working adjustment between the privileges of charity and the obligations of the community; but it was admitted also that in some districts such an arrangement would prove inadequate so that municipal aid on a larger scale would have to be supplied.[27]

'We offer no apology for referring again to the condition of the more neglected children, in the poorer parts of our great cities especially, who are compelled from hard necessity to attend school insufficiently or improperly fed', Macnamara wrote in a *Schoolmaster* editorial on 13 August.

Now he was looking for an effective remedy. Admirable ministration was being rendered by benevolent agencies. Teachers were giving time and money. But, he asked, was voluntary effort sufficient to meet the case?

> ... We frankly confess that for many years we held that it was. But longer experience and closer investigation has driven us to the conclusion – and with us we believe we have the great bulk of those engaged on this work day by day ... – that the matter will never be satisfactorily dealt with until it becomes the direct duty of the public authority charged with the supervision of the public elementary education.[28]

Through the *Daily News* he appealed to Education Committee members in the great urban centres to table motions based on the Inter-Departmental Committee's recommendations and to back them up with evidence derived from local first-hand investigations.[29] At the NUT Executive meeting on 3 September, Macnamara introduced a resolution, intended for the next annual conference, at Llandudno, that:

> legislation is urgently needed by which the Local Education Authorities shall be empowered (1) to make provision, if they deem necessary, whereby children suffering from lack of proper food shall receive the same; and (2) to take such action as may seem desirable for the recovery of the cost of such provided food from the parents or guardians of the children receiving the same.

He quoted both the Physical Deterioration Committee Report and also the Royal Commission on Physical Drill in Scotland which had reached the conclusion that, unless children received sufficient nourishment, they could not be expected to profit by the mental or physical training provided for them. The Executive was entitled to ask if the feeding of improperly and imperfectly fed children was defrayed by public expenditure, would parental responsibility be undermined? It was a question which naturally presented itself. Parents who could make proper provision for their children would be called upon to do so; those who through illness or misfortune could not make provision, should be assisted out of public funds. Those who were able to make provision, but, through thriftlessness and self-indulgence, neglected their parental duty, would, however, have to be punished for their negligence. He explained the plan he had described to the Physical Deterioration Committee: the poorer schools would be scheduled in groups of six and a school kitchen provided for each group. The kitchen would be under the control of a public official and a public office would be established at which parents could procure tickets free or on payment, the tickets all being in appearance the same. Some doubts were expressed by other Executive members about the plan and its effect on parents. A. W. Dakers commented that it would be a sorry state of things if the English working classes, like the Roman proletariat, came to care for nought but plays and games. He was, he said, in favour of stringent measures for recovering the costs so that the municipality or the Imperial

Exchequer was not weighted with the responsibility that parents ought to discharge. But an amendment to Macnamara's resolution by Jackman to the effect that grants should be given from the Central Exchequer towards local expenditure was approved and accepted by Macnamara himself.[30]

Macnamara had built a reputation as one of the best platform speakers of his day. Teacher audiences had shown him the need to master a subject, be pithy and forcible in style and logical in his conclusion. For political meetings he developed a talent for repartee particularly valuable in encounters with his constituents in the Old Kent Road, restless, elusive, easily wearied, delighting in the disconcerting interruption. Once, describing the defects of the Workmen's Compensation Act, he observed that if he were a painter, painting the outside of a ship, and fell into the water he would be classed as a sailor and therefore get no compensation. 'You ought to have fallen into fresh water!', a man in the front row inexplicably called out. 'Everybody laughed, and then waited for my retort', Macnamara recalled. 'You take care you don't fall into whisky and water', he responded, frankly conscious that he had perpetrated an equal absurdity. The cheers that followed showed, however, that he had hit the spot. Meetings in Scotland, Wales and the North of England took him often from home. In Yorkshire, on one occasion, he was reminded how his children missed him. He arrived in a big rough travelling coat. Throwing it over the back of a chair on the platform as he faced his audience he was disconcerted to hear what proved to be a handful of walnuts roll down the slope. His son Brian had secretly put them in the pocket for the journey.[31]

The speech Macnamara made at Llandudno moving the amended resolution on the feeding of children exemplifies his oratorical style. There was no need, he began, to argue there the extent to which unhappy little scraps of humanity (a favourite expression of his) were compelled to go to school day by day hungry and ill-fed (Hear, hear). If there was a class in the community who had that bitter story written deeply upon their heart, it was the class of the elementary school teachers to which they belonged (Applause). Out of his scanty purse and hard-earned leisure, the school teacher had ministered to the wants of those children in times gone by to an extent he need not now dilate upon. He need not argue the case that nothing whatever must be done to undermine parental responsibility (Applause) – that if school meal provision was to be taken up as a public obligation the work of carrying it out and supervising it must be done by others than the school teacher (Applause). He laid the greatest stress upon that (Hear, hear).

There was one outstanding point of controversy that he must discuss with them, he went on: was food still to be provided by charity, or should it be a public obligation guaranteed from the public purse? He would confine himself exclusively to a discussion of that proposition. He admitted frankly that when he began as a teacher in a slum school, he held the view that underfeeding could be dealt with by charity. He was grateful to Mrs

Burgwin, George R. Sims and W. H. Libby of the East Lambeth Teachers' Association who had ministered to the needs of children in the past (Cheers). But charity had disadvantages: it fluctuated and it undermined parental responsibility (Applause). He explained his scheme and how parents would participate. If a parent, as the result of ill-health, lack of employment, or misfortune, could not pay for dinner coupons, he would receive them gratuitously, without any suggestion of pauperisation (Applause). If he could pay for them he must do so, and the great bulk would pay (Applause). They knew better than any class of the community that the lives of the working classes in the great bulk of cases were one long self-sacrifice (Applause) and they would pay if they could. But if they could pay and would not, because of drunkenness, thriftlessness and self-indulgence -and there was too much of that amongst the working class – then they must be pursued with the utmost rigour of the law to recover the cost of the meal and if necessary sent to gaol (Applause). He explained how the system he was advocating had already been taken up in many continental cities. He knew that his colleagues the audience would say it sounded like socialism (Hear, hear). It would take a great deal more than that to frighten him, but whether it was Socialistic or not, it was first-class Imperialism ('Yes' and 'No'). It was true Imperialism, because it began at home. They loved their country (Applause) and believed in its mission among the peoples of the world. They wanted its future to be a transcendental reflection of its glorious past, but they must and did shudder as they contemplated the spectacle of the rickety, misshapen, helpless shoulders of tens of thousands of those upon whom the burden of this great Empire would ultimately rest (Hear, hear) ... Let him read an extract from a speech delivered on 24 October 1900 by Mr Joseph Chamberlain, much of which he entirely agreed with:

> Think of it, gentlemen, an Empire such as the world has never seen. Think of its area, covering a great portion of the globe. Think of its population, embracing 400,000,000 of the people of almost every race under the sun. Think of the diversity of its products. There is nothing that it is necessary or useful, or grateful to man which is not produced under the Union Jack (Applause).

Yes, but they had to think of several other things. They had to think of the spectacle of the future Imperial citizens of the world-wide Empire foraging in the gutters for the garbage that fell from the costers' carts (Hear, hear). They had not only to sing 'Rule Britannia', but they had to weave the burden of Rule Britannia into the clauses of many a new social statute which they hoped would be made law for the good and the betterment of the people of the country (Applause). They had not only to think of those flamboyant attributes of Empire and of the Arabs of the Soudan and Kordofan. They had to think of the little arabs of the slums of Liverpool, Birmingham, Manchester and London (Applause). They had to remember that the youth of the nation were the trustees of posterity (Applause). They had to remember, he concluded, as they spent their sixty millions year by year upon their far-flung navies, their massed battalions, their shrapnel, their cordite, and their engines of war, that it was not out of the mouths of the knitted gun nor the smoothed rifle, but out of the mouths of babes and sucklings that the strength was ordained that would still the enemy and the avenger. The next speaker, Walter Shawcross, seconding the motion, ruefully asked what he could say after such a speech (Applause).[32]

This was in April 1905. In the meantime, from the beginning of the Parliamentary session, Macnamara and Gorst repeatedly pressed the Prime Minister, the Parliamentary Secretary of the Board of Education and the President of the Local Government Board to state in what respects they intended to carry out the recommendations of the Inter-Departmental Committee on Physical Deterioration. 'Never was seen such a campaign', the *Practical Teacher* reported:

> They have stood like Mrs Squeers and Fanny, brimstone-and-treacle basin and gravy-spoon in hand, dosing the Ministers with the Deterioration and Food-lessness of the young ... And the House of Commons has sat by quietly, not rising in its wrath and squelching the gruellers ... What member of Parliament who proposes to submit himself for re-election, at a date which may be the day after to-morrow (for nobody can tell), likes to be marked down and black-listed as an enemy to the feeding of starveling children? [33]

On 21 February, Anson, responding to Macnamara, said that he had considered the recommendations; some of them would need legislation to bring them into effect, while others might be carried out through the agency of local or central administration. He went on:

> But I think that the hon member will see how impossible it is for me to state in answer to a question the view of the Board as to what is expedient or possible in respect of recommendations which are fifty-four in number and which, in some cases, touch on topics of a highly controversial character.[34]

It was clear that the Government proposed to take no action; instead, as the *Schoolmaster* commented, in an editorial entitled 'Imperialism and the Race', it proposed to stuff the magnificent report into one of its dusty pigeon holes. The editorial continued:

> We do not think it should be allowed to do this. Further, we believe that there are as many men on its own benches who will press for materialisation of the admirable reforms suggested by this Committee as there are on the benches opposite. It is with every confidence, therefore, that we decline to take the present as the last word on the matter. As it seems to us, here is a chance for the NUT, which ought to hold a demonstration in every great town, and particularly in London, in favour of the prompt carrying out of the main recommendations of the Physical Deterioration Committee.[35]

On the morning of Wednesday 15 March 1905, Macnamara paid a visit to the Johanna Street School, East Lambeth, which he had advocated as the centre for his school dinner experiment. He was accompanied by his new ally, Gorst,[36] the Countess of Warwick (the Socialist and former socialite who had assisted in the rural schools campaign five years before),[37] and Dr Robert Hutchinson, a physician of the Great Ormond Street Children's Hospital. A systematic inspection of the various classes was carried out with the assistance of the headmaster. The boys in the lower Standards were worst off. Two in Standard I, six in Standard II and nine in Standard III had not breakfasted. In Standard II, Dr Hutchinson found that forty-five out of the total of fifty-six were suffering from habitual underfeeding; thirty-four could not go home at midday because there would be no dinner for them. Dinner tickets provided by charitable agencies were available for only twenty-four. The girls appeared to be better fed though again the visitors encountered several who had not tasted food that morning. The headmistress explained how there were only twelve breakfast tickets for 252 children; she needed fifty. The following week, as a result of diminishing subscriptions, the number of breakfast tickets would be reduced by thirty per cent and the dinner tickets by fifty per cent.

The visitors moved on to Kennington, where the Lambeth Board of Guardians was in session. Invited to address the Board as a deputation, all four described what they had seen that morning at Johanna Street. When they had left, to draw up a report which they forwarded to the London County Council and the Board of Education, the Guardians empowered the relieving officer to visit the school and take action on pressing cases of destitution.[38]

An immediate effect of the Johanna Street School visit was that Anson, the Parliamentary Secretary to the Board of Education, hastened to Lambeth to see conditions for himself. As he may well have expected, he was closely questioned by both Gorst and Macnamara on the physical condition of the children. But by now the Government had decided how it would deal with the Physical Deterioration Committee Report. 'I cannot say that on the occasion of my visit any children were unfit to receive instruction owing to hunger', Anson responded, 'though I formed an opinion that, owing to long-continued unhealthy conditions of life, some of the children were backward in development and needed a simpler, and in some respects a different, course of instruction.' On the specific question of food he added:

> My inquiries on this subject have led me to believe that the wisdom of preparing and cooking meals on the school premises, as a mode of dealing with those cases in which children need to be provided with food elsewhere than at home, is seriously open to question.[39]

Failing government action, individual MPs attempted to advance the cause of school meals. A group of Labour members, led by Arthur Henderson, assisted by Burns, Gorst and Macnamara, had prepared a

Hungry Children Bill, cited as the Education (Provision of Meals) Bill 1905, by which Education Authorities under Part III of the 1902 Act could take steps to provide food for those children who, by reason of hunger, were judged to be unable to take full advantage of the education provided for them.[40] Then, on 18 April, Bamford Slack (MP for St Albans) introduced a private member's bill on the same lines.[41] But the Government had other ideas. Macnamara asked Balfour whether his attention had been called to Henderson's Bill and whether, having regard to the recommendations of the Physical Training Commission and the Physical Deterioration Committee, he would grant facilities during the session for further progress on the measure. The Prime Minister referred to a new Inter-Departmental Committee which had been appointed on 9 March to collect information about the medical inspection of elementary school children and the provision of meals for such children by voluntary agencies. Pending the report of that committee, he said, he could not make any statement on the subject.[42]

'Simply a bare-faced and rather unworthy scheme for wasting time and for furnishing a counter-blast to the Report of the Physical Deterioration Committee so far as it affected the question of the hungry child', the *Schoolmaster* commented, after the new committee published its findings in November and it emerged that its members had been instructed that no Treasury funds were available.[43] Gorst and Macnamara had been invited to give further evidence, but in the circumstances they declined. Apart from this fruitless exercise the Unionist Government's contribution to the solution of the under-feeding problem was limited to a Relief (School Children) Order from the Local Government Board, extending (without further subsidy) the powers of the Boards of Guardians in such cases. In the House, Macnamara welcomed the Order, but said that he feared it would be dead letter in London and elsewhere, since poor parishes under a heavy burden of rates would be unlikely to take action under its provisions.[44]

Child welfare was an issue that the Liberal Party could have taken up. Macnamara himself had provided a sketch for improved public elementary school health in the *Contemporary Review* of February 1905. The great Education Act of 1870 had acted like a social lever, inserted a little above the base of the social pyramid. As a result eighty per cent of working-class children were better off through the discipline and physical training provided in the schools. The remaining 1,500,000 were in the most hopeless condition with regard to food, clothing and housing. In towns, slum children habitually went to school improperly fed. In agricultural villages, Macnamara added, diet was similarly inadequate. He described 'tea kettle broth', the regulation breakfast in many a West Country labourer's cottage, consisting of bread crumbled into a bowl to which a little dripping, pepper and salt and boiling water were added. To meet these deficiencies he laid out once again the plans for school dinners he had described to the Physical Deterioration

Committee, adding proposals for the provision of continuous medical supervision in public elementary schools; development of continuation school courses for adolescents in nutrition and physical training, including compulsory evening drill for youths between fourteen and twenty (a Liberal response to pressure over conscription) and brief suggestions for building schools and housing outside rather than in the midst of congested manufacturing centres.[45] The party leadership failed to respond.[46]

Another important issue, the Government's policy over the provision of public secondary schools, in which the Liberals could have taken up the party's traditional line of opening up opportunities to the less privileged, was also neglected. One of the reasons why the NUT had accepted the terms of the 1902 Act was that the new administrative structure that it introduced seemed to promise the coordination of elementary and secondary education. The Higher Grade Schools of the 1890s and the sprinkling of scholarships to established secondary schools had enabled hundreds of public elementary school pupils to scramble on to the ladder that led to a university. What was now sought by the NUT was 'linkage' of schools to make it possible for the poor child to move uninterruptedly from grade to grade.[47]

The implementation of the Acts of 1902 and 1903 began promisingly for the children who were to pass through them. Every public elementary school, whether provided or non-provided, was given lofty and explicit aims, stated in the Code of Regulations for 1904 and reprinted for over thirty years afterwards: 'to form and strengthen the character and to develop the intelligence of the children entrusted to it'; teachers were encouraged to endeavour 'to implant in the children habits of industry, self-control and courageous perseverance in the face of difficulties' and the interest and cooperation of the parents and the home were invited.[48] All this was a tacit recognition of the work achieved by teachers since the Forster Act, but especially since the restrictions of Payment by Results had been lifted by Sir William Hart Dyke and Sir George Kekewich. But the distinction between elementary and secondary school was suggested by means of 'an important though subsidiary object' of the elementary school:

> ... to discover individual children who show promise of exceptional capacity, and to develop their special gifts (so far as this can be done without sacrificing the interests of the majority of the children) so that they may be qualified to pass at the proper age into Secondary Schools, and be able to derive the maximum of benefit from the education there offered them.

The Bryce Commission had not recommended that secondary education should be available to the whole community. It had, however, urged that ample provision should be made by every Local Authority to assist poorer boys and girls by means of a graduated system of scholarships. In 1899 Macnamara had expressed the hope that secondary education, if cast on genuinely national lines, could be made 'the instrument not only of a great educational advantage for the country, but also of a great social leavening that steadily, if silently, would lead to the obliteration of the class prejudices that eat so deeply into our national life'.[49] In the *Fortnightly Review* of July 1904 he called for an adequate national system of scholarships, pointing out that by comparison with the older cities of the country, most of the county areas and all the newer districts were by no means so well supplied:

> To-day many a potential Faraday is washing bottles in the public-house backyard; many a potential Herschel is scaring crows on the country-side; many a potential Watt is crying 'Xtra Speshul' through the gutters at midnight; and many a potential Arkwright is scavenging the floors of the Lancashire cotton-mill.[50]

Action through Local Authority initiative rather than through Board of Education diktat had apparently been Balfour's aim. Meeting an agricultural deputation on 13 June 1902, he had forecast that the Board would more and more recede from the position of the universal manager of all schools and become a great advisory body.[51] But Morant, the now well-established Permanent Secretary, began to display an increasingly directive tendency.[52] In his Regulations for Secondary Schools of 1904, he made clear that the Board had taken on the responsibility of superintending and promoting the supply, by Local Education Authorities, of education other than elementary and it had become a matter of urgency to place the administration of grants upon a wider and firmer basis.[53] The *Schoolmaster*, in an editorial entitled 'How Not to Organise Secondary Education', attacked the document fiercely:

> That these are cleverly compiled and scholarly in their style goes without saying ... But the fundamental consideration to be kept in view is the necessity so to organise public Secondary Education as that it shall form a constituent part of the general provision of National Education as a whole. With this in view the Board of Education would have remembered that the base of the pyramid is the public provision of Primary Education, and that public aid on behalf of Secondary Education should be so offered as to secure that the Secondary School shall be found to be linked organically to the Elementary School and be in effect more or less of a telescopic development of the educationally humbler institution below it. At the other end the scope of the Secondary School should be so directed as to cause it to dovetail easily into the institutions for Higher Education above it ... really these Regulations constitute a serious breach of faith with the public.[54]

Administrative enactment based upon the Regulations followed over the next few months. The *Schoolmaster* commented in March 1905:

> Not only has the Board of Education failed as we think to build wisely in this matter of the new provision of Secondary Education ... it has grossly broken faith with the new Local Education Authorities. According to the Government pledges of 1902, all publicly-aided education within each area was to be put

into the hands of the great Local Authorities then about to be created. Yet forsooth, these 'Regulations' insist that a Local Education Authority must not conduct a Public Secondary School itself! It can only do so through a separate and semi–independent board of 'Governors'!

Instead of a system of cheap, effective and democratically-based public secondary schools, the Board of Education was treating secondary education as a class issue. This was clear from the way in which the Board of Education was dealing with the vital questions of fees and scholarships. It had been writing all over the country, insisting upon a minimum fee of £3 per annum:

> Imagine the result upon a working-class Secondary School -known in the past as a Higher Grade School – where the fee is 6d, 9d or even 1s a week! What a climax of cynicism to call upon a working-man parent already sacrificing the immediate advantage to the home of the few shillings a week which the child might be earning – to pay £3 a year. Ah yes! We shall be told: There are free places. So there are. And the Board of Education has had, we think, the impertinence to tell Local Authorities that 'the number granted should in no circumstances exceed twenty-five per cent of the total number of scholars in the school'.[55]

In the House of Commons, on 30 March, a brief opportunity arose during the Third Reading of the Consolidated Fund (No. 1) Bill to discuss the new Regulations. George White (Norfolk, NW) ex-President of the Baptist Union said that he was jealous of anything that would interfere with secondary education in connection with the poorer children. The Board of Education should give the Education Authorities a spur in this matter and not obstruct them. Macnamara supported him. It was the first step that counted. If they went wrong and provided for a particular class as against the whole community, if they built secondary schools as a thing for a special class of the community and not for the whole nation, 'then they would have done something to cut more deeply the social differences which marked our people'. He hoped, he said, that the Government would leave the Local Authorities (subject to the veto of the Board of Education) absolutely unfettered to carry out secondary education not as a mere class or exclusive provision, but as a provision for the whole community.[56] What this amounted to was a declaration in favour of secondary education for all: ignored by the Liberal Party leadership, it had to wait another twenty years to be adopted by the Labour Party, a further twenty for realisation.

Whilst the idea of creating a new system of secondary schools failed to catch the interest of both Liberals and Conservatives, the old familiar issue of financial aid to voluntary schools retained its attraction. If Balfour, in his desire to assist these schools, had merely continued the Treasury grants which they had been able to claim for nearly seventy years, no new issue need have arisen. But the South African War had made such a move impossible. The Imperial Exchequer had been depleted by the expenditure of nearly £223,000,000. So the newly designated 'non-provided schools' were permitted to share in the rates. The matter had been vigorously taken up in August 1902 by the Rev. John Clifford of Westbourne Park Chapel, Paddington, President of the Baptist Union. He declared:

> The Prime Minister has driven through Committee an enactment by which the whole burden of Denominational Schools is to be placed upon the shoulders of the people, but from whose real management they are intentionally and expressly excluded. Two-thirds of the managers in schools the whole cost of which is to fall on the taxpayer and ratepayer are clerical. That is the fact. What does it mean? Nothing less than the denial by statute of popular control of institutions whose entire maintenance is derived from the people; that is nothing less than the violation of the vital constitutional right of citizens to govern themselves.[57]

Dr Robertson Nicoll, editor of the *British Weekly*, asked in the *Contemporary Review* in November what the Nonconformists were to do if the Act was passed. They had already pledged themselves in ever-increasing numbers to do their best to make it unworkable. This they could do in various ways, through their powers on the councils, through their refusal to send children into voluntary schools, but mainly through passive resistance, a policy supported overwhelmingly by Free Church Councils and Baptist and Congregational Unions.[58]

In his final speech during the Third Reading of the 1902 Act, Balfour had shown some apprehension about Nonconformist reactions:

> I do make this demand on the patriotism and public spirit of every class, clerical and non clerical, in this country, that when this Bill becomes law they shall do their best to work it while it is unamended, and, if it requires amendment, that they shall use constitutional means to amend it in conformity with the declared will of the people.[59]

Macnamara responded with an article entitled 'The New Education Act at Work' in the *Fortnightly Review* of January 1903. Examining the local management of schools clause, whereby only two of a former voluntary school's managers were to be publicly appointed (the other four being denominationalists), he suggested that an incoming Liberal government could amend it by a one-clause bill within a week. Ultimately, he concluded, a national system would emerge with all schools under complete public control and denominational school buildings rented to the authorities for the hours they would be needed. Religious instruction would take the form of an undenominational opening service, after-hours right of entry being conceded to denominationalists for teaching purposes. All teachers would thus be exempt from any theological test.[60] Similarly Augustine Birrell, the lawyer and former MP, declared in the first number of the *Independent Review* in October that, once a Liberal government was in power, a bill should be introduced not to repeal, but to modify the Acts of 1902 and 1903 so as to place all public elementary schools in England and Wales under the control of some public authority, with the natural consequence that all teacherships would be thrown open without sectarian qualification. But even modification, in Birrell's view, was a major issue. To achieve it would require a Parliamentary majority big enough to make the Government independent of the Irish vote and of the votes of the North of England because local management would activate opposition, both lay and ecclesiastical, within the House of Lords.[61] Nevertheless, in the same month Sir Henry Campbell-Bannerman, Leader of the Opposition, told a deputation of Liberals and members of religious bodies in Bolton that it would be a great dereliction of duty, not only to the party, but to the country, if Liberals did not at the earliest moment take in hand the work of redressing grievances so flagrant and injurious. 'You have been good enough to thank me for the strong stand we have taken on the subject', he said: '... and we are under great obligations to many of my comrades in the House of Commons ... we have some good fighting men, such as Mr Lloyd George, Dr Macnamara and others I can name – all zealous and very adroit and capable in putting your case before the House of Commons.'[62]

Nonconformists responded to the call for constitutional action. Furnished with copies of *The Education Act: A Hand Book for Free Church Workers*, put together by the Rev. Thomas Law, organising secretary of the National Council of Evangelical Free Churches, they moved enthusiastically into the constituencies. Between 1903 and the resignation of Balfour's government, the Liberals won sixteen seats and lost only one.[63] Political victories of this kind might well have ensured that the popular control of non-provided schools became merely one part of Liberal educational policy. Extra-constitutional action over the issue in Wales, on the other hand, concentrated all attention on this one issue and prevented the party from defining its intentions before it returned to power. Macnamara, asked about a 'no rate' movement in the autumn of 1902, had denounced the idea as unconstitutional in the extreme. In May 1903 the *Schoolmaster* reported that a passive resistance movement had begun against the payment of rates which might be deployed for the support of non-provided schools.[64] By October the tide of hostility was rising. Macnamara wrote in the *Fortnightly Review*:

> the greater part of Wales is in open revolt ... the 'Passive Resisters' now number some 50,000 persons: and in many a remote village where harmony previously reigned – born probably of pure indifference – there is now all sorts of acute trouble about the character of the religious instruction, the management of the school and so on. Meantime, the opportunity of a generation of school children is slipping away ...

Now the Tariff Reform question was beginning to convulse the Unionist Party. The education of the next generation, Macnamara argued, was far more important. Tariffs alone would not protect the future of the country. Without a proper education, no amount of fiscal juggling would save the British from being the hewers of wood and the drawers of water for their more highly trained competitors:

> that is why I wring my hands in despair while Chapel belabours Church, while Radical pulverises Tory, and while School Board member falls upon county councillor over this hopeless education controversy. The national loss involved in the continuance of the squabble would instantly – were it appreciated of the working classes themselves – compel a cessation of hostilities so that we might get on at once with the perfection of this communally vital line of national defence.[65]

Individual passive resistance declined in the face of law enforcement. In Wales other means were essayed. The 1902 Act, the so-called Church clauses of which had created the dissension, had also, by in theory devolving all educational powers and responsibility to the Local Authorities, provided the Government with some formidable antagonists prepared either to starve the non-provided schools or to ignore their right to rate income. Over the Welsh National Executive, which consisted exclusively of representatives of Welsh Local Education Authorities, hovered the figure of Lloyd George, drawing on strongly felt Nonconformist grievances in both Wales and England. During the Second Reading of the 1902 Bill he had claimed that it would rivet the clerical yoke on thousands of parishes in England; on 14 March 1904 he moved to reduce the Education Estimates by £500 as a protest against the implementation of the Act and held forth against the injustices suffered by Nonconformists in Wales, where, he said, the county councils had come to the conclusion that it would be fairer and braver to take upon themselves the responsibility of protesting than to leave it to their constituents. Later, however, pressed by Anson, he agreed that he had been considering compromise proposals put forward by the Bishop of St Asaph. He had encountered the Bishop accidentally on a train journey in February the year before. A meeting at the Westminster Palace Hotel followed, attended by representatives of the diocese of St Asaph and of the Welsh county councils. The plan that emerged was that, experimentally for three years, all public elementary schools would offer non-sectarian religious education; all, in theory at least, would admit outside clergy at fixed times, and all teacher appointments would be made by the Local Authority.[66]

Macnamara, having expressed his support for the compromise plan in the Estimates Debate,[67] took up the issue at the NUT Conference in Portsmouth in April 1904. Explaining the terms of the fixed times agreement, he explained that it was Lloyd George who had suggested that on two days a week the school timetable should begin at 9.30 am:

> the State teacher commences then ... let the other people have from nine

o'clock to half-past – technically outside the timetable; actually within the hours the children always go to school – for special denominational teaching by volunteers.

Despite his advocacy, the compromise failed to win Conference's approval. Yoxall, as General Secretary, said he could not allow Dr Macnamara to claim him as a supporter of any proposal which would involve tampering with the undenominational nature of the board schools and the freedom of the teachers in those schools (Applause). Jackman agreed. They had to look very carefully at any compromise which was going to take away their liberty.[68]

By now the Government was taking steps to deal with Local Authority passive resistance. The machinery set up under Section 16 of the 1902 Act, by which a defaulting Authority would first be the subject of a public inquiry, then, if appropriate, by compulsion under a writ of *mandamus*, was too slow. Therefore, on 26 March, Anson, under the Ten Minute rule, introduced the Education (Local Authority Default) Bill. By this one clause measure Local Authorities refusing to disburse rate-aid to non-provided schools would find the schools applying directly to Whitehall for financial support. Whitehall, having yielded to the request, would deduct the sums involved from the Exchequer Grants to which the Authority was entitled. 'We do not for a moment suppose that even Sir William Anson would look upon this as a happy issue out of the Welsh difficulty', the *Schoolmaster* commented. 'And it would be idle to imagine – in the classical language of the day – that the fighting Welshmen will take it "lying down"'.[69]

The Second Reading provided ample opportunity for Lloyd George to trumpet once again the injustices of Wales and to attack the Government for introducing what he called a spiteful little Bill. Macnamara agreed that it had been produced particularly for the purpose of dealing with Wales (though the London County Council was also withholding rates from voluntary schools); it was also futile, because it would only accentuate the irritation.[70] Nevertheless he did not join Lloyd George and twenty or so of his supporters when, during the Committee stage, they were named by the Chairman (the Deputy Speaker) for refusing to vote on the closure; he had already made clear that he was still supporting a version of the Bishop of St Asaph's scheme which, as the Education (Transferred Schools) Bill, had been introduced in the House of Lords on 9 May.[71] But while the Default Bill received the Royal Assent on 15 August, the Bishop's Bill did not survive the Parliamentary session. When his Education Act was under threat, Balfour was not interested in compromise.

The *Schoolmaster*, in an editorial at the beginning of September 1904, was not yet disposed to take the Welsh issue seriously:

The *Times* and other Unionist journals are getting quite anxious about it; column after column appears in the dailies generally about the fearful conflicts that are to come; and all sorts of quaking conjectures are put forth as to what terrible things the leader of the Wild Welshmen, Mr Lloyd George may dictate.

It offered its own forecast of what would happen. Welsh councils would put themselves in order, then apply pressure on the non-provided schools managers, insisting that buildings met Board of Education standards before rates were handed over. 'The simple outstanding question', it concluded 'will then be: "Can the Church in Wales find the money?" If not, the schools will be closed and provided schools will take their places.' This was the real situation; it was being obscured by loud and valiant protestations from both churchmen and Nonconformists about a fight to the finish.[72]

Loud and valiant protestations were what Lloyd George enjoyed and the Default Act had given him further opportunities to make them. Questioned in September, a fortnight before the Welsh National Convention, about what was going to happen in the coming autumn, he declared that the Government had made war upon Wales; it had proclaimed that the county councils were not to be trusted to handle the disbursement of rates. If the Act were invoked, the Welsh county councils would resign. This would make a Board of Education take-over financially impracticable since the only fund upon which it could draw was, according to the Act itself, the Exchequer grant due to operational councils for their own, provided schools. All teachers would be given three months' notice. 'But won't your scholars suffer by the loss of education this autumn?', he was asked. He replied:

> We shall open every Nonconformist church as a public elementary school, re-engage part of our teachers and you will see that three-fourths of the scholars now attending Church schools will leave them ... It will be the making of Young Wales. As for the funds, we shall raise the money with the aid of the English Nonconformists, who recognise that it may be good policy for them to make the Principality the area where the fight will be fought to a finish.[73]

Once the Convention had taken place, the tone of the *Schoolmaster* grew more cautious. It was now plain that the Welsh Resisters were planning not merely to replace the non-provided schools as, in time, they failed to meet Board of Education standards; it was now intended to make the 1902 Education Act a national issue by challenging the Government to invoke the Default Act with the effects that Lloyd George had described.[74] Macnamara, interviewed by the *South Wales Daily News*, responded carefully, avoiding direct reference both to the St Asaph compromise which the NUT conference had rejected and to the Default Act. The volunteers' schools project was one of enormous magnitude, he said, which would cause grave dislocation of the all too brief opportunity for a good education available to the working man's child. A peaceful settlement was still his aim. All along both he and Lloyd George had been prepared to concede facilities for specific denominational teaching on certain days in the week in the denominational schools once they had been leased to the public authority under a proper rental. The question was whether facilities should or should not be within the timetable. 'I believe I am right in suggesting that the whole difficulty, great as it is in bulk and ramified as it is in detail, has been narrowed down to this', he concluded. 'I think if pourparlers were opened, as there are such grim possibilities before both parties, that one outstanding difficulty can be solved.'[75]

Other voices were being heard in favour of a settlement. In Swansea, Arthur Thomas (a former member of the NUT Executive) warned, to applause, that children would be the sufferers if a struggle developed and urged that a parley should be held. Bryn Roberts, the Radical MP for Eifion, warned in Caernarfon that closing all Local Authority schools and replacing them with new ones in the chapel vestries was too great a sacrifice. On Lloyd George's home ground he was voted down.[76] Lloyd George himself, however, seemed at one moment ready to compromise. Approached by Tom John, the NUT Vice-President, he made it clear that he was prepared to negotiate with the Welsh bishops. Only the accident of the delayed publication of a 'no surrender' resolution by the Welsh National Liberal Council, which caused the bishops to draw back, prevented a round table conference from taking place.[77]

The *Schoolmaster* continued to report local developments in Wales, including the opening of the first of the handful of revolt schools,[78] but the column entitled 'The Situation in Wales' ceased to appear. Though Lloyd George offered the occasional challenge,[79] the crisis had passed. The NUT Annual Conference of 1905 took place at Llandudno; as President, Tom John, headmaster of Llwynypia Schools, Rhondda, described the controversy between the Welsh county councils and the Authorities of non-provided schools as:

> unhappy ... a matter of profound concern to the teaching profession, not only in Wales, but in England also ... Educationally, while this dispute holds the field, Welsh children are kept at a low standard of efficiency ... the teachers of Wales have shown a magnificent restraint, but they cannot stand an interminable stress ...[80]

Macnamara himself was weary of the issue. In his book *The Gentle Golfer* he confessed that only once had he been beguiled into an expression of that blasphemous frame of mind which had come to be associated with a bad shot: 'I was just addressing my ball to drive from the tee, when my opponent cut in with "Oh! by the way, Dr Macnamara, are you a Passive Resister?"'[81]

In the first of a series of accounts of a typical day's work by representative public men commissioned by the *Manchester Daily Dispatch* and published in July the previous year, Macnamara described how he had settled into public life. His day began with the milk cart in Rollscourt Avenue, rattling like a gun carriage in the old days. This was his automatic knocker-up at 7.30 am. His first task would be to look through *The Times*, the *Daily News* and the *Standard*:

> to read three dailies and mark passages in each with the big blue lead that is tied to my bedpost is a matter of from twenty minutes to half an hour. By and by my wife will cut out the marked passages and gum them into the dozens of books of reference which line my shelves downstairs.

At 8.00 am the postman brought a big bundle of letters and papers of all shapes and sizes. The Blue Books in the larger parcels showed where his interests lay: Transvaal Affairs, Physical Deterioration, Postmen's Conditions of Service, Police Superannuation, Housing Loans, Workmen's Trains, the Condition of the Militia Volunteers and Yeomanry, or Alien Immigration. Answering the routine letters could take half an hour or an hour. After breakfast with his wife at which, for a minute or two, he would have the only weekday glimpse of his children, one, and sometimes two, shorthand writers would arrive:

> For an hour or so I dictate the longer and more serious replies to the morning's correspondence not yet attended to, and put in some stiff journalistic work in connection with the *Schoolmaster* and other educational journals published by the Educational Newspaper Company of which I am general editor. As a rule, I can, inside a couple of hours, serve out to a first-class shorthand writer a big day's work and more.

Between 10.00 am and 11.00 am he might rush off to the House of Commons for the early (11.00 am to 2.30 pm) sitting, or if he was unusually free, put in ten to fifteen holes on the North Surrey Golf Course. After lunch in the House he would be tied to the Chamber from 3.00 pm to 7.30 pm and from 9.00 pm to midnight if the bill or motion was one in which he was interested. If not, he would 'hang about the premises ... in the Library, reading the Blue Books just issued, doing my heavier journalistic work – with the aid, again, of a shorthand writer who comes down and works in the secretary's room'. When the twelve o'clock rule was in operation, a division usually occurred at three or four minutes to midnight. It was then possible to dash out of the lobby, catch bus, tram or cab to Victoria and arrive in Herne Hill about 12.35 am. If he missed the last train to Brixton, it would be a cab ride all the way:

> So while the silent streets are being swept and flushed; while weary-footed, filmy-eyed herds of horribly done up cattle are being hustled along to their unhappy fate; and while the midnight crowds gather round the coffee stalls at Vauxhall, at Brixton, and at Herne Hill I rumble slowly past in a growler.[82]

The Blue Book on the Transvaal was evidence of Macnamara's continued interest in South Africa. In the aftermath of the Boer War an expansion of production in the Rand goldfields appeared to Lord Milner, Head of the British Administration in South Africa, to be a ready means by which the former prosperity of the region could be restored. He was persuaded by the mine-owners to support a scheme whereby, because of the shortage of black Africans, labourers (without their families) would be brought to Hong Kong from the various provinces of China, then transferred by sea to South Africa, where they would be indentured and segregated in special camps. The proposed importation, Herbert Samuel wrote in the *Contemporary Review* of April 1904, had attracted widespread attention and aroused a spirit of sincere and intense resentment. The question was not merely economic; it was a rebuff to the spirit of freedom. It also raised in a conspicuous way grave questions of race policy. So long as Transvaal was without representative institutions, the guardianship of its interests lay in the British Parliament.[83] The Liberal Party had come out against Chinese labour; on 16 February Samuel had moved an amendment to the Address with a speech lasting an hour and twenty minutes. The House had to arrive at a grave judgement, he concluded. It had to look to the future, to build up the greatness of a new British colony. It had to decide whether it would lightly permit a new community of serfs to be established under its flag.[84] He was supported by Major Seely (member for the Isle of Wight) who referred both to the people of the self-governing colonies and the people at home who had been caught up in the late war. 'They thought that we fought for great ideals', he said, 'but so surely as we imported 150,000 slaves into South Africa, so surely we would shatter these ideals.'[85] Macnamara, just before the adjournment, took up this point. The British soldier had not many ideals, he said, but he believed the British flag ensured freedom, fair play and justice for all. If after all this any self-respecting British soldier tore his South African medal from his breast and threw it in the gutter, he would have his complete and entire support.[86] Campbell-Bannerman summed up in the same vein: 'No more important issue could be put before the country', he declared, 'and I venture to say that if the Government commit the people of this country to this policy, a terrible day of reckoning will certainly come to them'.[87]

On 22 February, Macnamara moved the Adjournment of the House on the question of the promulgation of the Ordinance by which the indentured labourers were to be introduced into the Transvaal. The Ordinance, he said, had been hustled through the House with indecent haste; its regulations, the vital machinery to give it effect which, it appeared, were not even in their final form, had not been discussed at all. The regulations were at least as important as the Ordinance itself. He could find only one intelligible reason why the matter had been hurried through: the whole thing was so repugnant to the sense of the British people that the Government got it out of the way as quickly as possible.[88]

Almost a year later, moving an amendment to the Address, he returned to the question. Now there were 27,000 Chinese labourers at work; their numbers were rising. The Colonial Secretary (Alfred Lyttleton) had given assurances without which the Ordinance would not have passed. It had become painfully clear that these assurances were not being carried out. It had originally been agreed that the labourers might be accompanied by their wives; the mine-owners had raised objections but the condition had been reinstated after representations by the Bishops of Worcester and Rochester and the Archbishop of Canterbury. But, Macnamara went on, it had been ignored by Lord Milner and not included in the recruiting advertisements displayed in Tientsin. The result was that, among the thousands of labourers already in South Africa, only two had their wives with them. Apprehension had been expressed on the question of wages. The Colonial Secretary had said that he had no fear that the Chinese wage would be lower than that of the Kaffirs; once the Ordinance was passed he had been obliged to admit that while the minimum wage of the Kaffir was forty-five shillings a month, that of the Chinese labourer was only thirty. Then they had been assured, any number of times, that the Chinese were to be engaged wholly and exclusively on unskilled labour; once the Ordinance had been sanctioned the announcement was made that they could be overseers and gangers, jobs promised to whites in an attempt to persuade the British public of the opportunities available under the scheme. The Prime Minister had stated at an election meeting the previous July that the Chinese had gone to the Transvaal willingly and been introduced there at the express wish of the white population. This, Macnamara exclaimed, was the climax of effrontery. As a Colonial born, he ended his speech by reminding the House of protests received from Australia, New Zealand and Cape Colony about what he called 'the shameful sequel to a war in which our brothers across the sea freely and even eagerly spent their blood and treasure'.[89]

This time Macnamara's motion was seconded by Samuel. He described the Chinese labourers as a helot community: 'never in the history of the world had there been such an attempt as this to keep isolated and separated from the rest of the community a vast body of tens of thousands of labourers'. The Government had intended that the Transvaal should be treated as a self-governing colony: that policy had been frankly abandoned. He trusted that when a Liberal government came in, the importation of Chinese labour would cease at once.[90] In reply, Lyttleton denied all the charges.[91] 'Excellent speeches were made by Dr Macnamara and Mr Herbert Samuel', the *Liberal Magazine* reported, 'but the amendment was of course opposed by the Government and lost by 277 votes to 216.'[92] As Samuel had indicated, the Liberals, once in power, were to abandon the experiment, though it was four years after the change of government that the last Chinese labourers left South Africa.[93]

Throughout 1904 and 1905, Balfour's administration was continuously unhappy. In the *Review of Reviews* of July 1904, Macnamara foretold a majority for the Liberals, independent of all other parties, in the coming general election. The next Liberal Administration, he argued, could only justify its existence by persistent and steady democratisation of national institutions: of the electoral machinery (by making election expenses a public charge, by abolishing plural voting, by introducing a minimum residential voting qualification, by fixing an election on one day only, by applying the second ballot on obscure results and by allowing the payment of members); and of national finance, by taxing urban land values; and by introducing a progressive income tax. Democracy also required the repeal of the Chinese Labour Ordinances, the amendment of the Education Acts, the extension of Housing legislation, the introduction of Old Age Pensions and the extension of the Factory Acts. Whether or not the Liberals won a majority with Irish support, he concluded, 'it will remain the conscientious duty of every democrat to bear speedily forward towards Home Rule'.[94]

By the autumn of 1905, it was plain that the general election was imminent. Balfour had been depicted in the *Westminster Gazette* as Humpty Dumpty, clinging in apprehension to his wall, marked 'office'.[95] Soon gravity would take its toll. In November, W. T. Stead, from the Review of Reviews office, published a pre-election manifesto entitled *Coming Men on Coming Questions*. Chapter One was contributed by Churchill, Chapter Two by Earls Spencer and Rosebery, both unfortunate choices since the former had just been struck down by a mortal illness and the latter was to have no future in government. Chapters Three and Four were to have been furnished by John Burns and Lloyd George, but Burns, Stead explained, could not write it and Lloyd George could not choose a subject. Hence the third chapter, 'The Physical Condition of the People', was by Macnamara. Stead wrote in introduction:

> The question which he deals with ... is emphatically the Coming Question Number One, although ... I have given precedence to Free Trade upon which the daily bread of our people absolutely depends. Nor is there any member or candidate who is more conspicuously marked out for dealing with his supreme problem than Thomas James Macnamara.[96]

Macnamara's treatment of the issue can be taken as a claim for office on the Local Government Board, the precursor of modern departments of Health, Employment and Housing. The people he was concerned with were the seven millions of men, women and children, the inhabitants of the slums of great cities and agricultural villages, whose food, clothing and housing conditions were, in the great bulk of cases, hopeless. Hungry children and child toilers had occupied him since his teaching days in Bristol. Now, he estimated, there were 100,000 who were so horribly treated and their surroundings so squalid, that the State should at once step in and take them out of the hands of their unworthy parents. On housing he recommended that an incoming Liberal government should tackle the land problem:

> It must enable the Municipalities to acquire land promptly, simply and cheaply.

It must lend them monies for Housing purposes from the Treasury chest on easy terms. The nation that can cheerfully spend £250,000,000 on burning the homesteads of the Boer farmers over their heads must turn to the nobler task of providing sweet, wholesome dwellings for its own homeland people.

He concluded with a characteristic peroration:

> One of the ugliest thoughts which I ever have ... is when I see ricketty, neglected, haggard little scraps of humanity ranging the gutters, or down-at-heel, broken, dilapidated men and women filling the Embankment seats, or strewing like wreckage the green sward of the Park. Because I am instantly haunted by the remembrance that each is a steward of the heritage of the British people. I believe in the British Empire. I believe in its mission among the peoples of the world. But I shudder for its future when I think of the tens of thousands of those upon whose appallingly unfit shoulders the burden of its maintenance is falling. It is for the coming Liberal Administration to spare no effort in the endeavour to make those shoulders fit.[97]

In the meanwhile, the need for a Liberal Party policy on education had become urgent. Macnamara wrote regretfully in the *Schoolmaster* on 30th September:

> See where we stand. Other nations are feverishly sharpening their wits for the keen international brain and capacity struggle in which all the peoples of the civilised world now find themselves plunged. Britain, with the greatest commercial stake among them, cannot stand unless her intellectual equipment is the most modern and perfect. And yet what are we doing? Flying at each other's throats over forms of religious instruction and dropping sand into the Educational Machinery of the Country to the praise and glory of God! If it were not nationally so acutely serious it would be ludicrous.[98]

The *Schoolmaster* took up the task of policy drafting: 'How Should the Acts of 1902–3 be Amended?', readers were asked. If the Liberals were returned to power, it would follow that once more the educational machinery of the country would be in the melting pot; therefore, the teachers should endeavour to shape public opinion; there was a danger of drifting into another Parliamentary conflict without a clear indication of the line to be pursued. So free discussion was invited about the local government of education; on whether the distinction between provided and non-provided schools should be ended; on the status of teachers in non-provided schools and on the religious question. By the beginning of December, hundreds of letters had been received and it had been concluded that education should be mainly funded by the Exchequer; that the incidence of rates should be equalised as far as possible; that London and some of the largest towns should revert to an *ad hoc* administration and some of the administrative counties should be subdivided; that the dual system of provided and non-provided schools should be abrogated so as to make all teachers employees of the Local Authority. The question of religious instruction was left till last. Significantly, a phrase so often employed by Macnamara ten years before ('there is no religious difficulty in the schools') was now expressly set aside with the explanation that the conflicts in Wales and elsewhere showed that things could not remain as they were.[99] Finding a solution was another matter. The *Schoolmaster* stated on 13 January 1906:

> Only one conspicuous conclusion arises and that is that so far as the teachers of the country are concerned ... it is the view that the teaching of religion should continue to be in the future as in the past, a characteristic feature of the English system of public elementary education.

Religious teaching of an undenominational kind, as practised under the Cowper-Temple Clause in the 1870 Act together with a conscience clause, was favoured by the bulk of opinion; it was also felt that wherever parental demand was made for denominational teaching, it should be available in the existing non-provided schools conducted by the denominations themselves, at their own expense and in no way interfering with the conduct of the school.[100]

The *Schoolmaster*'s investigation merely emphasised the Opposition's unpreparedness on educational issues. At Newcastle on 14 November, Balfour commented contemptuously that there was not a man either on their side or the Government's side who really knew what they intended to substitute for the system created by the Act of 1902.[101] On 4 December he resigned. At the time it was considered shrewd to have taken this course rather than to seek a dissolution, because Sir Henry Campbell-Bannerman, the new Prime Minister, would be obliged to make appointments and indicate policies which would revive divisions in his party and thus restore the Unionists to public favour.[102] The election results in January swiftly discredited this view.

But over education in which Balfour, anxious to preserve the legislation of 1902, had a special interest, it is plain that his tactics were successful. Campbell-Bannerman's appointment of Augustine Birrell as President of the Board of Education in a Cabinet of which, the *Crusader* judged, ten of the nineteen members (including Birrell himself) were Nonconformists, was taken as a signal that the Act of 1902 was to be overturned, even though he had declared himself in favour of modification rather than repeal.[103] 'I had no notion what was in C-B's mind', he wrote later, 'nor was I conscious of possessing any special qualifications for the office.'[104] But he felt no hesitation in accepting it and was soon involved, perhaps to his surprise, in planning the Bill which brought with it a wealth of opportunities for the Unionist Party to re-establish itself.

The *Schoolmaster* reported that appointments to non-Cabinet posts in the new Ministry would not be made until the close of the year. It was also assumed that in accordance with the Board of Education Act of 1899, the Parliamentary Secretary to the Board would not be appointed from the same House as the President.[105] Nevertheless, Campbell-Bannerman selected Macnamara. He refused; the post was accepted by Thomas Lough, MP for West Islington since 1892.

The offer, of which there was no documentary proof, provoked speculation. 'AC', in the *Practical Teacher* the following May, expressing his grief that the capable Doctor had not taken the tide at the flood, concluded that the reason for his decision lay in some restriction placed on him by the NUT. 'I am glad to recollect', he added, 'that since this great chance was missed the Executive has made such arrangements as will enable any member of the Union to whom office is offered to accept the same without apprehension as to the immediate or distant future.'[106] Lloyd George, aware of Macnamara's limited enthusiasm for the Nonconformist campaign, wrote to his brother: 'Macnamara has refused a post under Birrell in the Board of Education. Delighted he has. Would not have trusted him there.'[107] Beatrice Webb, hostile to Macnamara because of his lack of enthusiasm for the London County Council (on the education committee of which her husband was now enjoying the plenitude of power), recorded his refusal in her diary: 'it is said he could not afford to take an inferior berth or give up the editorship of the *Schoolmaster*; and he was offered no position equal to his expectations, and in that sense he is a disappointed man'.[108]

Policy rather than personal considerations appear to have caused Macnamara's decision. The NUT had decided that the 1902 Act needed amendment, to establish popular control and the abolition of creed tests, rather than replacement. But the investigation of possibilities conducted in the *Schoolmaster* since September had made one point very clear. The limited amendments desired by the NUT could not be achieved without raising the issue of religious instruction, an issue which Macnamara had thought soluble by means of outside facilities but which had proved resistant to settlement. He was therefore faced with a dilemma: to accept office, suspecting that ill-judged legislation would at once be embarked upon, or to stand aside, knowing that when the Government pressed ahead, he himself would still be expected to lend his support. Neither choice was attractive but the latter was the more sensible. Having taken it he might, in time, be offered a post more to his taste.

In retrospect his absence from the group of Liberals who planned the Bill of 1906 may be regretted. Among them Lloyd George, who had diverted his party from the practical issues of education reform back into the well-trodden area of theological debate, was still to be active. The resulting Bill was to exhaust Liberal energies in their first year of office and open up dissension with the Lords. Teachers and pupils would draw little benefit from it; for the educationists in the House of Commons it was to be a bitter and almost complete disappointment.

11

Outside and Inside the Government, 1905–1908

For a statement of Liberal Party policy and intentions on the eve of the general election of 1906, no single Liberal Party manifesto exists. Reference needs to be made to the address to the voters of Stirling Burghs by Sir Henry Campbell-Bannerman, their representative in eight successive Parliaments since 1868 and now Prime Minister. It was largely concerned with the record of the late government which Campbell-Bannerman described as 'in the main a legacy of embarrassment, an accumulation of public mischief and confusion absolutely appalling in its extent and its ramifications' and with a critique of Unionist policy for the future which, he considered, embodied the most mischievous characteristics of their past. He concluded:

> Should we be confirmed in office it will be our duty, whilst holding fast to the time-honoured principles of Liberalism – the principles of peace, economy, self-government and civil and religious liberty – and whilst resisting with all our strength the attack upon Free Trade, to repair, so far as lies in our power, the mischief wrought in recent years, and, by a course of strenuous legislation and administration, to secure those social and economic reforms which have been too long delayed.

Education, which had provoked such strong feeling both in 1902 and in Wales thereafter, received only passing mention. Along with other domestic legislation, the manifesto suggested, it had been treated by the late government more with the aim of propitiating its powerful friends than in settling a problem of national consequence with due regard to its needs.[1] It was only as the election campaign proceeded that the issue received attention. At the Albert Hall on 21 December the Prime Minister spoke of the principle of self-government and popular control:

> We believe in that principle, not only on grounds of justice and on the grounds of effective administration but on this other ground – that it exercises a wholesome influence on the character of the people who enjoy the privilege ... this is the foundation of our educational policy – that the people of the district should control and manage the schools (Loud cheers).[2]

Here was the fruit of two years of public disturbance. Its main proponent, Lloyd George, triumphantly assured his audience at Caernarfon on 2 January that an amendment of the Education Act would be one of the first legislative measures undertaken by the new Government, that it would embody the two essential principles for which Wales fought, namely, complete and absolute popular control and the complete abolition of religious tests, as well as the establishment of a Welsh National Council of Education. Birrell, the new President of the Board of Education, at Bristol the same day, confirmed that he, too, regarded popular control and the settlement of the religious instruction issue as priorities. Balfour, at the Queen's Hall on 29 December, identified the policy that was emerging. In 1902, he said, his opponents had abused the Education Bill for every kind of fault, real or imaginary, 'but they have now concentrated their efforts upon that portion of the measure which deals with the maintenance of voluntary schools and the preservation of religious teaching in the primary schools of the country'.[3]

By now a Cabinet Committee had been appointed to give legislative shape to what the new Government was still in the process of deciding was its policy. It was a strange body. Apart from Birrell it included Lloyd George, now President of the Board of Trade, Sir Henry Fowler, Chancellor of the Duchy of Lancaster, Sydney Buxton, the Postmaster General, who had been a member both of the London School Board and of the Cross Commission, with Lord Crewe (Lord President of the Council) as Chairman and Morant, entrenched and retained against expectation at the Board of Education, as Secretary.[4] Crewe, at the first meeting on 3 January, called for a large educational measure, to give the Government the opportunity to claim that a denominational settlement was only one element in a programme of national improvement. But the revival of school boards was rejected; the restoration of women's voting rights dismissed as too big a matter; the Committee toyed briefly with the idea of improved endowment schemes for secondary education only to set it aside. Finally, as the election results came in,[5] the pressure built up by Lloyd George's campaign proved irresistible. National improvement became a marginal consideration. The Bill drawn up by the Cabinet Committee centred on the abolition of non-provided schools: the Liberal government of 1906 decided to bring to an end the dual system set up by its predecessor in 1870. But following prolonged debate in the Commons it was to be rejected by the Lords. After only a year in office Campbell-Bannerman found himself on the brink of a constitutional crisis.

At the end of January, however, such an outcome would have seemed inconceivable. The election had taken place over ten days. The first result, a win for the Liberals at Ipswich, marked the beginning of the Liberal landslide. The Government and its allies won 379 seats, with an overall majority of 88 over the Unionists (157), the Irish Nationalists (83) and the Labour Party (51). In North Camberwell during the 1902 debates,

Macnamara had received a firmly-worded protest from all the Noncon-formist ministers that he was not attacking the Bill with anything like the vigour that they thought it deserved.[6] Now, having been approached by the Secretary of the Camberwell Free Church Council, he forwarded a statement in which he expressed his support for public control of schools (involving the abolition of religious tests for teachers), adding that where specific denominational teaching by voluntary agencies was permitted, rents would be charged for the use of buildings.[7] This elicited an unfavourable response from a Roman Catholic priest. Posters proclaiming 'We All Love Mac' were to be seen throughout the constituency; the priest, Macnamara related later, felt constrained by his conscience to go into the houses of the Irish residents, take the posters out of the windows and consign them to the flames.[8]

Despite this intervention Macnamara was returned with a majority of 2,817. To have established his views in favour of the eligibility of women for a reconstituted School Board for London proved to have been a shrewd precaution. Women were active at the public meetings. Asked whether he was in favour of giving every woman a vote he risked the response that every woman should have either a vote or a voter. Another woman asked him if he was in favour of the repeal of the blasphemy laws. 'Madam, I am a golfer', he replied.[9] On Wednesday 17 January a crowd of thousands assembled outside the Camberwell Baths to hear the result announced. Then a band appeared, the horses of the open landau in which Macnamara and his wife had arrived were spirited away and the victor was paraded through the constituency with his supporters between the shafts.[10]

Birrell introduced the Education Bill in the House of Commons on 9 April. The abolition of non-provided public elementary schools (all such schools coming under Local Authority control with effect from 1 January 1908) appeared to settle at once both the question of control and the issue of the creed test since Local Authority school religious instruction was of the unspecific Cowper Temple type. But it had also been decided that exemptions would be afforded. Under so-called 'Ordinary Facilities' relig-ious education of a special character might be given (but not by the teachers) in some former non-provided schools on not more than two mornings a week at parents' request; under 'Extended Facilities' religious education of a special character might be given by the teachers in other such schools without time limit. These facilities would only be afforded, however, in urban areas of 5,000 population and above, where alternative schools were available and where the Local Authority had approved a request for such facilities from the parents of at least four-fifths of the children attending the schools.[11]

'Anybody can see in the Bill the inevitable growth of the Act of 1902', the *Practical Teacher* commented. It judged that the Bill would withdraw from non-provided schools the anomalies of private management, but leave them their general Christian teaching and specific theology; that it would enable teachers to move unrestrictedly between provided and non-provided schools, taking on specific theological teaching if they so wished; that, in depriving the parson of his 'freehold' in the school, it would offer a fair price or a right to lease in return; and that it would give parents in urban areas a choice of schools whilst making the single village school undenominational. It added its customary tribute to the NUT: 'What other brains demanded these things at the first except the brains of the National Union of Teachers? Demands which have become the commonplaces of politicians were first uttered at Conference and at Russell Square.' [12]

But the picture provided by the *Practical Teacher* was too rosy. The Bill raised difficulties for teachers. Those in provided schools, for long dominant on the NUT Executive, had dutifully accepted the 1902 Act as a means of securing the same levels of pay for all their colleagues; the 1906 Bill, it was assumed, would establish the same conditions of work. On examination, however, they found it unsatisfactory: its proposal that only one kind of public elementary school, free of the creed test, would be recognised was made considerably less significant by the 'facilities' clauses. These, on the other hand, by no means satisfied those teachers in non-provided schools who were also devotees of the religious group that employed them.

As one of the original supporters of the 1902 Act, Macnamara had no wish to see it overturned. To establish public control he favoured a one-clause bill by which governing bodies would be given a Local Authority, rather than a clerical, majority; his idea of satisfying denominational groups rested on the assumption that they would be satisfied with facilities outside the day's timetable. Birrell's Bill was much more extreme. With Clause 1 it seemed set to abolish the dual system which Macnamara wished merely to adjust into more perfect equilibrium;[13] then as if in compensation it offered facilities not only within the timetable but hedged around with conditions that would restrict the teacher. To defend the 1902 settlement, give support to his party and to represent the interests of a Union which might again split as it had done in 1896 was going to be a daunting task.

The First Reading debate, giving an opportunity for the discussion of general principles, enabled him to offer support to all three causes. Prefacing his speech with the remark that he had not yet seen the text of the measure, he expressed satisfaction that the machinery of the 1902 Act was to remain substantially the same and rejoiced that the dual system was to disappear, coupling its disappearance with the abolition of creed tests. On behalf of his non-provided school teacher colleagues he raised doubts about teachers in schools granted facilities for specific denominational teaching which he supposed were to be outside the hours of the timetable. If the State teacher were allowed to become the volunteer denominational teacher, he hoped that nothing in the nature of a creed test would arise. As for the restriction on teachers volunteering for specific denominational teaching in Ordinary Facilities schools, that was something he was not going to express an opinion about, because he was in conflict about it with some of his personal associates.[14]

As in 1896 and 1902, the introduction of a major Education Bill preceded the NUT Annual Conference, this year at Scarborough, by a matter of days. When Macnamara moved the first resolution on the Bill it was in general terms: 'that this Conference expresses approval of those principles of the Education Bill of 1906 under which all public elementary schools, their teachers and managers, are to be brought under complete popular control and under which creed tests for teachers are to be abolished'. He recalled how, at the Cambridge Conference of 1899, he had moved a resolution in favour of public control which had been agreed almost unanimously. The Act of 1902 put all public elementary education upon the rates and taxes in accordance with the Cambridge decision. Even then the Archbishop of Canterbury, Dr Temple, had foreseen what the consequences would be. Now the new Bill duly removed from the denominationalists every vestige of financial responsibility left to them by the 1902 Act. The constitutional sequel was therefore popular control. The abolition of creed tests followed inevitably: no teacher employed in a public elementary school would be required by a Local Authority to give sectarian religious instruction as a condition of appointment. If this great Bill had contained nothing but clause 7, subsection 2, he concluded, it would not have been introduced in vain.[15]

Immediately the clash of interest between teachers in provided and non-provided schools became apparent. W. J. Fleming, a Roman Catholic teacher from Oldham, supporting an amendment to retain non-provided schools 'as at present', said that the intellectual giants of the Union were there to try to convince members that a common denominational system of Christianity was the best course to adopt. He did not think Conference would accept that even from Dr Macnamara, with all his wealth of rhetoric and force of eloquence. In the name of the Catholic teaching profession he declared that, by their action on the Bill, Conference was going to punish the Catholic teachers, who deserved the opportunity to impart religious education in that religious atmosphere they considered absolutely necessary for the well-being of the children (Cheers). 'What we ask for ourselves', he said, 'we want the Church of England and the other denominations, even the Nonconformists, to have as well.'

Jackman, for the Executive, responded forcefully and the amendment was defeated. He declared that as a Union of teachers they had no right to stand there and plead for any denomination (Loud applause). He reminded them of the previous year's resolution:

> that this Conference is of opinion that a satisfactory solution of the education question, in accordance with sound constitutional and educational principles, can only be found in such an amendment of the law as shall secure for the country a national system of education based upon popular control and be freed from all tests but those of character and capacity.

'Throw all the schools open', he declared, 'let us all have the same chance, let there be no differentiation of salaries, no creed tests, and then they would be one great united profession.'[16] Later the same day Charles Hole moved that any denominational religious teaching in public elementary schools should be given by persons other than the teaching staff. They had voted for the abolition of the dual system, they had said they wished to abolish religious tests; let them, he urged, go to the logical issue that the teacher should not be called on by any man to perform that for which he was not trained – specifically trained. The Bill used the term 'permitted'. Next it would be 'persuaded'; then they would have some veiled compulsion. His aim was to shake the fetters off the teachers' wrists.[17]

It was also evident that some teachers in non-provided schools regarded religious instruction as a privilege rather than an imposition and that this was by no means the simple question that Hole had assumed it to be, but insufficient time was left at the Conference to reach a solution. Consequently at the Executive meeting on 5 May Jackman moved the Education Bill be amended to provide that no teacher appointed or transferred after 1 January 1908 would be allowed to volunteer to give denominational religious instruction. It was the Union's function, he said, to approach the question from a purely professional point of view. Some teachers were willing to carry on denominational instruction from purely conscientious motives, though they were also strongly opposed to creed tests. It was quite impossible to support both positions. If the first obtained, the second must go. He concluded:

> The truth is that freedom can only be obtained by the restriction of liberty. It was a safeguard in most cases to have one's course of action defined from without, as it prevents the operation of undue influences which the individual might find difficult to combat of his own free will.

He offered, as a compromise, that the prohibition should apply only to future teachers. Those teachers who had already been tested and were carrying on sectarian teaching should continue to do so.

The disagreement to which Macnamara had referred in the Commons had surfaced. This would never do, he said. To divide teachers into two groups would not work. It must be one thing or the other, and in his view the wisest and safest policy was to let the teacher please himself. He moved the rescission of the resolution to restrict denominational teaching in public elementary schools to persons other than the teaching staff, saying that if they persisted in preventing volunteering, what would happen would be that the clerical amateur would go into the school, to be followed by representatives of Nonconformity. That was to create pandemonium. But the move to rescind was voted down by twenty-seven votes to twenty. The Union's policy, despite strong feeling within its ranks, was now to withdraw all teachers from specific religious teaching, making non-denominational Bible teaching the norm in all public elementary schools.[18]

The following Monday, the Second Reading began. Macnamara, answering George Wyndham, the Opposition's main speaker, met his first objection, that non-provided school buildings were in effect to be confiscated, with the arguments of the Bishop of Hereford, who had said that under the Bill the Church schools in his diocese would be better off than ever before. The other main attack on the Bill, he said, raged round the eternal religious question. The Government, in dealing with this question, had put aside the possibility that denominational teaching for all was entirely impracticable. But to confine instruction to purely secular teaching was hopelessly out of touch with national sentiment. 'There remains', he concluded, 'only the system of the State's giving simple biblical teaching, leaving to outside teachers the task of adding a denominational superstructure. That is the scheme of the Bill ...' [19]

Described thus, the Bill had a simple logic, but the discussion at the Executive the previous Saturday had made clear that the 'facilities' offered to various denominations complicated the issue, dividing teachers into non-denominationalists and denominationalists and dividing even the denominationalists into those who wished to give religious instruction and those who did not. Despite the Executive's decision, both Macnamara and Yoxall chose to support the Bill as it stood. 'For the first time in the history of this country', Macnamara stated, '... no teacher will be compelled to give religious instruction unless he likes',[20] Yoxall adding (two days later) that it might be provided that there should be full liberty to do so, so long as the 'volunteer' was not compelled to become a 'pressed man'.[21] But, as Balfour perceived, to employ teachers on denominational religious teaching unavoidably involved a test, specifically abolished by Clause 7 (2) of the Bill. He said scornfully:

> I think they [the Government] are conscious of the extraordinary absurdity of getting teachers, whether to teach Roman Catholicism or Anglicanism or Wesleyanism under Clause 4, without making adequate inquiries as to whether they really heartily accept the teaching of the denomination whose children are to be committed to their charge.[22]

'Toujours the Bill. Three days a week. Three days of hard labour. Three sweltering days a week – dog-days; and sometimes the mental and moral thermometer higher than the Fahrenheit recorder', the *Practical Teacher* complained as the committee stage, begun on 21 May, finally drew to a close on 18 July:

> Very little about education in it, even to begin with, even in cold print; but now, in hot verbiage, how the education in it shrinks and disappears! Welsh National Council, endowments and trust deeds, postponement of Clause 1, deferring of date of operation; on these we heard the members orating, railing, raving for days and nights. Is it any wonder that we are all cynics up in the Press Gallery? [23]

But the *Schoolmaster*, discussing what it called 'the End of the First Chapter', expressed relief:

> Certainly the Opposition are to be congratulated upon their general attitude. There has been absolutely nothing in the nature of Obstruction ... the members of the Opposition as a whole have set themselves out to the honest endeavour to improve the details of the Bill.[24]

The Government's proposals on absorption, on the creed test and on ordinary and extended facilities, remained in place. So did the subclause forbidding teachers to give any religious instruction of a special character, which had divided the NUT Executive.[25] On 3 July, Sir Michael Hicks Beach moved that it be removed, arguing that the teachers valued the privilege of giving that instruction as much as any part of their duties and were by no means anxious to give it up. But the Jackman line was forcefully taken up by Francis Dyke Acland, the Liberal member for Yorkshire, Richmond. If it was omitted, he said, they must say goodbye altogether to the idea that they were getting rid of tests for teachers. When the amendment was put to the vote, the subclause was retained by 318 to 191, with Yoxall voting in favour. Macnamara was absent.[26]

One amendment, making medical inspections of children in public elementary schools not merely possible but compulsory, was acclaimed from both sides of the House. H. J. Tennant, the Liberal member for Berwickshire, had introduced it on 16 July. Sir William Anson observed how satisfactory it was for anyone who really cared for the education of the children that after the wearisome controversies of the last six weeks, they had now come to some solid ground. Macnamara, drawing on his knowledge of London children, recommended that every child on admission to school should be medically examined and a record kept. One sixth at least of poor children were almost hopeless, some with running eyes and ears full of matter, and not one per cent of them had sound teeth. If they could get the amendment carried, he concluded, it would be worth all the rest of the Bill put together. Balfour urged the Government to take counsel from the hon. member for North Camberwell and other hon. Gentlemen and accept compulsory medical examination. Birrell duly concurred.[27]

With the Commons' Third Reading and the Lords' First Reading on 30 July and three days' full-dress debate on the Second Reading in the Lords, the Bill was left hung up, as the *Practical Teacher* put it, to mellow like a piece of venison until the end of October.[28] Macnamara, in a speech during the Third Reading, observed what a remarkable change had come over the temper of the Opposition as the debate proceeded:

> It began with fury and passion and frantic thumping of the drum ecclesiastic; but it has steadily moderated its tune and tone, until today it is a half apologetic pianissimo ... There will be amendments in another place; there will have to

be a conference between the Houses and give-and-take; but the Bill is going to pass into law.[29]

Balfour spoke next. The hon. member for North Camberwell seemed to think that the opposition to the Bill on its introduction was more vehement than now, he said, and that our protests have weakened:

> I am not sure that I agree with the hon member. I admit that in hot weather it is difficult to give the same vigorous expression to one's feelings as in different climatic conditions. But I believe there is a more important cause for the change which the hon Gentleman finds in our debates. I think most of us have begun to feel that the real discussion ... must be elsewhere ... another place is going to deal with large tracts of the Bill which we have not found time even to touch upon, and ... it is in the highest degree improbable that the Bill will come back in the shape in which it leaves us.

He went on to imply that Macnamara's support for the Bill was not whole-hearted. The Government had brought it forward as a solution of the education question: 'About that the hon Gentleman the member for North Camberwell and I, who have fought this education question for many years, are less sanguine than the relative novices on the Treasury bench; we at all events take less sanguine views'. The Act of 1902 had left in existence the two great classes of schools recognised in 1870: they could not be left in existence and efficient under any other arrangement than that of the Act of 1902.[30] The former Prime Minister intended to preserve his own handiwork; the speech of the Archbishop of Canterbury, Randall Davidson, in the Lords on 1 August made it clear where his main support was to come from.[31] 'The Speech of the Primate on Wednesday leaves no doubt as to the fate of the Bill in the Lords', the *Schoolmaster* reported: 'It will be read a Second Time and then drastically amended in Committee.'[32]

Macnamara, as Balfour had perceived, would have preferred to improve the social provisions of the elementary school system than devote any more time to the religious question. Birrell's Bill now offered compulsory medical inspections; a private member's bill, introduced by W. T. Wilson, the Labour member for Westhoughton, made possible the provision of school meals. After its Second Reading on 2 March it was referred to a Select Committee which began its enquiries less than a fortnight later and continued in session till the beginning of July. With Macnamara amongst its members was C. P. Trevelyan, his former colleague on the London School Board. This was now the fourth Parliamentary investigation in as many years following the Royal Commission on Physical Training (Scotland) (1903), the Inter-Departmental Committee on Physical Deterioration (1904) and the Inter-Departmental Committee on Medical Inspection and Feeding (1905). The basic question remained whether the limited provision of meals (usually in the winter only) should continue to be the responsibility of voluntary agencies or whether the Local Education Authorities should be empowered to supersede them. As the Committee's report was to show, such a change was viewed with apprehension. It was perceived that the provision of meals out of the rates or from Exchequer grants would result in the extinction of all voluntary agencies. This was deplored: education itself might suffer retrenchments; the best that could be said for statutory authorities was that they would be more effective in recovering the cost of meals from parents able but unwilling to pay for them.[33] But already the limitations of the provisions of the Relief (School Children) Order issued by the Local Government Board in April 1905 were becoming apparent. The London County Council had begun to implement these powers with what appeared to be a neat little experiment whereby pupils learning cookery served up the results of their instruction to pupils who could pay. An unexpected operational difficulty arose. Teachers had long been accustomed to give help to the voluntary bodies, both organisationally and financially, if they wished to do so. Now the LCC was disposed to compel them to undertake the supervision of meals, taking as its precedent Article 113 of the old School Board regulations which had, in fact, merely laid down the requirement that pupils who brought food to school should not remain within the building unsupervised at dinner-time.[34]

Macnamara encountered some old friends among the eight witnesses: Mrs Burgwin, who had supplied evidence the previous year to the Inter-Departmental Committee on Medical Inspection and Feeding and who was now Superintendent of the London County Council special schools; his former London School Board colleague Father Brown, now the Right Reverend Monsignor Brown, Vicar General of the Diocese of Southwark; as well as Jackman, still headmaster of the Michael Faraday School, Walworth, and a Lambeth Metropolitan Borough Councillor as well as a member of the NUT Executive. All of them had been involved personally in the provision of meals: Mrs Burgwin as honorary treasurer and secretary of the *Referee* Children's Free Breakfast and Dinner Fund, Monsignor Brown in Camberwell, Vauxhall, Lambeth and Southwark, and Jackman in a scheme based on St Peter's Walworth, where in winter 200 meals per day were served in the crypt and many more dispatched, kept warm by hot water, to schools and mission halls for children in both provided and non-provided schools.[35] Macnamara asked all three about the rôle of voluntary agencies. Mrs Burgwin was questioned after George Newlands, Secretary and Treasurer of the Poor Children's Table Society of Glasgow, had told the Committee that the voluntary agencies there were adequate to meet the needs of the hungry children. 'Do I gather ... that you take that view as regards London?' 'Yes', she answered, 'with definition of the necessitous child.'

'Would you give that definition? ...'
'I say it is one who, through the neglect of its parents, or through extreme poverty, cannot be fed at home.'

'You think that under all ordinary circumstances the many excellent agencies in London for helping children by voluntary means cover the cases of all those children?'

'Yes, I think so.'[36]

Monsignor Brown did not agree. 'You have long held the view that charitable agencies are not adequate to meet the need?', Macnamara asked him. 'Certainly', he replied.

'That was the sense of your resolution of 1897 at the Board?'

'Yes.'

'We sat in the following year under the late Mr Costelloe, and went into the matter very painstakingly, and our first resolution was that public Authorities should be charged with the responsibility ...?'

'Yes.'[37]

Jackman was more specific. 'You take a very strong view that charitable agencies are not sufficiently covering the ground?', Macnamara asked him. 'I do', Jackman replied.

'Therefore you ask for the addition of public assistance?'

'Yes.'

'And a special grant from the Exchequer?'

'Yes; for not only the reason of assisting the localities, but because I think the work should be more properly carried out in all the districts.'[38]

For the sake of their pupils, teachers in public elementary schools had an interest in securing the regular income, in summer as well as in winter, that the assumption of responsibility by Local Authorities would bring. On the other hand, the survival of a voluntary service preserved for them the option of non-participation. Yoxall, as General Secretary of the NUT, expressed the prevailing apprehension in a letter to the Chairman:

In the debate upon the Feeding of Children Bill a good deal was said about the inadvisability of the paid teachers of a school being compelled or even expected to carry out work connected with the feeding of children. You are aware that teachers up and down the country have done a great deal in that way, in a spirit of voluntary and philanthropic service to the community. There is now some danger that the volunteers shall become pressed men ...[39]

With a member of the NUT Executive on the Committee and another among the witnesses, this issue was easily ventilated. Macnamara questioned Jackman on the evidence provided by Robert Blair, Executive Officer of the London County Council, that non-participation in dinner-supervision did not affect promotion:

'You are not in agreement with Mr Blair who definitely says that neither by the officials nor by members of the [Education] Committee are these questions put at the time of promotion?'

'They have been put by members of the Committee.'

'They have been?'

'Yes, so I am informed. I can give a particular case.'

'Is it your experience that the teachers have done and continue to do voluntary work outside the strict letter of their agreement on behalf of the children in all sorts of directions?'

'Yes, in all sorts of directions.'

'They give the most cheerful assistance?'

'Willingly.'

'And even in connection with this matter had it been left to them as a voluntary and goodwill offering you think they would have continued as they have done in the past to have given generous service?'

'I do not think they would have objected.'

'The irritation has arisen because of the suggestion that it is really part of their duty?'

'Yes.'

The NUT proposals for the foundation of a meals service now emerged. Jackman explained that what he had in mind was that henceforth the funds required for meals provision would be supplemented by Exchequer grants and the rates. Meals would be provided in central places outside schools so that teachers' participation would be voluntary.[40]

In its report, published at the end of July, the Committee stressed the importance of continuing the aid of private agencies, recommending that a Local Education Authority should be empowered to organise and direct the provision of midday meals in public elementary schools by means of committees composed of its own representatives, those of the voluntary agencies and, where appropriate, those of the Board of Guardians and the Society for the Prevention of Cruelty to Children. Power to raise rates not in excess of a halfpenny in the pound and to spend money for accommodation, organisation and preparation of food was to be granted, though not for the food itself, as well as powers to reclaim the cost of the meals from neglectful parents who were able to pay. Finally the Committee had been persuaded that taking part in dispensing school meals should not be made part of the conditions of employment of teachers.[41]

In July and August the *Schoolmaster* was accustomed to provide suggestions for its readers about places in which to spend their holidays. When an elementary headmaster earned £150 per annum,[42] Thomas Cook provided a week in Switzerland for five guineas or a fortnight's cruise round Great Britain for eleven.[43] Macnamara, whose salary was considerably more, preferred to stay in England. This year, having spoken many times both at the London School Board and in the House of Commons about how hungry children were fed in Paris, he decided it was time to see the system in action. So at the end of September, with the week's *Schoolmaster* ready for the press, he set off on the Night Mail. Saturday and Sunday were spent sightseeing, noting the mourning wreaths on the statue representing Strasbourg in the Place de la Concorde, the clean streets, balloons tethered in the Tuileries Gardens in preparation for an international race. French children to his expert eye seemed to be well treated: 'I haven't seen a bare-footed youngster yet. Threadbare clothes I have seen. But no rags, everything neatly stitched and mended – silent witness of care, thrift and industry.' Monday was spent negotiating for a school visit permit. The next morning he arrived at L'Ecole Communale Rue Jomard, with its headmaster, eleven class teachers, no pupil-teachers and 500 boys:

> ... no tousled hair – indeed most of the boys wore their hair cut astonishingly short – no rags, no bare feet, no tatters ... splendid work in the matter of supplying blouses, jerseys, socks and boots is being done by a voluntary society – Caisse des Ecoles. It did my heart good to see a store room filled with the boots, socks, jerseys and blouses bye and bye to be served out to the boys during the coming winter.

In the neighbouring girls' school the pupils were walking quietly downstairs, two by two, for the midday recess:

> Like the boys many are unduly pale-looking, but they are otherwise well-nourished. There is nothing of the pinched, hunted look of the East and South of London. The clothes are uniformly neat and appropriate.

Now it was 11.30, time for dinner, for which 107 boys and 65 girls remained. Each had brought a crust of bread, an apple and a bottle containing vin ordinaire, coffee, syrup or water. Soup, then stewed beef and two potatoes with their jackets on, were served. About half the pupils paid nothing for the meal. Macnamara concluded:

> So far as I could ascertain no steps are taken to inquire as to whether the parents of children receiving meals gratuitously are in a position to pay for the same. That is ... an essential feature of any practicable scheme for this country. But it must be remembered that with the French peasantry it may be to some extent different. There is far less of thriftlessness, drunkenness and dissolute living amongst them than amongst the similar class in this country.[44]

Back in England he visited an infants' school in Liverpool. From his arrival the contrast was marked. In the teachers' room were 35 children who had been selected from the school population of 345 for attention by the Red Cross sister. 'Don't hang your coat on the peg above those children', he was advised: 'they are all dreadfully verminous.' There they were, leaning against the wall, sick, ill-nourished, thin and ricketty. Meantime, he wrote in the *Daily Chronicle*, Christ's ministers were at odds over Clause 4 and Extended Facilities.[45]

What was referred to as the Hungry Children Bill reached its Committee stage in the Commons on 7 December. The proposal that the Local Authority might defray the cost of food in the case of a small proportion of necessitous children and draw on the rates to the extent of a halfpenny in the pound was found to be disturbing by a number of members, already worried by the fact that the Bill itself was so closely associated with the Labour Party. W. C. Bridgeman (later Home Secretary) a Conservative member of the Select Committee, argued that the issue was between socialism and family life. He was on the side of family life. The Bill would do harm: when the possibility of getting public money to provide meals for school children was put before people, an increasing number of parents, mothers as well as fathers, would take advantage of the fact, and at the same time many voluntary subscribers would cease to subscribe. Macnamara, speaking next, admitted that within the Select Committee a minority of three had voted against the disbursement of public money. But among the nine in favour was Sir Francis Powell Bt, the member for Wigan, 'who crowned half a century of honourable political life by supporting the proposal to do something for those unhappy little scraps of humanity, hedged round as the proposal was by conditions for preventing economic abuse. Was the hon Baronet a violent Socialist?' He himself had believed for many years that voluntary agencies were sufficient to meet the needs of hungry children, but he had been driven from it by the hard facts of the case. Voluntary aid was unreliable. When he and Sir John Gorst had visited the Johanna Street School, they found that a period of cold weather had placed a long and serious strain on the funds, with the result that both breakfasts and dinners were to be reduced by half the following week to eke out the money. This was a very good illustration of what happened everywhere. It had also been found, he added, deploying a Liberal rather than a Socialist argument, that voluntary agencies were indiscriminate. They had no means of following up those drunken, thriftless and careless parents who ought to be punished:

> With the Bill the machinery for that purpose would be set up, and gradually a conscience would be developed among those parents, just as the enforcement of the attendance of children at school by the Act of 1870 had developed from a legal to a moral obligation upon the parents.[46]

A fortnight later, on 21 December, the Education (Provision of Meals) Act permitting Local Education Authorities to provide land, buildings, furniture, apparatus, such officers and servants as might be necessary for the preparation and service of meals, but restricting expenditure on food to the amount which would be produced for necessitous children only, by the halfpenny rate, received the Royal Assent. The Board of Education also moved rapidly. On 12 January 1907, the *Schoolmaster* reported the publication of Circular 552 containing the Board's instructions to Local Education Authorities for its implementation.[47]

Few difficulties had been encountered by this measure, essentially a practical addendum to the 1902 Act. On 20 December, in sharp contrast, the Government's Education Bill, intended to overturn that Act, was abandoned. In Parliament at the beginning of August it was already plain that the Lords, both spiritual and secular, regarded it with hostility. Almost coincidentally a decision in the Court of Appeal redoubled their determination to deal very severely with it. The case had arisen from a Divisional Court decision making absolute a writ of *mandamus* against the West Riding County Council which had withheld a proportion of salaries due to teachers in relation to religious instruction in four non-provided schools (three Church of England and one Roman Catholic) since the end of April 1905. As the *Schoolmaster* explained, the case raised the question whether the Local Education Authority was bound, under the Act of 1902, to pay for denominational education in non-provided schools.[48]

The Court of Appeal verdict, delivered during the week ending 18 August, laid down that it was not. Perceiving the verdict as a justification of its campaign since 1902, the Passive Resistance movement in both England and Wales at once resumed its activities. This time it faced a counter-challenge voiced by Lord Hugh Cecil, who began to advocate passive resistance by churchmen. The *Schoolmaster* reported:

> He says they should pay the whole or part of their rates into a fund from which payments for denominational teaching may be made. That is an astonishing proposal to come from a legislator of such well-deserved standing ... Does he not know how easily ... his proposal ... would at once break up the whole scheme of common contribution for communal benefits? ... We have always objected to Dr Clifford's Passive Resistance; we object equally strongly to Lord Hugh Cecil's.[49]

The *Catholic Times* judged that while over 1,000 Roman Catholic schools might in theory be affected, very few Local Education Authorities would emulate the West Riding. Nor would the Government take action over the matter. Instead it would devote its utmost endeavours to getting its precious Education Bill through the Lords. 'Manifestly', it concluded, 'Catholics must push on with a determined agitation, must help the Lords to strangle the iniquitous proposals.'[50]

Macnamara, who had contributed an article on the Lords and the Education Bill to the *Nineteenth Century*, was obliged to add a postscript on the West Riding Court of Appeal decision. What it had done was to interfere with the operation of the 1902 Act: Local Education Authorities all over the country were now able to infer that no obligation rested on them to pay for denominational religions:

> Of course all this makes confusion worse confounded, and it is more than ever the duty of the Government to go ahead with its determination to straighten out this woeful education tangle ... My view ... is that when the Lords and Clergy come to look carefully into the Court of Appeal decision ... they will come to the final consideration of the Government Bill in a much more consenting frame of mind.[51]

For a while, Macnamara recalled in the debate on the Lords' amendments on 12 December, it appeared that he had been right. At Nottingham on 14 October, Lord Lansdowne, the former Foreign Secretary, declared that the Unionist Party did not object to popular control and did not wish to impose religious tests upon teachers. Lord St Aldwyn, the former Sir Michael Hicks Beach, repeated this view four days later. Even the Archbishop of Canterbury promised, as the Bill went into Committee on 25 October, that the amendments he would either propose or support would not, in any sense, be mischievous or wrecking amendments. In effect, however, the Lords had made the Bill a hopeless tangle of administrative impossibility, destroying or crippling the discretion and power of the great Local Authorities, insisting that all schools should provide half an hour of religious instruction each day and (as the NUT Executive had feared) restoring teachers' rights to volunteer specific religious instruction only to reintroduce religious tests.[52]

Birrell and Crewe prepared to compromise; but the debate was on the Prime Minister's motion of the previous day empowering the Commons to deal with the Lords' amendments en bloc. This was eventually passed by 417 votes to 107. The Parliamentary correspondent of the *Schoolmaster* concluded:

> I suppose no man living can forecast as to what is going to happen. Great influences are at work in the Lords ... in favour of a settlement. Amongst them it is safe to include the Archbishop of Canterbury, the Duke of Devonshire and, perhaps to a lesser extent, Viscount St Aldwyn. On the other hand it appears as if Mr Balfour, for some reason or other, desires to keep the controversy open.[53]

But the controversy had only one week more to run. The Archbishop of Canterbury, in the debate in which the Lords discussed the Commons' reaction to their amendments, made it clear that his long-held hopes for a settlement had been dashed. He denied Macnamara's charge that he and his colleagues had set out, after the Second Reading, to wreck the Bill. No educational system, he said, was truly representative of our national life unless it regarded, within due limits, the claim of the nation, the locality, the parent and the Christian community to which the parents belonged. The business of legislators was to assign to each of these its proper weight and influence. It was a complex and difficult problem and the Bill had, in particular, failed to recognise the attachment felt by hundreds of thousands of families and thousands of teachers to denominational schools and denominational teaching.[54]

Reporting the Lords' vote to adjourn future consideration of the Bill (which effectively killed it) and, coincidentally, the reversal of the West Riding judgement which had made the later stages of the debate more acrimonious, the *Schoolmaster* forecast that the Government would now abandon its Bill.[55] In the Commons the next day the Prime Minister who, as a result of the Lords' obstruction, was to revive the idea of the suspensory veto against the Second Chamber (eventually adopted as part of the

Parliament Act of 1911) asked bitterly whether the general election and its result were to go for nothing, pointing out that it was plainly intolerable that the Lords should act as a willing servant to the Unionist Party to neutralise and distort the electorally-approved policies of the Liberals. In Balfour's absence Walter Long responded. The object the Lords had in mind, he said, was to maintain an educational system in conformity with the wishes of the parents, a system which would make the children of the country good citizens, and give to all denominations equally the same opportunities and the same privileges. He did not believe that the member for North Camberwell, who knew as much about the education question as anybody in the House, would be prepared to say that the Bill would have settled controversy and maintained peace for the future.

Macnamara replied that he had thought the path was full of promise for peace, if not of a settlement at once. He summarised what the Government's objectives had been: to set up complete public control over every public elementary school; to establish that all school managers should be public nominees; to give teachers the right to opt out of religious teaching. All these would have been achieved; a great scheme of medical inspection had been added to them. He was filled with the bitterest disappointment, he said, and he deplored the absence of the Leader of the Opposition, not only for its cause (he was at home at Whittingehame with influenza) but because they would have liked to tell him what they thought of him.[56]

Macnamara had performed as his party would have wished: if Birrell had been the Moses of the Education Bill it was said, he had assuredly been its Aaron. But the effort had been vain; matters vital to the national education system, including the reduction of the size of elementary school classes, the improvement of teacher training, the establishment of continuation schools, the abolition of factory and agricultural half-time labour, the opening up of the Inspectorate and the reform of teachers' superannuation, had been sacrificed for the sake of a religious issue artificially revived in 1902 by Lloyd George.[57] Further attempts to deal with the status of the non-provided schools were to be made, twice by McKenna in 1907 and 1908 then again in 1908 by Runciman, without success.

So after months of assault the 1902 Act remained secure. Now, at last, the Liberal government, with the creation of the Welsh Department and the establishment of a schools medical service (both innovations saved from the wreckage of the 1906 Bill), began the process of refining and improving it that Macnamara and his NUT colleagues had advocated. More free secondary school places were made available; new regulations regarding staffing and the size of classes were introduced; after the Royal Commission on the Poor Law had reported, the advantages that continuation schools might offer were considered. As for the tidal wave of Nonconformist ire, it was soon dissipated. Macnamara had suggested that its origin lay less in religious conviction, more in the objection to the imposition of rates, avoided in one third of the country during the board era.[58] As many of Lloyd George's supporters had discovered between 1902 and 1906, avoidance of the education rate could prove expensive if alternative schools had to be provided.

In the last days of 1906, Campbell-Bannerman decided that Birrell must be replaced. The changes set in train brought Macnamara another opportunity of office, this time as Parliamentary Secretary to the Local Government Board under John Burns. This time he accepted. He wrote to the Prime Minister on 22 January 1907:

Dear Sir Henry,

I am very grateful to you for this second witness of your appreciation of whatever work I have been able to do. Both my wife and I agree though it will be a wrench giving up a life-long connection with the work of Education. I shall hope however to be able to take a hand now and again, in the country at any rate, with a subject to which I am so deeply attached.

I am especially grateful to you for putting me into harness with Burns. We are very old friends and my respect for him and his work is unbounded ... [59]

He wrote to Burns (whom he had not been able to see beforehand) the next day:

... I need scarcely say with what delight I shall work with so old and genuine a comrade; nor need I say how very grateful I am to you for the good word I know you have often put in for me.

Rachel and I are both greatly gratified that I should make my first venture at the work in your hands.[60]

The appointment was widely approved in the press. H. W. Massingham wrote in the *Speaker*:

the re-constituted Ministry gains clearly in strength and in youth. Dr Macnamara's further exclusion was impossible: no government could forget the character of his debating work on the Education Bill, which was nearly always contributed at the right time and in the right way. He is a personality of great force, which will be refined and strengthened by contact with the exacting duties of one of the most difficult of our great executive departments.[61]

Macnamara's appointment meant that he had to resign both as editor of the *Schoolmaster* and as a member of the NUT Executive. On 2 February, the Saturday morning meeting at 71 Russell Square was taken up with expressions of gratification on his achievement (which reflected the changed status of the teaching profession) and regret at his departure. A year ago, he said in response, he could not bring himself to do it. But everybody said that he ought to have accepted office when it was offered to him and that if he got the chance again he ought not to refuse. He was gratified to go as second in command to John Burns (Applause), a really great man and one of their own class (Applause) and a man whose sympathies were always with those from whom they had sprung.[62]

The *Schoolmaster* provided a handsome editorial entitled 'From Fleet Street to Whitehall'. Over forty years before, a small band of teachers had knocked timorously on the door of the Education Department Office in Whitehall, stung into action by the shameful breach of faith over superannuation. They were dismissed by their betrayer, Robert Lowe. Time had brought unexpected revenges:

> The elementary teacher has endured much and achieved something. In many quarters he has still to combat the unfortunate heresy that while he is a very worthy and, maybe, even excellent 'person' inside the schoolroom, he is a very poor tool in any other field of enterprise. This fallacy is so far from the truth that it is humiliating to feel called upon to confute it. In commerce and industry, in science and art, in business and administration, in the Church and at the bar, ex-teachers have risen to eminence. To Dr Macnamara, however, belongs the conspicuous distinction of being the first ex-elementary teacher to 'break his birth's invidious bar, And grasp the skirts of happy chance' by taking office as one of His Majesty's Ministers ... the dawn of democracy has arisen.[63]

Celebrations continued for weeks. On 14 February, Macnamara was presented to the King at the Levée at St James's Palace by Burns. Both were in Ministerial uniform with cocked hats. Eight days later Rachel Macnamara was presented at Court in a gown of ivory satin, with a train twenty yards long. The *Practical Teacher* published a photograph of the Macnamaras in their finery. On 15 March, the electors of Camberwell entertained them to dinner at the Criterion Restaurant at which the main toast of the evening was proposed by Andrew Bonar Law. Another dinner was hosted by the NUT Executive at the Inns of Court Hotel on 3 May.[64]

The climax was reached at the NUT Annual Conference, held in Oxford. On the second day Macnamara, with his wife and daughter, appeared on the platform to make his farewells. Arthur Pickles, the President, seconded by Jackman and supported by Mrs Burgwin, moved the resolution congratulating him on his appointment. In the history of the NUT, Pickles said, no name stood out more prominently than that of Dr Macnamara. His promotion had been acclaimed by friends and colleagues as well as by political opponents (Cheers). But Dr Macnamara had not yet attained the height of his ambition. He had once said that he would rather be a scratch golfer than a Cabinet Minister (Laughter) and as he had not yet recanted he took it that he was going to be both (Laughter and cheers). So generous had been the response to the appeal for subscriptions to a testimonial gift that he was able to hand to Mrs Macnamara a sum of money which would enable her to acquire the title deeds of the house in Rollscourt Avenue. Rachel Macnamara thanked his colleagues; then Macnamara recalled what the NUT had achieved during the twenty-one years in which he had been a member. It had broken down Payment by Results; fought for the mentally and physically afflicted children of the slums; striven for a higher standard of attainment amongst teachers; secured better school buildings and a better school atmosphere; raised the age for juvenile factory labour; and, generally, raised the level of the national importance of education as a factor in national defence. There was much more to be done, he added; his work at the Local Government Board lay with problems outside the school. Here the enormous influence of the teachers could be brought to bear in the cause of the child both before it reached school age and once it had earned exemption to enter the labour market. 'The whole speech', the *Practical Teacher* concluded, 'was a worthy swan song to a great Union career.' The next day, with Pickles and Yoxall, Macnamara appeared at the Sheldonian where each of them was invested with an honorary degree of Master of Arts.[65]

The Local Government Board to which Macnamara was now to devote his energies had been created by Act of Parliament in 1871 when it assumed the responsibilities both of the Public Health Board and of the Poor Law Board, which included the administration of workhouses and the education of workhouse children. It was also concerned with rating and local electoral reform, both issues with which Macnamara had been familiar through his work on the London School Board and with housing, in which he had taken an interest since he entered the House of Commons. Opportunities for radical innovation now seemed to be opening up. The Local Government Board was, or should be, he thought, the great central generating station for social reform and the well-being of the community.[66]

Burns, the President of the Board, was to all appearances the ideal senior partner for the new Parliamentary Secretary. Born in Battersea in 1858, he had been apprenticed as an engineer at the age of fourteen and had become one of the leading figures of the new trade unionism which aimed to meet the needs of less skilled workers. In the London dock strike of 1889 he had appointed himself strike leader and secured terms involving no victimisation and the award of the dockers' tanner. Safe in his Battersea base he had been politically changeable. He had moved into and out of H. M. Hyndman's Social Democratic Federation, been elected as an Independent Labour MP in 1892 but dissociated himself from the Labour Representation Committee in 1899, then finally drawn close to the Liberals over the Tariff Reform campaign of 1903–05, to be rewarded by his appointment as head of a department of which he had been a persistent critic.[67] 'John', Campbell-Bannerman said, 'I want you to join the Cabinet and take the Local Government Board.' 'Sir 'enry', Burns replied, 'you never did a more popular thing in your life.'[68]

Dealing with the specific problems of office, Burns had proved to be less confident, easy prey, it was suggested, for the officials of his department.[69] Where he and Macnamara worked together results were achieved; on the standing committee surveying Lord Robert Cecil's Bill requiring the notification of births within thirty-six hours rather than six weeks (to alert health visitors in the vital first days of life) they transformed it, in a single day, into a measure which the Local Government Board could utilise. But he postponed legislation on land valuation and resisted, with reason, changes in provision for the poor and unemployed whilst the Royal Commission on the Poor Law was in session.[70] Perhaps he resented the assumption that working men could be useful in government only in home affairs; his suggestion that he would prove a more than adequate replacement for Lord Cromer in Egypt had not been taken seriously.[71]

Fortunately, Macnamara found that he had the opportunity to work independently. All his recent work on the social conditions of children pointed to the fact that the way they lived conditioned the way they learned. He chose, therefore, to investigate the boarding accommodation furnished for pauper children under the Poor Law (their schools, inspected since 1863 by the Local Government Board, having been transferred to the Board of Education in 1904). In the first decade or so after the Poor Law Amendment Act had been passed in 1834, both accommodation and schools had been provided inside the workhouse confines. Soon the idea was mooted that schools would function better outside. In the 1840s, some Poor Law unions invested in so-called 'separate' schools of a residential character. The Royal Commission on Popular Education of 1858–61 recommended a further refinement whereby neighbouring Poor Law unions should combine to build district boarding schools. Except in London, however, few of these schools were built. The idea of the child living within the school gave way to proposals for cottage homes or boarding out which, under the 1870 Education Act, proved to be practical ways of taking care of children when they were enrolled in public elementary schools. Macnamara noted in the introduction to his report:

> To-day more than half of the children under the care of Poor Law Guardians attend public elementary schools. With regard to the remainder it may be said, generally speaking, that the policy of recent years has been directed towards the distribution of children in smaller homes rather than in large institutions; and this policy has been accompanied by the steady determination to abolish the workhouse schools. There has also been a growing extension of the system of placing children in homes and schools not under Poor Law authorities, the guardians making maintenance payments on their behalf.[72]

What Macnamara was undertaking in 1907 was the appraisal of the accommodation provided outside the workhouse for some of the 69,000 children chargeable in 1907 to the Poor Law; in particular the district schools, the cottage homes and the 'scattered' homes (small houses bought or rented by the Guardians and entrusted to a foster mother).[73] T. P. Sykes, his former colleague in the NUT, caught up with him at the Burnley Workhouse cottage homes at the end of October:

> It was the fifth workhouse which he had personally investigated during that week ... In each home the Doctor gathered the ten or twelve forlorn-looking children about his knees, asked them their names, and cheered them by a little breezy talk. In one of the homes this is what happened. The boys direct from

their household duties stood around. The master, matron, foster-mother and I stood behind. The Doctor sat on a bench.

'And now, my little chap,' he said to a boy of eleven, 'what is your name?'

'Neil____,' mumbled the boy.

'Spell it for me.'

'N E I L.'

'Now, Neil, my boy, do you know what that word means?'

'No, sir.'

'Very well, Neil, you look straight in my eyes and I will tell you. You other boys may listen.'

Neither Mr Swift, nor the matron, nor the foster-mother knew what I knew, that away yonder in Herne Hill Dr Macnamara has a little son called Neil, who is as the apple of his father's eye. So he said:–

'"Neil" means "chieftain," "leader." Say it.'

'Chieftain, leader,' said the boy.

'And what about your mother?'

'Dead, sir.'

'And your father?'

'Run away, sir.'

'Now, Neil, my boy, you start pretty low down, don't you? You don't realize that. But – Neil – Chieftain – leader.' A pat on the head and a shake of the hand and the Doctor rose.

Outside I clapped him on the back and said: 'Good old Mac.' That is what we teachers affectionately call him, because he is one of us and we are proud of him. And that is education, secular education, secular education of an entirely religious sort. [74]

Macnamara concluded his report with what he called a trite reflection: that in the case of the Poor Law child it was the character of the supervision that had the most potential for good or evil. A park with beautiful villa cottage homes, badly administered, might well fail to measure up to a derided 'barrack' district school with able people in charge. Against his admitted prejudice, he felt obliged to admit that a well-run district school possessed one signal advantage: it afforded children the benefit of technical instruction. But his own enthusiasm was for emigration, fired particularly perhaps by the fact that since 1883, when the Local Government Board had begun to arrange for the emigration of poor children, the majority (more than 7,000) had been sent to Canada.[75]

Children Under the Poor Law appeared at the beginning of February 1908; an investigation commissioned by the Board of Education into the schools attended by Poor Law children followed in July. Both were to be eclipsed the following year by the reports of the Royal Commission on the Poor Law. In the meantime, the Campbell-Bannerman Ministry was coming to an end. The Prime Minister, mortally ill, did not appear in the House of Commons after 12 February; as his life ebbed, support for the Liberals in the country seemed to decline. Mid-Devon had returned a Unionist in

January for the first time; the Ross division of Hereford followed its example soon afterwards; in South Leeds, Worcester and Hastings Liberal candidates were elected with reduced majorities.[76] In Peckham on 24 March, another by-election took place. Here the Liberal candidate was Thomas Gautrey, Macnamara's old friend from London School Board days. His campaign started badly. Gautrey had lived in the neighbourhood for years, but his party was slow to confirm him as their candidate. H. L. Gooch, the Unionist, had been nursing the constituency. From the start he was strongly supported by the licensed victuallers, keen to resist the Government's Licensing Bill. Again the Liberals were defeated; their former majority of 2,339 was transformed into a Unionist majority of 2,494. Gooch took his seat on 25 March to prolonged cheers from his supporters. From the Government benches the cry was 'Beer, beer'.[77]

'There are heroes of defeat as well as heroes of victory', *Picture Politics* reported later:

> When Mr Gooch took his seat for Peckham amid the deafening applause of the Opposition there were not a few members' thoughts turned to Dr Macnamara. 'Fighting Mac', as he is affectionately called by his friends, had borne the brunt of the battle in Peckham against the furious onslaughts of the Trade. His presence had been felt at every street corner, battling with the forces of reaction. Wherever he went he made his impression on the serried ranks opposed to him, like the swordsman who by sheer dint of blows hews his way through the enemy. Bad as the defeat of the Liberal candidate was, no one can say that it would not have been infinitely worse if it had not been for the heroic stand that Dr Macnamara made.
>
> To realise his force of character you must hear him address a London crowd. Whether they are opposed to him or not, he compels them to listen. For there is a magnetism in his energy, and the boisterous rush of his arguments carries his hearers with him. His courage and energy are the driving power for intense convictions, which, united to a singleness of aim and purpose, will carry him far as a leader of men.[78]

The turning point of Macnamara's political career was at hand. For all the qualities that he had displayed it was Asquith, Campbell-Bannerman's successor, who would now decide his future.

12

Financial Secretary to the Admiralty, 1908–1914

When the Liberals returned to power in December 1905, Macnamara's political prospects were thought to be rosy. After two or three years, W. T. Stead forecast, the older veterans would retire, and having served his apprenticeship, he would attain Cabinet rank:

> Dr Macnamara represents youth, energy, race, experience, character and ambition. He is like a machine made of gun metal, driven by a dynamo of inexhaustible energy. He is typical of the new generation. A self-made man promoted from the ranks for sheer merit, and destined to go far.[1]

But when Asquith succeeded Campbell-Bannerman in April 1908, Macnamara, because of his refusal of the post offered to him at the Board of Education, was only fourteen months into his ministerial career. The Government benches were crowded with ambitious young men. Macnamara always retained an affection for the old Prime Minister: 'one of the most large-hearted, kindly, simple and honest men I have ever met', he recalled fourteen years later.[2] Campbell-Bannerman, a wealthy Scot unconcerned with rank or with the ties of university and school so dear to so many early twentieth-century Englishmen, had admired and encouraged him. Asquith, in contrast, was drawn, especially through the ambition and influence of his second wife, into aristocratic circles. 'He enjoys the grand life', Sir George Riddell, the solicitor, director of the *News of the World* and Lloyd George's constant adviser between 1913 and 1922, wrote in his diary in May 1912: 'He likes to live amongst wealthy and fashionable people.'[3] When, in November 1913, Churchill and Lloyd George were discussing promotion to the Cabinet, the latter said that the Prime Minister had no sympathy with men of Macnamara's type and did not understand them.[4] 'His origin, his training, his equipment, his prejudices, his very appearance and outfit excited every antipathy in Mr Asquith's mind', Lloyd George wrote in his *Memoirs* of Bonar Law: 'He did not under-value his abilities; he placed no value at all upon them.' The observation could have applied equally to Macnamara.[5]

Asquith's first task was to find a replacement Chancellor of the Exchequer. Having approached Morley and Haldane, he finally appointed

Lloyd George. Lord Tweedmouth, the First Lord of the Admiralty, was replaced by Reginald McKenna, the former President of the Board of Education, whose post was taken over by Walter Runciman, lately Financial Secretary to the Treasury. Edmund Robertson, the Parliamentary and Financial Secretary to the Admiralty, retired, to be rewarded with a short-lived peerage. Two Financial Secretaryships thus needed to be filled. Lloyd George, at the Treasury, sought the appointment of Macnamara, but George Murray, the Joint Permanent Secretary, probably apprehensive about the conjunction of two Radicals, secured the post for Charles Hobhouse, MP for East Bristol.[6] Asquith then offered Macnamara the Admiralty vacancy. He accepted it. He was to occupy it for twelve years.

Hearty congratulations, by telegram, were sent to him by the members of the Sergeants' Mess of the Loyal North Lancashire Regiment. Old friends at the *Schoolmaster* hailed the move as a promotion. 'Some people may in a chaffing mood have asked what qualifications he has for this important post', the paper added a trifle defensively: 'Many of them will learn with surprise that his very name proves the appropriateness of the appointment. "Mac-na-mara" is really a Gaelic word meaning "Son of the Sea"; and in Elizabethan times the warships of the Macnamaras were a power in the estuary of the Shannon'.[7] What Asquith had in mind can only be guessed at, though he, too, chose to represent the appointment as a promotion.[8] Macnamara's interest in the army was well known; the Navy could be regarded as a near fit. It is, perhaps, plainer that the new Prime Minister did not want Macnamara at the Board of Education. Further activity in an already contentious area was unwelcome to him; to the day of his death, Lord Percy wrote fifty years later, he could see no point in the Act of 1902.[9] So the leading Liberal expert on educational matters was left literally to learn the ropes, and what had been the major issue of 1906 soon dwindled into insignificance.

The duties of the First Lord of the Admiralty, as defined in 1905, involved general direction and supervision of all business relating to the Navy. The Parliamentary and Financial Secretary was specifically responsible for:

1   Finance, estimates and expenditure generally, and all proposals for new and unusual expenditure;
2   Accounts – cash, store and dockyard expense;
3   Purchase and sale of ships, and of stores generally;
4   Payment of hire of ships as armed merchant cruisers, troop ships, colliers, freight ships etc.;
5   Questions involving reference to the Treasury financially, except as provided for under Civil Lord;
6   Exchequer and Audit Department questions.

The Civil Lord (George Lambert) was in charge of works, buildings, contracts, stores and land, civil staff of naval establishments, marine and dockyard schools and pensions.[10]

Macnamara's first official visit was to Portsmouth at the beginning of May, to see the dockyard, the steam factory, the Royal Naval barracks, the gunnery school and HMS *Impregnable*. Devonport was inspected at the end of the month; Pembroke and Queenstown in July. At the Welsh dockyard he surveyed the abandoned hut encampment in which he had lived nearly forty years before. He then embarked in the Admiralty yacht *Enchantress* for Ireland, returning to Portsmouth two days later.[11]

Both the new First Lord of the Admiralty and the Financial Secretary had been personally selected by Sir John Fisher, the First Sea Lord, who had been consulted in advance by Asquith about the appointments. He had responded jovially that he wanted the two Macs (then a famous music hall turn).[12] In April 1905, when Fisher had held office for only six months, doubts were already being expressed about the declining influence of the First Lord,[13] but the eccentricity of Lord Tweedmouth,[14] who held the post under Campbell-Bannerman, made it difficult to diagnose whether Fisher had consolidated his position in relation to the Navy's Parliamentary spokesman or not. Now the appointment of McKenna, a Treasury minister, and Macnamara, the Radical, neither of whom brought any specialist knowledge or experience to their new posts, was to mark the beginning of the dominant phase of Fisher's career.

From the periodicals (amongst them the *Contemporary Review*, the *Fortnightly Review* and the *Nineteenth Century*) to which Macnamara had contributed at the turn of the century, it can be seen that whilst social reform was emerging as an important domestic issue, the question of German intentions was increasingly dominating thinking about foreign policy. Since 1883 Germany, the greatest military power on the continent, had been assembling, against all tradition, a large navy.[15] On 1 January 1900, Kaiser Wilhelm II declared that it was his intention to develop it to stand on the same level as the army perfected by his grandfather. By October 1902, Lord Selborne, the then First Lord of the Admiralty, had concluded that the more the composition of the new German Fleet was examined, the clearer it became that it was designed for a possible conflict with the British Fleet.[16] Early that year the *Contemporary Review* reproduced in translation a pamphlet by Ernst Teja Meyer entitled 'Los von England' which, it noted, had enjoyed a great run in Germany. Meyer described how, at the suggestion of the Kaiser, details of the navies of the various powers were being posted up in town halls all over the country. No other enterprise, he observed, united in itself as shipbuilding did, all branches of industry:

> The trade of a nation which builds its great vessels, and especially its vessels of war, at home, must be in a condition of the most perfect completeness and productive power, and altogether independent of foreign countries. Moreover

the consciousness of such a mastery itself tends to produce the requisite manning of the ships; the iron body acquires a soul, and full of vigour launches out upon the ancient and eternal highway to all culture and national greatness; commands and enforces respect for the flag whereby her country is known. Where she is, there is a portion of her native land.

The Germans needed to preserve themselves from that evil and suicidal overweening national pride which was the mark of retrogression and decadence; nevertheless, Meyer considered, German shipbuilding was now taking a world lead. England had been held up as a model because it could hold its own against the allied fleets of any other two naval powers, but it could now serve Germans best as a warning of what they should not do. Defects of construction and boilers, imperfect manufacture of artillery and projectiles were resulting in constant mishaps in the much lauded and admired Royal Navy. German shipbuilding firms, for example Krupps, had superseded Armstrongs. Even the personnel in the Royal Navy could not match the deep moral seriousness with which German blue jackets had won hearts the world over. 'I am of opinion', Meyer observed, 'that in evil days too much reliance will not be placed on the English marine.'

The greatest problem for the English would be manning her gigantic Navy on a war footing. Reliable up-to-date boilers, first-class guns and other apparatus could be bought in due time, but no money would buy fit and trained crews. Against the Boers in South Africa the tenfold superior forces and immense resources of the British Army had been found completely wanting. The Fleet would be found wanting in the same way. Apart from the number of ships, Meyer concluded:

> England's Navy will find a superior enemy in the marine of every great power which is abundantly provided with all that gives force at sea ... the coming collapse in a war with a great European power will at last and for ever demolish the old boast: 'Britannia rules the waves' ... Then the adversary who has achieved this task will be able to dictate terms of peace in London.[17]

Already, however, the Royal Navy was being reformed. Through the inspiration of Fisher as, successively, Commander of the Mediterranean Fleet, Second Sea Lord, Naval Commander in Chief Portsmouth and, from October 1904, First Sea Lord, the whole machine was to be overhauled from top to bottom. Boilers, gunnery, long-range firing and mining were duly refined, torpedo warfare investigated, rapid manoeuvre practised and a wide-ranging programme of training in strategy, tactics, communications and supply rigorously pursued.[18] Improvement was accompanied by retrenchment. The 1905 Naval Estimates were £3,500,000 below those of 1904; a further reduction of £1,500,000 was projected for the following year. Hence the incoming Liberal government had no complaints about the direction of policy. The naval building programme was pared still further. Preparations were made to drop one battleship out of the four planned for 1907, to be followed by a second if the results of the international peace conference, to be held in the Hague during the summer, proved to be satisfactory.[19]

These hopeful developments were put at risk by the appearance of the *Dreadnought*.[20] Laid down only weeks before the resignation of Balfour's government, the biggest, fastest and most heavily gunned battleship in the world was launched on 10 February 1906 and underwent its steam and gunnery trials on 1 October. Stead commented in the August *Review of Reviews*:

> Most people scoffed in 1899 at the Russian suggestion of putting an international interdict upon new weapons of war. Few people to-day will deny that it would have been a good thing for us if some international authority had placed a veto upon the construction of the *Dreadnought* ... we are worse off than we were before. For our old ascendancy in other battleships no longer counts against the new monsters, in building which we have only one year's start and one ship to the good.

Throughout 1906, Stead enthusiastically recorded what he perceived to be fresh advances 'from the City of Destruction wherein the Jingoes dwell, towards the Celestial City in which all men are brothers'. In May, German burgomasters who, in 1902, had been pinning up details of the advance of the Imperial Navy, were welcomed in England by Dr Lunn and R. B. Haldane to study municipal institutions, receiving additionally assurances from the King downwards of the national desire for British-German cooperation which was duly echoed in Berlin. A few weeks later, on Stead's suggestion, a group of some forty newspaper editors, from Kiel, Danzig, Königsberg, Hamburg, Bremen, Cologne, Stuttgart, Munich, Frankfurt, Dresden and Leipzig, were given a princely welcome. But whilst on the face-to-face level British-German relations appeared to improve, the significance of the Franco-British entente, signed in April 1904, was becoming plain to the German government. With the destruction of the Russian Fleet by the Japanese at Tsu-Shima in May 1905 and the likelihood, after Britain's support of the French position in Morocco at the Algeciras Conference of January-March 1906, that the French Fleet would henceforth cooperate with the British, Britain's naval hegemony in the North Sea and North Atlantic appeared complete. The Germans felt challenged; the British, let down (in Stead's view) by the Foreign Office, failed to press the case for disarmament at the Hague Conference, which failed after three months in the autumn of 1907, and though the Kaiser was affably received in London in November, a new German naval programme was announced during his visit. Stead commented:

> Measured by ships it may not be great but the annual expenditure goes up from £14,500,000 to £17,500,000. The army expenditure also shows a rise of nearly £3,000,000 ... Of course there is no question as to what John Bull will reply to this programme, be it little or big ... He has no army to speak of; his

only defence is his Navy. The maintenance of its unquestioned supremacy is for him a matter of life and death ... when the Kaiser lays down one Keel we lay down two. That is the formula of safety.[21]

The British government did not react to the German programme. The Estimates of 1908–09, which allowed for an increase of only £900,000, seemed at first to indicate that retrenchment would continue. But on 19 April, Fisher wrote to Lord Esher that he had talked with McKenna for three hours and Macnamara for four and they had both said that they were convinced by all the reforms of the previous three-and-a-half years. McKenna had returned for a second dose and was 'fascinated'; Macnamara was 'infatuated'. He himself was well pleased: 'Our new First Lord is A1, and so is Macnamara', he wrote to the naval journalist Arnold White on 8 May: 'at last we are blest with two fighters'. A fortnight later he reported to Lord Esher:

> Yesterday with all Sea Lords present McKenna formally agreed to FOUR *Dreadnoughts* AND IF NECESSARY SIX *Dreadnoughts*, next year (perhaps the greatest triumph ever known!) As he says, he has to eat every word he has said of the Treasury and Cabinet.[22]

Macnamara was coming to terms with what would be needed to keep the Navy in what the Prime Minister referred to as a position of 'unassailable supremacy'. During the Supply debates in July he told the House that he did not mind confessing that in the three months that he had been studying naval expenditure he had frequently been filled with despair at the dreadful rivalry which civilised people were inflicting upon themselves:

> Everything is growing bigger and more expensive and is rapidly becoming more obsolescent and obsolete. Fifty years ago the rough standard of cost of a ship was about £1,000 a gun. A 120 gun battleship would cost £120,000 and a 36 gun frigate cost roughly £36,000. Ten years ago the first-class battleship *Caesar* cost £942,000. The *Dreadnought* cost £1,800,000 ... Ten years ago our total net actual estimates were twenty-six and a half millions. They are now thirty-two and one-third millions ... Germany's estimates ten years ago were six and three fifths millions. Now they are sixteen and three fifths millions ...

Heavy as costs were, he concluded, and rapidly as they had increased, battles cost more than battleships. Thus, deplore the expenditure as he might, he felt it was upon the unimpaired strength of the British Navy that trade, the Empire, the happiness and safety of the people and even the foundations of the peace of the world depended.[23]

Before the next Navy Estimates were presented to the House of Commons, the Kaiser, in his *Daily Telegraph* interview in the last week of October, increased the apprehension created by the German naval programme. Stead was shocked:

> to be told by the German Emperor that the majority of the German people

regard us with a hostility which is only kept at bay by his friendly disposition, and to be further told by him that his patience is wearing thin, is about the most menacing intimation any nation has ever received from its neighbour ... The only security against unfriendliness on the part of our neighbours is to have a fleet so strong that they will not dare to indulge their unfriendly sentiments at our expense.[24]

In the first few weeks of the new year the situation was transformed. McKenna, writing to Asquith on 3 January what he called 'a worrying new year letter', informed the Prime Minister of the results of investigations he had made into German shipbuilding. He concluded that Germany was anticipating the programme laid down by the Law of 1907; that she was doing so secretly; that she would certainly have thirteen big ships in commission in the spring of 1911 and probably twenty-one in the spring of 1912; and that Germany's capacity to build *Dreadnoughts* was at that moment equal to the British. This, he concluded, would give the public a rude awakening if it became known: 'If we have eighteen *Dreadnoughts* at the time when Germany has twenty-one, our total strength in battleships compared would not be more than as five is to four, and a single unfortunate battle might leave us inferior to her'.[25] Fisher, writing to McKenna on 21 February, told him that six *Dreadnoughts* were too few. Eight were needed.[26]

The First Lord presented the Estimates, the results of months of consultation with his colleagues, naval and civilian, on 16 March. Stead reported in the *Review of Reviews*:

> It was a case of 'Wake up! John Bull' with a vengeance ... the House of Commons was told plump and plain that in the near future it will be a case of *Dreadnoughts* only as decisive factors in naval war, if for no other reason, because the big guns of the *Dreadnought*, which can hit a moving target at a distance of four miles with every other shot, could smash up all lighter-armed battleships before they got within shooting range ... that the eight *Dreadnoughts* will be put in hand this year is certain ... It is ruinously expensive and sinfully wasteful. But we cannot help ourselves ... we must lay down two *Dreadnoughts* for each new *Dreadnought* that Germany begins to build.[27]

McKenna sought £35,142,700, an increase of £2,823,700 over the current year. Four *Dreadnoughts* were to be built; in a Cabinet meeting on 24 February it had been agreed that another four would be laid down in the next financial year if they were judged necessary.[28] 'We cannot take stock of our own Navy and measure our requirements', he told the House of Commons, 'except in relation to the strength of foreign navies.'[29] A speech from the Prime Minister was even more explicit. He referred to the enormous development in German shipyards, slips, gun mountings and armaments for *Dreadnoughts*, concluding that we could no longer take to ourselves, as we could a year ago with reason, the consoling and comforting reflection that we had the advantage in the speed and the rate at which ships could be constructed.[30]

Macnamara spoke the next day. His task, ironic in view of McKenna's January letter to Asquith, was to dispose of the idea that by the close of 1910 the Germans would have thirteen *Dreadnoughts* to Great Britain's ten. He said:

> In my opinion and upon my information ... the most gloomy prospect that we can consider is that at the close of 1910 – I am very doubtful about it, however – we shall have ten *Dreadnoughts* to the German nine ... In July 1911, however, we shall have fourteen, and in November 1911, we shall have sixteen. I assume that by that time all the four German 1909–10 ships would come in, leaving Germany with thirteen at the very outside ... If Germany accelerates her 1910–11 programme she possibly and conceivably might have seventeen *Dreadnoughts* by April 1912. If we confine ourselves to the first four in the Estimates ... we should have sixteen to Germany's possible seventeen. If we lay down the four contingent ships on 1st April 1910, by April 1912 we shall have twenty *Dreadnoughts* to Germany's possible seventeen. That is the situation.

He also reminded the House that the Navy had forty first-class battleships in reserve: two *Lord Nelsons*, eight *King Edwards*, two *Swiftsures*, five *Duncans*, eight *Formidables*, six *Canopuses* and nine *Majestics*, as well as thirty-five armoured cruisers.

Macnamara's responsibility for the correct and proper control of Admiralty finance and the maintenance of economy made him the natural target for questioners critical of the Government's naval policy. His reply to A. G. C. Harvey, MP for Rochdale, serves as an example. 'I know many members who deplore the necessity for the three millions of increase', he said. '... Personally, like my hon Friend, I pray for peace ... Like him, I harbour no ill-feeling whatever against any of the peoples of the world ... I want money for social reform.' But, he went on, they had a responsibility to protect not only the people of the Empire but also the nation's food supply, its imports of raw or partially manufactured materials and above all its system of government. After examining the situation calmly and dispassionately, he said, the Admiralty ministers had arrived at what they honestly believed to be a minimum of charge consistent with the national safety.[31] Their judgement was to prove correct. The four contingent *Dreadnoughts* secured the Grand Fleet's numerical superiority in the first six months of the war.[32]

Balfour was not satisfied. 'I do not believe it is in the power of the Admiralty or of any organisation, however well constituted, to know with certainty and security what is going on in Germany', he stated in a Vote of Censure debate at the end of the month.

> ... What is the deduction from that? The deduction from that is that it is perfect madness, from the national point of view, to depend for your national safety on a small margin ... The Government are depending on small margins ... a margin of one in this year, a margin of two in the other year, and

a margin of three in the third year. Is that the way national interests should be treated?[33]

The vote was lost but Macnamara took up what he called Balfour's formidable indictment, that the Government had neglected the interests of the Empire in its most important and most vulnerable point, in a speech to his constituents at the Old Kent Road Baths on 2 April. Balfour, he said, had argued that the Government ought not to allow the country's destinies to depend upon the nice balance of a *Dreadnought* more on one side, or a *Dreadnought* more on the other ... It had not done so. He repeated the points he had made in the House. At the end of the year, seven tried and tested *Dreadnoughts* would be in operation. Germany would have two untried *Dreadnoughts*. At the end of 1910, Britain would have ten to Germany's five; at the end of 1911, sixteen to Germany's nine. If the Government laid down the four contingent ships of this year's programme on 1 April 1910, Britain could reach 31 March 1912 with twenty *Dreadnoughts*; Germany would then have thirteen, at most seventeen. Where was the nice balance? His advice to his fellow-countrymen was to make ample security for national safety, then apply their spare cash to more productive ends than the building of unnecessary warships.[34]

Lloyd George's budget plans, by which the Government intended to raise revenue for old age pensions (introduced the previous year) and for his unemployment and sickness schemes, as well as discharging its naval responsibilities, occupied the Cabinet for the rest of March and almost the whole of April. The Opposition, determined to resist the Chancellor's domestic innovations, found the issue of defence an admirable means by which to attack him. 'The criticisms', Macnamara said, in the Estimates debate at the beginning of August, 'come to this, that we are guilty of having neglected the naval defences of this country. I resent that charge very deeply indeed.' He went on to show how dockyard personnel, and expenditure there on works, buildings and repairs had all risen; the shipbuilding construction vote, not including the four additional *Dreadnoughts*, was the largest since 1905–06; the estimate for ship repairs was the highest since 1903–04. As for the provision of cruisers and destroyers, the two-power standard (by which British capital ships were to equal at least the combined total of her two nearest rivals) was now to apply not only in capital ships, but also in armoured and unarmoured cruisers, destroyers and submarines.[35]

Expenditure on ships involved expenditure on docks. For Rosyth, acquired by the Admiralty in 1900, tenders had been sought for the supply of granite. The British tender was £134,055, the Norwegian £104,594. The latter was accepted. Pamphlets began to circulate in North Camberwell entitled 'Remember the Granite Contracts' and 'Dr Macnamara favours foreign workmen'.

Macnamara sought to answer this, as had become his custom, by a letter to his constituents. Foreign granite had been purchased on a regular basis over the past thirteen years. But the total expenditure on stores and materials (coals, armour, all stores and provisions, shipbuilding, engineering, gunnery and works contracts) amounted to a total sum of approximately £15,000,000. Out of this only £130,000 had been spent abroad, mainly on sugar and rum.

'Concerning Granite' was reprinted as the last of six *Letters to a Working Man* which Macnamara published in the autumn of 1909. Originally written in response to questions raised by constituents, they all touched to some extent on the issues raised by Lloyd George's People's Budget, which proposed to raise £14,000,000 to meet new responsibilities. Macnamara asked:

> What is a leading reason for the bitter opposition to the Budget now before the country? The money has to be found. Old Age Pensions have to be paid and *Dreadnoughts* have to be built. In raising the money we have been guided ... by three main principles ...:
>
> 1   We must add nothing to the cost of the necessaries of life.
> 2   We must arrange existing taxation so as to secure that the broadest back shall bear the heaviest burden.
> 3   We must make land bear its fair burdens.

But the prospect of an incremental land tax had alarmed the Tories. 'Surely Socialistic folly cannot go further than it has gone in the doings of the present Government with regard to land', Balfour had declared on 22 September. Macnamara put the Government's case. In March 1895, he recalled, the House of Commons had without dissent passed a resolution that no system of taxation could be equitable unless it included the direct assessment of the enhanced value of land due to the increase of population and wealth and the growth of towns. Land taxation bills had reached Second Reading stage in 1904 and 1905. To clinch his argument he quoted as an example the site near Temple Station on which the London School Board offices had been built. In 1865, covered with coal sheds and wharfing, it had been sold for £8,250. The Victoria Embankment, paid for by London ratepayers, had been created in 1869–70. In 1872 the Board bought the land for £26,420. Ratepayers thus paid first for the public works then for the enhanced value of the land. 'This particular proposal of the Budget is already in operation in a number of German towns, in some of our Australian colonies and in New York', Macnamara concluded. 'Don't you think it about time we took this thing in hand?'

As an alternative to the land tax, the Opposition began to reconsider Joseph Chamberlain's 1903 proposals for Tariff Reform (the replacement of Free Trade by Protection). The cry went up: 'Why not make the foreigner pay?' This had long been an attractive idea. Macnamara quoted a letter written in September 1881 by Lord Randolph Churchill about a speech he had made in Oldham. '"Fair trade and taxing the foreigner went down like butter", he boasted. But, he added, "how the latter is to be done I don't know".' Macnamara recalled how in 1902 Sir Michael Hicks Beach, the Chancellor of the Exchequer, had placed a small duty on corn. Bakers took the opportunity to raise the price of bread. So the following year the duty was removed and the Government refunded £362,389 1s 8d. 'To whom?' Macnamara asked:

> If the foreigner had paid the tax, surely to him! Nothing of the sort. To the dealers and merchants who had bought the corn from the foreigners! ... And yet some silly people will continue to tell me that, as the tax is only on foreign corn, it won't affect the price in the home market.

Nevertheless, Protection seemed to be gaining adherents. 'Why don't you give it a trial, Mac?', he had been asked at one of his meetings. In reply he drew from a speech which Joseph Chamberlain (then still a Liberal) had made in November 1885. He had recalled the Hungry Forties, when, he said, large towns appeared beleaguered, so dreadful was the destitution and misery. Within them bread riots occurred; in the countryside labourers were on the verge of starvation. Macnamara described how, recently, he had stood on the fringe of a great open air meeting in an industrial centre. The speaker drew attention to a nearby factory, closed, dilapidated and decayed. 'When you were boys', he had said, '£200,000 a year wages was earned in those works. What killed them? Foreign competition! What ought you to do? Keep the foreigner out; and once again happiness, prosperity, employment – and £200,000 a year wages.' The Tariff Reformer was at pains to assure his audience that, in respect of the things they made and sold, more work and higher wages awaited them. But he was silent, Macnamara argued, about the effects that protection would have on goods kept cheap by sixty years of Free Trade. Protection, he went on, was a snare:

> Your attention is directed to the presence of foreign manufactured goods in your shop windows. You are told that, if you keep these out, there would be higher wages and more work for *you*. On the first blush the thing looks probable. But do not forget that you pay for foreign imported goods with the British goods which are the work of your hands ... Restrict your system of Free Imports and you restrict your own opportunities for employment.

In 1908, in comparison with France, the USA and Germany, Great Britain achieved the highest total of exported goods and the highest total value per head. 'Surely', Macnamara concluded, 'you know the story of the dog who, crossing the bridge, dropped the bone, because he thought its reflection in the water looked more tasty!' Then again, in 1908, £513,000,000 worth of goods were imported for home consumption, but only £119,000,000 was on account of manufactured articles. The bulk, consisting of food, drink, tobacco, raw materials and articles mainly unmanufactured, went to factories for further processing:

Upon the bulk of this 394 millions' worth you depend for living and livelihood. 'Tariff Reform' would, so far as I can see, expose you to dearer prices for all these (as well as for the 119,000,000 worth of manufactured imports). Where would your mills, factories and workshops – to say nothing of your cupboards – be then?

The claim was also being made that there was less unemployment in countries which embraced Protection. Macnamara quoted the September 1909 Board of Trade figures: 7.4 per cent of Trade Unionists were unemployed. The rate in France was 10.9, in Belgium 12.0, in Berlin 14.1 and in New York State 33.0. The Unionist government had introduced an Unemployed Workmen Act in 1905. Since then the Liberals had dispensed growing sums to galvanise it into practical utility. A compulsory unemployment scheme was being devised for workers in the shipbuilding, engineering and building industries. 'Let us stick to Free Trade', he concluded, 'and accompany it with a similar care for our people, their health, their comfort and their well-being.'[36]

The Lords, voting down the Finance Bill 350 to 75 on 28 November 1909, precipitated the first of the two general elections of 1910. With its majority over the Unionists reduced from 220 to two, the Government took up the tasks of securing the Finance Bill and of reforming the House of Lords. But amongst the Conservatives returned in January was Admiral Lord Charles Beresford, since 1906 the acknowledged leader of a group of Navy malcontents hostile to Fisher's reforms. Buoyed up by his supporters, he had become ever more bold and insubordinate. Arthur Lee, the former Civil Lord, in a letter to *The Times* published on 6 July 1908, commented that the efficiency of the Navy was seriously imperilled by the strained relations between certain officers serving in the highest and most responsible positions and asked what steps the First Lord of the Admiralty, or the Cabinet, proposed to take to put an end to a grave scandal which constituted a serious menace to national security.[37] Consequently, Beresford was ordered to strike his flag; following his retirement on 24 March 1909, he wrote to the Prime Minister alleging that the Fleet was wrongly distributed and that the Admiralty had no war plans.[38] Having occasioned an inquiry[39] into the Navy which lasted from the end of April till mid-July, Beresford, who had, in turn, previously represented Waterford, East Marylebone, York and Woolwich in the House of Commons, now reappeared as the member for Portsmouth.

In March, McKenna presented the Navy Estimates for 1910–11. Again it was Macnamara's function to take up the points made by Opposition spokesmen. He was faced with Lee, determined and ambitious to prove (vainly as it turned out) his indispensability to the Conservative Party, and Beresford, former Commander in Chief of the Mediterranean Fleet (1905–07) and of the Channel Fleet (1907–09) who had entered the Navy in 1859. On 14 March the latter told the House:

All parties are agreed that the safety of the Empire depends upon our supremacy. I maintain that the Fleet is not strong enough at the present time owing to the shortage of units and that the provision in the Estimates for future additions is not adequate to maintain our supremacy. I also maintain that the Fleet has not been, and is not now, properly organised for war ... There is no question that we are face to face with a crisis in naval affairs.[40]

Macnamara first established that both Lee and Beresford differed from their party's policy on shipbuilding, which was to maintain the two-power standard. Lee was in favour of two keels to one regarding Germany, Beresford had his own programme and, as Macnamara reminded the House, had referred to those who wanted two to one for every ship of the *Dreadnought* class that Germany laid down as 'wild men', adding that 'there is no lunacy I have ever heard so great as that'. Macnamara then quoted in detail from the programme. The battleships, the ante-destroyers and the torpedo-boat destroyers that Beresford had demanded either had been built or were scheduled to be built. Beresford was obliged to agree. Then Macnamara took up the issue of stores.

Dr Macnamara:	Statements made as to stores are made on the platform and are extremely misleading. It is generally suggested that in our rather nefarious sort of way we have been living on stores ... to the vital detriment of the fighting efficiency of this force. Let me put the facts about the stores and I think the Noble Lord will be obliged. At the close of 1904 and the beginning of 1905 a very great change was made in Admiralty policy. There were 150 ships scrapped ... I should like the Noble Lord to hear this, because he has said in public that it is we who scrapped these ships.
Lord C. Beresford:	Never.
Dr Macnamara:	I think I have the Noble Lord's speech.
Lord C. Beresford:	I could not say what was not true.
Dr Macnamara:	At Pembroke Dock, 20th December, 1909: – 'This Government –' that is the present Government – 'scrapped 150 ships'.
Lord C. Beresford:	I never said anything of the sort.
Dr Macnamara:	I am quoting from *The Times*, 1st January 1910. Again, at Grimsby:– 'They –' that is this Government – 'had scrapped 154 vessels'.
Lord C. Beresford:	No, I never said that.
Dr Macnamara:	I believe the Noble Lord took exception in some journal to *The Times* report of the Pembroke Dock speech but not of the Grimsby speech, as far as I know: 'They had scrapped 154 ships –'
Lord C. Beresford:	I never said that.

Dr Macnamara:	'And that was a policy of the Unionists also –' Did the Noble Lord say that? '– which was a mistake'.
Lord C. Beresford:	It was the Unionists who scrapped them.
Dr Macnamara:	Now we have it definitely from the Noble Lord ...[41]

Fisher wrote to Lionel Yexley, editor of the *Fleet* on 23 March: 'Convict Beresford of one lie, he only tells another. How Macnamara did keep him on the run on the Navy Estimates debate!' [42] Soon Beresford was back on the attack. Lambert admitted that the question of docks had given the Admiralty a great deal of anxiety:

> ... You may vote money for building *Dreadnoughts*, but there is the collateral expenditure of providing docks for their repair and their upkeep. At Portsmouth ... when the *Dreadnought* was commenced, there was only one dock capable of taking her, and now that dock will be superseded owing to the size of the later *Dreadnoughts* and *Invincibles* ... Portsmouth is our chief naval base. We have only one dock there capable of taking the largest type of ship.

Beresford responded vigorously. The fact that there was only one dock was disgraceful and scandalous. Ten *Dreadnoughts* had been launched and ten were building and they could only get into dock on three days in the fortnight. Worse, none of them could enter the harbour till they had unloaded their ammunition, coal and oil. 'I described the management of our naval Service by this Government the other day as the most incompetent and the most extravagant we have had in this country', he declared, 'but of all their management the worst has been that with reference to docks.'[43]

Macnamara recast his speech in the form of a Liberal Party Pamphlet entitled *Concerning the Navy* which was published later in the year. First he showed how expenditure on dockyards, dockyard works (building and repairs) and shipbuilding had all risen since 1905. As for manning, provision in the current estimates was for 131,000 officers and men, the great bulk of whom were long service, with 55,000 officers on the reserve. 'With the exception of the USA', he stated confidently, 'there is nothing like this in the world. All other navies are manned by short-service men ... no navy has on its active service list a personnel half as strong numerically as ours.' His main purpose was to deal with a specific charge from Balfour and a series of rather less specific ones by Beresford. Balfour had alleged that, by 1913, Britain would have a superiority of only four *Dreadnoughts*. Macnamara, deploying the Navy League Annual, demonstrated that the margin was ten. Beresford had been advocating a great naval building programme, arguing from time to time that the Government had been irresponsibly scrapping or selling ships of the Fleet. Macnamara, describing these allegations as 'particularly odious and intolerable to those who are responsible to Parliament and the country for the state of the Navy', attributed Beresford's inconsistencies to a defective memory.[44]

As the constitutional crisis deepened into a collision between Commons and Lords (which necessitated the second general election of the year in early December), Balfour returned to the naval question in an hour long speech reviewing imperial defence at the opening of the new premises of the Imperial Union Club at Glasgow on 20 October. Offering a comparison between 1910 and 1905, the last year of Unionist government, he claimed that in no five, ten or twenty years of our history had there been so great a change in Great Britain's naval position, or one so ominous, as that which had taken place during the previous sixty months. 'Nobody pretended that the two-power standard had either been preserved or approximately preserved at the present time', he contended:

> It did not now require a combination of the two largest naval powers to put us in a numerical inferiority. One well-directed shot, one torpedo that reached its mark, one error in tactics on the part of an admiral in command, and our narrow margin of superiority of four ships in the year 1913 might be most seriously and materially diminished.[45]

It was a characteristic speech, Macnamara told the North Camberwell League of Young Liberals the next day. The Leader of the Opposition had never been strong on figures; seven years of Tariff Reform arithmetic scarcely strengthened the calculative faculty (Laughter). He had said that, in 1913, Great Britain would have a superiority of only four *Dreadnoughts* over the next great naval power; this must mean twenty-five to twenty-one. How did the matter stand now that the possibilities of 1909 were materialising into accomplished facts? The next great naval power would not have twenty-one *Dreadnoughts* in 1913 but seventeen at the most, whereas Britain, in April 1913, would have twenty-five plus the two Colonial *Dreadnoughts*. This took no note either of the 1911–12 programme which could be expedited whenever there was any necessity to do so, or of the great pre-*Dreadnought* fleet. What was it Toryism wanted?, he asked (Laughter). The British Navy, he concluded:

> is to-day, to an extent it probably never had been before, capable of performing its vital function of safeguarding British interests at home and abroad. Further, the man who suggests the contrary is either ill-informed or is seeking to exploit national sentiment for party purposes (Cheers). In either case, he casts a particularly odious and intolerable aspersion upon those who are associated with that great force, and whose patriotism is fully as sincere as his own (Cheers).[46]

In the Coronation Honours of June 1911, Macnamara, still described by the *Daily News* as 'a leading educationist', as well as 'a witty and effective platform speaker', was made a Privy Councillor along with Sir William Anson, Sir Rufus Isaacs, F. E. Smith, McKinnon Wood and Bonar Law, soon to become leader of the Unionist Party.[47] Two days after the Coronation, the Naval Review at Spithead provided evidence of the size and strength of the British Fleet after five-and-a-half years of Liberal government. Assembled for the King's inspection were thirty-two battleships, twenty-five armoured cruisers, nine protected cruisers, twelve depot ships, sixty-nine destroyers, twelve torpedo boats and eight submarines.[48] In the preparation of this massive display of naval power the McKenna-Macnamara partnership had been decisive. Yet in the Commons they remained on the defensive. In early July, during a debate on auxiliary armaments, Macnamara was obliged to rebut once more Beresford's customary allegation that the public had been misled again and again on the question of naval defence and his claims that necessary levels of shipbuilding were not being met. Macnamara pointed out:

> The programme for 1911–12 includes five large armoured ships – four battleships and an armoured cruiser ... three protected cruisers, an unarmed cruiser, twenty destroyers, six submarines, two river gunboats, a depot ship for destroyers, and a hospital ship.[49]

In March, he had encountered from his own side the suggestion that, Radicals as they were, the Government was setting the pace among the nations in naval armaments. He said:

> No charge could be further from the truth. It could only be made by persons of short memory. Let the House not forget that in the early days of the present Administration we gave the very best evidence of our genuine desire to arrest this crushing expenditure.

He had been told, he said, that the Civilian Members of the Admiralty had responded too confidingly to the pressure of the Sea Lords. He went on:

> The Sea Lords are experts, their views carry great weight, but if any hon Gentleman thinks the three Civilian Members ... do not play their part fully and patiently and thoroughly in setting the programme of the year I say he is woefully mistaken ... when I put my name to these Estimates I did not believe I was doing something which would be a menace to peace or to national security.

He quoted Sir Henry Campbell-Bannerman: 'If our fleets be invulnerable, they carry with them no menace across the waters of the world but a message of the most cordial good will'.[50]

Macnamara, at the Admiralty, had seen little of Lloyd George who, as Chancellor of the Exchequer, retained his Radical suspicion of armaments.[51] The National Insurance Bill, which began its progress through Parliament on 4 May 1911, re-established their association. Clause 36 (Special Provisions with regard to Persons in the Naval and Military Service of the Crown) was, Macnamara declared, a generous method of providing for the soldier or sailor, at a cost of 1½d per week per man, at the end of his service.[52] In *The Great Insurance Act*, published the next year, he included a personal tribute:

The genius, the industry, the faith, and the courage of the wonderful little man to whom we owe it all ... it will stand, a lasting monument to a man of humble extraction who, having reached the exalted rank of Chancellor of the Exchequer, failed not in the day of his great opportunity to remember the block from which he was hewn.

In Part I of the Act, dealing with sickness and invalidity, Lloyd George had drawn on the German system established by Bismarck in the 1880s. Unemployment insurance dealt with in Part II had much less certain origins. Macnamara wrote:

When I turn to the Unemployment Insurance Scheme my sense of the soundness of the lines along which we shall operate is in no wise shaken by the fact that we are here entering upon an endeavour for which there is no precedent among civilised communities. Though the scheme is novel it is comparatively speaking plain and straightforward.[53]

The original Act provided compulsory insurance in three scheduled trades: building, shipbuilding and engineering. Within a year some 2,500,000 workers, including 9,000 women, were included. Each paid 2½d per week, to which employers added a further 2½d and the State 1⅔d. Payment was made, as for Part I, by the stamping of cards or books. Benefit was to be available for those employed not less than twenty-six weeks in the preceding five years, who were capable of work though unable to find it, and who had not exhausted their right to it. Seven shillings per week, for fifteen weeks in the year following the first week of unemployment, was to be permitted.[54] The following year Macnamara wrote:

It isn't a flashy 'work for all' will o'the wisp. It is just a quiet, drab, unpicturesque piece of useful common-sense Radicalism. It hasn't given you one man running after two jobs where previously two men were competing for one job. Nothing so exciting. It has simply taken three great industries – Building, Ship-Building and Engineering – industries especially subject to grave fluctuations of fortune, and by the threefold cord of co-operation between the workman, the employer and the State it has furnished the means whereby the wolf shall be kept from the door during periods of unemployment.[55]

In July 1911 the naval magazine the *Fleet* proudly presented its readers with details of the Coronation Review. Two months later its tone had changed completely. Europe, it reported, had been within a hair's breadth of war:

Everything on the diplomatic and international horizon was as fair as fair could be when, lo, the *Panther* dropped anchor in Agadir Bay and war clouds rolled up as rapidly and ominously as thunderclouds out of a summer sky. Germany was playing her old game of bluff, and the only reason she did not succeed was because of the British Fleet and the fact that the Entente Cordiale and the Triple *understanding* remained 'in being' ...[56]

Later in the year the Moroccan crisis was interpreted differently. Stead, in the *Review of Reviews*, alleged that it was the French who, by seizing Fez against the provisions of the Treaty of Algeciras of 1906, had activated it. The despatch of the German gunboat *Panther* to Agadir on 1 July had, he considered, been a blunder; but so had the speech, inspired (in his view) by Sir Edward Grey, which Lloyd George had delivered at the Mansion House on 21 July.[57] Over Agadir, Britain had received no reply for seventeen days from the German Chancellor in response to the Foreign Secretary's enquiries. Now the Chancellor of the Exchequer declared that if in future:

> a situation were to be forced upon us in which peace could only be preserved by the surrender of the great and beneficent position Britain has won by centuries of heroism and achievement, by allowing Britain to be treated, where her interests were vitally affected, as if she were of no account in the Cabinet of Nations, then I say emphatically that peace at that price would be a humiliation intolerable for a great country like ours to endure.[58]

The German government reacted sharply. McKenna was warned by Grey that the British Fleet might be attacked;[59] though the crisis subsided, a special meeting of the Committee of Imperial Defence took place on 23 August. Here it emerged that, assisting the French over Morocco in 1906, the British had allowed the assumption to take root that they would supply an expeditionary military force should Franco-German hostilities begin. But the Admiralty's plans, as expounded by Admiral Sir Arthur Wilson, the First Sea Lord, did not allow for the transport of troops. At a further meeting in September, McKenna refused to guarantee it.[60]

The apprehensions created by the Agadir incident destroyed the First Lord's reputation in the Cabinet. Under pressure, from Haldane and Lloyd George, Asquith agreed that he be replaced. The Prime Minister was not prepared, however, to promote Macnamara. He decided that McKenna and Churchill, the Home Secretary, should change places.[61]

Within the Admiralty a reorganisation of responsibilities took place. Macnamara had described the McKenna trio as making decisions together over the entire range of Admiralty policy. In March 1912 Churchill defined the functions of the various members of the Board of Admiralty in specific terms. The First Lord, he said, stood in a special position, charged with the general direction and the assignment of all business; the First Sea Lord had the duty of making preparations for war and moving the Fleet, the Second Sea Lord working in association with him but having specific responsibility for the men of the Navy; the Third Sea Lord dealt with the Fleet's military construction, the Fourth Sea Lord with stores and ammunition. As for his Parliamentary colleagues, the Financial Secretary was responsible for the correct and proper control of Admiralty expenditure and the Civil Lord was responsible for works and other ancillary matters.[62] In the House, policy statements and the building, arming and fuelling of ships were reserved to Churchill who also responded, sometimes fiercely, to the interminable questions of Lord Charles Beresford; details of expenditure and on-shore issues were dealt with by Macnamara. Churchill and Macnamara often appeared together; Lambert appeared seldom.[63]

In Churchill's view he had been sent to the Admiralty to make a new and a vehement effort.[64] As a result of his predecessor's measures, he told the Commons in March 1912, there was no cause whatever for alarm and despondency. The Admiralty was prepared to guarantee absolutely the main security of the country and of the Empire for the next few years, and if the House would grant them what they asked for in the future, that prospect would be indefinitely extended.[65] So the three programmes of 1912, 1913 and 1914 comprised the greatest additions in power and cost ever made to the Royal Navy.[66] As the Estimates rose, complaints emerged from the Radical left (notably by Philip Snowden, the future Labour Chancellor of the Exchequer) that the new taxation they had fought for in 1909, supposing that it would be devoted to problems of old age, poverty, unemployment, the education question and better housing, was being spent on *Dreadnoughts* and more specifically that proper financial control was not being exercised.[67] Churchill, who was conscious of his own mathematical shortcomings in comparison with his predecessor, rebutted these charges. 'I am confident in my ability to prove to ... this House', he declared during the Supplementary Estimates debate in 1914, 'that it has never been more efficiently and rigorously maintained than it has been under my rt hon Friend the Financial Secretary to the Admiralty during the last two years.'[68]

Churchill made it clear that the Admiralty was now preoccupied with the intentions of Germany. The time had come to readjust standards in closer accord with the actual facts and probable contingencies; the Government had now to consider the growth and development of a very powerful homogeneous navy, manned and trained by the Germans, the greatest organising people in the world. He proposed a building moratorium for one year, warning, however, that British construction would be stepped up if further German increases took place.[69] The Kaiser rejected the approach,[70] hence the building programme was accelerated and £1,000,000 Supplementary Estimate duly presented to a generally sympathetic House of Commons. Macnamara, at the end of the debate, emphasised that, still, no menace was intended to any of the peoples of the world:

> The Members of the Admiralty have exercised all the care that was humanly possible in framing these Supplementary Estimates. They are 'penny wise' without being 'pound foolish'. They are sufficient. That is our deliberate view. They are not in any sense estimates of provocation; they are estimates of self-preservation ... Our great friendly neighbour, Germany are our greatest customers [sic] on the Continent of Europe, and I think we are almost their greatest customers, and I hope to live to see the day when international disputes

may be settled by peaceful arbitration. Certainly these Estimates are not inspired in any sense by any spirit of aggression. They simply provide that vital protection behind which we can quietly and soberly go on our way perfecting our institutions, curing our social evils. That is all.[71]

Again, in March 1913, Churchill proposed a moratorium, adding regretfully that he expected it to be refused.[72] Macnamara, reviewing expenditure over eight years, pointed out the consequential and continuous liabilities that arose from building *Dreadnoughts*:

More new ships mean more men, more men mean more money for pay, for naval stores, and establishment charges generally. New ships soon mean more charges for refits and repairs ... Not only have we been compelled to make new construction provision, but everything is bigger and costlier. Everything grows earlier obsolescent. Ships develop more speed, and more speed means greatly increased cost of machinery. They cost more as regards their sea service for fuel. Their guns cost more, and the guns cost more to fire. Longer, broader and bigger ships mean larger provision than we had hitherto to face for dock accommodation. Then comes oil fuel, tankers to carry it, land and tanks in which to store it ...

Now came the public demand for air protection. 'Either scrap the whole of the British Navy to-morrow, or see that your Navy is invulnerable; for to take any other course is ridiculous, wasteful and dangerous, and, may well be disastrous', Macnamara told the House.[73] His speech elicited a generous letter of thanks from the First Lord on 12 April:

My dear Macnamara,

I have been meaning for some time to write & thank you for the vy great aid wh you have given me in this office. It has most markedly contributed to any measure of success our admin has obtained. Whether on the Bd, or at the head of the Finance Ctee or in yr conduct of labour questions, or in the H of C, yr services to the Admy are of the highest value. Yr presence on the Bd enables me to leave the management of H of C business increasingly in yr hands, & I do so without the slightest anxiety. I also feel able with perfect confidence to follow yr judgment & adopt yr conclusions on an ever widening category of important questions.

Quite apart from personal friendships, I have felt it my duty to write in this sense to you, & I have also thought it proper to write the same thing to the PM.

Once more accept my warmest thanks. Don't bother to answer.

Yrs v sincly
WSC[74]

The post-Stead *Review of Reviews*, quoting Macnamara's comments, concluded that Churchill needed to take further action, arguing that Germany's attempts to reduce the British lead in warships would bear but a small comparison with the urgency and extent of the necessary efforts which needed to be taken if Britain was not to accede to Germany's mastership of the air.[75] But the first Lord needed no encouragement. Suspecting, as he prepared the Naval Estimates for 1914–15, that he would encounter opposition within the Cabinet, he began his campaign to increase the total spent by £3,000,000 to £50,694,800 with a powerful speech at Guildhall on 13 November in which he promised, to cheers, that the Government, once it was satisfied of the need for more men and money, would not hesitate to ask for them. Facing the Cabinet on 5 December, he argued that the German Navy Law, the increase in size, speed, armament, equipment and cost of warships, the introduction and development of oil fuel, the Air Service and wireless telegraphy and, in particular, a general rise in prices and wages made further expenditure unavoidable. Opposed by Samuel, Simon, Runciman, McKenna and, in the first weeks of what became a Cabinet crisis, by Lloyd George (who sought an assurance that 1915–16 expenditure would be reduced), Churchill refused to give way. On 12 January 1914, he argued that, far from reducing his demands, he needed a further £2,500,000 to cover the cost of three ships promised by the Canadian Prime Minister, which would now not be delivered.[76] The 1912 coal strike and shipyard congestion, he told Lloyd George a week later, had caused £4,800,000 of shipbuilding from previous years to fall into arrears and only now mature for payment.[77] Cabinet colleagues considering an enquiry into naval expenditure were challenged directly. On 16 January he circulated the report of the Finance Committee on the Naval Estimates for 1914–15:

> The zeal and industry of the Financial Secretary have been beyond all praise, and every portion of the naval notes has been subjected item by item to detailed scrutiny. In consequence of this there is no part of naval expenditure upon which I should not welcome the fullest enquiry by a Parliamentary Committee, free to discuss not merely administration but policy. Such a committee, if composed, of serious and reputable members of the House of Commons, however selected, would arrive at no conclusion except that increases were desirable under many heads ... [78]

Over the next fortnight, Lloyd George, who had at first concluded that the matter might involve a smash-up of the Ministry, moved slowly but surely towards Churchill's point of view. He consulted Macnamara both before and after the Cabinet meeting of 16 January;[79] ten days later he was disposed to accept Churchill's guarantee that expenditure would be reduced in 1915–16.[80] On 1 February, Asquith informed the First Lord that the critical pack had slackened their pursuit and invited him to make minor concessions on maintenance charges in the interests of conciliation. Churchill responded:

2nd February 1914   [Admiralty]

PRIVATE
COPY

My dear P Minister,

For the last four or five months I have been striving by every means in my power to reduce the cost of the maintenance votes. They have been searched and scrubbed by Macnamara & his Finance Committee as they have never been before. I am circulating today papers on the three points – fuel, practice, ammunition, & minor repairs – wh were specifically raised at the Cabinet. These will I believe be found conclusive ... there is no part of my admin of this office wh has not throughout been conducted with severe economy; & this can be proved by reference not only to facts but to my minutes & directions at every stage. I see absolutely no hope of further reductions in the cost of maintenance & upkeep ... I do not love this naval expenditure & am grieved to be found in the position of taskmaster. But I am myself the slave of facts & forces wh are uncontrollable unless naval efficiency is frankly abandoned. The result of all this pressure & controversy leaves me anxious chiefly lest the necessary services have been cut too low ...

Yours always,
W [81]

On 2 March, the Admiralty ministers presented Supplementary Estimates to the House of Commons. Churchill pointed out that oil prices had doubled over two years; higher dockyard wages, approved the previous May, had to be paid, shipyard contractors were working faster and pressing for payment; the three ships to replace those promised by the Canadian Prime Minister had to be paid for; eight airships had been ordered. 'The only new Service which involves an extension of programme, which involves a question of principle, which incurs an extension of liability is the £260,000 for aircraft', Churchill concluded. 'All the rest is either money which would have to be paid sooner or later under the existing commitments, but being paid now, will not have to be paid hereafter, or else it is an automatic increase through wages and prices which are a necessary consequence of market conditions.' [82]

Later the same day, Macnamara showed how the procedure followed over the Supplementary Estimates was the customary one, replicating four similar applications in the previous ten years. 'Then comes another charge which I feel bound to meet – the charge of careless estimating', he went on. 'Hon members say: "You ought to have foreseen this; you ought to have forecast that". Of course, when hon members talk of careless estimating, I am bound, as the result of my office, to meet the criticisms ...' He quoted from Churchill's speech on the Estimates of 1913–14 on 26 March 1913. The First Lord had referred to the extreme congestion in the shipyards arising from the extraordinary demands upon shipbuilding plant and skilled labour. He had made an estimate based not on the total nominal cost of executing the programmes but on the maximum which the contractors would in all probability be able to earn. If his hon Friends would leave out the variations announced by the First Lord in respect of the building contracts, and the oil, air, and increased dockyard expenses (all matters of policy) the difference between the original Estimate and the present position was comparatively small.[83]

The Supplementary Estimates were followed by the Estimates for 1914–15 which, at £51,000,000, were the largest ever presented to the House. But in the First Lord's view the prospects for 1915–16 were distinctly more favourable. Building arrears would have been worked off; the oil reserves were reaching their maximum; the reserves of ammunition were full. Some factors told in the opposite direction: in 1915–16 there would have to be more men and more officers; incremental scales of pay and pension schemes could not and ought not to be arrested and he added, 'there are always new services and new contingencies which crop up. Still, surveying the whole situation, I think it reasonable to predict that, in the absence of any new departure in policy, the Estimates for 1915 should be substantially lower than those of this year.'

Later in his speech, Churchill announced that the Admiralty had decided for 1914 to substitute a general mobilisation of the Third Fleet, calling up the whole of the Royal Fleet Reserve for a period of eleven days.[84] Consequently, at Spithead on 17 and 18 July, a grand review of the Navy took place which, as Churchill later asserted, constituted incomparably the greatest assemblage of naval power ever witnessed in the history of the world.[85] It was soon to be put to the test. On 24 July, Austria's ultimatum to Serbia was placed before the Cabinet. On 29 July, the First Fleet left Portland for Scapa Flow. Six days later, Great Britain, the time-limit on her ultimatum to Germany on Belgian neutrality having expired, entered the war.

13

Financial Secretary to the Admiralty, 1914–1920

When war began, on 4 August 1914, Macnamara had spent six years and nearly four months as Parliamentary and Financial Secretary to the Admiralty. A further five years and seven months in the post lay before him. It was to be the longest continuous tenure of one office by a member of the House of Commons since the Reform Act of 1832.

Two opportunities for promotion came and went. In February 1914, the post of Financial Secretary to the Treasury (which Lloyd George had sought for him in 1908) had fallen vacant, but Asquith had preferred Edwin Montagu, his former Private Secretary. A year later, the unfortunate C. F. G. Masterman, obliged to undergo re-election on appointment as Chancellor of the Duchy of Lancaster, was rejected by his constituents. He failed to find a safe haven elsewhere and was obliged to resign. 'There is real trouble about Macnamara', Asquith wrote to Venetia Stanley on 28 January 1915:

> When he was passed over for the Assyrian, he was assured that his 'political future' would not be prejudiced. He is a popular man in the party, having been for many years a keen wire-puller and favourite platform orator ... Winston thinks he will be mortally stricken if Montagu – much his junior – is now preferred to him for the Cabinet. LlG and I pointed out that, not only would he be of no real use in the Cabinet, but that it would look bad for him to leave his post at the Admiralty in the middle of the war. I must see him (he is really *au fond* a good fellow) and try to smooth things out, tho' I don't look forward with pleasure to the interview.[1]

Macnamara, however, made things easy for the Prime Minister, who reported the next day:

> McN [sic] behaved extraordinarily well. Nothing would induce him to forsake his quarter deck at the Admiralty during the war! Perish the thought! According to Lloyd George, his eye flashed & his bosom swelled with patriotic pride & self-devotion. He volunteered to go and see the Assyrian & assure him of his good will – which he did ...[2]

The realistic Riddell commented:

I wonder if he has done the right thing. He thinks himself almost indispensable at the Admiralty, but this opinion is not shared by others, although he is no doubt a very hard-working capable official. Whether he is exactly the right man in the right place some doubt. From his own point of view I have no doubt he has done the wrong thing. This is, I think, the third time he has missed his chance. Missing chances is dangerous in the greedy game of politics . . .[3]

Macnamara's decision proved, however, to be a fortunate one. The last Liberal government had only three months to run. As the newest member of the Cabinet, he would, in all likelihood, have lost his post and returned to the back benches when the first Coalition was formed. As it was, even though the epicentre of the explosion which toppled the Liberal administration was the Admiralty itself, he was too firmly established there to be dislodged.

On 15 February 1915, Churchill gave his account to the Commons of what, since the beginning of the war, the Navy had achieved. It was, he said, as sound as a bell all through, 'the product of good management and organisation, of sound principle in design and strategy, of sterling workmen and faithful workmanship, and careful clerks and accountants, and skilful engineers, and painstaking officers and hardy tars'. With its allies it had driven the Germans from the seas of the world. 'We have established for the time being', he stated proudly, 'a command of the sea such as we had never expected, such as we had never known, and our ancestors had never known, at any other period of our history.'[4]

Bertram Falle, the member for Portsmouth, remained sceptical. In Churchill's absence, he accused him of 'blowing'. In September, the First Lord had been in Antwerp, vainly telling the burgomaster that the British would save his city. He was continually running over to France. He bore personal responsibility for the loss of the *Cressy*, the *Hogue*, the *Aboukir* and *Hawke*, and also, Falle implied, for the loss of the *Good Hope* and the *Monmouth* off Chile. The subsequent victory off the Falkland Islands he ascribed to Fisher. 'The country', he concluded, '. . . is agreed that it is Heaven's mercy that Lord Fisher is at the Admiralty.'[5]

This observation, with its implication that the direction of naval policy properly lay with the First Sea Lord, heralded the collision of Fisher and Churchill which was to break up the Government in mid-May. Recalled to his former post at the age of seventy-three at the end of October 1914, on the enforced resignation of Prince Louis of Battenberg, Fisher found, to his dissatisfaction, that his place on the War Council was merely an advisory one and that, at the Admiralty, he was frequently overruled by Churchill on technical matters, as well as on fleet movements.[6] This was in sharp contrast not only to the preeminence enjoyed by Kitchener at the War Office,[7] but also to the dominance he himself had enjoyed at the Admiralty in his previous period as First Sea Lord, especially when McKenna had been his willing disciple. McKenna may also have stimulated anti-Churchill hostility of a personal nature. As First Lord he (and his young wife) had become very friendly with Fisher. The friendship survived both the latter's retirement and the former's replacement by Churchill, which the old Admiral viewed with regret.[8] Riddell, spending the day with the McKennas in November 1913, perceived, when the Churchills arrived for tea, that under the outward appearance of amity and goodwill there was no love lost between the couples. A year later, just after Fisher returned to the Admiralty, he recorded McKenna's comment that things there had been found in an unsatisfactory state.[9] By the end of January the First Lord and First Sea Lord were expressing grievances about one another to the Prime Minister. Already Fisher was frequently threatening to resign.[10] When in mid-April Churchill attempted to persuade Riddell that he and Fisher were in agreement, Riddell noted: 'He seemed very sure of Fisher. I wonder whether his confidence is justified? Fisher is very thick with the McKennas. I doubt if Winston and Fisher will be able to pull together ...'[11]

By now, in fact, the Dardanelles campaign was beginning to destroy their partnership. The possibility of forcing the straits and thereby offering relief to the Russians had occupied Churchill since September, weeks before Fisher's reappointment. The bombardment of the outer forts by the British and French Fleets, already essayed on 3 November, was begun in earnest on 19 February; by 2 March they had been destroyed. After this promising beginning, things began to go wrong. On 10 March, Kitchener, having previously resisted the idea, decided that a division should be sent out from Great Britain in support. Its commander reached the war zone a week later; his troops, Australian, New Zealand, French and British, were not assembled till mid-April. The naval attack on the narrows went ahead on 18 March, but four days later both naval and military commanders declared that troops were essential to force a passage. The military invasion began on 25 April.[12] What had been envisaged originally as a naval enterprise of limited cost and risk had become a military operation, lasting for the remainder of 1915, in which the Navy was merely an adjunct.

At the War Council, on 13 January, when the campaign had been authorised, Fisher had remained silent.[13] On 14 May, when Kitchener complained about the Navy's abandonment of the operation, Fisher responded that he had been against it from the beginning. The same evening he seemed to agree, in conversation with Churchill, to the idea of further naval support.[14] Later his long-suppressed rage against politicians' interference broke forth. The next day he resigned. Lloyd George, Asquith and McKenna tried in vain to persuade him to return and, according to Fisher, the Civil Lord (Lambert) went to him three times, offering him a seat in the Cabinet if he agreed to Churchill going back as First Lord. Finally, Macnamara appeared as Fisher was going to bed. He told them both to take back the thirty pieces of silver they offered him for betraying his country to the men who had sent them.[15]

On Sunday 16 May, Asquith refused Churchill's offer of resignation. The following afternoon, however, when the First Lord arrived at the House of Commons ready to defend his policy, he discovered from Lloyd George and the Prime Minister that he no longer held office.[16] A coalition was to be formed, with Balfour as First Lord of the Admiralty. Curiously, Fisher still felt that he might regain his former position. On 19 May, he despatched an ultimatum to the Prime Minister stating that if six conditions were agreed, he could guarantee the successful termination of the war and the total abolition of the submarine menace (which, in May 1915, was not yet serious):

1.   That Mr Winston Churchill is not in the Cabinet to be always circumventing me, nor will I serve under Mr Balfour.

2.   That Sir A. K. Wilson leaves the Admiralty and the Committee of Imperial Defence and the War Council, as my time otherwise will be occupied in resisting the bombardment of Heligoland and other such wild projects, also his policy is totally opposed to mine and he has accepted position of First Sea Lord in succession to me, and thereby adopting a policy diametrically opposed to my views.

3.   That there shall be an entire new Board of Admiralty, as regards the Sea Lords and the Financial Secretary (who is utterly useless). NEW MEASURES DEMAND NEW MEN!

4.   That I shall have complete professional charge of the war at sea, together with the absolute sole disposition of the Fleet, and the appointments of all officers of all rank whatsoever, and absolutely untrammelled sole command of all the sea forces whatsoever.

5.   That the First Lord of the Admiralty should be absolutely restricted to policy and Parliamentary procedure and should occupy the same position towards me as Mr Tennant MP does to Lord Kitchener (and very well he does it).

6.   That I should have the sole absolute authority for all new construction and all dockyard work of whatever sort whatsoever, and complete control of the whole of the Civil establishments of the Navy.[17]

Not surprisingly the ultimatum had no effect. In retrospect the Prime Minister blamed Fisher for the ministerial crisis and the formation of the coalition. 'He deserved to be shot', Asquith told C. P. Scott, editor of the *Manchester Guardian*, the following March: 'and in any other country he would have been shot.'[18] As for the sally against Macnamara, it was ignored. On 28 May, the Financial Secretary accepted reappointment in his post. The ultimatum itself was not made public till Asquith published his *Memories and Reflections* thirteen years later. 'Lord Fisher was undoubtedly a man with streaks of genius', the former Prime Minister then concluded, 'but he was affected with fits of megalomania, in one of which this extraordinary ultimatum must have been composed.'[19]

With Churchill and Fisher gone, the opposing fleets settled into a contest in attrition, interrupted briefly just over a year later by the battle of Jutland. Germany, its plans to wage war by sea frustrated, sought other means, amongst which submarines proved to be the most deadly, to break the stalemate. Under pressure of what, in Churchill's view, was 'in scale and in stake the greatest conflict ever decided at sea',[20] the Admiralty was placed on the defensive. Changes of personnel, which brought to its direction three First Lords and three First Sea Lords in three years, weakened its political impact. Balfour, Churchill's successor, occupied in Cabinet, on the Dardanelles Committee, on the War Staff Group as well as on the Board of Admiralty,[21] could spare little time for the House of Commons. Sir Edward Carson, appointed on 10 December 1916, announced that he knew nothing of naval affairs and would be guided in all things by his advisers.[22] Sir Eric Geddes, who replaced him after only eight months, had not yet been elected a member of Parliament. He, too, appeared rarely in the House, usually to read a prepared statement. In his maiden speech of 1 November 1917 cast in this mode, he referred to the kaleidoscopic change going on in warfare which, he said, was also occurring in workshop and shipyard. 'To the uninformed observer', he added, 'it must appear sometimes that there is no method in the madness of those who control these matters.'[23] During the long absences of Macnamara's immediate superiors, it was not the least of the Financial Secretary's functions for the rest of the war to attempt to explain to the Commons how this control was being exercised. Balfour expressed his gratitude in a letter that Macnamara always treasured:

> During all the critical period I was at the Admiralty you gave me the most important assistance. Your long experience ... was invaluable and your tact and judgment in dealing with the question in the House of Commons beyond praise. You did most excellent public service and the country should be grateful to you.[24]

Other duties came and went as the Government's activities extended in all directions. In the autumn of 1914, Macnamara's chief concern was the creation with Montagu and Harold Baker (Financial Secretary to the War Office) of a scale for pensions and separation allowances appropriate for war conditions. On 13 October, their report, over which they had not been in agreement, came before the Cabinet. 'Finally the question emerged whether a childless widow should get per week (as now) 5s (Montagu and Baker) or 7s 6d (Macnamara) or 6s 6d (proposed by Kitchener as a compromise)', Asquith reported:

> The argument in favour of not more than 5s is almost overwhelming, but as the childless widows are estimated to amount to no less than one-third of the whole, and they would be left as they are, a 5s rate would be genuinely condemned outside as mean and ungenerous. There was a long dreary desultory discussion, and in the end I said I would do what I have done (I think) only twice before in nearly seven years – take a division in the Cabinet ...

Only Churchill voted for 7s 6d; eight of his colleagues voted for 5s and ten for 6s 6d; though when the question was reconsidered on 4 November, 7s 6d was agreed.[25]

Four days later, on the eve of the publication of the scales in a White Paper, Macnamara sent for Riddell, to find out what the reaction of the press would be. 'I gave him my criticism which he did not agree with and did not like', Riddell recorded: 'The scale is drawn on generous lines, but many of the details are highly objectionable.'[26] This proved to be a shrewd comment. On 11 November, Parliament reassembled, and it was soon plain that the White Paper was not popular. Separation allowances and pensions constituted a very difficult question, Asquith admitted during the debate on the Address. The sort of problem which arose was one of the most intricate and most difficult with which any statesman could possibly have to deal:

> ... it would be impossible to have a scale of pensions or of separation allowances which is graduated according to the different earnings of the different people with whom we are dealing. The complications are infinite and the justice of it would be very doubtful.

Bonar Law agreed that the task was a colossal one. To avoid further delay he suggested that a small all-party committee be appointed to go into the matter. Asquith agreed.[27] On 18 November, the committee, consisting of Austen Chamberlain and Bonar Law (Conservative), George Barnes (Labour), T. P. O'Connor (Irish Nationalist), Reginald McKenna (Home Secretary) with Lloyd George as Chairman, was duly created. It began its investigations five days later. Among the twenty witnesses Macnamara himself appeared, to discuss with the committee the main features of the White Paper, including graduated pensions and differentiated separation allowances for Army and Navy wives and dependants, as well as the administration of the new schemes.[28]

By mid-February, when the issues were again taken up in the Commons, it seemed likely that both pensions and separation allowances would be increased. On the second day of what was to be the last debate on the Navy Estimates in which the Churchill-Macnamara partnership answered for the Admiralty, Macnamara confirmed the fact. He said:

> Although I was responsible, with others, for the rather less generous schemes of the White Paper it is not for me, the son of a non-commissioned officer, to complain of the greater liberality of the Select Committee ... But ... the Select Committee has followed in the main ... the general foundations for the administration of assistance laid down by those responsible for the White Paper schemes ... I do not forget the pension day that came once a quarter for the few and the long line of broken men and women outside, pathetically holding out basins into which their old comrades threw assistance with recklessly generous hands ... I greatly rejoice that under this provision those days are gone for ever.[29]

The Naval and Military War Pensions Act, passed in July, supplemented the scales through extra-Parliamentary means; local committees were also set up. Macnamara remarked at the end of November 1916:

> From the very beginning there has not been a day upon which some phase or other of this problem has not had to pass through my hands ... at the Admiralty ... we were very fortunate in having in existence when war broke out a piece of machinery tested by long experience. War subjected that machinery to no very serious strain.[30]

But now the establishment of a Ministry of Pensions was being proposed. At first the Navy was not included. Macnamara thought the omission appropriate. The Admiralty, he felt, had a duty to direct, to administer and to preside over the care of those who served them, which was not affected by the needs of the enormous New Army, for which the legislation had been designed:

> All our work is done under one roof. All Service records are under that roof ... The work is done by men, one and all, imbued by the fine sentiment that the Lords Commissioners of the Navy are the little fathers of the Fleet, and that their responsibility towards the sailor and those he leaves behind does not close when he is laid aside and broken, or when he has passed away.[31]

He was overruled. Hayes Fisher, during the Second Reading, referred to his powerful, very effective speech: 'We all know how much he has cared for the sailor under his charge, and how much he has tried to do for him. But although I admired the speech I am unconvinced.' When he observed the functioning of the new Pensions Ministry, under Barnes, Macnamara changed his mind. He wrote to Lloyd George on 6 June 1917:

> When the Ministry was formed, I tried, as you may remember, to stick to the sailors ourselves (there was really no need for them to be taken over by an outside authority; the real need arose from a great extension of War Office operations). But after six months' close touch with Barnes as one of his Statutory Advisers I am very glad indeed he has got the soldiers, and I am not altogether sorry that he has got the sailors. Watching his method of tackling matters I have had to confess, even to myself, that generations of dealing with the subject had perhaps caused us to be a little official in our methods.[32]

Another responsibility which fell to the Admiralty, to be transferred elsewhere once it had expanded, was the requisitioning of merchant ships. When the war began, more than one sixth of the world's merchant shipping was British. The needs of troop transport and coal and oil supply demanded immediate government action; hence, following a Royal Proclamation, the Admiralty, in combination with the ship-owners, set up a Board of Arbitration, with powers to requisition. Consequently, the Transport Department of the Admiralty met not only the immediate needs of the Army and Navy but also the urgent calls for assistance from Canada,

Australia, New Zealand and Britain's continental allies, as well as the demands of the Dardanelles campaign. By March 1916, 4,000,000 combatants, 1,000,000 horses and other animals, over 2,000,000 tons of stores and 22,000,000 gallons of oil had been carried to their destinations. Before the war the Department had employed fifty-five persons; now the figure approached 900. In the early days of its operations, ship-owners did not feel it a particular hardship to be what was subsequently styled 'over-requisitioned'. But market rates had risen considerably beyond what the Board of Trade was paying. The Admiralty began to incur criticism from ship-owners and their Parliamentary representatives. In the Debate on the Address, B. E. Peto, the Unionist member for Devizes, introduced an unsuccessful amendment regretting that measures had not been taken to utilise economically the available merchant tonnage of the country by placing it under the control of a central expert authority, with full powers to requisition and direct the movements of all vessels and fix and limit remuneration for transport services of all kinds during the war. Macnamara responded:

> What is said of us is that the Department could have done all that it has done without making such great inroads upon merchant shipping ... when ships are taken away it is only natural that both the shipowner and the general community, which is very seriously affected ... should regret it ... But it must be remembered that between these great warlike operations and the everyday peaceful operations of commerce there is an inevitable gulf fixed. It is quite impossible to conduct great warlike operations with the deliberation, the careful circumspection and the nice adjustment of interests with which peaceful commercial transactions can be carried out.[33]

Already a Shipping Control Committee had been set up under Lord Curzon to secure economy in the use of tonnage, to set a limit to the amount of tonnage supplied to Allies, to investigate import restrictions, port congestion and shipbuilding, but no action was taken to secure these aims. The Department of Transport continued its massive task until December when within hours of the fall of Asquith's government, Sir Joseph Maclay took over, first as President of the Shipping Control Committee, later as Shipping Controller. 'Hitherto the Admiralty had exercised a considerable measure of control over sea transport, and the new Ministry was thus relieving them of a very heavy and increasingly difficult task which lay strictly outside their ordinary routine and for the handling of which they did not possess the appropriate commercial and industrial experience', Lloyd George observed in his *War Memoirs*. 'Yet ... there was little gratitude at the lightening of burdens they were unable to carry. Sir Joseph Maclay got no friendly reception from the Admiralty.'[34]

The war had also robbed Macnamara of his main responsibility, the explanation and defence of Admiralty expenditure. Once hostilities had begun, the traditional processes of public debate could no longer be maintained, in the interests both of rapid action and of secrecy. An Emergency Standing Committee was at once set up between the Admiralty and the Treasury, by means of which the former was relieved of the necessity of obtaining the latter's sanction as a preliminary to urgent expenditure in the public interest.[35] In the debate on Supply (Navy Supplementary Estimates 1915–16) on 1 March 1916, Macnamara explained how the old procedures would henceforward be superseded. Details of the Estimates were now quite out of place. Hence, for each of the seventeen Navy Votes Parliament had been asked to sanction a token £1,000, with an Appropriation-in-Aid for each heading of £100. Discussion on particular votes, in abstract terms, would be permitted, so as to provide a statutory basis for each nominal amount; discussion on Appropriations-in-Aid would take place later in the year and Commons approval sought so that authorisation might be given to utilise these amounts either for a particular Vote or for another Vote.[36]

Starved of the details of naval expenditure, Commons critics sought reassurance from the Financial Secretary that Parliamentary control had not been completely lost. On 22 June 1917, Macnamara explained how, under the token system for 1915–16, the amount placed at the Admiralty's disposal was £18,700:

> By the Supplementary Estimate presented on 21st February 1916, a further sum of £10 was voted, plus £4,500,000 estimated substantive Appropriations-in-Aid, and that was made available by that Token Vote. Therefore, down to 21st February 1916, the total spending power of the Admiralty for the year 1915–16, so far as the Navy Votes was concerned, was £4,518,710. For the rest, we drew upon the Vote of Credit ... The Appropriation Account shows that in 1915–16 we actually expended a gross sum of £211,421,914 3s 3d. If I deduct from that the sum to which I have already referred ... there remains an excess of £206,903,204 3s 3d which has to be met out of issues from the Vote of Credit and out of Appropriations-in-Aid ...

The Appropriation Account for the year had been submitted to the Comptroller and Auditor General in summarised form, printed by order of the House on 1 March. Consequently, Admiralty officers had been examined before the Public Accounts Committee, which would report to the House later in the year. Full details would be published as and when the public interest permitted.[37]

Macnamara reinforced his points in a debate on House of Commons Control of National Expenditure a fortnight later. No one pretended that the Token Votes were anything more than the merest form, he admitted. No one would pretend that, in the slightest degree, they filled the place of the old detailed Estimates, but they were, in his view, the only thing possible in the circumstances. Some members seemed to think that when Navy Token Estimates showed less than £20,000 and Appropriation Accounts showed an expenditure of £200,000,000, Treasury or Parliamentary check had gone to the winds. But, though expenditure had enormously increased, the machinery of checking it after it had been made remained pretty much what it was in peace time:

> ... at the close of the financial year we still go to work ... to complete the Appropriation Account. We submit that account to the Comptroller and Auditor-General within nine months of the close of the financial year as usual. He reports upon it in the early part of the following year and submits his Report to Parliament as usual ... the Public Accounts Committee proceeds to examine the Report of the Comptroller and Auditor-General, examine Departmental officers upon it and submits its Report to Parliament as usual.

Hence, he concluded:

> I really cannot admit the proposition that the strain has broken down the machinery for checking public expenditure which we created before the war ... there remains at work precisely the same as ever the peace-time check upon expenditure after it has been incurred of the Comptroller and the Public Accounts Committee, and finally of the House of Commons itself.[38]

Churchill's resignation as First Lord of the Admiralty in May 1915 had coincided with the end of Germany's first submarine campaign, brought to a close after American protests about the sinking of the *Lusitania*. In Churchill's view it had created no alarm, and no substantial nor even noticeable injury was wrought upon British commerce. Commons questions on hostile attacks over the next twelve months, dealt with by both Balfour and Macnamara, concerned aircraft and Zeppelins. But in June 1915 Balfour had told Riddell that, in his opinion, his predecessor had rather underestimated the importance of the submarine and that many more casualties could be expected.[39] The second campaign, beginning in October 1916, confirmed the wisdom of this view. It was to become the British Government's chief anxiety. In December, Carson informed the House, 118 British, Allied and neutral vessels of over 1,000 tons had been lost; in January 1917 the figure had fallen to ninety-one, but in the first eighteen days of February it had risen to 134.[40] As fear spread, apprehension developed that the true picture was being concealed. Macnamara denied this in an oral answer on 16 March; on 29 March he provided details of British losses from submarines and mines; thirty in December; twenty-six in January, sixty-eight in February and fifty-five in March.[41] Eight days later, the United States declared war on Germany. To counter the German aim of bringing starvation to Britain before any American assistance could be given, the convoy system was introduced at the end of the month. On 27 July, Macnamara announced that over 3,000 merchant ships had already been armed and that the process was continuing, though it was not in the public interest to give exact details, nor to state the types of guns mounted.[42] The matter was now so serious that Geddes, in his first appearances as First Lord, refused to provide either in figures or in percentages, the gross register tonnage which had been sunk. It was left to the Prime Minister, on the eve of the summer recess, to assure the House that far from losses of 450,000 to 500,000 tons a month, as the German Government claimed, British monthly losses were now under 250,000 tons.[43] But the losses continued, well into the new year, and in the frequent absences of Geddes it was Macnamara who was obliged to deal with Parliamentary questions. On 5 December, for example, the following exchanges took place:

> Mr Tillett asked the First Lord of the Admiralty whether he is aware of the serious loss of mercantile tonnage, and the consequent serious loss of life and foodstuffs and supplies, owing to the lack of destroyers; and whether or not naval strategy should be reviewed to concentrate on more effective anti-U-boat warfare and the safer convoying of merchant shipping?

> Dr Macnamara: 'I can assure my hon Friend that the Navy gives all the protection its resources and duties permit.'

> Mr W. Thorne: 'Is there any truth in the statement that the major part of the ships that are now being sunk by the U-boats are in the Irish Channel, and does the rt hon Gentleman think that the Irish Channel is sufficiently protected at the present time?'

> Dr Macnamara: 'I cannot say anything as to the former part of the question, but the Navy is doing all it possibly can within its resources.'

> Mr G. Lambert: 'Has the rt hon Gentleman any available information with regard to the destruction of foreign hostile submarines?'

> Dr Macnamara: 'No; I cannot add anything to what has already been said ...'

> Mr Houston asked the First Lord of the Admiralty whether he is aware of the delay to ships and loss of the use of mercantile tonnage by the present system of convoy?

> Dr Macnamara: 'Yes, Sir. Some delay to shipping must necessarily result from any system of convoy sailings.'

> Mr Houston: 'I do not wish to be severe on the Admiralty, but is not the rt hon Gentleman aware that there have been many inefficient methods adopted up to the present, and that steamers are kept waiting at least ten days for convoys, and that convoys have been sent out ... with fast and slow ships running together, with the result that the convoys go along at the rate of four or seven knots an hour?'

> Dr Macnamara: 'If my hon Friend has any views as to convoys not being worked as efficiently as they might be, I shall be very glad to have them.'[44]

The establishment of the Ministry of Shipping in December 1916 had appeared to offer advantages in placing the overall control not only of requisitioning but also of the building of merchant ships in the hands of Maclay. As the toll of shipping, naval as well as merchant, exacted by submarines, rose, however, the disadvantage of separating naval and merchant shipbuilding began to be perceived. 'The answer to the submarine menace lies in the shipyards and the marine engine shops', Macnamara told the House of Commons during the Navy Estimates debate in February 1917:

> The Admiralty has at present in each shipbuilding district an admiral and a staff, and under him ... experts in the labour problem in connection with shipbuilding and repairs. And, again, in the shipyards we have technical officers not merely superintending Admiralty work, but also assisting in the development of commercial work ... I think we must look for a substantial acceleration in the output of merchant tonnage of the right sort.[45]

It was decided to place the control of all shipbuilding in the hands of an Admiralty Controller.[46] Consequently, on 11 May, Sir Eric Geddes was appointed to the post, charged, as he put it, with the whole business of the production of naval material as well as of the designs and production of ships for the Ministry of Shipping and craft for the War Office.[47] These responsibilities remained with the Admiralty when, on 17 July, Geddes succeeded Carson as First Lord. Now in addition to House of Commons questions on the submarine war, Macnamara was obliged to deal with the Admiralty's efforts to make up the tonnage lost through enemy action.

In his Navy Estimates statement of 5 March 1918, Geddes explained how, after the difficulties of the first nine months of 1917, the last three months had shown an upward trend in United Kingdom shipbuilding. In January 1918, however, a serious drop had occurred, for which the main reason appeared to be labour unrest.[48] This observation unleashed a series of attacks on the Admiralty. Had it dealt with the whole question with the utmost diplomacy that was possible? Had the Admiralty not the power to press on the employers of labour and make contracts with them? Would the rt hon. Gentleman who would reply say whether he was quite satisfied with the management and arrangement made for shipbuilding right at the very top, where there was constant chopping, changing and interference? Was the Admiralty satisfied that the national shipyards it was setting up at Benchley, Portbury and Chepstow were the best means of giving the maximum output of tonnage?[49] Macnamara responded:

> So far as the Board of Admiralty was concerned charged as they now are ... with the duty of new construction and repair, the more the House of Commons ventilates this subject the better they will be pleased. The more the public ventilation of the problem – the temper and determination of the people being what it is – the more it will put the right public spirit and resolve behind the problem, just as in 1915 it was put behind the problem of the supply of munitions ... If I were asked to name that date on which the new construction will balance the losses, I should say, indeed I must say, 'Ask the shipyards and the marine engine shops' ... It is in the hands of the employers and employed themselves in those yards and shops. Without their hearty co-operation and good-will the date must be postponed ... dangerously postponed, at which

tonnage losses and new tonnage put into service shall balance each other ... [50]

He was not prepared to blame the shipyard men, he said. The shortcomings were not of their own creation. The matters at issue and the disputes which had delayed output were no doubt of grave importance to themselves: but, he added:

> that importance rests, like everything else to-day, solely upon the assumption that when the war is over the Union Jack will be seen floating serenely in the skies. Take that away, and everything else is lost and what, then, will be the value of the rights and privileges, of 'private interests, prejudices and partial affections' about which all of us are so jealous? ...

He ended with an unusually passionate peroration:

> We have either to put our shoulders to the wheel or to put our necks under the yoke ... My appeal, therefore, consists of two words – Maximum Output – and I confess I never make that appeal – no one can – without thinking of those other men, the men of the Fleet, the men in the trenches, and the men of the merchant service, in the continued and loyal support of whom throughout this long struggle I gratefully recognise that the great majority of our people home here, men and women, have toiled so spontaneously and so faithfully and will continue to toil to the end ... [51]

Still the torrent of criticism went on. 'Why the Admiralty should ever have undertaken this avalanche of merchant shipbuilding which is contemplated I have never been able to understand', Commander Bellairs (Maidstone) complained during the Consolidated Fund Bill debate a week later. 'It has hindered the conduct of the war. It is not merely merchant shipping which has been hindered: Naval shipbuilding itself has been hindered.' But Macnamara was not to be moved:

> I observe that there is pretty general agreement in all quarters that one reason – in some quarters it is given as THE reason – for the failure is the defectiveness of Admiralty organisation at the top ... I am far less concerned with defending Admiralty organisation than I am to get tonnage ... It may very well be that we have not got the last word in perfect organisation on the Admiralty shipbuilding side. The Department is not twelve months old. We have already made changes ... If there are still defects they must be dealt with promptly and without respect for persons ... But if you make the machinery at the top as perfect as the most severe critic would wish – ... let the House and the country be under no delusion; you will not get the tonnage unless at the other end, in the yard and elsewhere, everybody pulls on the rope for all he is worth.[52]

Macnamara's responsibility for labour and conditions in the dockyards had earlier revived his personal connections with Lloyd George. When, in the Navy Estimates debate of mid-February 1915, Churchill had dilated on sterling workmen and faithful workmanship, careful clerks and accountants and skilful engineers,[4] Macnamara had been dealing more specifically with time-rates, overtime and Sunday work in the Royal yards.[53] With independent yards Admiralty relations had been less good. On 15 December 1914, he had met the Standing Committee of the Shipyard Trades at Newcastle (following conferences between it and the Shipbuilding Employers' Federation at York on 3 November and between the latter and the Unions at Carlisle on 9 December) and, later the same day, the Newcastle shipbuilders. The employees were looking for inducements; the employers complained about lost time and demarcation. Negotiations were judged to be in a state of deadlock; a month later a Committee of Production under Sir George Askwith began to investigate questions in dispute between engineers, shipwrights and boiler makers. Nevertheless, by the beginning of March 1915, it had become plain that no further progress would be made unless direct government intervention took place with a view to controlling employers and workers alike.

A new Defence of the Realm Act (planned at a Board of Trade Conference on 12 February at which Macnamara and Sir Frederick Black represented the Admiralty) gave the Government further powers to take over non-munition factories and require their owners to use them for the production of war material as directed by the Admiralty or the Army Council. On 11 March, the Cabinet decided to call a representative meeting with Trade Unionists with the aim of reaching agreement to suspend restrictive rules and practice. The Government was represented by Lloyd George, Runciman, Montagu and Macnamara. After two sessions at the Treasury, voluntary agreement appeared to have been reached,[54] but the fact that the bargain to limit profits and to remove restrictions needed to be embodied in the Munitions of War Act of July furnishes sufficient proof that the early negotiations had failed to secure their object.

As his grip on the munitions industry began to tighten, Lloyd George sought information from employers and government departments about levels of production. His question to Churchill about whether workmen in the North were refusing to work more than three days a week for government firms was referred to Macnamara, who replied in a secret letter on 3 February. He took the opportunity to state how, in his view, labour stood in relation to the national emergency. The men in the Royal Yards had worked with great assiduity, notwithstanding the sometimes excessive demands made upon their strength by overtime requirements. In the private yards all classes of mechanics had worked well, but, he added, 'I think it necessary to add the comment that I have recently noticed, even amongst these men, a tendency to stand out for a substantial increase in wages'.

The charge that only three days' work was being done was inspired, Macnamara concluded, by what in every yard was called the 'Black Squad', platers, drillers and riveters, always a minority, never remarkable for good timekeeping. There were also labourers engaged in connection with transports, colliers, squadron supply ships and so on. 'Here again, you deal with a class of labour some members of which cannot be said to be inspired by any very vivid sense of concern. There have been numerous complaints of carelessness, indifference and drunkenness, and, in certain cases, large demands for increases in emoluments.'

Lloyd George, who was now preoccupied with production, took up this information and a report he had received from the Shipping Federation, alleging high levels of drunkenness amongst the workforce. Macnamara wrote to Churchill on 2 April:

> In view of Parliamentary discussion I should like to have copies of statements made or forwarded to George as regards effects of drink on output … the King has prevented a nasty situation arising out of George's ready acceptance of the Shipping Federation's general charges. In the shipyards – with exceptions – the relations between Masters and Men are not exactly cordial at any time. And the men resent the masters' strictures upon a state of affairs which, as they say – greater solicitude and care and sympathy on the part of the latter would have been largely anticipated … While I am working let me say that what is needed among other things is a Buffet in each shop and yard where men can get every three or four hours supplies of hot soup, hot coffee and hot milk. Our Restaurants and Dining Halls have proved most acceptable in our yards.

The same day he supplied further comments to enquiries from the First Lord:

> … Paper A … I see refers to fitters and shows Monday the worst day. That is largely due to the double pay system of Sundays. As regards remedies I recommend:
>
> 1. Shutting down work a day or half a day a week
> 2. Establishing Buffets for the supply of hot soup, hot coffee and hot milk in every shop and yard once every three or four hours
> 3. No sale of intoxicants except during certain hours of day, say 12–2, 5–6, 9–10. (I think total prohibition out of the question.) I am not sure that government workers should only get drunk between 12–2 and 5–6 by Beer Tickets issued by foremen
> 4. Sharp punishment for bringing liquor into yards or shops engaged in government work
> 5. Every Labour Organisation to pledge itself to deal with any of its members who transgress excessive drinking
> 6. As regards Transport workers, if these enactments don't affect desired result there is nothing for it but enrolling the men in Special Corps …[55]

Lloyd George's plans to deal with the alleged drunkenness appeared to be developing into a great prohibition campaign, in which he proposed a heavy surtax on spirits and beer and the assumption by the Government of powers to close public houses. In the Commons on 29 April, he alleged that in some, though not all, of the centres of armament activities, time lost was mainly attributable to excessive drinking amongst workmen who were receiving very high wages. The Home Department, he said, had conducted an independent investigation. He quoted one observer who said that he had never seen so much drinking at all times of the day as he had witnessed in one of the most important districts for shipyards and ammunition in the whole country.[56] The Defence of the Realm (Amendment) (No. 3) Act of May 1915 secured control of liquor by State agencies in areas where war material was being made or loaded. This included powers to take over licensed premises to control liquor supply and (as Macnamara had advocated) provide refreshments instead or as well.[57] But Lloyd George's main purpose was secured by the Munitions of War Act, given the Royal Assent at the beginning of July. This was mainly a recapitulation, in statutory form, of the Treasury Agreements of March. It made the Board of Trade the supreme arbiter between employer and employee regarding wages, hours and conditions of work in the manufacture or repair of arms, ammunition, ships, vehicles, or any other articles required for use in war.[58]

In October, Macnamara addressed a personal letter to Lloyd George (now Minister of Munitions) on the newly implemented Defence of the Realm Act and on the Munition of War Act, on both of which, he argued, hope of securing necessary output rested:

> As regards the Liquor Traffic, the Board of Control has done wonders – far beyond my most sanguine expectation ... The effect of their operations on the Transport work has been most marked and it is telling in the Munition areas ... it is worth considering whether the public houses should not be closed on pay-day if that day is Saturday, as in Glasgow ... Further they should close certain public houses entirely. Outside Docks and Factories there are usually one or two public houses that do great mischief. Shut them up.

About the Munitions of War Act Macnamara had much to say. It had helped a great deal, he thought, but its fault lay in the fact that it was solely directed towards the men and (except for the limitation of profits) did not touch management supervision and organisation. Its defects were skilfully magnified by the small band of eager and tireless malcontents who sedulously spread dissatisfaction in most great industrial centres – especially on the Clyde. This small band should not be allowed to spread disaffection and incite to mutiny with impunity. He advised that officers of the Ministry of Munitions, the War Office, the Home Office and the Scottish Office should keep an eye on the firebrands and prosecute wherever definite cases of incitement to disorder, disaffection or stoppage of work arose.

Macnamara was convinced that emphasis should always be placed on the fact that restrictive and prohibitory rules came from the Government on behalf of the community and not from employers:

> You know the deep suspicion existing between Employers and Employed. In the Shipyards especially it is simply deplorable. On the Clyde ... men have got

it into their heads that the persons selected for prosecution under the Act are not infrequently selected also because they are well-known local Trade Union leaders and advocates ... That feeling leads to a very great deal of bitter resentment ... The tendency to 'get one in' for a man because he is what is styled an 'agitator' is very natural; and suggestions of it have not altogether been wanting in vague charges made to me at the hearing of workmen's petitions against our own Dockyard officers.

Wages, he considered, were getting into a hopeless tangle. Some contractors, to meet contract dates, had made concessions on all sides. Others had resisted. Since the Act tied men down to their existing yards, there was no end of discontent in the yards where less than the highest rates were being paid. Overtime had largely become the established order of the day and was looked upon by men as their due. The organisation of the shops and yards left a good deal to be desired in certain cases. Men complained that when on non-urgent work they were sometimes stood off for a day or more. Supervision in the shipyards, particularly of new entrants, was insufficient.

Summing up, Macnamara expressed the view that the great body of the men were sound enough:

... it is up to us promptly to meet and if possible remove legitimate grievances and sources of irritation. There are in their midst a comparatively small number of extremely active revolutionaries. They are doing and have done all the mischief, and you will never satisfy them ... On the one hand you must detach the men from them by the sincerity of your administration in the direction of promptly meeting legitimate claims for the removal of grievances, on the other you must, if necessary, lay these gentlemen by the heels.[59]

By November, Lloyd George was completing work on his Munitions of War Amendment Bill. Macnamara wrote to him on the last day of the month:

My dear George,

We sent you on Sunday night a letter on your ... Bill ... we strongly urged you to declare the building and repairing of Merchant Ships war work. Of course, if such ships are designed for Transport or any other direct war service no difficulty arises. But, in view of national needs, we are strongly of opinion that *all* Merchant Shipwork should be declared war work ... and I strongly commend this urgent proposition to you.

Very faithfully yours,
T. J. Macnamara [60]

The Bill, presented by Lloyd George, supported by Sir F. E. Smith, Dr Addison and Macnamara in December, duly placed the building of merchant ships (so far as the Admiralty considered it desirable) under government control, well in advance of the submarine depredations of the following year. It was also concerned with the limitation of profits, further controls over how munitions factories were run and with dilution, the principle that no skilled man should be employed on work which could be done by semi-skilled or unskilled male or female labour.[61] Macnamara had worked closely with Lloyd George. 'I am disclosing no secret when I say I have been in communication with my rt hon Friend on nearly every document he has issued on this matter', he told the House of Commons during the Navy Estimates debate at the beginning of March 1916:

> We fully agree that the Minister of Munitions cannot man his new factories and cannot get his guns and shells, and neither can we get all we want with these great operations going on, with the expedition which is vital, without every practicable effort in the direction of dilution being carried forward with earnestness and energy.[62]

His efforts brought no reward. Shortly after the Munitions of War Act was passed, Riddell was talking to Lloyd George about whether he would succeed Kitchener at the War Office if the Field Marshal went elsewhere. 'I said that in some quarters I had heard Macnamara suggested as Lloyd George's successor at the Munitions Department', Riddell recorded. But Lloyd George thought he would not be suitable. Bonar Law (then Colonial Secretary) would be a much better man.[63] Similarly when, at the end of the year, Lloyd George formed his War Cabinet, Macnamara, like most of his colleagues, was merely confirmed in his existing post. This Cabinet, with little division of function, was to run the war; elsewhere new men, often from business backgrounds like Geddes and Maclay, were inserted into ministerial posts, Maclay without entering Parliament. With Lloyd George in charge, the normal processes of political reward and promotion fell into disuse.[64]

Later in 1917 the Prime Minister found a use for Macnamara. On 12 June, Lloyd George had appointed a Commission of Enquiry into Industrial Unrest. Eight reports were assiduously and rapidly put together, dealing with North East, North West and South West England, Yorkshire and the East Midlands, the West Midlands, London and the South East, Scotland and (by far the longest) Wales and Monmouthshire. A summary by George Barnes was appended. The reports, he concluded, were practically unanimous. The main issues were high food prices, restriction of personal freedom (especially under the Munitions of War Acts), lack of confidence in the Government (particularly because it was felt that Trade Union rights would not be restored), delay in settlement of disputes, the operation of the military service acts, lack of housing in certain areas, restrictions on liquor, industrial fatigue, imperfect Union organisation, lack of communal sense ('this is noticeable in South Wales, where there has been a break-away from faith in Parliamentary representation'), inconsiderate treatment of women, especially regarding pay, delay in granting pensions to soldiers, the raising of the limit of Income Tax Exemption and the low rates of workmen's compensation.[65]

Hard pressed as he was by the effects of the submarine war, the battles of Passchendaele and Caporetto, Lloyd George asked Macnamara to visit and address meetings in the North West, the North East, Wales and the Midlands.[66] He despatched his report, entitled *The Civil Population and the War*, to the Prime Minister on 27 November. He had already been to Southport, Abertillery, Blaenavon, Pontypool, Tonypandy, Burnley, Wigan, Stockton and Coventry, with other places to follow. The mass of the industrial population, he concluded, was all right. They wanted to see the war through for their sons' sakes. But they were rather sorely tried and tempted in more than one direction. There followed an attack on the Independent Labour Party, which, he wrote:

> ... is always at their elbows fomenting grievances, distorting facts, putting sinister constructions upon everything. People talk about German Money ... But money, German or otherwise, isn't needed to start the typical ILP-ite. His vanity and superiority of intellect easily make him an 'international'. He sneers at patriotism as mere parochialism at its best, crafty greed at its worst. He probably isn't consciously pro-German. In fact he isn't pro-anything ... It is enough for him that our institutions are based on private enterprise and private ownership. He is their deadly enemy. From his point of view, I imagine, it is of little use to beat the Bosche unless he can also defeat Capitalism. By this process of reasoning, the German working man is a better friend of his than the British Capitalist. That's his starting point – though of course he takes care not to say so ... he is a fanatic ... tireless and unscrupulous ... to some extent discounted by the large-minded, easy-going tolerance of the British Working man. Still he is indefatigable in the way he lays hold of grievances that the workpeople do suffer under ... To-day it is Bonuses to Ship-Building firms for Acceleration ... To-morrow it is increased Rentals. The next day increased cost of coal and food. And always it is 'profiteering' ... no allowance whatever is made for the inevitable results of war. Everything is attributed to the Government and 'the governing classes'. They are capitalistic and probably not free from the suspicion that they and their kind are waxing fat out of war and the sufferings of the people ... the war easily becomes a Financiers' War ... Even if the Government isn't in this, they are muddle headed idiots, utterly indifferent to the claims of the workpeople and without the knowledge, the ability, or the inclination to deal with them.

The effect of this was telling with an increased momentum because the people were getting rather weary with the long continuance of the war. They threatened to down tools on the flimsiest pretext. Recently a twelve-and-a-half per cent increase in time rates had been awarded by the Ministry of Munitions to skilled fitters and moulders on time work. The claim of all other time workers for a similar increase had been natural enough and ought, Macnamara thought, to have been foreseen. But the alarming thing had been the peremptory and short-tempered way the further claim was put forward from all parts of the country. 'Closely familiar as I am with the Labour situation during the war', he concluded, 'the temper imported into this incident troubled me ...'

He offered a seven-point programme as the remedy:

1. By its policy and action, the Government must convince the people that it is determined to spare them any sacrifice not the direct consequence of the war.
2. It must treat all alike, and especially in the matter of Food Rationing. (I attach front page of a recent copy of the *Herald* giving a Ritz Menu with comments thereon. I am told that the greatest exasperation is caused upon the circulation of this in the workshops and yards. Of course it is.)
3. It must put its heel on profiteering ...
4. It must punish the holding-up, the hoarding of food supplies in the most summary and severe manner.
5. It must insist upon government Departments promptly and intelligently dealing with matters affecting the condition of the people. Delay in replying to complaints about Pensions, Allowances, Food Supplies, Food Prices, in the issue of Wage Awards, etc, etc, etc, is the best text for the ILP and the rebel orator generally ...
6. It must nail false charges to the counter. We are all so busy with our proper work that we let too much go by default ...
7. It must state War Aims in a manner understood by the people. And in so doing, it must give the lie direct and emphatic to the suggestion that this is in any sense an Imperialistic War and a War of Conquest ...

I have put these few thoughts on paper. They probably represent nothing new. But they do lead up to definite conclusions as to policy – for what they are worth.[67]

Sound though this advice was, its author was not yet needed by Lloyd George on a permanent basis. Ruling through the War Cabinet, the Prime Minister had reached the opinion that Parliament was not required in war-time and was often dangerous. Some of the members, he told Riddell on 17 June 1918, were now putting questions which were conveying information to the enemy.[68] His appointees from outside Parliament fulfilled his aims without exercising embarrassing representative functions. But the Maurice debate of 9 May, occasioned by the Director of Military Operation's charge that Lloyd George had misled the House of Commons about the size of the British army in France at the beginning of 1918, had already drawn his attention to the shaky political position he would occupy when the war was over; the following week the nucleus of a Coalition Liberal group was formed under Churchill (Minister of Munitions) and Addison (Minister of Reconstruction) and a chief whip appointed. Hence Lloyd George was prepared to admit that a general election (the first since December 1910) needed to take place before long.[69] A fortnight later the issue was discussed again:

LG said that many of the younger members of the Conservative Party favour an arrangement whereby LG would be placed at the head of a definite party and a definite organisation. His thoughts lie in the same direction, but he sees a difficulty with the Liberals – he feels that he can depend on a certain number of the Liberal members, but the creation of a new party with a new organisation would bring about an absolute and definite split.[70]

Within the next three weeks the agreement between the Unionists and Lloyd George's Liberal Whip had been drawn up. It pledged that 150 Liberals endorsed by the Prime Minister and Bonar Law would not be opposed by Unionists. As a result, Lloyd George was palpitating with energetic enthusiasm, strongly in favour of a November election.[71] From the Policy for Government Committee which met under Addison's leadership on 19 July emerged a programme for publicly provided housing, land settlement, the coordination of health insurance and medical services, the development of unemployment insurance, the establishment of a public assistance system to replace the Poor Law and a programme for devolution in industry.[72]

The issue, Riddell still thought at the end of August, would really be who was to run the war – Lloyd George, Bonar Law and their associates, or Asquith, Runciman and others who were acting with them.[73] In fact, the war was almost over. Bulgarian peace proposals at the end of September marked the beginning of the collapse of morale amongst the Central Powers which was to yield the Armistice on 11 November. The next day, at a meeting of between 150 and 200 Liberal MPs and others at 10 Downing Street, Lloyd George announced his intention of going to the polls. He wanted, he said, a united government representing all parties.[74] With Bonar Law and Barnes (who had just left the Labour Party) he opened the Coalition campaign at the Central Hall, Westminster, four days later. The letters described by Asquith as 'coupons' were then distributed, making public the existing Government's approval of 159 Liberal and 364 Conservative candidates.[75] Failing a government representing all parties (the Labour Party had withdrawn), the Prime Minister, as he made clear at Bristol on 11 December, wished to keep the men with him who had supported the Coalition steadily over the past two years.[76]

Macnamara had written to Lloyd George on 25 November, suggesting a public meeting in London. The Electoral Reform Act earlier in the year had yielded an additional seat to Camberwell; Macnamara was putting up for the new constituency in the North West which contained three wards from the former Camberwell North and two Unionist wards from Dulwich. Though he had the coupon, he was being opposed by a Unionist candidate who, having been adopted by his party the previous May, now refused to stand down.[77] Lloyd George decided to deliver his seventh and last campaign speech at the Old Kent Road Baths on Friday 13 December; by now, however, Macnamara had undertaken to make a speech in Huddersfield. He arranged for his wife to accompany the Prime Minister and sent him a letter three days before, setting the scene:

> [The] Chairman will be Capt Newton Knights, Coalition candidate for the Constituency in which you will be speaking (the new N Camberwell) ... You will no doubt be ready to make reference to the fact that I stood for the old Constituency ... for nearly twenty years, and that I have been throughout all that time one of your closest associates and, I think I may say, one of your most loyal supporters.
>
> In view of the very determined attack which is being made upon me, and the handicap under which I work in not having been able to attend to any party organisation work during the whole of the war, you might make some reference to my work at the Admiralty, and particularly to the fact that I have striven for all I know to see that the Soldiers, the Sailors and their dependants are equitably treated by the State.

He went on to suggest headings on allowances, pensions, unemployment and conscription (none of which, in the event, Lloyd George took up) and ended with a firm expression of personal opinion:

> ... it is up to the Coalition, promptly, with imagination and with courage, to meet the legitimate aspirations of the working people of the country that social problems – housing, health, sanitation, child welfare and so on – shall be taken in hand in a way which has not so far stood to the credit of any party in the State. You should frankly recognise that the people come out of this war eager in the determination and purpose to make the country a more fitting memorial to those who have died to defend it. You should frankly realise that, though Coalition is essential for the Reconstruction period, it needs to have a wider purpose and intention than that. It can only be fully justified to the people to whom you will be speaking by the frank assurance that in no quarter of its ranks will be found other than the most sincere desire to meet the aspirations of the people by dealing with all social problems with a largeness of grasp and a spirit of determination the like of which we have not seen before.
>
> Forgive me if I seem to be issuing commands. You get into that sort of way at the Admiralty ... [78]

At Camberwell, having begun his speech with an encomium on Bonar Law, his Unionist partner, Lloyd George provided, as requested, another on Macnamara:

> Dr Macnamara is a very old friend of mine. I know him well. I am a believer in his intense patriotism. I know his sympathies with all those who are suffering from wrongs and injustice. I very much regret that after the good work which he has done during the war it should have been thought necessary to oppose him (Hear, hear) ... I will tell you why. After all, preparations for an election take a good deal more time than the three weeks before the election, and it means attending in the constituency and organizing. Dr Macnamara has been as busy as if he had been in a ship in the North Sea during the whole of the

time and could not attend his constituency, and I think at any rate this election should have been passed without a challenge under these conditions. I think it would have been fairer. I should regard it as a bitter personal blow if the man who helped so much in the conduct of the war at the Admiralty were rejected by an important London constituency to-morrow ...[79]

At the Town Hall, Huddersfield, Macnamara explained that the Prime Minister had found it impossible to make the journey north and had arranged with him what in pastoral circles was called an exchange of pulpits. Let the first item of the new Government's programme be the continuing sympathy and care of the victims of this dreadful war, he said. Less than that would be the basest ingratitude. Then it was the duty of statesmanship to crown the victory won by the fighting men by laying down the terms of peace and, he added, let those terms provide that Germany should pay, farthing by farthing, for the cost of the war (Applause) and that stern, swift justice should be the portion of those who initiated that bloody attack upon the peaceful peoples of the earth. He turned next to the question of who should lead the post-war government. Surely the conduct of affairs during the war left them in no doubt whatever as to who ought to be their commander in chief, he asked (Applause). He would certainly say nothing in disparagement of his old chief, Mr Asquith (Applause), of whom he spoke with deep respect both on public and personal grounds, but anyone who had closely watched the course of events could do no other than pay the most profound tribute of gratitude to and admiration for Mr Lloyd George (Applause).

Discussing the aims of the Coalition, Macnamara emphasised his hopes for social reform:

> Some of my friends are frankly distrustful and suspicious of the ability and the desire of the Coalition as at present constituted – (Ah!) – to meet the proper and legitimate aspirations of the people. I submit that they are allowing prejudices, old predilections, old antipathies to blind them to the fundamental change that has come over all of us, all parties, all creeds, as a result of this dreadful war (Applause). There is no doubt that to the solution of all problems affecting the social condition of the people – wages, housing, health, child welfare, education and the like – a new motive power, a new impulse, a new kind of inspiration is coming. To my friends who are doubtful and suspicious I would say that here, as a result of war experience, is a great and pregnant impulse waiting to be called to the service of the country. In heaven's name let us turn it to good account. Some of you tell me that Mr Lloyd George has sold himself to the Tories (Hear, hear). To you I reply in the words of the old hymn: 'Ye fearful saints, fresh courage take, the clouds ye so much dread are big with mercies and shall break with blessings on your head (Laughter).[80]

Re-elected with a 3,000 majority, he wrote to the Prime Minister from the Admiralty on 15 December:

My dear George,

While it is fresh in my mind, a few words on the election – if you can find time to read them.

1. The Coalition will be all right & Reconstruction will go ahead under it.

2. But that alone is not sufficient justification: the people are ardent to see social problems tackled with a determination, a largeness of grasp & an imagination that do not stand to any party's credit up to date.

3. If this sentiment is not met the Coalition's life will be short & not merry & you'll be faced with another election at a very troublous time for the country.

    Bonar Law & his people no doubt fully realise this and will help to shove things along.

4. You'll need to get the same Labour men back into your govt – the Barnes's, Clynes's, Hodges, & the Walsh's. Barnes ought to have another seat if Maclean beats him.

5. Courageous tackling of social conditions will bring the women to your side every time.

6. The Departments dealing with Demobilisation (Fighting Forces and Munition Workers) will need to be watched all the time or they'll let you down. The man at the head of these must *drive* the coach or you'll have muddle & delay.

7. The same is especially true of the Pensions Ministry. No doubt the Discharged Soldiers & Sailors are loud in putting their demands. This is mainly due to the fact that the Socialists, Syndicalists & Bolsheviks are exploiting them and will exploit them, like they've exploited everything during the war. Here they've got the best card they've yet had. But the more I listened to these men's questions the more I was convinced that *delays, Departmental hanky panky, giving-with-one-hand-and-taking-with-the-other* have a lot to do with their utterly irreconcileable attitude. You've got to be prompt to see that real grievances are removed *or this agitation will be serious.* You want a big man on *Demobilisation* and a big man at *Pensions.* Of course you're aware of all this. But I thought to ease my mind by writing it.

Very faithfully yours,
T. J. Macnamara [81]

Lloyd George, at this stage, may well have been in full agreement with these views,[82] but the first task of the new Government was the framing of the peace treaty with Germany. With this in mind the Prime Minister retained his War Cabinet in operation till the following October, adding Sir Eric Geddes as Minister without Portfolio with the task of presiding over the demobilisation of the armed forces. Economies in the Navy began the day the war ended. On the morning of the Armistice, as the guns boomed outside and the bells rang, Macnamara had been at an emergency meeting of the Board of Admiralty, considering how at once they could slow down, reduce, cancel and abandon.[83] In January, the Prime Minister

informed the new heads of the great fighting and spending departments that, in the face of existing conditions and the immense burden of debt resulting from the war, they must, while retaining their efficiency, be severely economical.[84] Later the same month, Macnamara was put in charge of a committee to go into all branches of expenditure, examine it and report as to reductions. Progress was already being made. Though the Fleet needed to be kept in readiness till the peace treaty was signed and though action took place in the eastern Baltic against the Bolsheviks in the summer, demobilisation and the cancellation of shipbuilding contracts proceeded steadily.[85] On 11 November 1918, naval personnel totalled 407,317. By 20 February 100,000 had been demobilised, by November 257,000. Naval expenditure for 1918, Macnamara announced on 10 December 1919, had amounted to £325,000,000. For the current year it would fall to £157,000,000.[86]

The issue of naval pay complicated the economy drive. In October 1917 increased pay for able seamen and concessions regarding hospital stoppages, kit and pensions had been proposed by the Cabinet Committee on Sailors' and Soldiers' Pay [87] but unfortunately the news was not communicated to the lower deck. Consequently Yexley, editor of the *Fleet*, had written to Macnamara on 1 November calling for urgent action. The following day, Ben Tillett, standing in a by-election as an Independent on a programme of higher pay and better conditions for sailors and soldiers, was returned with a large majority over the Coalition candidate. This triggered a Cabinet response. Increases for able seamen and petty officers were announced on 4 December.[88]

In July 1918 lower deck pay dissatisfaction again made itself manifest. Riddell, after a conversation with Churchill and Rothermere, noted that Yexley had warned Geddes of the likelihood of monster demonstrations in the three home ports. he concluded that the Navy Pay Department was the most unsympathetic and archaic of all public departments and that Macnamara, the head of it, was quite incompetent. Churchill did not agree: in his view Geddes was responsible. Later Churchill and Lloyd George were discussing the Navy. 'I added my quote', Riddell recorded, 'by criticising the Pay Department and Macnamara ... two days later, I urged the Prime Minister to appoint a Committee to enquire into naval grievances. This is vital.' [89] Macnamara and Forster, his counterpart at the War Office, were not, however, disposed to recommend an all-round increase on the grounds that, since the Committee on Sailors' and Soldiers' Pay had begun its work, increases in general pay, separation allowances and parents' allowances had been made aggregating £88,000,000 in the first year and £92,000,000 in the second.[90]

But if Macnamara had advised delay in September, he was quick to act once the general election was over. On 27 December, he announced that a special war gratuity would be granted to chief petty officers, petty officers, men and boys of the Royal Navy and to warrant officers, NCOs, men and boys of the Royal Marines.[91] The same day, the Government published its intention of setting up a review of pay and conditions in both Services. Less than a fortnight later, a committee, under Admiral Sir Martyn Jerram, was reconstituted to inquire into pay, allowances and pensions of all ranks and ratings in the Royal Navy and the Royal Marines. It was to visit Portsmouth, Chatham and Devonport; at each port four lower deck ratings were to be appointed to the committee in an advisory capacity and to be associated with it in the final drafting of the report in London.[92]

These moves, prompt though they were, were in response to what was developing into a volatile situation. On 20 January, Basil Thomson, Director of Intelligence at Scotland Yard, forwarded a memorandum to J. T. Davies, the Prime Minister's principal private secretary (in Paris):

> A combination between the lower deck of the Grand Fleet, the various Depots and Royal Dockyards to force the Admiralty and the Treasury to concede to all ratings a revised increased scale of pay, as recommended by sub-committees representing the whole of the Lower Deck Societies, is actively at work. The Officers are said to be in sympathy with the movement, because they too will benefit financially. The whole of the lower deck are in deadly earnest. They contend that, as the British Navy has been the primary cause of the defeat of Germany, they should be paid a wage which would place them on a footing with skilled and unskilled labourers.
>
> They also demand the dismissal of Dr Macnamara from the Cabinet [sic], and state positively that unless he is dismissed and their demands acceded to, they will declare a general strike in which, on a given date, the whole of the men will leave their depots, ships etc, taking with them those Officers who are not in sympathy with their cause.
>
> They even suggest that attempts may be made to blow up certain ships, care being taken to avoid loss of life. The men say that they have been patriotic throughout the war, and they are now driven to the only resort which will obtain their just demands ... [93]

This proved to be inaccurate as well as alarmist. Macnamara pressed ahead, announcing all round increases, as a temporary measure, on 30 January and the appointment of a further committee, under Admiral Sir Lionel Halsey, to consider officers' pay on 5 March. In the Navy Estimates debates, members for the naval constituencies gave him their support. Sir Bertram Falle (member for Portsmouth since 1910) said that during the whole time he had been in the House he had always found the rt hon. Gentleman most sympathetic towards all the demands of the lower deck. He knew, he said, that at that moment that was not the opinion in some places. He thought, however, that the opinion of those places was mistaken.[94] G. F. Hohler (Rochester and Gillingham) agreed:

> I do deplore the view which the men of the Navy have taken in regard to the rt hon Gentleman the Financial Secretary. I can assure him that I have told

them that they have no better friend than the rt hon Gentleman, and that their resolution, if they only knew the facts as I know them was wholly wrong ... unfortunately the rt hon Gentleman is in a position of responsibility without power.[95]

As the information was assembled, the truth of this observation became plain. The Admiralty Board had received the Jerram Report on 2 March; Macnamara promised on 9 April that the Board's recommendations would be presented to the War Cabinet within the next few days. By 29 April, Falle was becoming impatient. He asked:

Is the rt hon Gentleman aware that there is very considerable dissatisfaction in the Navy because of the delay in the issue of this Report and that the men do not understand how it is that police strikes and miners' strikes involving enormous sums of money can be settled in a couple of days or a fortnight whereas they have had to wait months for this Report? [96]

Macnamara, two days later, assured Falle that the Jerram recommendations and government decisions would be published side by side in a Parliamentary paper.[97] In fact, that very day the report had been considered by the Cabinet. Walter Long, the new First Lord, had urged immediate acceptance, but a further delay had been agreed so that the War Office and the Air Ministry could be consulted. At last, at a conference held at the House of Commons on 6 May, attended by Austen Chamberlain (Chancellor of the Exchequer), Churchill, Long and Macnamara, it was agreed that the total sum allocated by the Jerram Report should be awarded but that rates for men under twenty-one should be kept lower. The sum so saved would be distributed among the higher ranks. But Admiral Sir Rosslyn Wemyss, the First Sea Lord, was also present. His threatened resignation ensured that the War Cabinet accepted the bulk of the Jerram recommendations the next day; Halsey's recommendations were accepted in July.[98] Lambert, the former Civil Lord, congratulated the Board on doing broad justice to the officers and men of the Navy. It was, he said, a long over-due reform:

I can associate him with that ... I can associate his colleagues on the Board with that work; and I know also, from my past experience, that in dealing with the grievances of the men of the Navy my rt hon Friend the Financial Secretary is always extremely sympathetic.[99]

Before the general election, Lloyd George had inveighed against the party system. 'I can hear sounds of elaborate preparations for setting up the same old merry-go-round, which gives men the illusion that they are prancing along at a terrific speed, when they are really circling around the same old crank engine to the same old tunes', he told his hosts in Manchester on 12 September, when he was presented with the freedom of the city: 'Let us have an open mind.'[100] But the election consensus, never as complete as the Prime Minister had hoped, did not last long.

The weakness of his position, as a Liberal Prime Minister dependent for his majority on the Unionists, soon became the subject of press comment.[101] The Spen Valley by-election campaign at the end of 1919 showed how even his Liberal support was a wasting asset. Up till now Lloyd George had supported Coalition Unionists against Asquith supporters but had avoided a direct confrontation. Now the local association adopted Sir John Simon, the former Attorney General and Home Secretary, who thus secured the only active Liberal Party local machine.[102] Coalition Liberals at first hung back, annoying the local Unionists (who were keen to contest the seat) first by their indecisiveness, then by suddenly adopting Colonel Fairfax, a raw war hero, as their candidate.

The campaign, which with proper organisation would in all likelihood have secured the seat for a Coalition Liberal, proved to be a disaster. On 10 December, Lloyd George was informed that Tom Myers, the Labour candidate, was forging steadily ahead, Fairfax was improving and Simon was just about holding his own. Eleven days later the Prime Minister was telling Riddell that the Coalition organisation had been very bad and that nothing had been done until he personally took the matter in hand and sent down some good speakers, including his wife, Hamar Greenwood, F. G. Kellaway and Macnamara.[103]

By New Year's Day Lloyd George was convinced that the Coalition would lose Spen Valley.[104] So it proved. Myers secured 11,962 votes, Simon was second with 10,244 and Fairfax third with 8,134. 'The result is a portent for the Prime Minister', *The Times* concluded: 'He deliberately challenged the Independent Liberals to a trial of strength, and he has been fairly and squarely beaten … It has been long suspected that the Parliamentary Coalition had no real counterpart in the country. Spen Valley shows that the suspicion was well founded.'[105] Macnamara had written to the Prime Minister from the Admiralty two days before:

Dear George,

Fairfax got Tory poll and little or nothing else. Simon got nine-tenths of Radical ditto … Myers got full Labour poll + one tenth Radical. It is a thundering pity Fairfax wasn't more experienced. I won't stay to speculate on the effects upon Coalition of this election. Cost of Living! Housing! There it is. It would be an impertinence to suggest that you are not aware of it, or that you don't mean in 1920 to put yourself behind each. But I should be disposed to let it be known. Good luck.

Very faithfully yours,
T. J. Macnamara [106]

Spen Valley brought Macnamara, at last, into the Prime Minister's inner circle of advisers. It also turned Lloyd George's thoughts, not for the first time, towards the formation of a new party. On 8 January the matter was discussed at a dinner at the house of the Lord Chancellor, Lord Birkenhead.

The guests comprised Sir Robert Sanders, Sir Archibald Salvidge, Sir Robert Horne, Churchill, Lord Edmund Talbot, Kellaway, Addison, F. E. Guest, Macnamara, Bonar Law and the Prime Minister. 'The discussion was fusion in order to strengthen resistance to Labour', Sanders recorded:

> Everyone thought it advisable in the course of the next few months. But several thought that a good excuse such as a big strike ought to be awaited. Bonar's attitude was the most hesitant. He considers we must fuse, but thinks that on doing so we must have an early election and does not want to hurry things. LG was anxious to state a programme that would last us for five or ten years. Winston also wanted a programme. Bonar deprecated a programme. All were pledged to secrecy.[107]

On 15 February, Lloyd George told Riddell that fusion had been discussed again at Cobham the previous week with six Liberal Ministers. Addison and Macnamara, who, he said, knew much more about electioneering than Edward Shortt, H. A. L. Fisher and Sir Gordon Hewart, had agreed with Kellaway that immediate action was necessary.[108] The next day Frances Stevenson noted that Sir Robert Horne was pondering whether to become Minister without Portfolio, to assist the Prime Minister. '... I know it would relieve D enormously', she wrote: 'I think Horne is inclined to accept. He suggests that Macnamara should take his place at the Ministry of Labour. It ought to be a good appointment.'[109]

In the event the idea of fusion failed to attract the Coalition Liberals. In June, Lloyd George put it to his colleagues for the second and last time. Lord Beaverbrook recorded in 1963:

> Ministers, Under-Ministers and colleagues, under the leadership of T. J. Macnamara, Ian Macpherson and Alfred Mond, were in opposition to the plan. They would not sacrifice their Liberal affiliations. The plan was defeated. From the meeting Lloyd George came to Cherkley, my Surrey home. He regretted the decision. Dame Margaret Lloyd George, who came with him, rejoiced. She never liked the Tories and never failed to say just so.[110]

Horne, instead of becoming Minister without Portfolio, had by now succeeded Sir Auckland Geddes as President of the Board of Trade. His former Cabinet post, however, duly fell to Macnamara. On 17 March, during the Navy Estimates debate, Long drily referred to newspaper reports that the Financial Secretary was to be transferred to some other field of labour. Commander Bellairs observed:

> We are very sorry to lose him but what is the Navy's loss will be the country's gain and, I hope, whatever position he occupies, he will have sufficient leisure to follow the universal habit, which is spreading, of writing his reminiscences. He has occupied the position of Financial Secretary to the Admiralty probably longer than anybody for years past, and he has been a Minister of the Crown longer, in one position, than any other Minister of the Crown. Possibly he has not been so long Financial Secretary to the Admiralty as ... Pepys, but if he

writes his reminiscences I hope they will rival those of that distinguished predecessor.[111]

Macnamara's ministerial by-election took place at the end of the month. He was duly returned. The long wait for Cabinet office was over.

14

Minister of Labour

The Ministry of Labour had been set up in 1916. After the war it exercised what Macnamara was to describe as both temporary and permanent functions. The former involved the resettlement in civil life of ex-Service men; the latter, negotiations with Labour leaders (though the Prime Minister continued to play a major rôle) with the Whitley Councils created since 1917 and the Trade Boards established under the Acts of 1909 and 1918, and responsibility for the operation of the Employment Exchanges and the Unemployment Insurance Acts. Unemployment and its consequences were to occupy most of Macnamara's time as Minister. In 1919, during the first months of peace, British industry experienced a boom that seemed to herald a return to prosperity. It was short-lived. Now, coincidental with his appointment, large-scale, persistent unemployment made its appearance.[1]

Before he assumed his duties, the new Minister took a holiday on the Kent coast. At Margate the golden jubilee conference of the National Union of Teachers was taking place. W. P. Folland, the retiring president, who had been a fellow student at Borough Road forty years before, invited him on to the platform to address the assembled teachers. Like a mariner who had come home after the longest and most adventurous cruise of his life, his mind, he said, was filled with old memories. He had joined the Union thirty-seven years before, he had maintained his membership and his subscription was paid for the current year (Applause). He hoped he could say the same for his audience (Laughter). Looking round for old and well-remembered faces he observed how, at his first conference, men and women had been present in proportion of about six to one. Now it looked as if they were about half and half. He turned to what had been achieved. In the late 1880s, teachers toiled in an atmosphere charged at its best with incredulous toleration, at its worst with active hostility to the idea that money could be applied to an enterprise as ridiculous as public education. At every turn they were met by quite honest, sincere people who insisted that in the complex organisation of modern society there were certain functions that could be performed satisfactorily only by ignorant people (Laughter). 'Thank God that day has long departed', he added, to applause, then cries of 'No!' 'Are there some of these people alive yet?', he responded. 'On Education Committees!', came the answer. He tried again with Payment by Results. How they all toiled in those days, he recalled, at the seemingly hopeless task of convincing the public that you cannot measure educational results by running a foot rule over the teachers' work and paying for it at so much a hundredweight. This time there was applause and laughter. Such an attitude, it was confidently felt in 1920, would never return.[2]

Another meeting, this time of the National Liberal Federation at Leamington on 7 May, proved less pleasant. The split between the Coalition Liberals and the Asquithian 'Wee Frees' remained unresolved; Lloyd George, impatient with old party loyalties but reluctant to call for fusion between the elements that made up the Coalition, now invited the Liberal Party of England and Wales to enter into what he called closer cooperation with the Conservatives. At Leamington, *The Times* commented:

> Every available Coalition member of Parliament was whipped up for the occasion. At their head was placed the second eleven of the Ministry, with the captaincy apparently in commission between Dr Addison and Sir Gordon Hewart, for the former opened the attack and the latter led the retreat. The party had the advantage of the active co-operation of Dr Macnamara and Mr McCurdy, who had recently submitted themselves to their constituents for re-election on their appointment to high office and emerged victorious ...

But when Macnamara and his colleagues took their seats on the platform, they were greeted with hooting and cries of 'Rats!' Far from acceding to the Prime Minister's proposals, the Executive Committee reaffirmed its confidence in Asquith as leader of the Liberal Party and moved a resolution that affiliated associations should remain independent. Following Addision, who had spoken amidst an almost continuous crossfire of taunts and interruptions, Macnamara rose to oppose the resolution and was loudly hissed. He went into the attack, his voice prevailing against cries of 'Spen Valley' and complaints that he had won his ministerial by-election through Tory intervention. The President, he observed, had said that he longed for reconciliation (Uproar, and cries of 'Go on, Mac'). He went on:

> Well, as conciliators, you beat the band. I used to learn at the Federation meeting that measures and not men was a cardinal faith with this assembly (Loud cheers). If to-morrow the present Coalition disappeared (Uproar) do you think the historic Liberal Party could form a government? Why, you would have at once to espouse the thing you profess to loathe.

By pursuing the course they sought to adopt, he concluded, they would make the Liberal Party not historic but prehistoric. Eventually, led by Sir Gordon Hewart, the Coalition Ministers and their supporters, numbering fifty-seven MPs and some twenty delegates, left the meeting amid derisive cheers. The Prime Minister's invitation was declined. *The Times* observed:

> After yesterday's vote, it is obvious that the Coalition has no title to be described as a combination of two parties. One historic party has decisively repudiated

it, and, whatever be the outcome, Mr Lloyd George and Mr Bonar Law will never again be in a position to broach a true fusion of Liberals and Unionists ... It is admittedly difficult for a Parliamentary party, which has the abnormal representation in the Ministry of one of every five of its members, to realize that it is, in the familiar phrase, only a transient and embarrassed phantom.[3]

Politically, the prospects for the new Cabinet Minister were far from promising.

With his new post Macnamara took over a government initiative renewing and expanding (providentially, as was soon to become clear) the existing legislation on unemployment insurance. Between 1911 and 1920, Lloyd George's innovatory Act had already been amended five times. The 1916 Act increased the number of persons covered from 2,500,000 to 3,750,000, incorporating workers in the munitions, chemicals, oils, soap, candles, metals, rubber goods and leather goods industries. By the end of the war the number had risen to 4,000,000; thereafter it declined slightly as the numbers of manual labourers and working women ran down. In December 1919, because funds at the disposal of the State had accumulated, the benefit rate was raised from seven shillings to eleven.[4]

In February 1920, Sir Robert Horne, then Minister of Labour, introduced what was now specifically designated an Unemployment Insurance Bill. Now all manual workers were to be included except those engaged in agriculture and in private domestic service; permanent civil servants, pensionable teachers, permanent employees of municipal authorities and railway companies' employees were permitted to remain outside, but the effect of the legislation was to extend cover to some 12,000,000 people. He stated at the beginning of the Second Reading:

> We have recognised the solidarity of industry, of all industries by making them support each other. But on the other hand we have provided a scheme of contracting out, which will enable an industry, if it thinks it can do better for itself than if it was under the general scheme, to provide a special scheme of its own.[5]

Women's contributions and their employers' were to remain at the 1911 level; men's contributions and their employers' were to be increased by ½d; the State's contribution was still to be one third. Benefit was to be increased to 15s per week for men and to 12s for women; each employed person was to be entitled to one week's benefit for every six contributions.[6]

The Bill was passed for consideration to a Standing Committee of which Macnamara was a member. When it returned to the Commons for the report stage at the beginning of July, the new Minister was in charge of it. The Bill had been modified; in its new form it was now proposed to increase benefit to 20s per week for men and 16s for women and to abolish the waiting period. But, as Macnamara made clear, the Government was not prepared to countenance the increased benefit; those who desired it, he stated on 9 July, would have to pay for it themselves. The abolition of the waiting period was also unacceptable; even with benefits fixed at 15s and 12s, the annual cost of unemployment insurance would be increased by £4,750,000. The Government proposed a compromise allowing for increased costs of £2,750,000: benefits of 15s and 12s would be coupled with a waiting period of three days, with a contribution of 4d per week from men and 4d from their employers; 3d from women and 3½d from their employers.[7] These were the terms finally established when the Bill was passed at the end of the month.

The Government was still assuming that the payment of benefit was a secondary consideration. The first object of the Bill, Macnamara had argued the previous week, was to see that there was effective touch between the various agencies involved in the administration of the Act (mainly trade unions or friendly societies) and the man in want of a job.[8] Nevertheless, unemployment of a specialised kind was already causing concern. On 7 July, he told the House of Commons that although some 5,250,000 ex-Service men had been reabsorbed in industry, 180,800 (of whom over ten per cent were disabled) were still registered with the employment exchanges as unemployed and 14,897 officers and other ranks of similar educational qualifications were registered with the Appointments Department as requiring employment.[9] On 4 August, he wrote to Lloyd George urging that two questions affecting his Department should be considered before the recess. The first was the case of the unemployed ex-Service men:

> Shortly we have round about 150,000 ex-Service men unemployed. Most of them are unskilled. Many have been unemployed for a long time ... We have handed them out donations, originally 29s a week with allowances for children: they are now in most cases 20s a week without allowances. Beyond that we have done nothing for them. No doubt some of them don't want to work. That is not true of the great majority. How far have we helped them? We tell them to register at the Local Employment Exchange ... [10]

By November, Macnamara estimated, these men would be leading unemployment processions. He therefore recommended that many of them should be absorbed into extended building operations, that as many as possible of them should be upgraded by means of training and that financial assistance should be given to Local Authorities to develop public works. Secondly, training allowances needed to be increased by 5s per week for disabled soldiers, to allow for the rise in the cost of living. He concluded:

> These men are generally extremely self-respecting, loyal men. They are making a gallant struggle to earn their own livings. My personal experience – and I have been in the closest contact with them now for nearly five months – is that no men's gratitude can be won by so little; no men get so intensely bitter if slighted and neglected.

The contents of this letter formed the basis of a joint memorandum presented to the Cabinet by Macnamara and Addison (Minister of Health) on 13 August. Consequently, three days later, on the eve of the summer recess, the appointment of a Cabinet Committee, empowered to examine measures to be taken to meet abnormal unemployment in the coming winter, was announced. Under the Chairmanship of Sir Laming Worthington Evans, it was to consist of Horne (now President of the Board of Trade), Stanley Baldwin (Financial Secretary to the Treasury), Sir Eric Geddes (Minister of Transport), Addison and Macnamara.[11] As it met, unemployment began to worsen. On 21 September, Macnamara informed the Prime Minister that, the following Wednesday, he was receiving a deputation from Poplar; two days later he was addressing a meeting at Middlesbrough, arranged in the hope of solving (with special reference to ex-Service men) the problem of unemployment in the area. He enclosed a draft speech which provided an indication of what he called the large schemes of really productive work of one sort and another with which it was hoped to absorb as many as possible of the fit ex-Service men during the early autumn.[12]

Now, another factor was emerging. 'In my short time here many local disputes have threatened', Macnamara had written to Lloyd George on 24 June:

> Most have been smoothed out ... Four big troubles have threatened: Cotton, London trams, Printers, Gas workers. Three of these have been similarly smoothed out. The fourth – the Gas Workers – has been tided over and I believe will ultimately be straightened out. You owe all this to David Shackleton and H. J. Wilson. If you have two minutes to-morrow morning & will let me know – by about 12–1 – I w[oul]d like to bring them over so that you might personally thank them. They are wonderful men.[13]

Settling the coal industry was proving more difficult. Like the railways, it remained under the Government control set up during the war. In January 1919, the Miners' Federation announced its post-war programme. Permanent nationalisation was to be accompanied by a six-hour day and a thirty per cent increase in total earnings. The Government's disinclination to settle led to a vote in favour of a strike; this Lloyd George foiled by setting up the so-called Sankey Commission to investigate the industry. Its reports, published on 20 March and 20 June 1919, expressed support for nationalisation, a reduction in working hours and for wage increases, but failed to command a majority amongst the Commissioners. Hence its positive results were few; its greatest achievement was to have kept antagonists occupied.[14] In early 1920, the miners, activated by the rising cost of living, again became militant. With one wage increase granted by Lloyd George at the end of March, they pressed for a second in June; by September it appeared that the old pre-war alliance of miners, railwaymen and transport workers would operate once more. The coal strike began on 16 October;

government action in the form of the Emergency Powers Act, passed between 22 and 27 October, checked the move to a wider strike, however, and the miners, agreeing to an increase of 2s per shift, called off their strike pending a settlement of output questions, on 28 October.[15]

What appeared to be a success marked, instead, the fact that the Coalition, elected less than two years before, was losing public support. Talking with Lloyd George and Hamar Greenwood during lunch at Trent Park on 3 October, Macnamara expressed regret that the Government did not contain men who really understood what the working class wanted, or had really risen from the working classes and urged that Labour members should be brought into the Government. Later, pressed further by Riddell, he responded that he did not think that Lloyd George had ever understood the mechanic class as he had only seen them from the outside. Riddell's diary for 3 October continued:

Macnamara is very apprehensive regarding the coming winter. He thinks there will be serious unemployment and ascribes this in some measure to the restriction of credit by the banks. I told him that several of the Trade Unions had proposed that they should be represented on the Board of the Bank of England in order that Labour's point of view might be considered. Macnamara said that this would be a most desirable innovation as financial, commercial and social problems were interwoven. Credit is restricted and men are thrown out of work in consequence. Then the Government and Local Authorities have to find work for them. Macnamara is strongly of opinion that, if there is trouble, ex-soldiers will be at the head of it. He said that they feel that their services have not been adequately recognised and that they are entitled to demand work ...

Macnamara has improved a great deal and seems to be doing his job well. He is one of the few Ministers who are in touch with the working and poorer classes. He lives in a little house in Camberwell, and is in constant touch with Labour and the lower middle classes. He agrees that housing is one of the chief causes of revolutionary sentiments and says that he thinks the campaign has been badly executed. He says that Addison is a good Liberal and a benevolent and right-thinking man, but that he has no drive and does not get things done.[16]

Parliament reassembled as the coal strike was being settled. The Prime Minister, questioned about the Government's plans for dealing with the difficulties of the coming winter, referred buoyantly both to the Cabinet Committee on Unemployment appointed in August and to the Cabinet Committee on Housing which had also been in session during the recess. The Government, he said, had concluded that a great opportunity of finding work for many thousands of the fit ex-Service men still unemployed was afforded by the building trades. There were 65,000 fewer skilled men in the building trades than there were pre-war and there was a shortage of at least 500,000 houses. Approaches had been made to the trade unions on 6 October. Further proposals had been approved by the Cabinet. The four-year programme of the Ministry of Transport for road-making and road improvement would be anticipated, and further schemes both in London and the provinces would be started immediately. Here, too, emphasis was placed on the needs of ex-Service men.[17] Much of this was over-hopeful. At a conference of ministers two days later it was reported that nothing had yet emerged from negotiations with the building industry for the admission of ex-Service men except that disabled men trained by the Ministry of Labour had been rejected. Ministers were warned, however, not to express hostility to trade unions whilst the negotations with the miners were going on.[18]

The same evening an unsuccessful vote of censure was moved on the Government. Proposing it, William Adamson (leader of the Labour Party) reminded the House of Commons of the promise made by the Prime Minister and numerous other people of importance to Service men, that when the war was over they would be living in a new world:

> One can very well understand that men in such a position are not in a mood to be trifled with ... The Labour Party hold the opinion that the true solution of the unemployed problem is a national one ... The unemployed are not looking for a dole; they want work ... The finances necessary to provide that work ... ought and could be found by the Government ... If the Government and this House do not deal with this question, I believe that we are rapidly reaching a point when those who are involved in all the sacrifices and the sufferings of unemployment will take some steps to deal with it themselves.[19]

Macnamara put the Government's case carefully. He thanked the various local worthies whose recent special efforts on behalf of disabled ex-Service men had practically discharged that part of his responsibilities. Elsewhere, he said, he was faced with a bad set-back. The registered unemployed had amounted to 283,058 on 27 August; by 8 October there were 338,242. The coal strike, the cost of living and the increased cost of travel had made things worse. Whilst the Government could never fully requite ex-Service men for what they had done for the country, it would not do to say that what could be done had not been done. Five million men and 210,000 officers had been demobilised and returned to civil life. Thirty million pounds had been provided, which he acknowledged was an expedient, for those who were still unemployed. Two million pounds had been spent on resettlement, five million on industrial training for the disabled and one million on apprenticeship completion. Five-and-a-quarter million had been spent on land settlement. But still, he admitted, there were 187,000 ex-Service men, most of them between twenty-five and thirty years of age, mostly unskilled and segregated in the artisan parts of London. Here he returned to the opportunities which he and his colleagues had concluded were available in the building trade. Resistance had been encountered, negotiations begun in July 1919 had been prolonged and disappointing:

By agreement with the building trade we have been training 4,331 disabled
ex-Service men to fill the ranks ... We have 771 disabled ex-Service men
awaiting training and now I am suddenly confronted with the resolution of the
National Federation of Building Trade Operatives, passed on 1st September,
stating they will not agree to take any more trainees.

But considering the road construction and road maintenance schemes
outlined by the Prime Minister two days before and the provisions of the
extended Unemployment Insurance Act, due to take effect at the end of
the month, Macnamara rejected Adamson's strictures:

... whilst it is one thing to table a series of general propositions, it is another
thing, and if I may say so, a more useful thing, to hammer out and put into
actual operation practicable, productive, workable, ready-use schemes which
will directly assist the unemployed.[20]

But by the end of November Macnamara became alarmed. He wrote to
the Prime Minister:

SECRET AND PERSONAL

My dear George,

I am very much concerned about the unemployment problem. I have been
about the country a fair amount recently, and almost invariably the outlook is
depicted as very gloomy. In a good many industries, apparently, manufacturers
are drawing to a full stop. I cannot put the situation better than this. Since
31st August the barometer has steadily fallen. The Coal Strike, of course,
involved a temporary further sharp fall. At its close the glass naturally went up
again. But all the time the steady fall continued. We seem to me to be now
reaching a point when the fall may be very rapid indeed ... we have not secured
the results which I expected after your answer in the House of 19th October.
For instance the total number of men actually at work on the Arterial Road
Schemes at the close of last week was 125 in London, and 706 in the Provinces.
I confess I had hoped by this time the number would have been ten times as
many. Then as regards Housing, the urgent necessity to absorb forthwith 50,000
men was placed before the Building Trades' Federation at Manchester on the
26th October. Well! We are still discussing the matter with the building trades.
Heaven knows, I am far from passing anything in the nature of censure upon
anybody. On the contrary, it would be ungracious not to recognise that
everybody is doing all they can. Nevertheless, I think it my duty to call your
personal attention to a situation which may rapidly become very serious
indeed ...

Very faithfully yours,
T. J. Macnamara [21]

On the eve of the Christmas recess Macnamara reported the very limited
results of all his efforts to the House. In addition to the 265,000 soldiers,
he said, the 87,000 civilian men registered out of work in August had

grown to 148,000; women from 54,000 to 131,000. Beyond those was a margin, perhaps a wide margin, of persons unemployed but not registered. The Government had only just put its proposals to the building trade for recruitment and training (with a grant of £5 per head to the unions and a guarantee, in principle, of a rate of pay during wet weather work); three sections of the new London arterial schemes were proceeding and fifty-one provincial authorities had in operation, or under consideration, schemes of new arterial work; the Minister of Transport was negotiating with boroughs about road repairs both in London and the provinces and the Ministry of Health had taken measures to expedite and expand work on housing schemes' roads and sewers. The Government itself had decided to appoint a Committee under Lord St Davids which, drawing on a sum of £3,000,000, would assist Local Authorities in other useful work. Preference in employment was still to be given to unemployed ex-Service men.[22]

J. R. Clynes, for the Labour Party, contested the unemployment figures. There were hundreds of thousands of people suffering the privation of unemployment who had never been near a Labour Exchange, he said. The Government's plans amounted to a few makeshifts, a few lines of relief that would keep the wolf from the door for a few weeks only. Over the building scheme he expressed some sympathy for Macnamara. There was no Department of State at that moment of more importance than the Ministry of Labour, but the Minister had insufficient power, especially in dealing with the building trades unions. As for the road construction and repair schemes, only 4,000 men had so far been found work. The initiatives of the St Davids' Committee in giving preference to ex-Service men he regarded as questionable. There were many young ex-soldiers who had neither family nor household responsibilities, whilst middle-aged married men who had remained at home working in the factory or workshop to make effective the work of the ex-soldier abroad were now in difficulties. So were war widows.[23]

Before the debate Macnamara had been petitioned by a number of members, including Clynes, to waive the four weeks' qualifying period for benefit under the Unemployment Insurance Act. Now he introduced a one-clause Bill, which passed rapidly through the House, amending Section 44 of that Act so that any person who had been in any employment now insured for not less than ten weeks since 31 December 1919, or for any four weeks since 4 July 1920, should be eligible for benefit. Clynes welcomed the proposal. In his reply, however, he indicated the direction in which Labour Party thinking had moved. The war had completely altered the mentality of masses of out of work people, he said. Hundreds of thousands of men who were called upon to save their country when its life was in the balance and, happily, had survived, now expected their country to do something for them. The test of a government in relation to unemployment in the future would be in regard to how far the State could secure the masses of the people in employment and in a state of contentment.[24]

The Christmas recess afforded no rest to the members of the Government most closely concerned with the unemployment issue. The Prime Minister on 22 December received a deputation representing the City of London and other municipalities, urging the Government to increase its contribution from thirty per cent to seventy-five per cent of the costs of local relief work. His reply made clear the limitations within which Macnamara was confined. The great difficulty, he said, was the restriction of cash; the Exchequer could not grant the deputation's request because the only way to raise the money would be through new taxation. As it was, there had never been such generous contributions before from the Exchequer towards the solution of the unemployment problem.[25] He and Macnamara attended a conference on the issue at 10 Downing Street on the afternoon of Christmas Day. Riddell noted:

> After dinner ... Macnamara was very gloomy about unemployment. He says that the next three months will put the Government to a serious test and that he doubts whether the Cabinet appreciate the strength of the feelings of the ex-soldiers, and that they will be the ones who will cause the most trouble. He added, 'They have the most justification!' He said that he was worn out with negotiations with the building trade, and that he was convinced that the trade unions did not mean to accept the offer made by the Government ... If the scheme fails, his policy is not to interfere with the trade union jobs, but to start fresh works with non-union labour trained by the Government ... He thinks this work should be done by Mond's department ...

Riddell took up the matter with Lloyd George when he played golf with him on 27 December. The Prime Minister did not take the same line as Macnamara. 'People always want the Government to bell the cat', he said. 'Mond says, why should he be a strike breaker? Why should he undertake such a task? If the masters want this thing done, we will help them, but why should we incur all this unpopularity?' Riddell rejoined: 'You will be a great deal more unpopular if you don't find work for the people and if you don't find them houses. Why should the selfishness of the building trade hold up the country?' [26]

Early in the new year, the Cabinet resolved to set up an advisory committee, with Macnamara as Chairman, to review unemployment. Labour Party leaders refused to participate. Instead, the party drew up its own manifesto, which declared that unemployment arose from the very nature of the capitalist system. It urged action on an international scale to extend credits, called for large-scale public works and unemployment benefit of 40s per week for each householder and demanded an investigation into the causes of unemployment.[27] Macnamara found this unhelpful. 'To embark upon such an investigation', he wrote to Arthur Henderson on 5 January 1921, 'would of necessity push into the background the problem of dealing with the present emergency – a problem which in the view of the Government cannot wait; and I greatly fear that any attempt to combine the immediate with the ultimate would only result in both issues being confused and nothing effective done.'[28]

On 16 February 1921, in the debate on the Address, Clynes moved an amendment referring to the Government's lack of preparedness in dealing with unemployment. Demanding the fullest information about efforts so far made, he recalled Lloyd George's 1918 assurances that the country would be made so fit that heroes could live in it. 'You cannot go halfway with this problem. You either accept full responsibility or none at all.' 'I am sure the rt hon Gentleman opposite will conceal nothing from us', he said, indicating Macnamara: 'We regret that so good a man should have to struggle under such adversity; but we shall not be content with a re-hash of the information we received before we adjourned at Christmas.'[29]

Macnamara, plainly on the defensive, began by giving the latest figures of unemployed men and women. In October, the total had been 350,000; in November it had risen to 473,000, in December to 582,000 and in January to 842,000. It now stood at 1,039,000, including 368,000 ex-Service men, but this figure excluded non-registered unemployed as well as dependants. The Government's policy, he said, had been as far as possible to see that relief work of a useful and productive character was put in hand. But his account of the measures taken in cooperation with the Ministry of Health, the Ministry of Transport, the Office of Works and municipal authorities, and of the initiatives taken by the St Davids' Committee amounted, as Clynes had suspected, to no more than further details of the limited programme outlined by the Prime Minister in mid-October, followed by an account of the difficulties he had encountered in negotiations with the National Federation of Building Trade Operatives. The only innovation offered by the Government was derived from a plan put before the Cabinet by Macnamara himself on 7 February, by which unemployment benefit was to be increased and the period of its availability extended. The measures appeared ungenerous; they were to be financed by increased contributions from employers, employed and the State.[30] Nevertheless, the Government emerged triumphantly from the two-day debate, largely through a cheerful and persuasive speech by Lloyd George, in which he argued that the unemployed of 1921 were far better treated than their counterparts in 1907–08, castigated the building industry trade unions and blamed the situation on international factors. 'If international trade fails', he said, 'I do not care what you do in this House by legislation, or by administration outside, or by expenditure of public money, you will have nothing but starvation and ruin.'[31]

The new unemployment Bill reached its Second Reading on 23 February. Since the Armistice, Macnamara explained, the Insurance Fund's obligations had very largely been met by the out-of-work donation (a special State subvention outside the National Insurance Act) to the extent of nearly £40,000,000 in respect of ex-Service men. Consequently, the Fund's accumulated balance had risen to £20,000,000. He now proposed, assuming an average of nine-and-a-half per cent of unemployment amongst insured persons, to draw upon the greater part of that balance to bring in the ex-Service men and to enable men and women who had been employed for twenty weeks since 31 December 1919 to draw benefit for sixteen weeks between the passing of the Bill and the coming October and for another sixteen weeks between October and July 1922 (instead of the existing entitlement of eight weeks). Thereafter, all insured persons would be entitled to twenty-six weeks' benefit per year instead of fifteen weeks under the existing Act. The amount would be increased from 15s to 18s for men and from 12s to 15s for women. To provide for the longer periods and the greater benefit, contributions would be increased by 1d from the employed, by 2d (men) and 1½d (women) from the employer and by ¾d (men) and ⁷⁄₁₂d (women) from the State.[32] During the Committee stage, Clynes duly moved an amendment to raise the benefit rate to the figure laid out in the Labour Conference Manifesto. Eighteen shillings, he said, was too low. The sum of 40s in 1921 was worth no more than 15s before the war. The Government should devise means of drawing not only on past but on future reserves which were certain to accrue on the basis of industrial prosperity and normal conditions of trade in the years ahead.[33] Macnamara, however, resisted his proposals. 'All our insurance schemes have been based upon the contributory principle', he responded:

> The employed person, the employer and the State have contributed ... My rt hon Friend wants to depart from that principle ... I am not quite sure ... where he would get his fund from ... I will assume, and I do not think I am far out, that it is in the mind of the rt hon Gentleman that this ought to be a State charge.

He recommended further study of Section 18 of the main Act, whereby, if it appeared that more satisfactory insurance could be secured in any industry than that provided by the Act, then employers and employees should cooperate in establishing a superstructure to provide it. Nevertheless, as the debate proceeded, he yielded to the argument that the 18s and 15s benefits should be increased to 20s and 16s respectively, at the price of using up all rather than most of the accumulated balance of £20,000,000.[34]

On 22 March Clynes took up the unemployment issue again, having put down an amendment to the Consolidated Fund (No. 2) Bill in order to secure further discussion before the Easter recess. From the Official Returns, he had found that 1,280,000 persons were now registered as unemployed, with 744,000 on short time, as well as hundreds of thousands of unregistered workless people. The solution of the problem, he said, did not lie in giving relief in extensions of Insurance Acts. Pending the return of Great Britain's export trade, the question was whether more could be done at home to provide productive remunerative, useful and beneficial work:

> ... I think, roughly, the position is that something over 100,000 people altogether have been found work to some degree or other ... That is less than one out of every twenty of the total number unemployed. We believe on this side of the House that sufficient has not been attempted, that we are allowing 'useful' and willing work to go to waste ... We demanded a level of 40s a week for men who are unemployed and unable to get work ... as this problem gets worse ... the Government will be driven to the figure of 40s ... I would sooner, myself, pay a man as wages 40s for two days' work ... than pay 20s, as we are now doing, for doing nothing at all ... [35]

In his response, Macnamara agreed that whilst 1,207,000 men and women were now out of work, only about 100,000 had been found work in the arterial road and road maintenance schemes and the Ministry of Health operations that he had previously described, and also through the St Davids' Employment Grant Committee. It was not so easy, he said, to make and to find productive work as Clynes had suggested. Nevertheless, progress was at last being made in the scheme for the absorption of ex-Service men into the building trade. The £5 training scheme had been abandoned, but in cooperation with the Federation of Building Trades Employers the Government now hoped to arrange for 50,000 men to be trained as craftsmen. 'I wish to take this final opportunity of making an appeal to the building trades unions to come into the scheme', he concluded.[36]

Now, however, the situation was exacerbated by another miners' strike. Declining coal prices were involving the Government in losses; a rapidly passed de-control Bill abruptly brought about de-nationalisation on 1 April. Negotiations between the Miners' Federation and the mine owners, mainly about establishing a national wage through a National Wages Board, were broken off and a strike began. Within a fortnight, the involvement of the Transport Workers' Federation and the National Union of Railwaymen raised the possibility of a general strike; it was averted on 15 April, with hours to spare, by the withdrawal of these organisations from strike action once news of negotiations between the General Secretary of the Miners' Federation and the Prime Minister appeared to have begun. But the miners' strike lingered on until 1 July.[37] The slump deepened without intermission; in 1920, 27,000,000 working days had been lost through industrial disputes; in 1921 because of the coal strike, the figure was 47,800,000 by the end of May. By 22 June it had reached 70,000,000. Factories, mills and workshops in coal-using areas began to close down. By 8 April, 1,500,000 people had been unemployed, with 964,000 on short time; by mid-June the figures were 2,185,000 and 1,144,121 and still rising.[38]

Macnamara's March plans were thrown into disarray; it was soon plain that the National Insurance Fund could not sustain the new demands made upon it. Worse still, the Cabinet, having already responded to a press campaign against government waste by Lord Rothermere's *Sunday Pictorial* by adopting plans to reduce military and naval expenditure, authorised (on 13 May) a Treasury circular directing all ministers to effect drastic economies without which, an accompanying Prime Ministerial letter suggested, the 1922–23 Budget could not be balanced.[39] Macnamara found himself on a special Cabinet Committee with Horne (now Chancellor of the Exchequer), Sir Alfred Mond (Minister of Health) and Robert Munro (Secretary of State for Scotland) with instructions to devise an emergency scheme of unemployment insurance, one which, as the Cabinet of 3 June decided, should fix the maximum debt that the Treasury would have to meet at any moment at £16,000,000. Austerity had begun.[40] At the beginning of August, on Horne's initiative, a strong independent committee to make recommendations for cutting down government expenditure, consisting of four leading businessmen under the Chairmanship of Sir Eric Geddes, was set up. Its reports, creating the notorious 'Geddes Axe', began to be published the following February.[41]

Though the 1911 Act allowed for a reduction of benefit and an increase of contribution without further legislation, so that Macnamara could have proceeded by means of an Administrative Order, he preferred, he said, to lay the facts before the House of Commons. On 8 June, under the Ten Minute Rule, he sought leave to bring in a bill to vary the rates of contributions and the rates and periods of benefit, and otherwise to amend the Unemployment Insurance Acts of 1920 and 1921. Recalling his plan of 3 March, whereby benefit was to be made available in two sixteen-week periods between March 1921 and July 1922, he pointed out that, given an average of nine-and-a-half per cent unemployment amongst insured persons for the whole of that period, July 1922 could have been reached with funds exhausted but free of debt:

> That was our reasonable hope and expectation. But all those calculations have been upset. To-day the percentage of unemployment amongst insured persons is twenty-three per cent. Two millions of men and women are wholly unemployed; another 1,000,000 are on short time. We are now paying benefit at the rate of two millions a week with an income from contributions of less than £350,000. The insurance fund, which in March last stood at twenty-two and a half millions, now stands at eight and a half millions. As things are going it will last us only for about another month.

Hence, he asked the House to approve extra contributions of 1d per week from men and employers, with benefit reduced to the rates of the 1920 Act, namely 15s for men and 12s for women. To meet the pressing needs of the unemployed he proposed to add six weeks to the sixteen-week periods of benefit, at the same time increasing the three days' waiting period to six. The maximum deficiency which these readjustments would give at any period would be about £16,000,000. That sum would have to be advanced by the Exchequer.[42]

Clynes in a brief but passionate speech promised the Bill every resistance. It was a most amazing step for the Government to take, he said:

> There never has been a bill involving such big considerations, financial and otherwise, which ever before in the history of Parliament has been introduced under the Ten Minute Rule ... The Government has chosen this method of dealing with the problem of unemployment. It has limited its action in relation to unemployment to insurance, and now we have the spectacle of unemployment becoming worse and daily deepening in every sense of the term, and at the very worst stage of the unemployment trouble, when great suffering is being endured, the Government comes forward to undo a good part even of the little which they have attempted in the way of providing relief or remedy.

Moreover, he concluded, the Bill would encourage further demands. It would make many employers believe that they could impose excessive wage reductions upon their workers. Industrial trouble would follow.[43]

Moving the Second Reading on 15 June, Macnamara provided further details of the difficulties in which the National Insurance scheme now found itself. The March Act had been based on the assumption that throughout the whole succeeding emergency period of sixteen months there would be a weekly average of 1,000,000 workers unemployed (nine-and-a-half per cent of the trade union workforce, when for fifty years before the war ten per cent was the highest level that had been reached) and £800,000 payment of benefits. 'I have no wish to overdo the effect of the coal dispute', he said, 'but I am bound to say that I think I could have got through if it had not arisen.' But with over 2,000,000 unemployed and with the prospect of an average figure of 1,250,000 over the year July 1921 to July 1922, if benefits, contributions and waiting period remained as they were, he would run into debt, to the tune of £41,750,000. Already it appeared that by the end of the year the fund would be £13,750,000 in debt but in apprehension of even worse unemployment figures he was seeking powers to borrow up to £20,000,000. He told the House:

> I have worried away examining every possible expedient that might be tried to meet the present situation ... All I can hope is that the clouds may soon break and that blue sky will prevail again. The sooner that takes place the sooner I shall be in the position to clear off the liabilities now resting upon my shoulders – liabilities, the direct consequence of unemployment graver than anything experienced in the modern history of our country at any rate – and the sooner I shall be able again to put this scheme of unemployment insurance on the permanent and satisfactory basis, upon which we would all wish to see it.[44]

In an ill-attended debate (Royal Ascot was in progress) it was the Government rather than the Minister that came under attack. The day before, benches had been crowded as the prospects of the Emir Feisal, to whom £28,000,000 was to be advanced, were discussed. The House was reminded that if pledges had been given to our Arab allies, they had also been given on recruiting platforms during the war to men who were now expected to keep themselves and their families on 15s per week. 'Whenever the Government has cared to settle upon a certain policy, and that policy has involved the expenditure of millions, they have always found the will, just as they have settled upon the way', Clynes declared. D. M. Cowan (Scottish Universities) took up the argument. He was sorry to think that a strong Coalition Government should lose its nerve owing to the threats of the so-called anti-waste Press:

> What does this mean, the lowered rate of weekly allowance to the men and the women? It means ... lowered vitality for every man, woman and child. I am old enough to remember the rt hon Gentleman the Minister of Labour speak outside this House, and make some of the most eloquent pleas to which I have ever listened on behalf of the children of this country.[45]

Twelve days later, during the Report stage, Lieutenant Commander Kenworthy, the Asquith Liberal member for Hull, addressed Macnamara personally:

> The rt hon Gentleman has told us that it pains and grieves him to reduce the benefit ... I know how sincere on this question the rt hon Gentleman always is, and I would ask him, therefore, why does he maintain his portfolio as Minister of Labour, if he does not agree with this reduction and if he realises what harm it will do to the working population, and especially to the children of working classes? Why is he not brave? Why does he not resign? ... He must know that if he were to resign on a question of this sort he would become one of the most popular ex-members of the Government.[46]

But on the day, a week later, that the Bill was read a third time and passed, Macnamara was able to justify his measure in terms of the proportion of unemployed who would receive assistance. There were now, he said, 2,000,000 men and women registered as wholly unemployed and nearly 1,000,000 registered for benefit as working short time. For all the 3,000,000, save some 60,000 or 70,000, his scheme found something. 'What effort has there been in this country or any other comparable with that?', he asked.[47]

From the peak figures of 2,170,379 men, boys, women and girls registered as totally unemployed and the 988,394 registered as on short time, a continuous though not very striking decrease occurred throughout July and August. On the eve of the summer recess, Macnamara, recalling once again what had been achieved, nevertheless conceded that, at the end of the previous week, 100,000 men and 27,000 women had run out of the newly extended period of twenty-two weeks' benefit which had begun on 3 March. 'How to help these people to carry on until the end of October, when the second period of benefit begins', he admitted, 'is the problem before the Local Authorities and the Government at the present time.'[48] Maintaining the network of Ministry offices was an essential element in his programme. 'I hope the Minister of Labour will not give way to the panic-mongers, who are at him day and night for spending too much on Labour administration', Lady Astor had commented during the supply debate of 4 August. He did not do so. Thanking the House for its generous measure of sympathy, he provided a brisk and telling account of the operation, under pressure, of the employment exchanges and benefit offices. 'Our economies', he said, 'must be always consistent with the speedy and sympathetic treatment of the cases of ex-Service men whom we have to train and place, and the prompt and smooth payment of unemployment benefit to those entitled to receive it.'[49]

The Irish truce and the prolonged negotiations between Lloyd George and de Valera (ending on 30 September with agreement to set up a British-Irish Conference) occupied much of the Cabinet's attention over the summer recess. At the meeting on 19 August, apprehension was expressed that by the end of October some 500,000 unemployed would be out of benefit;[50] Macnamara, writing on 3 September to Lloyd George, who was on holiday at Gairloch, laid emphasis on this prospect, pointing out that the rather larger decrease in numbers registered at employment exchanges from mid-August onwards was due more to unemployed workers who had exhausted benefit ceasing to register than to an acceleration in the rate of recovery of industry. He went on:

> You will remember that under the Unemployment Insurance Acts we were able to pay benefit for a period of twenty-two weeks in all from 3 March. This includes an extension of six weeks authorised under the Act passed last July. When these twenty-two weeks have been drawn there is no power to pay more to those workers who exhausted their benefit until 3rd November next, when a fresh maximum period of twenty-two weeks on benefit will begin for those workers who are then unemployed. The first week in which the first twenty-two weeks' benefit could be exhausted was that ended 19th August, and I estimate that at the present time the number who have exhausted benefit is about 200,000. This figure may be subject to some adjustment but, coupled with the fact that each week will see a steady increase in the number, it is sufficient to indicate the seriousness of the problem that is before us in dealing with unemployed workers between now and the beginning of November.

There was a real danger, he considered, that the unemployed and those who had exhausted benefit were congregrated in a few areas, of which he provided details. In a number of them what he called 'Unemployment Committees on communist lines' had been formed. These, in his view, represented the feelings of comparatively few, but they were an element of serious danger especially where, following the example of the Poplar Board of Guardians, they were beginning to agitate for higher rates. Hence he had proposals ready for the Cabinet Unemployment Committee and, having heard, against expectation, that the Cabinet itself was to meet, he asked for the matter to be raised.[51]

The Cabinet meeting of 7 September 1921 took place at Inverness, to save the Prime Minister the inconvenience of returning to London from his holiday retreat. With Irish business (in which he was, unusually, able to participate) dispatched, Macnamara took the opportunity to brief his colleagues on the serious situation that was developing in London and elsewhere. This led, disappointingly, to criticism of government policy both before and after his assumption of the Labour portfolio. The whole character of the Unemployment Insurance Act, it was now asserted, had been modified both by the grant of uncovenanted benefits to ex-Service men and of additional weeks of benefit to the insured. The result had been to lead large numbers of the unemployed to lean unduly on this form of State assistance rather than accept work at such reduced rates of wages as employers could afford to pay.[52] Back in London, however Macnamara found new evidence of public dissatisfaction. From a Dundee union official there was a telegram, a copy of which he sent to the Prime Minister:

Thousands of Dundee men and women workers foodless and virtually destitute. Government responsible for state of affairs through blockading, boycotting and in other ways impeding trade with trading neighbours. Insist upon Government dealing at once with urgent question. Situation serious, dangerous and clamant.[53]

The following week Macnamara, with Mond and Hilton Young (Financial Secretary to the Treasury), returned to the Prime Minister's rain-sodden retreat at Flowerdale House, Gairloch, for further consultation about unemployment. 'Much discussion', Riddell wrote in his diary. 'It was interesting to think that the fate of millions was being settled in such an informal way in this remote spot ... the Ministers evidently did not enjoy Gairloch and presented a somewhat disconsolate appearance.' Churchill, on holiday nearby and anxious about the reception he was likely to encounter in his Dundee constituency, was drawn in and it was agreed that he (as Secretary of State for the Colonies), the Home Secretary, the Minister of Agriculture and the Parliamentary Secretary to the Department of Overseas Trade (Lloyd Greame) should be added to the Cabinet Unemployment Committee.[54] Back in London, the Committee began to press ahead with plans for export credits. Macnamara, however, had reservations. 'I shall be glad when you are able to return', he wrote to the Prime Minister on 27 September. Statements made to the press over the previous week had raised public interest and expectation, particularly among the unemployed. Unless work was actually put in hand at once, he warned, the Government's last position was going to be worse than its first. His own concern was still with unemployment benefit:

We had 1,465,761 persons registered as wholly unemployed on 16th September. And undoubtedly a further 200,000 or more must be added to that figure as unemployed but not continuing to register, having exhausted their benefit. That gives, I estimate, at least 1,670,000 wholly unemployed in all.[55]

The Prime Minister told the Cabinet on 6 October that he regarded the unemployment situation as unprecedented. With Horne and Austen Chamberlain (Lord Privy Seal) he had met the Committee on Unemployment earlier in the morning; a Drafting Committee under the President of the Board of Trade had been convened, and its conclusions were now handed round for Cabinet approval.[56] The following week, the Cabinet agreed to reserve legislation in the forthcoming session to unemployment.[57] In practice, this meant that Lloyd George, Chamberlain, Birkenhead, Churchill, Worthington-Evans and others could devote themselves to the negotiations leading to the Irish Treaty, which was secured on 6 December whilst the legislative programme was placed in the hands of Horne, Mond and Macnamara.

In a brief speech on 19 October, the Prime Minister outlined the programme to the House of Commons. They were confronted, he said, by probably the worst period of unemployment that the country had seen for 100 years. Though there was nothing that the House, or any other House, could do to hasten a trade recovery, what the Government proposed was to amend the Export Credits Scheme; to activate engineering work in the colonies and to guarantee loans up to £26,000,000 to foreign governments, the Dominions and public authorities at home to buy British manufactured goods. 'There are undoubted signs of a revival', he asserted: 'The best we can hope for is a steady improvement, and I think we shall get it. But meanwhile there will be unemployment on a very considerable scale, and we shall have to provide for it.'[58]

Macnamara summed up on the benefit programme at the end of the two-day debate which, he said, was in general not wanting in generous recognition of the Government's endeavour to meet the most complex and baffling problem and full of solicitude for the condition of those who had fallen upon the evil day of unemployment. Over the previous three months things had improved. The figure of 2,170,000 wholly unemployed in June was now 1,750,000, of which 300,000 were women; throughout the winter he expected to have about 1,500,000 people wholly unemployed. Reviewing the efforts made over the previous year, he reported that work had been found, mainly on the roads, for some 200,000 men. With the assistance and cooperation of Local Authorities, every endeavour had been made to make work outside the ordinary channels of industrial activity. But large groups of people, namely all the women, clerks, and artificers engaged in intricate and highly-developed processes, could not be helped by a mere pick and shovel policy. He declared:

> The fact is, it is not easy to make productive work outside the ordinary industrial activities of the country for large classes of the industrial population ... it is common ground that there is only one way of permanently curing the disease

from which we are suffering, that is, if possible, stimulating trade and industry on an economic basis.

In the meantime the Government proposed to take further action under the Unemployment Insurance Act:

> We propose to take the whole of the employers and employed persons covered by the Insurance Act, and ask them for six months to bear a further contribution which, together with a substantial grant from the Exchequer, will go to the women and children ... What I am asking the man lucky enough to be at work to do is to find another 2d per week for six months ... and that is to be augmented by contributions from the employer, and the Exchequer will furnish during the winter 5s a week for the wives and 1s for the dependent children of the men in insured trades but out of a job.[59]

Macnamara moved the Second Reading of the Unemployed Workers' Dependants (Temporary Provision) Bill on 24 October. Calling on men to pay 2d a week, their employers 2d a week and women, boys and girls to pay 1d a week, with their employers paying 1d a week, the State would add, he said, 3d and 2d respectively. This contribution from the employed would give the fund about £5,500,000 over six months. It had been estimated that about 700,000 wives and nearly double the number of children (not more than four in a family) would be given assistance. The whole efficacy of the proposal was that aid would become available within the month; it would run until 7 March 1922. He concluded:

> We assume that if the average number of persons unemployed week by week in the period covered is not more than 1,500,000, the contributions received will by that date balance the expenditure. If, however, unemployment is more severe, there will be a deficit in the fund on 7th May 1922, and power is accordingly taken to make the contributions payable in such a case for a further period to meet the deficiency.[60]

The Government's evident determination to exercise a rigorous control over the disbursement of unemployment benefit was to make Macnamara's rôle in the further progress of the Bill very difficult. The sum suggested was far too low to form anything like a substantial amount of supplementary relief, Clynes, the next speaker in the debate, observed, and he asked, 'Is that all the State, at this moment of extreme working class urgency, can afford as its contribution for the relief of this distress?'[61] His colleague, George Barker (Monmouth, Abertillery), looked further ahead. Unemployment, he said, should not be dealt with by a temporary expedient; there was no evidence that it would be a temporary evil or a temporary difficulty.[62] But Macnamara had been cautious in his claims for the Bill. He summed up just before the House divided (Ayes 226: Noes seventy):

> I have tried in the most simple way and in the most expeditious way to set down something which will do the largest amount of good in the shortest

amount of time. The basis I have gone on is this: here is the Insurance Act, and here are the people in the Insurance Act. I will base this Bill upon that, and I will do it through the agencies which now deal with the Insurance Act in as simple and as expeditious a way as possible.[63]

The almost immediate applicability of the scheme was the argument he used again during the protracted Committee stage. Pressed to increase the wife's allowance from 5s to 10s and to broaden the system, he emphasised that the result would be to bankrupt the insurance scheme; further, the system could not be broadened or even altered without major legislation.[64] Meanwhile the pressure increased over the 1s child allowance. Clynes said that 1s was contemptible, about as much as an hon. member would think of throwing to a cabman or to a porter by way of a tip for some momentary service;[65] his colleague Neil Maclean (Govan) introduced an amendment to raise the allowance to 7/6d for the first child and 6s for every other child;[66] Sir Donald Maclean more realistically pressed for 2s rather than 1s.[67] Macnamara indicated that, procedurally, the moment had passed for discussion of the issue, but he promised to see what he could do about extending the allowance beyond four children in a family and about raising the age at which it would be discontinued from fourteen to sixteen.[68]

All four issues reappeared during the Report stage. Macnamara rejected the proposal to increase the wife's allowance from 5s to 10s flatly, saying that the Government had not got the money.[69] Doubling the child allowance proved more difficult to resist. Morgan Jones (Caerphilly) made the first of three appeals to the Minister's former calling:

> We are both ex-teachers ... From time to time it has been my unfortunate lot to address lessons to children who have had to come to school without breakfast, who are ill-clad and ill-fed, and I invite hon members opposite to tell me what sort of chance they have of getting an adequate return for the money which they spend upon education unless the child to whom the education is given is in a fit condition to receive it.[70]

The ex-headmaster of the Avon Vale Board School could not, and did not, yield, though the availability of the shilling to all the children in a family of more than four was conceded.[71] The Chancellor of the Exchequer was at hand to emphasise that a very depleted revenue was expected the following year and his task was to balance the budget.[72] A further call on the past was made by Macnamara's old NUT colleague Ernest Gray, now the Conservative member for Accrington:

> We are now so poor that for a period of six months we cannot find more than 1s per week for starving children. My rt hon Friend the Minister of Labour did not pretend in a single sentence or word that this grant ... was sufficient to sustain the child. I have known him for many years and I have known his deep interest in the welfare of the worker's child, and I ask myself what language he would have used had he been sitting ... in the Opposition and the

Government had offered him 1s per week for the relief of starving children ...
I can imagine not merely the words but the gesture with which he would have
thrust aside the arguments which to-day have been adduced by himself,
supported by his friend the Chancellor of the Exchequer.[73]

The 1s grant remained unchanged, but a third appeal brought about the
extension of the age at which it was available from fourteen to sixteen.
Macnamara had himself proposed to extend the age to fifteen; J. M. Hogge,
the Asquith Liberal member for East Edinburgh, successfully pressed him
further:

> We were talking in the war about our C3 population. If you stunt the physique
> of a boy or girl between fourteen and fifteen, you are stunting that physique
> permanently as an asset of the nation of the future. Most of us remember that
> the Minister of Labour ... came into this House as a representative of the
> teaching profession ... I used to admire the stand he made for the education
> of children in this country ... and I am perfectly certain he must feel ... rather
> chagrined that to-night he ... as the first representative and the first voice from
> teachers, should be in the position of Minister of Labour denying to boys and
> girls between fourteen and sixteen the necessary nourishment of 1s per week,
> or £2 12s per year ...[74]

Writing in the December edition of the *Lloyd George Liberal Magazine*,
Macnamara summed up what the Government had done in preparation
for the second successive winter of mass unemployment, with 1,750,000
out of work. Its first endeavour had been to do something to start normal
trade again. Hence, as a result of the recent Trade Facilities Act, an
extended Export Credits Scheme had been in operation since the end of
October; so far £300,000 had been handed out, with provisional sanction
for a further £488,000. Guarantees were to be available in respect of
£25,000,000 for capital undertakings at home. Local Authorities had been
offered government indemnification for a proportion of the loan charges
incurred in relief works. The St Davids' Committee was spending over
£2,000,000 on 143 schemes employing 12,500 men for five months. Additional work on roads, land drainage, afforestation and light railways was
being planned. Certain government contracts had been brought forward.
Further monies to provide free passage for ex-Service men and their families
to the colonies had been allotted. He concluded:

> But manifestly with the best will in the world, this work-finding and work-
> making policy cannot possibly cover the ground ... For those who cannot thus
> be helped the duty of finding other assistance, pending the return of trade
> prosperity, still remains. Here, again, the Unemployment Insurance Act is our
> sheet anchor. Benefit began again on 5th November and will be paid through
> the winter ... we paid the first instalment of ... Supplementary Dependants'
> Allowances with the Unemployment Benefit on 18th November ... Lastly ...
> Our plan provides ... for loans to help Boards of Guardians in necessitous

areas, to enable them to spread their present abnormal expenditure over a number of years.[75]

The New Year brought no relief. Macnamara wrote to Lloyd George on 18 January:

My dear Prime Minister,

I am sorry that we were unable at the Cabinet this morning to discuss unemployment, for I am quite sure that the position is so serious that an early discussion is essential. The fact that funds at the disposal of the St Davids' Committee are 'exhausted' is receiving wide publicity and is giving rise to discussions which I think will cause trouble. I realise the Chancellor's difficulties and it is, of course, the case that the previous limit of £10,000,000 was increased to £13,000,000; but look at the facts about unemployment at the moment. There was some hope during December that things were improving and our figures of registered unemployed fell from 1,834,000 on 2nd December to 1,813,700 on 22nd December, but since then there has been an increase and our latest figure shows a total of 1,933,000. This is bad enough, but I can see no promising prospects of any general revival ...

The St Davids' Committee have before them useful schemes amounting to about £5,000,000 more than they can sanction, which they must turn down unless some more money is available. The view is widely held – and I am convinced that it is the right one – that of the various devices which we have adopted to deal with unemployment, that of inducing the Local Authority to carry out works of practical utility is by far the best; and with practically 2,000,000 unemployed I can see no adequate answer to the plea that somehow or other we should continue to encourage Local Authorities to go on with their schemes by assisting them with some of the cost ... There is to be a meeting of the Cabinet Unemployment Committee to-morrow, but I am convinced that the whole question of unemployment is one which must be discussed by the Cabinet, and I very much hope that you will agree to have an early discussion.

Very faithfully yours,
T. J. Macnamara [76]

Lloyd George, however, was occupied with the possibility of a Franco-British Treaty and the prospects of a general election.[77] Cabinet discussion of unemployment was postponed until after Parliament had reassembled. The King's Speech on 7 February treated it as an international issue in anticipation of the Genoa Conference which the Prime Minister was to attend in April.[78] Two Labour members, Arthur Hayday and T. E. Naylor, the newly elected member for South East Southwark, took a different view, moving an amendment to the effect that the Government was ineffective in dealing with the causes of unemployment, in providing for useful productive work and lacking in intention to enable Local Authorities to take up the responsibility for benefit as the national scheme ran out.[79] Their party, formerly content to berate the Government for under-spending, was at last moving towards a distinctive and Socialist policy. Clynes, early in the debate, expressed admiration for the condition of workers in Russia. Could the Prime Minister say that they were worse off than the unemployed in Great Britain? When Macnamara gave his customary account of the number of men employed as a result of what the Government had hoped was pump-priming, adding that to place factories under State direction would have the effect of throwing other sections of the same industry into unemployment, the Labour leader accused him of trying to have it both ways:

> He must choose as to whether finding work through a statutory department or through the Local Authorities is beneficent work, proper and profitable work, or is it work which ... causes the unemployment of other workers who would otherwise not be unemployed? [80]

Macnamara, as usual, strove to emphasise the community of interest between government, employers and workpeople in dealing with unemployment.[81] Naylor observed that a Labour government would not be quite so much concerned about the interests of the private employer and the private capitalist. Instead, it would use capital to start productive work.[82] Thomas Griffiths (Pontypool) pressed the matter further. During the war, the Government had been compelled to admit that they could not trust private enterprise. Mines, munitions, steel and railways had been taken over. Now the mines, factories and land which were idle should be taken over by the 2,000,000 unemployed, who would be able to exchange the goods produced amongst themselves. 'I guarantee', he said, 'that they would work the scheme successfully.'[83]

The immediate needs of the unemployed remained to be considered. Benefit was due to finish on 22 February and the operations of the Workers' Dependants Act on 9 May and, as Macnamara had indicated in his letter of 18 January to the Prime Minister, unemployment was rising again. At the end of November the figure stood at 1,833,000 wholly unemployed, with 265,000 on short time. Post-Christmas holiday closures produced a material set-back: on 10 January there were 1,933,000 persons registered as wholly unemployed with 316,000 on short time. At the end of the month some alleviation had occurred. The figures fell to 1,904,300 and 280,000.[84] Extended benefit and aid for dependants was still needed. But the publication of the Geddes Reports and the debate that followed made their continuance unlikely. Twice on 8 March, Macnamara was asked whether he intended to reduce unemployment benefit. He refused to answer.[85]

In response to his proposals on 15 February the Cabinet had agreed to the extension of benefit for another six weeks, but the new austerity was already exerting its effect. Section 3 of the 1921 Act had obliged claimants to provide evidence of their entitlement under what was still an insurance measure; now the conditions for the extra six weeks were made more rigorous. Macnamara announced them in a written answer on 17 February. Workers under eighteen not entirely dependent on their earnings for their livelihood would be excluded, as would single adults who had exhausted all rights derived from payment of contributions, unless they secured a specific recommendation from their Local Employment Committee. The Committees were also to be directed to pay careful regard both to the earnings of short-time workers and to all cases where unemployment benefit had been drawn for long periods. The extension would not be granted to persons who were not prepared to accept work other than that to which they were accustomed, but which they were reasonably capable of performing. There were, the Cabinet agreed, manifestly vacancies available for women to which their attention should be directed. Such vacancies were domestic.[86]

By mid-March the main issues of benefit and aid had not yet been decided. Macnamara wrote to Lloyd George on 18 March:

SECRET

Dear Prime Minister,

As you know, one of the very urgent problems before the Cabinet is that of the extension of unemployment benefit, and, with Chamberlain's concurrence, I am writing to you in order to bring specially to your notice one or two very important points in the proposals on which we have provisionally agreed as a Cabinet Committee ...

Unemployment benefit is at present being paid at the weekly rate of 15s for men and 12s for women. In addition, under the temporary scheme for Dependants' Grants, unemployed persons receive 5s a week for a wife and 1s a week for each dependent child.

The benefit originally allowed in the period from last November to next July was sixteen weeks. This has recently been extended to twenty-two weeks, under the exercise of discretionary powers given to me by the Act. *As things stand, therefore, the benefit will begin to expire from 5th April next onwards ...*

We clearly must do something substantial to fill the gap now existing after 5th April. We also think that the Dependants' Grants Scheme cannot be allowed to come to an end on 9th May, and must in fact be continued as part of the Unemployment Insurance Scheme. *But in considering what can be done we are faced with great financial difficulties.* The amount of unemployment benefit now being paid week by week is about double the revenue from contributions, and the Unemployment Fund, therefore, is running into debt at the rate of something like half a million a week. There are statutory borrowing powers up to £19,000,000 or so, but £13,500,000 has already been borrowed, and there is every prospect that, even allowing for exhaustion of benefit rights, we shall come to an end of our borrowing powers or practically so at the end of June.

We propose that a new period of benefit shall begin on 26th April, *thus leaving a gap of three weeks after the date – 5th April – when benefit begins to be exhausted. By the end of this interval of three weeks the number of unemployed persons* without benefit rights may number 600,000 or more. That is the first proposal I think you should definitely have brought before you.

We propose further to reduce the weekly rate of benefit for single men from 15s to 12s and for single women from 12s to 10s. The Dependants' Grants which are at present temporary would be continued as part of the Unemployment Insurance Scheme, at their existing rates, viz 5s for a wife and 1s for each child. This reduction in benefit is the second proposal which you should definitely have brought before you ...

The effect as regards the Exchequer is that during the next financial year a sum of about £5,000,000 will have to be provided over and above what is required under existing legislation. In addition it will probably be necessary for the sake of security to increase somewhat – though probably not to any great extent – the existing borrowing powers ...

Very faithfully yours,
T. J. Macnamara [87]

On 29 March, Macnamara moved the Second Reading of the new Unemployment Insurance Bill. It was necessary, he said, because while the existing provisions were drawing to a close, unemployment remained widespread and, according to his calculations, an average of 1,500,000 unemployed could be expected for the next fifteen months. His aim now was to continue, until June 1923, emergency and uncovenanted benefit (which under the terms of the 1921 Act would, for many, be exhausted on 5 April) and the provisions of the Unemployed Workers' Dependants Act, due to end on 9 May. Macnamara's emphatic letter to Lloyd George on 18 March had produced decisive results. Benefit was to remain at 15s for a man and 12s for a woman; there would be fifteen weeks' benefit out of thirty between April and October and twelve weeks (with two possible extensions of five weeks) between November 1922 and the end of June 1923.[88] 'I think that, on the whole, the Minister of Labour may be congratulated upon having weathered an exceptional storm so far, and upon having brought in a proposal which has the appearance and promise of carrying us through an exceptional period again up to the middle of next year', George Barnes, the Labour spokesman, admitted. His colleague, James Sexton (St Helens) was similarly complimentary: 'I want to congratulate the rt hon Gentleman on having retained the very meagre benefit suggested in the Bill before us. It has relieved some of our anxieties, for our impression generally was that there was likely to be a reduction in the relief now being dispensed to the unemployed.'[89] Now criticism centred on the conditions (following the February guidelines) to be laid down for uncovenanted benefit. But Macnamara was unrepentant. He knew, he said, that the Labour Party advocated a non-contributory system, with benefit financed by the State. He himself was in favour of a contributory system.[90] Under it covenanted workers had a prior claim. As the Report stage drew to a close, he said:

I am not proposing to touch the covenanted side, provision for which is laid down in the Statute. I am proposing in regard to the uncovenanted side to have some discretion as to the conditions under which these benefits should be paid ... this benefit will be received by many people who have paid little or nothing into this fund. We are paying benefits in advance of contributions, and I think, in these circumstances, I am entitled to lay down reasonable and just conditions under which this free uncovenanted benefit should be granted ... I am bound to make such regulations as will secure that this fund shall be conserved for those who need it most.[91]

Benefit and aid now seemed to have been fixed until well into 1923. Nevertheless, a further adjustment proved to be necessary. On 10 July, the Prime Minister announced that, because of weighty representations made by the Poor Law Authorities, the intervals which, under the April 1922 Act, had to elapse between successive periods of uncovenanted unemployment benefit between July and October would be reduced from five weeks to one week.[92] Macnamara moved the Second Reading of the Unemployment Insurance (No. 2) Bill two days later:

I am asking in this Bill that the fifteen weeks' uncovenanted benefit from April to October may be twenty-two in order to avoid two more gaps of five weeks each. I do this because of the case made out by the Poor Law Guardians in the areas heavily hit by the long period of depression through which we have been passing. I can do it without asking for a further grant from Parliament, and without increasing my borrowing powers, but, of course, I am, to the extent of this additional seven weeks, postponing the date at which my scheme would otherwise again become solvent. I beg respectfully to ask the House to do what it can to give this Bill a speedy passage.[93]

Whether there was a need for a gap was questioned both from the Labour and Government benches. Clynes, accepting the Bill as an instalment of some further support, expressed the hope that the policy of gaps could be further debated.[94] Neville Chamberlain, noting that the Labour Party view now seemed to be 'We will take anything we can get from you, but we will give you no thanks. We will reserve to ourselves the right to point out how much more we should have done had we been in power', also expressed regret that Macnamara had not enlarged upon the necessity for it. 'I can only imagine', he said, 'that the object of my rt hon Friend is, so to speak, to pull up the men at certain intervals, to make them realise that they cannot go on for ever receiving benefits, and must look round to see if they cannot get work ... I confess I am very sceptical.'[95] But Macnamara, as the Bill moved rapidly through the Committee stage, was quite clear what his reasons were:

From the time of the original Insurance Act of 1911, the scheme of providing a number of weeks of benefit less than the calendar period to be covered, has been the established principle and rule ... whether as a moral corrective or not ... I do not enter.[96]

Now the Coalition had only three months to run. The Chanak crisis, in which it successfully resisted Mustafa Kemal's apparently irresistible move to occupy Constantinople, edged the Conservatives towards their withdrawal from partnership with Lloyd George and his Liberal supporters, finalised at the Carlton Club meeting on 19 October. Free of ministerial duties for the first time for fifteen-and-a-half years, Macnamara turned back to writing. He had occasionally contributed to the *Lloyd George Liberal Magazine*, set up in opposition to the Asquithian-dominated *Liberal Magazine* in October 1920. Now articles under his name appeared frequently, dealing at first with unemployment and the other issues with which his Ministry had been concerned, later with the whole range of policies.

With the general election over, Bonar Law's government undertook to examine afresh the ameliorative measures prepared by the late ministry to deal with unemployment. Macnamara reported the response to the Gracious Speech made by Ramsay MacDonald, restored to the House after an absence of four years and now leader of the Opposition:

> We are not interested in the ameliorative measures prepared by My late Government. We are interested in the blunders of the late government, which created the conditions out of which the unemployment arises. Our interests are concerned not with the ameliorative measures that the late government prepared. Who cares in the least about them?

'I confess I have always thought a good many people did', Macnamara commented, 'including not only the unfortunate workless themselves, but the Labour members in the late Parliament who certainly continuously pressed upon us the necessity to pursue and extend them.'[97]

On 8 December, with Macnamara's arrangements for unemployment benefit still in operation, Sir Montague Barlow, now Minister of Labour, declared the Government's intention to continue also the Coalition's measures for encouraging trade by credits and providing temporary work via the St Davids' Committee, government Department projects and loans to Local Authorities.[98] The Labour members, increased to 142 at the general election, were openly contemptuous: 'Neither in schemes of relief nor in plans of finding work can we accept these proposals of the Government as in any sense meeting the problem', Clynes declared:

> Its international aspects we do not touch. They have been discussed and they will be discussed again. Within the ambit of our own resources there are means and ways that are being neglected, until we are driven almost to the point of despair in bringing these matters before the House ... Scarcely a week in the past two and a half years, or perhaps the last three years, has passed without some reference to this problem. We cannot get away from it. It is the business of the Government to face it as something likely to remain with us for years, and to begin now such measures of reconstruction and profitable service as will pay the country better than dispensing each week immense sums of money without any return of any kind whatever.[99]

Macnamara, who had always been sympathetic to individual Labour members, did not conceal his hostility to what he judged was the party's increasing enthusiasm for Marxism. In a pamphlet entitled *Success in Industry*, published in 1920, he had already contrasted the tremendous appeal of socialism and the hopeless impossibility of its practical application:

> All our activities would be either municipalised or nationalised ... Socialism suffers among other things from a fatal constitutional defect ... It takes away the direct incentive to personal enterprise and endeavour.[100]

In *Labour at the Cross Roads: Two Camberwell Addresses* he marvelled how every social shortcoming was now regarded by the Socialist as proof positive of the evils of capitalism. Marxists, he wrote:

> want to upset the existing system and replace it by something entirely and fundamentally different ... I am profoundly convinced that ... Socialist policy is bound to prove ashes in the mouth for the very people on whose behalf it is put forward ... it is not at all necessary to upset the whole fabric of our industrial and commercial system, and re-cast it on the basis of public ownership, to secure what the average workman really wants ... the Socialist State is bound to be hopelessly anti-progressive in its industrial methods.[101]

'If I could bring myself to believe that the Labour Party's socialist policy would give us our heart's desire, I would ask nothing better than to be placed in the forefront of its advocacy', he declared in Camberwell on 21 June 1923:

> But all examination I have been able to make shows that though the Socialist's promise is extremely attractive and seductive so long as it remains in the prospectus stage, it comes to grief directly endeavour is made to carry it into practical effect. Applied to human nature it is a hopeless misfit ... And I would appeal to people whose lives are so hard that no one can blame them if they turn a ready ear to anyone who comes forward promising a quick way out of difficulty and distress, to remember that all isn't gold that glitters; to remember the fable of the dog who dropped the drab but solid substance for the more attractive but entirely worthless reflection in the stream below. The truth is – and all the experiences of the past enforce it in the most emphatic way – there is no short cut to the Social Millennium. There is nothing for it but slow step-by-step advance along the well-defined track of sane, practicable, well considered progress.[102]

Of course, he wrote in the *Lloyd George Liberal Magazine* in June, no sincere Liberal could do other than rejoice when the labouring man found his way to the green benches of the House of Commons. No sincere Liberal could do other than lend a hand when such a man asked that the cause of social reform be prosecuted with courage, with determination, and with imagination. But when the political Labour Party put Karl Marx and the doctrine of Class War in the forefront of its programme, then it was the duty of Liberalism to resist that policy ... Unfortunately, it was plain that some Liberals were reluctant even to seem to run counter to Labour's declared policy.[103] In August, he reminded readers that, on 2 March in Edinburgh, Lloyd George had urged the members of the divided party to confer and consult with a view to reaching a common decision which would revive and reinvigorate Liberalism. He observed:

> Five vital months have elapsed since that urgent invitation was extended. Everybody knows the result. Conference and consultation have been impossible ... The combined Liberal vote at the general election was within 100,000 of the Socialist vote. Yet the Socialist Party is the official Opposition to His Majesty's Government ... Now does anyone mean to tell me that if Liberalism had gone into the fight of 15th November a united body this enormously valuable strategic position need have been conceded to socialism? [104]

Already Liberals, including C. P. Trevelyan, Macnamara's former colleague on the London School Board, were moving to Labour. Liberal unity was almost accidentally restored when Baldwin, Bonar Law's successor, chose to fight another general election on the issue of protection on 6 December 1923, but it was already too late for them to recover their former position. MacDonald had long been speaking of the Labour Party as the inevitable and speedy successor of the Conservative government.[105] The election results provided him, probably to his own surprise, with his opportunity.

The Conservatives, with 258 members, remained the largest party; Labour secured 191 and the reunited Liberals 158. Baldwin did not resign, but on 15 January a King's Speech was delivered in the expectation that its plans would not be carried into effect. A Labour government, with nominal Liberal support, was poised to take office and square up to the unemployment problem. 'What remains for the successors of the present Government?', Macnamara asked on 18 January. 'There is nothing for them but to work along the lines which have been laid down from the beginning, developing, extending and adding to it as experience and the circumstances admit.'[106] This forecast proved to be just. Four days later, Baldwin resigned. As Prime Minister, MacDonald continued for a while with the lofty tone that he had employed the previous October on unemployment:

> Here again, we are faced with a problem at which, in my view, we have hitherto rather nibbled. Two things have to be secured, and these we are working at: first, work; secondly, an effective income which is being supplied by the scheme of insurance if work cannot be provided.[107]

Instead of being discarded, the principle of insurance was to be refined:

> I come to the point when we deal with 'doles', as they are called, or insurance. Two expedients have been adopted which never had any rational foundation, and sooner or later they have to be abolished. The one is the expedient of the

'gap', and the other is the expedient of selection in regard to uncovenanted benefit ... Does any hon member mean to say that a gap of three weeks in a long period of unemployment has any moral or economic value to the man himself? It has no value at all ... the Government propose to abolish both the gap and the selection ... the cost comes out of the Insurance Fund.[108]

Macnamara surveyed the Labour government's plans during the Estimates debate on 10 March. His approach was unmistakably critical. Though the 'gap' had been abolished, he could not find, in the new administration's handling of the distressing problem of unemployment, any evidence of that bigger, bolder and braver grasp which the country had been led to expect. Neither its members nor its followers would deny that they were under a special obligation with regard to finding or making work for the unemployed:

They will forgive me if I point out that they speak with something approaching contempt of the efforts of their predecessors [Hon. members: 'Hear, hear!'] ... They say that governments in the past have merely nibbled at this question. I use the phrase of the Prime Minister himself.

Yet despite the often-expressed opinion of the hopeless inadequacy of the efforts of both the Coalition and the Conservative governments and the impression that Labour was ready to tackle the problem in a way which would make its predecessors hang their heads with shame, the full Estimates for 1923–24 now made less provision for work finding and the relief of unemployment than the total for 1922–23.[109]

It was soon apparent that Labour's policy on unemployment benefit amounted to nothing more than the extension of the system to which Macnamara had devoted himself for two-and-a-half years. On 8 April, Thomas Shaw, the Minister of Labour, moved the Second Reading of what he called his small Bill which, he explained, was intended to secure uncovenanted benefit for forty-one weeks instead of twenty-six, and thus to give the House time thoroughly to consider, discuss and pass a larger measure.[110] Macnamara gave him his support. Already the three weeks' gap had gone. Single young people living at home had been admitted to benefit; so had aliens of all kinds. The larger Bill, he said, would provide eleven more weeks' benefit, bringing the total to fifty-two weeks in the year. There would be increased benefit for men, women and children and, later, boys and girls aged fourteen to sixteen. All this was to be done under the existing national insurance system. Macnamara commented:

When I look at this Bill and even more when I look at the larger Bill, I cannot help recalling the sharp change of front ... on the part of a number of Labour members in this House. When I came to the House again and again for extended benefit, what was the attitude taken up towards me? It was that I was all wrong, that I ought to find work, that money relief without service in return was waste ... Let me give one quotation ... from a statement by the present Prime

Minister in ... the *Review of Reviews* in September 1921 ... It is a statement developing Labour's policy, and the paragraph referring to unemployment is as follows:–

> 'The greatest risk that a Labour Cabinet will have to run in the development of its industrial policy will be the temptation to offer doles instead of prosperity. Fortunately, however, it can choose no Chancellor of the Exchequer who can afford to support doles wholesale and its general financial and trade policy will soon eliminate the conditions which make doles a tempting expedient for short-sighted and irresponsible politicians. It is altogether in the interests of the State that the Labour Party should be brought up against the practical impossibility of doles policy as a relief for distress, more particularly as its constructive economic policy will invigorate industry and enable it to deal with such problems as normal unemployment risks in a scientific way'.

> Well, well, well! If we were short-sighted and irresponsible politicians, we at any rate may take some comfort from this fact, that the policy set forth this afternoon by my rt hon Friend – the policy of this Bill and of the larger Bill – is an admirable illustration of the truth of the old proverb – 'Imitation is the sincerest form of flattery'.[111]

Macnamara's period as Minister of Labour had been crucial to the development of assistance for the unemployed. He himself, in the House of Commons and elsewhere, had always maintained that benefit was not a dole. He explained why this was so to a deputation representing the organised unemployed of the City of Birmingham on 17 August 1922, in response to the plea that gaps in benefit should be closed:

> If ... I undertake to give benefit from the fund continuously week by week without any limit or restriction, it is no use calling that an insurance scheme. It may be a scheme for giving relief, but you upset the whole scheme of insurance and it goes on the rocks as an insurance scheme ... Supposing I do say, very well, Gentlemen, I have carried this thing so far, there shall be no further restriction. I will pay week by week without any limit or restriction and the thing goes on the rocks, what have I to say to the people, hard working people, the men who pay up their 9d a week – many can ill-afford it – for the rainy day which may follow their present employment? What can I say to them? They have paid so that there may be something for them when unemployed. If this thing goes on the rocks and these men are paying as they are doing, so that they may have something for the day of unemployment, well, I should be doing them an ill service if that were the result.[112]

But even before he took office, the claims of unemployed ex-Service men, whom no government could resist, were being met by the out-of-work donation, so that the insurance principle had already been undermined. Macnamara himself absorbed the donation into the insurance scheme, only to readopt non-contributory benefit as a means to assist the uninsured and their dependants as the depression deepened. By the time the Coalition fell, the case for unconditional benefit, at least as far as the political left was concerned, was conclusive.

The reputation of the Lloyd George Coalition, long denigrated by both the Conservative and Labour Parties, has risen steadily as the century has progressed. Amongst its achievements, A. J. P. Taylor reflected, was the strange new system of unemployment insurance, which, despite its defects, took the edge off discontent and ensured that barricades were not set up in English streets. Taylor gave the credit for the stability to Lloyd George.[113] Lloyd George gave it to Macnamara. 'One and a half to 2,000,000 men won't go wandering through the street for three or four years without a crust', he said:

> ... between 2,000,000 and 3,000,000 insured ... was not enough after the war. Dr Macnamara raised the figure and covered 12,000,000 workers, raised the allowance and reduced the gap; started schemes for out-of-works, got great road schemes for new arterial roads ... the sum of £60,000,000 had been spent ... there was not one new idea, not a glimmer of one since ... When Dr Macnamara developed these daring schemes he saved the country from revolution.[114]

15

Exclusion

The first Labour government lasted only nine months. Parliament was dissolved on 9 October 1924; five days later Macnamara was formally adopted as Liberal candidate for North West Camberwell at a constituency association meeting in the Surrey Masonic Hall. It was twenty-four years since he had first been elected to Parliament. Throughout all those long years, he reminded his supporters, Camberwell folk had supported him with unbroken loyalty – loyalty for which he could never sufficiently express his gratitude:

> We have carried the flag of sane common sense progress to victory eight times. We have got to make it nine ... If you only realise the tremendous task before you, I am perfectly satisfied you will achieve it. But take nothing for granted, make up your minds that the task before you is far and away the biggest you have ever undertaken in the long years of our association with one another and to our eighth triumph we will add another and the greatest of all (Cheers).[1]

In October 1900, after his first campaign, the *South London Observer (and) Camberwell and Peckham Times*, the local Conservative newspaper, received Macnamara's 1,335 vote victory with resignation as an admittedly brilliant conquest of an unstable seat:

> The defeat of Mr Diggle is softened in bitterness by the recognition of the high abilities and exceptional personnel [sic] of his conqueror, and the chastening atmosphere of the House of Commons will speedily subdue the perfervid Radicalism of the redoubtable School Board champion. It would be ungenerous to withhold congratulations to 'Fighting Mac' on his hard-won battle and it is, moreover, pleasant to chronicle the fact that ... the contest has been fairly and squarely conducted.[2]

In 1906, the *Observer and Times* was resigned, at an early stage, to a Liberal victory. 'The ubiquitous and undoubtedly popular "Mac", with an army of willing workers is holding monster overflow meetings throughout the constituency', it reported on 13 January.[3] Four days later, some 20,000 people assembled outside the Camberwell Baths to hear the result. From a narrow ledge outside a top floor window, gripped from within by the Baths Superintendent, Macnamara himself announced his victory (with a majority of 2,817) to deafening cheers.[4] A month later, North Camberwell Liberals, joined by NUT colleagues and journalists from both Liberal and Unionist newspapers, assembled at a reception in the Surrey Masonic Hall to congratulate him. As an orchestra played, Macnamara, his wife and children received the guests. After a concert he was presented with a silver salver. Visibly affected, he thanked his supporters not only for the gift, which was costly and beautiful, but for the feeling behind it. He could say, quite honestly, that of all the candidates in the United Kingdom there never was one who was surrounded by such loyal, devoted and enthusiastic friends:

> ... During the last ten or twelve days of the election I was confronted everywhere with a poster which said 'We all love Mac'. When I saw that poster and remembered the very large number of pretty girls there were in North Camberwell, I felt I was not born in vain (Loud laughter). My wife and I – I feel I must mention my wife at this point (Laughter) – passed from triumph to triumph, from friendship to friendship, and you ended up by giving me a majority of nearly 3,000. What man could ask for more?[5]

By 1910, the year of two elections, the *Observer and Times* had become accustomed to the Radical member: 'Dr Macnamara is familiarly known as "Mac" and is exceedingly popular on both sides of the House ... One of the most versatile men in the Government ... is a musician, golfer, lecturer, singer, journalist and raconteur ...' The Unionist candidate at both elections, Sidney Hoffnung Goldsmid, strove to make the first contest a straight fight on Tariff Reform. Complaining afterwards that many of the electors had been influenced by the grotesque misrepresentations of Radical literature and canvassers, he claimed, with some justification, that his campaign had made many converts. Macnamara's majority fell to 1,032. Goldsmid had vigorously nursed the constituency throughout the year. The *Observer and Times* concluded, shortly before the second election, that he would prevail against the justly popular member who had represented the division for ten years.[6] But it was Macnamara who prevailed, though his majority was again reduced, this time to 982. The *Observer and Times* sought refuge from its error in a judicious speculation for the future:

> If general elections are to succeed one another in quick succession – as seems only too probable – and the Unionist cause in North Camberwell continues to progress as it has progressed during the last four years it is obvious that the day is not far distant when the undoubtedly popular doctor will no longer command permanence in the division.[7]

The Coupon Election of December 1918 introduced new hazards. Macnamara, the *Observer and Times* reported on 23 November, had received the coupon, but four days later it perceived a growing disposition amongst the more thoughtful of the electors to resent the attempt which was being made to compel them to accept, not the men whom they would prefer to represent them, but the labelled men who were sent to them.[8] Nevertheless, it was in favour of a Coalition:

Practically if we are wise in our day and generation, we shall build up a new and better Empire in which we shall retain all the virtues and none of the faults of the old. Clearly that task can only be accomplished by a Coalition government ... it is plain that the best men should be sent to the House of Commons by the constituencies. It is not equally clear that the best man is necessarily one who sat in the last House of Commons and who qualified himself for the Lloyd George-Bonar Law hall mark. It is because we feel so keenly that the electors should have perfect freedom of choice that we object to the dumping of candidates into the constituencies.[9]

But the Prime Minister denied that there was any wish to dictate to the constituencies: 'If you get any letters signed by Mr Bonar Law or myself', he said in a speech at the end of the week, 'they are simply the expression of our opinions as to the men who will give steady support. As British citizens we are entitled to express our opinion on a subject of that sort.' This disingenuous explanation did not satisfy the executive of the London Liberal Federation. It adopted a resolution inviting the thirteen Liberal members whose names appeared on the Coalition list to withdraw them and stand instead as unpledged Liberal candidates.[10]

Macnamara had no intention of following this recommendation. His candidature had run into difficulties for another reason. Because the electorate had been extended by the 1918 Representation of the People Act, constituencies had been recast, and the Borough of Camberwell had been granted an additional member. Macnamara had been approached some twelve months before by a delegation of the Radical Association for the old division asking him for which of the two new divisions he would like to stand. 'Whichever asks me first', he replied. Consequently, on 2 February he was adopted for North West Camberwell, only to find that there was a rival candidate.[11] At a Unionist concert and party meeting held in the last week of November, Guy Radford, a Unionist who had also been granted the coupon, explained that for seven years he had been prospective Unionist candidate for North Camberwell; he had left when Macnamara joined the Coalition and, he said, he had been adopted for North West Camberwell in May 1918. The wishes of local people had to be considered. If the executive committee desired him to stand, he would do so. He was duly adopted as Unionist Coalition candidate.[12]

Without Radford, Macnamara might have been returned unopposed. As it was, he was obliged to fight an unusual campaign against a candidate whose views, for the purposes of this election at least, coincided with his own. 'The Tory candidate has got his organisation right up to Concert pitch', he wrote to Lloyd George, on 25 November: 'I've got nothing and my old pals are sore about Asquith.' The Prime Minister responded on 5 December:

My dear Macnamara,

This is to wish you all success in your election. Your work throughout the whole war and for years before at the Admiralty has been of the greatest national service and I now think it due to you to say that when offered promotion to another office you preferred to stick to the fighting service which has contributed so magnificently to the success of the allied cause. I regret that you should be opposed by a gentleman who describes himself as being in favour of the Coalition policy outlined by Mr Bonar Law and myself. It seems to me that he would best support that policy by supporting, instead of opposing, you. I feel sure that North West Camberwell will stick to you.

Ever sincerely,

D. Lloyd George [13]

Macnamara, his candidature further supported by the Prime Minister's speech at the Old Kent Road Baths on 13 December, was returned with a majority of 3,037. But his devotion to the Coalition had already attracted public criticism. In the *Star* a copy of a letter he had sent to Sir Harry Samuel, the Conservative candidate in his home constituency, was reproduced with the comment that it was an ominous sign. Macnamara had stated that it was no time for a party tug-of-war:

> ... calmly ignoring the bald blatant fact that the Coalition wire-pullers have allotted forty-six Tories and thirteen Liberals to London. That is a 'party tug-of-war' in which the Tories have done excellently well for themselves, and we are amazed that it evokes no protest from Dr Macnamara.[14]

Macnamara's part in the Spen Valley by-election campaign at the end of 1919 extended the ill-feeling of the local Liberals. The North West Camberwell Liberal, Radical and Labour Association, concluding that his support for the Coalition candidate and opposition to the Asquith Liberal candidate was objectionable, informed him that he would no longer be regarded as its representative; J. C. Carroll, Chairman of the London Junior Liberal Association and president of the West Ham Liberal Association, was appointed prospective candidate in his place. A few weeks later, Macnamara's appointment as Minister of Labour, which necessitated a by-election, brought the matter to the test. G. A. Hardy, President of North West Camberwell Liberal Association, was unmistakably hostile. He was reported as saying:

> There is no Liberal split in Camberwell. It was through my own personal influence that the Association adopted Dr Macnamara at the general election. Many members of the executive are not enthusiastic about his candidature. He has lost Liberal support entirely now, and I believe he will be beaten.

Carroll, who had been endorsed by Asquith, was already into his stride. 'I am opposing Dr Macnamara', he said, 'first because he has ceased to be a Liberal and secondly because I am convinced that the electors are disgusted with the Coalition government's lack of principle and policy.'[15] Macnamara, however, was strongly supported by the Coalition leaders. Bonar Law sent a special appeal to Alderman E. W. Room, the local Unionist Chairman. 'I understand as well as any member of the party in the division how difficult it is for Conservatives to give their support to a man who has been their life-long opponent', he wrote. But the claims of the Coalition came first:

> In my opinion the Coalition is as necessary now in the national interest as when it was formed, and it can only continue if there is united action in the constituency as well as in the House. Dr Macnamara has been throughout a whole-hearted supporter of the Coalition and in supporting it he has shown great courage, as for example, in the part taken by him in the contest at Spen Valley against Sir John Simon. I feel sure, therefore, that you will do everything in your power to secure his return.

The Association duly pledged itself to support Macnamara's candidature and to place its organisation at his disposal.[16]

Macnamara received a joint letter from Bonar Law and Lloyd George:

Dear Macnamara,

> We warmly commend your candidature to the men and women of North West Camberwell.

> The by-election in which you are now engaged is in accordance with the law, which requires an appeal to your constituents upon your promotion to your new post of Minister of Labour with Cabinet rank.

> We cannot believe that the electors will do other than give you their hearty support at the moment when you have secured that promotion in rank which your long and faithful service so thoroughly merits.

> We know from day to day experience how faithfully you have discharged your work at the Admiralty. Your long tenure of office, including the whole of the war period is unprecedented, in recent times at any rate.

> So far you have preferred not to leave the Admiralty, but invited to take up your new office, for which your close and warm sympathy with Labour eminently suits you, you have agreed to do so.

> In the campaign which you are now conducting you have our most sincere and cordial good wishes.

Ever sincerely,

David Lloyd George/Andrew Bonar Law

At a meeting of local women, presided over by Rachel Macnamara, on 26 March, the principal speaker was the Prime Minister's wife. She was sure, she said, that the people of Camberwell were not going to turn their backs on Dr Macnamara after twenty years.[17]

But a new threat was emerging from the Labour Party and its candidate, the former London School Board member, Susan Lawrence. Macnamara wrote to the Prime Minister on 21 March: '... I have definitely challenged the Socialists. *They are* pretty busy. If everyone who is against them will take the trouble to vote it will be all right. Not unless.' At Cambridge Hall, on 26 March, Macnamara's meeting was disturbed by a loud thumping on the door. He himself opened it. A band of what the *Observer and Times* referred to as extremists rushed in and made a determined effort to stop the proceedings. Once they had shouted themselves hoarse Macnamara took the opportunity to make a sharp attack on Labour policies:

> The Socialist Party demands that all private ownership, all private profit, all private enterprise shall be abolished. It is a fantastically impracticable programme put forward by utterly impractical visionaries. It is put forward in glowing and attractive colours, but it would be disastrous to the community as a whole and a bitter delusion and a snare to the workpeople themselves.

By now the insurgents had recovered themselves: affairs reached such a pitch that the meeting had to be closed: when Macnamara's supporters attempted to sing the national anthem they were howled down. The wild men were left in possession, their leader delivering an extremist address from a chair in the centre of the hall.[18]

'Dr Macnamara's view of the forces influencing the Labour movement reflect those of the Prime Minister', *The Times* commented. 'He professes to see the spectre of communistic socialism lurking behind the skirt of Miss Lawrence.' Asquith took the opportunity to adopt a more lofty attitude. His telegram to Carroll, dated 29 March, ran:

> Please accept my best wishes for your success. I trust that the electors of North West Camberwell will reject the attempts which are being made to divide the nation on the lines of a class struggle and will endorse the policy of Liberalism for which you are standing, which seeks to secure the greatest measure of individual freedom consistently with the general well-being of the community as a whole.[19]

Polling took place on 31 March. 'I think I have done the trick', Macnamara wrote to Lloyd George in the last week of the campaign, 'but it's been a tremendous fight.'[20] Fortunately for the new Minister, who was now referred to by the *Observer and Times* as 'Camberwell's old and trusted public servant', he was returned with a majority of 1,885. But now his future in the constituency was in doubt. In the absence of a Conservative candidate he had secured 6,618 votes; Susan Lawrence was second with 4,733; Carroll was third with 3,386.[21] Should the Coalition break up and a Conservative candidate offer a challenge, Macnamara's chances would be small.

'Winston thinks that LG will remain with the Tories but will be compelled to bow to their will', Riddell had noted in his diary on 27 July 1917.[22] Having failed to reach some permanent accommodation with them, Lloyd George and the Coalition Liberals found themselves abruptly discarded by the Conservatives at the Carlton Club meeting of 19 October 1922 and obliged to face a general election. 'The case of Dr Macnamara is the most interesting London provides of an ex-Liberal Minister trying to hold his own in a changed political world', the *Manchester Guardian* observed. Local Asquithian Liberals, whose candidate was John H. Harris, an ex-missionary, had concluded that Macnamara had gone over to the Tories; Dr Morgan, the Labour candidate, was thought to have a good chance, so long as the Conservatives plucked up courage to attack the former minister.[23]

But the local Conservatives found the decision to sever ties with Macnamara difficult. The day after the Carlton Club meeting he was entertained by the North West Camberwell Coalition Association at the Grove Lane School. He expressed admiration of the Conservative ministers of the Coalition for their striking courage and splendid loyalty to the great ideal of national unity, adding, in unmistakable terms, a tribute to the displaced Prime Minister for his handling of the Chanak crisis:

> And what shall I say of Mr Lloyd George, that great statesman whose friendship I esteem it the highest privilege of my life to have enjoyed through the last twenty-five years? ... though I have ever been a devoted adherent of his I can most sincerely say that I have never admired him more than during the last few anxious weeks ... It is, in my judgment, nothing short of a national calamity that his leadership of public affairs has been brought, for the time being at any rate, to this sudden conclusion. And if I know my fellow countrymen and women aright there are vast numbers of them who think as I do.[24]

Macnamara's adoption took place at a meeting of what was still called the North West Camberwell Coalition Association, at Camden Church Hall, Peckham Road, on 27 October. In a fighting speech he provided a powerful justification and defence of the Coalition government. 'During the great war I stood for national unity in the hour of national emergency, country before party', he declared, to cheers:

> At the close of hostilities it was manifest that national unity was no less essential if the ship of State was to be safely steered through the troubled waters that would inevitably follow in the wake of the great gale. Those waters ... still toss about in ferment and confusion. Again, therefore, I stand emphatically for the policy of national unity (Cheers) ... Coalition has been, as I think, condemned unheard ... Although so much remains to be done isn't it abundantly clear, when you review the situation confronting us after the Armistice and consider where we stand four years after, that we have every reason to rejoice that we have been able to do so much and do it so smoothly? (Cheers). It is all very well to denounce Party Co-operation – Party conflict could not have done it (Hear, hear)! ... we have steadily sought and worked for peace among the peoples of the world ... We have made every effort to requite the profound obligation under which we rest to the ex-Service men: we have brought the problem of Ireland to the point of settlement; we have got national expenditure back to a normal peace time basis to an extent that few realise ... we have striven tirelessly for the re-establishment of trade and industry on sound economic lines; we have faced unprecedented unemployment with schemes of remedy and relief out of all relation to anything ever attempted in the past (Cheers).[25]

Macnamara had been asked by Alderman Room, still Chairman of the Association, to define his position regarding the Bonar Law government in writing. His response was that he had for years worked day by day with most of the ministers of the new administration. On all matters he and they had cooperated in general accord, agreement and amity. He could not believe that they would propose to depart from the national policy in the promotion of which they played so important a part. 'And if my view is correct', he concluded, 'they may be assured of my support.' A decision was taken by vote not to contest his candidature. At the same time the view was expressed that Dr Macnamara's letter was ambiguous. A more definite statement was requested. Macnamara again placed his views on record:

> I have carefully studied Mr Bonar Law's policy so far as it has been announced. It is, if I may say so, in all its main essentials a continuance and extension of the policy he and his colleagues worked with us to carry forward. In particular, I read with satisfaction his reference to the Irish Treaty, his reference to trade and unemployment, his insistence upon the necessity to do all that is practicable further to relieve industry from the burdens of taxation ... and his declared intention to do all that he can towards the development of trade within the Empire itself. Since these are objects to which I did my best to contribute as a member of the late government, of course they will have my support.[26]

This seemed to satisfy Alderman Room and his associates. On 15 November, Macnamara, supported by the Conservatives, secured 8,339 votes. Morgan was second with 5,182, Harris third with 3,270.[27]

Just over a year later, the electorate was again called to the polls. Baldwin, Bonar Law's successor, had, in Macnamara's view, blundered or been pushed by his wild men into a jack-in-the-box declaration that he could not help the unemployed without a general tariff, which he had then transformed into an election issue. With the Liberals finally separated from the Conservatives and at last reunited under Asquith in defence of free trade, Macnamara found no difficulty in regaining the full support of the local party.[28] Though he received a gracious telegram from the restored Liberal leader,[29] the centrepiece of his campaign was a packed meeting at the Camberwell Palace on 5 December, addressed by Lloyd George. Every time Protection had been submitted to the British people, the former Prime Minister said, they had turned it down definitely and emphatically:

> It is one of those things that looks glittering the first time you see it. I remember (I hope I am not giving away my friend, Dr Macnamara, in his own constituency) he and I went out yachting together. We were in the yacht of Sir Thomas Lipton. One evening we landed at a little seaport down in the South of England. We found there was a fair there, and we took part in it (Laughter) ... There was a trader there who had a most costly show of silver and gold, shining bright and splendidly made. Coffee pots and all sorts of things. All you had to do was to put sixpence down and have a fling (Laughter). They looked very

attractive. I tried my luck (Laughter) and I was a great failure (Laughter). I never got one (Laughter). But Dr Macnamara – he had been at it before – (Loud laughter) – and he went home (Laughter). I really thought he would sink the boat (Laughter). I asked him shortly afterwards 'What about them?' 'All poor stuff', he said. 'The silver was all tin'. That's the sort of thing you get if you go to the Protectionist fair (Applause).

The real method of dealing with unemployment, he concluded, was the method adopted by Dr Macnamara, of making provision for the extension of insurance, in order that there was no distress when a man was out of work, so that the burden on local rates was relieved. And it was Dr Macnamara who had started the policy of public works.[30]

The main threat in North West Camberwell now seemed to come from Morgan, the Labour candidate. On 29 November, Macnamara faced a strong attack at a two-and-a-half hour meeting in Boundary Lane. The *Daily Chronicle* reported:

> For over an hour he was bombarded with questions and sometimes abuse. But 'Mac' gives as good as he gets and many of his Labour friends willingly accepted his invitation at the end to sing 'God Save the King', though a minority persisted in showing their independence by chanting the 'Red Flag'. At lunch-time yesterday Dr Macnamara carried the war into the enemy's camp. Hearing that there were a good many Socialists employed at the big building construction yard of Trollope and Colls Ltd, 240 Camberwell Road, Macnamara sought them out during their dinner-hour and readily obtained permission as an old friend to speak to them ... He is easily the best candidate of the three. He thrives on heckling and the worst-mannered Socialist succumbs to his fluent handling.[31]

Voting took place on 6th December. Macnamara's majority fell to 80. He had 6,843 votes, Dr Morgan 6,763 and E. T. Campbell, the Conservative, 6,045.[32] North West Camberwell had become marginal.

Now, less than a year later, Macnamara was facing his ninth Camberwell campaign. In January 1924, the Liberals had been instrumental in enabling Labour to take office; once MacDonald's government had crumpled into dissolution their reward was to be treated by the electorate as outsiders in a two-party contest. When, for what was to be the last time, Lloyd George was welcomed to Camberwell by Rachel Macnamara (president of the North West Camberwell Liberal Association) and by the Macnamaras' daughter, Elsie Elias, who was the candidate for South East Southwark, the crowds and the cheers were as great as ever. But the tide had turned against Liberalism. On 29 October, Campbell, the Conservative, won the seat with 9,626 votes, a majority of 194 over Morgan, the Labour candidate (who was to prevail in 1929). Macnamara was third, with 5,138.[33]

On 22 November, he and his wife were entertained by their supporters at the Camberwell Baths. In response to a hearty welcome he struck an optimistic note. They had felt the wrench of 29 October pretty severely, he said:

> That is only natural after a long and unbroken association of nearly a quarter of a century. But of course we faced the situation with what philosophy and fortitude we could command. We managed to keep smiling ... our feelings were rendered all the more acute by the knowledge of the fact that so many loyal and devoted friends had striven so long and so affectionately for us, only in the end to find their labours in vain ... But now let us one and all enshrine the years that are past in the glad recollection of good work accomplished and in the splendid memory of the many lasting friendships made.

In response to musical honours he and his wife expressed their thanks. 'I am glad to hear I am a jolly good fellow', he responded. 'I have been in this hall sometimes and have heard quite the contrary (Laughter). You did well to include Mrs Macnamara. She has been my help and supporter for nigh on thirty-nine years. She has made the best of a bad bargain (Laughter).'[34]

Only forty-two Liberal members returned to Westminster. Asquith, defeated at Paisley, transferred to the House of Lords in January. He remained leader of a diminished and impoverished party; the Chairmanship of the Liberal Parliamentary Party fell to Lloyd George. As divisions again developed, exacerbated by Lloyd George's proactive policy initiatives,[35] Macnamara, keen to return to Westminister, seized the opportunity to contest a by-election. William Preston, the newly-elected member for Walsall, had been disqualified on the grounds that he had held government contracts (trivial in amount) with the Post Office at the date of the general election. Councillor Patrick Collins, the showman who had been the Liberal member for two years, was obliged to withdraw from the new contest through ill-health; consequently, on 13 February 1925, Macnamara, having been adopted by the local Liberal Executive Council in his place, arrived in the town to begin another vigorous campaign, in which his wife played her usual devoted part.[36] On 21 February, Lloyd George was welcomed by 2,500 people at a meeting in the Town Hall. Looking far from well, he admitted that nothing would have induced him to come from London but a desire to help his old colleague and fellow fighter. Though he struggled hard, his speech was a poor one, concerned with the past (including previously deployed reflections on the distress that had followed the Napoleonic wars) rather than the present or the future. As usual he paid a generous tribute to Macnamara's achievements, both during the more recent war and after it. One day, when the testimonials were examined, he concluded, it would be found that there was no more honoured or patient servant of the people than Dr Macnamara (Great cheers). As Minister of Labour he had foreseen and devised plans and pressed them upon the Cabinet. He asked any representative of the Conservative or Labour Party to point out one new plan that was introduced by either of them that was not invented by Dr Macnamara.[37]

The Conservatives, however, were confident of victory. Dr Macnamara's party was defunct, Roy Wilson, the member for Lichfield, declared at the Public Hall, Bloxwich on 25 February. As a force in politics it did not exist. It had no leader in the Commons; during the principal debates of the previous few weeks most of the forty members had been absent; it was also without a policy. In October, Preston's majority had been 2,552; the by-election reduced it by only 59. He was re-elected with 14,793 votes, Macnamara was second with 12,300, and the Labour candidate, Captain Small, third with 11,610.[38] '... It was a great campaign and will always remain a most pleasant memory', Macnamara wrote to Frances Stevenson, enquiring about Lloyd George's recovery:

> The people were kindness itself. And even opponents listened respectfully. What beat me in the end was the Tory machine. I had got together a very good improvised twenty HP machine that was just getting warmed up for the hill before it when an eighty HP machine came alongside and left me easily on the last lap. But I am deeply convinced that there is a volume of goodwill towards and belief in Liberalism that in six months could win any fight in Walsall if steadily and at once organised and trained.[39]

As Minister of Labour, Macnamara had reactivated his journalistic skills with frequent contributions to the *Lloyd George Liberal Magazine*, which he kept up throughout 1923 until (when the two wings of the party reunited) it ceased to appear. In December 1922, he began a weekly series of articles for the *Referee* on the depression, unemployment and socialism which lasted till February 1923; in early November he provided a similar series of six for the *Western Mail*. But, by early 1924, his financial future was beginning to look bleak. The loss of his ministerial salary had reduced his income by four-fifths; no Cabinet Ministers' pensions were paid after 6 April 1924.[40] Now his Parliamentary salary was in jeopardy. Lloyd George proved staunch and generous.[41] At the beginning of May, Macnamara received a cheque from J. T. Davies, one of the former Prime Minister's secretaries. He responded on 9 May:

> I am more than grateful to you for J. T. 's cheque. It is, I can assure you, rather timely. Meantime, I am casting about for work – outside the pretty crowded field of journalism. As regards the cheque J. T. handed me I do wish you would allow me to do some specific work for you. Since the closing up of the National Liberal Organisation I have felt a bit of a fifth-wheel; and, so far as Liberal Organisation is concerned, look like continuing so.[42]

Rachel Macnamara wrote in similar vein two days later, disclosing the origin of the gesture:

> I want to thank you very sincerely for your great generosity towards us. We are deeply grateful and appreciative of your kindness and ready response to my

appeal. Tom is doing his best to get on to something and I hope he will soon find something suitable. With kind regards and many thanks.[43]

With the loss of his Parliamentary salary, Macnamara's financial situation grew more serious. Lloyd George proved consistently supportive. In December 1925, Macnamara accompanied him on a holiday to Rome and Naples. 'May I be allowed to thank you more than I can express for your great kindness in sharing your holiday with my husband – we both sincerely appreciate the true friendship that lies behind it', Rachel Macnamara had written just before Christmas.[44] She wrote again a fortnight later, when he had hurried home because his daughter had been taken ill:

> It is difficult to find words in which to thank you for your wonderful kindness in arranging for me to go to Rome and for bringing home for me the exquisite shawl. I do thank you with all my heart for this and also for the splendid holiday you have given Tom. It is the best he has ever had and has done him no end of good. I hope you yourself are feeling much the better for it in spite of the unfortunate circumstance that hurried you home. However, we are more than thankful that dear little Megan is over the worst and doing well. With our united kindest regards and very many thanks ...[45]

At the beginning of 1927 she acknowledged a more substantial gesture:

My dear Mr Lloyd George,

> Words fail me in trying to express my feelings at the news brought home by Tom today. Your more than kind solicitude for our future and your great generosity in providing for it have touched me very deeply. I can only say very humbly and sincerely, thank you from the bottom of my heart. I may confess that, at times, I have been troubled about the future, but that anxiety is now banished by your generosity. It is particularly thoughtful of you to provide for me should I outlive my husband. I can only hope that this will enable us to be of greater service to yourself and to the great objects upon which our hearts are set. Please let me say again how grateful we are.

Yours very sincerely,
Rachel Macnamara [46]

But in the meantime Lloyd George's policy initiatives, paid for by his large and (as it was seen in some quarters) notorious fund provided some opportunities and openings. 'The first thing Liberalism has got to do, and it is a difficult thing for a beaten party, is to get rid of the paralysing psychology of defeat', the former Prime Minister declared in February 1926, 'and there is nothing better for that, when you are down on your luck, than to set a task before you and the bigger the task the higher your spirits will rise.'[47] He had already set in motion a series of investigations into the domestic political problems of the day in order to develop plans for their solution ahead of a Liberal return to office. *Coal and Power* had been published in July 1924. Next, from the Land Enquiry, set up in June

1923, emerged the *Green Book* (*The Land and the Nation*) of October 1925, containing plans for developing agriculture through the confiscation of neglected land and, the following month, the *Brown Book* (*Towns and the Land*), proposing town planning on regional lines. From his reflections on these and other policy developments Macnamara assembled *If Only We Would: Some Reflections on our Social Shortcomings with some Suggestions for their Removal*. The Liberal Committee of Enquiry had recommended that mining royalties and mineral rights should be acquired by the State and that the coal industry should be run by a public authority outside politics. This conclusion had been approved by the report of the Royal Commission on the industry (the Samuel Commission) published on 11 March 1926, but had not been acted upon in time to avert the General Strike. Now, in its aftermath, Macnamara again pressed for State acquisition, arguing that with its Mining Industry Act the Government had gone back on its contingent acceptance of the Samuel Report. Drawing on the *Green Book*, he pointed out that £200,000,000 worth of agricultural produce and £50,000,000 worth of timber was imported annually. 'What are we going to do about it?' he asked:

> ... extend the area of cultivable land by schemes of Improvement, Drainage and Reclamation, on a scale out of all relation to anything so far attempted. Our efforts in these directions, and also in the matter of Afforestation, are ludicrously inadequate compared with those of countries like Holland, Denmark, Belgium, France and Germany ... We've got to reform our system of Land Tenure so as to give every encouragement and every security to those who till the soil ... We've got to secure to the agricultural population fair wages and reasonable conditions, decent housing, and opportunities for education, recreation and social life ... We've got to open up a chance of advancement in status and prospects for the labourer ... the essence of the whole thing is simply the definite assumption by the State of the responsibility of seeing that our agricultural land is used to the best advantage.

On industrial relations, his view was that existing attitudes between employers and employed were unlikely to get the best and the most out of Britain's great industrial undertakings and activities. What he favoured were the Whitley Councils which, set up under the recommendations of the 1917 Reconstruction Committee, had been extended to fifty-four industries, covering 3,000,000 people, on the principle of cooperation between all elements within the work force:

> The fabric of Whitleyism should be crowned by the establishment by Parliament of a National Industrial Advisory Council to deal with questions referred to it by the Board of Trade, the Ministry of Labour, the Ministry of Education [sic], the Home Office, or by any of the Joint Industrial Councils; [it] should establish an Industrial Research Department which would work with the International Labour Office.

In the long run, he emphasised, the surest way to secure industrial peace lay with the Trade Unionists themselves. They had to take the lever, wherever necessary, out of the hands of the extremist and lay hold themselves. If they did this, the General Strike would not have been without its salutary effect. The direction taken by the Labour Party, however, did not help. At first it had claimed that the fundamental defect in economic and industrial organisation was private ownership, private profit, rectifiable only by public ownership of all the means of production, distribution and exchange. This explicit economic proposition was, in Macnamara's view, fantastic and utterly impracticable:

> It is a complete misfit applied to human nature. The stimulus and incentive of Private Enterprise must be maintained. If you succeeded in your endeavour to set it aside, stagnation and impoverishment must inevitably follow. I say ... that you might as well endeavour to abolish the Solar System itself as to try to abolish the human impulse that makes for personal initiative.

Private enterprise needed to be subordinated to the well-being of the community as a whole. He was, he declared, pro-Labour without being anti-Capitalist. Certain essential public services, namely schools, electricity and the Post Office, needed to be under public direction and control. But in the field of commerce and trade the public official, no matter how devoted, could not replace private enterprise. Unfortunately, the Labour Party was now moving on from a dubious economic proposition which a man could advance and still be a perfectly self-respecting citizen, into a deep and even menacing protest fuelled by notions of class war.[48]

As *If Only We Would* was being written the Liberal Party's Summer School Committee secured Lloyd George's active cooperation in setting up the Liberal Industrial Inquiry to investigate business organisation, industrial relations, national development and national finance. Its Executive Committee included Samuel, Simon and Masterman, the economists Walter Layton, H. D. Henderson, and Maynard Keynes and the social scientists E. H. Gilpin, E. D. Simon and Seebohm Rowntree. Among the twenty-five members of the special committees that met in the eighteen months during which the inquiry proceeded, Macnamara took part alongside Professor L. T. Hobhouse, the future Lords Jowitt and McNair, Sir Archibald Sinclair and Sir Josiah Stamp. Its report and recommendations, entitled *Britain's Industrial Future* (also known as the *Yellow Book*), was published at the beginning of February 1928 and approved at a special meeting of the National Liberal Federation's Council on Industrial Policy at the Kingsway Hall at the end of March. Macnamara, referring to the report as the most skilled and most detailed diagnosis of the condition of British trade, industry and commerce that had ever been given to the country, concentrated on the issue of industrial relations. Again he emphasised the positive rôle of the Whitley Councils. Already, he said, these worked wonders. What Liberals now had to do was to make the greater prosperity of the industry the manifest and paramount interest of both sides. Amongst further refinements, the report now proposed procedures to ensure full deliberation took place before stoppages occurred in the public health services, the water, gas and electricity industries and the main transport services. A new Council of Industry would now require negotiating bodies in those industries to draw up a full scheme of negotiation and conciliation, including a compulsory reference to a Court of Enquiry in the event of a deadlock. If no satisfactory scheme emerged the Council would itself prepare a scheme for submission to Parliament, including a provision that Trade Union privileges (peaceful picketing and freedom from actions for tort) should not apply in the case of any lock-out or strikes declared before the defined procedure had been carried out:

> Without those privileges no lock-out or strike could take place which might not involve those responsible for it in serious consequences clearly both in the criminal and civil code. The proposals of this Report, therefore, while not actually taking away the right to strike, do, in effect secure as far as is humanly possible that the public shall be protected in the public service industries against sudden stoppages of work ... it says, if you pass this, 'Look here, both sides, you must have an Enquiry before you break away, and if you do not, your funds may be attachable'.[49]

The Liberal programme, *We Can Conquer Unemployment*, also known as the *Orange Book*, was published twelve months later. Six years' preparation had produced a lucid and apparently practical series of plans ready for a general election which could not be held any later than October. This was to be Lloyd George's supreme effort to return to power; the famous Fund, which had supported the preparatory work, was now deployed in support of 512 candidates.[50]

In Walsall, Macnamara was selected as Liberal candidate at a meeting in the Cooperative Hall on 7 May. Councillor Leckie, the Chairman of the local association, expressed the hope that the election would prove to be one of the turning points in the country's history. A united Liberal Party was challenging with rare pluck and determination both reaction and revolution. He hoped the result would be the same as in 1906. Macnamara took up the theme. No serious and sustained effort had been made by the Conservatives since 1924 to deal with unemployment. They had let it drift on in the vain hope that it would cure itself. By their incompetence and incapacity they had let the country drift into the disastrous coal dispute which, unquestionably, could have been averted. Slum clearance remained to be tackled. Toryism was quite incompetent to meet and satisfy the needs of the time. Socialists, on the other hand, came forward with high-sounding doctrinaire theories including the replacement of capitalism by the Socialist Commonwealth, a fantastically impracticable proposal, the endeavour to apply which would leave the last end of the people worse than their first. The Liberals, in contrast to both, had remedial plans which represented the only fruitful reconstructive policy before the country.[51]

All three candidates, Macnamara, William Preston (the former member) and J. J. McShane (Labour), were well aware of the importance of the so-called flapper vote, the fruit of the 1928 Representation of the People Act, which had given voting rights to women between the ages of twenty-one and thirty and contributed to an increase in the electorate from 21,750,000 to nearly 29,000,000. On 25 May the *Walsall Times* addressed the implications of the innovation. It provided a cartoon, entitled 'Puzzle: Find the Winner' and some disclosures elicited from newly enfranchised women about their voting intentions. The first, leaving the tennis court, was unaware that an election was taking place; the second, following her parents' example and because she regarded the other two parties as too extreme, was a Liberal. The third intended not to vote. 'What can I possibly know about politics?' she said. 'I always leave such matters to my father and brothers. Politics are not playthings and require careful thought.' A fourth favoured Preston because he was a local businessman: 'Dr Macnamara is not a Walsall man, neither is Mr McShane a businessman'. A waitress favoured McShane because the Conservatives had made a sorry mess of things and because the Liberals seemed too antiquated for words. A young woman at a leather works blamed the Conservatives for the increase in unemployment, considered that the Labour Party would do no good in the matter and intended to try the Liberals. A seventh liked Billy Preston and because she thought the Conservative Party would bring her the most good, had decided to vote for him. The eighth favoured McShane on the grounds that everybody should have an equal chance of sharing in the world's goods. It was not right that a man who amassed a huge fortune by sweated labour should then start giving it to charities in order to be knighted. 'There is a lot to be said in favour of Dr Mac', remarked the last. 'He is a well educated gentleman and knows all that there is to be known about politics.'[52]

Macnamara was hopeful. After the Whitsuntide break, he resumed his campaign on 21 May at the Butts. Lloyd George had sent an encouraging message referring to his former colleague's brilliant record, gifts and wide experience of administration which, the former Prime Minister concluded, would be one of Liberal Party's greatest assets. Macnamara said:

> What it all comes to is this ... if you are satisfied with the state of the country and not very keen to get anything done, vote Tory.
>
> If you desire to enter a protest against evil conditions that ought to be remedied, and can be remedied, and make no practical contribution towards their solution, vote Socialist.
>
> If you agree that the state of the country is not satisfactory and want to see practical common-sense remedial measures at once applied, vote Liberal.[53]

But the election was disastrous for the Liberals. They had made the running, but they lost the race. The Labour Party won 287 seats, the Conservatives 261 and the Liberals 59. In Walsall, McShane secured the seat with 20,524 votes, Preston was second with 15,818 and Macnamara last with 15,425. 'Although they were beaten they were not disgraced', Councillor Leckie said at the Liberal Club immediately after the results had been made known. It had been a fine fight and if any candidate deserved to win it was Dr Macnamara:

> There was no comparison between the candidates or their policies ... I hope the day will come when we will redeem our good name. I do hope we shall live to see the day when Walsall regains its Liberalism and that Dr Macnamara will lead us to victory. We thank him for his magnificent fight.

Macnamara seemed unperturbed. He thanked all his election workers (who had included his wife and daughter) and dwelt on the courtesy he had been shown by the people of Walsall. His confidence in what he believed to be bold, far-seeing and above all practical plans to restore British prosperity was unshaken. 'Men go to extremes and they pass the things they will go back to in time', he said. 'In the end the cause we stood for must prevail. People will come back to quiet, sane, Radical reforms.'[54]

What soon became clear was that the Labour Party, which had fought the election on general principles,[55] had no practical plans to deal with unemployment and the economy. The new Unemployment Insurance Bill, introduced by the new MacDonald government in November, was still, seven years later, merely a further refinement and expansion of Macnamara's legislation. The Prime Minister entrusted the task of devising schemes for the reduction of unemployment to J. H. Thomas (the Lord Privy Seal), George Lansbury (Commissioner for Works) and two junior ministers, Tom Johnston and Sir Oswald Mosley. Of these the most energetic was the last. His memorandum, presented to the Cabinet in February 1930 and rejected (with catastrophic results for his political career) three months later, called for governmental intervention not only to take charge of short-term public works measures but also, on the assumption that the old staple industries would never again be able to reabsorb the out-of-work, to plan and finance new ones. Macnamara, in the *Liberal Magazine*, drew on the *Orange Book* and reached similar conclusions. He asked:

> Are we not ... tending to make the duty of providing assistance for the workless the first line in our national policy, instead of, as it should be, the second line? Our first and main objective should be the provision of permanent productive work ... Parliament ... has devoted since the slump developed twenty times the attention to shaping the amounts and conditions for the receipt of Unemployment Benefit than it has devoted to the problem of finding permanent employment ... this problem must be attacked both at short and at long range on ... bigger and wider lines.

In what was to be his last policy statement on the issue, he called, not for financing of new industries as Mosley had done, but for education, by keeping children at school for as long as possible and by insisting that every young person in receipt of Unemployment Benefit should attend technical or trade classes. Without decisive government action, he concluded, the 1,000,000 long queue of unemployed would still be there at the next general election.[56]

In fact, the number was to be much greater. In November 1929, it stood at 1,326,000, but the effects of the collapse of the international economy, signalled by the Wall Street crash, soon began to be felt. By December 1930, 2,500,000 people were unemployed. In February 1931, a Conservative vote of censure on wasteful expenditure and borrowing, especially for the unemployment insurance fund, was supported by a Liberal amendment for the appointment of an economy review committee.[57] Its report, published at the end of July, after bank failures in Austria, Germany, Hungary and Romania, led to the withdrawal of foreign funds and created the crisis which was to bring about the formation of the National Government on 24 August.

In Walsall, a few weeks after the 1929 general election, Macnamara called on the local Liberal Association for hard, continuous, untiring, systematic and well-organised effort:

> Socialism won Walsall because of the steady day by day work its supporters accomplished since the last election. Every Socialist voter is a Socialist worker. If the same were even approximately true of Liberalism the result would have been entirely different. You can have your Liberal MP for Walsall. But to get him you have got to give up the idea that his return can be secured by a fortnight's tremendous effort at election times. It can't. By that time victory is already in the hands of those who have been consistently at work since the poll was last declared.[58]

But the Macnamaras, after thirty-five years at Rollscourt Avenue, Herne Hill, moved to Redhill, not to Walsall.[59] As he approached his seventieth birthday, Macnamara's political ties were beginning to snap. Perhaps he hoped that his daughter, an experienced and effective campaigner, who appeared in his place at the Liberals' five-day Romany Fair Bazaar in Walsall in March 1931 and made a rousing political speech,[60] might succeed him as candidate. MacDonald's decision to hold a general election only two months after the formation of the National Government brought such speculation to an end. Lloyd George, convalescent after a prostate operation, had approved of the Labour leader's initiative in August even though he had been unable to join him. But he saw no need for an election, which he described as the most wanton and unpatriotic into which the country had ever been plunged, and he urged Liberals not to be deluded by the National label.[61] Of all his political associates, Macnamara was least able to resist such an appeal.

In Walsall, Leckie, now an Alderman, declined to state at first who the

Liberal candidate would be.[62] Then, on 8 October, he announced that he was standing as a National candidate with the support of both the Liberal and Unionist Associations. He felt strongly, he said, that at this crisis the efforts of the Cabinet to straighten out the national finance and to put the country on its feet again should be enthusiastically backed up by men and women of all parties.[63] For many months, he added at his adoption meeting, the Liberals had been asking him to be their standard bearer, but he had deferred his decision. He was very glad that he had done so because now they could stand shoulder to shoulder with Ramsay MacDonald and the National Government.[64] He was duly elected, defeating the Labour victor of 1929 by over 6,000 votes.[65]

Lloyd George left England on 19 November for a convalescent cruise to Ceylon. Four days previously, Macnamara was treated in a Wimpole Street nursing home for the same condition that had struck down his old friend. On 17 November, he was reported to be going on well.[66] But he did not recover. A relapse occurred and he died on 3 December. 'Just heard of poor Macnamara's death', Frances Stevenson wrote to Lloyd George two days later. 'It makes me feel very sad, but terrified too, to think of the danger you ran.' 'Poor Macnamara', Lloyd George responded from Colombo on 8 December:

> Never thought I would feel his death so much as I very seldom saw him. What happened? He seemed to be getting on so well. I am glad I asked him to Bron-y-de this last summer. He must have been ill then. He looked pinched, drawn and subdued. He had a notable career and left his mark on the lives of millions through his unemployment measures. For an ordinary school teacher to have reached a position where his death is recorded by wireless thousands of miles away is an achievement.[67]

C. F. G. Masterman, Macnamara's colleague in Asquith's first ministry, pointed out in *The Condition of England* (published in 1909) how a new type of elementary teacher had emerged who was everywhere taking the lead in public and quasi-public activities.[68] Macnamara had done better than any. Moreover, education had provided him with an issue with which to make his name in politics. Two years after he entered the Commons, the debates over what was to become known as Balfour's Act made him a national figure. Like Lloyd George in Wales, he had a secure base; among the teachers his progress was applauded weekly in the columns of the *Schoolmaster* and annually at the NUT Conference. From 1902 till the fall of the Unionist Government in December 1905, he was perceived to be in the vanguard of the younger Liberals and a man of the future.

In 1911, when he was made a Privy Councillor, the *Schoolmaster* commented on his distinguished career which, it added, 'sheds lustre on the profession to which at heart he still belongs'.[69] This was a shrewd insight. The fiasco of the 1906 Bill had put an end to the possibility of the major education legislation he had hoped for; by the time the next opportunity arose, the radical ideas of the first NUT MPs would have been displaced by the view, reinforced by the war, that the class system, in education at least, was immutable.[70] Meanwhile, Macnamara had been sidelined. In education he had been an expert, an ex-practitioner responding with confidence to the aspirations of an open profession. The move to the Admiralty transformed him into a novice, an outsider within a closed and secretive brotherhood. The zestful figure of the early years of the century was rendered down, as Riddell perceived, into a hard-working capable official.[71]

As the war ended, even his close association with Lloyd George was of no avail. As he stayed on at the Admiralty the new radical beginning that he had urged the Prime Minister to make was set aside in the interests of peace-making. Fortunately he was neither exhausted nor disillusioned; awarded the least desirable post in the Cabinet, he proved himself to be determined, equable, resourceful and successful in dealing with the first stages of what was to become a fifteen years' unemployment crisis. If by 1931 his work at the Ministry of Labour was discounted, it was not only because unemployment was by now worse than anything he had encountered, but also because the political equilibrium that he had done so much to secure could be taken for granted.

In December 1931 the national press, even though National Liberals held office in the new Government, was inclined to dismiss old Liberals as relics from a vanished age. 'Though not in the first rank of constructive statesmen', *The Times* concluded, 'Dr Macnamara was an invaluable asset to any political party by reason of his general popularity, his deserved reputation as a platform speaker, and the great energy which gained for him the nickname – always a sign of popularity in Parliament – of "Fighting Mac" ... at one time he was a prolific writer on social questions.'[72] The *News Chronicle*, the newspaper which, as the product of the merger between the once-powerful *Daily News* and *Daily Chronicle* exemplified the decline in Liberal fortunes, treated him as an historical figure:

> Those who knew Dr Macnamara in these last ten years may find difficulty in explaining the place which to the end he continued to hold in the regard and affection of Liberals. But those who remember him in the old days will have no such difficulty. He was a Radical of a type become now rather old-fashioned because the power of privilege and snobbery against which these men fought is now so largely broken. But it was not broken then; it took a courage which ... the younger generation has difficulty even in imagining to stand up to it fearlessly. And no one ever stood up to it with a higher heart or a purer zeal for the cause of the poor and oppressed than 'Dr Mac' ...[73]

Educationists still remembered him. When members of the Union who had grown grey in the teaching service talked of the early days, they nearly always mentioned a trinity of names, Yoxall, Macnamara and Gray, the President of the NUT told the Executive on 5 December, and this was an occasion when they reflected and paid their tributes to those who had served and built up their great organisation. 'He will be best remembered in the teaching profession as the passionate and unwearying advocate for better conditions for the child and the teacher', Arthur Thomas wrote in the *Schoolmaster and Woman Teacher's Chronicle*. 'Sympathy with the weak and oppressed was one of the deepest instincts of his nature, and it was this sympathy which attracted to him so many devoted friends among all sorts and conditions of men and women.' Looking back half a lifetime T. B. Ellery remembered how it was his superb confidence, his readiness in debate and his thoroughgoing determination to 'get down to business', as he frequently put it, that won all hearts.[74]

Since the 1920s many British politicians have sought to secure or enhance their reputations by publishing memoirs and by assembling and safeguarding appropriate political and personal papers. Macnamara took no such steps. No memoirs or reminiscences were written; forty years after his death it was clear that no political or personal papers had survived.[75] But unprocessed material existed; enough had been set down in his years as a journalist and in the official records of his public career to furnish an account of a life which, in the variety of its achievements, should not be forgotten. His favourite quotation, the *Schoolmaster* reported in November 1905, was from the *Rubaiyat of Omar Khayyam*:

> Ah Love! could thou and I with Fate conspire
> To grasp this sorry scheme of Things entire
> Would we not shatter it to bits and then
> Re-mould it nearer to the Heart's Desire?[76]

In reality his aims were practical, not utopian. 'Dr Macnamara looks at the dark places in our modern organisation and says "Let's get something done!"', Lloyd George wrote in 1926. 'Those who know him best have heard the sentence most often.'[77] It was the hopeful and confident cry of early twentieth-century Radicalism, proud of Great Britain's institutions, certain of their soundness, determined that, as democracy advanced, they would be refined and perfected. It still has the power to cheer.

Notes

Notes to Chapter 1

1. *Blackwood's Edinburgh Magazine*, XCI, January 1862, pp. 102, 105; Col. H. C. Wylly, *The Loyal North Lancashire Regiment*, Vol. I: 1741–1914, The Royal United Service Institution, 1933, p. 162.

2. Facsimile: Registre de référence, Ministère de la Justice, Québec.

3. 'In the Days of My Youth', *MAP* ('Mainly About People'), LXXIV, 11 November 1899, p. 452.

4. *Ibid.*; 'The School Boy of Today & of Yesterday', The *Schoolmaster*, 25 June 1904, p. 1350.

5. *MAP, op. cit.*, 452.

6. Devon Record Office, *Log Book of Exeter Wesleyan Boys' School*, 68/4/1/1, 12 May 1871.

7. J. Kay-Shuttleworth, *Four Periods of Public Education*, Harvester, 1973, pp. 309ff, 481–90.

8. See *Hansard*, 199, 17 February 1870, 444.

9. G. Sutherland, *Policy Making in Elementary Education, 1870–1895*, Oxford University Press, 1973, pp. 95, 99.

10. *Schoolmaster*, 31 October 1896, pp. 699–700.

11. *Ibid.*, 27 December 1902, p. 1058.

12. *Ibid.*, 1057.

13. E. G. Sandford (ed.), *Memoirs of Archbishop Temple*, Macmillan, 1906, pp. 345–6.

14. B. Marshall, *Emma Marshall, a Biographical Sketch*, Seeley, 1901, p. 99.

15. *School Board Chronicle (SBC)* 11 March 1871, p. 113.

16. Devon Record Office, *St Thomas Boys' School, Exeter, Log Book No 1, 1863–84*, 68/4/2/1, 20 November 1870.

17. *Ibid.*, 24 March 1871.

18. *SBC*, 18 March 1871, p. 147; 29 July 1871, p. 335; 16 December 1871, p. 144.

19. *Hansard*, 112, 30 July 1902, 202.

20. *Log Book*, 68/4/2/1, 13 January 1873. Under Article 32b HM Inspectors were entitled to make a surprise visit within six months. If requirements were not carried out, a deduction from the next grant could be made. (New Code 1872, *Report of the Committee of Council on Education 1871–2*, HMSO, 1872, p. lxxxiv).

21. '... the man in charge of a school, whether for young labourers or young lords, is a headmaster': *Board Teacher*, 1 September 1897, p. 174.

22. *Log Book* 68/4/2/1, 17 July 1873.

23. *Ibid.*, 11 August 1873.

24. *Schoolmaster*, 6 April 1907, p. 702.

25. J. S. Hurt, 'Drill, discipline and the elementary school ethos' in P. McCann (ed.), *Popular Education and Socialization in the Nineteenth Century*, Methuen, 1977, pp. 167–91.

26. *Log Book*, 68/4/2/1, 26 August 1873; 12 January 1874.

27. *Ibid.*, 13 March 1874.

28. *Ibid.*, 21 December 1874.

29. Reprinted in *Schoolmaster*, 25 June 1904, p. 1350.

30. *MAP*, *op. cit.*, 452.

31. *Log Book*, 68/4/2/1, 5 April 1875.

32. *Ibid.*, 26 April 1875.

33. *Ibid.*, 24 May 1875.

34. *Ibid.*, 9 June 1875.

35. *Education Department, New Code of Regulations*, HMSO, 1873, p. 12.

36. *Log Book*, 68/4/2/1, 25 July 1875; 26 July 1875; 27 August 1875; 20 October 1875; 28 October 1875.

37. *Ibid.*, 9 December 1875.

38. *Ibid.*

39. *Ibid.*, 17 January 1876.

40. *Practical Teacher*, 12, 8, February 1892, p. 426.

41. 'A Grateful Tribute to the Memory of a Great Schoolmaster', *Schoolmaster*, 25 January 1896, 158; *Minutes of the Proceedings of the School Board for London*, IV, p. 969; V, p. 1179; *SBC*, 29 January 1876, p. 111.

42. *Log Book*, 68/4/2/1, 25 January 1876; 26 January 1876; 23 August 1876; 31 October 1876; 2 June 1876; 29 July 1876; 22 September 1876.

43. *Ibid.*, 19 December 1876; 4 December 1876; 10 April 1877; 24 January 1877; 26 April 1877; 17 December 1877.

44. *Schoolmaster*, 25 January 1896, p. 158.

45. *Log Book*, 68/4/2/1, 3 November 1876; 8 January 1877; 1 July 1878; 25 September 1878; 8 November 1878; 27 January 1879.

46. *Ibid.*, 25 November 1878; 7 July 1879; 15 September 1879; *Hansard* 156, 7 May 1906, 1087.

47. British and Foreign Schools Society (B and FSS) Archives Centre: 6 February 1879; 7 March 1879; 10 March 1879; 6 March 1879.

48. *Schoolmaster*, 25 January 1896, p. 158.

49. T. J. Macnamara, 'Training College Student Days', *New Liberal Review*, 6, 32, September 1903, 227–28; P. B. Ballard, *Things I Cannot Forget*, University of London Press 1937, 34–35; H. B. Binns, *A Century of Education*, Dent, 1908, p. 217.

50. Macnamara, *New Liberal Review*, *op. cit.*, 228–29.

51. J. Runciman, *Schools and Scholars*, Chatto & Windus 1887, pp. 134–37.

52. Macnamara, *New Liberal Review*, *op. cit.*, pp. 231–32.

53. Binns, *op. cit.*, p. 213.

54. R. W. Rich, *The Training of Teachers in England and Wales during the Nineteenth Century*, Cambridge University Press, 1933, p. 179.

55. Ballard, *op. cit.*, 36; Macnamara, *New Liberal Review*, *op. cit.*, 230–31, D. Salmon, 'When I was at College, I', *Schoolmaster*, 9 August 1902, p. 194; Runciman, *op. cit.*, p. 146; *SBC*, 14 February 1880, p. 148.

56. *Schoolmaster*, 1 October 1898, p. 563; 6 January 1872, p. 8; Salmon, *Schoolmaster*, *op. cit.*, p. 194.

57. T. J. Macnamara, 'The Work of the London School Board', *New York Education Review*, June 1896, p. 12; B and FSS, 76th Report, Rider 1881, p. 28; *Educational Record, with the Proceedings of the British and Foreign Schools Society*, X, 128, January 1880, p. 317; XI, 132, January 1881, p. 33; XII, 136, January 1882, pp. 138–39.

58. B and FSS Archives Centre.

59. *English Teacher*, December 1888, p. 28.

60. B and FSS Archives Centre. This may have been the last time that he signed his name with a capital 'N'.

61. *Ibid.*

62. R. H. S. Randles, *History of the Friends' School, Lancaster*, Allan Sharpe, 1982, pp. 73–8.

Notes to Chapter 2

1. Father of the poet, Robert Graves.

2. *Report of the Committee of Council on Education (England and Wales) 1881–2*, HMSO, 1882, pp. 300, 304. Graves's report is dated 16 December 1881.

3. T. J. Macnamara, *Schoolmaster Sketches*, Cassell, 1896, p. 99.

4. *Practical Teacher*, 19, 2, August 1898, p. 106.

5. *SBC*, 11 December 1880, p. 610.

6. *Ibid.* Details of the speech were provided by Graves. See A. P. Graves, *To Return to all That*, Cape, 1930, p. 211.

7. *Practical Teacher* 23, 9, March 1903, p. 439; 15, 12, June 1895, p. 647.

8. *Ibid.*, 13, 8, February 1893, p. 411; *Schoolmaster*, 9 February 1907, p. 255.

9. *Hansard*, 167, 12 December 1906, 383.

10. Yorkshire Post, quoted in *Schoolmaster*, 9 February 1907, p. 256; *Teachers' Review*, June 1899, p. 128.

11. *Practical Teacher*, 12, 8, February 1892, p. 424; PRO, *ED* 21/6105.

12. T. J. Macnamara, 'Are Free Schools a Failure?', *Pall Mall Gazette*, 26 September 1891, pp. 1–2.

13. *Teachers' Aid*, 200, 27 July 1889, pp. 385–86; 218, 30 November 1889, p. 193; 210, 5 October 1889, pp. 1–2; 221, 21 December 1889, pp. 265–66; 224, 11 January 1890, pp. 337–38.

14. *Report of the Inter-Departmental Committee on Physical Deterioration, II, Minutes of Evidence*, HMSO, 1904 (Cd 2210) 12,517–18.

15. *Practical Teacher*, 12, 8, February 1892, pp. 424–26.

16. *Ibid.*, 9, 6, August 1889, p. 286.

17. *Ibid.*, 10, 4, June 1890, p. 197.

18. B and FSS Archives Centre: letter to the Secretary of the BFSS, 4 June 1886, signed T. J. Macnamara, thus establishing finally his preferred version of his name.

19. Quoted in P. Horn, *Education in Rural England, 1800–1914*, Gill & Macmillan, 1978, p. 243.

20. *NUT Annual Report 1920–1*, p. xxvi.

21. Harry Coward (President of the NUT 1903–04), reported in *Schoolmaster*, 9 February 1907, p. 255.

22. *NUET Annual Reports*: 1885–86, 17; 1888–89, p. 23.

23. MAP, 11 November 1899, p. 453.

24. *Teachers' Review*, June 1899, p. 128.

25. *South London Observer and Camberwell and Peckham Times*, 30 November 1910, p. 5.

26. *MAP, op. cit.*, p. 453.

27. *Schoolmaster*, 6 April 1907, p. 702.

28. E.g. 6 October 1888, reported in *Schoolmaster*, 20 October 1888, p. 501.

29. *Teachers' Review*, April 1898, p. 83.

30. *Schoolmaster*, 23 January 1904, p. 196; 24 March 1888, p. 419.

31. *Ibid.*, 31 March 1888, pp. 448–49.

32. *Teachers' Review*, April 1898, p. 100; *Schoolmaster*, 7 April 1888, p. 525.

33. *Schoolmaster*, 14 April 1888, p. 553.

34. *Teachers' Review*, April 1898, p. 100; *Board Teacher*, 1 May 1889, p.78.

35. *English Teacher*, February 1889, p. 67.

36. *Schoolmaster*, 14 April 1888, p. 553.

37. *Ibid.*

38. *Ibid.*, 21 April 1888, p. 582.

39. *Western Daily Press*, 16 April 1888, p. 3.

40. *Schoolmaster*, 12 April 1890, p. 571.

41. *Ibid.*, 12 April 1890, p. 577; see also T. J. Macnamara, 'Village Education under Popular Control', *Westminster Review*, 136, 1891, pp. 148–56.

42. G. A. Christian, *English Education from Within*, Gandy, 1922, pp. 183–84; *Teachers' Review*, February 1902, p. 20.

43. *Schoolmaster*, 26 April 1890, p. 634.

44. *Ibid.*, 27 September 1890, p. 417.

45. *Ibid.*, 11 October 1890, pp. 503–04.

46. *Ibid.*, 23 January 1904, p. 197.

47. *Ibid.*, 4 April 1891, p. 631.

48. *Ibid.*, p. 644.

49. *SBC*, 14 April 1888, p. 380.

50. *Schoolmaster*, 4 April 1891, pp. 618–19.

51. *Ibid.*, 11 April 1891, p. 659.

52. *Ibid.*, p. 660.

53. *Ibid.*, 7 April 1888, p. 496. The Union had met the expenses of George Collins, one of the editors of the *Schoolmaster*, when he unsuccessfully put up as Liberal candidate for Dulwich in 1885. It had not offered to provide maintenance should he have been elected.

54. 'Cheltenham Conference Conclusions', *ibid.*, 14 April 1888, p. 550.

55. *Ibid.*, 7 April 1888, p. 523.

56. *Ibid.*, 15 March 1890, p. 389.

57. *English Teacher*, April 1890, p. 64.

58. 'Another Florin', *Schoolmaster*, 22 March 1890, p. 426.

59. *Ibid.*, 26 April 1890, p. 636; 9 August 1890, pp. 174–75.

60. *Ibid.*, 28 March 1891, p. 561.

61. *Board Teacher*, 2 May 1892, p. 106.

62. *Schoolmaster*, 6 February 1892, p. 257.

63. *Ibid.*, 26 March 1892, p. 541.

64. *Ibid.*, 2 April 1892, p. 598.

Notes to Chapter 3

1. *Schoolmaster*, 7 January 1922, p. 16.

2. 'Twenty-one Years for Education and the Teacher', *ibid.*, 31 December 1892, p. 1161.

3. G. Christian, *English Education from Within*, Gandy, 1922, pp. 105, 61, 107.

4. *Schoolmaster*, 31 December 1892, pp. 1161–64; 2 January 1892, p. 14; 9 January 1892, p. 56; 6 February 1892, pp. 231–32.

5. Christian, *op. cit.*, 60; *Schoolmaster*, 7 January 1922, p. 14; 9 September 1893, p. 397.

6. 'Celebrities At Home', *The World*, 26 November 1902, p. 880.

7. *Schoolmaster*, 14 May 1892, p. 863.

8. *Ibid.*, 23 September 1893, p. 473.

9. *Ibid.*, 6 August 1898, p. 223.

10. *Ibid.*, 20 June 1896, p. 1140.

11. *Ibid.*, 25 March 1893, p. 558.

12. *Ibid.*, 22 April 1893, p. 755.

13. Between 1833 and 1839 the State's contribution to public elementary education was regulated by Treasury Minutes. From 1839 until 1860 the Minutes were issued by the Committee of Council on Education. In 1860 Robert Lowe, Vice-President of the Committee of Council, collated them into the original Education Code. From that year onwards the

Code was revised and tabled annually in the House of Commons, providing the rules by which schools were administered. See *Schoolmaster*, 24 March 1894, p. 505.

14. *Hansard*, 199, 17 February 1870, 444.

15. See G. Sutherland, *Policy-Making in Elementary Education 1870–1895*, Oxford University Press, 1973, Chs 7–8.

16. W. H. G. Armytage, *A. J. Mundella*, Benn, 1951, pp. 270–71, 369.

17. Cross Commission, *Final Report*, HMSO, 1888, p. 222.

18. *Schoolmaster*, 10 April 1920, p. 702. Kekewich was knighted in 1895.

19. *Ibid.*, 24 March 1894, p. 505.

20. Cross Commission, *Final Report*, pp. 220, 249, 333, 334.

21. *Schoolmaster*, 8 November 1902, p. 737.

22. *Ibid.*, 11 April 1891, p. 660; '*The Schoolmaster*: Reminiscences of Twenty-Five Years' Work Upon It', *ibid.*, 30 December 1905, p. 1371.

23. *Practical Teacher*, 13, 3, September 1892, p. 161.

24. 'Work Before the New Administration', *Schoolmaster*, 3 September 1892, p. 343.

25. Sutherland, *op. cit.*, p. 314.

26. *Schoolmaster*, 20 August 1892, pp. 266–67.

27. W. E. Forster (1870–74); Edward Stanhope (1885).

28. Christian, *op. cit.*, pp. 70–71.

29. 'A Chat with the Vice-President', *Schoolmaster*, 3 September 1892, p. 346; 'Awaiting the Thirty-Fourth Edition', *ibid.*, 18 February 1893, p. 298.

30. *Hansard*, 202, 1734–35.

31. Armytage, *op. cit.*, p. 74.

32. Education Act 1870, pararaph 74.

33. T. E. Heller, 'The Organisation of Elementary Education' in R. Cowper (ed.), *Proceedings of the International Conference on Education*, Vol. I, Clowes, 1884, pp. 157, 166.

34. Cross Commission, *op. cit.*, *Final Report*, p. 212.

35. *Schoolmaster*, 23 April 1892, p. 736.

36. *Ibid.*, pp. 749, 750, 751.

37. *Ibid.*, 15 April 1893, p. 707.

38. *Ibid.*, 23 December 1893, p. 1095.

39. *Digest of the Evidence taken before Group C of the Royal Commission on Labour*, HMSO 1892, paragraphs 3667–71; see also *Practical Teacher*, 12, 12, June 1892, pp. 651–52.

40. Royal Commission on Labour, *op. cit.*, paragraphs 3676–77, 3704.

41. *Practical Teacher*, 11, 23 May 1891, pp. 291–93; Cross Commission, *op. cit.*, *Final Report*, p. 212. Henry Matthews, later Lord Llandaff (1826–1913) '. . . had no political flair ... he seemed cold and indifferent'. See J. S. Sandars, *Studies of Yesterday*, Philip Allan, 1928, p. 156.

42. Sutherland, *op. cit.*, p. 320.

43. Notes and Jottings of the Week, *Schoolmaster*, 17 May 1894, p. 839.

44. *Schoolmaster*, 9 February 1895, pp. 255–64.

45. 'The Half-Timer', *ibid.*, pp. 238, 262, 263–64.

46. *Ibid.*, 9 March 1895, 423. R. W. Hanbury was to be Financial Secretary to the Treasury 1895–1900.

47. *Ibid.*, 20 April 1895, p. 700.

48. *Ibid.*, 27 April 1895, p. 772; 18 May 1895, p. 878.

49. *Westminster Gazette*, 6 June 1895, p. 2.

50. 'The Half-Timer', *Schoolmaster*, 6 July 1895, p. 18.

51. *Ibid.*, 28 September 1907, p. 507; 22 August 1908, p. 286. Half-time was ended under Fisher's Education Act of 1918 (*Schoolmaster*, 7 July 1922, p. 7).

52. Cd 4791, discussed in *Schoolmaster*, 7 August 1909, p. 422.

53. Cross Commission, *op. cit.*, *Final Report*, p. 200.

54. T. J. Macnamara, 'Free Schools', *Macmillan's Magazine*, 63, 1891, p. 284.

55. *Schoolmaster*, 12 November 1892, p. 867.

56. Sutherland, *op. cit.*, p. 322.

57. *Schoolmaster*, 18 March 1893, p. 497.

58. *Ibid.*, 27 May 1893, p. 929.

59. *Ibid.*, 17 June 1893, p. 1040.

60. 'Education: Facts and Figures for 1894', *Schoolmaster*, 8 June 1895, p. 990.

61. *Report of the Commissioners appointed to inquire into the State of Popular Education in England*, Vol. I, HMSO, 1861, p. 160.

62. *Sutherland, op. cit.*, p. 76.

63. *Hansard*, 242, 5 August 1878, 1233.

64. *Sutherland, op. cit.*, pp. 55, 75–76. Sub-Inspectors were Senior Assistants.

65. Cross Commission, *op. cit.*, *Final Report*, pp. 209, 238.

66. *Schoolmaster*, 23 April 1892, p. 738.

67. Sutherland, *op. cit.*, p. 311.

68. *Schoolmaster*, 23 April 1892, p. 739.

69. *Ibid.*, 28 January 1893, p. 174.

70. 'Within the Ring', *ibid.*, p. 166.

71. 'A Disappointment', *ibid.*

72. *Ibid.*, 18 February 1893, p. 318.

73. *Ibid.*, 30 December 1893, p. 1141.

74. *Ibid.*, 3 February 1894, p. 199.

75. *Ibid.*, 10 February 1894, p. 239.

76. *Ibid.*, pp. 230–31.

77. *Ibid.*, 10 March 1894, p. 425.

78. *Ibid.*, 12 May 1894, pp. 837–38.

79. T. Jones, MA, placed in charge of the Llanelli district. *Ibid.*, 19 May 1894, p. 881.

80. *Ibid.*, 9 June 1894, p. 1002.

81. *Ibid.*, 7 July 1894, p. 33.

82. *Ibid.*, 14 July 1894, p. 52.

83. *Ibid.*, 29 June 1895, p. 1099.

84. 'Raw Recruits for the Inspectorate', *ibid.*, 19 April 1902, p. 727. As the notorious Holmes-Morant Circular of 1910 was to show, however, the Education Department's successor, the Board of Education, continued to regard elemenatary school teachers as narrow and uncultured.

85. Cross Commission, *op. cit.*, *Final Report*, pp. 64, 260.

86. 'The Condition of the Fabric of the Older Primary Schools', *Schoolmaster*, 17 September 1892, p. 446.

87. *Ibid.*, p. 447.

88. *Circular 321.*

89. *Schoolmaster*, 18 February 1893, p. 291.

90. *Ibid.*, 4 February 1893, p. 214.

91. *Ibid.*, 29 July 1893, p. 167.

92. A. W. Jephson, *My Work in London*, Pitman, 1910, p. 127. Jephson was a member of the School Board for London from 1885–91 and from 1894–1904.

93. Christian, *op. cit.*, pp. 188–89.

94. Cross Commission, *op. cit.*, *Final Report*, p. 210.

95. *Schoolmaster*, 27 February 1892, p. 359.

96. *Ibid.*, 21 May 1892, pp. 905–06.

97. *Ibid.*, 4 June 1892, p. 999.

98. 'The Present Position of the Superannuation Movement', *Schoolmaster*, 10 December 1892, p. 1040.

99. *Ibid.*, 4 March 1893, p. 413.

100. *Ibid.*, 27 May 1893, p. 929.

101. 'The Last Lap!', *ibid.*, 9 March 1895, pp. 429–31.

102. *Ibid.*, 16 March 1895, pp. 470, 469.

103. *Ibid.*, 20 April 1895, p. 725.

104. *Ibid.*, p. 697.

105. 'The Manchester Conference', *ibid.*, 27 April 1895, p. 770.

106. 'All Things Come –', *ibid.*, 4 May 1895, p. 806.

107. 'Success Almost Assured', *ibid.*, 6 August 1898, pp. 221–22, 227.

108. *Ibid.*, 9 February 1895, p. 264.

109. *Ibid.*, 13 April 1895, p. 655.

110. *Board Teacher*, 1 May 1895, p. 112.

111. *Schoolmaster*, 24 March 1883, p. 356.

112. Cross Commission, *op. cit.*, *Final Report*, pp. 308, 219, 148.

113. *Schoolmaster*, 21 May 1892, pp. 921–22.

114. *Ibid.*, 31 March 1894, p. 545.

115. *Ibid.*, 10 March 1894, p. 425. That the secretary was described by Queen Victoria as 'Esquire' may also have come as a surprise.

116. Royal Commission on Secondary Education (the Bryce Commission), *Minutes of Evidence*, HMSO, 1895, paragraphs 8838–41, 8851, 8854–5, 8862, 8197, 8198.

117. Sutherland, *op. cit.*, 333–34.

118. *Schoolmaster*, 2 December 1893, p. 977.

119. 'The Educational Year', *ibid.*, 30 December 1893, p. 1150.

120. For example, on book charges. See *Hansard*, 14, 26 June 1893, 56–57; 15, 27 July 1893, 662–63; 18, 17 November 1893, 1141–42; 20, 27 December 1893, 248–49, 2 January 1894, 657–58; 21, 26 February 1894, 1036–37.

121. J. Wilson, *C-B: A Life of Sir Henry Campbell-Bannerman*, Constable, 1973, pp. 203–04.

122. 'The Political Situation', *Schoolmaster*, 29 June 1895, pp. 1105–06.

123. 'The New Vice-President', *Schoolmaster*, 6 July 1895, p. 18.

124. *Ibid.*, p. 10.

125. *Ibid.*, 13 July 1895, p. 70.

126. *Ibid.*, 27 July 1895, p. 130.

127. *Burns Papers*, BL 46295, 144b Add.

128. *Schoolmaster*, 20 July 1895, p. 104.

129. *Ibid.*, 27 July 1895, pp. 129–30.

Notes to Chapter 4

1. Member of the Board 1870–72; candidate for Chairman 1870.

2. T. Gautrey, *Lux Mihi Laus: School Board Memories*, Link House, 1937, p. 19.

3. T. A. Spalding and T. S. A. Canney, *The Work of the London School Board*, King, 1900, p. 29; *Board Teacher*, 1 October 1893, p. 196. The membership was increased to 55 in 1885.

4. P. B. Ballard's introduction to Gautrey, *op. cit.*, p. 9.

5. E. R. Robson, *School Architecture* (1874), Leicester University Press, 1972, pp. 315–16.

6. Gautrey, *op. cit.*, 35.

7. *Final Report of the School Board for London*, King, 1904: Lord Reay's Valedictory Address, p. xxii.

8. Gautrey, *op. cit.*, pp. 27–28.

9. *Ibid.*, p. 81.

10. *Ibid.*, p. 27.
11. *Ibid.*, p. 44. Diggle surrendered his holy orders in 1889.
12. *Schoolmaster*, 1 October 1892, p. 548. Members were, of course, unpaid.
13. *Ibid.*, 15 April 1893, pp. 707–08.
14. *Ibid.*, 10 December 1892, p. 1041.
15. Reproduced in *Schoolmaster*, 27 May 1893, p. 954.
16. *SBC*, 11 March 1871, p. 117.
17. Quoted in *Schoolmaster*, 4 February 1893, p. 222.
18. T. J. Macnamara, 'Three Years of Progressivism at the London School Board', *Fortnightly Review*, 74, 1900–01, p. 591.
19. *Board Teacher*, 1 May 1903, p. 104.
20. Gautrey, *op. cit.*, p. 60.
21. In *The Church Reformer*, January 1893, p. 16; quoted in D. Rubinstein, *School Attendance in London 1870–1904: A Social History*, University of Hull, 1969, pp. 29–30.
22. *Schoolmaster*, 4 February 1893, p. 222.
23. *Ibid.*, 4 March 1893, p. 392.
24. 'Is the Battle of the Adjectives to be Re-fought?' *ibid.*, 13 May 1893. The adjectives were 'board', 'voluntary', 'denominational', 'non-denominational', 'sectarian', 'unsectarian' and 'ad lib.' See T. J. Macnamara 'The Battle of the Adjectives', in *English Teacher*, March 1890, pp. 35–36.
25. Gautrey, *op. cit.*, 102.
26. *Schoolmaster*, 27 January 1894, p. 164.
27. Gautrey, *op. cit.*, p. 102 and *SBC*, 17 February 1894, p. 165.
28. *SBC*, 3 February 1894, p. 117.
29. See *Schoolmaster*, 12 October 1895, p. 582.
30. 'Religious Tests', *Board Teacher*, 1 February 1894, pp. 38–39.
31. *Schoolmaster*, 21 April 1894, p. 710.
32. *Ibid.*, 1 May 1894, p. 109.
33. *Schoolmaster*, 21 April 1894, pp. 709–10.
34. *SBC*, 5 May 1894, p. 477.
35. *Ibid.*, 12 May 1894, p. 502.
36. *Ibid.*, p. 503.
37. *Board Teacher*, 1 May 1894, p. 114.
38. 'The Crisis: Another Test Proposed', *ibid.*, 1 June 1894, p. 1334.
39. *SBC*, 16 June 1894, p. 663.
40. *Schoolmaster*, 19 October 1895, p. 627; 12 October 1895, p. 582; *SBC*, 19 October 1895, p. 391.
41. *SBC*, 14 July 1894, p. 30.
42. *Ibid.*, 29 September 1894, p. 313.
43. *Ibid.*, pp. 315–16.
44. *Ibid.*, 17 November 1894, p. 580–1.
45. *Board Teacher*, 1 December 1894, p. 242.
46. *Schoolmaster*, 1 December 1894, p. 924.
47. *Board Teacher*, 1 December 1894, p. 242.
48. *Ibid.*, 1 December 1894, pp. 240–42; 1 February 1895, p. 32; 1 March 1895, p. 63.
49. *Ibid.*, 1 June 1895, p. 148.
50. *Ibid.*, 1 December 1894, pp. 241–42.
51. Quoted in *Schoolmaster*, 1 December 1894, p. 918.
52. 'The London School Board Contest', *ibid.*, p. 924.
53. *Board Teacher*, 1 October 1893, p. 196.
54. *Ibid.*, 1 November 1893, p. 224.

55. *Schoolmaster*, 8 December 1894, p. 968.
56. *Ibid.*
57. *Final Report of the School Board for London, op. cit.*, 78; *School Board for London: Report of School Board for London for the year 1895–6*, Straker, 1896, pp. x, xiii, xi.
58. *SBC*, 15 December 1894, p. 691; *Schoolmaster*, 15 December 1894, p. 1013.
59. *SBC*, 22 December 1894, p. 728.
60. *Ibid.*, 2 February 1895, p. 112.
61. *SBC*, 16 February 1895, p. 172.
62. *Ibid.*, 2 March 1895, pp. 225–26.
63. *Schoolmaster*, 8 December 1894, p. 968.
64. *SBC*, 27 July 1895, p. 82; 4 May 1895, p. 486.
65. *Ibid.*, 16 March 1895, p. 286; *Schoolmaster*, 16 March 1895, p. 490.
66. *SBC*, 4 May 1895, p. 486.
67. *Ibid.*, 20 July 1895, p. 58; *Schoolmaster*, 20 July 1895, p. 112.
68. *SBC*, 27 July 1895, pp. 82–83; *Schoolmaster*, 27 July 1895, p. 145.
69. *Schoolmaster*, 5 October 1895, p. 555.
70. *Schoolmaster*, 12 October 1895, pp. 581–82.
71. *Ibid.*, 582.
72. *Ibid.*
73. *Ibid.*, pp. 582–83.
74. *Ibid.*, p. 583; *SBC*, 12 October 1895, p. 363.
75. *Schoolmaster*, 19 October 1895, p. 625.
76. *Ibid.*
77. *SBC*, 19 October 1895, p. 390.
78. *Ibid.*, pp. 390–91.
79. *Ibid.*, p. 391.
80. *Ibid.*, 391–2; *Schoolmaster*, 19 October 1895, pp. 626–27.
81. *SBC*, p. 392; *Schoolmaster*, 19 October 1895, p. 627.
82. 'The 2,886', *Schoolmaster*, 19 October 1895, p. 637.
83. 'Mr Riley renounced', *Board Teacher*, 1 November 1895, pp. 237–39.
84. Quoted in *Schoolmaster*, 26 October 1895, p. 678.
85. *Schoolmaster*, 7 March 1896, p. 425.
86. *Ibid.*, 26 October 1895, p. 679.
87. 'The Educational Year: Special Review of the Educational Activities of 1895', *ibid.*, 24 December 1895, p. 1111.
88. *Practical Teacher*, December 1891, pp. 307–11.
89. *Final Report of the School Board for London, op. cit.*, pp. 223–38.
90. *SBC*, 2 March 1895, p. 227.
91. *Ibid.*, 23 March 1895, p. 309; 1 June 1895, pp. 598–99.
92. *Ibid.*, 4 May 1895, pp. 485–86.
93. *Ibid.*, 1 June 1895, p. 599.
94. *Ibid.*, pp. 599–600.
95. *Schoolmaster*, 29 June 1895, pp. 1111–12: 'child' included girls, but the possessive adjective reverted to 'his'; *SBC*, 29 June 1895, p. 744.
96. *Ibid.*, 3 August 1895, pp. 106–07.
97. *Ibid.*, 12 October 1895, p. 362.
98. *Infants' Mistress* (reprinted from the *Echo*), 14 December 1895, pp. 1–2; cf T. J. Macnamara, 'Religious Teaching in the Elementary Schools', *Contemporary Review*, January 1896, p. 57.
99. *SBC*, 20 June 1896, p. 726; *Schoolmaster*, 20 June 1896, pp. 1128–29.
100. For Gorst's Education Bill see Chapter 5.

101. *Schoolmaster*, 13 November 1897, pp. 814–15; *SBC*, 13 November 1897, p. 531.
102. *Schoolmaster*, 20 November 1897, p. 848.
103. *SBC*, 17 February 1894, p. 166.
104. Gautrey, *op. cit.*, pp. 108–09.
105. *Board Teacher*, 1 January 1893, p. 17.
106. *Schoolmaster*, 6 July 1895, p. 73.
107. *Ibid.*, 13 July 1895, p. 34.
108. *Schoolmaster*, 21 December 1895, p. 1062.
109. *Ibid.*, 21 December 1895, p. 1069.
110. *SBC*, 21 December 1895, p. 717.
111. Gautrey, *op. cit.*, p. 70; *Schoolmaster*, 7 December 1895, p. 970.
112. *Schoolmaster*, 15 February 1896, p. 278.
113. *SBC*, 4 July 1896, pp. 5–6.
114. *Schoolmaster*, 4 July 1896, p. 22.
115. *Ibid.*, 11 July 1896, p. 54.
116. *Ibid.*, 5 December 1896, p. 910.
117. *Ibid.*, 29 May 1897, p. 985.
118. *Ibid.*, 24 July 1897, p. 135. The ironclad had been promised by the Prime Minister of Cape Colony at the Diamond Jubilee Colonial Conference. It did not materialise. (See Hansard, 50, 12 July 1897, 1601; R. C. K. Ensor, *England 1870–1914*, Oxford University Press, 1936, p. 241.)
119. *Ibid.*
120. *SBC*, 17 April 1897, p. 438.
121. *Board Teacher*, 1 April 1895, p. 76.
122. *Schoolmaster*, 24 October 1896, p. 668.
123. *Ibid.*, 19 October 1895, p. 630.
124. *Ibid.*, 22 May 1897, pp. 952–53.
125. *Board Teacher*, 1 September 1897, p. 175.
126. 12 October 1897, quoted in *Schoolmaster*, 16 October 1897, p. 638.
127. *Schoolmaster*, 20 November 1897, p. 850.
128. *Ibid.*, 4 December 1897, p. 935.
129. 'Education Triumphant', *Board Teacher*, 1 December 1897, p. 273.
130. *SBC*, 17 November 1894, p. 581.

Notes to Chapter 5

1. Royal Commission on Secondary Education, *Vol. 3, Minutes of Evidence*, HMSO, 1895, paragraphs 8081, 8138, 8131, 8155–56, 8158, 8191, 6 July 1894.
2. *Ibid.*, paragraph 8957, 11 July 1894.
3. *Ibid.*, paragraph 8194a, 6 July 1894.
4. *Ibid.*, paragraph 8880, 11 July 1894.
5. *The Times*, 7 September 1895, p. 13.
6. Royal Commission on Secondary Education, *op. cit.*, *Vol. 1, Part IV, II*, p. 31.
7. 'The Report of the Secondary Education Commission', *Fortnightly Review*, 1 December 1895, pp. 900–01, 899.
8. *Schoolmaster*, 12 January 1895, p. 64.
9. *Ibid.*, 20 July 1895, p. 106.
10. *The Times*, 20 September 1895, p. 5. The letters were dated 20 August 1895 and 22 August 1895.
11. *Schoolmaster*, 26 October 1895, p. 667.
12. *Ibid.*, 668.

13. *Ibid.*, 1 February 1896, p. 188.
14. *Ibid.*, 22 February 1896, p. 338.
15. *SBC*, 27 May 1893, p. 588.
16. *Schoolmaster*, 23 November 1895, p. 857.
17. 'Re-opening the Education Settlement of 1870', *Nineteenth Century*, January 1896, p. 57.
18. *Contemporary Review*, January 1896, quoted in *Schoolmaster*, 4 January 1896, p. 12.
19. B. Holland, *Life of Spencer Compton, 8th Duke of Devonshire*, Vol. II, Longmans Green, 1911, p. 274. His secretary was Almeric Fitzroy, later Clerk to the Privy Council.
20. 'After the Battle', *Schoolmaster*, 27 July 1895, p. 138.
21. *Pall Mall Gazette*, 17 December 1891, p. 3, drawing on *Review of Reviews*, 4 December 1891, pp. 575–78.
22. *SBC*, 1 February 1896, pp. 124–25.
23. J. S. Sandars, W. M. Short, Bernard Mallet, Sir Henry Craik and Lord Cranborne. See N. D. Daglish, 'Planning the Education Bill of 1896', *History of Education*, 16, 2, 1987, pp. 91–104
24. *A Bill to make further provision for Education in England and Wales*, 31 March 1896 (Bill 172).
25. A. S. T. Griffith-Boscawen, *Fourteen Years in Parliament*, Murray, 1907, p. 93.
26. *Schoolmaster*, 22 February 1896, p. 324.
27. *Practical Teacher*, 16, 10, April 1896, p. 531.
28. *Schoolmaster*, 21 March 1896, p. 540.
29. *NUT 27th Annual Report*, 1896–97, pp. xxxiii–xxxvi.
30. *Schoolmaster*, 11 January 1896, p. 73.
31. *NUT 27th Annual Report, op. cit.*, pp. xxxvi–xlv.
32. *Schoolmaster*, 11 April 1896, 678, pp. 705–06.
33. *Ibid.*, 714–16; SBC 11 April 1896, pp. 410–11.
34. *Practical Teacher*, 16, 11, May 1896, pp. 618–19; *Schoolmaster*, 11 April 1896, pp. 718, 682.
35. *Schoolmaster*, 11 April 1896, p. 676.
36. *Ibid.*, pp. 683–84, 682.
37. *Ibid.*, 18 April 1896, 745–46.
38. *Ibid.*, 23 May 1896, p. 979.
39. *Ibid.*, 30 May 1896, p. 1041.
40. *Ibid.*, 2 May 1896, p. 836.
41. *Ibid.*, 6 June 1896, pp. 1051–56. Jackman, the defender of the boards at Brighton, made only a brief appearance.
42. *SBC*, 18 April 1896, p. 437.
43. *Ibid.*, 25 April 1896, p. 469.
44. Quoted in *Schoolmaster*, 6 June 1896, p. 1059.
45. *Hansard*, 40, 5 May 1896, 570–71.
46. *Ibid.*, 12 May 1896, 1247.
47. *SBC*, 13 June 1896, p. 713.
48. *Schoolmaster*, 26 December 1896, p. 1068.
49. *SBC*, 13 June 1896, p. 713.
50. *Hansard*, 41, 11 June 1896, pp. 896–901, 928; *Schoolmaster*, 26 December 1896, p. 1068.
51. *SBC*, 27 June 1896, p. 772.
52. *Schoolmaster*, 26 December 1896, p. 1066.
53. 'The Position of Rural Duties', *ibid.*, 13 February 1892, pp. 289–90.
54. 'The Village Schoolmistress', *ibid.*, 4 February 1893, p. 212.
55. *Ibid.*, 31 March 1894, pp. 582–85; *Punch*, 7 April 1894, pp. 158–59.
56. *Schoolmaster*, 14 December 1895, p. 1024.

57. *Schoolmaster Specials*, No. 5, *ibid.*, 5 September 1896, pp. 361–66.

58. *Ibid.*, 21 November 1896, p. 826.

59. *SBC*, 26 September 1896, p. 302.

60. 'The Local Support of Education', *Nineteenth Century*, December 1896, pp. 919–20.

61. *Schoolmaster*, 9 January 1897, pp. 54–60.

62. *Ibid.*, p. 65. Macnamara had laid out the arguments in 'The Neglect of the Village School', *Westminster Review*, January 1897, pp. 38–46.

63. *Schoolmaster*, 8 April 1899, pp. 688–90.

64. 'In the Days of My Youth': 11 November 1899, p. 453.

65. T. J. Macnamara, *Schoolmaster Sketches*, Cassell, 1896, pp. 41, 143, 7–8.

66. *SBC*, 18 July 1896, p. 69.

67. *Phrenological Magazine*, 12, May 1896, pp. 206–07.

68. Quoted in *Schoolmaster*, 13 June 1896, p. 1100.

69. *Practical Teacher*, 22, 11, May 1902, p. 561; G. Christian, *English Education from Within*, Gandy, 1922, pp. 87–89; *Schoolmaster*, 2 April 1898, p. 611.

70. *SBC*, 25 July 1896, p. 90.

71. G. W. Kekewich, *The Education Department and After*, Constable, 1920, pp. 98–99, 96.

72. 'Higher Education and the State', *Nineteenth Century*, April 1899, p. 666.

73. H. W. Lucy, *A Diary of the Unionist Parliament 1895–1900*, Arrowsmith, 1901, p. 285.

74. *Schoolmaster*, 12 March 1898, pp. 443–54.

75. *Ibid.*, 27 December 1902, p. 1058.

76. Committee on the Pupil-Teacher System (National Society), *Report with Minutes of Evidence & Papers of Information*, National Society's Depository, Westminister, 1899.

77. 'A Pitiable Surrender', *Schoolmaster*, 22 April 1899, p. 772.

78. *Ibid.*, 30 December 1899, p. 1238.

79. *Ibid.*, 4 March 1899, pp. 385–86.

80. *Hansard*, 67, 1 March 1899, 976–77, 978–79; *Schoolmaster*, 4 March 1899, p. 386.

81. *Schoolmaster*, 20 May 1899, p. 951.

82. *Ibid.*, 24 June 1899, pp. 1147–48.

83. 'Education in 1899', *ibid.*, 30 December 1899, p. 1222.

84. *Ibid.*, 29 December 1900, p. 1218.

85. *Ibid.*, 21 April 1900, p. 802.

Notes to Chapter 6

1. 'A Word to the London Progressives', *Schoolmaster*, 4 December 1897, p. 944.

2. *Schoolmaster*, 4 December 1897, p. 937; Viscount Bryce, 'Lord Reay 1839–1921', in *Proceedings of the British Academy*, Vol. X, 1921–23, pp. 533–39.

3. G. Wallas, 'Lord Sheffield on the London School Board', in *Men and Ideas*, Geo Allen & Unwin, 1940, pp. 83–84; *Schoolmaster*, 31 December 1898, p. 1150.

4. *SBC*, 26 February 1898, p. 218; *Schoolmaster*, 31 December 1898, p. 1150.

5. Royal Commission on Local Taxation, *Vol. II, Minutes of Evidence*, HMSO, 1899, Appendix VIII, p. 294; paragraphs 18,412, 18,424.

6. *The Times*, 4 February 1896, p. 7.

7. *Royal Commission on Local Taxation Vol. II*, *op. cit.*, paragraphs 18,417, 18,418.

8. Cross Commission, *Final Report*, HMSO, 1888, p. 351.

9. *Schoolmaster*, 'Hungry!', 8 December 1894, p. 962.

10. School Board for London, *Report of a Special Committee on Underfed Children Attending School with Appendices: presented to the Board, 7 November 1895*, SBL 1468. The Rev Benjamin Waugh (1839–1909) was a member of the London School Board 1870–76; Founder of the National Society for the Prevention of Cruelty to Children.

11. *SBC*, 16 November 1895, pp. 555–57; *Final Report of the School Board for London 1870–1904*; P. S. King, 1904, p. 322; *Schoolmaster*, 16 November 1895, p. 837.

12. *SBC*, 18 December 1897, pp. 677–78; *Schoolmaster*, 18 December 1897, p. 1028; *Board Teacher*, 1 February 1898, p. 46. Fr Brown was a Roman Catholic convert, parish priest of the Vauxhall mission.

13. *SBC*, 24 December 1897, p. 714.

14. *SBC*, 9 July 1898, pp. 29–30; *Schoolmaster*, 9 July 1898, p. 63; *SBC*, 4 November 1899, pp. 474–75; *SBC*, 10 December 1898, p. 649.

15. *SBC*, 4 November 1899, pp. 474–76 and 11 November 1899, pp. 503–05; School Board for London: *First Report of the Sub-Committee on Underfed Children*, 24 October 1898, SBL 1469, paragraphs 38, 19, 22, 24, 35, 37.

16. *Board Teacher*, 1 December 1899, 285; *SBC*, 18 November 1899, p. 530; *Schoolmaster*, 18 November 1899, p. 922. Costelloe died on 22 December. Cf *Schoolmaster*, 30 December 1899, p. 1219 and B. Strachey, *Remarkable Relations: The Story of the Pearsall Smith Family*, Gollancz, 1980, pp. 116, 123, 192–93. His wife Mary, who had left him for Bernard Berenson in October 1891, wrote to her aunt: 'It is an awfully sad thing to go thus, leaving behind you confusion and bitterness, and almost no regret ... Alas, while testimonies to his cleverness and usefulness abound, there seems almost no one to mourn him as a friend'. Father Brown attended him in his last hours. His widow duly married Berenson, his brother-in-law Bertrand Russell referring to his death as 'a stroke of great good luck'.

17. *Board Teacher*, 1 December 1899, p. 285; *SBC*, 25 November 1899, pp. 558–59. See also Macnamara's editorials 'The Nation's Responsibility to its Children', *Schoolmaster*, 18 November 1899, pp. 929–31 and 'The School and The Hungry Child', *Schoolmaster*, 2 December 1899, pp. 1041–42.

18. *Board Teacher*, 1 December 1899, p. 285; *SBC*, 25 November 1899, p. 559; *Schoolmaster*, 4 November 1899, p. 812.

19. *Final Report of the School Board for London, op. cit.*, pp. 324–25; *Schoolmaster*, 18 August 1900, 150; 1 September 1900, p. 341; *SBC*, 5 January 1901, p. 14.

20. National Union of Teachers, *22nd Annual Report*, 1891–92, pp. cxxiii–cxxiv.

21. H. B. Philpott, *London at School*, T. Fisher Unwin, 1904, pp. 88, 90–91; National Union of Teachers, *22nd Annual Report*, 1891–92, p. cxxvii; *Final Report of the School Board for London, op. cit.*, p. 203.

22. *SBC*, 23 November 1895, pp. 587–88; *Schoolmaster*, 23 November 1895, p. 878; *Schoolmaster*, 12 December 1896, p. 976; *SBC*, 20 November 1897, p. 559.

23. *Board Teacher*, 1 January 1898, p. 14; cf M. Rutter, B. Maughan, P. Mortimore and J. Ouston, *Fifteen Thousand Hours*, Open Books, 1979, in which similar conclusions were reached about twelve Inner London comprehensive schools in the 1970s.

24. *SBC*, 11 December 1897, p. 651; *Board Teacher*, 1 October 1898, p. 230; *SBC*, 12 November 1898, p. 530; *SBC*, 19 November 1898, pp. 559–60.

25. *Board Teacher*, 1 October 1898, p. 230.

26. *Schoolmaster*, 9 July 1898, pp. 63–64; *SBC*, 18 February 1899, pp. 166–67; *Schoolmaster*, 18 February 1899, pp. 306–07.

27. *Schoolmaster*, 18 February 1899, p. 307.

28. *SBC*, 4 March 1899, p. 226; *Fortnightly Review*, 74, 1900, p. 798; *Schoolmaster*, 26 May 1900, p. 1034; *SBC*, 6 May 1899, p. 479.

29. *SBC*, 14 October 1899, p. 349.

30. *Schoolmaster*, 7 December 1895, p. 1000.

31. *Final Report of the School Board for London*, 1870–1904, op. cit., p. 132; *Schoolmaster*, 1 June 1895, p. 948.

32. *Schoolmaster*, 15 June 1895, p. 1041.

33. T. Taylor, 'The Cockerton Case Revised: London Politics and Education, 1898–1901',

British Journal of Educational Studies, XXX, 3, October 1982, p. 332; *Schoolmaster*, 7 December 1895, p. 1001.

34. Quoted in *Schoolmaster*, 15 May 1897, p. 911.

35. *Schoolmaster*, 22 May 1897, p. 938; *Board Teacher*, 1 June 1897, p. 133.

36. *Board Teacher*, 1 January 1898, p. 13.

37. *Schoolmaster*, 22 January 1898, p. 160; *SBC*, 22 January 1898, p. 82; *Schoolmaster*, 14 May 1898, p. 876; *SBC*, 14 May 1898, p. 502.

38. *SBC*, 14 May 1898, p. 502.

39. *Ibid.*, 23 July 1898, p. 78; 30 July 1898, p. 103.

40. *Ibid.*, 6 August 1898, pp. 130–31.

41. *Schoolmaster*, 26 November 1898, p. 922; *SBC*, 26 November 1898, p. 587.

42. *SBC*, 3 December 1898, pp. 617–18.

43. *Ibid.*, 10 December 1898, p. 650; *Schoolmaster*, 10 December 1898, p. 996.

44. *Report of Representatives of the Board to the London County Council's proposed application under Clause VII of the Science and Art Directory, 20 December 1898*, SBL 1435.

45. Departmental letter dated 18 December 1897: *SBC*, 24 December 1898, p. 714.

46. *SBC*, 24 December 1898, p. 714.

47. *Ibid.*, 28 January 1899, p. 82; 4 February 1899, p. 113; *Schoolmaster*, 4 February 1899, p. 219; B. M. Allen, *William Garnett, A Memoir*, Heffer, 1933, pp. 80, 86; W. Garnett, 'How the County Council became the Local Education Authority for London', *Educational Record*, XXII, 1929, p. 753.

48. *SBC*, 4 February 1899, p. 113; *Schoolmaster*, 4 February 1899, p. 219; *Practical Teacher*, 19, 10, April 1899, p. 577.

49. Garnett, *op. cit.*, p. 754; *SBC*, 18 February 1899, p. 165; *Schoolmaster*, 18 February 1899, p. 306.

50. Garnett, *op. cit.*, p. 754. Section I of the 1890 Act, which was obscurely worded, had enabled school boards to branch out into non-elementary evening instruction. See E. Eaglesham, *From School Board to Local Authority*, Routledge and Kegan Paul, 1956, p. 57.

51. School Board for London, *List of Members*, SBL 1356; *Hansard*, 66, 20 February 1899, 1445–46; *Schoolmaster*, 25 February 1899, p. 339.

52. Taylor, *op. cit.*, 334–37; *SBC*, 29 April 1899, p. 452; A. W. Jones, *Lyulph Stanley: A Study in Educational Politics*, Wilfrid Laurier University Press, 1977, pp. 122, 135; Eaglesham, *op. cit.*, p. 114.

53. 'The Reasons for the Auditor's Surcharge', *Schoolmaster*, 7 October 1899, pp. 622–23.

54. *SBC*, 25 February 1899, p. 197; *Practical Teacher*, 20, 3, September 1899, p. 123.

55. *Practical Teacher*, 20, 6, December 1899, pp. 292–93; *Schoolmaster*, 11 November 1899, pp. 874–75, 886.

56. 'The Higher Elementary School', *Schoolmaster*, 14 April 1900, pp. 723–24; Eaglesham, *op. cit.*, pp. 50–51.

57. *Final Report of the School Board for London*, *op. cit.*, p. 134; *SBC*, 30 June 1900, p. 729; *Practical Teacher*, 21, 4, October 1900, p. 182; *Schoolmaster*, 20 October 1900, p. 693; *SBC*, 20 October 1900, p. 381.

58. *Practical Teacher*, 21, 6, December 1900, p. 299; *Schoolmaster*, 29 December 1900, p. 1225.

59. Wills, quoted in Eaglesham, *op. cit.*, p. 131; Gorst, PRO, *Ed 24/29*, quoted in P. H. J. H. Gosden, *Educational Administration in England and Wales*, Blackwell, 1966, p. 173.

60. *Schoolmaster*, 24 November 1900, p. 953; *Schoolmaster*, 8 December 1900, p. 1038.

Notes to Chapter 7

1. *Practical Teacher*, 21, 4, October 1900, p. 182; *Schoolmaster*, 20 October 1900, p. 688; *Liberal Magazine*, VIII, December 1900, pp. 574–75.

2. *South London Observer Camberwell and Peckham Times* (*SLOCPT*), 29 September 1900, p. 5.

3. *Schoolmaster*, 13 October 1900, p. 632.

4. F. W. S. Craig, *British General Election Manifestos 1900–74*, Macmillan, 1975, pp. 4–5.

5. *Schoolmaster*, 13 October 1900, p. 631.

6. *SLOCPT*, 29 September 1900, p. 5.

7. *Ibid.*, 3 October 1900, p. 5.

8. *Ibid.*, 6 October 1900, p. 5.

9. *Teachers' Review*, November 1900, p. 187.

10. *Schoolmaster*, 13 October 1900, pp. 632–33.

11. *Ibid.*, p. 633.

12. 'Education in the New Parliament', *Schoolmaster*, 20 October 1900, p. 688.

13. *Hansard*, 121, 28 April 1903, 711.

14. 'Education at Arms: the Officers', *Schoolmaster*, 2 August 1902, p. 162.

15. Reproduced in *Schoolmaster*, 4 April 1903, p. 686.

16. *Ibid.*, 28 November 1908, p. 891; *Schoolmaster and Woman Teacher's Chronicle*, 12 May 1932, pp. 850–52.

17. *Schoolmaster*, 28 November 1908, pp. 891–92.

18. *Schoolmaster*, 28 November 1908, p. 891; *Journalist and Newspaper Proprietor*, XII, II, December 1902, p. 15.

19. See T. J. Macnamara, *The Gentle Golfer*, Arrowsmith, 1905, pp. 165–66.

20. *Schoolmaster*, 22 December 1900, pp. 1161–62; 5 January 1901, pp. 13–15.

21. Quoted in *Board Teacher*, 1 January 1901, p. 14.

22. *Ibid.*, pp. 13–14.

23. Quoted in *SBC*, 5 January 1901, p. 13.

24. *Ibid.*, 2 February 1901, pp. 102–04.

25. *Ibid.*, 9 February 1901, pp. 125–26.

26. *Ibid.*, 27 April 1901, pp. 453–55.

27. 'The Educational Muddle and the Way Out', *New Liberal Review*, 1, 4, May 1901, pp. 516–18.

28. 'Wanted: An Imperial Policy in Education', *New Liberal Review*, 1, 3, April 1901, pp. 366–68.

29. *Schoolmaster*, 23 February 1901, p. 302.

30. *Hansard*, 92, 1 April 1901, 374–75.

31. *Ibid.*, 92, 2 April 1901, 492.

32. *Ibid.*, 551–52.

33. *Schoolmaster*, 27 April 1901, p. 761.

34. Public Record Office (PRO) Ed 24/15/65, 27 March 1901. Jebb was Regius Professor of Greek in the University of Cambridge; Anson was Warden of All Souls' College Oxford; Sir Michael Foster was MP for the University of London. Jebb and Hobhouse had been members of the Bryce Commission; Bond and Peel were members of the London County Council. For a personal account of the Committee's work, see J. F. Hope, *A History of the 1900 Parliament, Vol. I*, 1900–01, Blackwood, 1908, pp. 161–64.

35. *Ibid.*, 24/15 and 24/15/65a, 2 May 1901.

36. *Hansard*, 93, 7 May 1901, 970.

37. *Ibid.*, 975.

38. *Practical Teacher*, 21, 12, June 1901, p. 605.

39. *Hansard*, 93, 7 May 1901, 993, 994–95, 996, 998, 1002.

40. Quoted in *Schoolmaster*, 18 May 1901, p. 880.

41. *Practical Teacher*, 22, 1, July 1901, p. 2.

42. *SBC*, 29 June 1901, p. 745.

43. *Board Teacher*, 1 July 1901, p. 157.

44. *Hansard*, 96, 8 July 1901, 1171, 1173–74, 1175, 1178.

45. A. S. T. Griffith-Boscawen, *Fourteen Years in Parliament*, Murray, 1907, p. 202.

46. *Hansard*, 96, 8 July 1901, 1180.

47. *Practical Teacher*, 22, 2, August 1901, p. 56.

48. *Hansard*, 96, 8 July 1901, 1185, 1189, 1190, 1196, 1198, 1199.

49. *Ibid.*, 9 July 1901, 1369, 1371.

50. *Practical Teacher*, 22, 3, September 1901, pp. 113–14.

51. M. Sadleir, *Michael Ernest Sadler*, Constable, 1949, 171–72; L. Grier, *Achievement in Education*, Constable, 1952, p. 74; B. M. Allen, *Sir Robert Morant*, Macmillan, 1934, pp. 154–56.

52. PRO, Ed 24/16/79a, 28 August 1901.

53. PRO, Ed 24/16/83.

54. *SBC*, 2 November 1901, p. 448.

55. *Board Teacher*, 1 December 1901, p. 273.

56. J. H. Yoxall, 'Our Educational Dux', *New Liberal Review*, 2, 2, December 1901, pp. 680–86.

57. *The Times*, 30 October 1901, p. 5.

58. *SBC*, 2 November 1901, p. 446.

59. *Ibid.*, 7 December 1901, pp. 569–70.

60. *Practical Teacher*, 22, 7, January 1902, p. 333; 22, 8, February 1902, p. 338.

61. *Ibid.*, p. 338.

Notes to Chapter 8

1. 'Doubtful Prospects', Schoolmaster, 8 March 1902, pp. 403–04; *Practical Teacher*, 22, 9, March 1902, p. 439.

2. 'The Government and the Education Problem', *New Liberal Review*, 3, 14, March 1902, pp. 187–89, 191–92.

3. *Hansard*, 105, 24 March 1902, 856–57.

4. *Ibid.*, 873–74.

5. *Ibid.*, 881, 884, 882–83.

6. *Schoolmaster*, 5 April 1902, p. 642.

7. T. J. Macnamara, *The Education Bill and its probable effects on the schools, the scholars and the school-teachers* (No. 1 in 'Burning Questions'), Swan Sonnenschein, 1902, pp. 17–18.

8. *Schoolmaster*, 5 April 1902, p. 644.

9. Reproduced in *Schoolmaster*, 26 April 1902, p. 760.

10. *Practical Teacher*, 22, 12, June 1902, p. 601.

11. *Hansard*, 107, 6 May 1902, 811.

12. *Ibid.*, 896.

13. *Ibid.*, 896–97.

14. *Ibid.*, 7 May 1902, 1013–14.

15. *Ibid.*, 6 May 1902, 903–07.

16. *Ibid.*, 8 May 1902, 1172–73.

17. *Practical Teacher*, 22, 12, June 1902, p. 602.

18. *Hansard*, 107, 7 May 1902, 1013.

19. *Practical Teacher*, 22, 12, June 1902, p. 602.

20. *Hansard,* 108, 26 May 1902, 555–56.

21. *Ibid.,* 569, 570, 572, 575–78, 579–80, 581.

22. *Ibid.,* 582, 596.

23. *Practical Teacher,* 23, 1, July 1902, p. 1.

24. *Ibid.,* p. 2.

25. Since the King's operation for appendicitis had already taken place, Balfour announced that the business of the House would continue as usual. *Hansard,* 109, 24 June 1902, 1513–14.

26. *Ibid.,* 108, 2 June 1902, 1202–03, 1205; 3 June 1902, pp. 1301–02.

27. *Practical Teacher,* 23, 1, July 1902, p. 2.

28. *Hansard,* 108, 3 June 1902, 1337, 1339.

29. *Ibid.,* 1341–42.

30. *Ibid.,* 109, 17 June 1902, 846–48, 854, 856.

31. *SBC,* 21 June 1902, pp. 659–60.

32. *Hansard,* 109, 23 June 1902, 1456–58.

33. *Ibid.,* 110, 30 June 1902, 407; 1 July 1902, 484–86.

34. *Practical Teacher,* 23, 2, August 1902, p. 56.

35. *Hansard,* 110, 8 July 1902, 1103.

36. *Ibid.,* 107, 8 May 1902, 1104; 110, 2 July 1902, 575–76, 579, 586. Macnamara's case against the Church Colleges appeared, in more detail, in the *Daily News* on 4 July.

37. *Hansard,* 9 July 1902, 1233–34.

38. *Ibid.,* 1246, 1248, 1250.

39. *Ibid.,* 1250–51.

40. *Ibid.,* 1252. (Philipps tried again, with the same observation, on 12 November: 114, 12 November 1902, 812–13.)

41. *Ibid.,* 110, 9 July 1902, 1254, 1255.

42. *Ibid.,* 1291.

43. *Ibid.,* 1295–98.

44. *SBC,* 19 July 1902, p. 71.

45. *Schoolmaster,* 16 August 1902, p. 207.

46. *Ibid.,* p. 208.

47. *Practical Teacher,* 23, 3, September 1902, p. 111.

48. *Hansard,* 111, 14 July 1902, 203–04.

49. *SBC,* 9 August 1902, pp. 133–34.

50. *Hansard,* 111, 21 July 1902, 853–54.

51. Cf C. P. Trevelyan, *Hansard,* 113, 17 October 1902, 152; A. J. Balfour, *ibid.,* 114, 11 November 1902, 611 and 115, 3 December 1902, 1179.

52. *Ibid.,* 107, 8 May 1902, 1102–03, 1111–12.

53. *Ibid.,* 110, 9 July 1902, 1283–84.

54. *Ibid.,* 1284, by W. R. W. Peel (Manchester S.), a member of the Parliamentary Education Committee.

55. *SBC,* 2 August 1902, pp. 108, 114.

56. *Schoolmaster,* 30 August 1902, p. 305.

57. *Ibid.,* 6 September 1902, p. 342.

58. Quoted in *Ibid.,* 18 October 1902, p. 593.

59. *SBC,* 18 October 1902, p. 378.

60. *Hansard,* 113, 27 October 1902, 884–86, 887.

61. *Ibid.,* 28 October 1902, 997–1000.

62. 'The Bill: Tenure and Extraneous Tasks', *Schoolmaster,* 1 November 1902, p. 692.

63. *Hansard,* 113, 28 October 1902, 1007–14.

64. 'The Bill: Tenure and Extraneous Tasks', *Schoolmaster,* 1 November 1902, 692.

65. *Practical Teacher,* 23, 6, December 1902, p. 270.

66. *Hansard*, 113, 31 October 1902, 1311–16; Kenyon Slaney 'became famous throughout the land as a Protestant champion and Ritualist slayer, but it was well-known that the real authors of it were the Government, and that he was moving it at their request'; A. S. T. Griffith-Boscawen, *Fourteen Years in Parliament*, Murray, 1907, p. 246.

67. *Practical Teacher*, 23, 7, January 1903, p. 322.

68. *Hansard*, 115, 3 December 1902, 1072–74.

69. *Ibid.*, 114, 11 November 1902, 617, 621, 623–24.

70. *Ibid.*, 640, 643–44.

71. *Ibid.*, 115, 20 November 1902, 71 (Education Act 1902, paragraph 14).

72. *Hansard*, 115, 20 November 1902, 74, 75, 77.

73. *Ibid.*, 77–78.

74. *Ibid.*, 83, 86, 93–94.

75. *Ibid.*, 97, 102, 98, 105–06, 108.

76. *Ibid.*, 25 November 1902, 389, 391, 395.

77. *Ibid.*, 406, 421–22.

78. *Ibid.*, 26 November 1902, 547–48, 549.

79. *Ibid.*, 581–82.

80. *Ibid.*, 2 December 1902, 936–37.

81. *Ibid.*, 3 December 1902, 1078; 2 December 1902, 938, 1046, 1043.

82. *Journalist and Newspaper Proprietor*, 11, December 1902, p. 15.

83. *Schoolmaster*, 21 February 1903, p. 375.

84. *Ibid.*, 28 March 1903, p. 639.

Notes to Chapter 9

1. *Schoolmaster*, 11 April 1903, p. 740.

2. *Nineteenth Century*, August 1897, pp. 235–44.

3. Inter-Departmental Committee on the Employment of School Children, *Minutes of Evidence*, HMSO, 1901, Appendix 1, pp. 306–07.

4. *Ibid.*, paragraphs 522–23.

5. *Ibid.*, paragraph 641.

6. *Ibid.*, paragraphs 503, 682.

7. *Schoolmaster*, 14 December 1901, pp. 981–84.

8. 'The Opening of the Session', *Schoolmaster*, 21 February 1903, p. 376.

9. *Hansard*, 118, 4 March 1903, 1425.

10. *Ibid.*, 1425–26.

11. *Ibid.*, 1428.

12. *Schoolmaster*, 9 May 1903, p. 920.

13. 'Out of School Labour', *ibid.*, 16 May 1903, p. 962.

14. Inter-Departmental Committee on the Employment of School Children, *Minutes of Evidence, op. cit.*, paragraphs 500–01, 578.

15. *Hansard*, 124, 3 July 1903, 1284–85.

16. *Practical Teacher*, 24, 2, August 1903, p. 55. By November 1905 only seventeen urban Education Authorities out of 268 had taken action; among the counties, only one. See T. J. Macnamara, 'The Physical Condition of the People', in W. T. Stead (ed.), *Coming Men on Coming Questions*, Review of Reviews Office, 1905, p. 62.

17. *1870 Education Act*, paragraph 37.

18. *Hansard*, 105, 24 March 1902, 862.

19. *Ibid.*, 121, 28 April 1903, 687.

20. *Ibid.*, 115, 25 November 1902, 469.

21. *SBC*, 29 November 1902, pp. 522–23; *Schoolmaster*, 29 November 1902, p. 862.

22. *SBC*, 6 December 1902, p. 545; 13 December 1902, p. 566. The term 'higher education' was still often used to denote secondary education.

23. *Board Teacher*, 1 January 1903, p. 14.

24. *Schoolmaster*, 31 January 1903, pp. 215–16; *School Government Chronicle*, 31 January 1903, pp. 99–100.

25. 'The London Bill', *Schoolmaster*, 31 January 1903, p. 221.

26. *Schoolmaster*, 7 February 1903, p. 284. The Secretary of State for Scotland was Lord Balfour of Burleigh.

27. *Practical Teacher*, 23, 10, April 1903, p. 487.

28. 'London's Opportunity', *Board Teacher*, 1 March 1903, p. 62.

29. *Schoolmaster*, 7 March 1903, p. 499.

30. *Practical Teacher*, 23, 10, April 1903, p. 488.

31. *Hansard*, 120, 7 April 1903, 1261–73; *Practical Teacher*, 24, 1, July 1903, p. 2.

32. *Hansard*, 120, 7 April 1903, 1276–77.

33. *Ibid.*, 1285–90.

34. *School Government Chronicle*, 11 April 1903, pp. 309–10.

35. 'The London Education Bill'; '"Ad Hoc" for London'; 'Useful Words from the *Standard*', *Schoolmaster*, 11 April 1903, pp. 729–31.

36. *Ibid.*, p. 731.

37. *School Government Chronicle*, 18 April 1903, p. 338.

38. *Ibid.*, pp. 338–39.

39. *Ibid.*, 339; *Practical Teacher*, 23, 11, May 1903, pp. 548–49.

40. *Hansard*, 121, 28 April 1903, 677–78.

41. *Ibid.*, 681.

42. *Ibid.*, 690.

43. *Ibid.*, 690–93.

44. *Ibid.*, 711.

45. *Ibid.*, 714–15.

46. *Ibid.*, 719.

47. *Ibid.*, 122, 18 May 1903, 1019–20.

48. *Practical Teacher*, 24, 1, July 1903, pp. 1–2.

49. *Hansard*, 122, 18 May 1903, 968, 999, 997, 999–1001.

50. *Ibid.*, 1022.

51. *Ibid.*, 1027, 1030, 1034–35.

52. *Ibid.*, 20 May 1903, 1274; 25 May 1903, 1653–55.

53. *Ibid.*, 1656.

54. *Ibid.*, 1675.

55. *Ibid.*, 1676.

56. *Ibid.*, 1677, 1681. The elimination of women, unless they were coopted from representative bodies responsible for education administration by the Acts of 1902 and 1903, may be counted as one of the reasons for the creation of the Women's Social and Political Union, founded on 10 October 1903.

57. 'A Pantomime and its Transformation Scene', *Schoolmaster*, 30 May 1903, p. 1042.

58. *Hansard*, 122, 25 May 1903, 1659.

59. *Practical Teacher*, 24, 1, July 1903, p. 1.

60. *Hansard*, 122, 25 May 1903, 1659; 'Transformed', *Board Teacher*, 1 June 1903, p. 138.

61. *Schoolmaster*, 30 May 1903, p. 1043; T. Gautrey, *Lux Mihi Laus: School Board Memories*, Link House, 1937, p. 170.

62. Reproduced in *Schoolmaster*, 22 August 1903, p. 317.

63. *School Government Chronicle*, 24 October 1903, p. 359; *SBC*, 12 October 1901, p. 366; *Schoolmaster*, 18 October 1902, p. 607.

64. *School Government Chronicle*, 24 October 1903, pp. 359–60.

65. S. Webb, 'London Education', *Nineteenth Century and After*, October 1903, pp. 561–62, 565–66, 567–72, 575.

66. B. Webb, *Our Partnership*, Longmans, 1948, pp. 284–85.

67. *London Teacher*, 1 May 1904, p. 114. Lord Stanley was the former Lyulph Stanley.

68. Gautrey, *op. cit.*, p. 172.

69. For example, during the Committee stage of the Birrell Education Bill: *Hansard*, 161, 23 July 1906, 822–25.

70. *Schoolmaster*, 21 May 1904, p. 1153. J. Williams Benn was the father of William Wedgwood Benn (Viscount Stansgate) and grandfather of Tony Benn.

Notes to Chapter 10

1. The *World*, 26 November 1902, pp. 880–81.

2. *Schoolmaster*, 18 April 1903, p. 800.

3. The *Yorkshire Post*, cited in *Schoolmaster*, 9 February 1907, p. 256. Sergeant Macnamara had died in February 1899 at South Molton, Devon. He served in the Army for thirty-six years, 217 days. 'His death', Macnamara wrote, 'was the biggest wrench I have had. His pride in my work was my big inspiration.' Cf *SBC*, 18 February 1899, p. 167; *MAP*, 11 November 1899, p. 452.

4. *Teachers' Review*, January 1901, p. 1.

5. *Schoolmaster*, 15 December 1900, p. 1095.

6. *Yorkshire Post*, cited in *Schoolmaster*, 9 February 1907, p. 256.

7. 'The Crimea and South Africa', *New Liberal Review*, 6, 35, December 1903, pp. 566–69, 571–72, 573–77.

8. 'Education at Arms', *Schoolmaster*, 19 July 1902, p. 82; 'Education at Arms – the Officers', *Schoolmaster*, 2 August 1902, p. 162.

9. The *Daily News*, 15 January 1904, p. 4; *Schoolmaster*, 23 January 1904, p. 195.

10. T. J. Macnamara, 'The Physical Condition of the People', in W. T. Stead (ed.), *Coming Men on Coming Questions*, Review of Reviews Office, 1905, p. 50.

11. *Schoolmaster*, 3 January 1903, p. 17; *Hansard*, 109, 9 June 1902, 97–98.

12. 'Notes on Women's Work: The New Drill Craze', *Schoolmaster*, 21 February 1903, p. 378.

13. *Hansard*, 118, 23 February 1903, 482.

14. *Schoolmaster*, 7 March 1903, pp. 495–96.

15. *School Government Chronicle*, 28 March 1903, p. 272.

16. *Schoolmaster*, 28 March 1903, p. 630.

17. *Report of the Inter-Departmental Committee on the Model Course of Physical Exercises*, Cd 2032, HMSO, 10 March 1904, p. 5.

18. *Schoolmaster*, 30 April 1904, p. 994.

19. *Hansard*, 124, 6 July 1903, 1324, 1328–29, 1336–37.

20. *Ibid.*, 1351.

21. *Hansard*, 132, 28 March 1904, 905–06, 910–11.

22. *Report of the Inter-Departmental Committee on Physical Deterioration*, *Vol. II*, Cd 2210, 1904, 11,834; 12,361; 12,362–64; 12,370; 12,372; 12,422; 12,541; 12,543.

23. *Ibid.*, 12,374; 12,377; 12,378; 12,381.

24. *Ibid.*, 12,407–08; 12,410–13; 12,501; 12,416; 12,418–20; 12,382.

25. *Ibid.*, 12,429; 12,431; 12,436.

26. 'The Publick Health', *Schoolmaster*, 6 August 1904, p. 236.

27. *Report of the Inter-Departmental Committee on Physical Deterioration*, *Vol. I*, Cd 2175, 1904, 91, paragraph 41; 59, paragraph 303; 39, paragraph 216; 72, paragraph 361.

28. 'The School and the Hungry Child', *Schoolmaster*, 13 August 1904, pp. 271–72.

29. *Schoolmaster*, 3 September 1904, p. 407.

30. *Ibid.*, 10 September 1904, pp. 446–47.

31. T. J. Macnamara, 'Platform Reminiscences', *T.P.'s Weekly*, 8 May 1903, p. 829.

32. *Schoolmaster*, 29 April 1905, pp. 884, 887.

33. *Practical Teacher*, 25, 11, May 1905, pp. 541–42.

34. Reported in *Schoolmaster*, 25 February 1905, p. 371.

35. 'Imperialism and the Race', *ibid.*, p. 378.

36. Macnamara, despite his frequent attacks on Gorst, had always given him credit for progressive views on public education, suspecting that his hands were tied. See, for example, *SBC*, 21 October 1899, p. 373.

37. A year later the Countess of Warwick was to publish an article on physical deterioration in the *Fortnightly Review* (March 1906, pp. 504–15).

38. *Schoolmaster*, 18 March 1905, p. 556; 25 March 1905, p. 620.

39. On 23 March 1905; reported in *Schoolmaster*, 25 March 1905, p. 619.

40. *Ibid.*, 8 April 1905, p. 716.

41. *Ibid.*, 22 April 1905, pp. 795–96.

42. *Schoolmaster*, 8 April 1905, p. 717.

43. 'Time', *Schoolmaster*, 25 November 1905, p. 1118; 30 December 1905, 1380–81; *Report of the Inter-Departmental Committee on Medical Inspection and Feeding of Children Attending Public Elementary Schools*, Cd 2779, 1905, *Vol. I*, HMSO, 1905, vii, paragraph 2; 33, paragraph 115.

44. *Schoolmaster*, 10 June 1905, p. 1158; *Hansard*, 147, 1 June 1905, 536.

45. 'In Corpore Sano', *Contemporary Review*, February 1905, pp. 239–41, 244–45, 247.

46. See T. W. Massingham, 'The Need for a Radical Party', *ibid.*, January 1904, p. 13. In Massingham's view there were only a dozen Radicals in the House of Commons. They included Lloyd George, Sir Charles Dilke, John Burns, Thomas Lough, J. H. Whitley, Henry Labouchère, W. R. Cremer, Macnamara, a handful of Scottish and Welsh MPs and the Labour members. (This amounted to more than a dozen.)

47. See O. Banks, *Parity and Prestige in English Secondary Education*, RKP, 1955, p. 27.

48. HMSO, 1904, Cd 2074, i. It was the work of Morant, its production supervised by Sir William Anson, W. R. Davies and Cyril Jackson HMI. See P. Gordon, 'The Handbook of Suggestions for Teachers: its origin and evolution', *Journal of Educational Administration and History*, XVII, I, January 1985, p. 43.

49. 'Higher Education and the State', *Nineteenth Century*, April 1899, p. 664.

50. 'A Chance for the Poor Man's Child', *Fortnightly Review*, 1 July 1904, pp. 164, 169.

51. *Liberal Magazine*, X, 1902, p. 348.

52. See 'Sir Robert Morant's Methods', *Schoolmaster*, 21 November 1908, p. 873.

53. *Regulations for Secondary Schools*, Cd 2128, HMSO, 1904.

54. *Schoolmaster*, 27 August 1904, p. 358.

55. 'For Class or Country', *ibid.*, 11 March 1905, p. 510.

56. *Hansard*, 143, 30 March 1905, 1789, 1790, 1798, 1800.

57. Quoted in *SBC*, 23 August 1902, p. 186.

58. 'The Education Bill and the Free Churches', *Contemporary Review*, November 1902, p. 644.

59. *Hansard*, 115, 3 December 1902, 1179–80.

60. *Fortnightly Review*, January 1903, 94, 99; cf also *Hansard*, 125, 9 July 1903, 208; 'The Future of the Act', *Schoolmaster*, 20 June 1903, pp. 1165–66.

61. Quoted in *Schoolmaster*, 10 October 1903, p. 629.

62. *School Government Chronicle*, 24 October 1903, p. 375.

63. S. E. Koss, 'Revival and Revivalism', in A. J. A. Morris (ed.), *Edwardian Radicalism 1900–1914*, RKP, 1974, p. 86.

64. R. Blathwayt, 'A Talk with Dr Macnamara MP', *Great Thoughts Vol. II*, 5th Series, 497, October 1902–March 1903, p. 88; 'Passive Resistance', *Schoolmaster*, 9 May 1903, pp. 919–20.

65. 'The Education Act in the New Parliament', *Fortnightly Review*, 1 November 1903, pp. 800–01.

66. *Hansard*, 107, 8 May 1902, 1110; 131, 14 March 1901, 1004, 1006, 1021–22; W. R. P. George, *Lloyd George: Backbencher*, Gomer, 1983, pp. 358–59; B. B. Gilbert, *David Lloyd George: A Political Life; I: The Architect of Change 1863–1912*, Batsford, 1987, pp. 236–37, 238.

67. *Hansard*, 131, 14 March 1904, 1045.

68. *Schoolmaster*, 9 April 1904, pp. 860–61; 'The St Asaph Bill', 14 May 1904, p. 1083: an example of adverse publicity for Macnamara from his own paper. Cf also *Fortnightly Review*, 1 November 1903, *op. cit.*, p. 808.

69. 'The Welsh Impasse', *Schoolmaster*, 30 April 1904, p. 994.

70. *Hansard*, 138, 15 July 1904, 206, 196, 198.

71. *Ibid.*, 139, 5 August 1904, 1266.

72. 'What will happen in Wales?', *Schoolmaster*, 3 September 1904, p. 406.

73. *Review of Reviews*, September 1904, quoted in *Schoolmaster*, 24 September 1904, p. 559; 'The Situation in Wales', *Schoolmaster*, 8 October 1904, p. 674.

74. 'The Welsh Crisis', *Schoolmaster*, 15 October 1904, p. 730.

75. 'The Situation in Wales', *ibid.*, 22 October 1904, p. 773.

76. *Ibid.*

77. *Ibid.*, 29 October 1904, p. 830; 'Why the Bishops did not confer', *ibid.*, 5 November 1904, p. 890.

78. *Ibid.*, 8 July 1905, p. 79.

79. For example about his campaign fund: *ibid.*, 2 September 1905, p. 440.

80. *NUT Annual Report* 1905, pp. xxiii–iv (24 April 1905).

81. T. J. Macnamara, *The Gentle Golfer*, Arrowsmith, 1905, p. 175.

82. Reprinted in *Schoolmaster*, 23 July 1904, p. 168.

83. Viscount Samuel, *Memoirs*, Cresset Press, 1944, p. 44; H. Samuel, 'The Chinese Labour Question', *Contemporary Review*, April 1904, pp. 465, 457, 467.

84. *Hansard*, 129, 16 February 1904, 1522–23.

85. *Ibid.*, 1532.

86. *Ibid.*, 1566.

87. *Ibid.*, 130, 17 February 1904, 107.

88. *Ibid.*, 22 February 1904, 631–34.

89. *Ibid.*, 141, 17 February 1905, 481–90.

90. *Ibid.*, 491, 499.

91. *Ibid.*, 533–34.

92. *Liberal Magazine*, XIII, 1905, p. 119.

93. R. C. K. Ensor, *England 1870–1914*, Oxford, 1936, p. 390.

94. T. J. Macnamara, 'A Friendly Lead for the Coming Liberal Government', *Review of Reviews*, July 1904, pp. 83–84.

95. *Ibid.*, February 1905, p. 113; August 1905, p. 113.

96. Stead (ed.), *op. cit.*, p. 43.

97. *Ibid.*, pp. 47, 51–52, 49, 64.

98. *Schoolmaster*, 30 September 1905, p. 621.

99. *Ibid.*; 2 December 1905, pp. 1155, 1159.

100. *Ibid.*, 13 January 1906, p. 66.

101. *Ibid.*, 18 November 1905, p. 1066.
102. Samuel, *Memoirs, op. cit.*, pp. 47–48.
103. Koss, *op. cit.*, p. 90.
104. A. Birrell, *Things Past Redress*, Faber and Faber, 1937, 183–84.
105. *Schoolmaster*, 9 December 1905, p. 1226.
106. *Practical Teacher*, 26, 11, May 1906, p. 567. 'AC' was Allen Croft, President of the NUT, 1902–03.
107. W. George, *My Brother and I*, Eyre and Spottiswoode, 1958, p. 207.
108. B. Drake and M. I. Cole (eds), *Our Partnership, by Beatrice Webb*, Longmans Green, 1948, p. 326 (15 December 1905).

Notes to Chapter 11

1. See A. K. Russell, *Liberal Landslide: The General Election of 1906*, David and Charles, 1973, ch. 1; F. W. S. Craig, *British General Election Manifestos 1900–74*, Macmillan, 1975, pp. 10–13.
2. *The Times*, 22 December 1905, p. 7.
3. *Schoolmaster*, 6 January 1906, p. 11.
4. PRO, Ed 24/116, 3 January 1906–17 January 1906.
5. Between 180 and 200 of the Liberals were thought to be Nonconformists: S. E. Koss, 'Revival and Revivalism', in A. J. A. Morris (ed.), *Edwardian Radicalism 1900–1914*, RKP, 1974, p. 92.
6. *Hansard*, 155, 9 April 1906, 1065.
7. *Schoolmaster*, 6 January 1906, p. 12.
8. *Ibid.*, 24 February 1906, p. 410; *Hansard*, 155, 9 April 1906, 1065.
9. *Schoolmaster*, 6 January 1906, pp. 11–12; 24 February 1906, p. 410; 9 February 1907, p. 256.
10. *Ibid.*, 20 January 1906, p. 118.
11. Education Bill 1906, reproduced in *ibid.*, 14 April 1906, pp. 749–54.
12. *Practical Teacher*, 26, 11, May 1906, pp. 555–56.
13. I.e. four out of six, instead of two out of six; 'The Government and the Education Problem', 'The New Education Act at Work', *Fortnightly Review*, January 1903, p. 94.
14. *Hansard*, 155, 9 April 1906, 1057, 1060, 1064, 1062–63.
15. *Schoolmaster*, 21 April 1906, 846/9. Clause 7, subsection 2 ran: 'A teacher employed in a public elementary school shall not be required as part of his duties as teacher to give any religious instruction, and shall not be required as a condition of his appointment to subscribe to any religious creed, or to attend or abstain from attending any Sunday school or place of religious worship (*Schoolmaster*, 14 April 1906, p. 750).
16. *Ibid.*, pp. 849–50.
17. *Ibid.*, pp. 861–62.
18. *Ibid.*, 12 May 1906, pp. 986–90.
19. *Hansard*, 156, 7 May 1906, 1090–92.
20. *Ibid.*, 1092.
21. *Ibid.*, 9 May 1906, 1377.
22. *Ibid.*, 10 May 1906, 1597. Clause 4 dealt with 'Extended Facilities'.
23. *Practical Teacher*, 27, 2, August 1906, p. 57; 27, 1, July 1906, p. 1.
24. 'The End of the First Chapter', *Schoolmaster*, 4 August 1906, pp. 195–96.
25. For amended text of the Bill see *Schoolmaster*, 11 August 1906, pp. 222–24.
26. *Hansard*, 159, 3 July 1906, 1645–47, 1689–90.
27. *Ibid.*, 160, 16 July 1906, 1376, 1386, 1382–83, 1394, 1397. Tennant was Asquith's brother-in-law and had acted as his private secretary from 1892 till 1895.

28. *Practical Teacher*, 27, 3, September 1906, p. 115.

29. *Hansard*, 162, 30 July 1906, 541, 544.

30. *Ibid.*, 545–47.

31. *Ibid.*, 1 August 1906, 921–43.

32. *Schoolmaster*, 4 August 1906, p. 186.

33. *Ibid.*, 28 July 1906, pp. 153, 152.

34. *Ibid.*, 17 February 1906, p. 343.

35. Select Committee on Education (Provision of Meals) Bill, *Minutes of Evidence*, 1906 (288), paragraphs 3350; 1038; 782–86.

36. *Ibid.*, paragraphs 3392–94.

37. *Ibid.*, paragraph 1021.

38. *Ibid.*, paragraphs 971–73.

39. *Ibid.*, Appendix No. 4, paragraph 220.

40. *Ibid.*, paragraphs 997–1002, 1003.

41. *Ibid.*, viii, paragraph 18; *Schoolmaster*, 28 July 1906, p. 154.

42. E.g. *Schoolmaster*, 28 May 1904, p. 1176.

43. *Ibid.*, 25 June 1904, p. 1380.

44. *Ibid.*, 6 October 1906, pp. 609–10; 13 October 1906, pp. 653–55; 20 October 1906, p. 684.

45. Reprinted in *ibid.*, 27 October 1906, p. 748.

46. *Hansard*, 166, 7 December 1906, 1378–80, 1381.

47. *Schoolmaster*, 12 January 1907, p. 85.

48. *Ibid.*, 28 July 1906, p. 166.

49. 'The Court of Appeal Decision', *ibid.*, 18 August 1906, pp. 262, 253.

50. Quoted in *Schoolmaster*, 1 September 1906, p. 327.

51. *Ibid.*, quoted from the *Nineteenth Century and After*.

52. *Hansard*, 167, 12 December 1906, 380, 384–5.

53. cf also 'The Lords and the Bill', *Schoolmaster*, 3 November 1906, pp. 781–82; 'The Struggle for the Teacher', *ibid.*, 17 November 1906, pp. 852–53; 'Test for Board (sic) School Teachers', *ibid.*, 17 November 1906, p. 859; *ibid.*, 15 December 1906, p. 1054; 'Peace or War', *ibid.*, 15 December 1906, pp. 1065–66.

54. *Hansard*, 167, 19 December 1906, 1393–94, 1400.

55. *Schoolmaster*, 22 December 1906, pp. 1093–94, 1096.

56. *Hansard*, 167, 20 December 1906, 1739–40, 1744, 1742, 1752–54.

57. *Schoolmaster*, 9 February 1907, p. 254; *ibid.*, 15 September 1906, p. 451; 'The Immediate Future', *ibid.*, 22 September 1906, pp. 493–94.

58. *Practical Teacher*, 28, 2, August 1907, p. 84; 'The New Code', *Schoolmaster*, 10 July 1909, pp. 274–75; 'A Report that Marks an Epoch', *ibid.*, 6 March 1909, pp. 411–12; 'Passive Resistance' (apparently by Macnamara), *ibid.*, 9 May 1903, p. 920.

59. *BL 41239 f 202 Add.*

60. *BL 46299/189 Add*, 23 January 1907.

61. *Speaker*, 2 February 1907, p. 525.

62. *Schoolmaster*, 9 February 1907, pp. 253, 255.

63. 'From Fleet Street to Whitehall', *ibid.*, 16 February 1907, p. 314.

64. *Ibid.*, 2 March 1907, p. 433; 6 April 1907, p. 702; *Practical Teacher*, 27, 10, April 1907 (cover); *Schoolmaster*, 23 March 1907, p. 570; 11 May 1907, p. 925.

65. *Ibid.*, 6 April 1907, pp. 701–02, 705; *Practical Teacher*, 27, 11, May 1907, pp. 560–61.

66. *Schoolmaster*, 23 March 1907, p. 571.

67. G. D. H. Cole, *John Burns*, Fabian Society/Gollancz, 1943, pp. 17–27.

68. J. Wilson, *C-B: A Life of Sir Henry Campball-Bannerman*, Constable, 1973, p. 463.

69. Cole, *op. cit.*, pp. 27–28; L. Masterman, *C. F. G. Masterman: A Biography*, Nicholson and Watson, 1939, p. 104.

70. K. D. Brown, *John Burns*, Royal Historical Society, 1977, pp. 132, 135, 153.

71. Lord Hardinge of Penshurst, *Old Diplomacy*, John Murray, 1947, p. 142.

72. *Children Under the Poor Law*, Cd 3899, 1908, p. 4.

73. *Ibid.*, p. 5.

74. In the *Yorkshire Daily Observer*, quoted in *Schoolmaster*, 2 November 1907, p. 767. Sykes was President of the NUT 1906–07. The 'little son' was more probably Terence, born in 1905.

75. *Schoolmaster*, 8 February 1908, pp. 267–68; *Children Under the Poor Law, op. cit.*, pp. 18–20; 7.

76. *The Times*, 25 March 1908, p. 11.

77. *Ibid.*, 13 March 1908, p. 12; 11 March 1908, p. 11; 14 March 1908, p. 14; 25 March 1908, p. 12; 26 March 1908, p. 7.

78. *Picture Politics*, August 1908, p. 8.

Notes to Chapter 12

1. W. T. Stead, *Coming Men on Coming Questions*, Review of Reviews Office, November 1905, p. 43.

2. *Reynolds News*, 29 October 1922, p. 2.

3. *Riddell* 62970, 11 May 1912, p. 101.

4. *Riddell* 62973, November 1913, p. 71.

5. David Lloyd George, *War Memoirs, Vol. II*, Ivor Nicholson & Watson, 1931, p. 1024.

6. E. David, *Inside Asquith's Cabinet*, John Murray, 1977, p. 72.

7. *The Times*, 15 April 1908, p. 10; *Schoolmaster*, 18 April 1908, p. 771.

8. Lord Oxford and Asquith, *Fifty Years in Parliament*, Vol. II, Cassell, 1926, p. 52.

9. Lord Percy of Newcastle, *Some Memories*, Eyre and Spottiswoode, 1958, p. 97.

10. *Statement* showing present distribution of business between the various members of the Board of Admiralty, dated 1 January 1904, Cd 2417, Board of Admiralty, 1905, pp. 5–6.

11. *The Times*, 7 May 1908, p. 11; 30 May 1908, p. 10; 22 July 1908, p. 18; 23 July 1908, p. 5; 25 July 1908, p. 9.

12. Lord Hankey, *The Supreme Command*, Geo Allen & Unwin, 1961, p. 147.

13. *Review of Reviews*, 31, April 1905, p. 343. This does not take account of the work of Lord Cawdor, appointed First Lord the previous month. See R. C. K. Ensor, *England 1870–1914*, Oxford University Press, 1936, p. 363.

14. R. Vansittart, *The Mist Procession*, Hutchinson, 1958, p. 77, describes Tweedmouth as 'patently potty'. He had responded to a private letter from the Kaiser about the German and British Navies in February 1908 and may even have sent him a copy of the Naval Estimates before they were submitted to Parliament. See also M. and E. Brock (eds), *H. H. Asquith: Letters to Venetia Stanley*, Oxford University Press, 1985, p. 300, note 4.

15. See H. W. Wilson, 'The Naval Situation', *Nineteenth Century*, 45, 1899, pp. 620–21; A. Eltzbacher, 'The Anti-British Movement in Germany', *Nineteenth Century and After*, 52, 1902, p. 196.

16. A. Marder, *From the Dreadnought to Scapa Flow: The Royal Navy in the Fisher Era 1904–1919, I: the Road to War 1904–14*, Oxford University Press, 1961, p. 107.

17. Ernst Teja Meyer, 'A German View of the British Navy', *Contemporary Review*, 82, 1902, pp. 23–38.

18. Hankey, *op. cit.*, 15–17, 27; W. S. Churchill, *The World Crisis 1911–1918*, Four Square 1964, pp. 60–1. Fisher remained First Sea Lord until January 1910.

19. G. L. Bernstein, *Liberalism and Liberal Politics in Edwardian England*, Allen & Unwin, 1986, p. 175.

20. R. Hough, *The Great War at Sea*, Oxford University Press, 1983, p. 1.

21. *Review of Reviews*, 34, August 1906, p. 117; 33, June 1906, pp. 455, 555–56; 36, December 1907, pp. 574, 555.

22. A. J. Marder (ed.), *Fear God and Dread Nought, the Correspondence of Admiral of the Fleet Lord Fisher of Kilverstone, Vol. II: Years of Power 1904–14*, Cape, 1956, p. 175.

23. *Hansard*, 192, 13 July 1908, pp. 480–82.

24. *Review of Reviews*, 38, December 1908, p. 510; November 1908, p. 399.

25. S. McKenna, *Reginald McKenna 1863–1943*, Eyre and Spottiswoode, 1948, pp. 72–73.

26. Marder, *Fear God and Dread Nought, op. cit.*, p. 222.

27. *Review of Reviews*, 39, April 1909, pp. 324–25.

28. Marder, *Fear God and Dread Nought, op, cit.*, p. 207.

29. *Hansard*, 2, 16 March 1909, 933.

30. *Ibid.*, 16 March 1909, 962.

31. *Ibid.*, 17 March 1909, 1091–94, 1099.

32. Marder, *Fear God and Dread Nought, op. cit.*, p. 208.

33. *Hansard*, 3, 29 March 1909, 141.

34. *The Times*, 3 April 1909, p. 10.

35. *Hansard*, 8, 3 August 1909, 1793–97.

36. T. J. Macnamara, *The Political Situation: Letters to a Working Man*, Hodder & Stoughton, 1909, pp. 52, 30, 32–34, 27, 12–13, 24, 7, 8, 18–20, 43, 38, 45.

37. Reproduced in A. Clark, *A Good Innings: The Private Papers of Viscount Lee of Fareham*, John Murray, 1974, pp. 99–100.

38. Marder, *Fear God and Dread Nought, op. cit.*, pp. 210–11, 240.

39. *Report of Sub-Committee of the Committee of Imperial Defence* (256), 1909.

40. *Hansard*, 15, 14 March 1910, 89.

41. *Ibid.*, 141–45.

42. Marder, *Fear God and Dread Nought, op. cit.*, p. 315.

43. *Hansard*, 19, 19 July 1910, 1146, 1152, 1149.

44. T. J. Macnamara, *Concerning the Navy*, Liberal Publication Department, 1910, pp. 4–5, 7, 11–12.

45. *The Times*, 20 October 1910, pp. 7, 9.

46. *Ibid.*, 21 October 1910, p. 8.

47. The *Daily News*, 20 June 1911, p. 1.

48. The *Fleet*, July 1911, p. 155.

49. *Hansard*, 27, 4 July 1911, 1000, 1008.

50. *Ibid.*, 22, 16 March 1911, 2549–50.

51. See, for example, *Riddell* 62974, 6 January 1914, p. 2; 17 January 1914, p. 18.

52. *Hansard*, 30, 7 November 1911, 1510.

53. T. J. Macnamara, *The Great Insurance Act: Addresses to Working Men*, Hodder and Stoughton, 1912, pp. xii, ix.

54. *Hansard*, 125, 25 February 1920, 1741; Macnamara, *The Great Insurance Act, op. cit.*, pp. 49–51.

55. T. J. Macnamara, *The Great Insurance Act: A Year's Experience*, Liberal Publication Department, 1913, p. 12.

56. The *Fleet*, July 1911, p. 155; September 1911, p. 201.

57. *Review of Reviews*, 44, December 1911, pp. 547, 551.

58. Quoted in F. Owen, *Tempestuous Journey: Lloyd George, his Life and Times*, Hutchinson, 1954, p. 211.

59. Churchill, *op. cit.*, p. 38.

60. David, *op. cit.*, pp. 105, 111–12.

61. *Riddell* 62975, 22 May 1915, p. 231; David, *op. cit.*, p. 108. Asquith had previously offered Churchill the post when he first became Prime Minister: see Churchill, *op. cit.*, p. 57.

62. *Hansard*, 35, 20 March 1912, 1982–83.

63. See, for example, *Hansard*, 46, 16 January 1913, 2277–79.

64. Churchill, *op. cit.*, p. 68.

65. *Hansard*, 35, 18 March 1912, 1555.

66. Churchill, *op. cit.*, p. 92.

67. *Hansard*, 59, 18 March 1914, 2132–33.

68. *Riddell* 62973, 26 September 1913, p. 31; Hansard 59, 2 March 1914, 95.

69. *Hansard*, 35, 18 March 1912, 1555, 1557, 1556–57.

70. Churchill, *op. cit.*, pp. 74–80.

71. *Hansard*, 41, 22 July 1912, 936.

72. *Ibid.*, 50, 26 March 1913, 1757–59.

73. *Ibid.*, 51, 31 March 1913, 166–68.

74. R. S. Churchill, *Winston S. Churchill, Vol. II: Companion 1901–14; Part 3, 1911–1914*, Heinemann, 1969, p. 1723.

75. *Review of Reviews*, 47, April 1913, pp. 355–56. Stead had been lost with the *Titanic*.

76. *The Times*, 11 November 1913, p. 9; R. S. Churchill, *op. cit., Vol. II, Young Statesman 1901–1914*, Heinemann, 1967 pp. 656–57, 658, 664, 669.

77. HLRO *Lloyd George Papers*, C/3/16/3, 19 January 1914.

78. R. S. Churchill, *op. cit., Vol. II, Companion 1901–14, Part 3, 1911–1914*, p. 1847.

79. *Riddell* 62974, 17 January 1914, 18; B. B. Gilbert, *David Lloyd George, A Political Life: II, Organizer of Victory 1912–1916*, Ohio State University Press, 1992, pp. 75–76.

80. David, *op. cit.*, p. 157.

81. R. S. Churchill, *op. cit.*, Vol. II: Young Statesman 1901–1914, pp. 678–80.

82. *Hansard*, 59, 2 March 1914, 83–98.

83. *Ibid.*, 178, 182–3.

84. *Ibid.*, 1906–07, 1917.

85. W. S. Churchill, *op. cit.*, pp. 112, 114, 130.

Notes to Chapter 13

1. M. and E. Brock (eds), *H. H. Asquith: Letters to Venetia Stanley*, Oxford University Press, 1985, p. 405. Venetia Stanley was the daughter of the Hon Lyulph Stanley, Vice-Chairman of the London School Board, who had become Lord Stanley in 1903 and Lord Sheffield in 1909. Montagu ('the Assyrian') was born in 1879.

2. *Ibid.*, pp. 408, 399.

3. *Riddell* 62975, 29 January 1915, pp. 42–43.

4. *Hansard*, 69, 15 February 1915, 933–34.

5. *Ibid.*, 959–60, 961–63, 959.

6. Brock, *op. cit.*, pp. 387–88.

7. Lord Beaverbrook, *Politicians and the War 1914–1916*, I, Thornton Butterworth, 1928, p. 105.

8. A. Marder (ed.), *Fear God and Dread Nought: The Correspondence of Admiral of the Fleet Lord Fisher of Kilverstone, II, Years of Power 1904–14*, Cape, 1956, pp. 310–11, 400.

9. *Riddell* 62973, 16 November 1913, p. 81; 62974, 5 November 1914, p. 229.

10. Brock, *op. cit.*, p. 405.

11. *Riddell* 62975, 15 April 1915, p. 159.

12. W. S. Churchill, *The World Crisis 1911–18*, Four Square, 1964, pp. 419–20, 423, 446, 456, 486; A. Moorehead, *Gallipoli*, Hamish Hamilton, 1956, pp. 116, 124.

13. Lord Hankey, *The Supreme Command*, Vol. I, Geo Allen and Unwin, 1961, p. 267.

14. Churchill, *op. cit.*, pp. 511, 514.

15. Marder, *op. cit.*, *Vol. III, Restoration, Abdication and Last Years*, 1959, 244 (letter dated 21 May to Admiral Sir John Jellicoe).

16. R. Blake, *The Unknown Prime Minister: The Life and Times of Andrew Bonar Law*, Eyre & Spottiswoode, 1955, pp. 245–46.

17. Lord Oxford and Asquith, *Memories and Reflections 1852–1927*, Vol. II, Cassell, 1928, p. 93.

18. T. Wilson (ed.), *The Political Diaries of C. P. Scott, 1911–1928*, Collins, 1970, p. 191.

19. Oxford and Asquith, *op. cit.*, p. 94.

20. Churchill, *op. cit.*, p. 831.

21. Dardanelles Committee, *1st Report*, HMSO, 1917, p. 10, paragraph 32; A. J. P. Taylor, *English History 1914–1945*, Oxford University Press, 1965, p. 44.

22. E. T. Raymond, *Uncensored Celebrities*, T. Fisher Unwin, 1918, p. 32.

23. *Hansard*, 98, 1 November 1917, 1668.

24. Quoted in *SLOCPT*, 9 December 1931, p. 3.

25. Brock, *op. cit.*, 276–77.

26. *Riddell* 62974, 8 November 1914, p. 235.

27. *Hansard*, 68, 11 November 1914, 30–31, 23, 33.

28. *Special Report and Second Special Report from the Select Committee on Naval and Military Services (Pensions and Grants) &c* (53/196), HMSO, 1915, pp. 18–34 (30 November 1914).

29. *Hansard*, 69, 16 February 1915, 1030.

30. *Ibid.*, 73, 6 July 1915, 318; 14 July 1915, 881; 88, 30 November 1916, 585.

31. *Ibid.*, 87, 14 November 1916, 688.

32. HLRO *Lloyd George Papers*, F 36/1/4.

33. *Hansard*, 75, 18 November 1915, 2063–64; 80, 7 March 1916, 1405; 17 February 1916, 345, 258, 347.

34. David Lloyd George, *War Memoirs*, Vol. III, Ivor Nicholson and Watson, 1934, pp. 1213, 1219–21.

35. *History of the Ministry of Munitions, Vol. 2, Part I*, Crown Copyright, 1922, pp. 13–14; *Hansard*, 90, 26 February 1917, 1748.

36. *Hansard*, 80, 1 March 1916, 1072–76.

37. *Ibid.*, 94, 22 June 1917, 2141–42.

38. *Ibid.*, 95, 6 July 1917, 1522, 1524–25, 1528.

39. *Riddell* 62976, 11 June 1915, p. 22.

40. *Hansard*, 90, 21 February 1917, 1366.

41. *Ibid.*, 91, 16 March 1917, 1430; 92, 29 March 1917, 619.

42. *Ibid.*, 96, 27 July 1917, 1603.

43. *Ibid.*, 97, 16 August 1917, 1478.

44. *Ibid.*, 100, 5 December 1917, 389–92.

45. *Ibid.*, 90, 21 February 1917, 1422–23.

46. *Ibid.*, 104, 20 March 1918, 1059–60.

47. Lloyd George, *op. cit.*, Vol. III, p. 1234; *Hansard*, 98, 1 November 1917, 1674.

48. *Hansard*, 103, 5 March 1918, 1876–77.

49. *Ibid.*, 6 March 1918, 2057, 2066–67, 2069.

50. *Ibid.*, 7 March 1918, 2205–06.

51. *Ibid.*, 2212–13.

52. *Ibid.*, 104, 12 March 1918, 251, 257.

53. *Ibid.*, 69, 16 February 1915, 1022.

54. *History of the Ministry of Munitions, op. cit., Vol. I, Part 2*, pp. 35–36, 56, 81–83.

55. HLRO *Lloyd George Papers*, C 3/16/22.

56. *Hansard*, 71, 29 April 1915, p. 881.

57. *History of the Ministry of Munitions, op. cit., Vol. II, Part I*, p. 283.

58. S. J. Hurwitz, *State Intervention in Great Britain: A Study of Economic Control and Social Response 1914–1919*, Columbia University Press, 1949, p. 96; *History of the Ministry of Munitions, op. cit., Vol. I, Part 3*, pp. 56–57.

59. HLRO *Lloyd George Papers*, D 17/13/3.

60. *Ibid.*, D 17/13/4 (?) October 1915. In Lord Beaverbrook's recollection, Lloyd George did not like being addressed as 'George'. See *The Decline and Fall of Lloyd George*, Collins, 1963, pp. 303–04.

61. *Hansard*, 76, 9 December 15, 1587, 2074, 2078; Hurwitz, *op. cit.*, p. 89.

62. *Hansard*, 80, 8 March 1916, 1613.

63. *Riddell* 62977, 16 January 1916, pp. 19–20.

64. Taylor, *op. cit.*, pp. 75, 77.

65. *Commission of Enquiry into Industrial Unrest*, Cd 8662, 8696, HMSO, 1917–18, pp. 8, 5–6.

66. PRO, *Geddes A145*, 13 October 1917.

67. HLRO *Lloyd George Papers*, F 6/2/49, 27 November 1917.

68. J. M. McEwen (ed.), *The Riddell Diaries 1908–1923*, The Athlone Press, 1986, p. 228 (17 June 1918).

69. *Ibid.*

70. *Ibid.*, p. 230 (30 June 1918).

71. *Ibid.*, p. 231, 28–29 July 1918; p. 234, August (no date).

72. K. O. Morgan, *Consensus and Disunity: The Lloyd George Coalition Government 1918–1922*, Oxford University Press, 1979, pp. 24, 29.

73. McEwan, *op. cit.*, p. 234, August (no date).

74. *The Times*, 13 November 1918, p. 9.

75. T. W. Wilson, *The Downfall of the Liberal Party 1914–1935*, Collins, 1966, p. 139.

76. *The Times*, 12 December 1918, p. 6.

77. HLRO *Lloyd George Papers*, F 36/1/8, 25 November 1918; *The Times*, 13 December 1918, p. 10.

78. HLRO *Lloyd George Papers*, F 36/1/9, 10 December 1918.

79. *The Times*, 14 December 1918, p. 6.

80. *Huddersfield Examiner*, 14 December 1918, p. 8.

81. HLRO *Lloyd George Papers*, F 36/1/10.

82. Morgan, *op. cit.*, p. 44.

83. *Hansard*, 122, 10 December 1919, 1465.

84. *Ibid.*, 126, 17 March 1920, 2297–98, W. Long, *Memories*, Hutchinson, 1923, p. 272.

85. *Hansard*, 122, 10 December 1919, 1371, 1377.

86. *Ibid.*, 112, 20 February 1919, 1157; 122, 10 December 1919, 1377, 1465.

87. *The Times*, 1 October 1917, p. 9; A. Marder, *From the* Dreadnought *to Scapa Flow, Vol. V, Victory and Aftermath, January 1918–June 1919*, Oxford University Press, 1970, pp. 212–13.

88. A. Carew, *The Lower Deck of the Royal Navy, 1900–1939*, Manchester University Press, 1981, pp. 5, 14, 16. Lionel Yexley, whose real name was James Woods, was an ex-petty-officer and coastguard who had founded the *Fleet*, a twopenny monthly, in May 1905. Though he was regarded by most naval officers as a subversive influence, he had been supplying the political ministers at the Admiralty with information since 1909.

89. *Riddell* 62982, 4–5–6 September 1918, p. 56.

90. HLRO *Lloyd George Papers*, F 87/10/2: Prime Minister from Cecil Harmsworth, 20 September 1918.

91. *The Times*, 27 December 1918, p. 3.

92. *Hansard*, 113, 12 March 1919, 1429; *The Times*, 18 January 1919, p. 9; Long, *op. cit.*, p. 272; Carew, *op. cit*, p. 102.

93. HLRO *Lloyd George Papers*, F 46/9/3.

94. *The Times*, 30 January 1919, p. 10; *Hansard*, 113, 5 March 1919, 373; 12 March 1919, 1381.

95. *Hansard*, 113, 12 March 1919, 1416.

96. *Ibid.*, 115, 29 April 1919, p. 19.

97. *Ibid.*, 115, 1 May 1919, p. 342.

98. Long, *op. cit.*, p. 273; HLRO *Davidson Papers*, 98, 6 May 1919; A. Marder, *From the Dreadnought to Scapa Flow*, V, *op. cit.*, pp. 216–17.

99. *Hansard*, 118, 24 July 1919, 1609.

100. *Manchester Guardian*, 13 September 1918, p. 6.

101. E.g. 'Who's A-Top?', *Daily Mail*, 6 January 1919, p. 4.

102. D. Dutton, *Simon: A Political Biography of Sir John Simon*, Aurum Press, 1992, p. 55.

103. HLRO *Lloyd George Papers*, F 21/4/28; *Riddell* 62984, 21 December 1919, p. 229. Sir Hamar Greenwood was Secretary, Department of Overseas Trade; F. G. Kellaway was Deputy Minister of Munitions.

104. *Riddell* 62985, 1 January 1920, p. 4.

105. *The Times*, 5 January 1920, p. 13.

106. HLRO *Lloyd George Papers*, F 36/1/13, 3 January 1920.

107. J. Ramsden (ed.), *Real Old Tory Politics: The Political Diaries of Sir Robert Sanders, Lord Bayford, 1910–55*, The Historians' Press, 1984, p. 134. Sir Archibald Salvidge, the Liverpool brewer, was a friend of Lords Birkenhead and Derby; Sir Robert Horne was Minister of Labour; Churchill was now Secretary for War, Addision Minister of Health; Lord Edmund Talbot and F. E. Guest were Unionist and Coalition Whips.

108. McEwan, *op. cit.*, p. 305, 15 February 1920. Edward Shortt was Home Secretary; H. A. L. Fisher President of the Board of Education; Sir Gordon Hewart Attorney General.

109. A. J. P. Taylor (ed.), *Lloyd George: A Diary by Frances Stevenson*, Hutchinson, 1971, p. 201.

110. Beaverbrook, *op. cit.*, p. 9, note 1. Ian Macpherson was lately Chief Secretary for Ireland; Sir Alfred Mond was First Commissioner of Works.

111. *Hansard*, 126, 17 March 1920, p. 2331.

Notes to Chapter 14

1. T. J. Macnamara, *The Work of the Ministry of Labour*, National Liberal Council, 1922, p. 1; Hansard, 145, 4 August 1921, 1676–90. See also R. Lowe, *Adjusting to Democracy: The Role of the Ministry of Labour in British Politics 1916–1939*, Clarendon Press, 1986, pp. 11–12. The salary was £2,000 per annum, as compared to the £5,000 of an established Secretary of State.

2. *Schoolmaster*, 10 April 1920, p. 702.

3. *The Times*, 8 May 1920, pp. 17, 10, 16; 10 May 1920, p. 12.

4. *Hansard*, 125, 25 February 1920, 1742–43; HLRO *Lloyd George Papers*, H 271: *Unemployment Insurance: 'Dr Macnamara's Memo'*, p. 4.

5. *Hansard*, 125, 25 February 1920, 1743, 1749, 1746; *Unemployment Insurance*, *op. cit.*, p. 5.

6. *Hansard*, 125, 25 February 1920, 1749–50, 1752. Previously, each employed person was entitled to one week's benefit for every five contributions.

7. *Ibid.*, 131, 9 July 1920, 1914, 1906, 1907, 1909–10.

8. *Ibid.*, 1865.

9. *Ibid.*, 7 July 1920, 1426; see also T. J. Macnamara, 'The Ex-Service Man, *Lloyd George Liberal Magazine*, I, 1, October 1920, p. 29.

10. HLRO *Lloyd George Papers*, F 36/1/25, 4 August 1920 (SECRET). The King was seeking information about the resettlement of soldiers and sailors: see F 36/1/26, p. 27.

11. *Hansard*, 133, 16 August 1920, 568; 136, 21 December 1920, pp. 1665–66; compare PRO, *CAB 23/22*, 13 August 1920, pp. 113–14.

12. HLRO *Lloyd George Papers*, F 36/1/28.

13. HLRO *Lloyd George Papers*, F 36/1/22 (PERSONAL). Sir David Shackleton, the former Labour MP, was the Permanent Secretary; H. J. Wilson (later special adviser to Neville Chamberlain) succeeded him in 1921.

14. C. Loch Mowat, *Britain between the Wars*, Methuen, 1955, pp. 31–33.

15. *Ibid.*, pp. 42–43.

16. *Riddell* 62986, 3 October 1920, pp. 107, 110, 111; cf 62983, 23 January 1919, p. 53.

17. *Hansard*, 133, 19 October 1920, 757–58.

18. PRO, *CAB 23/23*, 21 October 1920, p. 66.

19. *Hansard*, 133, 21 October 1920, 1116–17, 1119.

20. *Ibid.*, pp. 1120–28.

21. HLRO *Lloyd George Papers*, F 36/1/33, 22 November 1920.

22. *Hansard*, 136, 21 December 1920, 1573–80; see also H. A. Clegg, *A History of British Trade Unions since 1889: Vol. II: 1911–1933*, Clarendon Press, 1985, pp. 265–66.

23. *Hansard*, 136, 21 December 1920, 1587–96, 1614, 1617.

24. *Ibid.*, 1581–82, 1588–89.

25. *Annual Register 1920*, Longmans Green, 1921, pp. 146–47.

26. *Riddell* 62986, Christmas Day 1920, pp. 179–81; 27 December 1920, p. 182. Sir Alfred Mond was First Commissioner of Works.

27. *Unemployment: A Labour Policy: Report of the Joint Committee on Unemployment appointed by the Parliamentary Committee of the Trade Union Congress and the Labour Party Executive*, TUC and the Labour Party, January 1921; *Annual Register 1921*, Longmans Green, 1922, pp. 2–3.

28. HLRO *Lloyd George Papers*, F 36/1/35.

29. *Hansard*, 138, 16 February 1921, 112, 109–110.

30. *Ibid.*, 119–28; PRO, CAB *23/24*, 7 February 1921, pp. 57–58; 11 February 1921, p. 73.

31. *Hansard*, 138, 17 February 1921, 409, 414, 412.

32. *Ibid.*, 23 February 1921, 999–1000; 994–97; the Out-of-Work Donation had begun on 25 November 1918 (PRO, *CAB 23/22*, 29 July 1920, p. 72).

33. *Hansard*, 138, 24 February 1921, 1199–1204.

34. *Ibid.*, 1204–08; 1247–48. Twenty shillings had been agreed at the Cabinet meeting of 11 February 1921: see PRO, *CAB 23/24*, 11 February 1921, p. 73.

35. *Hansard*, 139, 22 March 1921, 2428–32.

36. *Ibid.*, 2461–62. See also outline of the scheme, 2567–69.

37. Loch Mowat, *op. cit.*, pp. 120–24; K. Middlemas (ed.), *Thomas Jones: Whitehall Diary*, I, *1916–1925*, Oxford University Press, 1969, pp. 132–51.

38. *Hansard*, 143, 22 June 1921, 1386; *Lloyd George Liberal Magazine*, I, 9, June 1921, p. 584.

39. PRO, *CAB 23/23*, 8 December 1920, p. 201; *23/25*, 11 May 1921, p. 257; HLRO *Lloyd George Papers*, F 36/1/39, 23 May 1921.

40. PRO, *CAB 23/26*, 1 June 1921, p. 2; 23/26, 3 June 1921, p. 18.

41. K. O. Morgan, *Consensus and Disunity: The Lloyd George Coalition Government 1918–1922*, Oxford University Press, 1979, pp. 104–05.

42. *Hansard*, 143, 28 June 1921, 2012; 142, 8 June 1921, 1875–77.

43. *Ibid.*, 1882, 1879–80, 1881–82.

44. *Ibid.*, 143, 15 June 1921, 453–55; 461, 454, 462.

45. *Ibid.*, 473, 497–98, 547, 556.

46. *Ibid.*, 27 June 1921, 1906.

47. *Ibid.*, 28 June 1921, 2017. The Bill received the Royal Assent on 1 July as the Unemployment Insurance (No. 2) Act 1921.

48. *Ibid.*, 146, 17 August 1921, 1510–11, 1513–14.

49. *Ibid.*, 145, 4 August 1921, 1722, 1675–76, 1696.

50. PRO, *CAB 23/26*, 19 August 1921, p. 330.

51. HLRO *Lloyd George Papers*, F 36/1/43, 3 September 1921. The 'few areas' were Cardiff, Middlesbrough, Sheffield, Bradford, Huddersfield, Birmingham, Coventry, Smethwick, Wolverhampton, Openshaw, Bristol, Glasgow, Edinburgh, Dundee and Belfast; in London, Borough, Camberwell, Clapham, Holloway, Poplar, Shoreditch, Stepney, Woolwich. Poplar's rate was 22s 10d when the average general rate in London was 14s 11d and £5,000 per week was being spent on poor relief. See also PRO, *CAB 23/27*, 7 August 1921, p. 144.

52. PRO, *CAB 23/27*, 7 September 1921, p. 7.

53. HLRO *Lloyd George Papers*, F 36/1/44, 8 September 1921. It was sent by J. Cunningham, Secretary, Calendar Workers' Union, 8 Overgate, Dundee.

54. *Riddell* 62988, 15 September 1921, pp. 92, 96; T. Jones, *op. cit.*, pp. 172–73.

55. HLRO *Lloyd George Papers*, F 36/1/45.

56. PRO, *CAB 23/27*, 6 October 1921, p. 15. Chamberlain had been Chancellor of the Exchequer until April; Stanley Baldwin had succeeded Horne at the Board of Trade.

57. *Ibid.*, 23/28, 12 October 1921, p. 62.

58. *Hansard*, 147, 19 October 1921, 75, 94, 85, 89–91, 83.

59. *Ibid.*, 20 October 1921, 396.

60. *Ibid.*, 24 October 1921, 474–75, 481.

61. *Ibid.*, 487.

62. *Ibid.*, 550.

63. *Ibid.*, 578.

64. *Ibid.*, 26 October 1921, 909–10.

65. *Ibid.*, 914.

66. *Ibid.*, 919.

67. *Ibid.*, 927.

68. *Ibid.*, 931, 934, 941, 952.

69. *Ibid.*, 1 November 1921, 1597.

70. *Ibid.*, 1640–41.

71. *Ibid.*, 1634.

72. *Ibid.*, 1657.

73. *Ibid.*, 1666–67.

74. *Ibid.*, 1636, 1682–83, 1678–79.

75. *Lloyd George Liberal Magazine*, II, 3, December 1921, pp. 199–203.

76. HLRO *Lloyd George Papers*, F 36/1/48.

77. Lord Beaverbrook, *The Decline and Fall of Lloyd George*, Collins, 1963, Ch. 7.

78. *Hansard*, 150, 7 February 1922, 7.

79. *Ibid.*, 9 February 1922, 345–58.

80. *Ibid.*, 383, 366, 374.

81. *Ibid.*, 362, 369–70.

82. *Ibid.*, 357.

83. *Ibid.*, 437.

84. *Ibid.*, 358–59.

85. *Ibid.*, 151, 8 March 1922, 1257.

86. PRO, *CAB 23/29*, 15 February 1922, p. 111; *Hansard*, 150, 17 February 1922, 1384–85.

87. HLRO *Lloyd George Papers* F 36/1/53.

88. *Hansard*, 152, 29 March 1922, 1375–77.

89. *Ibid.*, 1405, 1411.

90. *Ibid.*, 30 March 1922, 1607–08.

91. *Ibid.*, 6 April 1922, 2571–72.

92. *Ibid.*, 156, 10 July 1922, 817.

93. *Ibid.*, 12 July 1922, 1255.

94. *Ibid.*, 1259.

95. *Ibid.*, 1262–64.

96. *Ibid.*, 13 July 1922, 1575–76.

97. (*Ibid.*, 159, 23 November 1922, 52): *Lloyd George Liberal Magazine*, III, 3, December 1922, p. 172.

98. *Hansard*, 159, 8 December 1922, 2215–17. Barlow had been Parliamentary Secretary to the Ministry of Labour under Macnamara.

99. *Ibid.*, 2225.

100. T. J. Macnamara, *Success in Industry*, Harrison, 1920, p. 3.

101. T. J. Macnamara, *Labour at the Crossroads, Two Camberwell Addresses*, Hodder & Stoughton, 1923, pp. 10, 8, 33, 20.

102. *Lloyd George Liberal Magazine*, III, 10, July 1923, p. 799. Macnamara had deployed the dog fable in *The Political Situation: Letters to a Working Man* 1909: see Chapter XII, note 36.

103. *Ibid.*, III, 9 June 1923, p. 679.

104. *Ibid.*, III, 11 August 1923, p. 844.

105. cf Asquith, *Hansard*, 160, 13 February 1923, 29.

106. *Ibid.*, 169, 18 January 1924, 461.

107. *Ibid.*, 12 February 1924, 759.

108. *Ibid.*, 763–64.

109. *Ibid.*, 170, 10 March 1924, 1977, 1981, 1976, 1981, 1978.

110. *Ibid.*, 172, 8 April 1924, 289.

111. *Ibid.*, 301–02, 303, 305–06.

112. HLRO *Lloyd George Papers*, F 223/1/36.

113. A. J. P. Taylor, *English History 1914–1945*, Oxford University Press, 1965, p. 149.

114. Speech at the Town Hall, Walsall, 21 February 1925: *Walsall Times & South Staffordshire Advertiser*, 28 February 1925, p. 5.

Notes to Chapter 15

1. *SLOCPT*, 18 October 1924, p.5.

2. *Ibid.*, 6 October 1900, p. 5.

3. *Ibid.*, 13 January 1906, p. 3.

4. *Ibid.*, 20 January 1906, p. 5; *Schoolmaster*, 20 January 1906, pp. 117–18.

5. 'Presentation to Dr Macnamara MP', *Schoolmaster*, 24 February 1906, p. 410.

6. *SLOCPT*, 19 January 1910, p. 5; 3 December 1910, p. 5.

7. *Ibid.*, 7 December 1910, p. 5.

8. *Ibid.*, 23 November 1918, p. 3; 27 November 1918, p. 3.

9. *Ibid.*, 7 December 1918, p. 3.

10. *Ibid.*, 30 November 1918, p. 3.

11. *Ibid.*, 18 December 1918, p. 3.

12. *Ibid.*, 30 November 1918, p. 3.

13. HLRO *Lloyd George Papers*, F 36/1/8; *SLOCPT*, 14 December 1918, p. 3.

14. Quoted in *SLOCPT*, 30 November 1918, p. 3.

15. *Ibid.*, 27 March 1920, p. 5; *Daily Chronicle*, 30 March 1920, p. 5.

16. *SLOCPT*, 27 March 1920, p. 5.

17. *Ibid.*, 31 March 1920, p. 3.

18. HLRO *Lloyd George Papers*, F 36/1/17; *SLOCPT*, 31 March 1920, p. 3.

19. *The Times*, 30 March 1920, p. 16.

20. HLRO *Lloyd George Papers*, F 36/1/20 (no date).

21. *SLOCPT*, 17 April 1920, p. 5.

22. *Riddell*, 62980, 27 July 1917, p. 17.

23. *Manchester Guardian*, 1 November 1922, p. 11.

24. *SLOCPT*, 25 October 1922, p. 3.

25. *Ibid.*, 1 November 1922, p. 3.

26. *Evening Standard*, 28 October 1922, p. 7; 3 November 1922, p. 3.

27. *The Times*, 17 November 1922, p. i.

28. *SLOCPT*, 8 December 1923, p. 5.

29. *Ibid.*, 5 December 1923, p. 3. 'We look to Camberwell Liberals to vote unitedly for Free Trade and Liberalism and to spare no effort to secure your return in these great causes.'

30. *Ibid.*, 8 December 1923, p. 5.

31. *Daily Chronicle*, 1 December 1923, p. 3; 5 December 1923, p. 3.

32. *SLOCPT*, 8 December 1923, p. 5.

33. *Ibid.*, 29 October 1924, p. 3; 1 November 1924, p. 5.

34. *Ibid.*, 22 November 1924, p. 5.

35. M. Thomson, *David Lloyd George: The Official Biography*, Hutchinson, 1948, p. 381.

36. *The Times*, 11 February 1925, p. 7; 14 February 1925, p. 14.

37. *Walsall Times and South Staffordshire Advertiser* (*WTSSA*), 28 February 1925, p. 5; *Hansard*, 147, 19 October 1921, 75.

38. *WTSSA*, 28 February 1925, p. 10.

39. HLRO *Lloyd George Papers*, G 13/6/7, dated Sunday (22) February.

40. In 1922 only two ex-Cabinet ministers, Lord George Hamilton and Lord Chaplin, were receiving pensions. See *Hansard*, 151, 8 March 1922, 1307.

41. Lloyd George 'not only had no genius for friendship, but he could even say that he had no time for friendships which were not political'. See T. Jones, *Lloyd George*, Oxford University Press, 1951, pp. 279–80.

42. HLRO *Lloyd George Papers*, G 13/6/3, 9 May 1924. Macnamara had been Chairman of the National Liberal Organisation for a year when it ceased to function, at the end of 1923, on the reunification of the party.

43. *Ibid.*, G 13/6/12, 11 May 1924.

44. *Ibid.*, G 13/6/13, 20 December 1925.

45. *Ibid.*, 13/6/14, 9 January 1926.

46. *Ibid.*, G 13/6/15, 19 January 1927.

47. *Daily Chronicle*, 20 February 1926, p. 3.

48. T. J. Macnamara, *If Only We Would: Some Reflections on our Social Shortcomings with some Suggestions for their Removal*, P. S. King, 1926, pp. 81–82, 22–24, 53, 60, 50, 54–55, 48–49.

49. National Liberal Federation, *Report of the Special Meeting of the Council on Industrial Policy, held in the Kingsway Hall, London, on Tuesday, Wednesday and Thursday, March 27th, 28th and 29th 1928*, Liberal Publication Department, 1928, pp. 151–53.

50. Jones, *op. cit.*, pp. 229–30.

51. *WTSSA*, 11 May 1929, p. 7.

52. *Ibid.*, 25 May 1929, p. 7.

53. *Ibid.*

54. *Ibid.*, 1 June 1929, p. 7.

55. See A. J. P. Taylor, *English History 1914–1945*, Oxford University Press, 1965, p. 267.

56. T. J. Macnamara, 'The Unemployment Problem', *Liberal Magazine*, May 1930, pp. 225–26.

57. *Hansard*, 248, 11 February 1931, 449.

58. *WTSSA*, 13 July 1929, p. 4.

59. Limavady, Carlton Road, Redhill.

60. *WTSSA*, 14 March 1931, p. 6.

61. Lloyd George's Election Address, re-printed in the *Liberal Magazine*, November 1931, p. 504; Jones, *op. cit.*, p. 236.

62. *WTSSA*, 26 September 1931, p. 7.

63. *Ibid.*, 10 October 1931, p. 7.

64. *Ibid.*, 17 October 1931, p. 7.

65. *Ibid.*, 31 October 1931, p. 7.

66. *The Times*, 17 November 1931, p. 14.

67. A. J. P. Taylor (ed.), *My Darling Pussy: The Letters of Lloyd George and Frances Stevenson, 1913–41*, Weidenfeld and Nicolson, 1975, pp. 160, 163.

68. Quoted in A. Tropp, *The School Teachers*, Heinemann, 1957, p. 150.

69. 'The Coronation Honours', *Schoolmaster*, 24 June 1911, p. 1248

70. See H. A. L. Fisher's statement on the Introduction of his Education Bill, *Hansard*, 97, 10 August 1917, p. 800.

71. *Riddell*, 62975, 29 January 1915, pp. 42–43.

72. *The Times*, 5 December 1931, p. 14.

73. *News Chronicle*, 5 December 1931, p. 2.

74. *Schoolmaster and Woman Teacher's Chronicle*, 10 December 1931, pp. 892, 890, 888.

75. C. Hazlehurst and C. Woodland, *A Guide to the Papers of British Cabinet Ministers 1900–1951*, Royal Historical Society, 1974, p. 99.

76. *Schoolmaster*, 18 November 1905, p. 1067.

77. D. Lloyd George, in T. J. Macnamara, *If Only We Would, op. cit.*, p. vii.

Bibliography

A: Manuscript Sources

(i) Official Papers

Public Record Office:
    ADM 116 Private Correspondence of Sir Eric Geddes, First Lord of the Admiralty 1917–20
    CAB 23 Cabinet Papers
    Ed 24 Papers on Education

(ii) Private Papers

Bodleian Library, Oxford:
    Asquith Papers
    H. A. L. Fisher Diaries
    Rey Papers

British Library:
    Balfour Papers
    Burns Papers
    Campbell-Bannerman Papers
    Long Papers
    Riddell Diaries (typed version)

Churchill College Cambridge:
    McKenna Papers
    Churchill (Chartwell Trust Papers)

House of Lords Record Office:
    Historical Collection 187: Davidson Papers
    Historical Collection 192: Lloyd George Papers

(iii) Institutional Papers

Brunel University (West London Institute):
    Borough Road College Papers

Devon County Record Office, Exeter:
    Minutes of the St Thomas (Exeter) School Board
    St Thomas Boys' School Exeter, Log Book

London Metropolitan Archives:
    School Board for London Papers

B: Parliamentary Papers

(i)   Hansard's Parliamentary Debates, fourth and fifth series

(ii)   Reports of the Committee of Council on Education (England and Wales) 1839–99

(iii) Reports of Commissions, Committees, Departments &c

RC	Royal Commission
C	Committee
CN	Commission
DC	Departmental Committee
IDC	Inter-Departmental Committee
SC	Select Committee
JSC	Joint Select Committee
CC	Consultative Committee

1861	RC	Popular Education (Newcastle)
1882–84	RC	Technical Instruction (Samuelson)
1886–88	RC	Elementary Education Acts (Cross)
1892	RC	Labour
1892	SC	Elementary Education (Teachers' Superannuation)
1893	DC	School Attendance and Child Labour
1894	DC	Superannuation of teachers in public elementary schools
1895	DC	Maintenance and Education of Poor Law Children
1895	RC	Secondary Education (Bryce)
1897	C	Grants to Science and Art Schools
1898	DC	Pupil Teacher System
1899	RC	Local Taxation
1901–02	IDC	Employment of School Children
1902	C	Education and Training of Officers of the Army
1902	JSC	Housing of the Working Classes
1903	RC	Physical Training (Scotland)
1904	IDC	Model Course of Physical Exercises
1904	IDC	Physical Deterioration
1905–06	CC	Questions affecting Higher Elementary Schools
1905–06	IDC	Medical Inspection and Feeding
1906	SC	Provision of Meals Bill
1908		Children under the Poor Law
1909	IDC	Partial Exemption from School Attendance
1914–15	SC	Naval and Military Services (Pensions and Grants)
1917	CN	Dardanelles
1917–18	CN	Enquiry into Industrial Unrest
1917–18	SC	National Expenditure

C: Contemporary Newspapers and Periodicals

Annual Register
B's Hum: the Magazine of the Borough Road Students
Blackwood's Edinburgh Magazine
Board Teacher/London Teacher
Contemporary Review
Daily Chronicle

Daily Mail
Daily News
Educational Record with the Proceedings of the British and Foreign School Society
Educational Review
English Teacher
Evening Standard
Fleet
Fortnightly Review
Great Thoughts
Huddersfield Examiner
Infants' Mistress
Journalist and Newspaper Proprietor
King
Liberal Magazine
Lloyd George Magazine
London
Macmillan's Magazine
Manchester Guardian
MAP (Mainly About People)
National Review
New Century Review
New Liberal Review
New York Educational Review
Nineteenth Century
North American Review
Pall Mall Gazette
Phrenological Magazine
Picture Politics
Practical Teacher
Punch
Review of Reviews
Reynolds News
Saturday Review
Scholars' Own
School
School Board Chronicle/School Government Chronicle
School Guardian
Schoolmaster/Schoolmaster and Woman Teacher's Chronicle
South London Observer (and) Camberwell and Peckham Times
Speaker
Teacher (I and II)
Teachers' Aid
Teachers' Review
The Times
TP's Weekly
Vanity Fair
Walsall Times and South Staffordshire Advertiser
Western Daily Press
Westminster Gazette
Westminster Review
World

D: Academic Journals

British Journal of Educational Studies
Historical Journal
History of Education
History of Education Society Bulletin
Journal of Educational Administration and History
Proceedings of the British Academy

E: Published Papers

National Union of (Elementary) Teachers, Annual Reports 1882–1920

National Society, Committee on the Pupil Teacher System, Report, 1899

School Board for London:
    Minutes of Proceedings
    Annual Reports, 1891–1904
    Special Reports

F: Theses

N. D. Daglish, *The Educational Work of Sir John Gorst*, unpublished PhD, University of Durham, 1974

J. R. Fairhurst, *Some Aspects of the Relationship between Education, Politics and Religion from 1895–1906*, unpublished DPhil, University of Oxford, 1974

A. I. Taylor, *The Church Party and Popular Education 1893–1902*, unpublished PhD, University of Cambridge, 1981

G: Published Books

C. Addison, *Politics from Within, 1911–1918*, Herbert Jenkins, 1924

B. M. Allen, *William Garnett: A Memoir*, Heffer, 1933
    Sir Robert Morant, a Great Public Servant, Macmillan, 1934

W. H. G. Armytage, *A.J. Mundella*, Benn, 1951
    'W. E. Forster and the Liberal Reformers', in A.V. Judges (ed.), *Pioneers in English Education*, Faber, 1952
    Four Hundred Years of English Education, Cambridge University Press, 1964

Admiral Sir R.H. Bacon, *The Life of Lord Fisher of Kilverstone*, Hodder & Stoughton, 1929

P. B. Ballard, *Things I Cannot Forget*, University of London Press, 1937

O. Banks, *Parity and Prestige in English Secondary Education*, RKP, 1955

G. F. Bartle, *A History of Borough Road College*, Dalkeith Press, 1976

Lord Beaverbrook, *Politics and the War 1914–1916, Vol. I*, Thornton Butterworth, 1928; *Vol. II*, The Lane Publications, 1932
    The Decline and Fall of Lloyd George, Collins, 1963

G. Bennett, *Charlie B: A Biography of Admiral Lord Beresford of Metemmeh and Curraghmore*, Peter Dawnay, 1968

M. Bentley, *The Liberal Mind, 1914–29*, Cambridge University Press, 1977

G. L. Bernstein, *Liberalism and Liberal Politics in Edwardian England*, Allen & Unwin, 1986

F. G. Bettany, *Stewart Headlam: A Biography*, John Murray, 1926

H. B. Binns, *A Century of Education*, Dent, 1908

A. Birrell, *Things Past Redress*, Faber & Faber, 1937

A. S. Bishop, *The Rise of a Central Authority for English Education*, Cambridge University Press, 1971

R. Blake, *The Unknown Prime Minister: The Life and Times of Andrew Bonar Law*, Eyre & Spottiswoode, 1955

R. Blake and J. Louis (eds), *Churchill*, Oxford University Press, 1993

R. Bourne and B. McArthur, *The Struggle for Education, 1870–1970*, Schoolmaster Publishing Company, 1970

W. J. Braithwaite, H. N. Bunbury and R. M. Titmuss (eds), *Lloyd George's Ambulance Wagon: Being the Memoirs of William J. Braithwaite, 1911–1912*, Methuen, 1957

Britain's Industrial Future: Being the Report of the Liberal Industrial Inquiry, Ernest Benn, 1928

M. and E. Brock (eds), *H. H. Asquith: Letters to Venetia Stanley*, Oxford University Press, 1985

K. D. Brown, *John Burns*, Royal Historical Society, 1977

D. Butler and J. Freeman, *British Historical Facts 1900–60*, Macmillan, 1965

J. Campbell, *Lloyd George: The Goat in the Wilderness*, Cape, 1977

D. Cannadine, *The Decline and Fall of the British Aristocracy*, Picador, 1992

A. Carew, *The Lower Deck of the Royal Navy, 1900–1939*, Manchester University Press, 1981

D. Cecil, *The Cecils of Hatfield House: A Portrait of an English Ruling Family*, Constable, 1973

G. A. Christian, *English Education from Within*, Wallace Gandy, 1922

R. Church, *The Voyage Home*, Heinemann, 1964

R. S. Churchill, *Winston S. Churchill, Vol. II: Young Statesman 1901–1914*, Heinemann, 1967
Winston S. Churchill, Vol. II: Companion, Part 3, 1911–1914, Heinemann, 1969

W. S. Churchill, *The World Crisis, 1911–18*, Four Square, 1964
Thought and Adventures, Thornton Butterworth, 1932

A. Clark (ed.), *A Good Innings: The Private Papers of Viscount Lee of Fareham*, John Murray, 1974

P. Clark, *Liberals and Social Democrats*, Cambridge University Press, 1978

H. A. Clegg, *A History of British Trade Unions since 1889: Vol. II 1911–1933*, Clarendon Press, 1885

G. D. H. Cole, *John Burns*, Fabian Society/Gollancz, 1943

M. Cowling, *The Impact of Labour: The Beginning of Modern British Politics*, Cambridge University Press, 1971

R. Cowper (ed.), *Proceedings of the International Conference on Education: Printed and Published for the Executive Council of the International Health Exhibition and for the Council of the Society of Arts*, Clowes, 1884

F. W. S. Craig, *British General Election Manifestos 1900–74*, Macmillan, 1975

D. M. Cregier, *Bounder from Wales: Lloyd George's Career before the First World War*, University of Missouri Press, 1976

C. Cross, *The Liberals in Power (1905–1914)*, Barrie & Rockliff, with Pall Mall Press, 1963

E. David (ed.), *Inside Asquith's Cabinet: From the Diaries of Charles Hobhouse*, John Murray, 1977

J. Davies, *The Prime Minister's Secretariat 1916–20*, Johns, 1951

R. E. Davies (ed.), *John Scott Lidgett: A Symposium*, The Epworth Press, 1957

B. Drake and M. I. Cole (eds), *'Our Partnership' by Beatrice Webb*, Longmans Green & Co., 1948

D. Dutton, *Simon: A Political Biography of Sir John Simon*, Aurum Press, 1992

D. Dwork, *War is Good for Babies and Other Young Children*, Tavistock, 1987

E. Eaglesham, *From School Board to Local Authority*, RKP, 1956

H. V. Emy, *Liberals, Radicals and Social Politics 1892–1914*, Cambridge University Press, 1973

R. C. K. Ensor, *England 1870–1914*, Oxford University Press, 1936

Final Report of the School Board for London, 1870–1904, P. S. King, 1904

Admiral of the Fleet Lord Fisher, *Memories*, Hodder & Stoughton, 1919

Sir Almeric Fitzroy, *Memoirs, Vol. II*, Hutchinson, 1930

A. G. Gardiner, *Prophets, Priests and Kings*, Alston Rivers, 1908

W. R. Garside, *British Unemployment 1919–1939: A Study in Public Policy*, Cambridge University Press, 1990

T. Gautrey, *Lux Mihi Laus: School Board Memories*, Link House, 1937

D. Lloyd George, *War Memoirs*, Ivor Nicholson & Watson, 1933–36

W. George, *My Brother and I*, Eyre and Spottiswoode, 1958

W. R. P. George, *Lloyd George: Backbencher*, Gomer, 1982

B. B. Gilbert, *The Evolution of National Insurance in Great Britain: The Origins of the Welfare State*, Michael Joseph, 1966
British Social Policy 1914–1939, Batsford, 1970
David Lloyd George: A Political Life: I. The Architect of Change 1863–1912, Batsford, 1987; *II. Organizer of Victory, 1912–1916*, Ohio State University Press, 1992

M. Gilbert, *Winston S. Churchill: IV: 1917–1922: Companion 3, April 1921–November 1922*, Heinemann, 1977

P. H. J. H. Gosden, *The Development of Educational Administration in England and Wales*, Blackwell, 1966

A. P. Graves, *To Return to all That*, Cape, 1930

L. Grier, *Achievement in Education*, Constable, 1952

A. S. T. Griffith-Boscawen, *Fourteen Years in Parliament*, Murray, 1907

J. Grigg, *The Young Lloyd George*, Eyre Methuen, 1973
Lloyd George: The People's Champion, 1902–11, Eyre Methuen, 1978

R. B. Haldane, *An Autobiography*, Hodder & Stoughton, 1929

Lord Hankey, *The Supreme Command*, Geo. Allen & Unwin, 1961

Lord Hardinge of Penshurst, *Old Diplomacy*, John Murray, 1947

R. W. Harris, *Not So Humdrum*, John Lane, The Bodley Head, 1939
National Health Insurance in Great Britain 1911–1946, Geo. Allen & Unwin, 1946

C. Hazlehurst, *Politicians at War: July 1914 to May 1915*, Jonathan Cape, 1971

C. Hazlehurst and C. Woodland, *A Guide to the Papers of British Cabinet Ministers 1900–1951*, Royal Historical Society, 1974

E. P. Hennock, *British Social Reforms and German Precedents: The Case of Social Insurance 1880–1914*, Clarendon Press, 1987

History of the Ministry of Munitions, Crown Copyright, 1922

B. Holland, *Life of Spencer Compton, 8th Duke of Devonshire*, Longmans Green, 1911

J. F. Hope, *A History of the 1900 Parliament: Vol. I: 1900–1*, Wm. Blackwood, 1908

P. Horn, *Education in Rural England, 1800–1914*, Gill & Macmillan, 1978

R. Hough, *The Great War at Sea*, Oxford University Press, 1983

S. J. Hurwitz, *State Intervention in Great Britain: A Study of Economic Control & Social Response, 1914–1919*, Columbia University Press, 1949 (Studies in History, Economics and Public Law No. 546)

R. Rhodes James, *Rosebery*, Weidenfeld & Nicolson, 1963

A. W. Jephson, *My Work in London*, Pitman, 1910

A. W. Jones, *Lyulph Stanley: A Study in Educational Politics*, Wilfrid Laurier University Press, 1939

T. Jones, *Lloyd George*, Oxford University Press, 1951

Sir James Kay Shuttleworth, *Four Periods of Public Education*, Harvester, 1973

Sir G. W. Kekewich, *The Education Department and After*, Constable, 1920

S. E. Koss, *Sir John Brunner, Radical Plutocrat: 1842–1919*, Cambridge University Press, 1970
Nonconformity in Modern British Politics, Batsford, 1975
'Revival and Revivalism', in A. J. A. Morris (ed.), *Edwardian Radicalism 1900–1914*, RKP, 1974

'Linesman' (pseud. M. H. Grant) *Words by an Eyewitness: The Struggle in Natal*, Blackwood (11th edition), 1902

Viscount Long of Wraxall, *Memories*, Hutchinson, 1923

R. Lowe, *Adjusting to Democracy: The Role of the Ministry of Labour in British Politics 1916–1939*, Clarendon Press, 1986

H. W. Lucy, *A Diary of the Unionist Parliament, 1895–1900*, Arrowsmith, 1901
Later Peeps at Parliament, Geo. Newnes, 1905
The Balfourian Parliament 1901–1905, Hodder & Stoughton, 1906

R. B. McCallum, *The Liberal Party from Earl Grey to Asquith*, Gollancz, 1963

P. McCann (ed.), *Popular Education and Socialization in the Nineteenth Century*, Methuen, 1977

S. Maccoby, *English Radicalism 1886–1914*, Geo. Allen & Unwin, 1953

J. M. McEwen (ed.), *The Riddell Diaries 1908–1923*, The Athlone Press, 1986

S. McKenna, *Reginald McKenna 1863–1943*, Eyre & Spottiswoode, 1945

J. S. Maclure, *One Hundred Years of London Education, 1870–1970*, Allen Lane, 1970
A History of Education in London, 1870–1990, Allen Lane, 1990

T. J. Macnamara, *Schoolmaster Sketches*, Cassell, 1896
The Education Bill and its Probable Effects on the Schools, the Scholars, and the School Teachers (No. 1 in 'Burning Questions'), edited by Col Dalbiac, late MP for North Camberwell, London, Swan Sonnenschein, 1902
The Gentle Golfer, Arrowsmith, 1905
The Education Bill of 1906 Explained and Defended, The Liberal Publication Dept, 1906
School Room Humour, Simpkin, Marshall, Hamilton, Kent, 1907
'What Not to Do', in H. Seton-Karr (ed.), *Golf*, Greening, 1907
The Political Situation: Letters to a Working Man, Hodder & Stoughton, 1909
Concerning the Navy, The Liberal Publication Dept, 1910
Dr Macnamara's Messages to Working Men, Hodder & Stoughton, 1910
Let London Lead: The Mother City's Duty to the Empire & Herself, reprinted, with additions, from *The Daily Chronicle*, 1910
The Great Insurance Act: Addresses to Working Men, Hodder & Stoughton, 1912
The Great Insurance Act: A Year's Experience, The Liberal Publication Dept, 1913

Success in Industry, Harrison, 1920

The Work of the Ministry of Labour, National Liberal Council, 1922

Labour at the Cross Roads: Two Camberwell Addresses, Hodder & Stoughton, 1923

If Only We Would: Some Reflections on our Social Shortcomings with some Suggestions for their Removal, P. S. King, 1926

A. J. Marder (ed.) *Fear God and Dread Nought: The Correspondence of Admiral of the Fleet Lord Fisher of Kilverstone, Vol. II: Years of Power,* Cape, 1956, *Vol. III: Restoration, Abdication and Last Years,* Cape, 1959

From Dreadnought to Scapa Flow: The Royal Navy in the Fisher Era 1904–1919, Oxford University Press, 1961–70

B. Marshall, *Emma Marshall: A Biographical Sketch,* Seeley, 1901

L. Masterman, *C. F. G. Masterman: A Biography,* Nicholson and Watson, 1939

K. Middlemas (ed.), *Thomas Jones: Whitehall Diary: I: 1916–1925,* Oxford University Press, 1969

Politics in Industrial Society: The Experience of the British System since 1911, Andre Deutsch, 1979

A. Moorehead, Gallipoli, Hamish Hamilton, 1956

K. O. Morgan, *The Age of Lloyd George,* Geo. Allen & Unwin, 1971

'Lloyd George's Stage Army: The Coalition Liberals 1918–22', in A. J. P. Taylor (ed.), *Lloyd George: Twelve Essays,* Hamish Hamilton, 1971

Lloyd George: Family Letters 1885–1936, University of Wales Press and Oxford University Press, 1973

Consensus and Disunity: The Lloyd George Coalition Government 1918–1922, Oxford University Press, 1979

A. J. A. Morris (ed.), *Edwardian Radicalism 1900–1914,* RKP, 1974

C. Loch Mowat, *Britain Between the Wars,* Methuen, 1955

B. K. Murray, *The People's Budget 1909/10: Lloyd George and Liberal Politics,* Clarendon Press, 1986

National Liberal Federation, *Report of the Special Meeting of the Council on Industrial Policy,* Liberal Publication Dept, 1928

F. Owen, *Tempestuous Journey,* Hutchinson, 1954

Earl of Oxford and Asquith, *Fifty Years of Parliament,* Cassell, 1926

Memories and Reflections 1852–1927, Vol. II, Cassell, 1928

Lord Percy of Newcastle, *Some Memories,* Eyre & Spottiswoode, 1958

H. B. Philpott, *London at School: The Story of the School Board 1870–1904,* T. Fisher Unwin, 1904

J. Ramsden (ed.), *Real Old Tory Politics: The Political Diaries of Sir Robert Sanders, Lord Bayford, 1910–35,* The Historians' Press, 1984

R. H. S. Randles, *History of the Friends' School, Lancaster (now the George Fox School),* Allan Sharpe, 1982

E. T. Raymond, *Uncensored Celebrities,* T. Fisher Unwin, 1918

R. W. Rich, *The Training of Teachers in England and Wales during the Nineteenth Century,* Cambridge University Press, 1933

E. R. Robson, *School Architecture* (1874), Leicester University Press, 1972

D. Rubinstein, *School Attendance in London 1870–1904: A Social History,* University of Hull, 1969

J. Runciman, *Schools and Scholars,* Chatto & Windus, 1887

School Board Idylls, Longmans, Green, 1885

A. K. Russell, *Liberal Landslide: The General Election of 1906*, David and Charles, 1973

M. Rutter *et al.*, *Fifteen Thousand Hours*, Open Books, 1979

M. Sadleir, *Michael Ernest Sadler*, Constable, 1949

Viscount Samuel, *Memoirs*, Cresset Press, 1945

J. S. Sandars, *Studies of Yesterday*, Philip Allan, 1928

E. G. Sandford (ed.), *Memoirs of Archbishop Temple*, Macmillan, 1906

G. R. Searle, *The Quest for National Efficiency: A Study in British Politics and Political Thought, 1899–1914*, Blackwell, 1971

R. H. Sherard, *The Child-Slaves of Britain*, Hurst & Blackett, 1905

B. Simon, *Education and the Labour Movement, 1870–1920*, Lawrence & Wishart, 1965

T. A. Spalding and T. S. Canney, *The Work of the London School Board*, P. S. King, 1900

W. T. Stead (ed.), *Coming Men on Coming Questions*, Review of Reviews Office, 1905

F. L. Stevenson, *Makers of the New World*, Cassell, 1921

B. Strachey, *Remarkable Relations: The Story of the Pearsall Smith Family*, Gollancz, 1980

M. Sturt, *The Education of the People*, RKP, 1967

G. Sutherland, *Policy-Making in Elementary Education 1870–1895*, Oxford University Press, 1973

  (ed.), *Studies in the Growth of Nineteenth Century Government*, RKP, 1972

A. J. P. Taylor, *Lloyd George: Rise and Fall, The Leslie Stephen Lecture 1961*, Cambridge University Press, 1961

  English History 1914–1945, Oxford University Press, 1965

  (ed.), *Lloyd George: A Diary by Frances Stevenson*, Hutchinson, 1971

  Beaverbrook, Simon & Schuster, 1972

  (ed.), *My Darling Pussy: The Letters of Lloyd George and Frances Stevenson 1913–41*, Weidenfeld & Nicolson, 1975

  'Politics in the First World War', in *Essays in English History*, Penguin, 1976

M. Thomson, *David Lloyd George: The Official Biography*, Hutchinson, 1948

A. Tropp, *The School Teachers*, Heinemann, 1957

J. Turner, *British Politics and the Great War: Coalition and Conflict 1915–1918*, Yale University Press, 1992

Lord Vansittart, *The Mist Procession*, Hutchinson, 1958

G. Wallas, *Men and Ideas*, Geo. Allen & Unwin, 1940

We Can Conquer Unemployment: Mr Lloyd George's Pledge, Cassell, 1929

B. Webb, *Our Partnership*, Longmans, 1948

S. Webb, *London Education*, Longmans, Green, 1904

J. Wilson, *C-B: A Life of Sir Henry Campbell-Bannerman*, Constable, 1973

T. Wilson, *The Downfall of the Liberal Party, 1914–1935*, Collins, 1966

  (ed.), *The Political Diaries of C. P. Scott, 1911–1928*, Collins, 1970

C. Wrigley, *Lloyd George and the Challenge of Labour*, Harvester Wheatsheaf, 1990

K. Young, *Arthur James Balfour*, Bell, 1963

Index